Youth Gangs in American Society

FOURTH EDITION

RANDALL G. SHELDEN
University of Nevada, Las Vegas

SHARON K. TRACY
Georgia Southern University

WILLIAM B. BROWN
Western Oregon University

WADSWORTH
CENGAGE Learning®

Australia • Brazil • Japan • Korea • Mexico • Singapore • Spain • United Kingdom • United States

Youth Gangs in American Society, Fourth Edition
Randall G. Shelden, Sharon K. Tracy, and William B. Brown

Publisher: Linda Ganster

Acquisitions Editor: Carolyn Henderson Meier

Assistant Editor: Virginette Acacio

Editorial Assistant: Casey Lozier

Media Editor: Andy Yap

Marketing Manager: Michelle Williams

Marketing Communications Manager: Heather Baxley

Production Management: Lynn Lustberg, MPS

Composition: MPS

Art and Cover Direction: Carolyn Deacy, MPS

Manufacturing Planner: Judy Inouye

Rights Acquisitions Specialist: Don Schlotman

Photo Researcher: PreMediaGlobal

Text Researcher: PreMediaGlobal

Cover Designer: Riezebos Holzbaur/Tim Heraldo

Cover Image: Uli Seit/The New York Times

For product information and technology assistance, contact us at **Cengage Learning Customer & Sales Support, 1-800-354-9706.**

For permission to use material from this text or product, submit all requests online at **www.cengage.com/permissions.** Further permissions questions can be e-mailed to **permissionrequest@cengage.com.**

Library of Congress Control Number: 2012933331

ISBN-13: 978-1-133-04956-2

ISBN-10: 1-133-04956-7

Wadsworth
20 Davis Drive
Belmont, CA 94002-3098
USA

Cengage Learning is a leading provider of customized learning solutions with office locations around the globe, including Singapore, the United Kingdom, Australia, Mexico, Brazil, and Japan. Locate your local office at www.cengage.com/global.

Cengage Learning products are represented in Canada by Nelson Education, Ltd.

To learn more about Wadsworth, visit www.cengage.com/wadsworth

Purchase any of our products at your local college store or at our preferred online store www.CengageBrain.com.

Printed in the United States of America
2 3 4 5 6 7 16 15 14 13

Contents

Preface to the Fourth Edition

As we wrote in the preface to the first three editions of this book, it is hard to write a survey of the literature on a subject that cannot be precisely defined. We noted that young people cannot possibly create their own definitions of their world without some input from the outside. The terms *gang* and *gang member* continue to be problematic concepts. In this regard, nothing has changed since the first edition.

As in previous updates, in this edition we have attempted to provide as much updated material as possible. We have included the latest data on the number of gangs and gang members and the amount of crimes they are responsible for. This is no easy task, as anyone who conducts research on gangs can testify. We have updated the information concerning news reports about gangs, noting that gangs are back on the front burner in the news media. At the time we are writing these words (January 2012), the news is dominated by the current economic crisis (displacing the news on the wars in Iraq and Afghanistan, which was front and center when we wrote the third edition). As usual, the impact of this crisis is keenly felt in urban areas where gangs have always flourished. Chapter 8 ("Gangs in Context: Inequality in American Society") provides the details. As everyone knows, the news is not good.

What was once Chapter 1 has been divided into two chapters, the first of which (Introduction, "A Brief History of Gangs") is an introduction on the history of gangs, with much new material. Defining *gang* and *gang member* continues to be an important topic, which is discussed, with new research, in Chapters 1 ("What Is a Gang and How Many Are There?") and 2 ("What Do Gangs and Gang Members Look Like?"). Chapter 3 ("The Gang Subculture") has not been changed much, except for new material on gang graffiti. The crimes associated with gangs are discussed in Chapter 4 ("Criminal Activities of Gangs"), with a new section concerning gangs and the drug business called "Crack Dealing as a Business: The Black Gangster Disciples." This is based on a chapter in the best-selling book *Freakonomics*. New material has been added on girl gangs (Chapter 5,

"Girls and Gangs"), especially the research findings from Jody Miller's book on girl gangs in St. Louis, an update from her previous book *One of the Guys*. We have also added a brief section on the subject of the large number of girls who "hang out" with male gang members (mostly as girlfriends) but who are not technically members of girl gangs. In the previous edition, we mentioned this in passing in an endnote. Now we moved the endnote to the text itself and, more importantly, added a paragraph about a recent study in San Antonio by Valdez (2007b) who devoted a great deal of attention to those he called "hangers-on."

Chapter 6 ("Adult Gangs") is a new chapter covering adult prison gangs and motorcycle gangs. Prison gangs have existed almost as long as there have been prisons. Most gangs inside prisons are more or less reproductions of street gangs. So while we discuss youth gangs in the streets of urban areas, we need to keep in mind the fact that many if not most members of these gangs will end up in prison, where they are gladly welcomed by their prison counterparts. On the other hand, most people who group together in various motorcycle groups are not considered as gangs and do not commit crimes. In this chapter, we are discussing what are often called the "one percenters." This refers to the estimated 1 percent of motorcyclists who are involved in criminal activity—especially drugs—and who are considered as gangs by most people (e.g., Hells Angels).

Chapter 7 ("Why Are There Gangs?") has a new section on deterrence theory as it applies to gangs (this was not covered in previous editions). Each of the major theories discussed in previous editions have been updated with the most recent research. For instance, we note that the research from the Chicago School perspective (e.g., concentric zones) continues to be updated, with the recent examples of mapping done in many communities showing the spatial distribution of crime.

Chapter 8 ("Gangs in Context: Inequality in American Society") has been extensively updated with a new section concerning the recession that began in 2008 and continues to the present date (2012). A new section on the capitalist economic system has been added because this system directly relates to crime and gangs and the recent economic downturn. Among other updates, we cite Barbara Ehrenreich's update of her best-selling book *Nickel and Dimed*. The "Changes in the U.S. Economy" section has been completely updated with data up to 2010. The section called "The Development of the Underclass" has been updated with recent data from the Census Bureau and the Bureau of Labor Statistics. The section called "Poverty and Family Structure" has been updated with information up to 2010, including reports from the Children's Defense Fund on childhood poverty. The section called "How These Changes Relate to the Growth in Gangs" has been updated with research by a highly recognized expert on youth issues, Henry Giroux, plus recent studies on the situation in Chicago.

We are sad to report that the legal response to gangs, discussed in Chapter 9 ("Legal Responses to the Gang Problem"), has little new to offer except "old wine in new bottles." The most significant change is a new section on gang-related legislation produced by states across the country. This was based on a review of nearly 600 pages of current or recent legislation. The impact of this new legislation in addition to various responses on the part of the legal system has been negligible. Gangs continue to grow and develop.

Chapter 10 ("Community and National Intervention Strategies") has been thoroughly rewritten from the beginning to the end, with noteworthy additions of new gang-prevention programs. Many programs noted in previous editions have been abandoned either because of lack of funding or their failure to have an impact on gangs. We begin the chapter with a new section arguing for the need for a new paradigm, followed by a new section called "Gangs Are Not Just Criminal Justice Problems." Here we argue that the surrounding context of so-cial inequality must be addressed if we are ever to reduce gang involvement.

By any measure, the gang problem has become worse, but mostly because the social context we wrote about in previous editions has worsened. We have not discovered any promising programs that would alleviate social conditions within our inner cities where gangs flourish. Once again, we apologize to the reader if we cannot be more positive. In the previous edition, published in the early years of the war in Iraq, we noted that the enormous expenditures of money (now in the trillions of dollars), in addition to the many "tax cuts" (for the wealthy, as usual), left little left for the average American family. We also noted at the time that "virtually every state faces huge deficits, and cutbacks on social programs—especially education—are well under way." We further wrote, "For the most disadvantaged in our urban areas, gangs will continue to be a via-ble option. And selling illegal drugs will likewise continue to be an alternative source of income, although never enough to achieve the 'American dream.'"

In Chapter 11 ("Conclusions"), there is an update on the story of "Jimmy" plus an extension of the last section, "Some Final Words," focusing especially on the current economic situation.

ACKNOWLEDGMENT

Each of us would like to once again extend our appreciation to many people for their efforts to bring about the third edition of this book. We would like to thank Carolyn Henderson Meier and others associated with Cengage for giving us the initial "push" needed to get this done on schedule. There are many others, too numerous to mention, who also deserve our thanks. We would be remiss if we did not mention (which we failed to do in the first two editions) the work of all gang researchers who have preceded us, including some long ago dead. After all, we are mere "assemblers" who have taken the work of many others and put it between two covers. Where would any of us be without these researchers?

Finally, many thanks go to our respective significant others: Virginia, Rusty, and Judy. Their love and support has once again aided us in yet another excur-sion into the world of "gangs." This will be our last venture into the world of gangs, we promise!

About the Authors

Randall G. Shelden is Professor of Criminal Justice, University of Nevada–Las Vegas, where he has been a faculty member since 1977. He was the recipient of the UNLV Alumni award for Outstanding Teacher in 1982, 1984, 1986, 1987, 1992, and 1993. He is the author or co-author of 16 books, including *Girls, Delinquency and Juvenile Justice* (3rd edition), with Meda Chesney-Lind (which received the Hindelang Award for outstanding contribution to Criminology in 1992); *Crime and Criminal Justice in American Society* (with William Brown, Karen Miller, and Randall Fritzler; Waveland Press); *Controlling the Dangerous Classes: The History of Criminal Justice* (2nd edition, Allyn and Bacon); *Delinquency and Juvenile Justice in American Society* (Waveland Press); *Our Punitive Society* (Waveland Press); plus three previous editions of *Youth Gangs in American Society*. His Web site is www.sheldensays.com.

Sharon K. Tracy is a full professor and Director of the Crime and Delinquency Project at Georgia Southern University, where she has taught for more than 20 years. She received her degree in Public Administration (Criminal Justice Administration) from the University of Southern California. A member of the Georgia Gang Investigators Association, she serves as a consultant to numerous law-enforcement agencies and has written a number of articles on gangs, particularly those in suburban and rural communities.

William B. Brown is Associate Professor of Criminal Justice, Western Oregon University. He has conducted more than 10 years of ethnographic research in the area of youth gangs, which focused on the culture of inner-city youth in the Midwest. He has co-authored several books, including *Criminal Justice in America: A Critical View* (with Randall G. Shelden; Allyn and Bacon); *Introduction to Criminal Justice* (with Randall G. Shelden, Karen Miller, and Randall

Fritzler; Waveland Press); and the three previous editions of *Youth Gangs in American Society*. He is completing the manuscript for a book titled *Veteran Betrayals and Public Apathy: From Vietnam to Afghanistan and Iraq*, which addresses the cultural aspect of the Military Total Institution.

Introduction

A BRIEF HISTORY OF GANGS

Pre-Twentieth Century

Youths have formed groups (usually with their own-age cohorts) from at least early Roman society. Some of these groups have committed various kinds of activities that have been considered harmful and even criminal. Some have been called **gangs,** while many have been labeled rowdies, bad kids, trouble-makers, and other negative terms.

Youth groups known as "gangs" are certainly not inventions of twenty-first century American society; such groups have existed since at least the early four-teenth and fifteenth centuries in Europe. For instance, Davis recently wrote that gangs were a prominent feature of early Roman society and in "the city-state of Renaissance Italy" (2008: xi–xii). Descriptions of life in England during this period note that gangs committed various forms of theft and robbery, along with extortion and rape (Hay et al., 1975; Pearson, 1983). One report noted that in London during the fourteenth and fifteenth centuries, citizens were "terrorized by a series of organized gangs calling themselves the Mims, Hectors, Bugles, Dead Boys ... who found amusement in breaking windows, demolishing taverns, assaulting the watch.... The gangs also fought pitched battles among themselves dressed with colored ribbons to distinguish the different factions" (Pearson, 1983: 188). In France during the Middle Ages, there were groups of youths who fought with rival groups from other areas and schools and who also committed a variety of crimes. Youth gangs or groups reportedly existed in Ger-many during the seventeenth and eighteenth centuries (Covey, Menard, and Franzese, 1992: 90–91).

One report suggested that street gangs were known on the East Coast around 1783, just as the American Revolution was coming to an end, although they were not that serious (Sante, 1991).

Groups of youths considered **deviant youth groups** (and no one knows for certain the extent to which these groups were referred to as gangs) did not exist in any large number in the United States until the nineteenth century, although one report notes that they were found in some areas during colonial times (Sanders, 1970). During the latter part of the nineteenth century, with the rapid expansion of the capitalist system following the Civil War, some citizens in cities such as Philadelphia and New York expressed a concern about the problem of delinquency in general and gangs in particular. Herbert Asbury wrote about various youth gangs in and around the "Five Points" area of New York City in the late 1800s. Among the most famous gangs were the Plug-Uglies, Dusters, Bowery Boys, Roach Guards, Shirt-Tails, and Kerryonians (Asbury, 1927[1]). An early study by the Illinois State Police noted that a gang called the Forty Thieves was founded in New York around 1820; this is believed to be the first youth gang in the United States (Goldstein, 1991: 8).

A study of a Philadelphia newspaper covering the years 1836 to 1878 found 52 different gangs identified. The report noted that in the pre–Civil War era, Philadelphia was "plagued" by gangs. A report by the *New York Tribune* stated that the northern suburbs of Philadelphia during the years 1849 and 1850 were crawling with "loafers who brave only gangs, herd together in squads," and mark their names on the walls. In New York City in 1855, there were an estimated "30,000 men who owed allegiance to gang leaders and through them to the political leaders of Tammany Hall and the Know Nothings or Native American Party" according to one contemporary account (Spergel, 1995: 7). As will be noted in Chapter 7, in the 1920s Frederick Thrasher (1927) discovered more than 1,300 different gangs in the Chicago area alone.

The earliest gangs were mostly Irish. After the Civil War, there were Italian gangs and then Jewish gangs. Often there was a mixture of Italian, Irish, and even Scandinavian gangs (Riis, 1902/1969; Sante, 1991). Dutch, Welsh, Scots-Irish, Irish Catholic, and German youth would constitute most of the gangs later on in the century, in addition to many that were of mixed ethnicity (Adamson, 2000). Howell and Moore (2010) note that the emergence of gangs in both the Northeast and Midwest "was fueled by immigration and poverty, first by two waves of poor, largely white families from Europe." Poverty has been a recurring theme throughout the history of gangs. Where there is widespread poverty—regardless of race or ethnicity—there have been gangs.

Most of the earliest gangs of New York City were not generally criminal groups; many held jobs as common laborers, bouncers in saloons and dance halls, longshoremen and apprentice butchers, carpenters, sailmakers, and shipbuilders. Sante noted that "They engaged in violence, but violence was a normal part of their always-contested environment; turf warfare was a condition of the neighborhood." These gangs formed the "basic unit of social life among the young males in New York in the nineteenth century" (Sante, 1991: 198, quoted in Howell and Moore, 2010: 2). As poverty increased within the inner cities, so too did gangs. One of the most famous was the "Forty Thieves gang" that emerged around the 1820s. There were several competing gangs around the Five Points area of New York City, an area that was to become infamous as an impoverished and violent place (Asbury, 1927). In fact, a group called the **Five Points Gang** was to become one of the most famous in the area, as one of its earliest leaders, Johnny Torrio, became an important member of the Sicilian Mafia (La Cosa Nostra) and eventually recruited a teenage Brooklyn boy by the name of Alphonse Capone—better known as Al Capone (Howell and Moore, 2010: 3). Howell and Moore summarize this early history as follows:

> Four gang alliances were longest-lived gangs on the Lower East Side of Manhattan—for nearly two decades on either side of the turn of the 19th and 20th centuries: the Five Pointers, the Monk Eastman, the Gophers, and the Hudson Dusters. Territorial disputes and reorganizations were commonplace, but the Jewish Monk Eastman Gang was particularly notable for having "terrorized New York City streets." (2010)

Not surprisingly, these gangs emerged out of the horrible slums of New York City, created in part by greedy landlords who had built the tenements that became synonymous with poverty. As described by the famous photojournalist Jacob Riis, these areas were characterized by "dark, damp basements, leaking garrets, shops, outhouses, and stables converted into dwellings" (1969: 12, quoted in Howell and Moore, 2010: 4). Also at this time, Chinese gangs began to emerge, starting with the infamous **Tongs.** These gangs controlled "opium distribution, gambling, and political patronage" (Howell and Moore, 2010: 4; see also Chin, 1995).

Twentieth-Century Developments

During the ensuing several decades, public attention to gangs oscillated. For example, during Prohibition and its immediate aftermath (the Depression years), the public seemed enthralled with gangland activities and many of gangland's colorful characters (e.g., the Mob, Al Capone, Bonnie and Clyde, the Ma Barker Gang, and others). Several decades later, mass media glamorized those flamboyant characters.[2] Throughout much of the 1940s, Americans were distracted by World War II events in Europe and the Pacific and the healing process associated with the closure of a world war. Fascination with the gang was revitalized during the 1950s and early 1960s by academics who marched behind a theoretical banner that questioned lower-class allegiance to middle-class values (e.g., Cloward and Ohlin, 1960; Cohen, 1955; Miller, 1958; Short and Strodtbeck, 1965). During the 1950s, migration among blacks from the South and Hispanics[3] from Latin America caused resentment among young white males who did not welcome the intrusion. Both blacks and Hispanics formed gangs mostly as a defensive measure. The building of high-rise apartment buildings helped to segregate them from whites. Eventually called "the projects," these buildings became places where various gangs settled in (Howell and Moore, 2010: 5). By the 1960s, New York City became mostly comprised of Hispanics and blacks and so did the gangs. As Howell and More note, by the 1990s, "post-World War II urban renewal, slum clearances, and ethnic migration pitted gangs of African-American, Puerto Rican, and Euro-American youth against each other in battles to dominate changing neighborhoods, and to establish and maintain their turf and honor" (2010: 4).

Not surprisingly, gangs emerged in other parts of the country as people migrated in search of economic opportunities. Chicago, Milwaukee, and Los Angeles especially witnessed a tremendous growth in gangs. Later in the chapter, we will provide brief historical summaries of gang growth in these cities.

The fear of crime in general (including gang crime) has been linked to political phenomena that are related to ethnic heterogeneity and social change rather than to crime itself (Heinz, Jacob, and Lineberry, 1983). Similar circumstances, with corresponding relationships, may paint our current beliefs and fears about youth gangs. Ethnicity, race, and subcultural differences have been found to play major roles in the promotion of the public's fear of crime (Covington and Taylor, 1991). Youth gangs are intrinsic to American society. Since the mid-1980s, youth gangs have been found to exist in many small and midsized cities throughout the country, and, during the first decade of the twenty-first century, more are being reported in rural areas (the topic of rural gangs will be covered in Chapter 1). As they have throughout American history, gangs are more or less permanent institutions in large urban areas with a heavy concentration of the poor and racial minorities. Gangs exist, in some form, in all 50 states (National Gang Center, 2011), and, as we will see in Chapter 6, they are also permanent fixtures within the prison system. As the famous French sociologist Emile Durkheim once proposed, there is a certain inevitability of crime, and so there will probably always be some groups within society that are going to be, at the very least, labeled as "gangs" (1950).

While violence is not the innovation of contemporary youth gangs, during the past three decades, gangs have become more involved in illegal drug marketing, drive-by shootings, and the acquisition of more sophisticated weaponry. These changes in gang activities parallel economic, social, and technological transformations that shape social change in the greater society (e.g., declining employment opportunities, widespread acceptance of violence promoted by the mass media, social fascination with draconian modes of punishment, and the development and sanitized/impersonal use of high-tech war machinery). One gang member in Detroit stated, "Fuck, man, we don't make no 9 millimeters. Business makes 'em, and we make business with 'em. That's capitalism, ain't it?"[4] Substantive attributes of youth gangs may not have changed significantly since the days of Thrasher; rather, gangs may have simply taken advantage of modern technological advancements (the abundance of automatic weapons), become more willing to expand their business-venture options (drug dealing), and scaled up their level of violence to keep up with social trends and interests (drive-by shootings).

As always, gangs are an adaptation to "racial and ethnic oppression, as well as poverty and slums, and are reactions of despair to persisting inequality" (Hagedorn, 2008: xxiv).

Much of our concern about youth gangs is precipitated by an interest in issues germane to decaying urban areas. Our preoccupation with youth gangs almost exclusively targets black and Hispanic gangs; both are reflections of ethnic minority groups that the dominant class has perceived to be the most threatening to social stability. Historically, the dominant class has sponsored legislation that portrays concern for the general public. However, this legislation often results in the adoption of social-control policies over the lower classes, particularly ethnic minorities, while the real beneficiary is the privileged class.[5] Musto describes how support for the Marijuana Tax Act (1937) was obtained by painting Mexican Americans—believed to be the principal consumers of the drug—as potentially violent while under the influence of marijuana (1973). Studies have offered evidence that information linking blacks with cocaine use was employed (for political purposes) to solicit support from Southern legislators to make cocaine illegal. It was argued that black males under the influence of cocaine presented a potential threat to white women (Cloyd, 1982; Helmer, 1975; Provine, 2007).

Back to the Future: Late Twentieth- and Early Twenty-First-Century Developments

Looking at the social conditions of present-day America, with widespread inequality and poverty (see Chapter 8), it appears that we have, in effect, gone "back to the future." Not much has changed since the nineteenth century. Gangs are still with us, living in the same slums as their nineteenth-century counterparts, with mostly blacks and Hispanics. The inner city is frequently envisioned as an area constituted predominantly of these two minority groups. Policymakers communicate their concern about the plight of the inner city. However, one question continues to surface from the center of this political concern: Are policymakers actually concerned about the social conditions of citizens residing in our inner cities, or are they simply worried about their ability (or inability) to contain this lower-strata population (not to mention getting re-elected)? Perhaps this "concern" is little more than a superficial reflective response—catering to dominant-class demands driven by the fear that their domain is threatened by inner-city inhabitants who want to flee the gang-occupied territories.[6] How else might one explain, in a humanistic context, their reluctance to institute structural changes that offer real hope and opportunities to inner-city residents? Instead, they pass scores of legislative rubbish that foster the social control of an underclass, particularly those elements of the underclass who find themselves trapped within the inner cities of America—ethnic minority groups. For decades, American society has been successful in its geographic isolation of these disenfranchised groups (Harrington, 1962; Massey and Denton, 1993; Piven and Cloward, 1971; Wilson, 1987; Massey, 2007; Shelden, 2008).

One example of this segregation is provided by two studies conducted by Jonathan Kozol, who found abundant evidence of the isolation and segregation of inner-city schoolchildren. This is done with two of his books written 13 years apart: *Savage Inequalities* (1992) and his follow-up *Shame of the Nation* (2005). What is most important here is the subtitle of this latter book: *The Restoration of*

Apartheid Schooling in America. The data reported by Kozol in the latter book show that in places like Chicago; Washington, D.C.; St. Louis; Philadelphia; Cleveland; Boston; Los Angeles; and New York City, the proportion of public school enrollment that was black or Hispanic ranged from 78 to 95 percent. His research found that some specific schools were almost 100 percent black or Hispanic. In a New York City school where Kozol once taught, there were 11,000 children enrolled in 1997, and among these, only 26 were white—in other words, 99.8 percent were minorities. As Kozol notes: "Two-tenths of one percentage point now marked the difference between legally enforced apartheid in the South of 1954 [this was the date of the *Brown v. Board of Education* ruling] and socially and economically enforced apartheid in this New York City neighborhood" (Kozol, 2005: 8–9).

One of the important implications of these recent developments is the fact that today's gangs have become in one important way different from the gangs of years ago, especially those studied by the "Chicago School" (see Chapter 7). For those groups, the gang was a transitory experience of recent immigrant groups. Most members eventually matured out of the gangs and settled down to jobs and families.

Recent studies indicate that this is no longer the case. More and more gang members remain within the gang well into their adult years, as there are fewer opportunities available to them in terms of well-paying jobs. The most recent National Gang Center survey (2010) found that during the last 10 years of the survey, law-enforcement agencies reported that increasing numbers of gang members were adults. Whereas in 1996 about half were adults, in 2006 about two-thirds were adults. This distribution varied by size of the city: larger urban areas had a greater proportion of adult gang members, while juvenile gang members were more prevalent in smaller areas.

This has become especially true for those gang members who were sentenced to prison during the crackdown in the 1980s and who have recently been released. Part of an upsurge in gang-related homicides in Los Angeles during the late 1990s and early 2000s, for example, was attributed in part to gang members getting out of prison (following the passage of get-tough legislation in the 1980s), who face worse social conditions in their neighborhoods than when they were sentenced (*USA Today,* 2002; Leovy, 2003). Similar results have been found in other cities throughout the past decade (McGloin, 2007; Huebner, Varano, and Bynum, 2007; Blazak, 2009; Steiner, Markarios, and Travis, 2011; Pyrooz, Decker, and Fleisher, 2011).

In short, gangs are part of an underclass of marginalized minority youth. Virtually all of the research within the past 100 years has documented this (e.g., Shaw and McKay, 1942; Thrasher, 1927; Asbury, 1927; Hagedorn, 1998, 2008; Klein, 1995; Moore, 1991; Short, 1990b; Spergel, 1995; Zatz, 1985, 1987; Krohn, Schmidt, Lizotte, and Baldwin, 2011; Vigil, 2010). During a follow-up study of the original 47 gang founders in Milwaukee, Hagedorn found that over 80 percent of them were still involved in the gang although they were in their mid-20s, a time when most have typically matured out of the gang (Hagedorn, 1998).

Media Portrayal of Gangs

Public concern about gangs was reinvented during the 1980s and continues today. The rediscovery of gangs has been augmented by an escalation of media presentations about youth gang activities—particularly those gangs located within America's inner cities. The media have experienced great success in raising the public's level of fear about youth gangs. Gangs are a hot topic in the media, with the amount of coverage increasing tremendously during the past two decades, although with some fluctuations to be sure. Two gang researchers have noted that during the 1980s "newspapers, television, and films were suddenly awash with images of gun-toting, drug-dealing, hat-to-the-back gangstas. With the hue and cry came a massive mobilization of resources. Federal, state, and local funds were allocated to create antigang units in law enforcement and prosecution agencies." Then came the rapid deployment of technology, databases and the proliferation of gang experts (typically police officers or former gang members), and all across the country they went, spreading the word that gangs were everywhere. "In public schools across the country, gang awareness and resistance techniques were incorporated into the curriculum, gang-related clothing banned from campuses, and teachers instructed on how to identify gang members and spot concealed weapons" (McCorkle and Miethe, 2001: 4–5).

According to an analysis of the Reed Nexis Database, the number of articles on the subject of gangs between 1983 and 1994 increased from a mere 36 references in 1983 to more than 1,300 in 1994. Then there was a downward trend in media coverage in the late 1990s, picking up again by the 2000s.[7] According to the National Gang Center, between 2003 and May, 2011, there have been 14,336 news reports on the subject of gangs. This averages out to about 1,365 per year.[8]

Regardless of media coverage, surveys of law-enforcement agencies indicate steady growth in the number of gangs and the number of gang members. This demonstrates that media reporting of events does not always conform to reality, as demonstrated by many studies of the mass media (Herman and Chomsky, 2002; Bagdikian, 2004; McChesney, 2004).

A detailed study of the role of the media in Nevada (specifically in the two largest cities, Las Vegas and Reno) shows a similar pattern (McCorkle and Miethe, 1998, 2001). While media coverage has obviously declined since a peak in the mid-1990s, the number of gangs, gang members, and gang-related crimes, according to every estimate from official sources, has actually increased (see more information later in this introduction). In fact, media coverage of most major topics rarely conforms to reality but to the need for profits. There is abundant research showing how the media portray a reality according to the perceptions of groups in power who control the media.[9] The famous phrase, "If it bleeds, it leads," is an appropriate way of expressing this point. Media coverage of most major topics rarely conforms to the importance of an issue to the community; instead, it conforms to the need for profits. One of the major roles of the corporate-dominated media is to divert the public's attention away from real problems and to keep them entertained.

More often than not, the true causes and the surrounding social context of social problems like gangs are totally ignored. Debra Seagal's research about a prime-time television "real crime" show, which was based on videotapes of real police arrests, illustrates this problem. In her article, Seagal discusses how focusing on individual criminals diverts our attention away from the social context of crime and, indeed, communicates the idea that these offenders exist in a social vacuum. Seagal writes as follows:

> By the time our 9 million viewers flip on their tubes, we've reduced fifty or sixty hours of mundane and compromising video into short, action-packed segments of tantalizing, crack-filled, dope-dealing, junkie-busting, cop culture. How easily we downplay the pathos of the suspect; how cleverly we breeze past the complexities that cast doubt on the very system that has produced the criminal activity in the first place (1993: 52).

This is an example of what is known as symbolic politics (Gordon, 1994: 4). Similarly, TV crime shows constantly inform the public about the dangerous criminals in our midst, without any attempt to explain why. The viewer is left with the impression that these criminals come out of nowhere!

Throughout the 1980s and well into the 1990s, the media, with the generous help of law enforcement, created many myths about gangs and gang crime, which understandably created much fear among the public. Similarly, the "war on drugs" has been largely a media-driven event. For example, shortly after the 1988 election, public-opinion polls revealed that only about 10 percent of the public believed drugs to be a major problem facing the country. Following an intensive media blitz, this percentage soared to almost 40 percent within one year (Miller, 1996: 157; Reinarman and Levine, 1997).

It did not take long for citizens to become alarmed about the threat of gangs. In Salt Lake City, for example, a 1993 poll found that the "majority of Salt Lake County residents are increasingly anxious about expanding gang violence and would accept a tax increase to combat that problem" (Shellety, 1993). *U.S. News and World Report* (July 16, 1984: 108–109) noted that the city of Miami is faced with the problems of Cuban immigrants forming gangs, while Seattle has Asian immigrants in competition with both black and Hispanic gangs. Many reports on gangs are highly exaggerated and based more on anecdotal rather than scientific evidence. An example of such media exaggeration comes from a 1987 *Time* magazine article on the subject of gangs, which stated the following in grossly exaggerated form:

> Despite the fratricide among gangs, most of their victims are innocent bystanders. Gangs are prospering because crime pays in the ghetto. Many gangs have made the deadly transition from switchblade bravado to organized crime, serving as highly efficient distributors for Colombian cocaine dealers. Stiff competition has prompted bloody firefights in broad daylight over market share, while the influx of drug money provides topflight weapons, fancy cars and high tech surveillance equipment. Gang membership is now a full-time job, lasting well into the 20s and 30s (1987: 22).

Not surprisingly, the media usually rely on various official sources for good sound bites. Here is a rather typical description of a gang by the California State Task Force on Gangs and Drugs:

> Today's gangs are urban terrorists. Heavily armed and more violent than ever before, they are quick to use terror and intimidation to seize and protect their share of the lucrative drug market. Gang members are turning our streets and neighborhoods into war zones, where it takes an act of courage simply to walk to the corner store (Klein, 1995: 7).

Howell has argued that "leading newsweeklies consider 'gangs' to be a monolithic phenomenon and often do not distinguish among different types of gangs, such as prison gangs, drug gangs, and youth gangs" (2007: 40). Moreover, mainstream media reinforce the stereotype that gang members are all male and made up of minorities. Also, the media "portray gangs as an urban problem that has spread to new areas, as part of a conspiracy to establish satellite sets across the country." Further, "the pervasiveness of violence is exaggerated."

The next section of this introduction explores the recent growth of gangs and how such growth is linked to changing social conditions. Brief case studies of three cities—Los Angeles, Milwaukee, and Chicago—provide some insights into this phenomenon.

THE GROWTH OF GANGS: A FOCUS ON LOS ANGELES, MILWAUKEE, AND CHICAGO

There is little doubt that the number of gangs, as well as the number of gang members, has grown in recent years. What is not well understood, however, is how and why this has occurred. There has been an increasing amount of research during the past decade on this subject. This research is important because it provides some insight into the gang phenomenon that will be helpful in the years to come. It places the recent growth of gangs in a much larger social and economic context.

Los Angeles Gangs

Prior to World War II, gangs, as we understand them today, did not exist in Southern California, although some important changes in the 1920s began to set the stage for their emergence. The economic boom of the 1920s helped bring thousands of Mexican immigrants to the area. These Mexicans were primarily rural and poor and brought with them a tradition known as **palomilla** (in Spanish, this means "a covey of doves"), in which a number of young men in a village would group together in a coming-of-age cohort (Vigil, 1990: 118). During the previous century, Mexican youth began to form groups, often labeled as "gangs," following the Treaty of Hidalgo, which ended the war between Mexico and the United States (in 1848). For all practical purposes, the United States stole parts of

Mexico (then consisting of California, Nevada, Arizona, Utah, New Mexico, and parts of Colorado). Young Mexican gangs resented such a "theft" of their homeland (Valdez, 2007; cited by Howell and Moore, 2010: 10).

In the Los Angeles area, young Mexican males began to identify with a particular neighborhood or parish during the 1920s and 1930s. These groups, called "boy gangs" by an early researcher on gangs, were to be the forerunners of the modern Chicano gangs of East Los Angeles (Bogardus, 1943). It is important to note the tradition of such youths identifying closely with a specific geographic area, such as a village, parish, or neighborhood. These areas are now referred to as *barrios*.

Vigil notes a process of **choloization** (or **marginalization**) within the **cholo subculture.**[10] This is a process whereby various cultural changes and conflicts have made some Chicano youth especially vulnerable to becoming gang members. In the Southern California area during the Depression, thousands of Mexican immigrants were repatriated and deported. This process had a very negative effect on the Mexican American population, with many feeling that they were unwanted. Racist policies and widespread discrimination set in, culminating with the famous **Zoot Suit**[11] riots of 1943. About the same time, a death at a party in East Los Angeles (in an area called the Sleepy Lagoon) resulted in sensational press coverage (which included stereotypic descriptions of Chicano gangs). The police arrested 22 gang members from the 38th Street gang for conspiracy to commit murder, resulting in 12 convictions. The trial was described as a "kangaroo court" and began to galvanize Mexican youths. One writer described the impact this way: "Mexican street gangs changed forever because of these convictions. The jail sentences also acted as a glue to unite the Mexican community in a common cause, a fight against class distinction based on prejudice and racism, a fight against the establishment" (Valdez, 2007: 98, quoted in Howell and Moore, 2010: 12).

There was a second large influx of Mexicans starting around 1940 until around 1964. During this period, about 4 million Mexicans settled in the United States; this was followed by an additional 6 to 12 million in the 1970s (Vigil, 2002). Presently, 48 percent of the residents of Los Angeles County are Mexican.[12]

These two events, perhaps more than any others, helped bring youths closer together and transformed informal youth groupings or boy gangs into gangs (Moore, 1988, 1991: 1–2). In regard to the Zoot Suit riots, those "that fought the marauding sailors in East Los Angeles were seen by their younger brothers as heroes of a race war" (Moore, 1978: 62). In fact, one particular boy gang known as **Purisima** (the name comes from a local parish) began to call itself **White Fence** (named after the surrounding barrio). This gang is one of the oldest, most well-established gangs in Los Angeles, having offshoots in other cities, such as Las Vegas (Moore, 1988, 1991).

All of these events took place during a time when many positive male role models left the barrios because of repatriation. Thousands of other such role models were removed from the area because of World War II. Upon returning from the war, many took advantage of GI benefits and purchased homes in the growing suburbs of Southern California. Unfortunately, the males who remained in the barrios for the youths to look up to were those rejected from the service, those with criminal records, and typically those among the poorest of the poor (Vigil, 1990: 119). These gangs continue to flourish throughout Southern California and indeed throughout the West (including northern California, Nevada, and Arizona).

The origins of black gangs in Southern California are similar to those of the Chicano gangs, even though they emerged a generation later. The most popular of these gangs are the Bloods and the Crips and their various offshoots (called **sets**). Like their Mexican counterparts, blacks came from rural areas (mostly the rural South) to Southern California, a sprawling urban and industrial society. Their traditional way of life in the South was mostly church based with close family ties. However, the second-generation children (again like the cholo youths) faced many pressures in the new culture in Los Angeles. By the late 1960s, these black youths (concentrated in a few areas near downtown Los Angeles and in the San Fernando Valley) "found themselves alienated from the old rural values that had sustained their parents. They were racially locked out of the dominant Anglo culture and, in most cases, economically locked out of the black middle class. Their futures were as bleak as any cholo's, maybe bleaker" (Reiner, 1992: 5). They had come in search of the American dream of good-paying jobs in the booming aerospace, automobile, and construction industries, only to find the jobs filled by mostly whites. From the late 1950s to the time of the Watts riots, unemployment among blacks in south-central Los Angeles went from around 12 percent to 30 percent, while median incomes dropped by about 10 percent. In 1964, one of the major causes of growing discontent (leading to the Watts riots) occurred: the repeal of the Rumford Fair Housing Act (Davis, 1992: 296). What these blacks found, however, was discrimination in housing, education, and employment, plus restrictive housing covenants, all of which resulted in their being almost totally excluded from mainstream Los Angeles (Alonzo, 2004; Cureton, 2009).

One of the earliest references to a "gang problem" appeared in black newspapers during the late 1940s, and this was in reference, ironically, to *white* youths ("gangs"?) who attacked black people. There were reported "racial wars" in several Los Angeles area high schools during the late 1940s and early 1950s. Much like the response by Hispanic youths to the Zoot Suit riots, black gangs emerged as a *defensive* response. These black gangs defined themselves mostly in terms of school-based turfs. Some of the earliest of these gangs went by such names as the Slausons, Gladiators, Watts, Flips, Rebel Rousers, Businessmen, and the like. Some of these gangs modeled themselves after the white car clubs so common throughout Southern California (e.g., the Slausons and the Flips). Some of these groups divided themselves into two factions, one group on the West Side (usually with more money and more sophistication) and the other on the East Side (less money and less sophistication). Some of these gangs were merely the extension of intramural athletic rivalries, common in those days (Davis, 1992: 293–294).[13]

The **Watts riots** of 1965 did for black gangs roughly what the Zoot Suit riots did for Chicano gangs. One result of the Watts riots was that young blacks were seen in a more negative light by the media and by the rest of society. Also, black youths began to see themselves differently. It is important to note that although black youths did not have the palomilla tradition of their Mexican counterparts, they did have already-developed Chicano gangs to imitate. As Reiner notes,

"Given the emasculating circumstances of ghetto life a quarter-century ago, it is small wonder that the cocky, dangerous style of the Latino gangs had a strong appeal for black youths. It responded perfectly to the need for repackaging defeat as defiance, redefining exclusion as exclusivity" (Reiner, 1992: 5).

During the late 1950s, some black youths (and a few whites) began to imitate some of the cholo style of the Mexican American youths. They formed car clubs and other organizations and had such names as the Businessmen, the Slausons (named after a street in Los Angeles), the Black Cobras, the Gladiators, the Boozies, and others. These groups consisted of "guys who banded together for camaraderie and, to a certain extent, for protection" (Bing, 1991: 148–149). These gangs were different from today's gangs in many other ways. While they had certain neighborhoods where they lived, they usually did not consider such areas as their territory or turf. They did not usually fight other gangs; they had no colors; and they did not paint graffiti (Los Angeles County, 1992: 20).

During the mid- to late 1960s a transformation began with the emergence of groups that called themselves **Crips.** There is some debate as to the exact origin of this term; some say it came from a movie starring Vincent Price, *Tales from the Crypt,* while others say it comes from the word cripple because the original gangs crippled their enemies or suffered a similar fate. Another story was that it referred to a style of walking (i.e., walking like one was crippled in some way). The most popular story was that the Crips were founded by a group of youths from Fremont High School (a youth named Raymond Washington is generally credited as one of the founders) that had one member who walked with the aid of a stick and who was referred to as a "crip," short for cripple.

Some have suggested that the original gang used walking sticks as a sort of symbol and that the police and the media began to apply the name, so eventually the gang did too (Davis, 1992: 299; Los Angeles County, 1992: 5; Reiner, 1992: 6). Several imitators came from the city of Compton. One group called themselves the Westside Crips. It was founded in 1971 by Raymond Washington and Stanley "Tookie" Williams.[14] They borrowed one of the cholo traditions of wearing railroad bandannas and added to this the color of blue. Other Crip sets soon began to imitate them by wearing blue bandannas and other blue clothing, a color that set them apart from others. (Some of these sets currently wear the colors brown, purple, and black; Reiner, 1992: 6–7.)

Still another version is that the Crips emerged in the wake of the demise of the Black Panther Party; in fact, there is some evidence that both the Crips and the **Bloods** more or less took the place of the Black Panther Party, at least at first. It is well known how the FBI and other police organizations engaged in a systematic elimination of the Black Panther Party in the 1960s, largely under the infamous COINTELPRO program. This was an elaborate counterintelligence program established by the FBI to "disrupt, harass, and discredit groups that the FBI decided were in some way 'un-American,'" which even included the American Civil Liberties Union (Chambliss, 1993: 308; Davis, 1992: 298; Chomsky, 1999). This effort was largely responsible for infiltrating just about every black political organization in the country whose views were in any way militant, and it included committing murder. Many believe that "the decimation of the

Panthers led directly to a recrudescence of gangs in the early 1970s" (Davis, 1992: 298). In fact, Raymond Washington himself was influenced by some of the beliefs of the Panthers (Baker, 1988c). A slight variation is given by Cureton (2009), who argued that former Black Panther president Bunchy Carter and Raymond Washington formed the Crips in 1969 because they were disappointed that the Black Panther Party had not achieved its goals. At first, the Crips were a community-based organization set up to help local residents. However, Bunchy Carter was killed (many say by someone in law enforcement, either the local police or the FBI), and the Crips then began to deal in drug and gun sales.

This version of the story indicates that the first "set" of Crips was in part the result of the destruction of housing and of neighborhood ties with the building of the Century Freeway. Within this area was the original 107 Hoover Street Crips, who split off from a gang called the Avenues. The area around 107th Street was where Raymond Washington lived. In fact, one of the "O.G.s" ("original gangsters") of this gang told journalist Bob Baker that Crip originally stood for "Continuous Revolution in Progress" (Davis, 1992: 299). By 1972, there were 18 Crips and Bloods gangs in Los Angeles, and these were the largest of the more than 500 active gangs in the city in the 1970s (Vigil, 2002: 76). By the 1980s, the most popular of the Crips and Bloods were the Hoover Crips, East Side 40th Street Gangster Crips, Hacienda Village Bloods, and 42nd Street Piru Bloods (Miller, 2001). "Many of the Bloods and Crips gangs regarded one another as mortal enemies and engaged in a continuing blood feud. In succeeding years, hundreds of gangs in the Southwest—and also in other parts of the United States—adopted the Bloods and Crips names" (Howell and Moore, 2010: 14).

The next important development was a reaction to the emergence of the Crip gang sets, both on the East Side and the West Side of Figueroa Street. Such independent gangs as the Brims, Bounty Hunters, and Denver Lanes, among others, came together wearing red handkerchiefs, calling themselves Blood, and arose in defense of the Crips (Davis, 1992: 299). One group of black youths who lived on a street called Piru in Compton began to get together for protection from attacks by Crip sets. They called themselves the Compton Pirus and are believed to be the first gang to borrow the term **blood brothers** and apply it to their gang name. The term suggested, of course, the color red, which they selected as their gang's color. Soon Blood sets wore red bandannas, shoes, and jackets to set them apart from the Crips.

Within just a few years, Blood and Crip offshoots or sets spread throughout the Los Angeles area. These gangs began to borrow other traditions of Hispanic gangs—flying colors, defending their turf, using graffiti, hanging with **home-boys,** and **jumping in** (formally initiating) new members. By the 1970s, gang culture was firmly established in the Los Angeles area (Reiner, 1992: 6–7).

One interpretation of the Crips was that they were a "radical permutation of black gang culture" and "however perversely, inherited the Panther aura of fear-lessness and transmitted the ideology of armed vanguardism (shorn of its program)." Even some Crips insignia "continued to denote Black Power," but "Crippin'" eventually "came to represent an escalation of intra-ghetto violence to *Clockwork Orange* levels (murder as a status symbol, and so on) that was unknown in the days of the Slausons and anathema to everything the Panthers had stood for" (Davis, 1992: 299).

A turning point in the history of black gangs in Los Angeles came with an incident that took place outside a movie theater in Westwood, about two blocks from UCLA and near the wealthy neighborhood of Beverly Hills. Two members of rival gangs faced off, and a young woman who was standing in line was shot in the head and killed. Bing reports as follows:

> Her death snapped people into a new and horrified awareness: The beast had slithered out of its cage to prowl streets where insularity is the rule and privilege the norm. Suddenly the specter of South Central LA— a nightmare landscape where shadowy figures of young men stalk the streets and cars burn unattended in alleyways, where there is a nightly roar of wind from the rotors of the police helicopters that hover overhead at tightly spaced intervals, where everything is illuminated by the surreal beams of their searchlights ... descended like nuclear ash over a city that had not been more than marginally aware of its existence.... Suddenly the lead stories on local newscasts were about the latest gang-related shootings. (1991: xiv)

As of June 2011, according to estimates provided by the Los Angeles Police Department (LAPD), there are more than 250 gangs in the City of Los Angeles with more than 26,000 members.[15] According to a 2008 story in the *Los Angeles Times,* "conservative analysts estimate that as many as 40,000 people belong to the 700 or so gangs in the city of L.A. Countywide, there may be as many as 1,200 gangs with 80,000 members" (Rutten, 2008). The *Los Angeles Times* and other sources continue to document not only the continuous existence of gangs but also the futility of the criminal justice system to deal with the problem.[16]

Milwaukee Gangs

In Milwaukee, gangs emerged within the context of major economic and social changes in the midwestern and northern parts of the country. As factories began to close, more and more young males became marginalized as unemployment rates in Milwaukee increased. Most gangs emerged through conflict either with the criminal justice system or with other groups of youths. Some of Milwaukee's gangs evolved from ordinary street-corner groups, while others began as break-dancing and drill teams, which became fads within the black community. Very often fights broke out at these events. Negative police–minority relations, protests, sensational press coverage, and other conflicts helped solidify these gangs. A few gangs were offshoots of some famous Chicago gangs, but these were mostly formed when ex-gang members or their families just happened to move to Milwaukee rather than through active recruiting by Chicago gang members. Further, school desegregation ironically contributed to the problem by placing rival gang members in the same schools and in the process destroying some of the turf connections of these gangs (Hagedorn, 1998).

In Milwaukee, a study by Hagedorn identified 19 major gangs, only 4 of which originated in Chicago. In the latter case, former Chicago gang members moved their families to Milwaukee (which is about one hour's drive away from Chicago), where in time their own children formed gangs and named them after such Chicago gangs as the Kings, Cobras, and others (Hagedorn, 1998: 58–59). Hagedorn could find no evidence of any sort of "franchising" by these gangs— that is, Chicago gangs did not move to Milwaukee to "set up shop." (Later in this introduction, the problem of "gang migration" will be discussed.)

In most cases, gangs develop in a way described years ago by Thrasher (see Chapter 7), that is, through normal youthful group processes (Thrasher, 1927). In the majority of cases, gangs are formed only after some sort of conflict, either with other groups or, more often, as a result of the response by the criminal justice system. In Milwaukee, 4 of the 19 gangs studied by Hagedorn developed out of break-dancing groups, while 10 emerged gradually out of ordinary street-corner groups that selected their names based on either the street they lived on (e.g., the 2–7 gang was named after 27th Street) or their housing project (e.g., Hillside Boys was named after the Hillside Housing Project). Two other gangs were female auxiliaries (Hagedorn, 1998: 58–59).

Some gangs were originally both a dance group and a corner group. All 19 of the gangs Hagedorn studied started while most of the members were attending middle schools between 1981 and 1983. Each gang's roots were in a group of friends in a particular neighborhood, and each gang developed the same way. **Break-dancing** was one of the main social activities of black and Hispanic youths in the early 1980s, and the dance groups formed spontaneously. They practiced frequently, had dance contests, and were highly competitive. Often during these contests, fights would break out, and the groups would act as units (not unlike fighting during other sporting events, especially hockey). These groups formed all over Milwaukee (and other cities too), with each group assuming its own name and identity. Most simply disappeared.

Corner groups formed the same way: A few youths who were not in school (or were cutting classes) had nothing to do except hang out. Many adopted a name and eventually became strongly integrated through conflicts with other corner groups and gangs.

The Chicago gangs did not merely migrate as a gang. They left Chicago (or, rather, their parents moved) to escape the gangs and other problems in their neighborhoods. However, ironically, some of the youths found that they had to band together in Milwaukee for protection (a common scenario throughout the country).

Hagedorn reports that many gang members blamed the police both for the creation of gangs and for giving them their name. They reported that they used to play games in playgrounds but were often chased away by the police. Having nothing else to do, they resorted to stealing instead of playing (stealing, it should be noted, is often a form of play for youngsters). Also, the police often identified these groups according to the addresses, blocks, or street corners where they hung out.

The gangs studied by Huff in Cleveland and Columbus, Ohio, had similar origins. Many originated from break-dancing or rappin' groups (rather informal groupings of young men and women who evolved into gangs because of conflict with other groups). Others evolved from regular street-corner groups as a result of conflict with other street-corner groups. Some had moved to Ohio from either Chicago or Los Angeles and brought with them leadership skills learned in gangs in these cities. With these skills, they founded their own gangs (Huff, 1989).

Chicago Gangs

The gang problem in Chicago dates back at least to the period just before the Civil War, long before Thrasher did his classic study. However, they did not receive much attention until the end of the century. By the turn of the century, gangs began to be noticed as European immigrants began to move into the area. Most of the early gangs consisted of young males from the ranks of mostly Polish and Italian immigrants, who came from the ranks of the peasants in eastern and southern Europe (Howell and Moore, 2010; Perkins, 1987).

Many of these gangs developed out of so-called athletic clubs, which often masked their true intent, namely to take part in the huge patronage system in the city. Howell and Moore (2010: 7) point out that many of these athletic clubs "hosted gangs, and gangs also assisted union leaders and factory workers in the protection of their interests."

By the 1920s, these gangs began to decline as many immigrant families were able to move out of the inner city. However, this migration left the door open for the large migration of blacks from the South. More than a million blacks moved from the South during this time, with about 200,000 moving to Chicago alone. Most of them settled in segregated areas of the city known as the "Black Belt." Howell and Moore (2010: 7) note that "The origins of Chicago's serious street gangs can be traced to blacks' disproportionate residency in socially disorganized inner-city areas, dating back to the period between 1917 and the early 1920s." As with European gangs, black gangs started with various athletic clubs.

The famous race riot of 1919 did for black gangs what the Zoot Suit riots did for Mexican gangs in Los Angeles more than 20 years later. Perkins reports that black groups and white groups started to fight over turf and "each group declared street supremacy and control over streets, alleys, railroad tracks, storefronts, building stoops, and small waterfronts" (Perkins, 1987: 353, quoted in Howell and Moore, 2010: 8).

Some significant changes came after World War II, when membership in Chicago gangs became generally younger and more nonwhite. At this time, three major gangs had emerged: Devil's Disciples, Black P-Stone Nation, and the Vice Lords, two of whom (Black P-Stones and the Vice Lords) developed within the Illinois State Reformatory School at Saint Charles. Other gangs followed, including the Latin Gangs and three offshoots of the Devil's Disciples between 1960 and 1973: the Black Disciples, the Black Gangster Disciples, and the Gangster Disciples (Perkins, 1987: 353, quoted in Howell and Moore, 2010: 8).

As is so often the case, city planning played a role. In this case, about 50 high-rise apartment complexes were built, known popularly as "the projects," all of which were located in predominately black ghettos. As Howell and Moore report (2010), "This setting provided a strong base for gangs, but also brought them into regular and direct contact. Gangs not only grew stronger in the buildings but in several instances took control of them, literally turning them into high-rise forts."

What followed was the emergence of the so-called "super-gangs" during the 1960s, commonly known as People and Folk (Bensinger, 1984; Howell and Moore, 2010: 8). During the 1940s and 1950s, there was a large migration of Mexicans into the part of Chicago formerly occupied by European immigrants in the early twentieth century, leading eventually to the formation of gangs. By the 1990s, the two most prominent gangs were the Latin Disciples and the Latin Kings.

Presently, the largest gang in Chicago is the Black Gangster Disciples, with others close behind, such as the Cobra Stones, El Rukns (previously the Black P-Stone Nation), Blackstone Rangers, and Vice Lords, all of whom form the famous People Nation and Folk Nation, to be discussed in the next section.

People and Folk

This grouping actually began in the 1960s in Chicago when a "youth group" known as the Black P-Stone Rangers evolved into a criminal organization, largely through the efforts of Jeff Fort (Knox, 2004; Florida Department of Corrections, n.d.). He eventually organized a group of about 50 gangs into one "nation" called the Black P-Stone Nation. The leaders (21 in all) described themselves in a more positive light, saying they were a "socially conscious, self-help organization that would help uplift themselves and their community." They were able to obtain $1.4 million in federal antipoverty money, but the funds were used to finance their criminal enterprises. Eventually Fort was indicted by a federal grand jury, convicted, and sent to prison.

Shortly thereafter, two other Chicago gangs (Black Disciples and Gangster Disciples) combined to form the Black Gangster Disciple Nation. Throughout the 1970s, these two groups—Black P-Stone Nation and Black Gangster Disciple Nations—fought over control of the illegal drug market in Chicago. Many from each nation ended up in prison. At the end of that decade, the informal alliances and rivalries merged to form two major super-gangs (or nations) known as People and Folk (Bobrowski, 1988; Hagedorn, 1998). Gangs that were originally part of the Black P-Stone Nation became aligned with the People Nation; those that were part of the Black Gangster Disciple Nation aligned with the Folk Nation.

Among the gangs aligned with People were Black P-Stone, Latin Kings, Vice Lords, Spanish Lords, El Rukns, Bishops, and the Gaylords. Gangs aligned with Folk included Black Gangster Disciples, Black Disciples, Gangster Disciples, La Raza, Latin Disciples, and the Simon City Royals. The People Nation is often distinguished by the use of the five-point crown (Florida Department of Corrections, n.d.), and the Folk Nation is often associated with the six-point star and pitchfork (see Figure I.1).

Even when aligned with a nation, individual gangs retained their own distinguishing characteristics, tattoos, and symbols (e.g., Vice Lords use the top hat and cane).

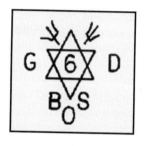

FIGURE I.1 The Folk Nation six-point star and pitchfork (on the left) and the People Nation five-point crown (on the right)

SOURCE: Florida Department of Corrections

According to the National Gang Intelligence Center (2009), there were about 10,000 gangs in the city of Chicago in 2008. The most prominent gangs (and the estimated number of members) were Gangster Disciples (6,000 to 8,000), Latin Kings (numbers in Chicago not given, but it was estimated that they and their sister gang Queen Nation had about 20,000 to 35,000 members and "make up more than 160 structured chapters operating in 158 cities in 31 states"), Vice Lords (based in Chicago, they had an estimated 30,000 to 35,000 members in 74 cities in 28 states), and Black P-Stones (6,000 to 8,000 members mostly in the Chicago area).

More than 30 Chicago gangs identified themselves as Folks (including the Spanish Cobras, Latin Disciples, Imperial Gangsters, Latin Lovers, Braziers, Insane Popes, and Simon City Royals); there were at least as many gangs identified as People (including Latin Kings,[17] Vice Lords, Future Stones, Gaylords, Latin Lords, Bishops, and War Lords). There are also numerous factions within each major super-gang, while an estimated 19 gangs are independent (National Gang Intelligence Center, 2009). According to the National Gang Intelligence Center, the numbers of gang members are almost equally divided between the People Nation and Folk Nation. In terms of racial distinctions, about 70 percent of Folks are Hispanics, while about 19 percent are black, and 10 percent are white. Among the People gangs, around 56 percent are Hispanic, 22 percent are black, and 19 percent are white. One of the most recent estimates is that in Chicago suburban areas, there are between 70 and 75 gangs with more than 100,000 members. This report does not mention People and Folk (U.S. Department of Justice, 2008). However, the Chicago Crime Commission (2009: 11) reported that in 2008 "the largest street gangs in Chicago appear to be the Gangster Disciple Nation (GDN), Black Gangsters/New Breeds (BG), Latin Kings (LKs), Black P-Stone Nation, Vice Lords (VLs), Four Corner Hustlers, and Maniac Latin Disciples (MLDs)" (quoted in Howell and Moore, 2010: 10).

Some Concluding Thoughts on the Recent Growth of Gangs

As indicated at the beginning of this chapter, the first known youth gangs in recorded history began to appear in London during the fourteenth and fifteenth centuries as England was shifting from an agrarian to an industrial society. As many scholars have noted, this revolutionary change displaced thousands of people, and they in turn flocked to the growing urban areas, such as London (Ignatieff, 1978; Marx, 1964; Marx and Engels, 1847; Rusche and Kirchheimer, 1968;

Shelden, 2008). Similarly, in several segments of American society, a very similar process has occurred. Displaced by the shift from an industrial to a service/information society with the corresponding need for better education and training, literally millions of minority youths have been displaced and become marginalized during the past 30 years. The growth of gangs can be seen as a method of adapting to such changes. The comparison between seventeenth-century London and late twentieth-century Los Angeles has not escaped notice. "Both cities were among the preeminent urban magnets of their time for huge rural populations displaced from the land (as was nineteenth-century New York). That status brings a city enormous benefits—growth, wealth, diversity. It also brings tremendous social dislocations—including gangs" (Reiner, 1992: 9).

There's another commonality that present-day gangs have with their nineteenth and early twentieth century counterparts: all have been natural byproducts of tremendous inequality and extreme poverty. Frederick Thrasher, in his classic study of gangs in Chicago (see Chapter 7 for details), found that gangs exist in what he called the *interstitial* areas of the city—areas that are found within the poverty belt of the city. This fact is what links the Bloods and Crips and People and Folk of the twenty-first century with the Mims, Hectors, Bugles, and Dead Boys of the nineteenth century. In this regard, nothing has changed in spite of the billions of dollars spent on suppressing gangs.

Along with the recent growth of gangs has come a flurry of research activity from both academic and nonacademic settings. Unfortunately, our knowledge base is still limited, and there is much disagreement about the nature and extent of youth gangs. In fact, there is little agreement about what a gang actually is, which will be the subject of Chapter 1.

SUMMARY

Gangs are not something new to the social arena. They existed in fourteenth- and fifteenth-century Europe and colonial America. Throughout the twentieth and well into the twenty-first century, social researchers have devoted extensive time and resources to the understanding of youth gangs in America. Many studies point out that discriminatory policies and practices by the government have contributed to the emergence of gangs in various parts of America. These policies and practices include the promotion of social disorganization in Chicago, the deportation of immigrants in Southern California during the Great Depression, and police brutality in Watts during the 1960s, among others.

Throughout this history, gangs have consistently existed within the margins of society, within what Thrasher called the *interstitial* parts of the city. In short, where there is extreme poverty and inequality (especially racial inequality), there have been gangs.

Public perception (and fear), crucial to policy development, is shaped largely by the mass media. It is clear that the media have done little to differentiate fact from fiction in their portrayal of youth gangs. Moreover, the media, over the past 30 years or so, have capitalized on the incidents of gang activities by significantly increasing their coverage of youth gangs. The media have contributed to the stereotypical images of how we think about gangs and gang members.

NOTES

1. A movie based partly on Asbury's book was released in 2002, called *The Gangs of New York,* earning several Academy Award nominations.

2. Just in the past decade, several movies have appeared that continue to glamorize various outlaws who formed "gangs." Examples include *Public Enemy* (with Johnny Depp as John Dillinger), *Pretty Boy Floyd* (starring Effie Afton), and *American Outlaws* (a movie about Jesse James, starring Colin Farrell), among many others, not to mention all the movies about the Mafia and other organized crime groups.

3. Several different terms are commonly used to describe persons of Hispanic or Mexican descent. Some prefer to use the more generic term *Hispanic,* while others prefer terms such as *Chicano, Latino,* or *Mexican-American.* Different sources cited in this book use different words to describe these gangs. We will be using all of these terms throughout the book, depending on the sources we are citing.

4. Interview by William Brown, one of this text's authors, of a gang member in Detroit, Michigan.

5. Enactment of the Chinese Exclusionary Act (1882) was encouraged by the American Federation of Labor and by the belief that opium use by Chinese immigrants facilitated production advantages for this minority group over white workers (Abadinsky, 1993; Latimer and Goldberg, 1981). Helmer (1975) points out that the 1875 economic depression in California was yet another motivating factor for this legislation.

6. This is similar to the "concern" about the so-called dangerous classes during the last half of the nineteenth century (e.g., Brace, 1872). For a complete history on the control of the "dangerous classes," see Shelden (2008).

7. Searches were conducted in January 1995, January 2000, and March 2003. The last two searches were conducted by Jennifer Dierick of Wayne State University. The authors extend their appreciation to her. Note that at the peak of gang coverage (1996), there were on average 3.6 stories per day; during 2001, there was an average of 1.4 items per day up until September 11. For the remainder of 2001, the average was 1.07 items per day, and during 2002, there were 1.5 items per day.

8. Source: http://www.nationalgangcenter.gov/Gang-Related-News.

9. See the following studies of the media that support our contention that gangs are portrayed in the media according to the perceptions of groups in power who control the media: Herman and Chomsky (2002); Bagdikian (2004); Chomsky (1989); Fox, Van Sickel and Steiger, (2007).

10. The term *cholo* is used to describe a Chicano gang member or the Chicano subculture itself. It is derived from a term used to describe a marginal position between two cultures—the older Mexican culture and the newer Mexican-American culture—thus the term *marginalization.* To better understand marginalization, think of the margins of typical notebook pages, and you will note that this part of the

page is literally off to one side and not part of the main body of the page. We can also speak of the marginalization of dissent, whereby alternative perspectives are not allowed within the mainstream press or political discourse. Chapter 3 elaborates on the cholo subculture in more detail.

11. The Zoot Suit riots in Los Angeles were an attack on several Mexican Americans (unprovoked) by a group of white sailors. The "zoot suits" were a unique style of clothing worn by some local Mexican males. This was an obvious racist attack (today it would be called a "hate crime"), and it provoked a counterattack by groups of Mexican Americans, who were subsequently labeled as "gangs" by the local press and the police. This was one of the first uses of the word "gang" to characterize Mexican American groups. The white sailors were not prosecuted, nor labeled as "gangs." See Moore (1978, 1991) for more detail.

12. Taken from the U.S. Census Bureau: http://quickfacts.census.gov/qfd/states/06/06037.html.

13. Davis provides a more complete history of black gangs, including an insightful analysis of the role of the Los Angeles Police Department in helping to perpetuate gangs—partly by trying to eliminate them—starting with Chief Parker in the 1950s and ending with Chief Gates in the 1980s and early 1990s. One example cited by Davis was the efforts by Chief Parker to engage in an "all-out war on narcotics" in both the south-central and east Los Angeles areas, which translated into a "war on gangs." This included an attack on the Group Guidance Unit of the Los Angeles Probation Department, which had been set up after the Zoot Suit riots to help young offenders. To Chief Parker, these were mere unreformable criminals who needed stiff prison sentences (Davis, 1992: 294–296).

14. The life of "Tookie" Williams took a turn for the worse when he was convicted of a murder committed in 1979. He was on death row until 2005, when he was executed (Warren and Dolan, 2005). He had become somewhat of a celebrity, having been nominated twice for the Nobel Peace Prize, based on the work he had done from death row, attempting to turn children away from the gang world. He even had his own Web page, with the advice column called "Tookie's Corner" (Mintz, 2003).

15. Retrieved from: http://www.lapdonline.org/get_informed/content_basic_view/1396.

16. See, for instance, this series of stories: http://www.sheldensays.com/gangs_in_los_angeles__updated.htm; see also Quinones (2007); Garvey (2005); Helfand (2008).

17. According to a member of the Latin Kings, the gang has left the People organization because of some conflicts with other gangs. "The Latin Kings Speak" (2002, March 28). Retrieved from: http://www.gangresearch.net/ChicagoGangs/latinkings/Reyx.html.

What Is a Gang and How Many Are There?

WHAT IS A GANG?

We must initially consider the problem of defining what exactly constitutes a gang and a gang member. If four youths are standing on a street corner or are simply walking down the street, is this a gang? If this same group of youths hang out together frequently and occasionally engage in some form of deviant activity, does this mean they are a gang? Suppose this same group invents a name for itself and even purchases special shirts or jackets and invents slogans or hand signs—does this mean it is a gang? If a young person is seen giving special hand signals or heard uttering gang phrases because he thinks it is cool or hip to do so, whether he may fully understand the implications, is he then to be considered a gang member? Or, if a youth who lives in a neighborhood inhabited by a gang (but no one in the gang considers him a member) just happens to be passing the time on a street corner with a gang member he has known for several years and is coincidentally questioned by a police officer, who subsequently fills out a field investigation card on him, is he therefore to be counted as a gang member? And how does race enter into the picture in the definition of gangs? If three or four *white* youths spend a considerable amount of time together, occasionally commit crimes together, and are often seen wearing the kinds of clothes typical of adolescents in general and some gangs in particular, are they considered a gang? We suspect that the average white citizen (and many police officers) would respond to this group differently than if they saw a group of three or four *black* teenagers hanging out together (e.g., at a shopping mall). Perhaps this is one reason why most official estimates of gangs and gang members tell us that less than 10 percent are white and the majority is black or some other minority group (usually

Hispanic). In other words, could it not be argued that the very definition of a gang is racially biased? Even these few examples illustrate the difficulty in defining gangs and gang members.

The term *gang* can have many different definitions. Gil Geis has provided one of the most interesting comments about the etymology of the term, noting that the early English usage of *gang* was "a going, a walking, or a journey" (quoted in Klein, 1995: 22). The definition given by the Random House College Dictionary provides similar meanings of a positive or neutral nature, such as "a group or band"; "a group of persons who gather together for social reasons"; "a group of persons working together; squad; shift; *a gang of laborers*"; along with the more negative meanings. The thesaurus of the word processing program used to type these words gives such synonyms as "pack," "group," "company," and "team." Not surprisingly, there has existed little consensus among social scientists and law-enforcement personnel as to what these terms mean. One writer defined gangs as "groups whose members meet together with some regularity, over time, on the basis of group-defined criteria of membership and group-defined organization" (Short, 1990: 3). In many studies, researchers have often used whatever definition was used by the police. Many researchers have apparently confused the term *group* with the term *gang* and have proceeded to expand the definition in such a way as to include every group of youths who commit offenses together. One of the most accepted definitions comes from the work of Klein:

> [A gang is] any denotable ... group [of adolescents and young adults] who (a) are generally perceived as a distinct aggregation by others in their neighborhood, (b) recognize themselves as a denotable group (almost invariably with a group name), and (c) have been involved in a sufficient number of [illegal] incidents to call forth a consistent negative response from neighborhood residents and/or enforcement agencies. (Klein and Maxson, 1989: 205)

The most recent survey by the National Gang Center more or less repeats what Klein said back in 1971, noting that there is a general consensus that these definitions have the following in common:[1]

- The group has three or more members, generally aged 12–24.
- Members share an identity, typically linked to a name, and often other symbols.
- Members view themselves as a gang, and they are recognized by others as a gang.
- The group has some permanence and a degree of organization.
- The group is involved in an elevated level of criminal activity.

The National Gang Center adds: "In general, law enforcement agencies report that group criminality is of greatest importance and the presence of leadership is of least importance in defining a gang."[2] Omitted from this definition were such groups as motorcycle gangs, hate/ideology groups, prison gangs, and "exclusively adult gangs."

The dominant law-enforcement perspective is that gangs are essentially criminal conspiracies with a few hard-core members (often described as sociopaths) and that arrest and imprisonment of these individuals are required as a viable social policy. An example is provided by the California Penal Code (Section 186.22), which gives a definition of a "criminal street gang" as (Spergel, 1990: 18–19):

> ... any ongoing organization, association, or group of three or more persons, whether formal or informal, having as one of its primary activities the commission of [specific criminal acts] ... having a common name or common identifying sign or symbol, and whose members individually or collectively engage in or have engaged in a pattern of criminal gang activity.... In order to secure a conviction, or sustain a juvenile petition, pursuant to subdivision (a), it is not necessary for the prosecution to prove that the person devotes all, or a substantial part of his or her time or efforts to the criminal street gang, nor is it necessary to prove that the person is a member of the criminal street gang. Active participation in the criminal street gang is all that is required.[3]

What is significant about this definition is that the actual legislation was called the "Street Terrorism Enforcement and Prevention Act, 1988" (California Penal Code sec. 186.22[f]).[4]

Many states use almost identical wording in their definitions of "criminal gangs."

Also missing from these definitions are other groups that technically may fit these standard definitions. For example, one writer noted that college fraternities might be included in the definition of "gang" (Venkatesh, 2003: 4–5). After all, all sorts of examples could be given that "lend credence to the notion that fraternities exist to perpetuate social transgressions." Continuing, the author says that "one should consider the weight of fraternal pedagogy—sometimes literally in manifestos and charters—around issues such as theft, vandalism, sexual conquest (read: harassment), and the imbibing of alcohol (read: underage drinking)." Given the recent frauds attributed to Wall Street, which resulted in literally trillions of dollars in losses to the American people (not to mention the trillions of dollars funneled away from the U.S. Treasury via tax havens), why not call this group a "gang" (and a "street" gang) too? (For documentation, see Scheer, 2011; Shaxson, 2011).

Modern researchers have argued that gangs and delinquent groups are significantly different, but most now generally agree that gang offenders are usually older; are more homogeneous with regard to age, sex, race, and residence; and tend to commit more violent crimes than ordinary delinquent groups. Spergel and Curry distinguish among the terms *gang, street gang, traditional youth gang,* and *posse/crew*. They define *gang* as

> ... a group or collectivity of persons with a common identity who interact in cliques or sometimes as a whole group on a fairly regular basis and whose activities the community may view in varying degrees as legitimate, illegitimate, criminal, or some combination thereof. What

distinguishes the gang from other groups is its communal or "fraternal," different, or special interstitial character. (1990: 388)

They define **street gang** as "a group or collectivity of persons engaged in significant illegitimate or criminal activities, mainly threatening and violent." The emphasis is placed on the location of the gang and their gang-related activities (Spergel and Curry, 1990).

The **traditional youth gang,** they note:

... refers to a youth or adolescent gang and often to the youth sector of a street gang. Such a group is concerned primarily with issues of status, prestige, and turf protection. The youth gang may have a name and a location, be relatively well organized, and persist over time. [They] often have leadership structure (implicit or explicit), codes of conduct, colors, special dress, signs, symbols, and the like. [They] may vary across time in characteristics of age, gender, community, race/ethnicity, or generation, as well as in scope and nature of delinquent or criminal activities (1990: 389).

Still another variation is the **posse** or **crew,** which, while often used in conjunction with the terms *street* or *youth gang,* is more commonly "characterized by a commitment to criminal activity for economic gain, particularly drug trafficking" (1990: 389).

Spergel and Curry also note that there are various kinds of deviant groups, such as "stoners, punk rockers, neo-Nazi skinheads, satanic groups, motorcycle gangs, prison gangs." These may resemble traditional youth gangs or street gangs. They also caution that these gangs should be distinguished from what have often been called **youth groups** and **street groups,** common in an earlier era (e.g., as when Thrasher wrote in the 1920s). These groups are often called *street clubs, youth organizations,* or *athletic clubs.*

Spergel and Curry also note that there are **delinquent groups** and **criminal organizations.** The former are far less organized and criminal than the gangs defined previously and do not have distinctive dress, colors, signs, and so on. The latter refers more to a relatively well-organized and sophisticated group of either youths or adults (often a combination of both) organized mainly around the illegal pursuit of economic gain. Finally, there are gang *cliques* or *sets* that are often smaller versions (or subgroups) of larger gangs, usually based on age (1990: 390).

Huff alerts us to another distinction, which has gained more significance in recent years, namely, that existing between gangs and organized crime. As he notes, **youth gangs** historically were largely groups of adolescents (mostly male) who engaged in a variety of deviant activities, especially turf battles and gang fights. Now they are increasingly involved in major crimes, especially those that are violent or drug related. **Organized crime** has meant *adult* criminal enterprises operating as businesses. Today such organized activities characterize many youth gangs. Huff defines a youth gang as a

... collectivity consisting primarily of adolescents and young adults who (a) interact frequently with one another; (b) are frequently and deliberately involved in illegal activities; (c) share a common collective identity that is usually, but not always, expressed through a gang name; and (d) typically express that identity by adopting certain symbols and/ or claiming control over certain "turf" (persons, places, things, and/or economic markets) (1993: 4).

In contrast, Huff defines an organized crime group as a

> ... collectivity consisting primarily of adults who (a) interact frequently with one another; (b) are frequently and deliberately involved in illegal activities directed toward economic gain, primarily through the provision of illegal goods and services; and (c) generally have better defined leadership and organizational structure than does the youth gang (1993).

There are several key differences between these two groups. First, they differ significantly in terms of age, with youth gangs being much younger than organized crime groups. Second, whereas the organized crime group exists almost exclusively for the purpose of economic criminal activity, youth gangs engage in a variety of both legal and illegal activities, with their illegal activities usually committed by individuals or small groups of individuals rather than by the entire group.

It is obvious that the majority of these definitions focus almost exclusively on delinquent or criminal behavior as the distinguishing feature that differentiates gangs from other groups. This is consistent with a strictly law-enforcement perspective. Several other researchers disagree and argue that gangs should not be defined as purely criminal or delinquent organizations (i.e., the reason they began in the first place and the reason they continue to exist is the pursuit of delinquent or criminal activity). In this context, it is important to consider one of Huff's most pertinent comments. He notes that:

> ... in analyzing youth gangs, it is important to acknowledge that it is normal and healthy for adolescents to want to be with their peers. In fact, adolescents who are loners often tend to be maladjusted. Because adolescents go to dances together, party together, shop together (and, in many cases, shop*lift* together), it should not be surprising that some of them join together in one type of social group known as a gang. Group experience, then, is a familiar and normative phenomenon in adolescent subculture, and gangs represent an extreme manifestation of that age typical emphasis on being together and belonging to something. (1993: 5–6, emphasis in the original)

Hagedorn believes that gangs are not merely criminal enterprises or bureaucratic entities with formal organizational structures. Rather, as other researchers have noted (e.g., Moore, 1978; Suttles, 1968), gangs are age-graded groups or cliques "with considerable variation within each age group of friends" (Hagedorn, 1998: 86).

It is difficult to conceive of gangs as purely criminal organizations. Most gang members spend the bulk of their time simply hanging out or engaging in other nondelinquent activities. Jackson notes that many researchers, accepting the popular imagery of gangs, have spent a considerable amount of time (perhaps months) "waiting for something to happen" (Jackson, 1989: 314).

It should be noted that at the end of 1999, a new category was invented. According to the 1999 National Youth Gang Survey, respondents were asked to identify how many **"troublesome youth groups"** they had in their jurisdiction. The new definition inserted "unsupervised peer groups" into the previous term "troublesome youth groups." Citing several sociologists (Sampson and Groves, 1989; Short, 1996; Warr, 1996), the report notes that these adolescent groups typically have three or four members and are not well organized and rather transitory (what adolescent groups are not?). Also, they occasionally get involved in delinquent activities (again, what adolescent groups do not?) but are not committed to a life of crime (once again, what adolescent groups are any different?). Despite any connection to full-fledged youth gangs, survey respondents were asked to estimate the number of these kinds of adolescent groups (how they were to identify them and what criteria were to be used are not spelled out in this report). Not surprisingly (given that those doing the data collection were all adults), the vast majority of jurisdictions reported the existence of such groups (U.S. Department of Justice, 1999). In the 2000 report, the term was dropped altogether.

An equally difficult task is trying to determine what constitutes a **gang-related offense.** If a gang member kills another gang member in retaliation for the killing of a fellow gang member, few would argue over whether this would be gang related. However, what if a gang member is killed as a result of some sort of love triangle, or if a gang member is killed by someone not in a gang, or if a gang member kills someone while committing a robbery on his own? Decisions about these kinds of incidents must be made, and police officials have procedures for such reporting. However, as Klein and Maxson observe, such procedures are conducted "not always according to reliable criteria, not always with adequate information regarding the motive or circumstances of the crime, not always with extensive gang-membership information on file, and—most clearly—not by the same criteria from city to city" (1989: 206).

Klein and Maxson reviewed this process in five cities around the country and found that each city had somewhat different methods for defining gang-related incidents; for example, in two cities, only violent incidents were counted. In one city, the policy was to include only gang-on-gang crimes, but the authors found that robberies where the offenders (but not the victims) were gang members constituted gang-related crimes. In another city, any offense committed by a gang member was counted as gang related (1989: 208).

A police official in Chicago expressed the following common view: "'Gang-related' simply means that the offender or victim has gang ties, either self-admitted or distinguishing tattoos" (Chaney, 2009). The Los Angeles Police Department maintains a Web site providing a citywide gang crime summary that lists gang statistics by month without providing a definition or a way to distinguish these crimes from crimes that are not gang related.[5] The National Gang Center states: "Larger cities were most likely to indicate regularly recording *any* [emphasis added] criminal offenses as 'gang-related,' although more than one-third reported not doing so in 2006. Of the other three categories of agencies, approximately half reported regularly recording any criminal offenses as 'gang-related.'"[6]

In short, there appears to be little consensus on what a gang-related crime is. Given the complexity of the problem, it is highly unlikely that such a consensus will ever be achieved. Quite often, we will find that a gang member is engaging in offending behavior by himself, without any assistance from his fellow gang members. Also, rarely will one find an entire gang (if, for example, there are 100 members) involved in a single incident. A method used by the Chicago Police Department seems as good a solution as any that has been offered or presented.

CHICAGO'S USE OF DESCRIPTORS TO DEFINE GANG-RELATED CRIME

Based on the definition of gang-related crime provided by Bobrowski (1988), the Chicago Police Department began using the term **descriptors** in the 1980s to aid in their recording of data on gang crimes (a system still in use today). These descriptors Bobrowski defines as "certain features which serve to distinguish street gang related cases from those which are not." Based on the research by this police department, there "emerges a finite set of descriptors which can be thought of as trademarks of the street gang crime" (1988: 15). (Data from the Chicago Police Department based upon this method of collecting data on gang crimes was used in a study by Curry, 2000.)

Descriptors imply more than just motives, as it suggests a certain "commonality of circumstances" of street-gang crime. The Gang Crimes Section of the Chicago Police Department chose seven specific descriptors "which serve to categorize the event data found in case narratives." The seven are representing, retaliation, street fighting, vice related, recruitment, turf violations, and other. The first four descriptors together constituted about 94 percent of all street gang-related crimes during the period under study (January 1, 1987–July 31, 1988). The seven descriptors are summarized as follows (Bobrowski, 1988: 17–29):

1. *Representing*—denotes any incident in which, in the process of committing a crime, the offender represents himself as being a member of a particular gang. This can be a verbal statement, a hand sign, a display of colors, or any other similar symbolic gesture. In a recent period of time (January 1, 1987, through July 31, 1988), Chicago police noted that this descriptor was found in 32 percent of all street-gang-related cases.

2. *Retaliation*—denotes when one gang resorts to some form of violence to solve certain conflicts with one or more other gangs. Examples include attempts to protect its own interests, uphold its interests, and seek revenge (for example, for a harm done to one of its own members). Such behavior arises out of insults, chance altercations, and infringements on one's criminal activities. This descriptor was found in about 8 percent of gang-related activities in Chicago.

3. *Street Fighting*—similar to the classic rumble, whether it be spontaneous or planned, an execution or hit, or simply a fair fight. The most common are "spontaneous assaultive engagements among small groups (three to five persons), random encounters among antagonistic rivals, and small bands of two or three persons assaulting non-gang victims" (1988: 22). These actions constituted 24 percent of gang-related crimes in Chicago.

4. *Vice-Related*—this category accounted for 30 percent of all the street-gang-related offenses. About 92 percent of these were narcotics, liquor-law violations, gambling, and prostitution offenses. It should be noted that less than 1 percent of all nonvice offenses involved drug activities (for example, evidence of vice activity was found in only 2 out of 82 homicides during the period under study).

5. *Recruitment*—refers to activities in which a gang member in some way attempts to force a nonmember to join the gang. Usually it is a type of "join or continue to pay" situation. Recruitment is probably grossly underrepresented in these statistics. Victims are often fearful of further actions against them by the gang and simply distrust the police; therefore, reporting does not occur. Also, if the youth joins the gang, the likelihood of the incidents being reported to the police is almost nil. Statistically, recruitment efforts constitute only 3 percent of the reported gang crimes.

6. *Turf Violations*—include the defacing of gang graffiti and passing through a designated gang territory, frequently a favorite hangout of a particular gang (for example, a restaurant, street corner, or bar). These events are also woefully underreported for basically the same reasons as noted in recruitment. Officially, these violations accounted for only 1.5 percent of all street-gang crimes in Chicago.

7. *Other Descriptors*—include such crimes as extortion (mostly forcing people to pay turf tax to cross into and through gang territory), personal conflicts among gang members, and prestige-related crimes, which may be greater than reported. These offenses "may include acts committed to satisfy membership initiation; to establish a special reputation, a position of responsibility, or a leadership role; to respond to challenges or avoid reproach; or to prevail in internal power struggles" (1988: 27). Together all of these constituted only 4 percent of the officially reported gang crimes in Chicago.

Reiner (1992) notes that there are two different ways of defining gang crimes. On the one hand there are **gang-related crimes,** and on the other hand there are **gang-motivated crimes.** The former is the broader definition that states if either the criminal or the victim is a gang member, then the crime is gang related. This is known as the **member-based** definition. This makes it a lot easier for law-enforcement authorities to count gang crime. However, some believe that it will tend to overstate the amount of crime attributed to gangs because many, if not most, of the individuals involved would probably commit crimes and/or be a victim whether or not they were in a gang (Klein, 1995: 15).

A more recent study distinguished two subcategories of gang-motivated crimes. One is known as **self-directed crimes.** These are crimes that are initiated by individuals or groups within the gang. The second is **gang-directed crimes.** These are ordered or otherwise set up by gang leaders or the gang as a whole. As for gang-motivated crimes, there are two types. One is "instrumental" actions that are "intended to advance the material interests of the gang or its leaders." Another is "expressive actions," which are meant to "show gang pride and demonstrate that the group is more fearless than its rivals by defending turf, avenging past injuries, and so on" (Greene and Pranis, 2007: 51–52).[7]

Some believe that focusing on motivation is using a more narrow view. From this perspective, gang-related crime is caused by *gang activity*. Supporters of this view claim that one of the main virtues of using the motive-based definition is that it eliminates unrelated kinds of crime and focuses on crimes that are "clearly due to the presence of gangs" (e.g., drive-by shootings), although it may understate the gang problem (Reiner, 1992: 95–96).

Using the motive-based definition may in effect obscure the extent of the gang problem in an area, perhaps hoping that the problem will "just go away" (Knox, 1991: 343). Indeed, there are significant differences in the amount of gang-related crime, depending on which definition one uses. Klein (1995) compared homicide rates in Los Angeles and Chicago. In Los Angeles, with a member-based definition, there were about twice as many gang-related homicides as in Chicago, which uses a motive-based definition.

Part of the problem in arriving at a consensus definition of *gang* and *gang-related crime* is that we are dealing with widely accepted stereotypes of gangs, most of which are derived from the biased information of law enforcement and the media. From many years of research, Joan Moore has compiled the following list of the most common stereotypes:

> (1) They are composed of males (no females) who are violent, addicted to drugs and alcohol, sexually hyperactive, unpredictable, and confrontational; (2) They are either all African-American or all Hispanic; (3) They thrive in inner-city neighborhoods where they dominate, intimidate, and prey upon innocent citizens; (4) They all deal heavily in drugs, especially crack cocaine; (5) "A gang is a gang is a gang"—in other words, they are all alike or "you see one and you see them all"; (6) There is no good in gangs, it is all bad (a corollary to this is that anyone who would want to join a gang must be stupid or crazy); (7) Gangs are basically criminal enterprises and that youths start gangs in order to collectively commit crimes; in other words, there is a tendency to confuse individual and group criminality; (8) The "West Side Story" image of aggressive, rebellious, but nice kids has been replaced in recent years by the "gangster" image of a very disciplined criminal organization complete with "soldiers." (1993: 28–29)

According to Moore, stereotypes shape the definitions of gangs and therefore determine policies structured to deal with gangs. Especially important is the stereotype of gangs as criminal enterprises, which confuses individual and collective criminal activity. Quite often, the police, as well as the media and the public, will label criminal behavior that is individually motivated as gang-related. It should also be noted that stereotypical thinking is a common phenomenon in the world. To stereotype is to think in terms of rigid and inflexible categories. Most of the time, such thinking is normal and harmless, but when it is associated with anxiety or fear, it is very different.

HOW MANY GANGS AND GANG MEMBERS ARE THERE?

Gangs can be found in all cities with populations of 100,000 or more. Gangs are also found within both the federal and the state prison systems and in most juvenile correctional systems. Gangs are found within practically every major urban high school in the country. At least this is the official version, according to the National Gang Center, which consistently shows growth in the number of gangs and gang members over the past 20 years or so (National Gang Center, 2011). However, the data depend solely upon reports from local law-enforcement agencies. Greene and Pranis note that police "estimates of local gang membership can fluctuate from year to year based on changes in police practices." They give Detroit as an example, noting that: "The number of active gang members reported by the Detroit Police Department nearly doubled between 1996 and 1997, rising from 2,000 to 3,500 before plunging to 800 the following year" (2007: 34). It has also been observed that once federal dollars begin to flow into a department, the number of gangs and gang members starts to rise significantly. This was noted by one of the co-authors of this book (Brown) for Flint, Michigan. It was also noted for Indianapolis (Green and Pranis, 2007).

Gang activity inside schools, however, fluctuates quite a bit. For example, one study noted that between 1995 and 1999, gang activity within schools declined and that the claim of high rates of gang activity within schools is highly exaggerated (Beres and Griffith, 2005). In January 2010, state lawmakers in Washington were debating how to deal with gangs in schools. A Department of Health survey conducted by the state reported that 25,000 students responded that they were "gang members or affiliated with a gang." Lost in the concern to do something about the gang problem was that there were about 1 million students in the school system at that time—2.5 percent of all students admitting being a gang member or "affiliated" with a gang. A Washington legislator introduced two bills aimed at suppressing gangs. One defined the circumstances under which schools could suspend or expel students who engage in gang activity or hate crimes on school grounds. It would also allow schools to reject a student who had a record of gang involvement to transfer from another district. As noted earlier, the sticking point is that there is no clearly defined way to define gang involvement. A task force that researched the rise in gang activity at Washington schools in 2009 had noted: "Despite research and years of experience that demonstrates the relative ineffectiveness of suppression as a long-term solution to gangs, programs designed to reduce gang activity in this country and our state lean heavily toward police suppression" (Slovan, 2010). The proposed legislation was a reaction to a problem that has been exaggerated by the media. Rather than helping to prevent a problem, it would be far more likely to introduce other problems, including profiling of students for expulsion.

Exactly how many gangs and how many gang members there are in the country is presently not known with any degree of certainty. In fact, there are as many estimates as there are estimators! In the 1920s, Thrasher estimated that there were 1,313 gangs in Chicago alone (Thrasher, 1927). Miller's nationwide survey in the 1970s estimated anywhere from 700 to almost 3,000 gangs in the largest cities in the country (Miller, 1975, 1982). Estimates come almost exclusively from law-enforcement sources. Until 1997, the estimated numbers showed yearly increases. During those years, the amount of money going to police departments increased as well, in addition to the number of "gang units" and police officers assigned to these units. As noted earlier, in virtually every survey in recent years, the definition of "gang" and "gang member" has been left entirely up to the reporting law-enforcement agencies. This enables local criminal justice agencies to vary their estimates depending on their goals. Some provide conservative estimates to preserve a safe image of their city or to promote tourism, while others exaggerate the numbers to obtain more funding.

In 2008, there were an estimated 27,900 gangs and approximately 774,000 gang members. As noted in Table 1.1, the estimated number of gang members has fluctuated a great deal, ranging from a high of 840,000 in 1999 to a low of 710,000 in 2003; the number of gang members increased by a modest 9 percent since 2003. Similarly, the estimated number of gangs has fluctuated over the past dozen years. Whereas in 1996 there were just over 30,000, in 2003, the number had declined to 20,000; in 2008, however, the number of gangs had risen to 27,000 (Egley, Howell, and Moore, 2010).

In the late 1970s, the Los Angeles Police Department created specialized antigang units called CRASH (Community Resources Against Street Hoodlums). These units were eventually assigned to each police division, including the Rampart division, which covers almost 8 square miles just west of downtown Los Angeles. It is the city's most densely populated community and has a heavily immigrant and transient population of about 300,000. The community had a history of high crime rates; by the mid-1980s, it was the city's most violent community. In addition to CRASH units, the city instituted a controversial tool to fight street gangs—gang injunctions. The injunctions prohibited named gang members from congregating or carrying pagers within certain geographic boundaries. Sworn statements from police officers—usually officers in CRASH units—identified the gang members targeted for injunction. CRASH officers enjoyed a great deal of discretion, and many abused their powers. The Rampart corruption scandal involved officers making false arrests, extorting money from drug dealers, giving perjured testimony, and falsely accusing many individuals of being "gang members." In March 2000, the CRASH units were disbanded (replaced by Special Enforcement Units). The Rampart scandal casts doubt on the authenticity of the gang data for Los Angeles. For example, of the alleged 112,000 gang

TABLE 1.1   **Estimated Number of Gang Members, 1996–2009**

Year	No. of Gang Members
1996	846,500
1997	816,000
1998	780,000
1999	840,500
2000	772,500
2001	693,500
2002	731,500
2003	710,500
2004	760,000
2005	789,500
2006	785,000
2007	788,000
2008	774,000
2009	731,000

SOURCE: National Gang Center: http://www.nationalgangcenter.gov/Survey-Analysis/Measuring-the-Extent-of-Gang-Problems#estimatednumbergangs; 2008 data source: Egley, Howell, and Moore, 2010.

members in Los Angeles County, 62,000 of them had been identified by a disbanded CRASH unit. Police officials and police gang "experts" claimed that the data were accurate, but this is a dubious claim. At least 100 convictions of "gang" members have been overturned, and 20 officers have been fired or have quit (O'Connor, 2000; Jablon, 2000).

The percentage of youths who self-report being in a gang or engaging in gang-related behavior has not changed significantly during the past two decades. Typically, no more than 10 to 15 percent of all youths report being in a gang (and this estimate includes areas with a high rate of crime and gang membership). According to the 1997 National Longitudinal Survey of Youth (unfortunately, the latest survey available) only 8 percent of a representative sample of 9,000 youths between the ages of 12 and 16 had belonged to a gang by age 17 (Snyder and Sickmund, 2006).

A word of caution is in order. It must be stressed that the numbers coming from law-enforcement sources should be treated with some skepticism because there is no way to verify them independently. Field researchers emphasize that local politics shape gang intelligence and record-keeping on gangs in law-enforcement agencies. The National Youth Gang Center cautions that gang problems can be exaggerated or denied in law-enforcement reporting, depending on local political considerations. The Justice Policy Institute observes:

> It is difficult to find a law enforcement account of gang activity that does not give the impression that the problem is getting worse by the day.... The most comprehensive survey of law enforcement data on gang activity shows no significant changes in estimated gang member-ship or the prevalence of gang activity—both of which are down sig-nificantly since the late 1990s. Further, law enforcement depictions of the gang population are sharply at odds with youth survey data when it comes to the geography of gang activity as well as the race and gender of gang members (Greene and Pranis, 2007: 33).

GANG MIGRATION

Quite a bit of controversy revolves around the issue of "gang migration," with suggestions that gangs have engaged in a nationwide **"franchising"** operation. The term **migration** often gets confused with a similar term, **proliferation.** The latter term signifies the increase in the number of communities in the nation reporting that they have gang problems. While it is true that more communities report having gang problems in recent years, this is usually the result of social conditions within the communities themselves that have caused gangs to grow. On the other hand, we would also suggest that such an increase may stem from changing definitions of *gang* and *gang member* and the tendency for law-enforcement agencies to exaggerate the problem in order to obtain more fund-ing. We are not the only researchers who have raised this issue, for Cheryl Max-son argues that some of the increase in gang proliferation may stem from a "heightened awareness of gang issues, redirection of law-enforcement attention, widespread training, and national education campaigns" (Maxson, 1998: 2).

On the other hand, the term *gang migration* suggests something entirely different. This term suggests "the movement of gang members from one city to another." Maxson's study of gang migration defined migration rather broadly to include 1) "temporary relocations" (e.g., visits to relatives); 2) "short trips to sell drugs or develop other criminal enterprises"; 3) "longer stays while escaping crackdowns on gangs or gang activity"; 4) "residential moves (either individually or with family members)"; and 5) "court placements" (1998: 2).

Much research has documented the proliferation of gangs in many commu-nities and even noted some connection to gangs in other cities, but for the most part, the exact nature of this connection had not been explored often until Maxson and her colleagues began to study the issue in depth (Maxson, 1998; Maxson, Woods, and Klein, 1996; see also Curry and Decker, 1996; National Drug Intelligence Center [NDIC], 1996).

What emerges from more recent studies is a very complex picture of gang migration. First, according to Maxson's survey, out of 1,000 cities, 710 had expe-rienced gang migration by 1992. Second, gang migration has been concentrated in just a few large cities, especially in the San Francisco Bay area, Southern California, Chicago, and southern Florida. In fact, almost half (44 percent) of the migration was in the western part of the country. Third, almost all of the cities that have experienced gang migration also have gangs that have been homegrown (only 45 of the 710 cities had no homegrown gangs). Fourth, most cities already had a gang problem before new gang migration began, which clearly contradicts the notion that gang problems are the result of franchising. (Maxson notes that the majority of those interviewed, 81 percent, disagreed with the statement "Without migration, this city wouldn't have a gang problem." Most reported that migration was not the major cause of the gang problem, contradicting reports by the media and by politicians.) Fifth, "emergent" gang-problem cities (gang problems have emerged during the past 20 years or so) and "chronic" gang-problem cities (those with gangs dating back several decades) are about equally as likely to report gang migration.

What is most important from Maxson's study was what she found when she asked law-enforcement officials what they thought were the major reasons why gang members move to their cities from another area. The most common reason (stated by 39 percent) was that gang members simply moved with their families. Another major reason was to stay with relatives and friends. Combined, these social causes of migration constituted more than half (57 percent) of the cases. Drug market expansion was cited in 20 percent of the cases, with another 12 percent citing other criminal opportunities (for a total of 32 percent)—what Maxson calls *pulls*. Finally, in about 11 percent of the cases, the reason given was that the gang member was forced out in some way—either by police crackdowns, court order relocation, or simply a desire to escape gangs. It was also discovered that these gang members are about equally as likely to join already existing gangs in their new city as remain with their original gang (Maxson, 1998: 7–9).

This complex picture suggests that gang members move mostly for the same reasons that others move—moving with their families or to be closer to friends or relatives. What is also clear is that most of these moves are by individual gang members rather than large segments of one particular gang. Clearly, there is little evidence to suggest that gangs migrating from one city to another are the major source of the gang problem. Nor is there any evidence of franchising or the outside agitator hypotheses. Maxson (and many other researchers) suggests that the popular perception of gang franchising stems mostly from "the diffusion of gang culture in the media." The nation's youth "are hardly dependent on direct contact with gang members for exposure to the more dramatic manifestations of gang culture, which is readily accessible in youth-oriented television programming, popular movies, and the recent spate of 'tell-all' books from reputed urban gang leaders" (Maxson, 1998: 9). What is perhaps most interesting from Maxson's study is the fact that the only sources are those in law enforcement. Perhaps a more complex picture will emerge when others are interviewed about such moves, especially the gang members themselves, their families, school officials, and so on.

The most recent surveys reinforce these conclusions. According to the National Gang Center's most recent survey in 2004 (the latest reported year) "the majority of gang-problem agencies in each area type reported that none or few (less than 25 percent) of the documented gang members in their jurisdictions had migrated from other areas, including more than two-thirds of the rural counties." The survey concludes that "these findings support empirical research which has demonstrated that a community's gang problem—however affected from other areas—is primarily and inherently homegrown and localized in nature" (National Youth Gang Center, 2012). The survey also found that the bulk of the migration took place for purely social reasons, as already noted (see also Egley and Ritz, 2006). The report concludes that

> Most of the remaining agencies serving suburban counties and smaller cities were unable to provide gang-member migration information, perhaps suggesting a marginal effect of this issue on the overall local gang problem. Additional analysis reveals that areas with emerging gang problems are less likely to report gang-member migration than areas with chronic gang problems. (National Youth Gang Center, 2012).

Gangs in Rural Areas

While we are on the subject of migration, something should be said about gangs in rural areas of the country. We should approach this particular subject with a good deal of caution, given the problems with defining gangs and gang members noted earlier. The senior author had an interesting experience in the early 1990s that may shed some light on this subject. He was invited to conduct a special class on gangs for continuing education credit through his university, University of Nevada at Las Vegas, in a rural area called Pahrump, about 60 miles west of Las Vegas. There were some rumors that gangs were active in the area, as evidenced by some graffiti in several locations, including some large gang letters painted on one of the streets. Local school teachers wanted some information about gangs. Prior to the start of class, Shelden drove around the area and began with a visit with the local sheriff. When asked if he knew of any gangs, he said to the best of his knowledge there were only rumors, but he had no evidence of any gangs. Visits with a few local shopkeepers resulted in the same answer. Finally, talks with some local high school students as they were leaving school for the day came up empty, although a couple of them said there were some "wannabes" trying to "look and act tough" and sport gang colors. Upon further investigation, the gang drawings on one of the local streets turned out to belong to one of the many Crip sets in Los Angeles, who were apparently just passing through on a recent weekend.

Admittedly, this incident was about 20 years ago, and there are no doubt a few gangs and gang members active in this particular area. In fact, a good deal of recent research confirms that there are gangs in rural areas, but the extent of the problem is not really known with any degree of certainty. There have been numerous reports of rural gang problems during the past 10 years or so. Although little is known about nonmetropolitan gangs, there are reasons to believe that our understanding of urban gangs will not automatically apply in nonmetropolitan areas. Weisheit and Wells (2001) found that while the variables used by urban gang researchers could predict gang activity in metropolitan areas, they had little predictive power in nonmetropolitan areas. Furthermore, wide variation exists among different social observers within the same community regarding what the term "gang" refers to and what it means to say that a community has a gang problem. As we have already noted, part of this difficulty hinges on the fact that the definition of a gang is so elusive and that few researchers agree upon any one set of descriptors to aid in that definition (Weisheit and Wells, 2001: 171).

In Takata's study (1987), the Kenosha (Wisconsin) Gang Project underscored the difference in official versus neighborhood youth perception of "the big-city gang connection" and its significance for youth gangs in this smaller-sized community. Based on content analysis of newspaper articles and interview data, the findings strongly suggest that when the presence of gangs in Kenosha could no longer be denied, police, school, and other local officials used the convergence of a set of factors to impose on the community an interpretation of the gang situation consistent with their vested interests (Zatz, 1987). Local officials used Kenosha's proximity to generate fear that Chicago street gangs were branching out across the Illinois-Wisconsin border. This perception enabled them to minimize and contain the potential damage to the image of their agencies and the city, which was threatened by the realization that Kenosha street gangs consisted of homegrown neighborhood youths.

The experiences in both Kenosha and Racine (small cities where Takata studied gangs) are repeated in one regional community after another, where minority youth gangs are defined by, and their existence attributed to, metropolitan gang connections. Media sensationalism and gang squad development abound. Age-graded corner groups of black and Hispanic youths are being labeled and dealt with as gang members. The findings in this research add to the literature that identifies wide variations in the way in which the gang phenomenon is interpreted. The literature suggests that this variation may be related to vested interests as well as the sources of information from which these interpretations derive.

Some researchers believe that the reports of the presence of gangs in small cities or rural areas are not highly reliable. This may be true as police reporting varies significantly from one jurisdiction to another. Also as Weisheit and Wells report, it is possible that nonmetropolitan gangs persist, but they don't consistently pose problems for local authorities, effectively "dropping out of sight." Weisheit and Wells then pose the question of whether or not this means the gang is still a gang (2001: 177).

Some rural jurisdictions have problems that are serious by any standard, whereas for others, the problems are rather minor. It is important to recognize this variability across jurisdictions when describing rural gangs and when establishing policies for responding to them. Asking police agencies if they have gang problems does not provide much specific information (Weisheit and Wells, 2001: 181).

Some have assumed that gangs spread from urban to rural areas through a process in which urban gang members themselves migrate to rural areas, whereas others have argued that only the symbols and culture of the gang are exported to rural communities. Although it is sometimes assumed that rural gang problems are almost entirely imported, there were a few jurisdictions in which the gang problem was completely homegrown (Weisheit and Wells, 2001: 181).

Further, even when outsiders moved into the area, continued gang activity was frequently reported to depend on the cooperation of local youth. In most nonmetropolitan jurisdictions reporting gang activity, the majority of gang members were local youth. In the Weisheit and Wells study, economic growth and prosperity in rural areas appeared to perhaps encourage the appearance of gangs because job opportunities draw families with gang-involved youth from larger urban communities. The observation that in rural areas gangs are more likely to emerge in conditions of economic growth has also been offered by the National Youth Gang Surveys (Weisheit and Wells, 2001: 181–182, 186–87).

Research conducted by Tracy (2003) on nonmetropolitan communities found support for the literature of Donnermeyer (1994) and Weisheit, Wells, and Falcone, (1994) in explaining the rise of gangs in rural areas. The following general themes have been identified in this literature: 1) *Displacement*—when urban gang members move into rural areas in response to enforcement pressure from urban police; 2) *Branch office*—when an urban gang sets up a drug operation in a rural area because prices are good and pressure from local police is expected to be minimal; 3) *Franchise*—when small-town drug dealers seek to expand their business by linking up with urban drug gangs; 4) *Social learning*—when local youth learn about gangs and make gang connections while incarcerated in a state or regional facility; 5) *Urban flight*—when families, including gang-affiliated youth, move into rural areas to escape gangs or violence in the cities (Weisheit and Wells, 2001: 183); 6) *Social reasons*—when migration is driven by employment, social programs, or other factors. When migrant workers move into the area for a short time and seem to bring gang-related activities with them; when local military bases provide an influx of gang activities as the family members of military personnel move into the area; and when the spread of public housing creeps into rural areas, placing urban gang youth into rural areas through social programs (Weisheit and Wells, 2001: 185).

How the gang phenomenon in the country occurred illustrates the way rural and urban areas have become more closely linked and interdependent, as well as how the social forces that explain urban crime can be applied to rural areas. Donnermeyer agrees with Weisheit and Wells that one model of urban-to-rural migration can be described through displacement, branch office, the franchise, and social learning. He, however, adds hate groups to this model (1994: 43).

Donnermeyer explains this category as when "[s]kinheads and young members of the Aryan Nation and other white supremacist groups (many of whom grew up in rural areas) establish their base of operations in a rural area. From this base, they move some or all of their activities to the fringe of a large city or even into the city, where minority groups can be targeted" (1994).

The perpetration of violence and victimization occurs at much higher rates among the youth who are identified with a gang for all community sizes. This connection is particularly strong for situations involving the use of a weapon. Of particular note is that the reported incidence of all types of violence is significantly lower across community size among youth who are *not* gang involved. In general, the highest rates were reported by youth in the smallest community (Edwards, 1994: 8). This finding is contradicted, however, by Osgood and Chambers (2000) (see material later in this section).

Regardless of community size, high and moderate drug involvement is much more prevalent for youth who are affiliated with gangs. Although the number of gang-involved youth in the rural community is small, almost all of those youth who are either in a gang or hanging around with a gang are drug-involved (i.e., high and moderate drug involvement), even more so than their urban counterparts (Edwards, 1994: 8).

The links among gang involvement, drug use, and violence hold true regardless of community size. Living in a rural area may provide some protection from some forms of violence—for example, robbery—perhaps because the perpetrator in a robbery is more likely to be a stranger to the victim, and rural areas have fewer strangers. Living in a rural area does not, however, isolate youths from violence (Edwards, 1994: 12).

A study by Evans et al. (1999) of rural gangs in Nevada found that, when compared to their urban counterparts, rural youths were about equally as likely to admit belonging to a gang. At the same time, the rural youths were significantly less likely to have friends in gangs and to be threatened by gangs. Also, those in rural areas had less concern for their personal safety from the threat of gang violence. More importantly, perhaps, is the finding that most of the rural gang members grew up in their own communities, rather than being gang transplants from urban areas.

Several differences were found when rural and urban gang members were compared by gender. Among the females, urban gang members reported being threatened by other gang members and were composed of minorities significantly more than their rural counterparts. Rural female gang members reported significantly more friends that were in a gang. This could be due to the smaller social environments of rural settings, where gang-involved rural youth are more likely to know one another. As with the females, the rural male gang members reported significantly more friends in a gang and were less likely to be composed of minorities. They also reported more physical fighting and were more likely to live with both of their biological parents compared to their urban counterparts (Evans et al., 1999: 278).

Although results indicate that rural students are becoming increasingly vulnerable to the spread of gang culture, we still know little of how gang-tolerant or favorable attitudes among youth lead to developmentally hard-core gang membership or gang-infested, violent communities (Evans et al., 1999: 280).

While not exclusively focusing on gangs, a study testing social disorganization theory examined rates of juvenile violence in 264 nonmetropolitan areas of the country (Osgood and Chambers, 2000). The researchers found that violence was far less likely to occur in counties with the smallest juvenile populations. This suggests that, while there may be gangs in rural areas, such gangs may not resemble their urban counterparts as far as violence is concerned.

SUMMARY

The only agreement about what constitutes a gang, its members, and its activities is disagreement. Often, this discord is linked to location (e.g., type of neighborhood), age (e.g., adolescent versus young adult), and purpose (e.g., play group, organized crime, drugs). We have found that one of the major problems associated with the study of gangs is the identification of gang-related crime. Each jurisdiction seems to create its own criteria to determine whether a crime is gang related.

This chapter addressed the issue of *how many*. How many gangs are currently active in America? How many individuals are in these groups? There are a significant number of projections and estimates related to these questions.

Frequently, the argument is raised that because gangs come and go, it is difficult to determine accurately the number of gangs and gang members. It is our contention, however, that in order to determine how many gangs or gang members are active in America, we must first determine what exactly a gang or gang member is.

Finally, the subject of gang migration was explored, especially the suggestion that there is a sort of franchising method working here. Contrary to popular belief, gang members who move do so for the same general reasons that young people in general move—with their families. The growth of rural gangs has often been linked to the migration issue. Most rural gangs are homegrown, with little evidence of huge cases of franchising. Contrary to popular opinion, gangs remain a mostly urban phenomenon.

NOTES

1. National Gang Center: http://www.nationalgangcenter.gov/About/FAQ#q1.
2. Retrieved from http://www.nationalgangcenter.gov/Survey-Analysis/Defining-Gangs.
3. On a fairly new Web site, a group called The "East Coast Gang Investigators Association" defines a gang this way: "A group or association of three or more persons who may have a common identifying sign, symbol, or name and who individually or collectively engage in, or have engaged in, criminal activity which creates an atmosphere of fear and intimidation." http://www.ecgia.org/faq.asp. Retrieved on February 13, 2010.
4. http://www.nationalgangcenter.gov/Survey-Analysis/Defining-Gangs. Retrieved on March 12, 2010.
5. Retrieved from http://www.lapdonline.org/get_informed/content_basic_view/24435.
6. National Gang Center, "National Youth Gang Survey Analysis." Retrieved from http://www.nationalgangcenter.gov/Survey-Analysis/Gang-Related-Offenses#gangrelated.
7. We will explore the subject of gangs and crime in Chapter 4.

2

What Do Gangs and Gang Members Look Like?

A WORD OF CAUTION

It is uncertain whether an accurate profile of the typical gang and typical gang member can be presented. As was noted in the first chapter, there is little consensus among professionals of what a gang is and how a gang member is identified. Therefore, the present chapter should be read with this caveat in mind. Also, this chapter should *not* be interpreted as a tool to identify who is or who is not a gang member or what group is or is not a gang. Unfortunately, any such typology presented is going to be used by some (e.g., law enforcement) merely to control or even eliminate the groups and individuals so categorized. We do not want to contribute to this kind of control.

AN OVERVIEW OF GANG STRUCTURES

It is important to emphasize that there is not only a variety of *gangs* but also a variety of gang *members*. Gangs and gang members come in many forms and can be differentiated by several criteria, including age, race, or ethnicity (all Hispanic or all black, Asian, or mixed), gender composition (e.g., all male, all female, or mixed), setting (e.g., street, prison, or motorcycle), type of activity (e.g., social, delinquent/criminal, or violent), purpose of the gang activity (e.g., defensive versus aggressive, turf defense), degree of criminality (e.g., minor or serious), level of organization (e.g., simple or corporate, vertical or horizontal), and group function (e.g., instrumental or cultural) (Spergel, 1990: 60).

Most common gangs are rather loosely structured groups who "come together for periods of weeks, months, or as long as a year, but then disintegrate" (Klein and Maxson, 1989: 209–210). The most recent research has reiterated these conclusions, with Klein and Maxson (2006: 163) concluding that in the overwhelming majority of street gangs "leadership is ephemeral, turnover is often high, and cohesiveness only moderate." Further, many gangs "are more a loose collection of cliques or networks than a single, coherent whole." The same conclusions have been reached by other researchers (e.g., Decker, Katz, and Webb, 2008; Decker and Curry, 2000, 2002).

One of the most common types is the traditional, vertical, or area, gang. Characterized by a common territory, these gangs are **age-graded,** typically all male, often with female auxiliary groups, and mostly ethnic minorities (usually black and Hispanic but often Asian). Another variation is the horizontally organized group. These usually include divisions that cut across different neighborhoods and include youths in different age brackets. Many have spread across cities, states, and even countries. Often they are referred to as super-gangs and nations. Examples of these horizontal alliances include the Crips and Bloods (who started in Los Angeles) and the People and Folk (who started in Illinois). It should be emphasized that these large groupings often consist of gangs with very little in common with one another other than their name. To a gang member, what is most important is the particular set or neighborhood of origin. As a gang member told Bing, "See, 'Crip' doesn't mean nothin' to a membership. Like 'I'm a Crip, you're a Crip—so what? What set are you from? What neighborhood are you from? What street do you live on? I may live on Sixty-Ninth, he may live on Seventieth'" (Bing, 1991: 244).

An example of the vertical type of gang organization could be found in New York City in the early 1960s. The age groupings there included Tots (11 to 13 years of age), Juniors (13 to 15 years of age), Tims (15 to 17 years of age), and Seniors (17 and older). But these age groupings are not consistently the same from one point in time to another, as evidenced in New York City. For example, by the 1970s, the most common groupings included the Baby Spades (9 to 12 years of age), the Young Spades (12 to 15 years of age), and the Black Spades (16 to 30 years of age). In Philadelphia, the following age groupings were recently identified: Bottom-Level Midgets (12 to 14 years), Middle-Level Young Boys (14 to 17 years), and Upper-Level Old Heads (18 to 23 years). Members of these gangs usually can be divided into such categories as hard-core, fringe, cliques, and wannabes, with the latter grouping reserved for the very young, usually 12 or younger (Spergel, 1990: 55–56).

Regarding **gang leadership,** gangs "present a shifting, elusive target, permeable and elastic, and thus inherently resistant to outside intervention. It presents not a cohesive force but, rather, a sponge-like resilience" (Klein and Maxson, 1989: 211). Gang leadership tends to shift over time "with changes in age, gang activity levels, and availability of members (owing to marriage, work, or incarceration, for example)" (Klein, 1995: 62). The stereotype of the gang leader is someone who is tough, with a long criminal history and strong influence over the members. To the contrary, the typical leader does not maintain influence over a long period of time. Leadership tends to be very situational, and contrary to the belief that to eliminate the gang all you need to do is "cut off the head" and the rest will die off, someone else will generally take his place. This is because gang leadership is, as with most groups, a function of the group rather than individuals (Klein, 1995: 63). In other words, gang leadership fluctuates. It is normally undertaken by youths who are the most stable members, who possess good verbal skills, who are cool under pressure, and who are generally looked up to by other members. But, like life in general, it constantly changes. All of the preceding points have continued to be reinforced by the most recent research (for a good review, see Klein and Maxson, 2006; see also Decker, 2007; Decker, Katz, and Webb, 2008).

One of the most important distinguishing features of gangs continues to be that of territory, or **turf.** However, this must be interpreted with caution, for there have been many changes in recent years (even since the first edition of this book). Klein's most recent research notes that most cities that he surveyed reported the existence of "single or autonomous gangs." These are gangs that occupy smaller territories than was once the pattern, such as single blocks, a school, a "project," and so on. They tend to have shorter histories and fewer ties to traditional neighborhoods, or barrios, than the more traditional gangs. Many of the more recent gangs are what Klein describes as "geographically connected gangs." These are more like branches of the same gang but located in a neighboring territory or totally separate areas and sharing an affiliation, but not the residence (Klein, 1995: 102). No doubt part of the declining importance of turf is because of the growing sophistication of some gangs and their greater involvement in criminal activities (which means that the actual physical location becomes less important) and the ubiquitous use of the automobile.

Among the more traditional gangs (those who have been in existence for the longest time), the notion of turf or neighborhood remains of critical importance. In many areas, especially in Los Angeles, the term *gang* is often synonymous with *barrio* (sometimes spelled *varrio*) or *neighborhood* (Moore, 1978, 1991). The notion of turf centers around two important ideas—identification and control—with control being the most important. At least three types of turf rights can be noted. The first is that of *basic ownership rights,* in which a gang "owns" a particular area and attempts to control practically everything that occurs there. The second is *occupancy rights,* which means merely that different gangs share an area or tolerate one another's use. The third is *enterprise monopoly,* in which a certain gang is said to have control of certain criminal activities occurring within a specified area (Spergel, 1990: 71–72). It should be noted that turf is less important to gangs now, with the exception of Hispanic gangs, who still define themselves as protectors of their own neighborhoods (Vigil, 2007, 2010).

Age seems to be one of the most important characteristics of gangs because the clique is one of the basic building blocks of gangs. "Gangs are loosely organized into small age/friendship cohorts or cliques. These groupings are called 'klikas' in cholo gangs and 'sets' in black gangs, where they are somewhat less rigidly age-bound" (Reiner, 1992: 38–39).

ILLUSTRATIONS OF GANG TYPOLOGIES

When it comes to categorizing gangs, two methods are generally used: types of *gangs* and types of gang *members*. The distinction is important because not only are there a variety of gangs in existence (more than a dozen specific "gang types" have been identified), but there are about an equal variety of gang members. This idea is consistent with a point made in the first chapter, namely, that there are a variety of adolescent groups existing at any one time. In fact, the adolescent subculture itself is famous for the infinite variety of groupings.[1] In the next two sections, we will review some of the more common typologies, starting with gang typologies and ending with gang member typologies.

For many years, researchers have attempted to typologize gangs, starting with Thrasher in the 1920s (1927) through the research by Cohen and others in the 1950s and 1960s (Cohen, 1955; Cloward and Ohlin, 1960; Spergel, 1964). Most typologies have been based upon behavioral rather than structural aspects of gangs. Structural typologies included those noted by Klein (1971), such as the aforementioned age-graded subgroups or cliques, horizontal and vertical gangs, and so on. As Klein and Maxson have noted, the more recent typologies (noted later in this section) are not articulated well with each other because they all used different methods to arrive at their conclusions.

The following typologies should be considered as *ideal types,* to use Max Weber's famous concept.[2] Ideal types are used frequently by researchers in all fields of study to help make sense and organize a vast array of research findings. Ideal types do not necessarily reflect reality in that there are no pure types of anything (e.g., no person is a pure authoritarian personality type, and there is no such thing as pure capitalism or democracy) since human life and nature itself can fit perfectly into any types. These ideal types merely serve as ways to clarify one's investigation. What normally happens is that the researcher suggests that a phenomenon tends to fit into one or another type more often than not. For example, using democracy as an ideal type, a researcher can compare different political systems in terms of the extent to which they are democratic, realizing that there will be no perfect democracy. Or, to use gangs as an example, there may not be a pure hard-core gang member or a pure "predatory" gang, but a particular individual may come close to the pure type of hard-core but also have certain characteristics that could place him into the category of peripheral member. Likewise with a predatory gang in that a gang may have some characteristics of this type of gang and yet have some characteristics of a territorial gang as well, but it is more predatory than territorial.

Types of Gangs[3]

Types of gangs can be based on many different criteria. The most commonly used criteria seem to be certain behavioral characteristics, especially deviant and/or criminal behavior but also certain nondeviant or traditional group behaviors. Research in six different cities by three different researchers uncovered the following major types of gangs:

- *Hedonistic/social gangs*—With only moderate drug use and offending, these gangs are involved mainly in using drugs (getting high) and having a good time, with little involvement in crime, especially violent crime.

- *Party gangs*—A group with relatively high use and sales of drugs, but with only one major form of delinquency (vandalism).

- *Instrumental gangs*—Those whose main criminal activity is that of committing property crimes (most members use drugs and alcohol but seldom engage in the selling of drugs).

- *Predatory gangs*—Those heavily involved in serious crimes (e.g., robberies and muggings) and seriously involved in the abuse of addictive drugs such as crack cocaine; some with much lower involvement in drug use and drug sales than the party gang. Some may engage in the selling of drugs, although not in any organized fashion.

- *Scavenger gangs*—Loosely organized groups of youths who are described as "urban survivors," preying on the weak in the inner cities, engaging in rather petty crimes but sometimes violence, often just for fun. The members have no greater bond than their impulsiveness and the need to belong. They have no goals and are low achievers, often illiterate, with poor school performance.

- *Serious delinquent gangs*—With heavy involvement in both serious and minor crimes, but with much lower involvement in drug use and drug sales than the party gang.

- *Territorial gangs*—Those gangs associated with a specific area or *turf* and who, as a result, get involved in conflicts with other gangs over their respective turfs.

- *Organized/corporate gangs*—Heavy involvement in all kinds of crime and heavy use and sales of drugs; they may resemble major corporations, with separate divisions handling sales, marketing, discipline, and so on. Discipline is strict, and promotion is based on merit.

- *Drug gangs*—These gangs are smaller than other gangs, much more cohesive, focused on the drug business, and have strong centralized leadership, with market-defined roles.[4]

Many prefer to describe most of these gangs (except for drug gangs) by using the term *street gang* (Klein, 1995: 132). This is a rather all-inclusive term that refers to most of the preceding typologies.

More recently, Klein and Maxson (2006: 176–178) provided yet another typology of gangs. They distinguish among five types as follows:

- *Traditional*—Large gangs (100+) that have existed for 20 years or more; many subgroups (e.g., O.G.s, Seniors, Juniors, Midgets, etc.); territorial; long age range (from 9 or 10 to 30s).

- *Nontraditional*—Like the traditional but has not existed for as long; medium size (50–100); subgroups; territorial.

- *Compressed*—Small size (up to 50 members); small age range (less than 10 years); no subgroups; in existence less than 10 years.

- *Collective*—Like the compressed but larger and with an age range of 10 or more years; no subgroups; in existence for 10–15 years.

- *Specialty*—Focus is on a few offenses and becomes known by their specialty; usually small and in existence fewer than 10 years; territorial; narrow age range.

Types of Gang Members

The most common method of distinguishing among different gang members is to base it on the degree of attachment to, and involvement in, the gang. It might be useful to think of a continuum from complete involvement and attachment to very little attachment and involvement. To use an analogy, think of attachment to and involvement in a local church. At one extreme are those who rarely attend church services or any church-related activity, except perhaps for weddings, Easter Sunday, or Christmas Eve services. Otherwise, you may seldom see them at church. Next on the continuum are those who attend Sunday services perhaps once a month on the average and on occasion will participate in a church-related activity (a picnic, a lecture, or a play sponsored by the church). Then there may be another type who attends church services almost every Sunday but rarely participates in church-related activities. Closer to the other end of the continuum are those who attend church every Sunday, get involved in many church-related activities during the course of the year, and who have several friends that are also similarly involved in the church (but they have many friends not involved in the church). At the extreme end of the continuum are those who not only attend every Sunday but also may serve as elected officials of the church (may even teach Sunday school) and participate in church-related activities almost on a daily basis. However, in addition to these characteristics, they literally have no friends who are not connected with the church in some way. In short, the church is, for all practical purposes, their life. They have no identity apart from their roles within the church.

Gang members may be similarly classified. The following gang member types have been discovered by researchers:[5]

- *Regulars/hard-core*—Those who are strongly attached to the gang, participate regularly, and have few interests outside of the gang (in other words, the gang is practically their whole life). Vigil describes these individuals as having "had a more problematic early life. They became street oriented earlier. They became gang members sooner, and they participated in the destructive patterns over a longer period of time." These individuals also lacked a consistent male adult in their lives, which made the streets even more attractive as they began to emulate other gang members. For these persons, getting into the gang was seen as a rite of passage. They also began experimenting with drugs and engaging in street fighting at a much earlier age than other kinds of members (Vigil, 1988: 66, 81–85). The *hard-core,* or simply *core,* members of the gang tend to be a smaller number of members who are the most influential and active members of a particular gang. These are the members of the inner clique who "interact frequently and relate easily to each other." They may be "those few who need and thrive on the totality of the gang's activity." These individuals "may make key decisions, set standards, and provide support and sanction for the action of the leaders. They are the key recruiters" (Spergel, 1990: 64–65). The hard-core are "the most gang-bound in terms of lifestyle. For these young men, life outside pretty much ceases to exist. They have few friends outside the gang and recognize no authority beyond its existence" (Reiner, 1992: 42).

- *Peripheral* (also known as *associates*)—These individuals have a strong attachment to the gang but participate less often than the regulars because they have other interests outside the gang. This person is "just as intense as the regulars once he is a member of a gang, but his level of commitment is mediated less by a problematic early life and more by a life-turning event (for example, incarceration), which causes him to contemplate pursuing another lifestyle" (Vigil, 1988: 66). The *associates* are sometimes called *fringe* members. They may belong to the gang but are not considered part of the hard-core group. Using the fraternity analogy, these may be like those students who only recently completed "hell week" and were formally initiated into the fraternity.

- *Temporary*—These are only marginally committed, join the gang at a later age than the regulars and peripherals, and remain in the gang only a short period of time. This individual "is neither as intense nor as committed as the others and primarily associates with the gang during a certain phase of his development" (Vigil, 1988: 66).

- *Situational* members—These are very marginally attached and join the gang only for certain activities (avoiding the more violent activities whenever possible).

- *At risk*—These are not really gang members but are *pre-gang* youths who do not as yet belong to a gang but have shown some interest. They live in neighborhoods where gangs exist. They often fantasize about being members and also might have friends or relatives who belong to the gang and whom they admire. Often they begin experimenting with certain gang attire and/or language. This may begin as early as the second grade (Reiner, 1992: 40–44).

- *Wannabe*—This is a term gangs themselves often use to describe "recruits" who are usually in their preteen years and know and admire gang members. They are perhaps one notch above the at-risk youths in terms of commitment and involvement. They have already begun to emulate gang members in terms of dress, gang values, and so on. Such young people are mentally ready to join a gang and perhaps just need an invitation or opportunity to prove themselves in some way. They may be called *Peewees* or *Baby Homies*. An analogy may be made to freshmen college students aspiring to join fraternities. One researcher called this type an *emulator* (Taylor, 1990a).

- *Veteranos/O.G.s*—This group usually consists of men in their 20s or 30s (or even much older) who still participate in gang activities (sometimes referred to as *gang banging*). There are two major subtypes within this category. *Veteranos* have traditionally been regarded as a type of elder statesmen who are somewhat retired but still command respect. The title is more honorable within Chicano gangs than black gangs. O.G.s are *original gangsters* and are those referred to in black gangs as men who have earned respect through a combination of longevity and achievement. Often they are expected to teach younger members the ways of the gang and/or to straighten out younger members causing trouble within the gang. Sometimes they are literally the founding member or members of the gang.

- *Auxiliary*—These are members who hold limited responsibility within a gang. This is a very common role for female members. These individuals do not participate in all gang activities. A related type is the *adjunct* member, who is a permanent part-time member by choice, often because of holding down a regular job (Taylor, 1990a).

Some gangs have formed unions to achieve certain uniform objectives (especially self-protection) and have thus formed so-called super-gangs. Still others have simply been described as gang nations or gang sets. Examples of the latter often include the famous (or infamous) Bloods and Crips that began in the Los Angeles area. However, the most popular grouping of gangs into gang nations or super-gangs are known as People and Folk, originating in Chicago in the 1970s.

NATONAL-LEVEL GANGS

People and Folk

Until the late 1970s, there were several alliances, mostly informal, and many rivalries among the gangs of Chicago. However, a turning point came when informal alliances and rivalries came together to form two major super-gangs (or nations), known as **People** and **Folk,** at the end of the decade (Bobrowski, 1988: 30; Hagedorn, 1998: 67).

This formation began within the Illinois prison system when the mostly white Simon City Royals agreed to provide drugs to inmates who belonged to the Black Disciples in exchange for protection; this group came to be called Folk (represented in graffiti by a six-pointed star). Shortly thereafter, and in response to this alliance, the Latin Kings aligned themselves with the Vice Lords and the El Rukns and became known as the People (represented by a five-pointed star).

According to the National Gang Threat Assessment report (2009), the People Nation and Folk Nation consist of the following major gangs:[6]

People Nation Sets

Latin Kings	Bishops
Vice Lords	Gaylords
Spanish Lords	Latin Counts
El Rukns	Kents
Black P-Stones	Mickey Cobras

Folk Nation Sets

Black Gangster Disciples	Latin Disciples
Black Disciples	Maniac Latin Disciples
Gangster Disciples	Simon City Royals
Imperial Gangsters	Spanish Gangster Disciples
La Raza	Two Sixers
Spanish Cobras	International Posse
Latin Eagles	

Presently, there are more than 30 Chicago gangs that identify themselves as Folk, including Spanish Cobras, Latin Disciples, Imperial Gangsters, Latin Lovers, Braziers, Insane Popes, and Simon City Royals. There are at least as many gangs identified as People, including Latin Kings, Vice Lords, Future Stones, Gaylords, Latin Lords, Bishops, and War Lords. Also, there are numerous factions within each major super-gang (the Latin Kings have more than 13 different factions, and the Black Disciples and Vice Lords reportedly have about 20), while an estimated 19 gangs are independent (Bobrowski, 1988: 34). In terms of the actual number of gang members, these numbers are almost equally divided between People and Folk. In terms of racial distinctions, about 70 percent of Folks are Hispanic, while about 19 percent are black, and 10 percent are white. Among the People gangs, around 56 percent are Hispanic, 22 percent are black, and 19 percent are white.[7]

These two nations have apparently spread into different parts of the country. One report noted that the Folk Nation has a chapter in the city of Atlanta. They are apparently well organized, as they even provide a somewhat formal application for membership that asks potential members about their qualifications, asking them, among other questions, "What can you do for our organization that we can't do for ourselves?" According to the Atlanta police, out of a total of approximately 1,500 gang members, 1,000 are members of the Folk Nation. The police also report that numerous gangs are in the Atlanta area vying for territory. A police official is quoted as saying that "The South is wide open. It's brand new virgin territory. It's like taking Coca Cola to Russia, like a great new market. There's more accessibility and it's easier to recruit" (Speir, 1994: 7–9).

Hybrid Gangs

A recent concept has been introduced that may explain some newer type of gang formation. Known as **hybrid gangs,** these groups tend to have the following nontraditional features (Starbuck, Howell, and Lindquist, 2001): 1) they may or may not have an allegiance to a traditional gang color. In fact, much of the hybrid gang graffiti in the United States is a composite of multiple gangs with conflicting symbols. For example, Crip gang graffiti painted in red (the color used by the rival Blood gang) would be unheard of in California but has occurred elsewhere in the hybrid gang culture; 2) the gangs may adopt the symbols of large gangs in more than one city. For example, a locally based gang named after the Los Angeles Bloods may also use symbols from the Chicago People Nation, such as five-pointed stars and downward-pointed pitchforks; 3) gang members may change their affiliation from one gang to another; 4) it is not uncommon for a gang member to claim multiple affiliations, sometimes involving rival gangs. For example, in Kansas City, Missouri, police may encounter an admitted Blood gang member who is also known in the St. Louis, Missouri, area as a member of the Black Gangster Disciples gang; 5) existing gangs may change their names or suddenly merge with other gangs to form new ones; 6) although many gangs continue to be based on race/ethnicity, many of them are increasingly diverse in both race/ethnicity and gender. Seemingly strange associations may form, such as between skinheads, whose members frequently espouse racist rhetoric, and Crips, whose members are predominantly black; 7) gang members who relocate from California to the Midwest may align themselves with a local gang that has no ties to their original gang; 8) some members of rival gangs from Chicago or Los Angeles frequently cooperate in criminal activity in other parts of the country.

Youth in these sorts of gangs often "cut and paste" bits of Hollywood's media images and big-city gang lore into new local versions of nationally known gangs with which they may claim affiliation. Other hybrids are homegrown and consider themselves to be distinct entities with no alliance to groups such as the Bloods/Crips or Folk/People. Because these independent gangs can be the most difficult to classify, they frequently pose the biggest problems for local law enforcement (Starbuck et al., 2001: 5).

ETHNIC AND RACIAL TYPOLOGIES OF GANGS

Another common method of characterizing gangs is by ethnicity or race. The most utilized is the distinction among black, Chicano/Hispanic, and Asian gangs. This section explores some of the differences among these types of gangs. It should be noted at the outset that there may be much more ethnic heterogeneity today than in the past, although for the most part ethnic homogeneity is still the norm

(Klein and Maxson, 2006; National Gang Center, 2010). In some cities, there are a few gangs that are ethnically mixed; usually these are white plus Hispanic.

Chicano Gangs

Greene and Pranis (2007: 38) report that currently Latinos accounted for almost half (49%) of the estimated youth gang population in 2004, "even though they make up just 17 percent of 12- to 24-year-olds in the United States." It goes without saying that there is a serious flaw in the way law enforcement defines and counts "gangs."

Chicano gangs consist of Puerto Ricans, Central Americans, and Mexican Americans (Valdez, 2003). Puerto Rican gangs are concentrated mostly in the midwestern and northeastern part of the country, areas that have been particularly hard hit economically during the past several decades because of deindustrialization. Consequently, these gangs have turned increasingly to drug dealing and other illegal economic activities. In contrast, Central American gangs have been spared the devastation of deindustrialization and are more concerned with territory or "turf" and much less organized. Mexican American gangs are also concerned with territory but more importantly are concerned with family and traditions passed through many generations. Yet they too have been hard hit by the recent economic problems (Valdez, 2003: 17).

Chicano gangs in Southern California have perhaps the longest history of any gang in America; they have been in existence for more than 50 years. It has recently been estimated that there are more than 500 Chicano gangs in Los Angeles County, constituting about half of all gangs in this area.[8] They appear to be more geographically distributed throughout the region than other gangs, in all likelihood because of so much geographic mobility during the past several decades throughout Southern California. These gangs emerged from a preexisting Mexican culture in the Southwest. Their growth was fueled by a huge Mexican migration to places like El Paso, Albuquerque, and Los Angeles. They brought with them a kind of "pre-gang" culture that was transmitted by youth known as the "pachuchos," named after field hands from a Mexican city of that name (quoted in Klein, 1995: 22). These pachuchos grew up with other Mexican youths in the streets of urban areas (Vigil, 2002). Currently, they are found predominantly in the San Fernando Valley, San Gabriel Valley, Long Beach (and other beach communities), and in south central Los Angeles (Vigil, 2002, 2010; Klein and Maxson, 2006).

Family and community ties are most apparent among these gangs, which may often be traced back several generations. The individual gang member is expected to assist other gang members in times of need and to uphold the neighborhood gang name. Those who join these gangs are among the most marginal youths within this area. There are economic, social, cultural, psychological, and ecological stressors in the barrios. Most barrio residents suffer from at least one of these, but those who suffer from more than one of these stressors constitute those who are victims of *multiple marginality,* and these are the most likely to become Chicano gang members (Vigil, 1988, 2010).

Most of these gangs do not identify with specific colors the way Bloods and Crips do. However, some colors favored include black, white, browns, and tans ("Dickie" pants and Pendleton shirts are favored). Some use red bandannas, which stand for northern California Hispanic gang allegiance, signified by the notation *Norte 14* (from the California prison subculture); others wear a blue bandanna, which stands for Southern California Hispanic gang allegiance, signified by the notation *Sur 13* (from the California prison subculture) (Vigil, 2002; Valdez, 2003).

Several other differences have been noted. Unlike the gangs Thrasher studied in the 1920s, Chicano gangs (particularly in Los Angeles) are not a transitory phenomenon, because they are based in neighborhoods where Chicanos have lived for several generations. These gangs are Mexican American, meaning that they have not assimilated into mainstream American society as did the Europeans. Also, some Chicano gang members remain affiliated with their gang well into middle age (Moore, Vigil, and Garcia, 1983; Vigil, 2002, 2010).

Chicano gangs can be divided into two distinctive categories: institutionalized and noninstitutionalized. Two of the more important institutionalized extensions of membership are intertwined with the very nature of the Chicano traditions of kinship and alliance. The first is self-explanatory; the second occurs when others come to the rescue or exhibit loyalty and an interest in friendship with gang members. Other categories include an expansion of boundaries (absorbing small nearby barrios) and the formation of branches (occurring when gang members move into new neighborhoods). Noninstitutionalized categories include family motives for moving out of the barrio, ecological displacement (making way for public improvements), and factional struggles within a particular group or *klika/clique* (Moore, et al., 1983; Klein and Maxson, 2006; Vigil, 2002, 2010).

Moore's study, which concentrated on three major Chicano gangs in the Los Angeles area, reaffirms some of these findings and reinforces some traditional sociological theories, especially those of Thrasher. She observes that "the age-graded gang is one among many barrio structures in which boys play a role; it may be the only structure in which they play a reasonably autonomous role" (Moore, 1978: 52). She also notes that the Chicano subculture is more than just machismo, as there is a sense of belongingness, a feeling of family. "The isolated individual is a rarity in the barrios…. It is no accident that gang members refer to each other as homeboys. Even in adulthood, when two strangers discover that they are homies, they open up to each other as if they were, in fact, members of the same family" (Moore, 1978: 53).

Two of the oldest gangs in East Los Angeles are White Fence and El Hoyo Maravilla. As described by Moore, the White Fence gang began during the 1930s as a sports group for young men and was associated with a local church. The younger brothers and cousins of these boys started the gang after most of the original group got drafted into World War II. By the time they began (1944), there were already several established gangs in the area. White Fence was considered more violent than other gangs, probably because they challenged older boys from other gangs (such as the *veteranos* from El Hoyo) (Moore, 1993: 25–34; see also Moore, 1991).

In the Maravilla neighborhood, there were several gangs, mostly named after streets (Arizona Maravilla, Kern Maravilla, Ford Maravilla, and others). The first clique of El Hoyo was actively involved in sports and often competed with White Fence neighborhood kids. The early El Hoyo gang was more like a modern gang than the original White Fence group. These were the zoot suiters, or pachucos, and their neighborhood was one that was invaded by white servicemen during the Zoot Suit riots in 1943. As in the original White Fence group, the war separated them and left many younger kids to carry on the tradition (Moore, 1991: 27). More recent research has documented the existence of at least 19 different offshoots of this gang, including Arizona Maravilla, Fisher Street Locos Maravilla, Lote Maravilla, and Pomeroy Maravilla, among others (Moore, 1991).

By the late 1940s, the gangs became permanent fixtures, more or less institutionalized agents of socialization in the form of peer groups. An age-graded structure developed as the older members matured and broke with the gang, and younger kids formed their own cliques. For example, the White Fence Monsters gang, which was formed in 1946, was followed by a gang called the Cherries in 1947, which in turn was followed by the Tinies in 1949. Later cliques went by such names as the Santos, Locos (and the girls' branch of Las Locas), Jokers, and Cyclones. The *veteranos* in El Hoyo Maravilla were formed in 1933 and were followed by the Cherries, Jive Hounds, Lil Cherries, Cutdowns, Midgets, Lil Spiders, and Winitos (Moore, 1991: 31). These cliques and their respective formation dates are denoted in Table 2.1.

Their counterparts in Chicago emerged during the early part of the twentieth century with the start of northern migration of Mexicans in search of work (Valdez, 2003, 2007). By the 1940s, gangs began to emerge in the barrios. Especially notable were the Latin Disciples and the Almighty Latin King and Queen Nation. Eventually, the Latin Disciples and the Latin Kings would become part of the largest Chicago gangs in the 1990s, part of the People and Folk Nation (Howell and Moore, 2010). Similar patterns of Chicago gang growth have been noted in other large cities, most notably New York (Greene and Pranis, 2007).

Asian Gangs

Reading recent surveys gives us the impression that Asian gangs are almost an afterthought. For instance, the most recent National Gang Survey gives a breakdown of gangs by race/ethnicity and shows that as of 2006, Latinos constituted 49.5 percent, blacks were 35.2 percent of the total, whites were 8.5 percent, and "all other" were 6.8 percent. Asians were not mentioned by name in this source (National Gang Center, 2011). However, reading certain recent Web sites, one might conclude that Asian gangs are taking over, especially in Southern California (reminiscent of the hysteria over Japanese Americans during World War II). For instance, on a Web site called "Terror in our Streets," there was a story called "Asian Gangs Latest Threat Sweeping the Neighborhood" (Gonzales, 2004). Another Web site contained an article called "A Rising Threat from the Far East."[9] Both based their stories on anecdotal evidence, which is typical of the news media. However, according to the California Department of Justice, in

T A B L E 2.1   Names and Beginning and Ending Dates for Gang Cliques in East Los Angeles

Hoyo Maravilla	Dates	White Fence	Dates
"Originals"	1935–1945	*"Originals"	1944–1952
Cherries	1939–1950	*Honeydrippers (girls)	
Vamps[a] (girls)	?	*Monsters	1946–1954
Jive Hounds	1943–1953	*Lil White Fence (girls)	
Lil Cherries	1945–1954	Cherries	1947–1960
*Cutdowns	1946–1956	WF Cherries (girls)	
*Jr. Vamps (girls)		Tinies	1949–1961
*[Big] Midgets	1950–1955	Spiders	1953–1960
Lil Cutdowns	1951–1969	Chonas (girls)	
Las Cutdowns (girls)		Midgets	1957–1966
Penguins	1954–1960	Peewees	1960–?
Lil Midgets	1958–1965	Los Termites	1964–1970
*Las Monas (girls)[b]		Lil Cherries	1964–?
Dukes	1958–1966	*Monstros	1968–?
Tinies	1958–1963	*Monstras (girls)	1970
Santos	1960–1963	*Lil Termites	1972–1981
Peewees	1961–?	*Lil Termites (girls)	
*Locos	1964–1968	Locos	1973–1981
*Las Locas (girls)		Lil Locas (girls)	
*Chicos	1967–?	Lil Spiders	1974–1981
*Las Chicas (girls)		Winitos	1974–1976
Ganzos	1969–?		
*Las Ganzas (girls)			
Jokers	1970–?		
Cyclones	1973–?		
Las Cyclonas (girls)			

*Indicates cliques chosen for sampling.
[a]Most of the Vamps lived in El Hoyo Maravilla, which counts them as one of their cliques, even though they were not formally attached either to the neighborhood or to any boys clique.
[b]Las Monas was an independent girls clique, contemporaneous with but not an auxiliary of the Lil Midgets, the Dukes, and the Tinies. At the outset of our study, we believed that it was attached to the [Big] Midgets.
SOURCE: Moore, 1991: 28.

2005 there were an estimated 839 Asian gang members in 32 gangs; the total population breakdown at that time was 246 Hispanic gangs (21,790 members), about 158 Crip and Blood gangs (15,000 members), 16 stoner gangs (537 members), and 11 white gangs (600 members). Asian gangs constituted just 2 percent of all gangs and gang members.[10] Thus, contrary to news media hype, Asian gangs are hardly a "rising threat."

Many Asians have struggled to "adapt to a new country and social environment and challenges of making a living, whether they are immigrants themselves, U.S.-born children of immigrants, or whose families have been in the U.S. for several generations." They have often felt "overwhelmed, frustrated, depressed, and even angry as they try to adjust to living in the U.S." Quite often, they lack the skills or English fluency to find decent jobs. This has been especially true for Vietnamese, Cambodian, and Laotian immigrants, who are more often poor compared to other Asians (Le, 2011).

Asians immigrating into the United States enter gang life and often pursue the same kind of activities that they pursued in their native countries. In general, the crimes they commit are much more often property offenses than other types of gangs. What little violence they commit is mostly of the instrumental variety (e.g., threats, retaliation, warnings, and paybacks) (Klein, 1995: 110; Pih et al., 2008). Police find that Asian gangs are difficult to penetrate because they are extremely secretive. Also, most members are clean-cut and polite and act with respect toward law enforcement. They are highly entrepreneurial in nature (Reiner, 1992: 46; Pih et al., 2008). Asian gangs generally victimize people from their own culture; therefore, the victims usually fail to report the crimes to the police, a fact reinforced by the latest Department of Justice report on victimization, which notes that Asians are the least likely to report being a victim (Truman, 2011).

In the United States, there are several varieties of gangs of Asian descent. Among the most common Asian gangs are Chinese, Japanese, Korean, Vietnamese, Cambodians (including Mien, Hmong, and Eurasian), Pacific Islanders (most notably the Filipinos, but also Samoan, Tongan, Fijian, Guamanian, and Hawaiian), Haitian, Cuban, Jamaican, Guatemalan, Salvadoran, Taiwanese, and Honduran. There are probably some other examples, but these are cited most often (Klein, 1995: 106–109; Pih et al., 2008; Klein and Maxson, 2006). Space does not permit a complete discussion of each of these varieties, so we will concentrate on the most common: Chinese, Vietnamese, and Filipino.

Vietnamese Gangs. In recent years, these gangs have been widely publicized in the press, especially in Southern California towns such as Garden Grove, San Gabriel, and Westminster. They are also found in such cities as Atlanta, Houston, New Orleans, St. Petersburg, Washington, Boston, New York, Denver, St. Louis, Chicago, and Vancouver, British Columbia (Klein, 1995: 109–110; Nguyen, 2002; Long and Ricaud, 1997; Yarborough, 2005; Van Do, 2002).

Due partially to the American desire to provide a safe haven to South Vietnamese who wanted to emigrate as the Vietnam War escalated, the U.S. immigration policy was changed. Subsequently, a large number of Asians entered the United States. Many were young, unskilled, and unable to speak English. Many were the sons and daughters born to American soldiers who had brief relationships with Vietnamese women while serving during the Vietnam War. Many came to America but never knew who their real father was. Often called "Children of the Dust," they came in search of greater opportunities, but many were denied this opportunity (see, e.g. Nguyen, 2002; Long and Ricaud, 1997; Yarborough, 2005; Van Do, 2002). As Long and Ricaud note, "Many children who were high achievers in Vietnam have failed here, and failure in school drives too many of these youngsters into gangs. Embarrassed, humiliated, lacking self-esteem and self-confidence, students on the edge of families begin cutting classes" (1997: 95).

Lam notes that Vietnamese gangs have become a permanent part of Southern California life, and although the first generation of gangs has died or been sent to prison, there is not a "very prominent Vietnamese and Asian American youth gang phenomenon that is more 'street'-socialized than their predecessors." These gangs "are not necessarily 'street' as traditionally defined, given that they have very different residential and settlement patterns than other racialized populations" (Lam, 2009: 13).

The ages of Vietnamese gang members range from mid- to late teens to the early 20s. They have been described as youths who are frustrated by their lack of success in both school and the community and their inability to acquire material goods. Also, many were picked on by neighboring Chicano gangs when they were growing up and thus began to form gangs as a method of protection (Lam, 2009: 14).[11] These gangs are unlike their black or Hispanic counterparts. They do not claim turf, nor do they adopt particular modes of dress and often do not have a gang name. They tend to be very secretive and loyal so that it is difficult to obtain good information about them. Fighting is infrequent, and drug dealing, wearing tattoos, and using hand signs are avoided, as attention would be drawn to their activities. They are organized very loosely, and membership changes constantly (Chin, 1990: 139; Goldstein, and Huff, 1993: 15–16; Vigil and Yun, 1996: 160: Kent and Felkenes, 1998). Unlike Chinese gangs, they have few ties to adult groups, although they often develop relationships with protection and extortion operations of the more established organized crime groups (Spergel, 1995: 139).

Money is the focal point within these gangs, for they have been extremely entrepreneurial, as have been most other Asian gangs. Their crimes include mostly auto theft, burglary, robbery, and extortion, and they travel rather extensively. They are very pragmatic in that they victimize other Vietnamese citizens because of this group's inability to understand and/or utilize the American legal system. (About half of the strong-arm robberies go unreported; Reiner, 1992: 48). Vigil and Yun note that many Vietnamese Americans "keep large amounts of cash and gold within their homes. Knowing this, the youth gangs will survey a residence and in small groups (usually four or five persons) will enter the home armed with handguns. Victims are beaten and coerced into revealing the location of their valuables" (1990: 157). Keeping valuables at home rather than in banks or other businesses is very common among many Asian families (Le, 2011). Many of these gangs have become very mobile when it comes to the crimes they commit, often traveling from city to city and sometimes going on nation-wide crime sprees (Spergel, 1995: 139).

The story of one Vietnamese gang member vividly illustrates the often tragic backgrounds they come from.[12] "Huc" was a product of the Vietnam War as he and his family fled the wartorn nation in an old, dilapidated boat that eventually capsized, resulting in the drowning of his mother (who was pregnant at the time), all of his siblings, and an aunt (a common story among the boat people). He and his father were lucky to survive. They were coming to America, where they had heard that the streets were paved with gold. They arrived poor and with little education. (In contrast, the first wave of Vietnamese refugees were much more educated and were thus better prepared to succeed in America.) It was not too long before Huc's relationship with his father became strained (his father was absent through most of Huc's childhood because he was imprisoned in one of the government's so-called reeducation camps). The streets of Southern California, where they eventually settled, were not, of course, paved with gold. Huc was placed several grades below his age because of his lack of English (a common experience for these youth). As a result, Huc's involvement in school activities was minimal, and he eventually lost interest and dropped out. His relationship with his father became more strained, and his belief in the American dream turned rather cynical. The gang became a way out, a way of fitting in. Huc eventually ran away and spent his nights with his new family, the gang, "as they traveled from city to city on the West Coast." In due course, the gang gave him a "shortcut to his American dream" and a "new value system," which was "emblazoned on his thigh in the form of a tattoo that depicts four T's, representing the Vietnamese words for love, prison, crime, and money" (Vigil and Yun, 1996: 144–145).

Chinese Gangs.   Chinese gangs have strong roots in China, Taiwan, and Hong Kong, tracing back to the famous tongs and triads. They are the most likely to have connections to organized crime groups (Spergel, 1995: 139; Huang, 2007; Kim, n.d.). They can now be found in San Francisco, Los Angeles, Boston, Toronto, Vancouver (British Columbia), and New York City (Chin, 1990; Toy, 1992; Huang, 2007). In the 1960s and 1970s, most Chinese gang members were from Hong Kong. After the passage of the Immigration and Naturalization Act in 1965, thousands of Chinese Americans sent for family members, who started immigrating to the United States. Thus, a second generation of Chinese youths were either born in this country or brought here at an early age. As with other second-generation adolescents, many formed gangs, often simply to protect themselves from other students in local schools. Most of the youths who are recruited are vulnerable and are not doing well in school or have dropped out. Their English is usually very poor, and they have few job skills. Many who dropped out of school began hanging out on street corners (like so many other gang members), whereupon they began to be recruited by adult Tong groups (hiring them to run errands for gamblers and to provide protection for gambling places). Thus, unlike other groups, Chinese gangs already had an existing organized crime network to emulate or operate within (Reiner, 1992: 49; Spergel, 1995:

139–140; Kim, n.d.). Since the mid-1960s, gang members of new Chinese gangs have included not only Chinese immigrants but sometimes Vietnamese-born Chinese and both Korean and Taiwanese youths as well.

Between 80 and 90 percent of Chinese businessmen pay these gangs on a regular or occasional basis for protection. Four distinct types of extortion are common among Chinese gangs: monetary gain, symbolic (used as a display of power to indicate control of a territory), revenge, and instrumental (to intimidate the victim into backing down in certain business or personal conflicts) (Chin, 1990: 134, 142).

Several characteristics of Chinese gangs distinguish them from other gangs: 1) They are closely associated with powerful community organizations; 2) they tend to invest in legitimate businesses and spend a lot of their time in these pursuits; 3) many have national and even international networks; 4) they have been heavily influenced by Chinese secret societies; 5) they are involved in serious forms of mostly property crimes and control large amounts of money; 6) monetary profit is their main goal; and 7) they victimize most local businesses (Chin, 1990: 137).

Chinese gangs are different from black and Hispanic gangs in that 1) they are not based on youth fads or illicit drug use and are closely related to their community's social and economic life; 2) they do not operate in deteriorated, poor neighborhoods; and 3) they are embedded in the legendary Triad subculture and so are able to claim legitimacy in the Chinese community (Chin, 1990: 137). (Triad secret societies date back several centuries in China.) Chinese gangs are composed predominantly of males whose ages range from 13 to 37, with an average age of 22. Each gang has between 20 and 50 hard-core members. Gangs tend to have a hierarchical structure nearly parallel to that of the Mafia or other organized crime groups. Many gang members are used as muscle by older gang members and, in this sense, "may be seen as the first rung on the ladder of Chinese organized crime" (Reiner, 1992: 48–49). Most gangs have two or more cliques constantly at battle with each other, so the inter-gang conflicts are more threatening (gang members are most often killed by other members of the same group) than attacks from external sources such as rival gangs or the police (Chin, 1990). There are some exceptions, however. A study of Chinese gangs in Vancouver, British Columbia, found that they engaged in a lot of street fighting over such things as status and turf (Joe and Robinson, 1980).

Still another recent study reveals a great deal of violence, heroin trafficking, and even human smuggling (Chin, 1996). This particular study focused on Chinatown in New York City and was based on interviews with 62 males who were either current or former gang members. They represented 10 different Chinese gangs in New York City. Most were between the ages of 16 and 21. The majority were born in another country, most commonly in either Hong Kong or China, although 35 percent were born in the United States. Their ethnicity was mostly Cantonese. It was reported that only a slight majority were ever arrested (52%) and that only 15 percent were ever in prison. Most reported that their gangs were only somewhat or not at all organized, that most of their gangs had rules, and that almost all (98%) had their own territory. They also reported that most had a division of labor within the gang and that a clear majority (three-fourths) of the gangs were involved in legitimate businesses. These gang members were also heavily involved in criminal activities. (More will be said about the criminal activities of these gang members in Chapter 4, which covers the subject of gangs and crime.)

Filipino Gangs.   Unfortunately, there has not been a lot of research on these gangs in recent years. The research that has been done has found that these neighborhood gangs are similar in structure and operation to Hispanic gangs and so affiliate largely with the latter in the western United States. They are located mostly in Los Angeles and San Francisco but also in cities in Alaska, Washington, and Nevada (e.g., Las Vegas). The largest gangs include the Santanas, Taboos, and Temple Street Gang. Their crimes include burglaries, muggings, drug sales, and assaults (Jackson and McBride, 1992: 50).

A mid-1990s study in Hawaii found that although Filipinos constitute only 14 percent of the population of that state, they made up almost half (47%) of the gang members in Oahu (Chesney-Lind et al., 1994). In a much later study, Guerrero et al. (2010) found strong correlations between the risk factors of acculturative stress, low cultural identification, and adverse peer influences and delinquency. These risk factors were in turn correlated with absent or ineffective adults in their lives, along with socioeconomic hardships and low self-esteem.

Filipino gangs began in the 1940s in the California prison system. However, many came from the Philippines in the 1970s and early 1980s during the height of the political unrest in that country. As the children of these immigrants began to attend school, they met with cultural confrontations and street gangs. In defense, they began to form their own gangs with other members of their families. These family groupings became cliques or sets within each gang (Los Angeles County, 1992: 47–49). The Santanas remain the largest Filipino gang in the Los Angeles area. This gang emerged in the 1970s as mostly a car club and more generally a group of male friends (known as "barkada"). They were located in an area known as the Temple-Rampart district, which is near the Historic "Filipinotown" in the central Los Angeles area (Alsaybar 1999).

Black Gangs

A study of Chicago's black street gangs by Perkins raises the issue of institutional racism as a major role in the development and perpetuation of these gangs. He also suggests that black youths are drawn into gangs to develop a sense of belonging, identity, power, security, and discipline, consistent with Maslow's theory (1987: 54–55).

The two major gang types in most cities are the Bloods and the Crips. Crips and Bloods have so influenced black street gangs in Los Angeles that the only distinction between the thousands of gang members is the blue and the red colors (Lavigne, 1993: 54–55; Alonzo, 2004). The most recent information is that in Los Angeles, Crips outnumber Bloods by about a 2:1 ratio. There are more than 100 different Crip gangs within the city of Los Angeles (one large division is between the "east coast" and "west coast" divided by the Harbor Freeway);

there are several groups named after Hoover Street in south central Los Angeles and several groupings of Gangster Crips. Then there are several in outlying areas of Los Angeles County, such as Long Beach and Compton. As for Bloods, there are about 30 within the city of Los Angeles, plus about 15 in Compton, and several in Pasadena, Covina, and Inglewood.[13]

In recent years, black gangs have struggled for economic survival and as a result have engaged in a great deal of drug trafficking (Kontos, Brotherton, and Barrios, 2002; Alonzo, 2004; Coughlin and Venkatesh, 2003). One of the most famous black gangs is the Black Gangster Disciples of Chicago. This group is one of the few that fit the stereotypic "organized gang" stereotype (Klein and Maxson, 2006: 154; for a discussion of gang involvement in organized drug trafficking, see Chapter 4).

White Gangs

It was once believed that white youths constituted about 10 percent of the nation's gang population (Reiner, 1992). However, recent research has contradicted this estimate. For instance, according to two different sources, about one-fourth of school-aged adolescents who are in gangs are white; 31 percent are black; 25 percent are Hispanic; and the rest are of other racial and ethnic groups (Esbensen and Lynskey, 2001; Howell, Egley, and Gleason, 2002).

In Los Angeles, white gangs began to become noticeable in the 1970s, and they emerged partly in response to "the growing encroachment of black families in south Los Angeles" (Decker, Gemert, and Pyrooz, 2009). As of 2005, there were an estimated 11 white gangs with 600 members, plus an additional 16 stoner gangs with 537 members in Los Angeles.[14]

Usually, white youth gangs express their delinquent behavior in different ways from those of most other street gangs. White youths typically join gangs of other ethnic groups, such as Hispanic or multiracial groups. Some are involved in the skinhead movement, identified as a militant racist organization. This organization provides a family link, much the same as with other gangs. A closer look at skinheads follows.

Skinheads

Skinheads have been described by some as "the kiddie corps of the neo-Nazi movement."[15] Youths have belonged to skinhead organizations since the early 1980s. However, skinhead groups are not all avowed racists; they can be divided into both racist and nonracist subgroupings. The racist skinheads advocate white supremacy, but the nonracist skinheads have a multiracial membership. They are rivals and often engage in violent confrontations. These groups are scattered, with erratic membership, although in some areas they claim territory and are classified as street gangs (Los Angeles County, 1992: 33). One example of a nonracist skinhead gang is a group known as SHARPs (Skinheads Against Racial Prejudice) or SARs (Skinheads Against Racism) (Wooden, 1995: 131). A variation is the kind of group known as a separatist group. These youths consider themselves to be "survivalists, concerned only with their own personal welfare and survival in the likelihood of a nuclear holocaust or natural disaster." These groups do not care too much about what is going on around them and try to avoid overt racial violence (Wooden, 1995: 136).

A group similar to the racist skinheads is known as political skinheads. These are youths who tend to take orders from such groups as WAR (White Aryan Resistance) or the Aryan Brotherhood. Perhaps the most avowedly racist gangs, and very critical of the U.S. government, these groups claim that minorities are given preferential treatment over whites. These skinheads are common in most prisons and frequently join forces with the White Aryan Brotherhood or the Ku Klux Klan (KKK) (Wooden, 1995: 136).

Skinhead gangs in the United States have their roots in a similar movement in England during the late 1950s. Those youths, known as Teddy Boys, were working-class males who wore distinctive Edwardian coats and tight pants and were viewed by British society "as threatening to everything the traditional family stood for." Some described them as folk devils. However, by the 1960s, the Teddy Boys had evolved into a more moderate group, sometimes referred to as "mods" because they wore a type of flashy clothing similar to that worn by young blacks (Wooden, 1995: 132).

However, according to Wooden, the original skinheads were actually black Jamaican immigrants to England who were called the Rude Boys. Their close-shaven heads and music style were eventually adopted by white working-class youths in Britain. While not avowedly racist, these skinheads adopted a very conservative, working-class view of the world. By 1972, with police harassment and political pressures, the British skinhead movement diminished, only to be replaced with the emergence of punks as the new form of skinheads. These groups were even more flamboyant than the original skinheads, sporting boots, jeans, and suspenders and adding the swastika as a prominent tattoo (Wooden, 1995: 133).

The skinhead movement in the Southern California area began in the late 1970s. These early groups were not just kids hanging out in local malls, for they soon began to develop a collective identity around shared interests that included various dress styles, such as Doctor Martin (steel-toed) boots, blue jeans, military flight jackets, short-cropped hair, T-shirts, Ben Shermans (similar to polo shirts), and specialized slang language. Additionally, they not only engaged in "garden variety" delinquent activities but also attended music shows, dances, and partying. Race emerged somewhat later as they began to develop close ties with both domestic and international adult white supremacist organizations. Although they held a variety of views on social issues, one of the most important was the perception that white youth were victimized by several outside social forces (e.g., minority street gangs, affirmative action programs, etc.) (Simi, 2003).

Other groups in Southern California played a part in the formation of the skinheads. The most important were the punks. So-called "punk rock" provided a subcultural foundation for the development of skinheads. In fact, most of the original skinhead groups came directly from the punk scene. Other groups included surfers, skaters, bikers, stoners, and peckerwoods. All of these groups were white youth subcultures. But the punks were the most important connection.

Punks can be viewed as a sort of rejection of left-wing political movements and represented a result of the anxiety of a rapidly changing world that tended to leave out the white working class. The shaved heads of many of these individuals was a strong statement to the "hippies"—a sort of "in your face" protest. Much of the punk subculture evolved into a more aggressive attitude, often expressed through random violence. The punk rock music reflected this aggressiveness, with very loud and hard music tones (Simi, 2003). Skinhead music is as important to these youths as rap is to black youths. This music is radical and often reflects the racial and political attitudes of the skinheads (Los Angeles County, 1992: 39).

Eventually, skinheads began to construct a racist ideology that included, in part, neo-Nazism. Some of the early skinhead gang members became involved with Nazism when they were punks and long before they shaved their heads and became skinheads. Furthermore, some of the surfers, such as those living in La Jolla (a very upscale town just north of San Diego) were sort of "Nazi punks" (Simi, 2003).

The first skinhead groups in Los Angeles modeled themselves after British skinheads. The music was an important component, with music bands such as Sham 69, Skrewdriver, and The Four Skins. They were not very organized at first, and many groups dissolved quickly. Eventually they became very aggressive groups with shared interests, which was pivotal in their development. The swastika tattoo was very significant as a symbol of what they stood for. These groups resembled other gangs in that they identified with specific "turfs." So, for instance, among the earlier skinheads were the Huntington Beach Skins, Chino Hills Skins, South Bay Skins, Norwalk Skins, and the like. Sometimes they marked parks as their turf and used graffiti "tags" to identify themselves (Simi, 2003).

The skinheads in Los Angeles were reacting to some very specific trends that they perceived as threatening to them and their class and especially their race. Increased immigration was one of the most important of these changes occurring in Southern California. Immigrants from the Middle East were especially hated and used as convenient scapegoats for the problems of working and middle-class whites. Not all of these gangs embraced a political stance, and others splintered and formed antiracist gangs. The most highly visible skinheads who espoused neo-Nazism drew the most attention and repression by the police. As a result, some skinhead gangs began to deemphasize overt political activities. Some of these shifted their attention to profit-making activities, not unlike many black gangs. Part of the reason for their less visible activism stems from increasing incarceration of their members. While law-enforcement efforts were sometimes successful in breaking up some of these gangs, putting them in prison tended to further solidify their commitment to skinhead values, mostly from their association with powerful and notorious prison gangs, such as the Aryan Brotherhood (AB), who were already a strong force within the California prison system before the skinheads emerged (Simi, 2003).

Eventually, two skinhead groups, the Nazi Lowriders (NLR) and Public Enemy Number One (PENI) developed a close relationship with the ABs. Thus, as has been noted by Klein (1995), attempts to break up skinhead gangs have helped to bring them closer together, especially within the prison system. Many skinheads have been recruited from within the California Youth Authority

(CYA), starting in the late 1970s and early 1980s. The CYA was the subject of many critical analyses finding extremely high rates of recidivism and numerous problems (Lerner, 1986), eventually resulting in the closure of most of their institutions (Shelden, 2012: Chapter 12).

The modern American skinheads usually wear a polo shirt or T-shirt, suspenders (often the color matches that of their shoelaces), pants (usually Dickies or Levi's) that are rolled up or tailored so that the entire boot is exposed, flight jackets (often with personalized graffiti), and boots (Wooden, 1995: 36–38). If a skinhead's boot has been scuffed on the steel tips, he is considered to be tough; the more scuffs on his boot, the tougher he is considered to be. If he is seen with his suspenders down, this means he is ready to fight. If he wears white laces in his boots, this means that he upholds white pride, while red laces stand for a more aggressive type of white power, and yellow laces signify hatred for the police or a claim that he has killed a police officer.

Skinhead graffiti is similar to that of other street gangs, with the addition of a racial and political orientation. Hand signs are given as well. Tattoos are common, appearing on the face, neck, and inside of the lips. American skinhead gangs have jumping-in initiations for new members, during which the recruit is attacked with fists by between 4 and 12 other members for a certain period of time (Los Angeles County, 1992: 39).

Skinheads are highly likely to engage in violent acts and to direct such acts against those they perceive as the most different or a threat to the white majority—homosexuals, racial and ethnic groups, and religious minorities. According to one source, during one period of time in the early 1980s, skinheads were responsible for 121 murders, 302 assaults, and 301 cross burnings (Wooden, 1995: 134).

Quite often some skinhead groups are characterized as kind of urban terrorists or hate groups. One report (Phillips, 2007) noted that "Skinheads and other hate crime groups terrorize members of targeted groups for intimidation and physical attacks. Racist skinheads—whose trademark appearance consists of shaved head, combat boots, bomber jacket, and neo-Nazi and white power tattoos—has [sic] become a fixture in American culture according to the Southern Poverty Law Center's (SPLC's) Intelligence Project." This report further noted that it had "tracked more than 844 cases of hate crimes that involved such hate groups as the Ku Klux Klan, neo-Nazi, Black Separatist, neo-Confederate, Racist Skinhead, and Christian Identity."

According to the Web site of the Southern Poverty Law Center:

> Most large police departments have bias-crime detectives, and many
> focus on skinheads as part of their gang enforcement strategies. Racist
> skinheads have also become a regular element in prisons and juvenile
> corrections facilities. The threat of a skinhead rally can lead whole
> communities to mobilize in opposition. The U.S. military has had to
> contend with racist skinheads in its ranks. Hate rock from racist skinhead
> bands has bled into the flow of rebellious teen music. And skinheads
> have taken their "boot parties" from the street to the Internet, targeting
> young people for recruitment into their supposed movement.[16]

Randy Blazek, the director of the SPLC, writes that "Racist skinheads are more a counterculture rather than a coherent political movement. Indeed, no segment of the white supremacist community is better characterized by disunity than the skinheads" (2011).

Stoners

Youths known as **stoners** are distinguishable from traditional street gangs by their secretiveness and the difficulty in identifying them. Often referred to as cults, they engage in many ritualistic activities. They are white suburban youths from a higher socioeconomic background than that of most other gangs. According to the California Youth Authority, stoner gangs constitute only about 5 percent of all gangs in the state and an even smaller percentage of all white youths in the correctional system (Wooden, 1995: 160–164).

A survey of 52 stoners in the CYA by Wooden found that the majority (62%) had an income level in their homes described as either "adequate" or "more than adequate." The majority (72%) scored above average on standard intelligence tests, and almost all had some work history prior to their most recent incarceration. Despite their high intelligence, none had graduated from high school, while two-thirds had been placed in special education classes. More than 40 percent had dropped out of high school. Most were described as either low achievers or nonachievers. Most had been heavily involved in the abuse of both alcohol and drugs, with the majority (69%) beginning their drug use before the age of 13. All except two were white. Their most common offense was burglary (70% were incarcerated for this offense). Most (81%) came from Southern California (Wooden, 1995: 164–165).

Stoner gangs are heavily involved in the use of various kinds of drugs (e.g., speed, LSD, rock cocaine, PCP) and have an especially high rate of toxic vapor use. They are almost always into heavy metal music. They generally do not have any organized leadership, are antiestablishment, and often dabble in Satanism, participating in animal sacrifice and ritual crimes (e.g., grave or church desecrations). These gangs are made up of lower- and middle-class white youths of junior and senior high school age who typically have a higher scholastic and economic status than found in other street gangs (Jackson and McBride, 1992: 42–45).

Stoners typically dress in red or black clothing, with athletic jersey tops portraying heavy metal music stars; metal-spiked wrist cuffs, collars, and belts; earrings; long hair; and tattoos. They often wear Satanic relics or sacrilegious effigies. Stoners use graffiti to mark territory, not necessarily geographic, but musical—to claim music groups or types of music (Jackson and McBride, 1992: 42–45).

Taggers

It seems that a form of graffiti known as **tagging** can be seen everywhere in urban and suburban areas. Such graffiti is not done to mark turf. Rather it is a way these mostly white middle-class youths call attention to themselves. Wooden, who has studied these groups extensively, quotes one 17-year-old

tagger: "It's addictive, once you get started. It's like a real bad habit." Wooden comments that:

> The addiction has drawn thousands of teenagers—who call themselves and their rivals "toys," "taggers," or "pieces"—to devote their time to "getting up" to attain "fame" by tagging poles, benches, utility boxes, signs, bridges, and freeway signs in the San Fernando Valley with graffiti. (Wooden, 1995: 115)

In the mid-1990s, police estimated that in Los Angeles County, there were at least 600 tagger crews, with about 30,000 youths. One crew, who call themselves NBT (Nothing But Trouble) claim a membership of 400 or more. These groups are also referred to by such names as graffiti bands, posses, pieces (so called because they believe that they draw masterpieces of art), housers (because they like to tag houses), and snapers. What specifically is tagged varies by age. Younger taggers (ages 10 to 15) usually tag around school grounds. Older youths will go after bigger targets, such as freeway overpasses or bridges, public transportation (especially buses), streetlight poles, and so on. "Less geographically bound to protecting a particular neighborhood turf than are ethnic and inner-city gangs, the taggers spread their marks far and wide on their nightly runs" (Wooden, 1995: 117–118).

Taggers, like regular street gangs, have their own slang. For example, a *toy* is someone who is a novice or amateur tagger, to "kill a wall" is to cover a wall completely with graffiti, a "bombing run" involves members of a crew going out and trying to mark as many places as possible with their "tag names" and the names of their crew, and sometimes crews will "slash" or cross out rival crews' or taggers' names, which is considered an insult or challenge (Wooden, 1995: 119).

To distinguish taggers from others, it is helpful to note three distinct types of graffiti vandalism and motivations (Barnard, 2002). *Hate crime graffiti* is motivated by personal or group prejudice, hatred, or racial or religious discrimination and is the rarest type. *Gang graffiti* is generally perpetrated by members of street gangs whose primary purpose is to make some sort of announcement (e.g., the superiority of a specific street gang in a specific neighborhood, the gang's turf). *Tagger graffiti* is committed by individuals and groups of kids for the sole purpose of establishing identity and recognition for themselves among their peers, generally other taggers. Putting their tag names up in highly visible areas or dangerous places increases the recognition, or "fame" value, of the effort (see Chapter 3 for more on graffiti).

Among some of the more common names, or monikers, of taggers in Southern California are AAA (Against All Authority), KNP (Knock Out Posse), ABC (Artist By Choice), ACK (Artistic Criminal Kings), DCP (Destroying City Property), and CMC (Creating Mass Confusion). Many of the names suggest a form of rebellion typical of many suburban white teenagers (Wooden, 1995: 120).

Tagger pseudonyms, or nicknames, can have up to six letters or numbers but usually have three. They usually adopt a name comprised of two or three words, for example, Clever Writing Kings, Phantom Causing Krime, or in the form of numbers, such as OPU, or Oxnard Piecers Unite, which is written as 678K–

corresponding to the letters OPU on the telephone. The K is for crew or "krew." A tagger can have two nicknames and may belong to several tagging crews at once. There may be several tag names and/or crew names put up by the taggers in the same incident (Barnard, 2002).

One explanation given for the rise of these tagger groups is that middle-class, suburban white youths have been influenced by the ethnic gangs of the inner cities and their "gangsta rap" and have tried to emulate them or even compete against them. However, taggers did not suddenly appear in the 1990s.

There was a crew in New York City in the early 1970s who called themselves Tough Artist Group (TAG). There were even a few tagger crews in Southern California in the 1980s (Wooden, 1995: 121). Wooden's interviews with tagger crews found that they typically do not have much of a formal organizational structure, that most members are not jumped in or do not otherwise go through a formal initiation process, that members often drift in and out of the groups, and that they often change their names (monikers) when they get tired of the old ones. Often these groups will "do battle" with each other, which is merely a contest to see who can have their name up the most often (1995: 124).

Although more and more are carrying weapons, mostly for protection from rival crews, for the most part tagging is a form of fun and play. Most do not choose to call what they do a crime, but merely an art form and a way to express themselves. They are insulted when others (e.g., the police) call their work graffiti. On the other hand, many become increasingly destructive in order to achieve some form of notoriety with other taggers. Many are merely trying to outperform their competitors (Wooden, 1995).

In many cities, police departments have created special task forces to deal with tagging and other forms of graffiti. In Santa Anna, California, a special task force was created in 1993. The Graffiti Task Force identified an estimated 500 different tagging crews in that city alone. The police in that city maintain that the situation has worsened and that "many of today's tagging crews are active in criminal gang activity." Moreover, they maintain that there is a fine line "between taggers and traditional criminal gangs." They state that "Today's tagger may be armed, may be involved in violent and/or drug related crimes, and may associate with or be a rival with gangs that have been long associated with serious criminal activity."[17] Similarly, the Los Angeles County Sheriff's Department has a special task force dealing with taggers and graffiti in general,[18] and Atlanta has also recently created a special task force on the problem (Wheatley, 2011). Also, the City of Los Angeles recently started a "tagger database" to keep tabs on tagging and graffiti in that city (Romero, 2011). After all these years and literally millions of dollars spent dealing with this problem, tagging seems to be just as common as ever.

Taggers have drawn the ire of many citizens and criminal justice officials. Some citizens, however, have taken matters into their own hands. In Los Angeles, during the winter of 1995, many people applauded the actions of a man named William Masters after he shot two graffiti taggers in the back. One of the youngsters died. There was conflicting testimony about whether the taggers really threatened Masters. A report containing an interview with Masters (*Chicago*

Tribune, February 16, 1995) revealed that he had been in this sort of trouble before and that he apparently was urging citizens to "take matters into their own hands" with the use of weapons. There was a time in this country when such behavior would have been considered an act of cowardice and/or murder. However, the Los Angeles district attorney stated that Masters had acted "reasonably." Among the most recent incidents was a report by the *Los Angeles Times* about a man who was shot by a tagger after he confronted a group of them outside his home (Blankstein, 2011).

Growing up in such communities can also lead to another characteristic, namely, a resignation to one's own death, even at an early age. In the final section of this chapter, we will explore a somewhat different perspective on gangs and gang members, a kind of typology that no one else has considered when studying gangs. We contend that gang members can be both victims and victimizers.

GANG MEMBERS AS VICTIMS AND VICTIMIZERS

Alex Kotlowitz (1991), in his penetrating book about youths growing up in a Chicago housing project, makes the following observation about 9-year-old Diante McClain, whose older brother, William, was fatally shot at Chicago's Henry Horner public-housing project. During the gunfire, Diante remained glued to a playground swing. His friend pleaded with him to take cover. Instead, Diante continued swinging, repeating over and over again, "I wanna die. I wanna die" (Kotlowitz, 1991: 54).

A 13-year-old gang member told one of the authors, "Man, I don't give a fuck if I die—it don't mean nothing" (Brown, and Shelden, 1994). What is often lacking in recent research on gangs is a close look at the immediate environment of gang youths as they are growing up, long before they even begin to think about joining a gang. This is not to say that researchers never address the social sources of gang delinquency, for indeed most have done this. However, what is the long-term impact of a very violent environment on young children? By a violent environment, we mean both inside and outside the home, where millions of children are exposed to an incredible amount of violence. Whether or not they are directly harmed in a physical sense is not the issue, although many are harmed in this manner. What needs to be looked at is how much indirect harm is done and how this exposure to violence tends to produce, over time, youths who not only act in aggressive ways but also are desensitized to violence.

The typical gang member has been a persistent victim of violence, both directly and indirectly. We also believe, as argued by Deborah Prothrow-Stith (1991) in her book *Deadly Consequences,* that many of these youths have suffered a form of posttraumatic stress syndrome.[19] The statements at the beginning of this section are typical of those who suffer this problem. The statement by the 13-year-old gang member reminds us of what many soldiers in Vietnam experienced. During this war, many combat soldiers used the phrase "It don't mean nothing" to reflect a self-defensive mechanism that reduced the impact of disappointment and dangerous situations. This expression was not an indication that the individual was resigning from life, nor did it mean that the individual was going to commit suicide. Rather, it was a response to a set of circumstances in which the individual felt little or no control over the outcome. Many would argue that such an attitude is irrational, and in a normal situation they would probably be correct. However, many Vietnam soldiers frequently found themselves, very much like many inner-city youths, in abnormal settings where such an outlook is very rational. There is still another analogy with Vietnam soldiers that applies to inner-city youths. Some of these veterans have been described as "tripwire" veterans. This term refers to those who suffered so much from the war that they developed a sort of siege mentality, or an "us versus them" outlook on life. They would go far into the woods in the Pacific Northwest, set up trip wires or booby traps, and hide from the world, fully armed and ready to defend themselves.

Alex Kotlowitz (quoted at the beginning of this section) has written extensively about some very young black males living in the Henry Horner projects in Chicago, in a book with the poignant title *There Are No Children Here*. He describes two youths, one a 12-year-old named Lafayette Walton, the other his 9-year-old brother Pharaoh, as living in a war zone. Lafayette "knows how to fling himself to the ground at the sound of gunfire. He knows how to crawl on his belly through the dirt to safety. He knows how to distinguish a .357 caliber Magnum from a .45 caliber revolver.... There is no one to protect Lafayette or his five siblings from violence. To live in the project is to live outside a protected circle. Inside the circle are middle-class people, middle-class neighborhoods, and middle-class institutions. Outside are the very poor, the very powerless.... During the summer, someone is shot, stabbed, or beaten every three days at Henry Horner Homes." This reality cannot be captured in mere words. Kotlowitz describes one occasion when 9-year-old Pharaoh found himself in the middle of a drug-gang gunfight while walking home from school (aren't children supposed to feel safe walking home from school?). One of the gang members had a submachine gun, and Pharaoh just barely escaped the gunfire, which occurred literally outside the door to his home. But, as Kotlowitz notes, "Other kinds of shootings, beatings, stabbings, and rapes occur more frequently. Weapons are ubiquitous, and family disputes often end in violence. Women as well as men resort to physical force, and project residents are often the victims of crime" (quoted in Prothrow-Stith, 1991: 66–67).

We believe that every Diante McClain, every Lafayette and Pharaoh Walton, and every other child growing up in such an environment are victims of crime. Yet with few exceptions, their names do not appear on police reports as crime victims, and the environment, such as that described by Kotlowitz, is not typically what people have in mind when they speak of crimes or criminals. (More often than not, the image of the victims is an innocent middle-class white person, and the perpetrator is a black gang member.) But the effects are the same as if they had been raped or assaulted.

Prothrow-Stith writes that many "mental health providers have begun to see signs of posttraumatic stress syndrome in crime victims, in the victims of terrorist attacks, and *in the children chronically exposed to violence in their homes and communities*"

(Prothrow-Stith, 1991: 68, emphasis added). We all know the data on the victimization of young black males: the most common cause of death is now homicide, and this group has the highest rate of victimization by violence in general. The fact that this same group has the highest rate of offending is also nothing new to us. But why do so many not see a connection here?

Given the violent environment most of these children grew up in, it should come as no surprise that one of the main reasons they give for joining a gang is for protection. And there is some research that is beginning to show the extent to which gang members have been victims—and we are not talking only of drive-by shootings. Studies have shown that gang members have had plenty of experience with violence while growing up. Such youths have seen and have been victimized by violence in their homes and in their communities.

Recent research has confirmed the close connection between being in a gang and being a victim of a crime. It is well understood that girls in gangs have experienced an enormous amount of victimization from males in general and male gang members in particular (see Miller, J., 2001, 2008). What is not commonly realized is that being in a gang (regardless of gender) is strongly correlated with being the victim of a crime, and actively being in a gang increases the likelihood of being the victim even further. A study by Decker (2007) proves this point. (Studies of delinquents in general have found that the delinquent lifestyle itself increases the risks of being the victim. See Laub and Sampson, 2006; Peterson, Taylor, and Esbensen, 2004).

The study by Decker was based upon interviews with detained juveniles (both males and females) in two counties in Arizona. What they found was that both current and former gang members were not only highly likely to have been a victim of a violent crime but also were the perpetrator of a violent crime. For instance, 75 percent of the current gang members and 62 percent of the former gang members had been threatened with a gun, while 74 percent and 57 percent, respectively, had been shot at (14% and 11%, respectively, had been shot); 82 percent of the current and 71 percent of the former gang members had been "jumped" or beaten up (Decker, 2007: 13). They also found strong correlations between violent offending and violent victimization (a study by Taylor, Freng, Esbensen, and Peterson, 2008, arrived at similar conclusions).

These experiences have shaped the attitudes of these young people toward perpetuating violence. Gang youths have accepted violence as the normal and appropriate way to resolve minor and major disputes. These youths have come to believe that there is no nonviolent method for dealing with daily disputes and other problems of life. Further, as our own research shows, these gangs reinforce what their environment has taught them by encouraging and even praising a gang member's willingness to engage in violence.

Data from 77 Detroit gang members were collected over an 18-month period by Brown through unstructured interviews and observations. Some of the interviews were conducted in the homes of the participants, on street corners, in alleyways, in the backseats of automobiles ("ride-arounds"—the equivalent of "ride-alongs" with police officers), and in crack houses. The concept of "interviews" is used rather loosely here because many of them were simply recordings of conversations in a variety of situations in which several participants were in-volved. Although there were specific research questions for this study, an unfet-tered interview schedule was used to prompt subjects to volunteer information on selected topics.

The majority of the gang members (74%) had been involved as a perpetrator in gang-related violence, and an almost equal number (70%) had been a victim in some kind of gang conflict. The gang members gave various reasons for why they engaged in the gang-related violence, and some of their responses indicated that many were not altogether willing participants. For example, two members said they faked involvement in the violence, while another four individuals said that they had protested but engaged in the violence anyway. Six members bluntly said that they did not want to be involved at all but did it anyway. The largest number (40%) said, in so many words, that they had no choice but to get involved in gang violence because they were members of the gang and felt that this was a basic requirement. Only 5 percent had actually initiated the violence. The remainder were admittedly willing participants in the violence.

It would be safe to say that just about every member of this gang had expe-rienced some form of victimization during his lifetime. For example, more than one-third (36%) had the experience of losing someone close to them from a ho-micide, and an almost equal proportion (35%) had actually seen someone dead following a gang-related homicide. However, when asked if they were ever con-cerned about being killed or seriously injured through violence, the vast majority (84%) said no. When asked why they were not concerned, they gave some fascinating reasons. About one-fifth (19.5%) said it "doesn't matter"; another 18 percent said, "I don't worry about it"; and 13 percent said, "Who cares?" About one-fourth (24.7%) responded that they "don't think about it," while an equal number said, "Someone will get even."[20]

Clearly gang members are not strangers to the world of violence. But to conclude, as many do, that they themselves are violent people is misleading. We wonder how others (including everyone who reads these pages) would re-spond if they grew up under similar conditions. When so many young men and women accept violence and accept even the inevitability of their own deaths from violence (some as young as 12 or 13), how can anyone say that they have not been victims and that this victimization is not a causal factor in their own violence against others?

We now turn to a consideration of the question "What do gang members *do* with their time"? The stereotype (constantly reinforced in the media, especially in full-length movies, and by "war stories" told by some police officials) is that all gangs do is engage in drive-by shootings, drug deals netting thousands of dollars, robberies, and other crimes. Actually, the life of a typical gang member is rather boring. Our favorite line is from a 30-year veteran of gang research, Malcolm Klein, who writes that during the years of research he and his colleagues have engaged in:

> We learned much about gang member life which, with the occasional
> exception of a boisterous meeting, a fight, an exciting rumor, is a very

dull life. For the most part, gang members do very little—sleep, get up late, hang around, brag a lot, eat again, drink, hang around some more. It's a boring life: the only thing that is equally boring is being a researcher watching gang members (Klein, 1995: 11).

However, they do commit crimes—a lot of crimes, compared to the average delinquent. (The reader should not jump to the conclusion that gangs commit the bulk of *all* crimes committed in your typical city. They just tend to commit more than nongang members their age.) Chapter 4 will be devoted to this subject.

SUMMARY

It is impossible to provide a profile of a gang member that is inclusive; it is equally difficult to identify a gang precisely. From scavenger to corporate gangs, with vertical to horizontal structures, any attempt to identify a typical gang falls short. Similarly, gang members cross gender, racial, and ethnic boundaries. There is evidence not only of the fairly traditional notion of gangs but also of a relatively new phenomenon—taggers—which further expands the parameters of a definition and further challenges the drive of social scientists to capture a universality of theme. Further, gangs in the United States are composed of youths from a wide variety of ethnic origins, including Chinese, Japanese, Vietnamese, Filipino, Korean, Mexican, and Cuban.

Viewing gang members as victims as well as victimizers was suggested. Although few researchers probe beyond the surface of this thesis, we are convinced that the overwhelming majority of those youths involved with gangs have indeed been victims themselves, both of specific persons who inhabit their social world and of the environment that surrounds them.

NOTES

1. There is plenty of literature on adolescent groups and subcultures. For a good review, see Schwendinger and Schwendinger (1985).
2. German-born Max Weber (1864–1920) was one of the earliest and most famous sociologists in history. Perhaps most famous for his work *The Protestant Ethic and the Spirit of Capitalism* (1958), he was a very prolific writer and wrote several books covering such wide-ranging subjects as law, economy, and religion. Within the academic world, he is also popular for developing the notion of the *ideal type*.
3. These typologies are taken from Huff (1989), Fagan (1989), and Taylor (1990a).
4. This definition comes from Klein (1995: 132).
5. Based mostly on Vigil (1988, 1990), Vigil and Long (1990), and Reiner (1992).

6. Information obtained from the following Web site: http://www.dc.state.fl.us/pub/gangs/sets.html.

7. Bobrowski (1988: 31). Although this reference may seem out of date, information provided at the 1999 National Youth Gang Symposium in Las Vegas (attended by the senior author) confirms that not too much has changed.

8. See this Web site for details: http://www.streetgangs.com/hispanic.

9. http://www.ipsn.org/asg08107.html.

10. Taken from the following Web site: http://www.laalmanac.com/crime/cr03v.htm.

11. Lam (2009: 17) states that he grew up in a neighborhood in San Gabriel (a suburb to the northeast of Los Angeles) where there were both Asian and Chicano gangs. He had friends who were part of a gang called Westside Asian Boyz (this stood for West San Gabriel Valley).

12. This story is told by Vigil and Yun (1996: 142–145).

13. http://www.streetgangs.com/crips; http://www.streetgangs.com/bloods.

14. http://www.laalmanac.com/crime/cr03v.htm.

15. Wooden (1995: 129). Other than Wooden's book cited here, there has been very little systematic research done on the topic of so-called white hate groups such as the skinheads. The bombing at Oklahoma City in the spring of 1995 apparently awakened many people to the existence of these kinds of groups, which may be more prevalent and dangerous than the typical minority gangs discussed in this text. A very comprehensive study was done by Pete Simi, a dissertation project at the University of Nevada–Las Vegas (the senior author was a member of his committee). Some of his findings will be reported in this section of the book (Simi, 2003).

16. Taken from this Web site: http://www.splcenter.org/get-informed/intelligence-files/ideology/racist-skinhead.

17. Taken from the following Web site: http://www.ci.santa-ana.ca.us/pd/documents/GraffitiTaskForce.pdf.

18. See this Web site: http://sheriff.lacounty.gov/wps/portal/lasd/graffiti/.

19. *The Diagnostic Statistical Manual* (DSM-IV) used by psychologists and therapists includes the following features associated with "posttraumatic stress syndrome": ambivalence, self-destructive and impulsive behaviors, attention seeking, needing to be around others, despair or hopelessness, feeling victimized, hostility, social withdrawal, feeling constantly threatened or unsafe, and impaired relationships with others.

20. In a special report on gangs called "Lives in Hazard" (about the filming of *American Me,* starring Edward James Olmos), Father Greg Boyle, a priest in East Los Angeles, said that every time he attended the funeral of a gang member, he cautioned other gang members that "this could happen to you," and there were two typical responses that he heard over and over again. One was "You gotta go sometime," and the other was "Why not?" A fascinating look at Boyle's work is shown in Fremon (2004). See also Boyle (2010).

3

The Gang Subculture

Youth gangs constitute a unique subculture in modern society. Like other subcultures, gangs are not only distinct from, but also part of, mainstream American culture. In other words, while they have much in common with the wider society, they also have their own unique set of values, norms, lifestyles, and beliefs. This chapter explores certain key aspects of the gang subculture, beginning with an examination of its origins (focusing especially on Chicano gangs in Los Angeles and a Puerto Rican gang in Chicago) and how youths growing up within these areas become, in effect, socialized into the gang subculture beginning at a rather early age.

THE NATURE AND ORIGINS OF AND
SOCIALIZATION INTO THE GANG SUBCULTURE

The Chicano gang subculture, often referred to as **cholos** (meaning marginalized), has evolved in Southern California during the past 50 years. The people that are part of it continue to renew it. As Vigil states, "Every few years a new cohort picks up the mantle of the barrio to defend it from intruders and to preserve and continue its street traditions" (2007: 56).[1] This subculture allows youths to adopt clothing styles, slang, hairstyles, and so on that set them apart from adults (Vigil and Long, 1990: 56). It is an adaptation to the poverty that surrounds the people in these barrios (see also Brotherton and Barrios, 2002). Vigil and Long describe it in these words:

> The Cholo subculture of Southern California was born in marginal
> urban areas where small houses exacerbated the crowded living
> conditions for large families. Poverty and discrimination in employment
> generated continual stress within these households. Few parks and
> playgrounds existed in such areas. The youths who created the Cholo
> subculture and those who have maintained it have been excluded by

distance and discrimination from adult-supervised park programs. They have fared poorly in school because of language and cultural differences and limited encouragement from school personnel who expect little of them and parents who often are preoccupied with day-to-day economic crises. It is no wonder that the streets have held such attraction for these youths (Vigil and Long, 1990: 60).

Vigil has added that "the process of multiple marginalization... continues to churn out youth from the most stressed immigrant families" (2007: 57). Moore has noted that success in the male Chicano world "is an idealized version of male strength and male responsibility that the people around them can rarely approach." Moreover:

> This success requires belonging to the group. Thus the gang represents a means to what is an expressive, rather than an instrumental, goal: the acting out of a male role of competence and of "being in command" of things. With the police quickly defining a separate and identifiable group of Chicano adolescents as a group and as dangerous, the gang will tend to at least partly redefine its competence in terms of increasing violence (1978: 53).

The barrio gang provides an arena for age- and gender-role formations and for role enactment and self-empowerment. For example, gang initiation rites and fighting and drinking behaviors allow young males to prove their manhood (machismo). The gang also includes a cholo front (described later in this section), a set of role prescriptions that include certain clothing styles, nicknames, tattoos, speech patterns, styles of walking, and so on. Deviations from these prescriptions exist among gang members, and the gang usually allows these deviations so that all members can be themselves without suffering any strong disapproval (Vigil and Long, 1990: 63–66).

The term *cholo*, according to Vigil (1988), reflects a unique "cultural transitional situation of Mexican Americans in the Southwestern United States; it is a process strongly affected by underclass forces and street requisites. This subculture has been developed over a period of several decades and includes a social structure and cultural value system with its own age-graded cohorts, institutions, norms and goals, and roles." This subculture "functions to socialize and enculturate barrio youth." It also involves many of the old customs of Mexican Americans, including the adolescent palomilla tradition that "includes many daring and bravado male patterns, and an anti-authority attitude" (1988: 3–7). An important part of this heritage is the age-graded clique, which Vigil and Long describe as "the nexus of the gang structure" (Vigil and Long, 1990: 92). Chicano barrio gangs consist of individuals of about the same age (hence age cohorts, or klikas), with each clique being separated by two or three years.

These gang members tend to be drawn disproportionately from the poorest households within a community. More specifically, they come from households with incomes lower than other inner-city, barrio families and with a much higher incidence of family stressors. In short, they are the poorest of the poor

(Vigil, 1988: 5; see also Moore, 1993; Vigil, 2010). Also, the lives of the street youths who make up the barrio gang reflect what Vigil calls a status of multiple marginality, which "derives from various interwoven situations and conditions that tend to act and react upon one another." Moreover, the lifestyle within that gang subculture is merely a response to the "pressures of street life and serves to give certain barrio youth a source of familial support, goals and directives, and sanctions and guides" (Vigil, 1988: 1–2).

In the urban setting of Los Angeles, most Mexican American families suffer economic problems revolving mainly around unemployment. As Vigil notes:

> Economic struggles taxed the parents' energies and affected the time they could spend monitoring their children's behavior, especially under crowded conditions and in large families. Disruptions in family life, moreover, often brought a high incidence of broken homes, where the mother had to take on the dual role of breadwinner and breadmaker. As a result, children spent more time outside the home, where there was more space to play and cavort. Here they began to learn the ways of the streets under the aegis of older children, with minimal adult supervision. The outcome was often early exposure to and induction into the gang. (1988: 36)

In this context, the supervision of children can be seen not merely as an independent variable that causes delinquency but also as a dependent variable. Thus the degree to which children are supervised may vary according to such factors as the number of children in the home, the number of rooms in the home, the type of residence the home is (e.g., government housing project versus single-family residence), the family income, and the presence of a father. In families experiencing multiple stresses, especially those with many children, there is a loosening of control networks. One result of this is that children spend more and more unsupervised time in the streets with other similarly situated youths. As Vigil notes, such "street peers, some slightly older and a few in their early teens (frequently including older siblings), become major agents of socialization. In fact, "street socialization of youths by one another and by slightly older youths becomes common" (Vigil, 2007: 1). Concomitantly, school behavior and performance also tend to suffer when parental guidance is lacking. School problems and the influence of street-based peer groups reinforce one another in a youth's increasingly marginal development; one can witness the same small group together in both schoolyards and the streets" (Vigil, 1988: 43).

Vigil defines "street socialization" as

> … an aspect of the barrio (and other ethnic conclaves) that undergirds established gangs and is conducted, to a considerable degree, away from home, school, and other traditional institutions. The most multiple marginal youths are often the most unsupervised and reside in crowded housing conditions where private space is limited. These youngsters are driven into the public space of the streets where peers and teenaged males, with whom they must contend, dominate. These peers and older males provide a new social network and models for new normative behavior,

values, and attitudes. They also make youngsters feel protected from other combative gang members who pose a possible threat (Vigil, 2010: 6).

So the street subculture becomes a significant and powerful presence in the lives of barrio youths. Similarly, in Chicago, the Diamonds studied by Padilla (1992) grew up in an area where gangs were an ever-present part of the terrain. In fact, the youths studied by Padilla "were unable to recall a day when the gang was not part of the neighborhood." One youth reported to Padilla that the gang was "a natural fixture of his neighborhood." The youth stated "Like the apartment buildings, the sidewalks, and trees of the neighborhood, we [the gangs] were all part of the same thing. You can't get the gangs out. They were there when I was a kid, and now we are here for the new kids" (1992: 61).

Most of the gang members Vigil interviewed in his study came from families with a history of stress. One of the main reasons these youths became involved in gang life was to get the kind of support they did not get at home. The absence of a father was especially significant (Vigil, 1988: 44). Prothrow-Stith (1991: 159) notes that the presence of fathers is of critical importance in determining the extent to which a child becomes involved in antisocial activities. Specifically, she notes that "children who spend a great deal of time with their fathers are more likely than other children to grow up to be highly empathetic adults. This is important because empathy is such a socially desirable trait: people who feel for others tend to be good parents, good citizens." Greg Boyle, a Jesuit Priest who has spent the better part of three decades in direct contact with gang members in East Los Angeles, says that virtually every male gang member has not had a father in his life. He described two "homies" as being "YA babies," having essentially grown up in Youth Authority facilities (referring to the California Youth Authority; Boyle, 2010: 77). Boyle says that the "great encounter with the 'father wound' is every homeboy's homework" (2010: 91).

Most of the gang members Vigil has studied began their association with the **street subculture**—that is, they began to hang out in the streets with their peers—between the ages of 7 and 9. The majority of these kids hung out with a brother, uncle, or other older male role model. These "early associations provided a sense of friendship and mutual trust that later proved useful in gang circles," especially in "backing up" friends (Vigil, 1988: 48). Vigil (2007: 57) also notes that "youth in such communities spend most of their time being street socialized and learning the values and norms of the street to survive and maintain their lives as street people." Another way of putting this is to say that when conventional institutions of social control "do not function as they should, street subcultures rise to fill the void" (Vigil, 2010: 7).

The general pattern Vigil found was that most gang members "become involved with street life early and additionally spend a great deal of time there, starting off as mischief and adventure seekers. Most of the street habits and customs are normal cohorting behavior, but other deviant activities are also learned. The experiences, good and bad, are bonding events that solidify trust and closer relations among the participants. Learning to back your friends is an early street lesson and, later, a core requirement for gang membership" (Vigil, 1988: 52–53).

Another thing they learn is a "defense of the barrio and protecting one's street friends," which becomes their *raison d'être* (Vigil, 2007: 58; 2010: 8). Not unlike what happens in the military, such personal qualities as sharing resources with others and backing up one's friends become prerequisites of gang membership and, incidentally, are learned early, before becoming a regular member (Vigil, 1988: 82).

The influence of peers in the lives of the gang members Vigil studied can be divided into three types: friendship, direct confrontation, and psychological disposition, with friendship being the most common. The most committed gang member (i.e., the hard-core) generally experienced peer pressure in the following way. First, friendships developed during elementary school years, and if the person remained in the same barrio, such friendships became more solidified during the adolescent years, at the time when the probability of gang involvement is highest. Direct peer pressure (e.g., helping a friend make a decision about joining a gang) was also common, but not as much as friendship. Psychological disposition, such as fear or the tendency toward loco (crazy) behavior, was rarely found among the gang members studied by Vigil (1988: 82).

It is important to note that each of the three types of gang members Vigil monitored (regular, periphery, and temporary) have much in common, such as growing up in barrios and adopting a **cholo front**—that is, the dress, demeanor, talk, and so on of gang members. It is relatively easy to look like a gang member by adopting this front. The regular gang members are distinguished by their earlier and more intense street experiences. What this does is to make them more embedded within the street subculture. Vigil describes what happens when **carnalismo,** or a strong support system among one's peers, "is sometimes the only human support system they have." Thus it is out of the question for such youths to avoid or reject this peer group, which is why so many have trouble leaving the gang. To them it might be like rejecting and leaving their own family (1988: 84).

In his study of the Diamonds in Chicago, Padilla noted that youths in this neighborhood grew up with the gang culture, learning many aspects of this culture from an early age. One important lesson they learned was that, as one gang member said, "Those guys got along so well…. They cared for each other. They were brothers…. They cared about each other more than a lot of other people who are not in gangs do" (Padilla, 1992: 62). In short, the attitude toward these gangs on the part of these youths as they were growing up became more and more positive as time passed. They slowly began to define gang members as straight, cool, and together—in short, "people to be admired and not resented." As one gang member put it, "The gang forces you to always be cool, together. You know, this is your homey, and brother, so take care of him, don't rat on him. That's what makes the whole thing cool, like a family. Everybody is a friend and brother. You treat people like a brother, like family" (1992: 67).

School became a problem for many second-generation Mexican Americans in Southern California (as well as for the majority of gang members in other parts of the country). A great deal of research has confirmed the importance of school and that one of the key variables distinguishing gang members from other youths from similar backgrounds is school failure (Curry and Decker, 1998; Padilla, 1992;

Shelden, 1995; Shelden, Snodgrass, and Snodgrass, 1992; Spergel, 1995: 118–120; Klein and Maxson, 2007; Vigil, 2007, 2010). A high incidence of dropping out and/or exclusion or expulsion from school resulted in "a situation in which significant numbers of barrio youngsters are socialized to a considerable degree in the streets" (Vigil, 1988: 37). The majority of the gang youths Vigil studied began to withdraw from school life by the third or fourth grade. For many, their "school careers began with skepticism, limited parental encouragement, and early exposure to street experiences that did little to promote self-discipline. It is clear that by the third or fourth grade they had not effectively adapted to the school situation" (1988: 57). Long before they officially dropped out (usually around age 16), they had been turned off by school. Some began to have problems as early as kindergarten, with the language barrier being the predominant cause. Many had experienced a great deal of prejudice and discrimination. Most of the problems at school began long before any involvement with a gang (1988: 61). The school experience "has often been a process of disengagement and dropping out" (Vigil, 2010: 46).[2] For most, the "transition to middle school means that youths must encounter and react to a new environment and group of students from other neighborhoods or barrios, setting in motion other events" (Vigil, 2010: 15). Most of these youths directly encounter conflicts with rival gangs for the first time in middle school, since rival gangs from other neighborhoods are thrown together (2010: 16). Vigil also has found that for many of these youths, school problems began in the elementary school years (Vigil, 2007: 59).

A typical experience in school is related by Padilla. He describes the gang members he studied as being labeled deviants and troublemakers by school officials, usually during their elementary school years (some as early as the fourth grade), long before they joined the gang. These youths responded (as if their labels were a self-fulfilling prophecy) "by joining with others so labeled and engaging in corresponding behavior." These youngsters began to develop various forms of oppositional behavior (fighting, cutting classes, and not doing homework). Many began to develop "a distinctive subculture within which they could examine and interpret what was going on in their lives and in school." In short, very early in their lives, these youths began to respond in ways that were almost identical to gang behavior. In effect, says Padilla, "they were undergoing early preparation for a later stage in their teenage years (during high school) when they would finally join the gang" (Padilla, 1992: 68–69). It is important to note that these particular youths experienced a form of public humiliation from some of their teachers (and some of their own peers). Such experiences were quite painful, and they quickly sought out others who were similarly branded. (It should be noted that part of their humiliation was from the various negative evaluations of their own Puerto Rican culture on the part of both teachers and peers.) "These youngsters began to recognize the common fate they shared with others like themselves" (Padilla, 1992: 69). A quote from one of Padilla's gang members summarizes this problem:

> If the teachers and everyone else thought that we were bad, we started
> to show that we were. So, we started doing a lot of bad things, like

hitting some kids and even talking back to the teacher and laughing at her. In a way, it was kind of fun, because here are these teachers thinking we were nuts and we would act nuts. That made them feel good (1992: 74).

Another response to these problems was that most concluded that it was better to simply stay out of school than be victimized by the constant verbal assaults by their teachers, so they began skipping school, most as early as elementary school. This became a regular experience, one in which they found pleasure. Padilla observes that "during their adolescent years the institution of education and its agents, the administrators and teachers, were already experienced as antagonistic elements in their socialization rather than as facilitators of their goals" (Padilla, 1992: 78).

As Padilla found with Puerto Rican youths, Vigil notes that there was a conflict between the Mexican American and white cultures that resulted in the marginalization of many youths. This conflict has created problems for Mexican American families, which in turn has meant that these families have lost some of their effectiveness as a social-control institution. As a result, schools and the police have taken over this function.

For gang members, a lack of strong attachment to the home and to the school has created an environment in which the gang provides answers. It is here, in the gang, where they associate and identify with similarly marginalized youths. Vigil comments that

> ... the gang has constituted a secondary "fringe" organization to resocialize members of the group to internalize and adhere to alternative norms and modes of behavior. Such gang patterns play a significant role in helping mainly troubled youth acquire a sense of importance, self-esteem, and self-identity. In short, rather than feeling neglected and remaining culturally and institutionally marginal, the gang members develop their own subcultural style to participate in public life, albeit a street one (Vigil, 1988: 63–64).

Padilla's gang members indicate that one of the turning points in their lives came during high school. Prior to this time, most of these youths were marginal members of the gang, engaged mostly in hanging out on the street corners or at school; **turning** (becoming regular and committed gang members) came during their early high school years. Throughout their elementary school years, most of the gang members referred to themselves as neutrons—that is, those with no affiliation to any of the many gangs within their neighborhood. However, this status was constantly being challenged by members of the various competing gangs. The punishment that they received from these gangs was aimed not so much to pressure them to turn but rather "to insure [sic] that they would remember the importance of remaining neutrons." Among gangs, there is constant fear that these neutrons might become informants for another gang or, even worse, be informants for the police (Padilla, 1992: 65). The decision to turn came rather informally without much thought. As one of Padilla's gang members put it:

> When I joined, like, four or five other guys that were like my neighbors, right there by the crib, they turned too, and we all joined at one time. Since we were friends we all decided to join—because we used to hang with the gang, but we were neutrons, and we just decided that we might as well become something since we hung out on the corner and gangbanged anyway, and so we just decided to go for it. We just did it just like that. We didn't think about it or think, "Wow, what is this?" We just slid into it (Padilla, 1992: 79).

While there are several specific reasons youths give for becoming gang members (discussed in the next section), the point here is that becoming a gang member is a gradual learning process that occurs over a considerable period of time as youngsters become embedded in the subculture of the gang. Over time, this street subculture has become an institutionalized or permanent fixture within many poor communities. The streets provide youths with networks of support that are not available to them in the family, the school, or the church.

Moore has noted that in cities where gangs have existed for a long time, they have become **quasi-institutionalized** (Moore, 1991: 6). In this sense, some gangs have functioned to help "order adolescents' lives. They have provided outlets for sociability, for courtship, and other normal adolescent activities." More importantly, the legitimate institutions of socialization, such as schools and families, have become less important in their lives, and street socialization has begun to compete with, and often replace, these institutions (1991: 6). She also found that, whereas in many communities gangs have disappeared as a result of the surrounding populations being integrated into the host culture (this happened with most of the gangs Thrasher studied), in many Chicano communities in Los Angeles constant immigration and the persistent problem of integrating the population into the mainstream mean that "the legitimate institutions remained comparatively marginal and the alternative structure—the gang—could become institutionalized" (1991: 6).

Vigil describes the gang subculture as a *lifeway* for youths, because early life experiences appear to be the most important determinants of whether someone will become a gang member. Also, the existence of age-graded cliques means that "there is a place for everyone, even the youngest member" because this "allows for gang regeneration with the inclusion of each new generation" (Vigil, 1988: 87).

About half of the gang members Vigil studied cited the important influence of a male relative who was, or had been, a gang member. This individual provided the youngster with an image or role model to emulate. Many wanted to follow in the footsteps of a relative. Brothers were especially important because they usually had lived under similar background circumstances and "it appeared that very little else was available to them except to follow suit" (Vigil, 1988: 89). Sometimes youngsters followed a family tradition. Vigil quotes one gang member who related that because his own father had been a Chino Sinner (the name of the gang), he would be too, because "it's been in the culture of my family for years. It's kind of like when white boys are brought up to play football or something else" (1988: 89).

The gang members Padilla studied gradually learned about different elements of the gang subculture throughout their youth. For example, many witnessed fights and learned that the way youths from different gangs settle their differences is by **throwing down** (fighting), especially if it was over their **hood** (neighborhood). As one member recalls, "To me the fights were started because some guy was in some neighborhood where he did not belong." What this youth learned was that the most important thing is his neighborhood. "Youngsters learned to accept the neighborhood as something that was very personal, for its identity and character were believed to originate directly from all of its residents" and that "maintaining neighborhood social harmony was an essential responsibility of gang members" (Padilla, 1992: 62–63).

As with any other subculture, the gang has many unique features that distinguish it from other groups. In many ways, the typical behavior of gang members is identical to that of adolescents in general, such as hanging out, joking (including playing the dozens, a game in which youths see who can come up with the best ways of putting down other youths), seeking out the opposite sex, drinking, using drugs, and, of course, partying. Gang members, not unlike other adolescent groups, want to distinguish themselves with their own styles of dress, a certain kind of walk, a way of talking, and so on.

JOINING A GANG

There appear to be two major ways of considering the process of joining a gang. On the one hand, as noted previously, most youths are informally socialized into the gang subculture from a very early age so that they do not so much join a gang as evolve into the gang naturally. Actually turning or being jumped is little more than a rite of passage. Vigil (2007: 58) states it this way:

> If you have lived in the barrio most of your life and grown up with the children your age, experienced attenuated parental and schooling influences, and undergone street socialization with them, then you are inclined to be informally "walked" into the gang. Some of the youth with such a background have mentioned that when they do have an initiation, it is usually a pro forma affair—a couple of punches by close friends and they are in.

Conversely, many researchers have found that there are often more formal mechanisms for joining the gang. In both cases, there is some degree of decision making by the youths along the way. No one suddenly wakes up on a Saturday morning in June and decides, "Hey, I think I'll join a gang!" Likewise, none of us suddenly decides to be a college professor, police officer, congressman, attorney, and so on. The point here is that it is a very complex process.

Jankowski (1990: 37–62) offers perhaps one of the most detailed discussions of the more formal processes whereby an individual is recruited by a gang and why some individuals choose to join and others choose not to join. Jankowski argues that kids join gangs for a variety of reasons, and a determining factor is whether the gang wants a particular youth as a member. Thus there are two rational decisions: one by the potential member and the other by the gang itself.

Reasons for Deciding to Join a Gang

Jankowski notes that because gangs already exist in virtually all low-income areas, the question facing a youth is not whether to start a gang but whether to join one. However, many of the reasons why youths join gangs are the same reasons why gangs are initiated. Jankowski (1990) lists six main reasons for joining a gang:

1. *Material reasons*—The most often-cited reason for joining a gang in Jankowski's study was that the youths believed that doing so would increase their chances of making money. They also believed that being in a gang meant not only a steady source of income but also assistance for their families in times of need. Thus the gang serves as both a bank and a social security system. One gang member stated that "they are there when you need them and they'll continue to be" (1990: 42). Further, in pursuing various illegal ventures within the context of gang membership, they would not have to work quite as hard to earn money, and moreover, the gang would provide a form of protection. In another study, Skolnick (1990: 14) noted that "it now seems that youths are increasingly interested in joining the gang for the economic benefits conferred by such membership," especially the economic benefits of dealing in drugs. One of Skolnick's respondents (a prison inmate at the time of the interview) used this analogy in explaining the benefits of joining a gang: "[Being a gang member] is just an easier way to get in [to drug dealing]. It's like if you going to get a job and you have a high school diploma. If you don't have one, you ain't goin' to get the job" (Skolnick, 1990: 16).

2. *Recreation*—The gang provides entertainment, not unlike a fraternity or a lodge (e.g., Elks, Masons, etc.). While in the gang, the individual has plenty of things to do, such as partying and meeting women. One member, talking about the gang he joined, said that "all the foxy ladies were going to their parties and hanging with them" (Jankowski, 1990: 43). The gang also provides a source of drugs and alcohol. It must be stressed, however, that most of the gangs frown on members getting hooked on drugs or alcohol because they could then become unreliable to the organization.

3. *A place of refuge and camouflage*—A gang provides its members with a cover and the protection of group identity. Some use the gang to hide from the police or others who may be after them. As one gang member put it, "It [the gang] gives me refuge until the heat goes away" (1990: 44).

4. *Physical protection*—Many dangers exist within low-income communities. There are predators everywhere. The gang provides some protection to its members. Those in a gang do not have to be on the alert constantly and therefore can devote more time to pursuing illegal ventures. Vigil notes that the element of fear is paramount in many cases. He quotes a 14-year-old Latino who said, "It was either get your ass kicked every day or join a gang

and get your ass kicked occasionally by rival gangs" (1988: 154). In a study of the recruitment into black gangs in Chicago, Johnstone (1983) found that one of the variables most significantly related to joining a gang was that of being the victim of a crime. In comparing active members, new recruits, and youths who were not connected in any way to gangs, Johnstone found that both recruits and active members were far more likely to have been victims. This fact supports the notion that protection is an important reason for joining a gang, especially because there is so much inter-gang rivalry. Protection was also cited in a study by Hochhaus and Sousa (1988). Several of the gang members studied by Padilla reported that while in high school, they encountered many rival gangs. Many of these rival gangs were in the same school primarily because of busing (see also Hagedorn, 1998, for a discussion of a similar phenomenon). Thus the school environment was tense. Members of different gangs were constantly harassing those who were neutrons, asking questions such as "Where do you live?" and "What you be?" or "What gang are you with?" Eventually many said, in effect, "If they are going to keep this up, I may as well turn!" (Padilla, 1992: 82).

5. *A time to resist*—Joining a gang gives members an opportunity to resist becoming like their parents. That is, most members come from families whose parents are either unemployed or underemployed or, if employed, are trapped within the secondary labor market in dead-end jobs. Most gang members "have lived through the pains of economic deprivation and the stresses that such an existence imposes on a family. They desperately want to avoid following in their parents' path, which they believe is exactly what awaits them." By joining a gang, the youth is able to resist and is able to say to society, in effect, that "I will not take these jobs passively" (Padilla, 1992: 45). One gang member was quoted as follows: "My parents work real hard and they got little for it.... If I don't make it, at least I told the fuckers in Beverly Hills what I think of the jobs they left for me" (1992: 46). Jankowski (1990) makes an interesting point when he says that many wrongly believe that these youths are having problems forming an identity and that they join a gang to gain this. He states that, more than a new identity, these gang members simply want better living conditions.

6. *Commitment to community*—In some communities, gangs have existed for many generations, and in many ways belonging to a gang is seen as a commitment to a person's own community. Such a desire represents a type of local patriotism. This is especially the case for Irish and Chicano gangs. Vigil and Long (1990), along with Moore (1988), have similarly noted that in some communities there are a few households or families with several generations of gang members: "In such households, one or both parents continue to participate more or less overtly in illicit activities while raising their children. Their children are thus virtually preselected to associate and unite with other troubled and disaffected barrio youths in emergent cliques, often at far younger than typical ages" (Vigil and Long, 1991: 67). The same is often found in some black families (Bing, 1991).

Jankowski concludes that most gang members join gangs for a combination of one or more of the previously stated reasons. Whatever the specific reason(s) for joining, it was a well-thought-out decision, based on what these youths believed was in their own best interest at the time. The literature on gangs has cited other reasons youths join gangs. For example, Hochhaus and Sousa (1988) cite the need for companionship and excitement in addition to the need for protection. There may be several deep-seated, underlying motives for joining gangs: "Those who join gangs are struggling with the classic, desperate needs of adolescence: for an end to childhood; for acceptance as an adult; for sexual, social and economic identity; for status and success; for respect and a sense of belonging" (Reiner, 1992: 22). They join gangs simply because the existing institutions of society that are supposed to meet many of these needs or provide opportunities to meet such needs—the family, the school, the church, the community—have become dysfunctional.

Gang Recruitment

Many gangs go through some process of recruitment, whereby new members are sought out. Gangs have their own reasons for accepting a new member. Gangs also use one of a number of different recruitment strategies. Jankowski cites three of these:

- *The fraternity type of recruitment*—As a fraternity might do, the gang using this will present itself as an organization that is the "in" thing to belong to, that is hip or cool. It advertises through word of mouth. Usually there is a party, and potential members are invited, at which time gang members and potential members size each other up. The potential member is evaluated according to his potential as a good fighter, his courage, and his commitment to assist other gang members. The most important factor, however, is the potential gang member's ability as a fighter—more specifically, whether he will come through when the gang is threatened or whether he will turn tail and run off. If he is already known as a good fighter, then he will be admitted without further testing. However, if his reputation is not known, then his ability will be put to a test by having a member purposely pick a fight with him to see how he reacts. This becomes an initiation ritual (Jankowski, 1990:49–50). Some gangs also look for other skills, such as military skills (e.g., the ability to build incendiary bombs).

- *The obligation type of recruitment*—As implied by the term, the gang using this type of recruiting tries to convince the potential member that it is his duty to join. This is especially common in areas where gangs have existed for many generations and therefore where everyone must "uphold the tradition of the neighborhood." One potential member was told that he had an obligation to "give something back" to the community (Jankowski, 1990: 52). One member told a potential recruit that "I want you to know that your barrio needs you just like they needed us and we delivered" (1990).

In some cases, if youths join a gang, some members of the community may help them find a job later. They are also told that women in the community look up to gang members; thus the recruit is promised access to many women. The prospective member is also told that if he fails to join, he will lose the respect of others in the community and even perhaps that of his own family (especially true for Chicanos and Irish).

- *The coercive type of recruitment*—This method of recruitment is used most often when gangs need more members quickly (not unlike a nation instituting a draft during a time of war). Often this is because a gang wants to expand some illegal operation into a new territory or wants to take over control of a new neighborhood not already under control of a gang. Other times, it may be because the gang faces possible takeover from a rival gang.

The types of coercion employed are both physical and psychological intimidation, the latter being the most preferred method. Typically, psychological intimidation involves threats to the individual or members of his family. Physical intimidation involves actual attacks on the individual or family members, in addition to the destruction of personal property.

Additional Comments on Gang Recruitment

Fagan (1990) examined the various social processes within gangs that might influence the nature of the gang's structure and the extent of gang cohesion. Specifically, four processes were examined: the process of getting involved in the gang (e.g., being recruited by leaders, partying with members, hanging out), the reasons for joining the gang (e.g., status, protection from other gangs, a family feeling), violations that provoked sanctions (e.g., taking someone's woman, ripping off a fellow gang member), and sanctions (e.g., defending the gang's name, stealing for the gang) for breaking rules.

According to Fagan's research, there were no consistent recruitment patterns within any of these gangs. Few gang members reported that they were actively recruited by gang leaders, and the process of initiation into the gangs took many different forms. The most common reason they joined was that they had friends who were in the gang, and they merely hung out with them on a regular basis. No specific reason was associated with any of the four types of gangs (social, party, serious delinquent, and organization—see Chapter 2).

Many gangs have developed somewhat elaborate rites of passage, or initiation ceremonies. Most of these rituals involve some form of physical confrontation with other members. Padilla describes one kind of initiation ritual with the Diamonds, the Puerto Rican gang he studied in Chicago. Known as the *V*-in, this initiation ritual is described by Padilla as a process that

> ... most poignantly demonstrates the kind of physical torture these young people are willing to suffer in order to "turn," that is, to become official members of the gang. Youngsters' willingness to undergo and endure this vicious physical onslaught suggests the high appraisal they

give to the organization. The agonizing course these youngsters are determined to cross also points to the limited opportunities they believe to exist in the larger society. Members of the Diamonds have come to accept the idea that, since society cannot offer them the means with which they can make something positive of their lives, the physical punishment of the gang's violation ritual is not too big a price to pay. They have taken physical punishment before—it comes with living in the inner city—so, why not take more, particularly when it can open doors that have been shut to them during an entire lifetime? (1992: 59)

However, as noted earlier, the initiation is merely a formal procedure and really the final stage of a long process of socialization into the gang subculture. The acceptance of the new members of this initiation rite follows several years of conditioning through a number of contacts with individual gang members. This results in a perception that the gang has something very positive to offer them so that, as a result, they are willing to walk through the *V*-in line to become official members of the gang (1992: 59–60).

It is often the case that gangs use a form of subterfuge to get members through a misrepresentation of what the gang really is and what it stands for. Recruiters sometimes use lies and schemes to convince teens that this is a club or a group of close friends dedicated to protecting themselves from a powerful enemy. For kids with unstable family lives, this group will love you even though your family doesn't. Similarly, some potential members can be seduced into gangs (just like being seduced into the military). Gangs have often used glorified myths about the gang. These include money, sex, and glamour. The graffiti, hand signs, colors, tattoos, and so on also pose a visual attraction for a group that is organized and powerful. Parties, where drugs are in abundance, offer an opportunity to get high, have fun, and forget problems (Marshall, Tuttle, and Laurenzano, 2002).[3]

Initiation into the gang has typically been formalized as a "rite of passage." As Vigil notes, "If not earlier, by middle school a prospective gang member is initiated into the gang by being 'jumped in'—that is, surrounded and beaten by two, three, or more other gang members." Vigil describes such an ordeal as a kind of "street ceremony, or baptism, that confirms how interested the novitiate is in joining the gang and also provides an opportunity for older gang members to assess the potency of the new member whom they *are allowing* into the gang" (2010: 17, emphasis in original).

Who Does Not Join a Gang?

Not everyone who grows up in an area where gangs flourish becomes a gang member. Why is this the case? Jankowski (1990) gives two answers to this crucial question. First, some youths see no advantage to joining a gang. These individuals constitute two groups: (1) those who possess all of the characteristics of defiant individualists but do not believe that being in a gang is to their advantage at the present time (most are already involved in illegal economic activity and see no advantage to joining but will eventually join), and (2) those who not only see no advantage to joining but also see many disadvantages (e.g., the risks of going to prison would be too great). These individuals have usually developed their own strategies for escaping from their ghetto environment (some will try to escape via sports, getting an education, or developing a legitimate skill). Jankowski maintains that these individuals do not possess all of the characteristics of the defiant individualist character structure. The second reason is that gangs do not want everyone who wants to be a member.

Despite popular beliefs, many youths who live in gang territories, are invited to join a gang, and refuse for various reasons, do not suffer any negative consequences. Huff's (1998) research on a sample of gang and nongang youth in several parts of the country found that of those who refused to join, fully two-thirds suffered no physical harm.

Jankowski (1990) suggests that there are seven possible outcomes for those who become gang members: 1) Some stay in the gang indefinitely; 2) some drop out and pursue illegal activities alone; 3) some move on to other organizations (e.g., Irish social clubs, organized crime); 4) some become involved with smaller organizations known as crews and continue to pursue illegal activity; 5) some end up doing long and/or frequent prison terms; 6) some die (e.g., from drugs, from violence, or merely from the risks of being in the lower class); or 7) some drop out of the gang and take the jobs and live the lifestyle they were originally trying to avoid (the most common outcome).

Most gang members will drift in and out of the gang most of their lives. Thus, coming and going is a normal part of the gang organization (Klein and Maxson, 2006; Vigil, 2010; Thornberry et al., 2003). This leads us to consider some of the reasons why a member leaves or quits the gang and some of the processes of doing so.

LEAVING THE GANG

Research by Thornberry of large samples of youth in three cities (Rochester, Denver, and Seattle) revealed that for most members, participation in the gang is limited to no more than a year (Thornberry et al., 2003). For the most hard-core gang members, there has been a trend lately whereby an increasing number remain with the gang longer than normal so that leaving the gang is becoming less and less common. Among the factors that account for this are a real increase in the age of the population; the changing structure of the economy, resulting in the loss of millions of unskilled and semiskilled jobs; and increasing opportunities to commit crime, especially in the lucrative drug markets (Reiner, 1992: 27).

As the study by Reiner notes, there is not a lot known about the process of leaving the gang, but many members do leave. There are any number of specific reasons: the influence of a girlfriend or adults, including parents; frequent arrests and incarceration (leading to burnout, or battle fatigue); a family move to another neighborhood or city; or a job (1992: 26). The key seems to be the availability of jobs. As Reiner notes, "Nothing can make a young man quit before he is ready. But if no work is available at the critical moment, he may not quit even when he is ready" (1992). It is also important to note that the availability of illegal opportunities may cause a person to leave the gang to pursue these sorts of activities. This method of leaving the gang is becoming increasingly popular.

Leaving the gang brings increased risks because there is so much emphasis on loyalty within the gang. Leaving is often seen as betrayal. As noted by Padilla (1992), one can get jumped out just as well as one can get jumped in. As will be described in a later section, the *V*-out is a common form of leaving the Diamonds (the Chicago gang Padilla studied).

The danger of leaving may actually be the greatest for those who have been the most successful and visible within the gang. As Reiner (1992) notes, "They cannot simply fade away unnoticed. Even if their colleagues acquiesce, they remain (not unlike gunfighters in the Old West) prestigious targets for rival gangs—especially those looking to build a 'rep'" (1992: 29). Gang members wanting to get out are often advised to begin engaging in other activities, such as getting a job, going back to school, starting a family, and so on. Such activities can provide a "graceful cover for gradually dropping out" of the gang. Conversely, youngsters can resist joining a gang by participating in such activities. In each case, they can legitimately save face by telling gang members they do not have the time to participate (1992).

Decker and Lauritsen (1996) interviewed a group of 24 ex-gang members, asking them about why they left the gang. The most common reason (given by two-thirds of this group) was because of the level of violence they experienced. Many left because of direct experience as a victim. For many, it was a rather sudden realization that, as one ex-gang member put it, "It wasn't my type of life. I didn't want to live that type of life" (1996: 109). Another stated that he became concerned because many of his friends were getting killed and he might be next: "When I really woke up was when my friend died because we got in there together.... We was in the eighth grade together [and] freshman year" (1996: 110–111). Another reason given was of "maturational reform," with one stating that he had two children to live for, while another stated that "I wasn't spending time with my daughter." This same person also stated that he obtained a job, which would help him take care of his daughter (1996).

What is perhaps most interesting from the Decker and Lauritsen study was what they discovered when they asked these ex-gang members *how* they left the gang. Contrary to popular conceptions, most just simply quit and said that they did not have to give a reason to anyone. This should come as no surprise to experienced gang researchers, for it has been said all along that most gangs are very loosely organized, with few close ties, few formal rules, very little structure, and few formal leaders. Typical was one gang member who responded to the question of "How did you leave?" with "I just walked away" (Decker and Lauritsen, 1996: 113). A total of 5 of these 24 ex-gang members left by moving away. One moved from California to St. Louis.

Another interesting finding (paralleling Huff 's research, noted previously) is that most of the active gang members, when asked why others left the gang, mentioned the same reasons: violence, maturational reform, and just plain quitting. One respondent told the researchers that an ex-member left the gang because "One of they [sic] friends got killed." Another said an ex-gang member got his girlfriend pregnant and "he said fuck that shit [the gang]. I'm just going to lay low with my gal, I ain't got time for that" (Decker and Lauritsen, 1996: 116).

These researchers conclude that while violence is a big part of gang life, there are contradictory consequences: "The very activity that often keeps gangs together appears to have provided the impetus for the majority in this sample to leave the gang" (Decker and Lauritsen, 1996: 117). They suggest that gang-prevention programs may want to seize the opportunity that presents itself when a gang member and/or someone close gets killed or seriously injured from an act of violence (1996: 121).

Many organizations have offered various suggestions and in some cases assistance for those who want to leave gangs. The National Alliance of Gang Investigators Association (NAGIA) suggests not even telling the gang that you plan to leave and instead gradually beginning to spend time doing other things and associating with people not in gangs. The youth should always try to find supportive people, especially adults, that they can depend on when there is a problem or advice is needed (National Alliance of Gang Investigators Associations, 2003). In many parts of the country, Boys and Girls Clubs sponsor a program called "Getting Out," among other programs to help kids.

A CASE EXAMPLE OF THE GANG SUBCULTURE: THE CODE OF THE STREETS

In a fascinating study, Anderson (1994) explores what he calls "the code of the streets," based on his observations of ghetto streets over several years. He echoes Cohen, Thrasher, and many others when he notes that in such poor environments, the negative influences are everywhere and have become part of an oppositional culture, which he refers to as "the streets." The street subculture contains norms opposed to those of mainstream society. This culture is in direct contrast to what inner-city residents refer to as decent families who are "committed to middle-class values." The existence of such an oppositional culture means that even those youths from decent homes "must be able to handle themselves in a street-oriented environment." The parents of such youths actually encourage them to at least become familiar with these norms (Anderson, 1994: 82). One of the main reasons behind this is that the street culture has created a code of the streets or a "set of informal rules governing interpersonal public behavior, including violence. The rules prescribe both a proper comportment and a proper way to respond if challenged. They regulate the use of violence and so allow those who are inclined to aggression to precipitate violent encounters in an approved way" (1994).

The heart of the code is respect, which is defined as being treated right, or with proper deference. Unfortunately, the precise definition is not consistent. Moreover, respect is something that is "hard-won but easily lost," and thus one must be ready to guard against its being taken away. If someone has respect, then he can go about his business without being bothered by others. But if he is bothered in public, it means that he may not only be in physical danger but be disgraced, or, as in current slang, be **dissed,** or disrespected. While many of the examples of what constitutes dissin' (e.g., maintaining eye contact for too long) may seem trivial to middle-class people, to those involved in the subculture of the gang, these events are of major importance. Why is this so? Anderson suggests that the reason can be found in the fact that so many inner-city blacks (especially the young) feel totally alienated from mainstream society and its institutions. The code is nothing more than a subcultural adaptation to the lack of faith in the justice system (especially the police), which they believe does not respect or protect them. Many residents have taken on the responsibility of protecting themselves from those who would violate them. The code of the streets, therefore, takes over where the police and judicial system end.

Anderson distinguishes between two polar extremes among families in the inner city—the decent and the street family, which are titles used by residents themselves. (They may even exist simultaneously within the same family.) The decent families accept mainstream values and try to instill them in their children. Most are among the working poor, and they place a high value on hard work and self-reliance. They want their children to stay in school and better themselves. They tend to be strict parents and warn their children to be on the lookout for bad people and bad situations.

In contrast, street parents tend to show a lack of consideration for others and are often unable to cope with the demands of parenthood. They strongly believe in the code and try to instill it in their children. Their lives are often disorganized, and they often engage in self-destructive behavior, largely as a result of their lowly status and their frustration over bills, lack of jobs and food, and so on. Many of the women get involved in drugs and abusive relationships with men. They often become bitter and angry, and they have short fuses, causing them to lash out at anyone who irritates them (Anderson, 1994: 83).

The women (too often at home with children and no man in the house) can be very aggressive with their children, yelling and striking at them with little or no explanation. Such verbal and physical punishment teaches children a lesson: "that to solve any kind of interpersonal problem one must quickly resort to hitting or other violent behavior." These mothers may love their children, but this is the only way they know how to control them. Many of these women believe, for example, that there is a "devil in the boy" and that this must be "beaten out of him" or that "fast girls need to be whupped" (1994).

The children are often ignored by their mothers, so they often learn to fend for themselves at a very early age. They become children of the street, and as a popular saying goes, they "come up hard" (this has also been noted by Vigil, 1988, 2007, 2010). Many become employed by drug dealers and learn to fight at an early age. In such environments, says Anderson, these children learn that "might makes right" and that to protect themselves "it is necessary to marshal inner resources and be ready to deal with adversity in a hands-on way. In these circumstances physical prowess takes on great significance" (1994: 83).

In the most extreme cases, a street-oriented mother may leave her children alone for several days. This is most common among women with drug and/or alcohol problems (especially crack addicts). For these children, a very harsh lesson is learned: "Survival itself, let alone respect, cannot be taken for granted; you have to fight for your place in the world" (1994: 86).

Beginning at a very early age, these children begin to hang out on the streets. They will come home after school and then walk right out the door and spend the afternoons and evenings (often until as late as 9 or 10 p.m.—much later for teenagers) on the streets with their peers. Children from decent homes are more closely supervised, with curfews imposed on them and lessons given by their parents on how to avoid trouble. When children from decent families meet children from street families, there is always tension and a social shuffle in which the decent children are tempted. Their choice depends on how well they have already been socialized by their parents. Street children rarely develop the values of decent families; when they do, it is almost always from sources in another setting, such as church or school, and often as a result of involvement with a caring adult (Anderson, 1994).

In the street, these children continually witness disputes, and the resolution of such disputes reinforces the might-makes-right belief already mentioned. They see that "one child succumbs to the greater physical and mental abilities of the other.... In almost every case the victor is the person who physically won the altercation, and this person often enjoys the esteem and respect of onlookers." The children learn that "toughness is a virtue, while humility is not" (1994).

While growing up, these children get these messages reinforced verbally by other family members, neighbors, and friends. They are told "Watch your back," "Don't punk out," and "If someone disses you, you got to straighten them out." Some parents even impose sanctions if their children do not live up to these norms. "Don't you come in here crying that somebody beat you up; you better get back out there and whup his ass. If you don't whup his ass, I'll whup your ass when you come home." Even some decent parents give similar warnings about the need for self-defense.

Although youths are ambivalent about fighting, they feel pressured to fight by the code. Looking capable of taking care of oneself as a form of self-defense is a dominant theme among both street-oriented and decent adults who worry about the safety of their children (Anderson, 1994).

The essence of the code centers around the presentation of self. The major requirement is for the person to prove to others that he is willing and able to use violence and that he can take care of himself. He communicates this message through facial expressions and a certain way of walking and talking (including the words he selects). Physical appearance is also important—jewelry, certain kinds of clothing (jackets, sneakers, etc.), and the way he is groomed. To be respected, he must have the right look (1994: 88).

There are always going to be challenges to his respect, or "juice" (as it is often called). If he is assaulted or otherwise challenged, he must avenge himself. According to the code, maintaining his honor or respect is crucial, and to do this, it is necessary to show others he cannot be messed with or dissed.

There is much pressure from peers to wear the right kind of clothing, jewelry, and so on (especially the most expensive items), and if a person displays these things, he is likely to be robbed by someone who wants what he has. Yet if he does not wear the right stuff, then he may be teased by others or even assaulted. Not having the right stuff is often translated into being socially deficient (Anderson, 1994).

By obtaining material things, a person improves his identity, but such an identity is very delicate, which results in a "heightened sense of urgency to staying even with peers, with whom the person is actually competing." He is able to maintain respect mostly by displaying his possessions. However, the precariousness of such an identity means he must constantly be involved in maintaining it and is thus very prone to deal violently with even a minor slight or put-down (1994).

Stealing from others, the ability to get in someone's face, to dis someone, and to take away another person's honor or someone else's girlfriend are methods of enhancing worth. In other words, according to the code, he must often put someone else down to feel up. These are trophies, showing others he is important (not unlike professional people showing off their awards, degrees, certificates, etc., indicating that they too have made it), and it is important to note that the open display of these trophies can provoke others into challenges. "This game of who controls what is thus constantly being played out on inner-city streets, and the trophy—extrinsic or intrinsic, tangible or intangible—identifies the current winner" (1994: 89).

There is a widespread feeling that within this environment there is little respect available, and thus "everyone competes to get what affirmation he can of the little that is available." These individuals crave affirmations, and a show of deference can enhance self-esteem tremendously. If one violates another, and there is no response, it merely encourages further violations against that person. Thus he must be constantly on guard against not only direct violations but even the appearance of potential violation. This is especially true among teenagers, whose self-esteem is by definition already vulnerable.[4] There are many young males who so desperately want respect that they are willing to die to maintain it (1994).

The issue of self-respect is therefore important to understand because it is related to the extent to which a young person has the potential for violence. Most individuals in mainstream society are able to retreat and not seek revenge against an attack because they have enough self-esteem from other sources (e.g., education, jobs, and family). For inner-city youths, however, other sources of self-esteem are absent; thus, they have to seek revenge (even going so far as to enlist the aid of relatives or fellow gang members).

The concept of manhood within this subculture is defined in terms of concerns over one's identity and self-esteem. To be a man within this subculture is to be concerned with one's level of respect. But the irony (a "chicken-and-egg" aspect) is that a person's safety is more apt to be threatened in public because manhood is associated with respect. Manhood and respect, therefore, are two sides of the same coin—"physical and psychological well-being are inseparable, and both require a sense of control, of being in charge" (Anderson, 1994). In short, being a man means being in control, in charge. This is not to say that within middle- and upper-class society being a man does not mean the same basic thing; the main difference (which Anderson does not mention) is that within the inner city it comes down to the physical aspect of this equation and that so much violence is involved (stemming from the fact that there are few nonviolent means to maintain respect and to prove that one is a real man).

One major assumption is that every man should know this code. Thus even the victim of a mugging who does not act according to the code may cause the mugger to feel justified in killing him and feeling no remorse. After all, the mugger reasons, this person "should have known better" (1994: 89). Because even youths from decent families are familiar with the code, they too may have to resort to violence to defend their honor or respect.

One of the core beliefs associated with this concept of manhood is that one of the best ways of gaining respect (therefore proving one is a real man) is to exhibit nerve. The concept of nerve refers to the ability to take someone else's possessions, mess with someone's woman, get in someone's face, or fire a weapon. The show of nerve, however, is a very forceful method of showing disrespect—it can very easily offend others and result in retaliation (1994: 92).

A recent court case reported in the *New York Times* reveals how important this code can be and how it acts to make it extremely difficult to prosecute gang-related crimes. The case involved the murder of a female member of the Latin Kings in Trenton, New Jersey, in August of 2004. She was killed because other members questioned her loyalty since she was dating a member of a rival gang. There were witnesses set to testify and to turn state's evidence in return for a reduced sentence. However, they were reluctant to do so because of the code concerning a snitch. One potential witness, placed in "protective custody" inside the Trenton jail, was severely burned. The inmate who admitted the attack said, "I heard he was a snitch."

SOCIAL CONTROL IN THE GANG

One of the unique functions of gangs is that they tend to provide a great deal of structure for members. Indeed, most gang members get from gangs something sorely missing from their families—consistent rules and sanctions. The effects of various economic hardships experienced by barrio and ghetto inhabitants have undermined traditional social institutions, which are supposed to provide social control. Over time in these barrios and ghettos, the streets and older street youths have become primary agents of socialization (Moore, 1991: 137–138). According to Vigil (1988: 12), the gang has become "a type of street social control institution by becoming in turn a partial substitute for family (providing emotional and social support networks), school (giving instructions on how to think and act), and police (authority and sanctions to enforce adherence to gang norms)."

Jankowski (1990) has argued that gangs are formal and cohesive organizations. Jankowski further argues that they have developed systematic methods of control and recruitment. All but one of the gangs Jankowski studied were very cohesive, largely because of the establishment of mechanisms for control. (The gangs who disappeared had lost these mechanisms.) Control was maintained through the use of both formal and informal codes and by reference to a particular ideology.

Formal codes (22 of the 37 gangs Jankowski studied had such codes) pertain to the following six areas: 1) regulatory behavior (e.g., fighting with one another); 2) personal relations between members and female relatives and lovers of other members (this was the most sensitive issue); 3) behavior of members while in the clubhouse (e.g., violence, use of drugs); 4) heroin use; 5) leaders abusing power; and 6) punishment for various offenses (i.e., what types of punishment are most appropriate). Informal codes consist of unwritten norms everyone is expected to follow, including being respectful to other members and observing dress codes.

Fagan's (1990) study of four types of gangs in Chicago, Los Angeles, and San Diego found that the most common violations that would provoke sanctions were to rip off a gang member and to snitch on a gang member. The two most delinquent gangs (the serious and the organization gang types) were the most likely to have specific sanctions for violating rules. The most common included having to fight another member of the gang and getting beat up by other gang members. Yet fewer than one-half of the respondents agreed with any of these sanctions (the highest percentage was 47.5).

A Puerto Rican gang in Chicago (heavily involved in the selling of drugs) studied by Padilla has developed some very strict rules, and the penalties are often harsh. If an individual ventures out on his own, he risks avoidance by the gang if he should get arrested—in this case, they will not come to bail him out, as they would if he were still part of the gang. One of the penalties involved what they called the violation ceremony, or simply the *V*. This involves using violence against members as a form of punishment for rules violations. One specific ceremony is the *V*-out penalty, which is used when a member who is leaving the gang knows a lot about the gang's drug-dealing operations. The *V*-out is also used against those "who have been nothing but trouble for the gang"—that is, they have been constant troublemakers and have not been committed team players (Padilla, 1992: 56–57). There is also a *V*-in ceremony, used as part of the initiation ritual for new members, described earlier in this chapter (see Padilla, 1992: 105).

GANG GRAFFITI AND TATTOOS

As unique subcultures, gangs can be described as exaggerated versions of normal adolescent groupings. As every parent knows, adolescents have a need to create their own unique world, separate and distinct from the adult world. In so doing, they often devise elaborate methods of distinguishing themselves and devise their own methods of communication. Modes of dress and the words used to communicate help them draw the line between themselves and adults. With gangs, there is the added attraction of two unique forms of communication—graffiti and tattoos.

Graffiti is the primary form of communication used by gangs today, although historically a wide variety of groups have used graffiti. Not all graffiti is the product of gangs. As several studies have shown, many respectable artists began with graffiti. The goal of such artwork (e.g., that is displayed in many

New York City subways) is to establish an individual artist's reputation and to display one's own style of art (Hutchinson, 1993: 139). In contrast, the purpose of gang graffiti is usually (but not always) to expand the reputation of the gang rather than that of an individual. Gangs use graffiti to identify their existence (to tell others who they are), to mark a specific area as their turf (e.g., by writing on a wall, a building, or other structure), to challenge rival gangs, and to commemorate members who have died in battles (it is common for gang members to draw the letters RIP [rest in peace] on a wall or other structure, along with the name of the deceased). Graffiti can be described as a kind of "newspaper of the street" (Fradette, 1992: 1) or a "poor people's memo."

One recent study noted that "Graffiti writers write in order to get fame and respect for their deeds, and therefore they write in places where their work is more likely to be seen by their intended demographic." The study also noted that graffiti is not always restricted to the poorest areas of a city. In the New York City area, there are places "where young people from all over the city are likely to congregate, and thus the East Village, the Lower East Side, and SoHo are the places where most of the illegal New York City graffiti can be found. These are not poor, crime-ridden neighborhoods" (Chan, 2009).

Gang graffiti may be viewed as a form of artistic expression because it follows established styles and makes use of sophisticated principles of graphic design (Hutchinson, 1993: 139–140). According to Alonzo (1998) the word "graffiti" means "little scratchings," and "it comes from the Italian *graffiare*, which means to scratch." There is a consistency in style in much of the gang graffiti today. The style of gang graffiti in Los Angeles, for example, especially the form of lettering used, is quite similar to the styles used in the 1960s. Much of it, in fact, has been appropriated by commercial artists and the adolescent subculture in general (Hutchinson, 1993: 139–140).

Tattoos serve a similar purpose. The use of tattoos is ancient in origin and is not limited to gang members or even to criminals in general. It is very popular among many segments of the population (at the present time, it can be seen on many youths who are not in any way affiliated with gangs or any other deviant group). For years it has been used by men in the military. In gangs, tattoos are a form of identification and communication, mostly to indicate to others the gang or set to which one belongs. In addition to the gang name or initials (or perhaps in place of the gang name) may be the gang logo (usually some type of symbol, such as a pitchfork, crown, stars, dots, etc.).

Purposes and Styles of Graffiti

Modern gang graffiti takes on a variety of styles and serves several different purposes. One of the most common styles is the use of large block lettering. This is especially common when writing the name or initials of the gang. Figure 3.1 contains a photograph of gang graffiti in Detroit, Michigan.[5] This photo represents graffiti of a gang called the Cash Flow Posse (part of the Folk Nation). Their initials (CFP) are shown on the left; the drawing in the middle that looks like a teepee stands for the Folk Nation; and the words "Cash Flow" appear in block letters on the far right.

FIGURE 3.1 Graffiti of the Cash Flow Posse.
SOURCE: William B. Brown

Graffiti can be classified into several different types, which include the following:

- *Identifying the neighborhood of the gang*—Usually, graffiti will identify a neighborhood, or varrio (*barrio* is Spanish for neighborhood; *varrio* is slang for *barrio*), often by merely the letter *V* or *B*. One example was found in a suburb of Los Angeles, the city of La Puente, where *VP-13* was used to identify a local gang. The *13* refers to the 13th letter of the alphabet, or *M,* and within the gang subculture has normally referred to Sur, or Southern, California. This method of gang reference is believed to have originated with prison gangs in California as a way to distinguish gangs in the southern part of the state from those in the northern part. (The number *14* stands for the 14th letter of the alphabet, or *N,* and refers to Norte, or Northern, California.) A variation of this usage is to place the word *barrio* or *varrio* before, after, or in the middle of the gang name. For example, a gang in south-central Los Angeles located in the area of Grape Street is known as Watts Varrio Grape. Another example is illustrated as follows:

BHGR

POS

-13-

L's

In this illustration, on the first line, the *B* stands for Barrio, the *HG* stands for the name of the gang (in this case Hawaiian Gardens City), and the *R* is street slang for *Rifa*, or to rule, control, or reign. In other words, this gang is making a statement that they control or rule this specific area. (In reality, this is typically an exaggerated boast, as they do not literally control every aspect of the entire area. They are claiming to be the only gang in this area and declaring that other gangs should stay out.) On the second line, the letters *POS* stand for the actual clique from this gang, in this case the Pequeños. The *13* stands for Southern California (as noted previously), and the *L*'s stands for another gang slang—Vatos Locos— meaning crazy ones or brave ones (the Spanish term *loco* is often used to mean wild and crazy).

- *Making certain pronouncements*—Gangs use graffiti to communicate with one another. One of the most common messages is to use the letter *R* (see previous example) or to simply write out the words *Rifa, Rifan,* or *Rifamos,* followed or preceded by the name of the gang. One of the most common pronouncements is to challenge or to show disrespect for a rival gang. Often gang members will travel into a rival's territory and cross out graffiti of the rival. (The police study this process to measure the extent of conflict between gangs or to predict a pending battle.) An example is noted in Figure 3.2. A variation of this is the targeting of a rival gang for retaliation. Figure 3.3 illustrates this (the number *187* stands for the California Penal Code number for murder and is often used by gangs in their graffiti to target

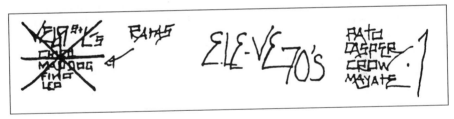

FIGURE 3.2 Crossed-out graffiti.

SOURCE: National Law Enforcement Institute, 1992: 28

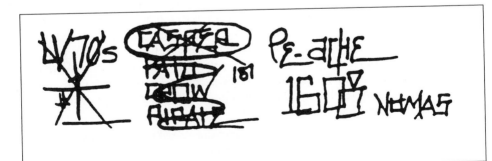

FIGURE 3.3 Targeting for retaliation.

SOURCE: National Law Enforcement Institute, 1992: 28

F I G U R E 3.4 Two recent examples are from Hispanic gangs in Texas, posted by Operation No Gangs.

SOURCE: Operation No Gangs (http://www.operationnogangs.org)

a rival). Sometimes a gang will put down one of their own members, as when they write the word *Lokos* next to a member's name. This means that the member is being given the silent treatment because of associating with another gang, talking bad about the gang, or some other infraction. An example of this is shown in Figure 3.4.

■ *Commemorating the dead*—Gangs often provide methods of grieving for fellow members who have died. Death is an ever-present reality for gang members, and much of their graffiti is used to commemorate their fallen brothers. Figure 3.5 shows an example of this, as the Village Boyz are commemorating MVP. Printing the letters *RIP* (rest in peace) is a common method of honoring the dead on walls and buildings in their neighborhood. Also common is the drawing of a flower (shown here in the middle of the photograph).

■ *Using numbers*—Much gang graffiti involves the use of various kinds of abbreviations, typically letters or numbers that stand for something related to the gang. The numbers may be in English, Spanish, Roman numerals, or a combination of these. Numbers usually refer to a specific street where most of the gang members live. This becomes part of the actual gang name, such as 18th Street or XVIII Street. A variation is to replace numbers with words, especially common among black gangs. Thus, the numbers *1, 2,* and *3* are replaced by *Ace, Deuce* (often written as *Duce*), and *Trey* (or *Tray*). In Los Angeles, for example, 73rd Street is written as 7 Trey St., and 101st Street is written as 10 Ace St. Specific examples are Eight Tray Gangster Crips (found on 83rd Street), Eleven Deuce Crips (located on 112th Street), and Ace Deuce Crips (found on 12th Street).

In El Paso, Texas, Operation No Gangs discovered the use of numbers by some gangs in the area. In the example in Figure 3.6, this gang uses "584" to display its gang abbreviation. The number 5 may represent any of the letters on the "5" telephone keypad, such as J, K, or L. The number 8 in the number set may stand for letters T, U, or V; and the number 4 for G, H, or I.

FIGURE 3.5 Commemorating the dead.
SOURCE: William B. Brown

FIGURE 3.6 The use of numbers to signify gangs.
SOURCE: Operation No Gangs (http://www.operationno-gangs.org)

- *Subgroups, cliques, and sets*—Gangs are often subdivided into age-graded cliques or sets, and graffiti often reflects this. For example, *TDS* would stand for the Tiny Dukes (a younger version of the Dukes gang), *MLS* would refer to the Midget Locos, and *LL* or *LxL* would stand for Little Locos. Also, Spanish names differentiate male from female gangs—thus *Chicos* = male, and *Chicas* = female.

- *Location*—The location or turf of a gang is often extremely important. Gangs often identify with either a small area (e.g., a housing project or a park) or a very large area within a city. Typically, they use names like *West, Westside, South, Southside, North,* and so on to refer to a wide area of a city. Then they will follow this location with the actual name of the gang itself. A common method is to use letters to stand for the location, or the side, of the area within which they are located. Thus the symbol *n/s* or *n* will stand for the northside, and *s/s* or *s* will stand for the southside. This notation will be followed by an abbreviation of the gang name. Some examples are as follows: *w/s V13* = Venice 13, a gang on the westside of Los Angeles, within the city of Venice near 13th Street; *e/s BP* (Eastside Baldwin Park) and *n/s BP* (Northside Baldwin Park) are two rival gangs within the same city. Often, as in the Baldwin Park example, landmarks are used to differentiate east and west and north and south. These can be streets, canals, rivers, freeways, railroad tracks, and in Los Angeles, washes (dry riverbeds). For example, the Harbor Freeway in Los Angeles separates east from west for black gangs. In Las Vegas, I-15 separates the West Coast Bloods from the East Coast Bloods.

- *Black gang graffiti*—Gangs of different racial and ethnic groups have their own unique style of graffiti. In the case of black gangs, there are noteworthy differences between the Crips and the Bloods. Crip gangs often use the word *Cuz* or *Cuzz* as a salutation. They also use the letters *BK* (often written as *B/K*),which stand for Blood Killer. Blood gangs will use the letters *CK,* which stand for Crip Killer. Both gangs often refuse to use the letters that stand for their rivals. Thus, for example, a Blood gang from the Citrus Heights suburb of Sacramento will call themselves Bitrus Heights (replacing the *C,* which stands for Crips, with a *B*). Sometimes a gang will include a rival's name followed by a *K* (which stands for Killer). For example, the Lime Hood Bloods (LHB), whose rivals are the Broadway Gangster Crips (BGC), may write on a wall the letters *BGC/K.* The Broadway Gangster Crips may in turn write *LHB/K.* These gangs may simply write *C/K* or *B/K,* respectively. Black gangs often use the dollar sign in their graffiti, which is reflection of their emphasis on making money (what they describe as "clocking dollars").

- *Taggers*—The phenomenon of tagging has been growing rapidly in most urban areas in recent years (see Chapter 2 for a more detailed discussion). This form of graffiti is not usually associated with specific gangs, although some people refer to groups of youths who do this as gangs. Tagging is usually a method of announcing who they are (typically by using a nickname). Some common examples in Las Vegas include the following names: ACME, BNEE, ASTRO, DAZE, POUR, TRASH, LEEN, REAM,

FIGURE 3.7 Examples of tagging.
SOURCE: National Law Enforcement Institute, 1992: 29.

and SMIRK. Figure 3.7 illustrates some tags on walls in San Diego. According to Alonzo (1998: 10), tagging is all about "getting up" in as many locations as possible. Also, marking one's name in the "most obscure place adds to the writers recognition and fame." Some examples of tagger crews from various parts of the country are presented by Savelli (2007: 78–99), such as: ATF (Artists for Fame, Phoenix), BTT (Big Time Thugs, Los Angeles), DEC (Destroying Everything Crew, Denver), TSC (The Sick Clique, Miami), CAP (Criminal Aerosol Posse, Atlanta), UMC (Union Mob Crew, Boston), CWB (Crazy White Boys, New York City), HMC (Heavy Metal Crew, Seattle).

- *Chicano gang graffiti*—Chicano gangs use a lot of Spanish words in their graffiti. The graffiti used by these gangs is often referred to as *placas* (literally translated as *plaques*) and is a form of public tattoos (Vigil, 1988: 113). Placas typically give the name of the gang member, the gang name, and the location of the gang. Hutchinson (1993: 141–158) provides the following example, written in large letters on a wall in Los Angeles: *Lil Bobby SS 38 St. CXS*. Lil Bobby is the name of the gang member writing the graffiti. The *SS 38 St.* stands for the Southside 38th Street gang. The *CXS* stands for "con safos," or "the same to you," which serves as a threat to anyone who might want to deface this message. Within Chicano neighborhoods, gang graffiti is a way of gaining attention and recognition from the public. Vigil quotes one gang member, who said, "I always wonder what people think of when they ride by and see the name 'Puppet' [his nickname] there. Do they think of me?" Another stated, "I know the guys from that barrio know who I am. They've seen my placas in their neighborhood" (1998). Some of the more common words and acronyms used include *Puro* (pure); *VNE* (Varrio Nueva Estrada, a local gang); *P/V* (meaning "for life," as in "I'm in the gang for life"); *R* or *Rifa* (meaning "control," "We control the neighborhood," or "We're number one"); *C/S* (con safos, which means "back to you" or, more commonly, "There's nothing you can do about it," as in "We are in control and you can't do anything about it," an obvious challenge to another gang); *TOL* or *TO* (meaning united or total); and *CONTROLLA* (control). An example of Chicano gang graffiti is shown in Figure 3.8.

FIGURE 3.8   18th Street Gang in Los Angeles.
SOURCE: Copyright ZUMA Wire Service/Alamy

FIGURE 3.9   Various forms of graffiti used by the People and Folk gang nations.
SOURCE: Florida Department of Corrections

- *Graffiti of the People Nation and the Folk Nation*—Figure 3.9 provides some examples of the various forms of graffiti used by the People and Folk gang nations. Note the six points used by the Folk gangs and the five points used by the People gangs. Note also the use of the pitchforks for both. Each representative of these two nations has its own forms of graffiti.[6]

SUMMARY

This chapter captured the characteristics of the gang subculture—from dress style to graffiti, to membership requirements.

The beliefs of a gang and the commitment to a gang are similar among gang members despite the differences in race and/or ethnicity. There are no greatly significant differences for black, Hispanic, or white gangs. Taggers (a fairly recent youth-group phenomenon) reflect the same commitment and loyalty to the group as do members of long-established gangs. Asian gang members exhibit somewhat less loyalty to the group. This is not particularly surprising because their reasons for joining the gang center around economics rather than personal relationships.

Much of the discussion in this chapter has focused on the works of Moore and Padilla and their detailed observations of the structure, style, and language within Chicano gangs. This language includes the very artistic graffiti employed by these individuals.

Attention has also been given to Jankowski's theories of gang recruitment and membership. While the reasons for joining a gang may vary somewhat, one compelling factor appears to be universal—the sense of self-worth and belonging. The authors believe self-worth and the need to belong are so intertwined that it is not possible to separate the two concepts. These concepts indeed may define the entire identity of the individual, making the gang member not so different from the rest of humanity.

NOTES

1. Part of Vigil's research for his book was an area called Cuatro Flats, which is located close to the center of Los Angeles and Union Station. Some of the settlements (which started in the 1920s) in the area, including the Flats, were known as "cholo court" (Vigil, 2007: 56–57).

2. Dropping out of school pushes most kids into gangs and subsequently into the juvenile justice system and eventually into the prison system. This has been called the "school to prison pipeline," a topic we will cover in Chapter 9.

3. Two of the authors have been in the military and see some parallels here as far as exaggerating what it is like to "serve your country." We both learned very early that much of what we were told was nonsense. We have also learned over the years from many police officers that this also applies to recruitment they experience. Could one not conclude that, in many ways, the police and the military can be considered "gangs"?

4. Co-author Shelden heard a good example of this that occurred at a local alternative school. A gang member attacked someone else merely because he heard a rumor that this other person was out to get him for some reason, and the code he lived by dictated that he attack this person before he was attacked in order to not be embarrassed or dissed. In case this belief and corresponding action sounds familiar, note that the U.S. government engaged in a "preemptive" attack against Iraq in

2003, based upon the assumption that Iraq may, in the future, attack us with "weapons of mass destruction." We suppose that in this case, one "gang" (the U.S. government and its military) is attacking another "gang."

5. Unless otherwise indicated, photos of gang graffiti from Detroit were taken by co-author Brown.

6. This was adapted from a figure on the Florida Department of Corrections Web site: http://www.dc.state.fl.us/pub/gangs/chicago4.html.

4

Criminal Activities of Gangs

The stereotype of the gang member and the gang revolves around criminal activity, as if they do nothing else. This is in part perpetuated by both the media and the police. In the case of the media, this is no doubt because the daily activities of the typical gang member are rather boring, with little or no crime occurring (much less the stereotype of the "drive-by") and thus not newsworthy. As for the police, their historic role in this society is to catch people who have committed crime, and they usually have little interest in what the person does the rest of the time. Moreover, largely because of this role, information from the police about gangs (printed up and handed out at literally hundreds of "gang workshops" throughout any given year) tends to focus almost exclusively on the criminal activities of gangs and methods of identifying gang members (e.g., graffiti, dress styles, hand signals, gang slang) to help officers make arrests or engage in proactive policing (i.e., keeping tabs on gang members). It is important to keep this in mind as we discuss the various crimes committed by gang members. Most of their time is spent doing other things—sleeping, eating, going to school, hanging out, and so on—that occupy the time of adolescents everywhere.[1]

As with information on the number of gangs and gang members, there are serious problems with the data collected by law enforcement, which is by far the most commonly used. Klein and Maxson (2006) received data from several police departments around the country and quickly discovered a serious problem. While some agencies sent information on a variety of crimes (both violent and property, serious and minor crimes), some departments included mostly the most serious crimes, and a few even reported no larcenies, petty thefts, and status offenses. The agency that had the most offenses listed (a total of 1,022) reported that 40 percent were classified as "other offenses" and another 21 percent were status offenses. They reported only two homicides and one drug sale.

Greene and Pranis also discount the widespread belief that gangs do little more than sit around and plan their crimes. They note that "gang-directed, instrumental activities are the exception, not the rule." Further, while many gang members commit violent acts, it is mostly of the expressive variety and often against the wishes of gang leaders. Further, while drug sales are common, such activity "generally ranges from a completely disorganized pursuit of individuals to loosely organized cooperative endeavors" (2007: 52).

HOW MUCH CRIME DO GANG MEMBERS COMMIT?

Recent reports by the National Gang Intelligence Center seem to indicate that gangs do nothing but commit crimes and that they commit most of the crimes in a given area. For example, consider the latest information from their Web site, which states the following:

> Gangs are responsible for an average of 48 percent of violent crime in most jurisdictions and up to 90 percent in several others, according to NGIC analysis. Major cities and suburban areas experience the most gang-related violence. Local neighborhood-based gangs and drug crews continue to pose the most significant criminal threat in most communities. Aggressive recruitment of juveniles and immigrants, alliances and conflict between gangs, the release of incarcerated gang members from prison, advancements in technology and communication, and Mexican Drug Trafficking Organization (MDTO) involvement in drug distribution have resulted in gang expansion and violence in a number of jurisdictions. Gangs are increasingly engaging in non-traditional gang-related crime, such as alien smuggling, human trafficking, and prostitution. Gangs are also engaging in white collar crime such as counterfeiting, identity theft, and mortgage fraud, primarily due to the high profitability and much lower visibility and risk of detection and punishment than drug and weapons trafficking. U.S.-based gangs have established strong working relationships with Central American and MDTOs to perpetrate illicit cross-border activity, as well as with some organized crime groups in some regions of the United States. U.S.-based gangs and MDTOs are establishing wide-reaching drug networks; assisting in the smuggling of drugs, weapons, and illegal immigrants along the Southwest Border; and serving as enforcers for MDTO interests on the U.S. side of the border (National Gang Intelligence Center [NGIC], 2011).

What sources do they have to back up this statement? They give the following reference to this: "The assessment is based on federal, state, local, and tribal law enforcement and corrections agency intelligence, including information and data provided by the National Drug Intelligence Center (NDIC) and the National Gang Center." In other words, local law-enforcement agencies say this is so; therefore, it must be true! Yet, law-enforcement estimates are contradicted by other reports. For example, a report from the Justice Policy Institute noted that "A large majority of rural counties and small cities reported no gang problems at the turn of the century, and among those reporting gang problems, 80 percent reported no gang-related homicides." They also reported that "Gang-related homicides are a serious problem in a number of cities, but nationally just one gang homicide occurs annually for every 18 gangs and 570 gang members" (Greene and Pranis, 2007: 56, citing Egley and Ritz 2006; see also Klein and Maxson, 2006). Moreover, most law-enforcement agencies reported no gang-related homicides between 2002 and 2004 (Egley and Ritz, 2006). As research has shown for decades, most homicides involve family members or acquaintances.[2]

Green and Pranis (2007: 51) conclude that both ethnographic and survey research has shown the following:

- The seriousness and extent of criminal involvement varies greatly among gang members.

- Gang members who engage in crime nonetheless spend most of their time in noncriminal pursuits.

- Gang members account for a small share of all crime (including violent crime), even within communities and neighborhoods where there are gang problems.

- Much of the crime committed by gang members is self-initiated and is meant to serve personal rather than gang interests.

The typical crimes committed by gangs have consistently been a garden variety or cafeteria style of offenses (e.g., burglaries, petty theft, vandalism, fighting, and truancy). The major victims of gang violence are other gang members. Innocent bystanders are rarely the victims despite claims from law-enforcement and other officials to the contrary (Klein, 1995: 22).

Two theories have been offered to explain why the crime rate is higher among gang members (Kaufman, 2010). One theory is called the "selection model." According to this view, those most likely to join gangs are "already predisposed toward delinquency and violence." The other perspective is known as the "facilitation model." This view argues that "gang members are no more disposed toward delinquency and violence than others are and would not contribute to higher crime rates if they did not join a gang. However, when they do join a gang, peer pressures promote their increased involvement in delinquency" (Kaufman, 2010). The overwhelming evidence gives support to the latter view.

Gang violence differs in significant ways from nongang violence. An analysis by Klein and Maxson of more than 700 homicides in the Los Angeles area found that gang violence is much more likely to occur in the streets (in contrast, most other homicides occur inside people's homes) and tends to be associated with the use of guns and less often associated with a robbery. Gang-related homicides are more likely to involve a larger number of participants and involve strangers, and the suspects are more often youths (Klein and Maxson, 1989: 223–224). However, when considering the overall rate of involvement in criminal behavior, there is little question that gang members commit a disproportionate amount of crime, as several studies have shown (Shelden, Snodgrass, and Snodgrass, 1992; Klein and Maxson, 2006; Green and Pranis, 2007).

A study of a sample of youths from neighborhoods (both high school students and dropouts, mostly black and Hispanic youths) in three parts of the country (Chicago, Los Angeles, and San Diego) is instructive. The offending (or participation) rates (of involvement in such offenses at least once during the past year) were higher among gang members for all behaviors (felony, minor assault, robbery, and extortion) except violence. However, for all offenses (including drug possession and drug sales), gang members committed these crimes more frequently than nongang members. Specifically, gang members were about five times more likely than nongang members to commit a crime during a given year, and more than half of the gang members had committed more than one offense during the year (Fagan, 1990).

Among the Chicago gangs, most of the crimes committed during the period under study by Bobrowski (January 1, 1987, to July 31, 1988) were intraracial and involved Part II offenses[3] (it must be stressed that these data are based on those known to the police and are therefore subject to underreporting). Crimes were about equally divided between personal and property crimes (49.7% were personal). The largest category was vice offenses (mostly drugs), which accounted for almost 30 percent. The next most common offense was aggravated battery (22%), with simple battery ranking third (15.6%).

What is most interesting is that Part I gang offenses[4] constituted less than 1 percent of all Part I crimes in the city of Chicago. However, when considering homicides and serious assaults, gang offenses accounted for as much as 18 percent of the homicides during certain months. Furthermore, in certain neighborhoods, this percentage was even higher, with gang homicides accounting for 28 percent in one particular area (Bobrowski, 1988: 42–44).

A study by McCorkle and Miethe (1998, 2001) challenged the notion that gangs are responsible for most of the crimes in a given jurisdiction. Examining court records in Las Vegas, Nevada, for the years 1989–1995, they discovered that the proportion of defendants charged with index crimes who were identified as gang members was quite low. For violent index crimes, for example, the proportion who were gang members ranged from 2 to 6 percent. Gang members were most often involved in murder cases, but even here, their percentage of the total murder cases ranged from 10 to 23 percent during this period of time. As for property offenses, gang members constituted from 2 to 7 percent of the total; they were most likely to be involved in motor-vehicle theft (ranging from 4% to 12%). The myth that gangs dominate the drug scene was shattered by this study, as the researchers found that gang members constituted from 2 to 8 percent of all felony drug defendants. These figures were in stark contrast to local media and law-enforcement reports that gangs had taken over the drug market.

Similar findings have been reported for studies covering Dallas (where only 8% of the crimes were committed by gang members; Fritsch, Tory, Caeti, and Taylor 2003) and in Westminster, California (7% were committed by gang members; Kent et al., 2000).

In the most recent National Youth Gang Survey (NYGS) covering the period 2002–2007, more than half of the jurisdictions did not report a single gang-related homicide—this includes 77 percent of the rural counties and 80 percent of the smaller cities reporting gang problems.[5] Most gang-related homicides occur in larger cities.

> Excluding Chicago and Los Angeles (which, on average, have accounted for roughly one-quarter of all gang homicides recorded in the NYGS over the past seven years), gang homicides increased 8.5 percent in very large cities (with populations of 100,000 or more) from 2002 to 2008. To illustrate the difficulties associated with making generalizations about gang homicide trends, the annual number in Chicago increased 22.5 percent, while the annual number in Los Angeles decreased by 52.3 percent in the 7-year time frame.[6]

A recent study in Toronto sheds new light on the subject (Wortley and Tanner, 2006). This study compared youths in what was described as "social gangs" (not involved very much in criminal activities) and "criminal gangs" (heavy involvement in crime). They found that about half of the "criminal" gang members sold drugs, compared to none of the social gang members and 2 percent of the nongang members. Also, just over one-third (35%) of criminal gang members said they broke into a home or business, compared to 2 percent of social gang members and 2 percent of nongang members. With respect to violence, 90 percent of the criminal gang members reportedly got into a physical fight, compared to just 27 percent of social gang members and 26 percent of nongang members.

The use of weapons is common in many gangs. In Chicago, for example, handguns were used in about 16 percent of all crimes and in about one-fourth of all crimes against the person (murder, rape, robbery, and assault); but they were used in 93 percent of all homicides and 42 percent of all serious assaults. Other kinds of weapons were used in the majority (55%) of all other crimes reported. It should be noted that included in the term *weapon* was "hands/feet." The use of hands or feet accounted for 29 percent of all crimes in which a weapon was used; hands or feet were used in 86 percent of the simple batteries involving a weapon, and hands or feet were involved in 93 percent of the strong-arm robberies involving a weapon. In fact, hands and feet were the most commonly used weapon (constituting 15.9% of all cases, compared to 15.7% for handguns), according to the Chicago data (Bobrowski, 1988: 42–44; Appendix D, Table 21).

It should be emphasized that for most gangs, the bulk of their time is not spent committing crimes. Hagedorn's gangs spent most of their time partying and hanging out (Hagedorn, 1998: 94; a similar finding was reported by Huff, 1989: 530). As noted in Chapter 2, Malcolm Klein has commented on how boring gang life is. When they hang out, it is usually by a park or a taco stand, and they are "smoking, drinking, roughhousing, playing a pickup ball game, messing with a few girls, or sauntering up a street in a possessive, get-outta-our-way fashion" (Klein, 1995: 22). More recently, Klein and Maxson (2006) have reiterated these observations.

When they do get involved in crime, it is either fighting (mostly with other gangs) or hustling, which included petty theft and drug sales. Drugs will be discussed in a later section, but it should be noted here that, as Hagedorn found for Milwaukee gangs, selling drugs "for most gang members is just another low-paying job—one that might guarantee 'survival,' but not much else" (Hagedorn, 1998: 103; see also Padilla, 1992; Klein, 1995). The minimal amount of violence actually engaged in by gangs has been corroborated by other studies (Horowitz, 1983a, 1987; Keiser, 1969; Miller, 1975). Property crimes remain the major type of offense committed by gangs.

Having said this, as already noted, gang members do in fact commit more crime than nongang members. This has been demonstrated in numerous studies, such as a study by Huff (1996, 1998) as part of a project funded by the National Institute of Justice that included gang and nongang but "at-risk" youth in three parts of the country (Colorado, Ohio, and Florida). Not surprisingly, the gang members were found to be more involved in criminal activity. Gang members were significantly more likely to engage in drug selling, assault, theft, weapons-related offenses, shoplifting, and a host of other crimes. One of the most interesting findings was that the first arrest for gang members typically came *after* becoming a gang member. In fact, in each of the areas where the research was conducted, the pattern was as follows: The youths began hanging out with the gangs at around age 12 or 13, joined the gang around 6 to 12 months later (between ages 13 and 14), and incurred their first arrest at around age 14. Typically they experience their first arrest about six months after they join the gang (Huff, 1998).

The findings from a widely reported survey in Rochester, Seattle, and Denver further reinforce these findings but add one more important fact, namely that being in the gang results in more criminal activity. In this study, it was found that gang members committed the bulk of serious violent offenses, serious property offenses, and drug sale offenses and did so *while they were gang members* (Thornberry, Huizinga, and Loeber, 2004). Also, when comparing levels of offending between those who were in a gang and those who were not, the gang members had a much higher rate of offending (Thornberry et al., 2007).

All of these findings are corroborated by other researchers on U.S. gangs (Battin et al., 1998; Esbensen and Huizinga, 1993; Thornberry et al., 1993; Esbensen and Lynskey, 2001; Decker and Curry, 2002) and European gangs (Bradshaw, 2005; Esbensen and Weerman, 2005) in addition to Canadian gangs (Gatti et al., 2005; LaCourse et al., 2003).

Why do gang members commit more crimes than nongang members? According to research by Reiner, part of the reason is that gangs tend to attract individuals who are in the highest at-risk group in society—adolescent males who live in urban areas. However, Reiner also notes that there are "three realities of life in the gang subculture which drive the crime rate: fighting, partying and unemployment" (Reiner, 1992: 55).

In the first instance, most gang homicides are the result of "gang fights over turf, status and revenge." They "are the results of traditional gang codes which require members to fight to prove their honor, manhood and loyalty" (Reiner, 1992: 55). Reiner further notes that

Boys who are toying with the gang lifestyle—hanging around with friends, perhaps, and timid or slow about speaking out—may suddenly, and unintentionally, become targets or accessories to drive-by shootings. There is a finality to such episodes, even when they do not end in death. For they can drag young men over the line and leave them there— exposed to arrest and imprisonment; fearful of retaliation from other gangs; wary of any action which would trigger rejection by friends they need now more than ever. Each attack thus creates a chain reaction of complicity, vengeance and commitment (1992: 55).

Partying tends to increase the likelihood of crime because, first, it corresponds with heavy drinking and drug use, both related to crime. Also, there is a need to obtain drugs for parties, costing money, which in turn brings gang members into contact with the illegal drug world. Because most gang members are without work (either because it is unavailable or because they have never been socialized into good work habits), crime becomes a part-time job. The most common crimes tend to be robberies (because they can produce money fairly quickly) and drug dealing.

It is important to note that the commission of these crimes is rarely a gang activity as such but rather the product of a small group of gang members. The gang, it should be noted, does not condone such activity, and in fact most discourage it. Moreover, "the crimes themselves are not committed on behalf of the gang, nor are proceeds shared. The individuals (or groups, which may include nongang members as well as homeboys) who commit such crimes do so for their own reasons and by their own rules—and that includes drug dealing" (Reiner, 1992: 58–59). This fact is important to underscore because it contradicts the theory underlying most gang-enhancement statutes (that increase the punishment if the crime is gang related), which suggests that gang crimes are committed on behalf of the gang.

One of the most recent studies (Decker, Katz, and V. J. Webb, 2008) was based on interviews with gang members in three different booking locations in Arizona. The aim of this study was to determine the relationship between the degree of gang organization and criminal activity (in this case, violent crimes and drug offenses). What is interesting about this study is that they considered the relationship between victimization and the degree of gang organization. Their findings are summarized as follows: "Individuals who were members of more organized gangs report higher victimization counts, more gang sales of different kinds of drugs, and more violent offending by the gang than do members of less organized gangs" (2008: 15). They also note that the strongest correlation was "between the degree of gang organization and violent offending" (2008: 16). Further, even though these gangs were not highly organized, they concluded that "what organization does exist is related to increased involvement in drug sales, violent offending, and violent victimization" (2008). Another recent study arrived at almost identical results that gang members are more likely than nongang members to be victims of crime.

Prior to moving on to the next section of this chapter, it is important to keep in mind something we have already said, namely that the vast majority of gang activities do *not* revolve around criminal activities. Nor is it the case that most gangs are involved in any systematic, highly organized criminal activities.

GANG VIOLENCE

There was a surge in gang-related violence in the 1980s and early 1990s. Moore's follow-up study of her first study of East Los Angeles gangs (Moore, 1978) is instructive and warrants discussion in some detail. She began by noting that gang violence was on the rise in the Los Angeles area. Whereas between 1970 and 1979 gang homicides accounted for 16 percent of all Hispanic homicides, gang homicides accounted for only 7 percent of the homicides among other ethnic groups (Moore, 1991: 57–58).

Moore cites the following reasons for gang fights: invasion of gang territory by a rival gang, rivalry over dating, fights related to sporting events, and personal matters in which the gang is brought in to support someone. During the 1970s, there were more deaths among gang cliques than in the 1950s. Moore offers two explanations for this. The first has to do with weapons. Not only were there more guns available in the 1970s, but those who used them were more likely intending to hurt someone rather than just to intimidate. Second, a greater degree of impersonality entered the picture, especially with the emergence of the drive-by shooting. This is related to the demise of the fair fight, whereby when the fight ends, the fighters shake hands and go their separate ways.

Moore comments that "younger members often want to match or outdo the reputation of their predecessors. Respondents from the more violent cliques were significantly more likely to believe that their clique was more violent than its immediate predecessor" (1991: 60).

It may be tempting to explain the increase in gang violence by pointing to exaggerated masculine behavior, or machismo. However, this term, says Moore, refers just as much to control as it does to aggressiveness. Increased violence by the younger cliques has been described as a reflection of members being loco (crazy) or *muy loco*. Moore states that "locura is the 'craziness' or wildness that is stereotypically associated with Chicano gangs and their *vatos locos* (crazy guys)" (1991: 62). It is especially related to unrestrained conduct on the part of a member. But even the definitions of *locura* have changed over time, often becoming linked to violence among the younger members.

Also, more of the recent clique members described themselves as either *loco* or *muy loco* (81% versus 65% of the older members); they also were more likely than the older members to emphasize violence in describing themselves. And it is the more extreme *locos* in a gang who are most likely to start fights.

Moore concludes by saying, "In general the elevated level of violence over time had some relationship to each clique's sense that it must outdo its predecessor and also with some elements of the changing definitions of *locura*. Violence also puts the gang under considerable strain. This is a consequence of the 'code of the barrio.' In part, this translates into a norm that homeboys back one another up in all situations, especially fights.... This 'code of the barrio' is one of the prime sources of lethal violence, especially in more recent times when guns replaced one-on-one fighting to establish a pecking order" (1991:65).

There is little question that the level of violence was related to the increasing availability of guns, especially the high-powered, semiautomatic weapons that, in the words of Reiner, "have profoundly altered the balance of power on the streets" (1992: 87). Much of this is a direct result of more money being made selling drugs, so that there is a decreasing need to steal guns. As one gang member put it, because of involvement in drug selling, "now you can just go buy a Mac 10 [an assault weapon] if that's what you want, instead of burglarizing somebody's house to get a weapon" (Bing, 1991: 223, quoted in Reiner, 1992: 87–88). The more weapons that are available, and the more powerful the weapons are, the more violence there will be. An increasing number of gang members carry guns with them all the time. One result of this is an increase in spur-of-the-moment shootings. Finally, with many of the new weapons, poor marksmanship is no longer a problem. Reiner concludes that "fewer constraints on violence, more shootings, fewer misses, and a greater chance of killing bystanders—that's a sure-fire recipe for accelerating the classic action/reaction cycle of gang attack and revenge" (Reiner, 1992: 89).

The violence committed by gang members was often shocking in its ferocity and is incomprehensible to ordinary citizens. Reiner notes that many rival gang members grew up in the same general area (perhaps a block or two is all that separated them) and went to elementary school together. But upon entering early adolescence, when the gang becomes more salient in their lives, they begin to drift apart. "Perhaps it is this very familiarity which yields such intensity of feelings. It also explains, incidentally, why gang members are usually very accurate (bystander casualties notwithstanding) about who they attack. These battles take place within small, fairly intimate local communities. In that sense, they are reminiscent of blood feuds from other cultures" (Reiner, 1992: 57–65). As with violence among acquaintances in general, violence can erupt over minor insults. One ongoing conflict, so far involving the deaths of at least two dozen people, is between two Crip gangs: the Rollin' 60s and the Eight Tray Gangsters. It allegedly started over a junior high school romance (Reiner, 1992).

Gang violence is also enhanced because gangs often attract young men who, frankly, enjoy violence. Reiner makes the following assessment: "The stark reality is that Los Angeles is producing an extraordinary number of dangerous, alienated young men—and, one way or another, there is a price to be paid for that in terms of crime. It may even be that gangs should be seen as symptoms rather than causes. After all, if gangs disappeared tomorrow, there is no reason to believe their members would join the Boy Scouts" (1992: 59).

Speaking of drugs, the assumption that gang leaders order members to commit violence to secure control of drug markets and other criminal enterprises is not true. Several studies have found that homicides are not very closely related to drug dealing but rather "are associated with external challenges to group solidarity and internal challenges to group norms" (Greene and Pranis, 2007: 59). Among Chinese gang members, one source noted that the police often assume that they commit violence because of drugs. However, interviews of Chinese gang members by Chin found that only around 15 percent were involved in drug sales and that violence with rival gangs stemmed from "staring" during encounters in public locations (this was mentioned by 45% of the members Chin interviewed) and fights over "turf" (mentioned by 32%). Fights with their own gang members were mostly over girls and money. Among these gang members, the use of violence was discouraged (Chin, 1996).

One exception to this research is found in a study by Bellair and McNulty (2009). They found that gang members who sell drugs are significantly more violent than those who don't. Moreover, it was found that "the gap between those groups is larger in disadvantaged neighborhoods."

Violence results from the connection between the emotions of fear, ambition, frustration, and testing of skills and the encounters during which such emotions are apparent. Fear is one emotion that instigates this specific kind of violence. It is manifested through the concepts of respect and honor, concepts that are particularly relevant within the Chicano culture (as noted in Chapter 3). Violence occurs most often against those who show a lack of respect or challenge the gang's honor, at least as perceived by the gang. This is very important because gang members firmly believe that if there is not respect, honor, and reputation, there is nothing (and the gang member comes to believe that he is a nobody). Also, attacking a member of one's own gang may be a way of advancing in the organization.

Violence is often associated with frustration and anger, which emerge from three main sources. First, violence may be a result of verbal combat, also referred to in street language as the **dozens.** A common occurrence is that the dozens routine simply gets out of control, and someone's honor or respect is challenged or offended. A second source is over women. From the perspective of the gang members Jankowski studied, the women are often viewed as property, and sexual advances to someone else's woman will result in violence. The women he studied had apparently resigned themselves to a level of subordination. A third source is the result of physiological reactions to food deprivation, inadequate rest, and taking drugs. A poor diet, consisting of too much fat and carbohydrates and low protein, plus the ingestion of drugs and lack of good sleep and rest (gang members usually stay up most of the night and therefore have to sleep in the day, which is difficult because others are up and about making noise), often caused them to be tired and irritable. Moreover, the buildings in which they live are poorly insulated or have poor climate control (either too hot or too cold).

The fights between members of the same gang are often more intense and serious than fights with others. Jankowski suggests that fellow gang members are not really viewed as brothers. They are "loners who have chosen to participate not because the gang represents a family (with brothers) but because they perceive it to be, at least in the short run, in their best interests" (Jankowski, 1991: 148).

Horowitz (1983b: 81) succinctly summarizes the important relationships among insults, honor, and violence. She suggests that public humiliation causes a person to question his own competence or weakness. This is especially important for young men without many personal accomplishments or valued social roles to protect their own self-worth when they are insulted. In a culture (such as the Chicano one about which both Horowitz and Jankowski have written) that emphasizes machismo and "defines violations of interpersonal etiquette in an adversarial manner, any action that challenges a person's right to deferential treatment in public ... can be interpreted as an insult and a potential threat to manhood." This situation demands that the offended male be able to respond. Horowitz states that this situation is particularly acute for youths because of their lack of educational and occupational success (1983: 247). Further, dishonor is something that is perceived as a loss of manhood, and the response to this, according to this subculture, must be physical. In short, "violence is triggered by the norms of the code of personal honor" (1983: 82; see also Anderson, 1994).

Violence by gang members is, as already noted, more prevalent than violence among nongang members of the same general age group and similar socioeconomic backgrounds. There are no known jurisdictions where gang homicides outnumber nongang homicides, however, because most homicides are committed by adults in totally different contexts. Klein's research documents the many differences between gang and nongang homicides. For example, homicides committed by gang members are more likely to be committed on the streets, with the use of guns and with a greater number of participants, and to involve victims with no prior contact with their assailants and where both the suspects and the victims are considerably younger (Klein, 1995: 114–115). Speaking of the streets, one study found that street corners dominated by gangs have a much greater level of crime than corners not dominated by gangs, and this includes violence (Ratcliffe and Taniguchi, 2008).

Gang-related homicides in Los Angeles are interesting because of the fluctuations during the 1980s and 1990s. Klein and Maxson collected data covering the years 1980 through 1997 (figures through 1992 found in Klein, 1995: 120; figures from 1993 to 1997 from Maxson, 1999).

Gang-related homicides really took off in the mid-1980s, exactly during the time when crack was introduced into the streets of Los Angeles. There was also a noteworthy increase in the availability and lethality of weapons during this time (Klein, 1995: 116). The number of gang-related homicides went from 212 in 1983 to more than 800 by 1992; the percentage of all homicides that were gang related went from 10 to around 45 during that period of time. A more detailed analysis revealed that part of this increase was directly related to the increase in drive-by shootings. Between 1989 and 1991, the number of these incidents went from 1,112 to 1,543, with the number of victims increasing from 1,675 to 2,222, and the number of deaths going from 78 to 141. The average number per day went from 3.0 in 1989 to 4.2 in 1991 (Klein, 1995: 118).

The good news is that there was a drop from 1992 to 1993, followed by a slight increase to 1995, which in turn was followed by a very significant decrease after 1995. Several possible explanations have been offered to account for this sudden drop, with the most plausible centering around the decrease in crack dealing, the improvement in the overall economy, and an increase in gang truces in the wake of the rioting following the Rodney King decision (Maxson, 1999). A report from the Office of Juvenile Justice and Delinquency Prevention noted that between 1996 and 1998, half of the cities surveyed reported a decrease in homicides, while 36 percent reported an increase, and 15 percent reported no change. There was an overall decrease in homicides nationally, which was strongly influenced by trends in Chicago, Los Angeles, and a few other cities with large numbers of gang homicides (Curry, Maxson, and Howell, 2001).

However, as already noted, gang-related homicides were on the rise in Los Angeles in the late 1990s and early 2000s. Part of the reason for this is the fact that so many gang members who were sentenced to prison in the late 1980s and early 1990s have been released. Following many years of what amounted to "warehousing" in California's gang-dominated and violent prisons, these men return with virtually no skills and no hope. And they are returned to the same communities, with the same problems (most of these problems have worsened over the years) and hence the same motives to commit acts of violence (*USA Today,* 2002).

However, the most recent data show that homicides by gang members are a very small proportion of all homicides nationwide. The latest report from the National Gang Center notes that in 2009, out of 167 cities (population over 100,000) that reported homicide data, one-third reported no gang-related homicides while the other cities reported a total of 1,017 gang-related homicides. This was only a 2 percent increase over 2002 (Egley and Howell, 2011: 1–2).

GANGS AND DRUGS

There is little question that drug usage and violent crimes are closely related. What is still in doubt, however, is the relationship between drugs (both usage and sales) and gangs. As far as drug use is concerned, studies spanning three decades have noted that gang members are more likely than nongang members to use drugs and to use them more often (Fagan, 1989; Vigil, 1988; Bobrowski, 1988; Mieczkowski, 1986; Moore, 1978, 1991; Maxson et al., 2011; Harper et al., 2008, Voisin et al., 2008; Swahn et al., 2010; Bjerregaard, 2010).

What is most controversial is the relationship between gangs and drug selling. Most law-enforcement sources contend that gangs control the trafficking of drugs. However, the sources that are cited to support such a view come from surveys of law-enforcement agencies. For example, the latest survey from the National Gang Threat Assessment concludes, "Gang members are the primary retail-level distributors of most illicit drugs. They also are increasingly distributing wholesale-level quantities of marijuana and cocaine in most urban and suburban communities." On the other hand, according to the latest National Gang Center report (Egley and Howell, 2011: 2), about 60 percent of "agencies in jurisdictions with gang activity do not record local drug crimes as gang related—in fact, with the exception of graffiti offenses, nearly half of these agencies as a matter of practice do not record any local crime as gang related." Also, "organizational control of the local drug distribution by gangs is uncommon." Egley and Howell note that several recent studies (e.g., Decker, 2007; Howell, Egley, and Gleason, 2002; McGloin, 2005) "find that most youth gangs lack the necessary organizational structure and capacity to effectively manage drug distribution operations." They also note that "drug use and drug sales have been shown to increase after joining a gang, and then decrease after leaving the gang" (Egley and Howell, 2011: 2–3).

After a careful review of the findings from scholarly research, Greene and Pranis conclude that

> Studies of several jurisdictions where gangs are active have concluded that gang members account for a relatively small share of drug sales and that gangs do not generally seek to control drug markets. Investigations conducted in Los Angeles and nearby cities found that gang members accounted for one in four drug sale arrests. The Los Angeles district attorney concluded that just one in seven gang members sold drugs on a monthly basis. St. Louis researchers describe gang involvement in drug sales as "poorly organized, episodic, nonmonopolistic [and] not a rationale for the gang's existence." A member of one of San Diego's best-organized gangs explains: "The gang don't organize nothing. It's like everybody is on they own. You are not trying to do nothing with nobody unless it's with your friend. You don't put your money with gangs." (2007: 6)

There is little doubt, however, that some gangs are heavily involved in the sales of drugs, even though they are in the minority. The next section covers this issue in more detail.

Drug Dealing among Gang Members

A study by Fagan (1989) reported that although gang members are far more likely to engage in drug selling than are nongang members, most of them sell drugs on a relatively infrequent basis. Generally, most gang members who sell drugs can be described as small-time dealers (Reiner, 1992: 61). This is not to say that some members of some gangs do not get heavily involved in the drug trade. Gang involvement in the drug-dealing business increased tremendously after the introduction of crack cocaine in Los Angeles in the mid-1980s. As Reiner notes, the change was most dramatic in the black community. From a "trendy but expensive specialty," it shifted "to a low-cost, high-volume product for the mass market. Suddenly, a greatly expanded market had room for countless local 'franchises.' Almost overnight, a major industry was born—with new outlets in every neighborhood, tens of thousands of potential new customers and thousands of available jobs in sales" (Reiner, 1992: 62).

Some reports give a rather exaggerated account of the gang–drug involvement. One report, for example, argued that the Crips and Bloods "have gained control of 30 percent of the crack cocaine market in the United States" (Spergel, 1990: 46). However, the spread of the crack problem as a gang-related problem "is generally attributed to market forces and normal migration patterns of individuals and families seeking economic opportunities [rather] than to a centralized, bureaucratic franchising campaign" (1990: 48).

Klein and Maxson (1990: 6) also take exception to the gang–drug linkage. They offer several reasons why the gang–drug sales connection is not as strong as media reports would have us believe. First, the greater degree of cohesiveness and organization that would be required for a sophisticated drug trafficking network does not normally exist in the typical gang. Also, such a business venture would require a gang "to overcome its own age-group compartmentalization, inter-member suspicions, inter-clique rivalries, age-specific leadership, and a focus on inter-gang rivalries." Second, if a gang were to specialize in profiting from drug sales, it would have to compensate its members. However, because membership fluctuates so much, such compensation would "require far more altruism, fellow-ship, and organization than is typical for street gangs." Third, strong and effective leadership would be required. The leadership within the typical gang "tends to be age-related and specialized for different functions." Fourth, because drug use and sales are generally combined and because users cannot be trusted (and trust is essential for any efficient business), it seems unlikely that most gangs could be successfully involved in the drug trade. Fifth, and finally, is the issue of violence. A successful drug trade requires instrumental violence, the kind that involves the "enforcer role, or takeover of rival territories," which is quite different from normal gang violence, which tends to be sporadic, retaliatory, unplanned, and expressive. As Klein and Maxson note, "It is no mean trick to convert 'normal' gang violence to that said to be demanded by drug distribution" (Klein and Maxson, 1990: 6).

A study by Skolnick (1990) questioned the conclusions reached by Klein and Maxson. His study, based on detailed interviews with more than 100 inmates (in both adult and juvenile correctional facilities in California), concluded that only a certain type of gang—the entrepreneurial gang—is likely to become heavily involved in drug dealing.

Skolnick wanted to focus on, among other things, the conflicting perspectives of Southern California convicts and the findings of Klein and Maxson on the extent of gang involvement in drug dealing. Law-enforcement sources claimed that it was increasing, while Klein and Maxson said such claims were exaggerated.

Skolnick argues that neither theory is totally accurate. He offers a **cultural resource theory** instead. To Skolnick, there is a gang culture that "generates values, understanding and trust relationships which facilitate, but do not direct, drug selling or the migration of members. Cultural gangs are initially organized horizontally, stressing values of neighborhood, loyalty, and the equality that obtains among members of a family" (Skolnick, 1990: 7). This applies particularly to Southern California gangs.

The northern California gangs are organized vertically, "with status in the gang dependent upon role performance" (1990: 7). As with any other capitalist organization, the organization of these gangs "is motivated by profits and the control of a particular market or markets. But unlike many capitalist enterprises, not all drug organizations strive for growth or expansion. They often perceive themselves as local businesses. Some may merely seek to control drug sales and distribution within delimited territorial boundaries, such as part of the city or housing project" (Skolnick, 1990: 5). (Padilla's [1992] study of a Puerto Rican gang in Chicago arrived at similar findings.) This may help explain why the gangs in the San Francisco Bay Area rarely travel (not even to Sacramento), while the Bloods and Crips of Los Angeles travel extensively. Skolnick claims that his research has discovered the paradox that those gangs originally organized for social purposes have more resources at their disposal to support their travels, more than entrepreneurial groups organized to sell drugs.

Skolnick concludes that it is the "cultural and structural organization of gangs, rather than law enforcement or market pressures" (1990: 47), that best explains why some gangs migrate and some do not. The horizontal gangs tend to migrate the most because of the greater loyalty and trust developed within this structure and because these gangs furnish their leaders with more resources to conduct their drug business.

LIMITATIONS OF SKOLNICK'S STUDY AND SOME COUNTER-EVIDENCE

It should be noted that the Skolnick study has some limitations. The most important of these limitations is the fact that the data come from interviews with a small and unrepresentative sample of prison inmates. The gang–drug connection discussed in this study has so far not been supported by most other research (with the exception of Padilla's [1992] work). However, as Reiner (1992: 70) notes, the Skolnick study "may document the rise of independent drug gangs rather than the transformation of traditional turf gangs." Even so, as Reiner suggests, some police officials believe that the gang–drug connection is more valid for black gangs than for Chicano gangs. It may be too early to tell the extent to which black gangs will make a transition to drug-dealing gangs. Reiner arrived at several conclusions regarding the gang–drug connection (1992: 70–75): 1) Gangs are highly likely to exercise at least indirect control over the selling of drugs in their own neighborhoods, but it is incorrect to say that gangs control the supply of drugs; 2) many original gang members (O.G.s) may take on major roles in drug selling, although most gradually drift away from the gang; 3) large-scale operations are generally conducted by "individuals and small groups acting on their own rather than for the gang" (1992:72); 4) gangs often recruit younger members as street-level dealers, and these members continue to engage in other gang-related activities simultaneously; 5) most gang members do engage in some amount of drug dealing, mostly of a limited nature and on their own rather than on behalf of the gang; 6) as with other kinds of businesses, a few gang members make a lot of money dealing drugs, while the majority either make a small amount or fail altogether; 7) gang members who sell drugs usually do not use them and even look down on those who do; and 8) some members of Los Angeles gangs have formed national drug-distributing networks. One report suggests that some ex-members of Crip sets have been identified as selling drugs in a total of 46 states (Reiner, 1992: 76).

Maxson's research provides a counter to the perspective offered by Skolnick and even suggests that those who are *not* in gangs are more involved in drug dealing. Her study compared two cities in the Los Angeles area, Pasadena and

Pomona (Maxson, 1995). Maxson examined a sample of arrest reports by the police and conducted interviews with gang members to assess the connection between gangs and drug sales in the two selected cities. Both of these are rather large suburban areas in Southern California, about 130,000 people each, and both have had a long history of gang and drug problems. In comparing these two cities with 37 other midsized cities around the country, Maxson found that they were close in terms of the number of gangs (e.g., an average of 24 in other cities and 32 in Pasadena and 14 in Pomona), number of gang members (2,200 and 2,000 in Pasadena and Pomona, respectively, and an average of 1,243 nationally), and the number of both Hispanic and black gang members.

Maxson compared drug sale arrests for three years: 1989–1991. What she found was that the majority of those arrested for drug sales were *not* gang members (definitions of gang member and drug sales were based upon law-enforcement sources). Specifically, during the three-year period, there were a total of 916 cocaine sale arrests in Pasadena, of which only 30 percent were gang members; in Pomona, there were 645 cocaine sale arrests, and only 21 percent were gang members.

In her report, Maxson noted that the percentage of gangs involved in cocaine arrests were similar to the percentage for Los Angeles cocaine cases as a whole in 1985 (25%). She also discovered significant racial differences between gang members who were arrested for cocaine sales and their nongang counterparts. Specifically, while 91 percent of the gang members were black, only 76 percent of the nongang members were; in contrast, 20 percent of the nongang members arrested were Hispanic, compared to only 7 percent of the gang members. Over 90 percent of those arrested in both cities were males. Further, in both cities, the majority of drug transactions (about 80%) involved only two participants, few involved any form of violence (5% in Pasadena and 6% in Pomona), and most drug transactions were done in open areas on the streets. Another interesting finding from this research is that while about half of those arrested in each city had cash on them, the average amount was $393 in Pasadena and $235 in Pomona. As for the sale of other drugs, the gang connection was similar, except in Pomona the proportion of arrestees who were not in gangs was considerably higher (92%).

Maxson cautions that many drug sales go undetected and that the data on gang members in police department files are often incomplete. Nevertheless, the data she reports contradict the common belief that gangs are heavily involved in the illegal drug trade. Her findings were even supported by the police chief of Pomona who said that "drug usage, as opposed to drug sales, is a more dominate aspect of gang involvement" (Maxson, 1995: 11).

Some gangs have been rather heavily involved in the drug distribution business. The next section summarizes some of the research on this question.

Gangs as Entrepreneurs: Organized Drug Dealing

Many observers have noted that those who live in impoverished areas are deprived of what Bourdieu (1986) has called "capital," consisting of three types: economic, cultural, and social (see also Field, 2003). Economic capital refers to material resources available to people; cultural capital refers to skills and knowledge that an individual possesses (education, vocational training, etc.); social capital includes a wide variety of social relationships with family, friends, and other people that together may be referred to as "connections." Normally these three types are associated with legitimate forms of capital, but they can also refer to illegitimate forms. Access to drug markets, gangs, and so on can be included. The lack of access to legitimate economic, cultural, and social capital leaves many poor people, such as gang members, with little chance in advancing in legitimate pursuits. As strain theory (see Chapter 7) suggests, those caught in this position have little recourse but to pursue illegitimate forms of capital. This was found to be the case in a study of Latino and Asian gang members (Pih et al., 2008).

In Jankowski's (1990) study of gang members in three large cities, we see evidence of the result of the deprivation of capital. Here he found that they had a strong "entrepreneurial spirit." This spirit encompassed a set of favorable attitudes toward accumulating money. One source of these attitudes is tensions between the consumer culture and the scarcity of resources in low-income neighborhoods. One message these youths receive is that activities not requiring cash are unsatisfying.

Many gang members do not want to take risks, so not all volunteer to participate in implementing plans. Often they have to be coaxed to do so. Many feel that there may be a strong possibility of being arrested and going to jail if they participate in a certain activity. However, fear of incarceration varies. Chicano gangs are far less likely to have such a fear because going to jail enhances their status. "So many Chicano gang members have gone to jail that imprisonment has ceased to be something feared and has become something expected" (Jankowski, 1990: 116).

Moore's study of Chicano gangs in East Los Angeles corroborates this. In fact, her data strongly suggest that for most gang members, the prison is experienced as a climax institution. In other words, going to prison is not a dramatic departure from their prior existence in the real world. Moore notes that "prison is no very big change for a man who walks a lifelong slack-wire between the highly personalized and emotionally consuming worlds of the barrio and of the institutional agencies" (Moore, 1978: 105–106).

As the preceding description makes clear, some of the characteristics of these gang members are not unlike the "spirit of capitalism" so common among those in the legitimate business world. In a similar vein, Taylor (1990a, 1990b) argues that drugs have become a unifying economic force for today's gangs, just as alcohol was during Prohibition. The intense demand for drugs has created an economic opportunity for gangs to act as suppliers. The gangs of the 1990s are no longer the same as those of the 1950s or 1970s, says Taylor. Today's gangs are entrepreneurs engaged in a corporate, albeit illegal, enterprise. They are, continues Taylor, the illegal counterparts of IBM and other legitimate corporations. As a result, a great number of today's gangs are highly organized and extremely deadly.

One of the best illustrations of the "spirit of capitalism" as it applies to gangs is described by the authors of the best-selling book *Freakonomics* (Levitt and Dubner, 2005). This is the subject of the next section.

Crack Dealing as a Business: The Black Gangster Disciples

The title of the chapter in *Freakonomics* (Levitt and Dubner, 2005) is "Why Do Drug Dealers Still Live with Their Moms?" The short answer is because they earn poverty wages dealing drugs on the street corners.[7]

As Levitt and Dubner explain it, the story begins with a young India-born man by the name of Sudhir Venkatesh who in 1989 began to pursue his PhD in sociology at the University of Chicago. His advisor, the prominent sociologist William Julius Wilson, sent him into the field to conduct a survey in one of the poorest neighborhoods in Chicago. What Venkatesh discovered was a gold mine of data provided by the leader of a drug gang that was a branch of the Black Gangster Disciple Nation. Venkatesh was trying to distribute a questionnaire when he was befriended by the leader of the gang, who happened to have a college degree in business. Venkatesh proceeded to practically live with this gang for about six years. He eventually was given a complete set of notebooks that consisted of a record of the gang's financial transactions covering four years. The records included drug sales, wages paid to workers, dues paid by some of the members, and even death benefits paid to the families of murdered members!

Venkatesh eventually earned his PhD and ended up at Harvard as a fellow. It was here he met Steven Levitt and together they took advantage of the financial books of the gang. The books provide a fascinating glimpse of the world of illegal drug dealing, and it turns out that this business was run like a lot of other American businesses. In fact, as the authors note, "if you were to hold a McDonald's organizational chart and a Black Disciples org chart side by side, you could hardly tell the difference" (Levitt and Dubner, 2005: 96).

It was discovered that the leader ("J.T.") reported to a board of directors (about 20 men), to which he paid about 20 percent of his earnings. Below J.T. were three "officers" who reported directly to him. One was called an "enforcer" (in charge of providing security for the gang), a "treasurer" (obviously one who looked after the "liquid assets" of the gang), and a "runner" (in charge of transporting the drugs to and from the supplier). Under these officers were "street-level salesmen" called "foot soldiers." The ultimate goal of a foot soldier was to someday become an officer (not unlike millions of workers of American businesses); there were around 25 foot soldiers, depending on the season of the year (the fall was the best time for sales). At the bottom of the organization were people known as the "rank and file" (numbering up to around 200). They were not so much "employees" but rather young males who paid dues (some for protection and some hoping someday to become foot soldiers).

Perhaps the most interesting part of this study was the "notebooks" and the information they provided. The total monthly revenues during the first year came to $32,000 ($24,800 in drug sales, plus $5,100 in dues, and $2,100 in "extortionary taxes"). The "extortionary taxes" were paid by other businesses that operated in the gang's territory (e.g., grocery stores, pimps, people selling stolen goods, etc.).

As with any business, there were expenses, which came to $14,000 per month, broken down as follows: 1) wholesale costs of drugs = $5,000; 2) board of director's fee = $5,000; 3) mercenary fighters = $1,300; 4) weapons = $300;

5) miscellaneous = $2,400. Mercenary fighters were those that were not members of the gang but were hired on a temporary basis to help fight during gang wars. The cost of weapons was low because the gang had a side deal with the local gun runners in the area whereby the gang provided protection. Among the miscellaneous expenses included legal fees, bribes, gang-sponsored "community events," and, perhaps most interesting, money paid to families of gang members who were murdered (this included funeral expenses plus a "stipend" of up to three years' wages paid to the families). A gang member told Venkatesh that "we grieve when they grieve. You got to respect the family."

After all the expenses were paid, J.T. took in $8,500 per month—$100,000 per year tax free. Not bad, providing you don't get killed or sent to prison. (J.T. eventually went to prison after a federal indictment broke up his gang.) In fact, about one-third of the board of directors (who could earn up to $500,000 per year) did time in prison. Then came J.T.'s three officers who collectively earned $2,100 per month or an average of $700 per month; then came the 50 foot soldiers who collectively earned $7,400 per month ($148 each). Now comes the reason why they lived with their moms: these foot soldiers earned about $3.30 per hour!

Finally, the ultimate "bottom line" of this "capitalist enterprise" that makes it different from mainstream businesses was the high probability that a member (including the board of directors) would be arrested and sent to prison, be seriously injured, or be killed. Over the four-year period covered by the financial notebooks, the typical fate of each member was to be arrested around six times, receive just over two nonfatal injuries, and have a one in four chance of being killed. You read that right: a 1 in 4 chance of being killed on the job! Compare this to the most dangerous occupation in the country, that of timber cutters, who have only a 1 in 200 chance of being killed on the job (Levitt and Dubner, 2005: 101).

Knowing this, one might reasonably wonder why anyone in this area would want to be a member of this gang. Looking at the demographics of the community surrounding this gang (typical of most gangs) provides an answer: more than half (56%) of the children live in poverty, less than 5 percent of the adults went to college, and only around one-third worked; the median income was $15,000 a year (2005: 102).

Levitt and Dubner summarize the situation as follows:

> The problem with crack dealing is the same as in every other glamour profession: a lot of people are competing for a very few prizes. Earning big money in the crack gang wasn't much more likely than the Wisconsin farm girl becoming a movie star or the high-school quarterback playing in the NFL. But criminals, like everyone else, responded to incentives. So if the prize is big enough, they will form a line down the block just hoping for a chance. On the south side of Chicago, people wanting to sell crack vastly outnumbered the available street corners (2005: 103).

Another example of the entrepreneurial activities of gangs is illustrated by a gang studied by Padilla (1992), called the Diamonds.

Another Chicago Drug Gang: The Diamonds

The Diamonds were originally a musical group, but the killing of one of their members by a rival gang was the catalyst for changing them into a violent gang. This act occurred in 1971, and for the ensuing six years, this gang engaged in violent confrontations with rival gangs. The gang gradually became more of a business in the mid-1970s. The Illinois Controlled Substance Act of 1971 increased the penalties for adults who sold heroin and cocaine, making the sanction for such selling a mandatory 20-year prison term. The adults in the area, aware that juveniles received light sentences, began to use them in their drug-dealing ventures. In effect, these youngsters became an instant source of cheap labor for adult drug dealers. Several members of the Diamonds were hired by adult drug dealers because they were juveniles. It was not too long before several members of the gang began to think about starting their own drug-dealing business. So, like a new company issuing stock, they asked other members to donate money to start the business (Padilla, 1992: 95–97).

During the 1970s, there was an increasing demand for drugs, especially cocaine. In fact, the demand was greater than the supply. "There was simply too much money to be made to forgo this economic opportunity, as more and more people began to use drugs; it was almost a natural act for the youth gang, which already controlled the streets of different neighborhoods, to become involved in this type of business. Youngsters realized that, by taking control over street-level drug dealing, they would have a long-lasting clientele desiring to purchase their goods" (1992: 15). What helped the Diamonds, first, as suggested previously, was that they already had control of their own neighborhood. Second, gang alliances that brought about the People Nation and the Folk Nation were aimed at reducing inter-gang violence. The alliance resulted in a better environment in which to conduct business. "Each gang was permitted to operate its business from a relatively safe turf or marketplace, selling only to those customers who voluntarily frequented there" (1992: 101).[8] After all, with so much demand for drugs, it made good business sense. (This is similar to what occurred as a result of the passage of the Eighteenth Amendment, prohibiting the sale of alcoholic beverages—namely, the rise of organized crime.)

Part of the motivation for these youths was their belief that traditional jobs did not pay enough to enable them to purchase the goods they wanted. These youths were also very pessimistic about the future of the economy. They rejected the traditional middle-class norm of success and, because of the strain from the lack of legitimate opportunities, became, in effect, innovators, as Merton (1968) predicted they would (Padilla, 1992: 101–103). "The youth gang as an ethnic enterprise came to represent an economic strategy with which they would create a niche for themselves outside a system that denied them equal participation. In brief, the youth gang became these youngsters' reply to a system of opportunity they believed to be closed" (1992: 14).

The gang became a sort of counter-organization or counterculture. The most important part of this culture was a collective ideology that bound them together as a whole, much like a family, and somewhat like a partnership in a business venture. Their business was analogous to a local mom-and-pop grocery store, as they catered to a "base of local consumers or people who are referred by friends." As one gang member told Padilla, "People from the neighborhood know that they can get smoke, cane, and other things from us" (1992: 107–108). They also believed that they could not succeed individually but could succeed if they acted together as a group.

The gang business of the Diamonds is run like any other business with a bureaucratic structure. At the top of this structure are the cocaine and marijuana suppliers or distributors. These are the leaders of the gang, often called the "older guys" or "mainheads." The distributor, says Padilla, "embodies the dream which the larger society had denied Puerto Rican youngsters." The distributors resemble an exclusive club and are not unlike the superstars of the NBA. But, like these superstars, only a few make it that far (1992: 112).[9]

This business enterprise is also typically capitalistic in another sense. Most of the workers within the gang hierarchy are street-level dealers. The goal of these individuals is to become independent businessmen, but success is rare. The average profit is only about $100 to $150 per week. However, the profit for the distributor is from $1,000 to $2,000 per week (Padilla, 1992: 135).

At the bottom of the hierarchy are youths who make money stealing. They are called Peewees or Littles. Most often, this stealing is a way to prove loyalty to the gang (1992: 113). These individuals are the youngest members of the gang, generally between 13 and 15 years of age. Older gang members take advantage of these youngsters because they realize that, if they are caught, the juvenile justice system will be lenient toward them. Also, the Peewees are perceived by older members as a little crazy—that is, with little regard for their actions and a desire to demonstrate their commitment to the gang. Some of these individuals already have a reputation for stealing and want to display their talent. Most of the stealing is done in groups or crews (Padilla, 1992: 118–119). It is important to note that it is the policy of the gang to never steal in its own neighborhood, so they burglarize homes and businesses in other areas (1992: 124).

Stealing cars is a common crime the gang commits. Quite often, they steal specific types of cars as requested by those who operate "chop shops." Gang members become familiar with several of these operations in the Chicago area. Many times, chop shop operators tell members of the gang where a specific car is located. Contrary to popular stereotypes, however, the amount of money the car thieves earn is rather small, usually between $20 and $50 per car. Most of the time the money is spent on each other or on girlfriends (1992: 126–127).

Eventually those who have proven themselves good at stealing will be given an opportunity to take on jobs as street-level drug dealers working for the drug distributors. This job is in many ways like any job in the legitimate world of work. Padilla writes that "street-level dealers are not independent workers; rather, they are employed by the gang's distributors, or "mainheads," and perform their jobs in accordance with job rules established by their superiors" (1992: 129). They become street-level dealers with the ultimate goal of becoming distributors, but this turns out to be a dream few realize.

Most of them begin working as *runners* or *mules.* "The job description for these individuals entails making deliveries, or drops, of merchandise for various customers of the distributors, not unlike someone who drives a beer truck for a distributor and delivers to bars and restaurants (Padilla, 1992: 130). As with any other job, the employers are looking for people who can be trusted and who are hard workers. Unlike legitimate work, however, this work is often irregular, with many downtimes when the "heat is on." Many of the gang members interviewed by Padilla continued stealing to supplement their income while working as runners.

Working as a runner provides a person with some valuable training in good business skills. For example, they learn how to manage customers, not letting them take advantage of their youthfulness and inexperience, and learn how to show who is in control. They also learn that most of the profits go to the distributors and that as long as they remain runners, their wages will be low. Yet, like wage earners in the legitimate business world, most of these runners do not realize they are being manipulated and kept as part of an "army of reserve workers" that Marx once wrote about (Marx, 1964). Padilla notes that these youngsters believe what the distributors tell them—that their low wages are due chiefly to the fact that not enough people are buying or are not buying in large enough quantities. The runners believe that "this form of labor exploitation could be best resolved once they had achieved the occupation of street-level dealer" (Padilla, 1992: 132).

The job of *street-level dealer* is the next stage in the occupational hierarchy, in which runners become hired dealers for the distributors and work on a consignment basis—that is, they are given the drugs on credit, not unlike salesmen in legitimate businesses. Those who have worked their way up to this position have proven themselves to be competent and trustworthy workers. Still, the money they make is small compared to the money made by independent dealers or distributors. One gang member interviewed by Padilla stated that his biggest profit in a week's time was between $100 and $200, while the distributor he was working for made as much as $1,000 to $2,000 off his sales (1992: 135).

The method of operations is quite sophisticated, again not unlike in legitimate businesses. Usually street-level dealers claim a specific block or corner (called their turf or marketplace) and ply their trade at this location. This is, of course, risky, because they always face the possibility of being invaded and taken over by rival gang members. It is little wonder that violence is often common as competitors try to take over a marketplace (1992: 137). One of the main differences between this scenario and legitimate businesses (aside from the obvious legal difference) is that competitors in the legitimate world have lawyers who do battle in a courtroom rather than in the streets.

When the police attempt to break up their marketplace, the gang members, knowing that they have customers to satisfy, will learn of this beforehand and establish their turf at a different location.

After they have established a turf, the next order of business is establishing a clientele. As customers continue to consume the drugs, they become, in effect, salespeople for the product because they tell others where to purchase good drugs (not unlike in the legitimate business world when one customer tells another where to buy a certain product). But actually it is more accurate to use the phrase "controlling the customer," because the dealers never know if the individual is a legitimate customer or working for the police. Also, dealers usually work in groups on the various street corners and blocks to provide protection not only from the police but also from customers who may want to rip them off.

Another common practice is to "control the law." What this means is that the gang members "must contend with the ever-present possibility of police detection," for there is the danger of becoming a victim of a buy-bust, when the police working undercover will buy drugs from street-level dealers and then proceed to arrest them. Many of the street-level dealers learn that certain police officers can be bought for the right amount of money (Padilla, 1992: 146). One method of avoiding getting busted is to simply ask a suspicious-looking customer to step out of the car and test the merchandise, for example, by smoking a joint. They also find several good hiding places for their drugs within their neighborhood.

The labor within the gang is highly exploitative, with few moving into their own businesses as independents. Not unlike in the mainstream labor market, the pay is low. They earn mostly survival income. One gang member told Padilla that, after working from about 4:00 in the afternoon until around 10 p.m., he earned between $250 and $300 for his employer but only $70 to $80 for himself and sometimes less than this (1992: 171). Another said he often earned around $25 out of $200 worth of sales. Despite hard work, dealers rarely venture beyond their own little corner in the neighborhood. Most believe they will become distributors, just like most playground basketball players believe they will be in the NBA. The street-level dealers are a cheap and permanent supply of labor. The distributors help keep it this way. In short, it is pure capitalism. The money is sporadic, with peaks and valleys. The majority of the youths Padilla studied spent most of the day and well into the night "working the block" or standing on the corner because a sale could occur at 6 a.m. or at midnight. Such a scenario is similar to that of a car salesman who stands around all day long waiting to make a sale.

After a period of time, disillusionment set in for many members of the Diamonds. As Padilla concludes, "For these youngsters the gang did not serve as the leverage necessary for improving their life chances in society, as they had earlier envisioned. Instead of functioning as a progressive and liberating agent capable of transforming and correcting the youngsters' economic plight, the gang assisted in reinforcing it" (1992: 163). They soon learned that the business of the gang was established to benefit mostly the chiefs and mainheads. As one gang member put it, "I used to see guys with the big cars and the ladies, and I thought everyone was like that. But those guys are the mainheads. You know, they are the suppliers, and there are only a few of them around" (1992: 165).

The gang members interviewed by Padilla dreamed of one day establishing their own business and could never anticipate (perhaps because as they were growing up, they got only bits and pieces of the whole story) "being relegated to the status of a dependent class of workers" (1992: 166).

The gang–drug connection will continue to be a topic of disagreement among both researchers and law-enforcement officials. One thing is certain—as long as there is such a high demand for drugs in our society, someone will supply the product. And some of these individuals will be affiliated with gangs because so many gang members are from the most disadvantaged segments of society and are therefore seeking methods of making money outside of the traditional labor market, which has been closed to them for so long.

SUMMARY

Gang members commit a variety of crimes, although the extent to which they contribute to the overall crime problem is not known with any degree of certainty. The crimes they tend to commit are similar to the kinds of crimes committed by other delinquent individuals—that is, mostly property and drug offenses. The extent of the violence committed by gang members is not nearly the level portrayed by the media, and, in fact, gang members' contribution to the overall rate of violence is relatively small. There is little question that the presence of drugs also accounts for increased criminal activity of youth gang members.

Drug dealing on the part of gang members is significant, but not to the extent that is portrayed by the media. As has been noted in this chapter, the extent of their involvement is in dispute, as is the claim that gangs are involved as an organized business. The studies reviewed here confirm this view. For the most part, drug dealing is a small-time activity in which the majority of dealers work long hours and receive little money, including the major examples seen in this chapter, both dealing with Chicago gangs. Most of the profits go to the suppliers and distributors.

NOTES

1. The stereotypes have often become so ludicrous that adolescents are mistaken for gang members simply because they "look like one." Much gang attire, plus slang, tattoos, and so on, have been borrowed by millions of teenagers all over the country, perhaps trying to mimic the rebellious image of gangs. Each of the authors has had students in his or her classes who "looked like" gang members—for that matter, many really once were gang members. Shelden gets many from Southern California who have moved to Las Vegas with their families and will tell him that they were once in this or that gang. Likewise, Tracy gets former gang members from Atlanta, while Brown, when he was at the University of Michigan-Flint, had many Detroit gangs and currently sees ex-gang members from Portland, Oregon. In all likelihood, the reader is sitting in a class with a few ex-gang members. These observations reinforce one of the key findings from gang research: Many gang members leave the gang eventually and lead normal lives, including going to college and majoring in criminal justice.

2. This research can be traced back as far as the classic study by Wolfgang (1958) and to the most recent studies (e.g., Miethe, McCorkle, and Listwan, 2005; Miethe, Regoeczi, and Drass, 2004; Beeghley, 2003).

3. Based on categories in the FBI's annual report, Part II offenses include fraud, drugs (sales and possession), vandalism, driving under the influence, possession of stolen property, and minor assaults, among others.

4. Based on categories in the FBI's annual report, Part I offenses include murder, rape, robbery, aggravated assault, burglary, larceny, motor-vehicle theft, and arson.

5. National Gang Center. Retrieved from http://www.nationalgangcenter.gov/Survey-Analysis/Measuring-the-Extent-of-Gang-Problems#homicidesnumber.

6. National Gang Center. Retrieved from http://www.nationalgangcenter.gov/About/FAQ#q5.

7. A more detailed look at this gang is provided by Venkatesh (2008). See also Bourgois (2002).

8. Padilla notes that, in the area where the Diamonds operated, drug dealing was "the most widespread and visible informal business establishment" with "nearly a dozen gangs and/or sections of the same gang carrying out drug-dealing operations in the community…. Drug dealing can be found on most street blocks, corners, and schoolyards" of this part of Chicago (1992: 48).

9. It goes without saying that the illegal drug business is not only one of the largest businesses in the United States but also an international business (for documentation of this see http://www.drugwarfacts.org/cms/Economics). And like legitimate international businesses, a few garner the bulk of the profits, operating seemingly without fear of government prosecution. This fact did not escape the attention of one of the members of the Diamonds, who told Padilla, "I don't know, but it seems like a setup. We work selling drugs, but have you ever stopped to wonder why it's people like, you know, people like Latinos, Puerto Rican people, and black people that are selling the drugs? I know that these drugs come from places far away from here. We don't grow this shit here. Maybe we should so we can keep all of the profit. You know, maybe all the money could belong to us. Have you thought about how the smokes and the cane get into the country, into our community, into the community of black people? You know, the government talks about guards who patrol the borders and shit like that. And on television, yeah, you see people talking about how the government made a large bust. And they say that's because of those guards on the borders. That's all bullshit. They are letting all the shipments of drugs come in because it's all political. People are making huge amounts of cash. But, then, we are the ones that pay. We can't get jobs, but we can certainly get our hands on as much reefer and cocaine that we want" (1992: 54).

5

Girls and Gangs

Beginning in the early part of the 1990s, there was a resurgence of interest in female offenders who engage in nontraditional, masculine crimes—particularly their involvement in gangs. The purpose of this chapter is to critically assess whether girls are becoming more like their male counterparts in relation to gang activities.

Girls' involvement in delinquent gangs has never been of the same magnitude as their male counterparts. When girls and women are mentioned, it is often through media stereotypes of bad, evil, or even overly masculine girls, ignoring the social context, especially that for young minority women (Joe and Chesney-Lind, 1995: 3; see also Chesney-Lind, 1993). Traditional discussions of gang delinquency, from Thrasher's work in Chicago in the 1920s (1927) to those in the 1950s through the 1990s (Cohen, 1955; Cloward and Ohlin, 1960; Short and Strodtbeck, 1965; Keiser, 1969; Dawley, 1992) stress the image of girls as playing auxiliary roles to boys' gangs, if they are involved in gang activity at all. In fact, in his study of more than 1,300 gangs in Chicago, Thrasher (1927) discovered only 6 female gangs, and only 2 of these he called true gangs. The stereotypical gang role for girls was "to conceal and carry weapons for the boys, to provide sexual favors, and sometimes to fight against girls who were connected with enemy boys' gangs" (Mann, 1984: 45). Most of the earlier accounts of girls' roles in gangs were based on data given by male gang members to male researchers and then in turn interpreted by male academics, which no doubt reinforced traditional stereotypes (Campbell, 1990: 166). More often than not, girl gang members have been portrayed "as maladjusted tomboys or sexual chattel who, in either case, are no more than mere appendages to boy members of the gang" (Joe and Chesney-Lind, 1995: 8; Miller, 2001).

Such impressions were often reinforced by male studies of girl gang members. Walter Miller's nationwide study of gangs in the mid-1970s, for example, found fully independent girl gangs to be rare, constituting less than 10 percent of all gangs. He also noted that about half the male gangs in the New York area had female auxiliary groups and that of all the gangs known to exist in the Bronx and Queens areas of New York City, there were only six independent female gangs. Further, he reported that the crimes committed by girl gangs were far less serious than those committed by boy gangs and were no more violent than in the past (Miller, 1975). In contrast, Joan Moore's research on gangs in East Los Angeles estimated that about one-third of the gang members were female (Moore, 1991: 8).

Given the range of estimates, one might wonder whether girls and their involvement with gang life resemble the involvement of girls in other youth subcultures, where they have been described as "present but invisible" (McRobbie and Garber, 1975). Certainly, Moore's higher estimate indicates that she, and her associates, saw girls that others had missed. The long-standing gendered habits of researchers has meant that girls' involvement with gangs has been neglected, sexualized, and over-simplified.[1] So, while there have been a growing number of studies investigating the connections among male gangs, violence, and other criminal activities, there has been relatively little parallel development in research on female involvement in gang activity. The recent study by Jody Miller (2001) is a welcomed exception.

When female researchers have studied female gang members, a different perspective emerges, one that suggests that girl gang members do *not* fully accept such conceptions of their roles and positions. Jody Miller notes that many scholars have argued that "gender is no longer relevant on the streets" (Miller, J., 2001: 5). This will become evident when we review some of these studies later.

Taylor's (1993) work marked a complete reversal in themes where girls are the central focus but from a male-centered perspective. His study provides a facade of academic support for the media's definition of the girl gang member as a junior version of the liberated female crook of the 1970s. Other studies of female gang members stress the image of girls as having auxiliary roles to boy gangs (Miller, 1975, 1980a; Rice, 1963; Brown, 1977). Miller (1980a) also conducted an in-depth analysis of a Boston gang known as the Molls. This gang consisted of a core membership of 11 girls whose ages ranged from 13 to 16. They were white and Catholic (mostly Irish). These girls seemed to fit the stereotype of inner-city working-class girls, as they spent most of their time "hanging out" around street corners and looking and talking tough. They were known in the neighborhood as "bad girls." Their illegal activities included truancy, theft, drinking, property damage, sex offenses, and assault, in order of decreasing frequency. Truancy was by far their most common offense, occurring about three times as often as the next most common offense, which was theft (predominantly shoplifting).

Similar findings have been reported in Philadelphia (Brown, 1977) and in New York City (Campbell, 1984). Overall, these studies portray girls who are part of gangs as either the girlfriends of the male members or "little sisters" subgroups of the male gang (Bowker, 1978: 184).

Early studies tend to report that a girl gang typically emerges after a male gang has been established, and it "often takes a feminized version of the male name" (Campbell, 1990: 177). Examples of the latter include the Egyptian

Cobrettes (related to the male gang called Egyptian Cobras), the Lady Rocketeers (affiliated with the male Rocketeers), and the Vice Queens (related to the Vice Kings).

The area of East Los Angeles provides a fascinating glimpse of how gangs emerge and change with the times. Gangs in this area first emerged during the late 1930s and early 1940s; girl gangs came along with male gangs. Many gangs started in an area known as El Hoyo Maravilla (translated roughly as "the hole" in Spanish). The girl gangs in Maravilla (going by such names as Black Legion, Cherries, Elks, Black Cats, and others) were small groups not tightly bound to the boy gangs and not as closely bound to a specific barrio as were the boys. They often partied with boys from different gangs (Moore, 1991: 27–28).[2]

In the mid-1940s, there were some girl gangs that were auxiliaries to the boy gangs (e.g., Jr. Vamps, who were associated with the Cut-downs). The girl gangs from the White Fence area were more like the traditional auxiliary girl gangs. Many offshoots of these gangs continue to flourish today, some 70 years later. The fact that they have existed so long may contribute to the continued fascination with girl gangs by the media. It is unfortunate that the vast research on these and other girl gangs (showing the incredible diversity of these groups) is often ignored by the mass media. Instead, we are often presented with stereotypic images.

TRENDS IN GIRL GANG MEMBERSHIP

Media portrayals of young women suggest that they, like their male counterparts, are increasingly involved in gang activities. Typical of media presentations of this issue was a special in *Newsweek* called "Bad Girls Go Wild" claiming that there has been a "significant rise in violent behavior among girls," which was described as a "burgeoning national crisis" (Scelfo, 2005). Several sources of information are available to look at this issue.

Official estimates of the number of youth involved in gangs have increased dramatically over the past decade, as noted in Chapter 1. But what is the role of gender in gang membership? The latest report of the National Gang Threat Assessment Center (National Gang Intelligence Center, 2009) noted that "in high-risk, high-crime neighborhoods, 29.4 percent of girls and 32.4 percent of boys claimed gang membership when self-definition was used as a measure." On the other hand, a 2007 Florida survey of law-enforcement agencies noted that female gang members accounted for less than 15 percent of all gang members. The report concluded, "Although female gang membership in male-dominated gangs is increasing, the prevalence of predominantly female gangs continues to be a rare phenomenon." It should be noted that the National Gang Intelligence Center report devoted exactly two short paragraphs to female gangs! So much for "intelligence"!

Other recent estimates suggest that between about 10 percent and 50 percent of gang members are females (Esbensen et al., 2001; Esbensen, Deschenes, and Winfree, 1999; Esbensen and Winfree, 1998), which is quite a large range. One researcher concluded that females, "although still marginalized and largely relegated to secondary and supportive roles in mixed sex gangs, are moving towards equality in gang roles and activities" (Gover, Jennings, and Tewksbury, 2009: 2; see also Anderson et al., 2003). Estimates from earlier years range from about 6 percent in Los Angeles (Reiner, 1992: 111) to 25 percent in Denver (Esbensen and Huizinga, 1993). Moore (1991) reported about one-third of gang members in East Los Angeles were female. Some self-report studies put the percentages much higher, such as the 38 percent figure reported in an 11-city survey of eighth graders (Esbensen and Osgood, 1997).

A detailed look at differences between male and female gang members in police databases can be obtained from a study that analyzed files maintained by the Honolulu Police Department (HPD). The study found patterns consistent with the national data. For example, only 7 percent of the suspected gang members on Oahu were female, and surprisingly, the vast majority of these young women were legally adults (70 percent); the median age for the young women was 24.5, and the median age for men was 21.5 for the sample (Chesney-Lind et al., 1994). Virtually all of the youth identified as gang members were drawn from low-income ethnic groups in the islands, but these ethnic differences were also found between male and female gang members. The men were more likely than the women to come almost exclusively from immigrant groups (Samoan and Filipino); the women, by contrast, were more likely to be Native Hawaiian and Filipino.

One major difference between girls and boys is the length of time they are involved in gangs. Several studies have noted that boys are more likely than girls to remain involved in a gang well into young adulthood. For girls, however, gang membership is much more likely to last until late adolescence, and they tend to join gangs at an earlier age (Hunt, Joe-Laidler, and MacKenzie, 2005; Miller, 2001; Moore and Hagedorn, 1996; Peterson, Miller, and Esbensen, 2001; Williams, Curry, and Cohen, 2002).

CRIMINAL ACTIVITIES OF GIRLS IN GANGS

Previous research has found that in every offense category, female gang members have a higher rate of delinquent offenses than nongang females (Bjerregaard and Smith, 1993; Fagan, 1990; Howell, 1998). Most studies of gangs show that gang membership tends to increase rates of delinquency after individuals join gangs and tends to decrease after they leave. Girls are involved in very few homicides, and the homicides differ significantly from those committed by boys (Curry, 1998; Loper and Cornell, 1995). The research is also clear that male gang members commit far more crimes than their female counterparts. A study by Esbensen, Deschenes, and Winfree (1999) found that gang girls, while to a significantly lesser degree in number of incidents, are very similar to gang boys in the types of illegal acts they commit. These researchers concluded that their findings did not support the idea that gang girls are only ancillary members or that they are excluded from the illegal and violent activities in which male gang members are exposed. "They are involved in assaults, robberies, gang fights, and drug sales at substantial rates" (1999: 48).

The Honolulu study referred to earlier found that youth suspected of gang membership were matched on ethnicity, age, and gender with youth who were in the juvenile arrest database but who had not been labeled as gang members. A look at offense patterns of this smaller group indicates no major differences between girls suspected of gang membership and their nongang counterparts. The most serious offense for gang girls was status offenses, and for nongang girls, it was other assaults.[3]

More recent studies show that gang-related delinquency among girls is related to the gender mix of the gangs. For example, Fleisher and Krienert (2004) found that having a large proportion of males in their gangs increases girls' participation in delinquency and violence (see also Miller and Brunson, 2000). Peterson, Miller, and Esbensen (2001) found that delinquency, particularly of a serious nature, was less likely within primarily female gangs than all-male gangs or mixed gender gangs. Also, girls in mostly male gangs had higher delinquency rates than boys who are in all-male gangs. Jody Miller's study (2001) of gangs in St. Louis, Missouri, and Columbus, Ohio, found that girls in gangs did not participate in the most serious forms of gang crime mainly because the male members excluded them and because many of the girls did not want to be involved in activities they considered either dangerous or morally troubling. There are also gender differences in norms supportive of violence and delinquency (Joe and Chesney-Lind, 1995; Campbell, 1993). Also, compared to male gang members, girls in gangs are less likely to engage in fighting, and they are less likely to carry weapons (Morash, Park, and Kim, 2010: 5000; see also Joe and Chesney-Lind, 1995; Miller, 2001; Molnar et al., 2004).

Jody Miller found that girl gang members report higher levels of carrying concealed weapons (79% compared with 30% of nongang members), ever being in a gang fight (90% vs. 9% of nongang members), and ever "attacked someone with a weapon to cause serious injury" (69% compared to 28% of nongang members) (2002: 85). She also found that for most kinds of offenses, girls in gangs committed far more offenses than girls not in gangs, especially serious crimes. Likewise, the use of both alcohol and drugs was far greater for the gang members than the nongang members. Drug sales were especially more prevalent among the girl gang members, as they were almost six times more likely to sell marijuana and nine times more likely to sell crack cocaine. Miller also found significant differences between the St. Louis gang members and their Columbus counterparts as far as the frequency of participation in delinquent activities. The Columbus girls were more likely than the girls in St. Louis to be involved in minor, moderate, and serious delinquency, while the St. Louis girls were far more likely to be involved in drug sales (Miller, J., 2002: 124–128). What is truly unique about Miller's findings about gang crime is that when comparing male and female gang members, there were no significant differences in their levels of crime: girls were about as likely as boys to steal things, joyride in stolen cars, damage or destroy things, intimidate or threaten people, attack people with the intent to seriously hurt them (62% of the males and 55% of the females participated in this offense), and sell drugs (2002: 133). Consistent with prior research, most of the girls' crimes were "spur of the moment" with little advanced planning.

Miller also found that making money by selling drugs was more pronounced in St. Louis than in Columbus. Most of the proceeds of drug selling were used to party. Also, the drug selling was sporadic rather than a daily event. One girl told Miller that "I ain't never really made it a career or nothing like that" (Miller, J., 2002: 144).

Being bad, crazy, or wild earns respect and status within the gang. Harris found that there were four motives for engaging in gang violence—honor, local turf-defense, control, and gain. "Machismo, even for girls, is involved in the value system that promotes the ready resort to violence upon the appearance of relatively weak provoking stimuli" (1997:158). The same macho themes emerged in a study of the female age sets found in a large gang in Phoenix, Arizona (Moore, Vigil, and Levy, 1995).

Laidler and Hunt, who note that female gang members are often characterized as being "wild, hedonistic, irrational, amoral, and violent," present a somewhat different interpretation. These girls challenge the traditional gender roles and are therefore deemed to be more troublesome than male gang members. They suggest that there exists a "punitive policy response to the grimness of street life, like the stiffening of sentences, criminalizing drug addiction among pregnant women, remanding juveniles to adult courts, and reducing monies for diversion" (1997: 148).

Laidler and Hunt found that "gang-banging is an ideal arena for studying the way in which gender is accomplished because the streets—like mainstream society—are typically organized along patriarchal lines" (Messerschmidt, 1993; Joe and Chesney-Lind, 1995). As Messerschmidt (1995: 174) succinctly put it, "gender is a critical organizing tool in gangs" (quoted in Laidler and Hunt, 1997: 149).

In the Hawaii study, the majority of both male and female gang members had extensive arrest records, with about one-fourth of each group having 10 or more arrests. Their offenses were mostly property offenses, but many (about one-third of the girls) had been arrested for violent offenses. Not surprisingly, girls were about equally as likely to have committed status offenses[4] as any other type of offense. Peer pressure was cited by both groups as a reason for their criminal behavior, but boys were more likely to cite economic reasons (e.g., they needed money) (Joe and Chesney-Lind, 1995).

It is important to note, once again, that the bulk of a gang member's time is not spent committing crimes. Furthermore, most crimes happen rather spontaneously, much of it because of just plain boredom. In the Hawaii study, Joe and Chesney-Lind (1995) found that to fill the time, gang members join together to hang out and have fun and develop makeshift strategies to fill the time void.

They engage in sporting activities and various activities on the state's many beaches. The girls, in contrast to the boys, handle the solution to the boredom of their lives somewhat differently. Many of their activities correspond to traditional gender roles—the girls often engage in singing, going to dances, and learning the hula from their families, while the boys spend a lot of their time cruising. This cruising is not unlike similar teenage activities in any city or town in America. As is typical for males, such activity often includes such expressions of masculinity as drinking, fighting, and petty theft (e.g., ripping off the tourists). A typical day of a male is described as follows by an 18-year-old Samoan:

> After school there is nothing to do. A lot of my friends like to lift weights, if there was someplace to lift weights. A lot of my friends don't know how to read, they try to read, but say they can't, and they don't have programs or places for them to go.... There are no activities, so now we hang around and drink beer. We hang around, roam the streets.... Yesterday we went to a pool hall and got into a fight over there. (Joe and Chesney-Lind, 1995: 20)

In contrast, girls are not usually involved in much drinking or fighting, although this occasionally happens. When it does happen, it is due either to unsubstantiated rumors (e.g., that someone in a rival gang threatened a girl gang member) or to the boredom in their lives. A 15-year-old Samoan girl explained it this way: "Sometimes we like cause trouble, yeah, 'cause boring, so boring, so we like make trouble eh, to make a scene" (Joe and Chesney-Lind, 1995: 21).

The Hawaii study found significant gender differences in the nature and extent of crime. Generally speaking, the girls were found to be much less involved than the boys in most areas of criminal behavior. It is interesting to note that one of the major activities of the boys was fighting, but when the girls were in their presence, they did not engage in much violence. Drug dealing was another major difference between the boys and the girls. The involvement among the boys in drug using and selling was far more frequent than among the girls. However, even among the boys, only a few were involved in the selling of drugs. Mostly it was using drugs and drinking that occupied the time of both boys and girls.

For girls, arrests for running away and other status offenses (e.g., staying out beyond curfew) were more common. Usually such arrests stemmed from the double standard of enforcement—boys were allowed to engage in this sort of behavior.

These quantitative data do not provide support for the rise of a new violent female offender. Yet we still have an inadequate understanding of the lives of girl gang members. There have been a small but growing number of excellent ethnographic studies of girls in gangs, which suggests a much more complex picture where some girls solve their problems of gender, race, and class through gang membership. As we review these studies later in this chapter, it will become clear that girls' experiences with gangs cannot simply be framed as breaking into a male world. They have long been in gangs, and their participation in these gangs, even their violence, is heavily influenced by their gender.

Types of Female Gangs

There are three types of female gang involvement: 1) membership in an independent gang, 2) regular membership in a male gang as a coed, and 3) as female auxiliaries of male gangs. Most girls are found within the third type.

Auxiliaries usually form after a male gang comes into existence and, as mentioned earlier, usually take a feminized version of the boys' gang name. They often reflect the age grouping found in male units. They have no formal leader but usually have some members with more clout than others. Girls are not coerced to join. Rather, they come into the gang through regular friendships and families. Wannabes are informally screened for acceptability. Initiation usually involves an intense fist fight with a regular (girl) member of the gang to prove the wannabe has courage. Initiation ceremonies are not unlike those experienced by sororities or fraternities or even country clubs (Campbell, 1993: 136). "The gang will not accept just anyone, and this fact alone augments the members' self-esteem, which has taken such hard knocks from teachers, social workers, police, and families. The gang rejects 'prospects' whose aim is merely to avail themselves of the gang's fighting ability for their own ends" (1993:136).

Even these auxiliary gangs are more than mere appendages of the male gangs, for many of the girls have some control over their own gang. They collect dues, hold meetings, expel members for violating rules, and so on. Strong normative control is exerted over members of the gang. For instance, once a girl becomes involved with a boy, she must remain loyal while the relationship lasts. Remaining loyal to the boy is important because suspicion and jealousy are extremely disruptive, and a norm of fidelity seeks to prevent this. Girls usually fight other girl gangs (sometimes even boy gangs). However, girls generally do not use guns but, rather, fight with fists or knives. There is recent evidence that this may be changing for some gangs, as more and more guns become available and as fewer and fewer legitimate opportunities become available for underclass women.

Many of these young women are becoming less and less attached to male gangs. Campbell's study (1984a) of independent female gangs in New York illustrates this. She found that these gangs exist as their own unique subculture in an attempt to survive within the larger capitalist society. Similarly, Taylor's study (1993) of Detroit gangs focused on female gangs whom he describes as much more independent and more willing to use force than earlier girl gangs. Much of the violence, especially utilizing weapons, is an effort at survival in a difficult and cruel world. Kitchen (1995: 43) notes that many female gang members "are rejecting the roles as mere extensions of male gangs, and working for males as drug runners and prostitutes. These females see the only way out of the ghetto life, while keeping their self-respect, is through the creation of their own crews, with their own rules and values."

In the first three editions of this book, we noted that there is another type of gang involvement on the part of girls and young women. We noted at that time that, as far as we could determine, this had not been noted in the literature. This remains true with the fourth edition. This involvement is in the everyday relationships of girls with males who happen to be in gangs, either as steady girlfriends, occasional dates, lovers, wives, or just friends. Should these girls also be called auxiliary gang members? Is this not similar to the situation of many young males who, because they happen to know regular gang members or are occasionally seen in the company of them, are therefore labeled as gang members (associates, wannabes, etc.) by the police? If we want to extend the often vague definition of a gang member to its logical conclusion (i.e., to include everyone who knows a gang member or is seen with them), then there are probably just as many female "gang members" as there are males.

A recent study of Mexican American girls by Valdez (2007b) makes this exact same point. The study devoted a great deal of attention to those he called "hangers-on." His field studies in San Antonio, Texas, documented the relationships these girls had with males who happened to be in gangs. These males have become a major part of the context of the girls' lives. These girls are not "gangs"—either as the traditional "auxiliaries" or independent groups. These girls live in the same neighborhoods, go to the same schools, and become influenced by and fully integrated into male groups.

MOVING BEYOND THE STEREOTYPES: THE SOCIAL CONTEXT OF GIRL GANGS

During the past two decades, several firsthand accounts of girl gangs have been conducted in a wide variety of settings, literally covering the breadth of the United States, from Hawaii to New York. Several themes emerge from these studies: 1) the importance of class and race; 2) drug use; 3) reasons for joining the gang (including some benefits); 4) their relationship with male gangs and males in general (including being victimized); 5) family-related issues; and 6) school and work issues. We will cover each of these issues in the following subsections.

Class and Race

Kitchen's study in Fort Wayne, Indiana, revealed some strong feelings about race and racism. Her respondents had some very strong feelings about the society they lived in, expressing the belief that racism was fundamental. One gang member expressed her feelings this way: "I think people are racist, because they always stop and look at me funny, and think I'm going to rob them or beat them up. Everyone is scared of you if you black" (1995: 100).

Kitchen's study demonstrates the dual problems faced by black women: racism and sexism. The world they inhabit does not afford many legitimate opportunities to succeed. It is a world filled with poverty on the one hand and the ready availability of drugs on the other hand. Selling drugs becomes an accepted part of an informal economy that has become institutionalized over many years. It is capitalism in its purest form—a product is in demand, and there are many willing to provide the goods. Whereas black women face many barriers in the legitimate world of work, including the consternation of males who do not approve of women who are in any way tough and assertive, they find acceptance and respect in the world of drug dealing.

Miller's study of Columbus and St. Louis gangs found that both class and race were of paramount importance. Both race and class was even more crucial in St. Louis, as there were more living in poverty than in Columbus, and almost all of the girls were black (89 percent), while the rest were other racial minorities. In Columbus, where the poverty level was not quite as high as in St. Louis, about one-fourth of the gang members were white (Miller, J., 2001: 93).

A study by Joe and Chesney-Lind of girl gang members in Hawaii found that these gang members come from many different ethnic backgrounds from those normally found on the mainland. Honolulu, its major city, currently has around 171 different gangs, with an estimated membership of 1,267. The majority of the girls were either Native Hawaiian or Filipino, whom the authors describe as part of the have-not ethnic groups (Joe and Chesney-Lind, 1995: 14).

A study of 65 female gang members in San Francisco (Lauderback, Hansen, and Waldorf, 1992) found that race was of critical importance, as the majority of the seven gangs studied were Latinas (78.5%), with blacks (15.4%) and Samoans (6.2%) comprising the remainder. Some noteworthy differences were found when comparing Latina and black gang members. Black female gang members were less likely to be affiliated with male gangs, while Latinas were more likely. Latina gang members were also more likely to be involved in activities with their male counterparts, while the black female gang members were more likely to engage in activities (e.g., drug sales) on their own. All of the black gang members were actively involved in selling drugs. For the total sample, however, less than one-half were involved in selling drugs.

A study of Hispanic girl gangs in Southern California shows that there are few economic opportunities within the barrio. As a result, families are disintegrating and are unable to provide access to culturally emphasized success goals for young people about to enter adulthood. Not surprisingly, almost all activities of young people occur within the context of gang life, where they learn how to get along in the world and are insulated from the harsh environment of the barrio (Quicker, 1983).

Harper and Robinson (1999) demonstrated the importance of social class in a study. Those girls who identified themselves as current (7.1%) or past (14.3%) gang members had the following characteristics: 96 percent of their families were receiving unemployment or welfare benefits; 56 percent were receiving food stamps; 71 percent received reduced-cost or free lunches at school; 48 percent were from single-parent families.

The economic context of gangs in general, both male and female, cannot be ignored, especially the occupational structure of America. Kitchen's study (1995) provides additional documentation of the economic deprivation that underclass women, especially black women, face today. The specific area she studied (south-central Fort Wayne) had a poverty level that was higher than the city as a whole and higher than the national average (almost 40% of all persons were below the poverty level and 27% of all families). For blacks, the percentages were even higher (38.5% of all black persons and 39.5% of all black families).

Black females in this part of Fort Wayne fared even worse: over half (54.2%) of black female-headed households lived under the poverty level (Kitchen, 1995: 84). The gang members Kitchen studied had some job experience, but most were in low-paying service industries.

A study by Laidler and Hunt (1997) found that most of the girl gang members either grew up in the same housing project or knew a relative associated with their group. The majority of these females were immigrants. Thirty-five percent of the fathers were absent; others were semiskilled or unskilled laborers. Their mothers were in the service industry or in unskilled jobs; 25 percent were homemakers and/or babysitters. And this was long before the economic crisis that hit the country in 2008.

What is important to emphasize is the social context of poverty within which girl gangs exist and to examine what it means to be a young girl growing up in such an environment. Campbell notes that female gang members "seek to resolve the intractable problems of class by simultaneously rejecting and opposing some aspects of community and mainstream values while incorporating and internalizing others. Their resulting identity is often apparently contradictory or incoherent" (1990: 172). Campbell argues that, at least for the young female gang members she studied in New York, there are five major problems such poverty-class girls face and try to seek answers for within the gang:

- "A future of meaningless domestic labor with little possibility of educational or occupational escape." Indeed, most are from welfare families and have dropped out of school and thus have few marketable skills.

- "Subordination to the man in the house." Especially within the Hispanic culture, the woman must submit to the man and has no say in the matter.

- "Responsibility for children." This job is hers and hers alone, which further restricts her options.

- "The social isolation of the housewife." She becomes trapped within the home with, at best, a few friends who are also housewives.

- "The powerlessness of underclass membership." As a member of this class, she is not only removed from the social and economic world, but is potentially a victim of crime within her own neighborhood. (1990: 172–173)

When Campbell made this assessment, it was the late 1980s. Has anything changed? In brief, it has become worse. Consider the assessment by Jody Miller, whose research has focused on girls living in St. Louis in the late 1990s and early 2000s. The neighborhoods in which the subjects in her study lived are characterized as follows (2008: 17):

- Median family income = $24,806
- % African Americans = 82.6
- % Female-headed families with children = 43.1
- % Poverty = 33.8
- Unemployment rate = 18.0

Miller notes that the city of St. Louis experienced the typical "white flight" during the past several decades. Whereas the population of St. Louis was greater than 850,000 in the 1950s, by 1990 it had dropped to less than 400,000; by the year 2000, it had lost an additional 50,000 residents. Meanwhile, racial segregation increased, and most of the youths she interviewed lived in neighborhoods where more than 90 percent were black. And these neighborhoods became typical of urban blight in other major cities as manufacturing jobs disappeared. Typical comments from the youths she interviewed described where they lived using words like "noisy," "dirty," "abandoned homes," "burned up houses," and so on (Miller, 2008: 19–20).

The youths are exposed to violence almost every day. Miller reports that virtually all of them witnessed fights, the majority of both boys and girls witnessed shootings and robberies, and about one-third saw people getting killed. Constantly witnessing such violence has been proven to have a negative impact on youths, causing them to become more aggressive and suffer emotional and psychological distress (Miller, 2008: 34).

Predictably, the public school system has deteriorated. Schools in St. Louis have been described as "crumbling," "failing," "in decline and decay," and "underperforming and violence-plagued." Not surprisingly in 2005, only 6 percent of high school graduates in the St. Louis public school system were proficient in English, while just 3 percent were proficient in math, and only 2 percent were proficient in science (Miller, 2008: 243). In the "alternative schools" where most of Miller's subjects attended, the dropout rate was 82 percent (2008: 68). St. Louis is not alone, as many studies in recent years show an almost identical pattern in virtually every major urban area (Kozol, 2005; see also Kozol, 1992).

Drug Use

Both male and female gang members (and many nonmembers living in the same areas) spend a lot of their time "partying," "kicking it," and just "hanging out," and the use of drugs and alcohol is common.

Moore's study of girl gangs in East Los Angeles reveals drugs to be a major problem. She noted that heroin has been a consistent feature of Chicano life for many years. Moore commented that in the 1980s, there was a heroin epidemic that was barely noticed in the press, no doubt because of the focus on crack cocaine. The lifestyle that revolved around the use of heroin was known as the **tecato** lifestyle. As the life history of one gang member revealed, this was a life filled with a sporadic work history and characterized by frequent jail and prison terms. By the age of 20, about half of the male gang members studied—but less than 25 percent of the females—were using heroin. By this age, most had already been labeled tecatos by their gang and had withdrawn into their own subculture. To give an idea of the importance of heroin in their lives, Moore reported that 39 percent of the men and 16 percent of the women mentioned "heroin, drugs, narcotics" as being "the major happening during their teens" and "it was during their teens that they were initiated into the world of heroin and its usually disastrous life consequences" (Moore, 1991: 107).

These individuals did not differ significantly from nonheroin users as far as family characteristics were concerned. However, they were significantly more likely to have grown up in a family where an addict lived in the home. Also, they were significantly more likely than nonusers to answer yes to the question, "Are you all for your barrio now?"

There were significant differences between men and women tecatos. Men were more likely to begin heroin and to continue the tecato lifestyle within the context of the gang. Also, the men were more likely to spend a greater part of their lives in and out of jails and prisons.

The women were more likely to be preoccupied with their children, while the men tended to lose contact with their children, a not altogether surprising finding. Also, the women were more likely to grow up in a family with another addict in the home and were most likely to begin using heroin with a boyfriend or husband. The world of the streets dictated that "a tecata's next boyfriend will also be a heroin user" (Moore, 1991: 109).

In the San Francisco gang study (Lauderback et al., 1992), drug use was widespread among these young women (marijuana was the most popular). They are not generally bothered by the police (half of those interviewed had no arrest record), primarily because they do not wear the usual gang attire. One member stated, "Basically we just wear our little beads and braids and stuff so they [the police] just think we are some girls hanging out." Another member stated, "We not in the gang bang shootings and all of that" (1992: 63). The Potrero Hill Posse gets its supply of drugs from their own homegirls (usually a senior member of the gang), while the Latina gang members get their drugs from both homegirls and homeboys. Most of their crack sales are conducted in rock houses. These houses are usually a neighbor's residence that is rented in exchange for drugs.

Drug use can also be explained as a response to trauma, which is a common feature in the lives of girls living on the margins. Much of this trauma is from abuse at home and it becomes magnified for runaways who end up on the streets, a common theme among gang girls. Additionally, girls in mixed sex groups, which often include older men, are often given drugs by those men producing the odd anomaly that, in some studies, more girls than boys were exposed to expensive drugs such as methamphetamines (Pasko, 2010; Pasko and Chesney-Lind, 2010).

In delinquent girls more generally, and particularly those with histories of aggression, depression is a major problem. In fact, girls in general are more likely to report problems of depression and anxiety than boys, and these trends are magnified among girls in the juvenile justice system (Belenko, Sprott, and Petersen, 2004: 21). Drugs are often used to cope with these problems.

One study (Kataoka et al., 2001) found that girl offenders were three times more likely than girls who were not in the system to show clinical symptoms of anxiety and depression. As has been reported by many researchers (for a review see Chesney-Lind and Shelden, 2004), girls in the juvenile justice system often have extensive histories of both physical and sexual abuse, which can certainly explain girls' choices to self-medicate in response to that traumatic history. The links between post-traumatic stress disorder (PTSD) and drug use are certainly more pronounced in girls than in boys. Deykin and Buka (1997) found that almost half (40%) of substance-abusing girls showed current prevalence of PTSD compared to slightly more than one-tenth of boys (12.3%).

Reasons for Joining the Gang

Girls in gangs are not generally recruited in the normal sense of the term, nor are they pressured or coerced. Members come from normal friendship groups in the neighborhood and through family ties (Harris, 1988). The reasons girls join a gang are much the same as their male counterparts: a sense of belonging (family-like), power, protection, respect, fear, and, sometimes, paranoia. In addition, with membership comes prestige and identity, guidance, and ample access to drugs and cash.

Fewer factors distinguish girls who join gangs from those who do not. This might be because gang girls are "less distinct from other girls than gang boys are from other boys"; most of the risk factors that relate to girls also hold for boys. For example, six out of the nine risk factors that Thornberry et al. (2003) identified for girls also applied to boys; what distinguishes girls from boys are the risk factors of lower involvement in sports, less attachment to teachers, less likelihood of receiving an award in school, and more neighborhood disorganization. However, no family variables are unique to girls (2003: 151; also Maxson and Whitlock, 2002).

The Hawaii study by Joe and Chesney-Lind (1995) illustrates a common theme among both male and female gang membership: many, if not most, gradually "grow into" gangs rather than merely "join." For the Hawaii youths, gangs had been a constant presence in their neighborhoods while growing up, and the majority of both boys and girls had another family member (usually a sibling) who had belonged to a gang. Girls tended to join at an earlier age (12) than the boys (14). Few reported having been jumped-in or otherwise initiated into the gang. The boys' gangs were generally larger than the girls' (45% of the boy gangs had 30 or more members, whereas about half of the girl gangs had between 10 and 20 members).

The need for protection should not be dismissed lightly, for this has always been one of the most common reasons cited to explain male gang membership, and it may apply equally to girls. Jody Miller notes that young women join gangs partly "as a means of protecting themselves from violence and other family problems and from mistreatment at the hands of other men in their lives. Within the gang, girls' friendships provide an outlet for members to cope with abuse and other life problems" (2001: 13).

The gang becomes a sort of family. Girls get involved in gangs as a result of abuse at home, and the gang becomes an extension of their family (Morash et al., 2010: 5101). The pseudo community of a gang "provides a haven for sexually abused and battered girls who have no genuine sense of safety, of being significant, or of the promise for a better life away from their neighborhood or community" (Davis, 1999: 257). However, in joining the gang, she is becoming more apt to be subjected to cruel treatment, injury, or death. Expected to do the bidding of the gang, activities that are for the most part criminal, she may find herself even more isolated if she is arrested and incarcerated.

Females, like males, generally go through some form of initiation, not unlike initiations into other groups in society (e.g., fraternities and sororities, military boot camps, etc.). Some of these initiations may include being beaten and kicked by gang members, participating in a robbery or drive-by shooting, getting tattoos, having to fight 5 to 12 gang members at once, or having sex with multiple male gang members. In addition, stealing sprees, muggings, or mental tests administered by other gang members are common requirements for initiation. Jody Miller (2002: 445) noted that one kind of initiation was "sexed in" which consisted of "having sexual relations with multiple male members of the gang....Other gang members, both male and female, viewed young women initiated in this way as promiscuous and sexually available and were more likely to mistreat them."

Laidler and Hunt (1997) found that one other type of initiation was that girls might be required to fight with a male, unlike the independent female gang. They were also targets for violence by other male gangs and/or the females in similar gangs (male-dominated). The Latinas self-reported fighting among themselves usually because of disrespect from another girl or because of a male; much of the conflict arose after drinking heavily. These fights were fistfights and did not include weapons (1997: 160).

Moore found that a clear majority of the males (89%) lived in the gang territory and sort of drifted into the gang through friends in the neighborhood and at school. For the girls, whereas 65 percent lived in the neighborhood and naturally drifted into the gang like the boys did, a significant number got into the gang through relatives and close friends, including boyfriends. One of the most common differences between the male and female gang members was the existence of problems within the home, which served as a major reason for joining a gang. One of the major problems that the girls had that the boys did not was the experience of being sexually abused (Moore, 1991).

Fishman's study of the Vice Queens (in Chicago) noted that they lived in a predominantly black, low-income community characterized by poverty, unemployment, deterioration, and a high crime rate. Joining the gang came quite naturally, and participation in the gang functioned to give them companionship, status, and protection (Fishman, 1988). Fishman concluded that the Vice Queens deviated somewhat from the traditional female gang that has been portrayed in the literature. The key to understanding this difference may be that this group was black and had experienced socialization practices distinctly different from those of their white counterparts. Specifically, they were "socialized to be independent, assertive, and to take risks with the expectations that these are characteristics that they will need to function effectively within the black low income community. As a consequence, black girls demonstrate, out of necessity, a greater flexibility in roles." The girls in this study used their participation within this gang "as a means to acquire some knowledge of such adaptive strategies as hustling and fighting in order to be prepared to survive as independent adult women within their community" (Fishman, 1988: 26–27).

Harris' study of female gangs in Southern California found that females join gangs much the same as they would any other group of their peers, but that the gang becomes a way of life, "a total institution, much like a commune or military unit completely absorbing the individual into the subculture" (Harris, 1997: 151–152). She found that certain values become internalized in a gang girl, and any girl who exhibits the qualities of being willing to fight, to be bad and/or crazy, to have great stamina and fortitude, and to use drugs is a welcome addition to the group (Harris, 1997: 152). Also, in Mexican American female gangs, which are perhaps the most uncommon within the varied ethnic groups, the requirements for joining a gang is to be of Mexican American descent and to live in, or near, the barrio (1997: 152–153).

Harris found that the reasons for joining a gang were centered around belonging and seeking an identity. Their perception of the gang was that with these other girls, they had "a common destiny ... a need for group support and cohesiveness, and a need for revenge...." (1997: 154–155). The violent nature of their own lives also appeared as a commonality among the Mexican American female gang members. The abusive relationships they had witnessed or experienced themselves created the necessity for an outlet for their emotions—often their anger and their rage.

As a member of the gang, the girl will be willing to exhibit risk-taking behavior to maintain her status and to prove her loyalty. "Supporting the 'hood' and identification as a gang member are two norms of great consequence, with strong sanctions applied if a girl is shown to be disloyal" (Harris, 1997: 156–157). The everyday lives of girl gang members and the neighborhood context of marginalization made joining or forming gangs an answer to their problems. Joe and Chesney-Lind put it this way:

> At one level, the boredom, lack of resources, and high visibility of crime in their neglected communities create the conditions for turning to others who are similarly situated, and consequently, it is the group that realistically offers a social outlet. At another level, the stress on the family from living in marginalized areas combined with financial struggles created heated tension, and in many cases, violence in the home. It is the group that provides our respondents with a safe refuge and a surrogate family. (1995: 17)

These young people lived in areas without recreational activities, no jobs, no vocational training opportunities, no money to pay for what entertainment was available, and "nowhere to go and nothing happening for long stretches of time." Many of the respondents said, "There is nothing to do" (Joe and Chesney-Lind, 1995: 19).

For both the boys and the girls, the gang serves as an alternative family. Some of these youths come from families in which the parents are overemployed (working at two working-class or service jobs) just to make ends meet in an area with an extremely high cost of living. Many youths are on their own much of the time, without any supervision, mostly due to being in a single-parent household where that parent (usually the mother) is working full-time.

In other cases, there are family stresses due to frequent periods of unemployment or underemployment. Thus the gang takes the place of their families in terms of having someone to share problems with and give support. One girl, a 15-year-old Samoan, stated it this way: "We all like sistas [sic] all taking care of each other." Another girl belonged to a group called JEMA, which stands for Just Every Mother's Angel. She describes the origins of this group as follows: "We chose that because all the girls I hang out with, yeah, all their mothers passed away, and during elementary days, we all used to hang and all our mothers were close, yeah, so that's how we came up with that name" (Joe and Chesney-Lind, 1993: 23).

Campbell's study of a Hispanic gang in New York concluded that for these girls, the gang represents "an idealized collective solution to the bleak future that awaits" them. These girls have a tendency to portray the gang to themselves and the outside world in a very idealized and romantic manner (1990: 173). Like their male counterparts, the gang offers girls solutions to two important needs noted by Maslow: acceptance and safety (1990: 136). These girls develop an exaggerated sense of belonging to the gang. In reality, they were loners prior to joining the gang, having been only loosely connected to schoolmates and neighborhood peer groups. The gang closeness, as well as the excitement of gang life, is more of a fiction than reality. Their daily street talks are filled with exaggerated stories of parties, drugs, alcohol, and other varieties of fun.

Jody Miller (2001), who compared girl gang and nongang members in two cities (Columbus, Ohio, and St. Louis, Missouri), found three underlying themes in the lives of the girls who joined gangs. First, the neighborhood contexts of these girls contributed to their joining gangs (and most of them joined the gang before age 14). These contexts included important peer and other friendship networks, the presence of gangs, plus the extreme poverty in their neighborhoods.

Secondly, Miller found that there were serious family problems (a theme mentioned in virtually every other study of gang contexts, especially for girls), including violence and drug abuse, all of which led them to avoid their homes whenever possible.

Finally, Miller found that for most girls, a strong influence came from gang-involved family members (such as older siblings and cousins). Each of these three themes typically overlapped in the lives of the girls Miller studied.

Reference should be made to Miller's discussion of the "neighborhood context" of the girls who joined gangs. Most telling is the extreme poverty. In Columbus, for instance, while the median income of the entire city was $26,651, within the gang members' neighborhoods, it was $19,625; while about 17 percent lived in poverty in the general Columbus area, 29 percent lived in poverty where these girls lived; and while the unemployment rate in the greater Columbus area was 5.9 percent, in the girls' neighborhoods it stood at 13.2 percent. In St. Louis, the situation was even worse, as just over 40 percent lived in poverty and 18 percent were unemployed (Miller, J., 2001: 39).

Miller also found that for girls who joined gangs, there was a significantly greater amount of gang activity around the neighborhood and more gang members who lived on the same street than girls who did not join gangs. In other words, gangs were a constant presence in the lives of these girls (2001: 41).

Not surprisingly, the girls in her study who joined gangs typically "hung out" with gang members for "some time"—often for as much as a year—before finally making a commitment to actually become a regular member (2001: 35).

Girls not only age-in but also they age-out of gangs at earlier ages than do boys. According to Harris, girls are most active in gangs between 13 and 16 years of age. She suggests that "by 17 or 18, interests and activities of individual members are directed toward the larger community rather than toward the gang, and girls begin to leave the active gang milieu" (1994: 300). Others "mature-out" of gang activity when they have children or go to jail. Jody Miller (2001: 35) found that the majority (69%) of the girls in her study joined the gang when they were under 14 years of age.

However, for many girls, leaving the gang life constitutes much the same activity as initiation into the gang. It is not uncommon for female gangs to "beat-out" members, with other members taking turns beating each girl who has asked to quit the gang. In some instances, members kill those who want out or force the girl to kill a member of her family in order to leave the gang, but these instances are rare (McNaught, 1999).

McNaught (1999) suggests that some girls who are drawn into gangs through sexual relationships and become pregnant are especially problematic. Often the children's fathers are incarcerated and cannot provide assistance, and their fellow gang members, their only friends, indeed, their family, often reject them. In addition, these girls have no skills or education to help themselves and their children. These girls realize that their gang membership can no longer help them, so they drift away from the gang.

In the Laidler and Hunt study, the girls joined gangs for the family-like relationships; however, they found that these feelings were different for girls in the independent female gang and the other female gangs. In the independent gang, the group "served as a surrogate family; providing a fictive kinship network and resource to draw upon for emotional and economic support." The females also joined together to make money. This was done largely through drug sales and shoplifting; viewing their actions as a way to make life better for themselves and their children (Laidler and Hunt, 1997: 153–154).

The conclusions reached by Joe and Chesney-Lind echo the words of Thrasher (1927) and many others (see chapter 5) and can be used to summarize the other studies noted earlier. They state the following for both the girls and the boys:

> The gang is a haven for coping with the many problems they encounter in their everyday life in marginalized communities. Paradoxically, the sense of solidarity achieved from sharing everyday life with similarly situated others has the unintended effect of drawing many gang youth—both boys and girls—into behaviors that ultimately create new problems for them.... The gang provides a needed social outlet and tonic for the boredom of low income life. The gang provides friends and activities in communities where such recreational outlets are pitifully slim. Gender, though, shapes these activities. For girls, the list of pro-social activities is

longer than boys. For boys, getting together in groups quickly moves into cruising instead of hanging out and that, in turn, leads to fights and confrontations with other groups of boys. (1995: 29–30)

For the girls, the abusive relationships within their families and in their communities lead them to seek protection within the gang, which in turn gives them skills for fighting back. But the violence the girls do engage in, which violates traditional notions of femininity, is hardly evidence of any sort of liberation from patriarchal controls. As Joe and Chesney-Lind note, the life of girls in gangs is not an expression of liberation, but rather "reflects the attempts of young women to cope with a bleak and harsh present as well as a dismal future" (1995: 32).

Relationship with Males and Male Gangs

Sexism was a topic that Kitchen (1995) explored with her respondents. Women (especially black women) do not appear to get much respect within the legitimate business world, but in the informal economy of drug dealing, they command respect as long as they are tough and do not sell themselves. As one put it, "The only girls not respected around here are the ones that are givin' it up for drugs, or are sellin' themselves to buy. Most women get respect if they sellin' drugs, but not if they using. It's ok for guys to use, but not us" (Kitchen, 1995: 104). This double standard did not go unnoticed among some of the female gang members Kitchen interviewed. One commented, "I think it is harder for girls to earn respect than guys. Guys just beat someone up, or carry a gun, and they got respect. But girls, if they mess up, they get treated like a ho [whore]…." Another stated that, "Guys get more attention, and women do not get the same amount of respect on jobs. Males have better opportunities. The bosses think 'cause they guys they will do a better job." Still another said that, "Guys around here don't respect women much. I think it is because of all the rap music bashin' women. I listen to some of this music calling women bitches and ho's and it upsets me. I think the guys around here think sex is all we're good for" (Kitchen, 1995: 104).

Campbell (1984a: 70) states: "These types of roles tend to suggest a no-win situation for gang girls. As Sex Objects, they are cheap women rejected by other girls, parents, social workers, and ironically often by the boys themselves. As Tomboys, they are resented by boys and ridiculed by family and friends who wait patiently for them to 'grow out of it.'"

Harris's study of the Cholas, a Latino gang in the San Fernando Valley (in Southern California), echoes this theme. She notes that, while the Cholas in many respects resemble male gangs, the gang did challenge the girls' traditional destiny within the barrio in two direct ways. First, the girls reject the traditional image of the Latino woman as wife and mother, supporting, instead, a more macho homegirl role. Second, the gang supports the girls in their estrangement from organized religion, substituting instead a form of familialism that "provides a strong substitute for weak family and conventional school ties" (Harris, 1988: 172).

Fighting protects female gang members from this victimization. The gang provides a "number of discrete functions" that serve as a "bulwark against a very hostile environment" (Davis, 1999: 256). The girls are most often from families that pay little, if any, attention to them, and they are starved for familial relationships; they long to have a close circle of people on whom they can depend and trust.

The girls in the Laidler and Hunt study described their boyfriends as "possessive, controlling, and often violent." This differed from the relationship with their other members with whom they kept a close and supportive relationship and did not fight, but rather "talked out" their problems (Laidler and Hunt, 1997: 157). While the males in these gangs were often protective of the females, they also victimized them, unlike the independent female gang members. This victimization took the form of verbal, physical, and sometimes sexual abuse. Their boyfriends used similar actions to control their girls; many of these males did not approve of the girls "hanging out" on the streets (1997: 161). Laidler and Hunt concluded that any type of female gang affiliation presents girls with violence-prone situations and places them at high-risk for abuse.

Most of the girls in Moore's study (1991) denied that the gang boys treated them like possessions. Three themes emerged from the male views. First, they believed that the gang was a male preserve and "any girl who joins is worthless and deserves whatever happens to her." A second theme centered around male dominance over women. As one young man said, "When you're young you want to be on top. You don't want no girls telling you what to do" (1991: 54). The third theme had to do with sexuality, one of the developmental imperatives of adolescent males. One male gang member stated that 90 percent of the girls were "treated like a piece of ass.... We just used them as sexual need things, and companions...." In more recent cliques, sexual activity began at an earlier age—14.5 years was the median age of the first sexual experience of younger cliques, whereas it was 15.2 years for older cliques (Moore, 1991: 55).

Moore also notes that the practice of dating partners from other gangs (which the majority of both boys and girls do) often caused gang fights. One gang member said, "many wars started with other neighborhoods because of a love affair" (1991: 56). On the other hand, there were times when the women helped prevent a fight with a rival gang.

In the earlier cliques, it was not unusual for gang members to have friends outside of the gang; in fact, Moore found that two-thirds of the earlier gang members had such friends. However, in more recent cliques, this percentage dropped to only one-third. Additionally, significant gender differences were found. Girls were more likely to date boys from gangs; in contrast, boys were more likely to date girls who were not in gangs, who were "squares." The boys reported that they enjoyed dating nongang girls and believed that these square girls "were their future," as they would be a stabilizing influence. One male gang member said, "you know that they were going to be good. You know they going to take care of business and in the house, be a good housewife, you know what I mean" (Moore, 1991: 75). Another change noted by Moore was that the men from more recent cliques were more likely to report that their girlfriends disapproved of their gang membership.

Latino gang girls have had to negotiate within a Mexican American culture that is "particularly conservative with regard to female sexuality" (Moore, Vigil, and Levy, 1995: 29). In their neighborhoods and in their relations with the boys in the gang, the persistence of the double standard places the more assertive and sexually active girls in an anomalous position. Essentially, they must contend with a culture that venerates "pure girls" while also setting the groundwork for the sexual exploitation by gang boys or other girls. One of their respondents reports that the boys sometimes try to get girls high and "pull a train" (where a number of males have sex with one girl), something she clearly rejects for herself—even though she admits to having had sex with a boy she didn't like after the male gang members "got me drunk" (Moore et al., 1995: 32) (see also Portillos and Zatz, 1995).

In the San Francisco study (Lauderback et al., 1992), most of the girl gang members have children of their own, who are brought along to many of the picnics. The fathers of their children are not involved in their children's lives, nor are many other members of their families. Also, their experiences with the men in their lives have been mostly negative. The men in their lives "are generally abusive, verbally and physically, and controlling." One member commented on her child's father, "They just get you pregnant and they go on about their business with somebody else" (1992: 69). However, these girl gang members would like to have a man in their lives, one that would be working and would be a family man.

Miller's study of gangs in St. Louis and Columbus arrived at almost identical findings noted previously. She found that being affiliated with a male gang or being part of a mixed sex gang (the overwhelming majority of gangs in both cities were mostly male) provided "at least a semblance of protection from, and retaliation against, predatory men in the social environment" (Miller, J., 2001: 157). The dependency upon men is clearly stated by one girl gang member who said, "You feel more secure when, you know, a guy's around protectin' you," adding that "not as many people mess with you" (2001; 157).

Ironically, notes Miller, while being a gang member offers some protection, at the same time it tends to open up possibilities of being victimized by rival gangs and the violence often associated with gang life in general. However, in contrast to family violence, gang violence is more "structured" because it is governed by various rules and regulations in that "they know which situations put them at risk, that there are known methods for response, and that they aren't in it alone." Thus, violence within the context of gangs is "perceived as more palatable for many young women," and it gives them some sense of empowerment that they did not have in their families (Miller, 2001: 158). Nevertheless, girls still get victimized, both by males in rival gangs and by some male members of their own gang. In fact, compared to nongang members, girl gang members are more than twice as likely to be sexually assaulted, twice as likely to be threatened with a weapon, and 15 times more likely to be stabbed (2001: 152).

One of the most glaring examples of girls' victimization within mostly male gangs is the "sexing-in" initiation practice. Although there was an unwritten rule prohibiting talking openly about this practice, Miller's respondents gave vague references to being sexed-in to the gang. She discovered that getting sexed-in to the gang placed them in a very vulnerable position that "increased their risk of ongoing mistreatment at the hands of their gang peers." Such mistreatment included both verbal and sexual abuse (2001: 172).

Family-Related Issues

Females most at risk for gang involvement come from homes in crisis. Virtually every study has noted that their homes most often are those which have marital discord, are headed by a single parent, and display prevalent alcohol and drug abuse; physical and/or sexual abuse often occur, and there is often sibling or parental gang involvement. Little wonder that girls usually become active in gangs in early adolescence. Moore has noted that "neighbors, family and—for the men —girlfriends all tended to have been more actively opposed to gang membership in recent cliques as compared with older cliques. The gangs of the 1970s, then, were operating both with less involvement with square friends and in a climate of disapproval: They were defined as deviant groups, and conventional neighbors, parents, and girl/boyfriends tried to discourage membership" (Moore, 1991: 76). Not surprisingly, girls had more restrictions placed upon them.

Moore reports that 29 percent of the women said that someone in the family had molested them. Incest was more common among the earlier cliques than in more recent ones. Not surprisingly, incest was associated with the patriarchal family system. Fathers who molested their daughters were also more likely to assault their wives, who were more likely to be strict with and to devalue their daughters. The victims of incest were more likely to report that their fathers were alcoholics (1991: 96). Another finding, not unexpected, was that most of the girls never told anyone about the incest and received no help (1991: 98).

Moore also reports that girls were more likely to run away from home than boys, which is not surprising given the fact that they were more likely to be the victims of incest. Boys from more recent cliques were more likely to run away than those from earlier cliques. For the girls, no difference was found between the two generations.

There was a lot of stress in the families of these gang girls, which caused many problems in childhood. Alcohol was one of several concerns. In one-fourth of the men's homes and in almost half of the women's homes, someone was either physically handicapped or chronically ill. In most homes, some member of the family died when the gang member was growing up, usually a grandparent, but in 30 percent of the homes it was the father (Moore, 1991: 100–101).

Moore also discovered that there was the additional problem of deviance of other family members. A heroin addict (usually a brother) lived in the home of 20 percent of the men and 45 percent of the women. Also, the majority of the respondents (57% of the men and 82% of the women) reported that they witnessed a member of their family being arrested when they were growing up. In over half, it was a brother, while in 28 percent of the homes, it was the father (1991: 101).

Moore concludes that, first, the problems in these families were varied, and there were few significant differences between earlier and more recent cliques. Second, it is clear that more of the women came from troubled families than the men. They were more likely than the men to come from families with an alcoholic, a chronically ill relative, someone who died, someone who was a heroin addict, or someone who had been arrested. For the girls, the gang may have been more of a refuge or escape than was the case for the boys (Moore, 1991).

Some of these earlier family problems were repeated in the girls' own relationships with men. Almost all of the girls Moore studied (both addicts and non-addicts) had been married at least once. But the marriages did not last very long, especially for men who had used heroin early in life. A term in prison usually ended the marriage (1991: 111).

There were gender differences in heroin use, as the women were twice as likely as the men (42% versus 21%) to live with someone at age 16 or younger, in contrast to only 7 percent of the nonusing men and 8 percent of the nonusing women (Moore, 1991: 112).

Even among nonusers, marriage (and relationships in general) was unstable. One main reason was that so many of the men continued to hang out with their gang after getting married. Hanging out with the gang led to problems for the family because the gang remained of central importance to the man, even more than the marriage. Also, when there were problems in the marriage, the gang became a convenient escape. A third source of problems was that so many marriage partners were both gang members; hence, there were two people, not one, unwilling to give up the gang (1991: 112–113).

Most of them had children, and, in most cases it was the women who were responsible for raising their children. Most of the women the men married were not in a gang; therefore, square mothers brought up most of their children. In contrast, the gang tradition (whatever this may be) was more likely to be found in the gang woman's household because she was more likely to marry a gang member. Most of the respondents said they did not want their children in gangs (Moore, 1991: 114).

Similar findings were reported in the Hawaii study (Joe and Chesney-Lind, 1995). Here the majority of both girls and boys live with both parents. Also, most of them reported being physically abused (55% of the boys and 62% of the girls).

Jody Miller's study sheds additional light on this subject while underscoring the previously discussed research findings. In comparing girls who joined gangs with those who did not, she discovered that those who joined gangs were more likely to 1) witness physical violence between adults in the family, 2) be abused by a family member, 3) live in a home where drug use was common, or 4) have "multiple family problems" (violence, abuse, alcohol or drug abuse, family member in jail or prison, etc.). Additionally, over half of the gang members reported being sexually assaulted, mostly at the hands of either family members or men whom these girls were exposed to through family members (Miller, J., 2001: 46). One girl gang member told Miller that "My family wasn't there for me. My mom smokin' crack and she act like she didn't want to be part of my life...." Another said she joined the gang at a time when she was "fighting with my mama 'cause she was on drugs" (2001: 47). Miller also describes girls like Erica, who was raped by both her father and uncle, and witnessed her own mother being raped. She said she joined the gang "just to be in somethin'" and so it would be "like a family to me since I don't really have one of my own" (2001: 49).

As already noted, Miller found that girls who joined gangs were more likely to have a member of their family already in a gang. Specifically, half of the gang members, but only 17 percent of the nongang members Miller studied had siblings already in gangs, and 60 percent had more than one family member in a gang, compared to only 28 percent of the nongang members (2001: 52).

One interesting finding from Miller's study is that the involvement of other family members in gangs was more salient in St. Louis than in Columbus. Recall that the social conditions were more severe in St. Louis (poverty, unemployment, etc.) than in Columbus. These differences led Miller to conclude that there was a much greater influence of extended family members on the lives of girls in St. Louis than was the case in Columbus. One of the reasons Miller cites is the fact that 72 percent of those living in gang members' neighborhoods in St. Louis were black, compared to only 59 percent in Columbus. This led Miller to conclude (based on a great deal of research) that "African American families living in poverty often rely to a greater degree on extended family for economic, social, and emotional support." This may explain why girl gang members in St. Louis spend more time with relatives who are outside the immediate family, such as cousins, uncles, and so on (Miller, 2001: 53).

In a study that centers on the relationships between black mothers and their gang-affiliated daughters, one of the authors of this book (Brown, 1999) alluded to individual cases that were analyzed in their larger social context, which also considered the fathers of these daughters and the historical legacy of the devaluation of black males and the structural barricading from mainstream society black males have experienced since the days of slavery. Such consideration is consistent with the work of several researchers (Higginbotham, 1983; Bell, 1987; Gordon, 1994), which is in direct contrast with the work of others who see this situation as symptomatic of "cultural pathology" among these groups (Fleisher, 1995; Herrnstein and Murray, 1994; Taylor, 1993).

Brown's study (1999) explores the relationships between these young women and their mothers, and demonstrates how these young women's gang affiliation affects those relationships. This study also shows how these mother–daughter relationships impact the daughter's gang activities and their individual behavior within the context of the gang. Because social phenomena never occur in a vacuum, Brown offers a historical backdrop of Detroit, Michigan, where the girls and mothers live. This history is filled with examples of racism that influence the social, economic, and political landscape, which contribute to the social realities of the mothers and their daughters. There is a long history of racial discrimination and poverty for blacks in Detroit and throughout America. This history sets blacks apart from other racial and ethnic groups in our society.

The girls in Brown's study ranged in age from 14–17 years. All were hard-core gang members, and all had been beaten into the gang rather than opting to be sexed into the gang. According to Brown (1999: 109), "this was a conscious decision made by each of these young women, since part of what they all were seeking through their gang affiliation was respect." For instance, one 17-year-old proclaims, "Any bitch can give it up to become accepted. But then her commitment is as loose as she is. I was beat into the family so that my commitment means something." A 16-year-old girl says, "I got beat into the family because, well, I wanted to be a family member, not a family whore." According to Brown, these motivations for being beating into the gang rather than sexed into the gang stem from the mothers who attempt to impress upon their daughters the importance of independence and survival.

The more than 20 mothers and their gang-affiliated daughters included in this study tend to share many common characteristics. To illustrate, all of the girls live in families located near the poverty line. In some cases, the family may qualify as officially poor, and in other cases they are located along the margin of poverty. All of the girls are currently enrolled in school and attend a predominately black school in northeast Detroit. Each of the girls has had some form of negative contact with law enforcement. This contact ranges from vandalism and truancy to theft and alcohol and drug violations. Finally, all of the girls share a legacy common to all black women—they all must contend with a society that devalues women in general and women of color even more. These girls are forced, in order to survive, to learn how to exist in "interlocking structures of race, class, and gender oppression while rejecting those same structures" (Collins, 1990: 124).

Like their daughters, many of the mothers share common threads of life. All of the mothers experienced early pregnancies. Two of the mothers were pregnant before they reached their fifteenth birthday. All of the mothers had experienced some form of racism in their life. All had experienced some type of institutional racism, while others had experienced a more direct form of racism. All of the mothers had to take responsibility for raising their family. Finally, all of the mothers share the history of black mothers who have been taught that they must provide physical protection for their daughters while teaching them how "to fit into social systems of oppression" (Collins, 1990: 123). Brown centers attention on the unique difficulties facing black mothers:

> Imagine the difficulties associated with a mother informing her daughter
> that a system operates in an oppressive way that can harm her because of
> her gender and race or ethnicity. Imagine further that, simultaneously,
> you must teach your daughter that in order for her to survive (e.g.,
> avoid the welfare trap and criminal justice sanctions, and the stigmas
> associated with both), she must also learn to become a part of that
> oppressive system. Thus, one element of the history of African-
> American women survival is part of the glue that bonds the African-
> American mother–daughter relationship. (1999: 110)

Scholars have argued that many mothers with children in gangs encourage their children to become involved in gang activities (Fleisher, 1995), or they turn their heads when they discover that their children belong to a gang (Taylor, 1990a, 1993). They often suggest that the mother's interest in their own personal economic gain is one reason for such tolerance. Brown found no substantiating data to support claims that black mothers knowingly capitalize on their daughters' gang affiliation, nor do these data support notions that these mothers ignore their daughters' gang involvement. In fact, all of the mothers consider such claims to be insulting and contradictory to the historical legacy between black women and their daughters. One mother captures the position of the other mothers when she states, "I am not working like a dog so that Latrese has to go out and sell drugs to support us. I may not have a lot of money to buy things, but I have my pride" (Brown, 1999: 111).

The mothers in Brown's study are aware of their daughters' gang affiliations but do not encourage them to become members of a gang, nor do they turn their heads and condone their daughters' illegal activities within, or outside, the context of the gang. All of the mothers are frightened of the potential dangers of their daughters' gang involvement, and in all cases there is a fear that someday they will receive a telephone call informing them that something has happened to their daughter. The mothers all concede that survival is enhanced in many cases through numbers and solidarity.

Thus, the gang, which is often bound by solidarity, is a form of survival. One mother, who also is concerned about her daughter's safety, is aware of her daughter's gang affiliation. She readily admits that black women must be stronger than men and women who are members of other racial or ethnic groups. "I try to impress on Sophie [the woman's daughter] that she has got to be strong and continue to fight and never give up. I can only pray that she has learned this," says the mother, who quickly adds, "I think I have given her values that will help her, and God will have to guide and protect her." This mother works long hours. She has problems with her back but cannot seem to get out of the "minimum-wage rut." Four years ago, she attended a community college because "I wanted to learn something so that I could get a job that didn't make my back hurt, but I had to stop because I couldn't afford to go to that school no more" (Brown, 1994). Clearly, this mother is the symbol of the strength for her daughter.

Family, as defined and shared by many black communities, "traditionally included those who nurture and help to support a child, regardless of the household residence or degree of biological relatedness" (Coontz, 1997: 120). Throughout the course of Brown's study, participants supported the idea that trust and loyalty shored up the foundation of a family. One participant proclaimed, "Trust is when you know the shit is going to hit, but you know someone is always there to be for you. Loyalty is like when you always put family first" (Brown, 1999: 115).

One 16-year-old girl in Brown's study says, "My mother is someone that I can always count on. Sometimes I can't talk to her about some of the things that I do, but I can always count on her. She has always been there for me, and I will always go down for her" (1999: 115). The mother of the 16-year-old champions her daughter's words. "I know Denise is no angel, and I know that from time-to-time she is going to step out across the road, but if something happens to me, she will take care of her brother and sister because they are family" (1999: 115). A 17-year-old girl, who is very close to her mother, says, "My mother has had a hard life. She lost her husband, my father, ten years ago, and my brother was killed in this neighborhood almost five years ago. ... If something happens to my mother, well, then I will just have to take care of them kids my own self. My family is my responsibility." Her mother, Gloria, is quite confident that her oldest daughter will look after her younger brother and sister if something were to happen to her.

Many of the families in Brown's study include children with different biological fathers. In addition, all of the households included in Brown's study, at various points in time, have taken in other children who had no biological connection to the family, and "In each instance, those nonbiologically connected children were treated as family members" (Brown, 1999: 115). One 16-year-old girl lives with her mother and two younger brothers. All have different biological fathers. Her youngest brother has diabetes and requires insulin injections. Because her mother works at two jobs, this 16-year-old devotes much of her time to providing care for her youngest brother. It is quite common for other youngsters (male and female), who are also gang affiliated, to be in the house because they understand her responsibilities to care for her younger brother. The 16-year-old girl says, "They [fellow gang members] are my all-around family. They are members of my family in the street, but they have become family members here at home too" (1999: 115). Her mother says, "Some days I think that I am just not going to make it, but then I have to. When I get home in the evening there are usually several kids in the house. They're always polite, and they always offer to help out when something needs to be done. Sometimes it seems like I got a dozen kids to watch out for" (1999: 115).

The meaning of family transcends much of the popular belief about gangs, and this meaning is adopted by most members of the gang. All of the gang members in Brown's study refer to their gang affiliation as a family affiliation. In fact, most participants reject the term *gang* completely, and argue that this term is used by various social institutions (e.g., mass media, criminal justice practitioners, and many researchers) because they want to focus only on the negative activities of the members. One girl argues that most people who use the term *gang* "want to have an excuse to fuck with us. A lot of them know that we love and protect each other, but they want to make us out as being something evil. Saying that we are a gang seems to give them an excuse to put us down" (Brown, 1999: 116). The youngest member of Brown's study says, "Being in the gang is like always being with family. One family is in my home, and the other family is in the streets. Sometimes I have a hard time seeing them as being different, because I am loved and protected in both families" (1999: 116).

Each of the young women and their mothers in Brown's study were asked to describe the neighborhood in which they live. Of particular interest was the girls' perceptions of their neighborhood, as well as their perceptions of how the neighborhood influenced their lives. One girl stated:

> It is my neighborhood, and that is really all I can say about it. Look around us. You can see what I mean. The houses are old and falling apart. There are drugs everywhere. People get killed on the streets. Everybody is poor around here. Oh they usually have food and things to get by on but they are still poor. The people who stay here are always going to be poor. Someday, I am going to get the fuck out of here. Someday, I've got to get out of here because I'm tired of being poor (Brown, 1999: 116).

When asked her how she plans to get out of her neighborhood someday, she replied, "Anyway I can. I just don't care. Someday I'm getting out" (1999: 116). When asked to explain what she meant by the term *anyway*, she replied:

> I mean just what I said. Whatever it takes…. My momma says to me that I can get something for myself if I do good in school…. When she says this to me, I usually say, 'yes momma, I know that,' but I know that is all bullshit. I see other brothers and sisters who graduate, and I see the others who don't. It makes no difference. The ones who graduate and the ones who drop out, they can't get a good job, so a lot of them, they deal drugs and steal…. Me, I'm going to take care of business and do whatever I got to do so that I can get out of here. Meanwhile, I'm going to kick with my family until I leave. (Brown, 1999: 116–117)

Most of the young women in Brown's study share the previous girl's perception of the neighborhood. For example, one girl, exhibiting a remarkable level of insight as she describes her neighborhood, stated, "My neighborhood is a place that encourages people that have nothing to take from others who have nothing. In the end, everyone who lives in this neighborhood, and other neighborhoods like this, will end up losers. It's a place that we have to try to survive in" (1999: 117). One 17-year-old girl began her description of the neighborhood by saying, "I have lived here all of my life."

Like, their daughters, many of the mothers find it difficult to speak favorably about their neighborhood. Some mothers plant flowers around the yard. "I don't do it so much for neighborhood pride," says one mother. Continuing, she states, "I think I like to plant flowers so that when I see them bloom I can pretend I am somewhere else" (Brown, 1999: 117).

School and Work

It should not be too surprising that gang members have had problems in school. Indeed, numerous studies of delinquency in general have found school problems are strong predictors of chronic delinquency (for a good review, see Shelden, 2012: ch. 10). Researchers have noted that school problems are of critical importance for male gang members (Miller, Jody, 2001; Morris, 2005). Thus, we have still another illustration of the common themes among both male and female gang members.

Gang members, as a general rule, are highly likely to drop out of school. For instance, the study of San Francisco gangs by Lauderback et al. (1992) found that the median number of years of education was 10, and only about one-third were actually in school at the time of the interviews. Lauderback et al. conclude, in a statement that echoes Campbell, that "the prospects for these young women, unmarried, with children, less than a high school education, and few job skills, can only be considered bleak" (1992: 70).

Many have noted that school is often deemed as totally irrelevant to the lives of gang members and presents a motivation to drop out and become part of a gang. Davis, for instance, has concluded, "In lives filled with boredom, the gang interjects excitement and 'something happening.'" For most girl gang members, success is elusive; "[s]chool is a road that leads to nowhere, and emancipation and independence are out of reach, given their limited family and community networks … avenues of opportunity for urban underclass girls are blocked by several sobering realities" (Davis, 1999: 257). These include lack of education, training, access to meaningful employment, and few, if any, career possibilities.

Many young women report that their teachers routinely stereotype them, ethnically, and police and punish black girls for being "loud" and "insufficiently feminine" (Morris, 2005), while Latinas are ignored and assumed to be headed for dropping out and early motherhood (Kelly, 1993).

Harris's study of the Cholas found that the bonds to both family and to school were weak (see our discussion of the "social bond" theory in Chapter 7). None of the females in her study completed high school. The gang therefore became the source of status and identity; "the most prevalent peer group association in the barrio, the one most readily available, and [it] provides a strong substitute for weak family and lack of conventional school ties" (Harris, 1997: 156).

Closely related to school problems are, quite naturally, work-related problems. As a general rule, gang members of both sexes have not had good work records. However, contrary to popular myths, most gang members, especially girls, have had plenty of experience in the workforce, although mostly in the very low-wage service economy. Moore (1991) found that there were several differences between earlier and later gang cliques concerning employment. In the earlier ones (before downsizing), 61 percent of the men and 44 percent of the women had jobs; in the more recent cliques, the figures were 48 percent and 61 percent, respectively. Those who used heroin were the least likely to have a job.

Of those working, about one-third (both men and women) worked in semi-skilled factory jobs; about one-third of the women but a fraction of the men were unskilled workers. Neither the men nor the women earned much—the median was $1,200 per month, although some earned more than $1,800 per month. Most found jobs through personal connections, such as friends, relatives, and gang members. Most were reasonably happy with their jobs and, interestingly, most recognized that they would need more education and/or training to advance themselves (Harris, 1997: 116).

In most households, at least one person was working. Roughly one-third of the men had received some form of government assistance (welfare, unemployment compensation, etc.), whereas women were less likely to receive it. Approximately one-fourth (no gender differences) got income from illegal sources, mostly from small-scale drug sales and hustling (Harris, 1997: 117).

Another area explored in Brown's study of girl gang members in Detroit (noted in the preceding section) centers on the impact of school on the lives of these girls. All of the mothers, with varying degrees, stress the importance of education. Several mothers indicated that they had tried to contact school administrators from time to time in order to check on their children's progress. Most of these mothers indicate that those attempts were either futile or were met with extreme criticism by administrators, but they continue to believe that a positive relationship exists between education and escape from poverty. However, they also believe that this relationship is not nearly as strong for their black daughters as it is for youngsters of other races.

SUMMARY

Girls' involvement in gangs has never been as frequent as that of their male counterparts. When they have been involved, it has usually been as so-called auxiliaries to male gangs. However, the extent to which girls have been involved in gang life may be understated because of the vague definitions of *gang, gang member*, and even *gang involvement*. As has been stated in this chapter, most male gang members have relationships with females, and this, almost by definition, makes every such female at least an associate gang member.

Media images of girl gangs continue to reflect the common stereotypes typical of how the media works in general. The images are exaggerations of "violent women" who have reached the level with males in just about everything. Largely ignored is the larger social context of poverty, class inequality, and racism that pervades their lives.

There is a general consensus in the research literature that girls become involved in gang life for generally the same reasons as their male counterparts— namely, to meet basic human needs, such as belonging, self-esteem, protection, and a feeling of being a member of a family. The backgrounds of these young women are about the same as those of male gang members—poverty, single-parent families, minority status, and so on.

The case studies of girl gang members in many different parts of the country reveal the common circumstances in their lives. The crimes that they commit are for the most part attempts to survive in an environment that has never given them much of a chance in life. Most face the hardships that correspond to three major barriers—being a member of the underclass, being a woman, and being a minority. The gang, while not a total solution, seems to them a reasonable solution to their collective problems.

NOTES

1. For exceptions see Brown, 1977; Bowker and Klein, 1983; Campbell, 1984a and 1990; Ostner, 1986; Fishman, 1988; Moore, 1991; Harris, 1988; Quicker, 1983; Giordano, Cernkovich, and Pugh, 1978.

2. Moore's 1991 study was a follow-up to her original study completed in the 1970s (Moore, 1978). The more recent study compared an earlier generation of gangs (those growing up in the 1940s through the 1950s) with a more recent generation (1960s and beyond). This is what we mean when we refer in this chapter to "earlier" and "later" gang cliques.

3. In addition, similar studies, using comparison groups in Arizona (Zatz, 1985) with Hispanic gangs and in Las Vegas (Shelden, Snodgrass, and Snodgrass, 1992) with black and Hispanic gangs, while not focusing on gender, found little to differentiate gang members from other "delinquent" or criminal youth.

4. Status offenses are applicable to juveniles only, such as running away, truancy, and other offenses.

6

Adult Gangs

INTRODUCTION[1]

Although this book focuses on youth gangs, there is little question that a great deal of influence on these groups comes from adult gang members. This is particularly true of black and Latino gang members who are released from prison and return to the "old neighborhood." With little, if any, marketable skills, these adult gang members hang out on familiar streets offering "sage" advice to the younger gang members—often with the same pre-prison affiliation. These O.G.s (old gang members) are typically respected and admired by the younger crowd.

Much of this is also true of Outlaw Motorcycle Gangs (OMGs), many of whom have served time in prison. Both those on the "outside" and those on the "inside" often use street gangs to "move their product"—methamphetamine. The common threads in these relationships are drugs and money. Whether in prison or "on the road," these groups can both intimidate and terrorize whole institutions and/or neighborhoods.

PRISON GANGS

The United States is currently the leader of incarceration among other industrialized nations, as it has been estimated that 1 in 100 citizens are now incarcerated (Shelden, 2010), totaling nearly 2.2 million people in 2009 (Glaze, 2010). The mass rate at which the correctional population has exploded has created a myriad of problems, both in society at large and within the microcosms that are prisons and jails. One of these notable consequences is the emergence of prison gangs, which have become increasingly prevalent in recent years (National Gang Intelligence Center [NGIC], 2011) and pose stark challenges to prison staff, administrators, and fellow inmates due to their disruptive and violent nature. Based on available data, it has been estimated that there are now at least 147,000 confirmed gang members imprisoned in local, state, and federal institutions (NGIC, 2009). Though prevalence estimates vary considerably by facility and the sample studied, researchers have found that roughly between 12 and 17 percent of inmates are members of gangs in state prisons (Griffin and Hepburn, 2006; Krienert and Fleisher, 2001), while approximately 9 percent of federal prison inmates are gang members (Gaes et al., 2002). According to Ruddell, Decker, and Egley (2006), prison administrators estimate that 13 percent of jail inmates are members of gangs.

The presence and prevalence of prison gangs is alarming because they are the source of various crimes and serious prison misconduct, including drug trafficking and drug use (NGIC, 2009; Krienert and Fleisher, 2001; Shelden, 1991), assaults and various violent acts (Griffin and Hepburn, 2006; Gaes et al., 2002; DeLisi, Berg, and Hochstetler, 2004), and assaults on staff as well as fellow inmates (Huebner, 2003). Prison administrators have expressed that prison gangs are responsible for a great deal of incidents that occur within prisons (e.g., Carlson, 2001). Also of concern is the fact that not only are incidents of disruption a threat to the security and stability of the prison environment, they are also costly; in a study of a medium-security facility, it was estimated that each violation cost approximately $970, with 90 percent of disciplinary costs spent on serious incidents due to investigations, judicial processing, and resulting disciplinary action, such as segregation and a loss of good time (Lovell and Jemelka, 1996). Yet, the best practices for the management of prison gangs are still, aptly put, a work in progress, as the effectiveness of current strategies (i.e., placing gang members in secure housing units [SHUs]) has not been empirically evaluated. Unfortunately, the threat posed by prison gangs extends well beyond correctional facilities, as roughly 95 percent of inmates will eventually be released from custody (Hughes and Wilson, 2005).

The following sections will separately discuss prison gangs and OMGs because they are distinct in several ways. First, the available literature regarding the definition of prison gangs and their organization and structure will be discussed. Next, the available research regarding the violent and disruptive behavior gang members display while incarcerated will be reviewed with a focus on more recent literature. In the following section, the five major prison gangs that are found in prisons and other groups (i.e., hate groups and terrorist organizations) and their characteristics will be briefly discussed. Finally, an overview of the classification processes and management strategies used to deal with members of prison gangs will be presented.

The Basics of Prison Gangs

The question "Exactly what is a prison gang?" can be difficult to answer, as definitions of prison gangs vary by geographic region and facility. For example, in a large-scale survey of prison inmates by the Bureau of Justice Statistics, Becker et al. (1993) defined prison gangs as

... groups that commit illegal acts and have [at least five of] these characteristics: formal membership with a required initiation or rules for members, a recognized leader or certain members whom others follow, common clothing (such as jackets, caps, scarves, or bandannas), or group colors, symbols, tattoos, or special language, a group name, members from the same neighborhood, street, or school, [and] turf or territory where the group is known and where group activities usually take place. (1993: 20)

In another study of prison gangs, Gaes et al. (2002) noted that for particularly disruptive groups, the Bureau of Prisons uses a three-tier system to define membership based on the level of involvement in a prison gang:

A member is viewed as a full-fledged, core gang member. In a few gangs, this means "blood in, blood out." Someone has to kill to become a member; someone has to be killed to "leave" the gang. A suspect is thought to be a gang member whose credentials have not been fully established. An associate is someone whose actions indicate he is conducting business or looks out for the interests of a gang but has not joined the gang or by virtue of race, ethnicity, residence, or cultural background cannot join the gang. All other inmates, except inmates associated with organized crime [are considered] unaffiliated. (2002: 362–363)

However, to account for gangs and other groups that do not necessarily fit the criteria associated with traditional prison gangs, yet another, more inclusive umbrella category, Security Threat Groups (STGs), was developed to classify inmates (Trout, 1992) and has become increasingly popular. STGs are loosely defined as

... any group, gang, or inmate organization that poses a threat to the safety, security, and orderly operation of the facility, its staff, and/or public safety. Furthermore, these individuals may be considered predatory to the safety and health of other inmates. (Newhouse, K., 2009, p. 33)[2]

Compared to typical street gangs, prison gangs are particularly dangerous, as they have been characterized as a more streamlined, efficient version of gangs that are present on the streets due to their superior organization and leadership structure (Pyrooz, Decker, and Fleisher, 2011; NGIC, 2009). According to Pyrooz et al. (2011), prison gangs operate in a more sophisticated, secretive manner to avoid intervention by prison staff, display goal-directed violence and group-style drug trafficking (vs. drug dealing by individual members in some street gangs), and most notably, members are undeniably loyal to the gang at all costs. Prison gangs tend to contain slightly older (mostly age 25 and above), more seasoned members that are likely to be racially and ethnically similar (Orlando-Morningstar, 1997). In contrast, street gangs may have a less sophisticated leadership structure, younger members, comparatively diminished levels of loyalty, and less organized displays of violent behavior. Although prison gangs are in many ways an extension of street gangs, as street gangs migrate to jails and prisons through the incarceration of their members, the conditions in prison require gangs to adapt and evolve to survive. Additionally, prison gangs maintain a defined presence outside of the walls of a prison, as members that are eventually released return to their communities of origin and may serve the gang in the form of recruiting new members and committing crime (NGIC, 2009). Needless to say, prison gangs present an inherent risk to the operation of prisons due to their structure and prevalence.

Prison Gangs and Misconduct

As noted, a body of research suggests that in addition to the unique features of prison gangs, membership leads to many forms of disruptive behavior. In one of the largest studies to date, Gaes et al. (2002) examined the records of 82,504 inmates to determine the nature of the relationship between gang affiliation and misconduct, predicting that individuals who are particularly involved in a gang may display particularly disruptive behavior. Gang membership was measured using official records and was coded on a continuum based on how involved in the gang an individual was; members are central to the gang and often must kill to gain such a title, while associates are involved in the affairs of a gang but are barred from officially joining (Gaes et al., 2002). The authors classified gang membership according to 27 distinct gangs, unlike most other literature in this area. Based on Bureau of Prison infraction records, the authors analyzed inmates' acts of violence (e.g., murder, rioting, and extortion), injuries resulting from acts of violence, and other miscellaneous forms of misconduct (e.g., drugs, insubordination, damaging property, and generally disruptive behavior).

The results indicated that gang membership was, in fact, related to increased misconduct in regard to drugs and property offenses. Additionally, in 18 of the 27 gangs studied, more serious violence was related to gang affiliation, while in 20 of 27 gangs, general violence was associated with gang affiliation. The authors also revealed that increased time in the gang resulted in less infractions for violence, suggesting that gang members may change their behavior after adjusting to life in prison or otherwise "age-out" of offending (Gaes et al., 2002). There was also a significant relationship between involvement in the gang and the frequency of infractions; members were the most likely to be involved in violent misconduct, followed by gang affiliates, while nonmembers were the least likely to accrue infractions for violence. These findings demonstrate that the relative threat an inmate poses is likely directly related not only to his degree of participation in a gang but also to which specific gang he is a member of; for example, the authors found that the Border Brothers were the most likely to commit violent acts. Thus, it is important not only to accurately classify gang members but also the activities of their respective gangs.

In a related vein, DeLisi, Berg, and Hochstetler (2004) used a sample of 1,050 inmates from a prison located in a southwestern state to assess the relationship between gang membership (street gangs, prison gangs, and membership in both) and violent behavior in prison. The authors anticipated that inmates with a continuity of gang membership (being a gang member on the street and then joining a gang in prison) may be particularly disruptive once incarcerated. To this end, inmate data were collected and analyzed based on official classification records, including gang affiliation (membership in a street gang, prison gang, and both), criminal career (history of confinement, violence, substance abuse, escapes, and offense severity), demographic data (e.g., age, race), sentence length, and acts of violence committed in prison (e.g., sexual assault, murder). In contrast to non-gang members, inmates that had either prior membership in a street gang or current membership in a prison gang were more likely to engage in violent misconduct. Unexpectedly, the relationship between inmates that were involved in both street gangs and prison gangs and infractions for violent behavior was insignificant. Though counterintuitive, the authors speculated that this finding may stem from increased correctional control of inmates heavily involved in gang activity (e.g., segregation in a SHU or solitary confinement), impacting their ability to commit violent offenses while incarcerated (DeLisi et al., 2004).

In a subsequent study of prison misconduct and gang membership, Drury and DeLisi (2011) hypothesized that inmates with histories of homicide and street gang affiliation would accumulate a greater amount of institutional infractions than those who had committed a homicide but were not involved in a gang. The authors examined each inmate's initial risk assessment, which is a tool used by the Department of Corrections to determine an inmate's classification and placement within an institution based on the inmate's background (e.g., offense history, drug use) and disciplinary records. Infractions were measured by six dependent variables—insubordination with correctional officers, destruction of property, holding a deadly weapon, holding illicit materials, committing three or greater insignificant infractions (e.g., presence in a restricted portion of the prison, roughhousing, faking illness), and committing major infractions (e.g., homicide, rape, breaking out of a facility)—and were compared across the two groups (homicide offenders without ties to a gang and "gangkill" inmates who had committed a homicide and were involved with a street gang). It was found that gangkill inmates were significantly more likely to commit *all* types of prison misconduct, while homicide offenders without prior gang afflation were actually less likely to commit prison misconduct. These findings suggest that gang members who have killed may, in particular, pose a safety threat to both fellow inmates and prison staff and should be monitored accordingly.

In a slight departure from the these studies of gang membership and its impact on prison violence, Griffin and Hepburn (2006) examined inmates who had been in prison for 3 years or more, positing that inmates may behave more violently and disruptively when they are first incarcerated and are acclimating to the prison environment. The authors examined the disciplinary records of 2,158 inmates during the 36 months following their initial imprisonment. The authors examined several independent variables, including demographic characteristics (e.g., age, ethnicity), sentence length, offense severity, and gang membership (street gang membership, prison gang membership, and nonmembership). The dependent variable, violent misconduct, was measured by infractions in the following categories: assault, fighting, threats, weapons, and other types of major violent misconduct (Griffin and Hepburn, 2006). The results indicated that overall, inmates who were affiliated with either a street or prison gang were significantly more likely to incur infractions for violence compared to nongang members, even when controlling for other factors such as age and ethnicity. Inmates involved with prison gangs were also significantly more likely to be involved in fighting offenses than those involved with street gangs and nonaffiliated inmates. Interestingly, inmates involved with street gangs and prison gangs were otherwise largely similar in terms of the amount of violent offenses committed, suggesting that any type of gang membership, regardless of its point of origin, may increase violent offending in penal institutions.

Aside from increased disobedience in a prison setting, there is also evidence that gang members are qualitatively different from nongang members in other areas such as social equity, which may partially explain their gang affiliation. Krienert and Fleisher (2001) compared 704 inmates (gang members and non-members) to determine if there are other forms of social deficiencies present in gang members, such as a lack of employment and increased drug use. During intake, inmates were systematically selected and were asked to participate in a structured interview. Inmates were asked questions about the 36 months prior to their arrest in the following areas: gang membership, demographics, offense history and acts of violence, employment, and substance use. Compared to nongang members, gang members disclosed a greater amount of arrests (72% vs. 53%). Additionally, gang members reported increased involvement in criminal activity at a younger age, committing a greater amount of robberies and assaults, and greater drug use than nonmembers, particularly in regard to marijuana.

Gang members also reported dismal educational and employment opportunities; not only did they earn less than their nongang member counterparts, even when taking into account illegally earned income, but they also possessed substantially lower levels of education (64% of gang members did not have a high school diploma or GED compared to 34% of nongang members). These findings demonstrate that given the relative severity of their criminal histories and degree of social disadvantage, gang members are not only in need of greater monitoring but also increased access to programming in order to address their needs and deficits (Krienert and Fleisher, 2001). Rather than focusing solely on security, drug addiction and life skills, such as educational and vocational training, need to be addressed to increase the likelihood that members will seek out other opportunities once released. It is paramount that efforts be made to modify the behavior of gang-involved inmates, as it has been demonstrated that such individuals are more likely to recidivate and engage in acts of violence upon release than nongang members (Olson, Dooley, and Kane, 2004).

Major Prison Gangs

Prison gangs have undergone a considerable metamorphosis over time, becoming increasingly commonplace. The first prison gang, the Gypsy Jokers, emerged in the 1950s in Washington (Orlando-Morningstar, 1997). Today, there are an estimated 20,000 gangs that exist both in the streets and in correctional facilities across the United States, with a total of 147,000 gang members behind bars (NGIC, 2009). Currently, there are five main groups that have been identified by the Bureau of Prisons as being "Certified Disruptive Groups" and, therefore, are monitored more closely than other prison gangs because of their menacing behavior (Orlando-Morningstar, 1997; Gaes et al., 2002). These gangs are formally known as the Mexican Mafia (La Eme), La Nuestra Familia, the Texas Syndicate, the Black Guerilla Family, and the Aryan Brotherhood. Though less prolific, there are also other groups in prisons that are considered STGs, such as hate groups and terrorist organizations. Each of these factions will be briefly discussed in this section.

The first prison gang with national ties, **the Mexican Mafia** (also known as La Eme, or the Spanish letter M) was developed in 1957 by 13 Latino gang members from the Los Angeles area (Valdez, 2009; Orlando-Morningstar, 1997). The 13 founding members were housed at the Deuel Vocational Institution located in Tracy, California, and unified for the goal of self-defense against other rival inmates (Valdez, 2009; Orlando-Morningstar, 1997). Currently, Eme members continue to hail predominantly from the barrios of Southern California and are at least 200 members strong (NGIC, 2009). However, the Eme's true power and influence comes through its control of approximately 50,000 to 75,000 Sureños (Southerners), a separate melting-pot gang comprised of Southern-affiliated Mexicans who were gang involved on the streets and unite once incarcerated (NGIC, 2009). The Sureños are known to commit crimes on behalf of the Mexican Mafia; for example, Sureño street-level drug dealers are required to give a share of their income to the Mexican Mafia (Montgomery, 2008). The Eme strives to intimidate the Sureños, as noted by a former member:

> A Sureño... knows that if he's engaged in a criminal activity on the streets, at some point he's going to go to jail, or going to go to prison... Because the Mexican mafia has such influence within the prisons and the jails, that street gang member knows, "If I don't do what I'm told to do on the streets, that when I hit the jail, or when I hit the prisons, there are those who are so loyal to the Mexican mafia that they're going to assault me." (Montgomery, 2008, para. 30)

The Eme and the Sureños detest the Northerners, as they perceive them to be simple farmers (NGIC, 2009). Members of the Mexican Mafia are known as "Carnales," Spanish slang for brothers (Rafael, 2009). The Eme enforces several rules, such as a policy of "blood in, blood out," and punishes offenses such as homosexuality, telling others about the activities of the gang, and drug addiction (Rafael, 2009).

The Mexican Mafia is well known for its brutality, which has been confirmed empirically; Gaes et al. (2002) found that the Mexican Mafia had one of the highest rates of serious violent offending (violence resulting in injury or the use of a weapon) in their sample of gangs. The Mexican Mafia requires obedience and discipline of its members and leaders; if Carnales refuse, for instance, to go through with a contract killing, they will instead be marked for death (Federal

Bureau of Investigations [FBI], 2011). This discipline is likely related to the fact that some of the members of both the Mexican Mafia and the Sureños have been involved in the military, and, thus, have received military training (NGIC, 2009). This gang is mainly involved in drug trafficking (cocaine, meth-amphetamine, heroin, marijuana) through their ties to contacts in Mexico but has also been involved in gambling and same-sex prostitution (NGIC, 2009; FBI, 2009). The Eme often display tattoos of a black hand on their chest or the number 13, which represents the letter M (Valdez, 2009).

La Nuestra Familia (Spanish for "our family") was founded by a group of Latino individuals in the 1960s for the purpose of aiding inexperienced inmates and defending against the dominance of the Mexican Mafia, an intense, violent rivalry that endures to this day (Valdez, 2009; Orlando-Morningstar, 1997). While the Mexican Mafia represents Latinos from Southern California, La Nues-tra Familia is affiliated with northern California, originating in Soledad State Prison, and currently has 250 members (Orlando-Morningstar, 1997; National Drug Intelligence Center [NDIC], 2005). Paralleling the Mexican Mafia, La Nuestra Familia works closely with the Norteños (Northerners), a gang of vari-ous Hispanics from northern California that coalesces in prison and contains 1,000 or more members (NGIC, 2009; NDIC, 2005).

La Nuestra Familia has a sophisticated structure in terms of leadership, as well as a comprehensive constitution; Skarbek (2008) noted that the organization has tried to develop a "system of checks and balances" to promote fairness and reduce predation between leaders and soldiers (2008: 202). The organization is headed by a supreme leader called the Nuestro General, who has the power to declare war, followed in order by a Regimental Captain, Lieutenants, and Famil-iano Soldados, or Soldiers (Nuestra Familia, n.d.). Members accept the following oath: "If I go forward, follow me. If I hesitate, push me. If I am killed, avenge me. If I am a traitor, kill me" (Fuentes, 2006, preface). Membership is also "blood in, blood out":

> All new members must spill the blood of the enemy to prove their
> NF loyalty, as the NF will not hesitate to spill the blood of a member
> who turns coward, traitor, or deserter. Blood in, blood out is, in fact, an
> NF ritual, not a myth. Blood in relates to the blood spilled during
> initiation, and blood out alludes to the consequences of trying to depart
> from the gang. (Fuentes, 2006: 2)

La Nuestra Familia is involved in various types of crime but predominantly supports itself through the business of drug distribution. The gang sells drugs inside and outside of prison; it is also involved in intimidating and controlling drug dealers, homicide, and robbery (NDIC, 2005). This gang is distinguished by the use of the number 14, which stands for the letter N's place in the alphabet (the letter N in Spanish is referred to as "Ene"), while tattoos may feature a Mexican sombrero and a blood-soaked dagger or a sword alongside the initials NF (Valdez, 2009).

The Texas Syndicate was established in 1978 in Folsom Prison by Hispanic inmates based out of Texas and currently has about 1,300 members

(Valdez, 2009; NDIC, 2005; Fong, 1990). This gang has a strict membership policy that adheres to ethnic segregation, as most members are Mexican Americans (NDIC, 2005). According to Fong (1990; see also Texas Syndicate, 2012), the Texas Syndicate is highly structured, with a president and vice president that are elected, as well as captains, lieutenants, sergeants of arms, and soldiers who facilitate the gang's operation. The gang is democratically run, and members are permitted to voice their opinion to approve ideas (as well as contract killings). The Texas Syndicate originated in 1973 at the Ellis state prison in Huntsville, Texas. They subsequently "declared war on all of TDC's inmate building tenders, AKA 'turn keys.'" These prisoners were despised by most prisoners because they received favors from prison staff in return for helping to keep gangs in check. The Texas Syndicate and other gangs began jockeying for power and prison soon became a war zone (Texas Syndicate, 2012). According to the special prison Web site on this gang:

> The Texas Syndicate is controlled by a president and vice president who are elected by the vote of the gang's majority. In the prison system level, the gang is ruled by a chairman who orders the vice chairman, captain, lieutenant, sergeant, and soldiers. The Texas Syndicate also has a Board of Directors whose duty is to monitor the gang's funds, approve of new members, and authorize war. Joining the gang is a lifetime commitment, and all members are required to produce money for the gang. (Texas Syndicate, 2012)

The Texas Syndicate maintains relationships with Mexican drug-trafficking organizations (NDIC, 2005). The gang primarily supports itself by smuggling large quantities of drugs (methamphetamine, cocaine, heroin, marijuana) through the Mexican border and selling them to both inmates and citizens in the community (NDIC, 2005), but it is also involved in other activities such as gambling, coercion, and prostitution (Fong, 1990). The Texas Syndicate is also known for its disruptive behavior in prison, both anecdotally and empirically. Gaes et al. (2002) found that with the exception of the Border Brothers, this gang was the most likely to be involved in all forms of misconduct (as measured by infractions for violence and drugs) compared to 26 other gangs. The Texas Syndicate is represented by the letters T and S, which may be displayed openly in tattoos or hidden by other symbols and pictures (Valdez, 2009).

The Black Guerilla Family was founded in 1966 by a former member of the Black Panthers who was held at San Quentin prison (Valdez, 2009). Compared to other major prison gangs, it is the most politically charged, known for its endorsement of extreme anti-government and anti-authority attitudes (Orlando-Morningstar, 1997). This gang was originally geared toward black individuals who felt they had been victims of white oppression and were incarcerated as a result; it also aligned itself with radical beliefs, such as Marxism, Leninism, and Maoism, and solicited members from other revolutionary groups, such as the Black Liberation Army, to join the gang (Valdez, 2009; Orlando-Morningstar, 1997). Currently, the gang contains approximately 100 to 300[3] members and is predominantly seen in California and Maryland. The Black

Guerilla Family is extremely structured and displays paramilitary characteristics, pledging obedience to a "supreme leader" and "central committee" (NGIC, 2009: 29). Members are also bound by national guidelines (NGIC, 2009), which prohibit certain activities (usage of heroin, aiding enemies) and the following oath that denotes lifelong dedication to the gang:

> If I should ever break my stride,
> And falter at my comrade's side,
> This oath will kill me.
> If ever my world should prove untrue,
> Should I betray this chosen few,
> This oath will kill me.
> Should I be slow to take a stand,
> Should I show fear to any man,
> This oath will kill me.
> Should I grow lax in discipline,
> In time of strife refuse my hand.
> This oath will kill me (Knox, n.d.)

The Black Guerilla Family is mainly involved in drug trafficking in the form of cocaine and marijuana (NGIC, 2009). La Nuestra Familia and the Norteños maintain a cooperative relationship with the Black Guerilla Family and, thus, provide the gang with drugs. In contrast, however, the Mexican Mafia is a fierce enemy, as they have reportedly initiated a "green light," or an order to attack and potentially kill, for all members of the Black Guerilla Family (Mock, 2006). Black Guerilla Family members commonly display two tattoos: "a prison watchtower surrounded by a dragon with a quarter moon depicted in its body" and "the silhouette of a rifle with a sword lying over it to form an X [with the] initials BGF" (Valdez, 2009: 42).

The Aryan Brotherhood (AB) was formed in 1960 by white supremacist inmates (Valdez, 2009) who sought to defend themselves against other ethnic groups, namely blacks and Mexicans (Orlando-Morningstar, 1997). Its members are concentrated in correctional facilities in California, namely San Quentin and Folsom, although the gang has also spread to Texas and currently has approximately 15,000 members (Valdez, 2009; NGIC, 2009; Bamhart, 2009). The AB has established its presence and reputation because of its penchant for violence (NGIC, 2009). Despite the fact that the AB represents a small proportion of gang members, it has committed up to 18 percent of murders in prisons (Holthouse, 2005). Members of the AB feel they are fighting on behalf of Rahowa (Racial Holy War) and live by the words, "We must secure the existence of our people and a future for white children" (Holthouse, 2005: para. 11). Typically, in each facility a council leads members of the gang, known as kindred (Bamhart, 2009). When individuals join the AB, they recite the following oath, which binds them to the gang for life:

> An Aryan brother is without a care
> He walks where the weak and heartless won't dare

For an Aryan brother, death holds no fear
Vengeance will be his, through his brothers still here (Holthouse, 2005: para. 7)

Some members of the AB are highly trained, having served in the military, likely adding to their level of organization and skill in regard to violence (NGIC, 2009). Generally, the AB finances itself through the sales of illicit drugs and also engages in contract killings to maintain their control over the drug trade (Jaffe, 2006). As is the case with some gangs, Mexican drug traffickers supply select AB members with illegal drugs. The AB is also tolerant of the Mexican Mafia; this partnership has extended as far as cooperatively committing crimes together, such as contract killings (Valdez, 2009). AB members often sport tattoos such as clovers, bolts of lightning, Nazi swastikas, phrases referring to "White Power," the numbers "666," and "AB," (Valdez, 2009: 42).

Overall, it has been estimated that approximately 10 percent of inmates are members of racist prison groups and gangs (cited in Blazak, 2009; Anti-Defamation League [ADL], 2001). White inmates who find themselves in prison may congregate with such groups, finally expressing previously dormant prejudice and racism (ADL, 2001). Aside from the AB, a bevy of other racist gangs have formed in prison, such as the Confederate Knights of America (one member is part of the group charged with the high-profile lynching of James Byrd Jr.) and the Nazi Low Riders (NLR). The NLR is known for its historical ties to the AB and its hatred of minorities, emphasizing "white pride." Like the AB, the NLR is involved in the business of drug distribution, among other forms of crime in and out of prison, such as the harassment of blacks (ADL, 2001). Racist groups attempt to reach out to prospective members through written propaganda in the form of publications and magazines. Some members of these groups also consider themselves "prisoners of war" or otherwise seek to bolster their status through their imprisonment (ADL, 2001). However, white groups are not the only racist factions that exist in prisons; one such example is the Nation of Islam, a group headed by Louis Farrakhan, an outspoken anti-white minister. The gravity of such extremist beliefs is considerable, as many of these individuals will, at some point, be released into the community. Thus, it is imperative to investigate methods to assist individuals that want to drop out of such groups (Blazak, 2009).

Finally, Muslim extremist groups are perceived as yet another growing threat in the correctional system. Islam has become increasingly common in jails and prisons, and it has been estimated that anywhere from 10 to 20 percent of prisoners identify as Muslim (Warren and Krikorian, 2005). This trend has somewhat toed racial lines, as Islam is said to be rapidly growing among younger black inmates; it has been estimated that one in three blacks in federal facilities identify as Muslims (Silverberg, 2006). While some insist that an association with Islam does not necessarily equate with a propensity for terrorist activities and are weary of the repercussions for the rights of Muslim inmates, others, such as the FBI, feel that there is reason to be concerned about the risks of radicalism within Muslim prison groups. For instance, officials fear that there has been an increase in the incidence of Wahhabism, an extremist sect of Islam that is embraced by organizations such as Al Qaeda (Silverberg, 2006). Additionally, due to the conditions in prison (e.g., reduced programming and vocational training) and the lack of opportunities that await prisoners after they are released, there may be an increased opportunity for prisoners to radicalize (Warren and Krikorian, 2005), which is something that extremist groups may be attempting to exploit:

> An Al Qaeda training manual found by police… instructs operatives to set up "Islamic programs" if they are incarcerated and to try to recruit "candidates." Such candidates, the manual said, include those "disenchanted with their country's policies." (Warren and Krikorian, 2005: para. 23)

Hamm (2008) authored a study that focused on the conversion of prisoners to various religions, including Islam. It was found that it was a rarity for inmates to become radicalized to the point of inciting terrorist actions, something that usually occurred in "fresh converts, the newly pious, with an abundance of emotion and feeling" (Hamm, 2008: para. 33). Hamm observed that most prisoners converted to religion in pursuit of spiritual discovery and were advised to do so primarily by people they socially connected with (e.g., family, friends, and cell mates). It was noted that a charismatic leader may influence the process of radicalization by targeting embittered inmates and preaching extremist beliefs. As one chaplain surmised:

> Today's inmates are more dissatisfied with the government than they were 10 years ago or even 20 years ago. The seeds of dissatisfaction are everywhere. Inmates display more aggressive posturing. They cluster on the yard by religion. Racism is rampant. They find a new religion in prison [that] reinforces their opposition to authority. Some of these inmates are very fertile ground for jihad. (Hamm, 2008)

To combat extremist beliefs that may turn into dangerous behavior, Hamm (2008) recommends several actions, including hiring more chaplains to increase access to moderate perspectives, incorporating Muslim employees in the system so that prisoners feel more accepted, increasing staff knowledge of religious groups and gang activities, and further investigation of the processes that lead to radical, extremist beliefs and terrorist groups developing in prison. While it is possible that inmates may radicalize and develop a terrorist organization in prison, it is also possible that they may do so when released and are no longer under the watchful eye of a correctional institution, underscoring the need for preventative action to curb radical beliefs.

Classifying and Managing Prison Gangs

The first step in impacting the operation of prison gangs is to properly identify gang members when they enter into a correctional institution. Most institutions do not use a formal, objective instrument to determine if an individual is a gang member (Austin and McGinnis, 2004). Instead, prisons enlist the expertise of staff members who are trained in gang intelligence to recognize the signs of gang membership (e.g., gang tattoos, associations with gang members, identification by other inmates). Inmates may be interviewed, have their tattoos photographed, and have their law-enforcement records examined for previous affiliations when they are initially processed in an institution to document current gang involvement (Holvey, 2005). Based on a survey of 134 jails in 39 states, most administrators indicated that gang membership was usually determined using tattoos, displays of gang affiliation and colors on one's clothing, hand signals, or previous law-enforcement designation as a gang member; roughly 82 percent of administrators indicated that they also based gang identification on an individual's admission of gang membership (Ruddell, Decker, and Egley, 2006). Some states as well as the Federal Bureau of Prisons use a more objective process in the form of a point system to aid with the identification of gang members (Austin and McGinnis, 2004). Selected characteristics are worth points (e.g., gang tattoos and ties with a known STG), and if inmates accrue enough points, they are positively identified as active gang members.

However, the issue of gang classification remains a contentious issue within both academic and law-enforcement circles. For instance, questions surround the effectiveness and accuracy of gang databases (e.g., Barrows and Huff, 2009; Jacobs, 2009). This is problematic because prisons use law-enforcement records and databases on previous gang affiliations during initial processing (Austin and McGinnis, 2004). The collection and classification of gang membership data may differ across jurisdictions, and law-enforcement agencies may misclassify individuals or provide incomplete information that distorts the true nature of an individual's gang membership (Jacobs, 2009). Individuals may also fail to be identified as a gang member because of the increasing presence of "hybrid" gangs, or groups that are more loosely associated and do not behave in ways that can be readily classified by law-enforcement agencies (e.g., failing to "fly their colors" or sport classic gang tattoos, switching gang alliances) (Starbuck, Howell, and Lindquist, 2001). Illustrating the wide gap between local and national classification schemas of gangs and their subsequent crimes, in 2009, the FBI nationally attributed only 835 murders to gang-related circumstances, despite the fact that research has demonstrated at least half of city-wide murders are committed by gang members (Kennedy, 2009).

Such disparities in gang classification both in prisons and on the streets are cause for concern. As pointed out by Kennedy (2009), the negative effects stemming from a flawed gang classification system are manifold:

> Wrongly designating, or not designating, a group as a gang or an individual as a gang member can mean that it and he gets undeserved law-enforcement attention, fails to get deserved attention, does or does not trigger statutory sentencing enhancements, does or does not lead to segregation in jail and prison, as well as causing a host of other consequences. (2009: 711)

If there is a break in the system, a potentially dangerous situation could arise once a gang member is incarcerated (e.g., rival gang members are unknowingly placed together in a cell and attack one another). Additionally, the consequences of a false positive identification are also considerable. The stigma that surrounds a mistaken label of gang membership may be difficult to escape because it is sometimes difficult to remove an individual from a gang database due to information sharing between agencies and the increasing use of electronic databases that can be accessed with relative ease (Jacobs, 2009).

Managing the disruptive behavior of prison gangs day to day is also a daunting task because of their overall prevalence and efforts by members to operate covertly and avoid staff detection. Based on the available research, prisons have enacted several management strategies to quell prison gangs and disrupt their leadership, including the use of solitary confinement and SHUs; transferring gang leaders to different facilities (Pyrooz et al., 2011); "jacketing," or noting in an individual's file that he is associated with a gang (Decker and Fleisher, 2001); and programming aimed at encouraging individuals to leave their respective gangs (Trulson, Marquart, and Kawucha, 2008). It should be noted, however, that these strategies have not been empirically assessed in terms of their effectiveness (Pyrooz et al., 2011; Trulson et al., 2008; Decker and Fleisher, 2001).

Isolating gang members appears to be one of the more preferred management tactics (Winterdyk and Ruddell, 2010; Ruddell et al., 2006). Trulson et al. (2008) noted that in Texas, in response to the rising incidence of gang members and associated misconduct, 60 prison units were added during the 1990s in combination with intensified efforts at gathering gang intelligence. Gang members were placed into SHUs and were locked down. Though a direct causal link could not be established, in the years following the aforementioned policy changes, the number of gang incidents has continued to stay relatively stable, despite an increase in the overall prison population. However, this strategy was financially costly and may have contributed to other issues such as an increase in staff assaults and psychological problems resulting from constant isolation killings (Trulson et al., 2008). From a pragmatic viewpoint, it is probably not advisable to implement widespread isolation of gang members due to these problems because inmates may become even more problematic if they become mentally ill as a result of prolonged solitary confinement (see Haney, 2003, for a review), and many facilities likely do not have the finances to build additional housing specifically for gang members. In addition, members of prison gangs may still find ways to communicate with one another, even if segregated (Klivans, 2008). In the case of La Nuestra Familia, it was uncovered during a large-scale law-enforcement operation that members still managed to commit various criminal acts while residing in SHUs, including drug trafficking and contract killings (Trulson et al., 2008).

Other efforts, such as programming, have also been applied to manage and suppress gang activity in prisons. As noted by Fleisher and Decker (2001), gangs may form out of a desire to create a social group and protect themselves:

> If prisons want fewer inmate tips and cliques and by extension prison
> gangs, management must step forward proactively and offer inmates a
> meaningful alternative to prison gangs and gang crime and offer inmates
> treatment for personal issues such as addiction. (2001: 6)

Therefore, it is vital that gang members are offered alternatives to feeling that they need to be a part of a gang to be safe during their time in prison, and interventions must address other components aside from security. Even though such programming has not always been successful (Carlson, 2001), it is in the best interest of correctional facilities to continue such attempts in light of the costs associated with prison gangs, both in terms of disruption within prisons and the community at large. As noted by Carlson (2001), adult facilities have moved toward "deganging" (also called "debriefing") programs that strive to educate members so they will drop out of their respective gangs, sometimes involving giving offenders an ultimatum to do so (i.e., they must commit to dropping out in order to do the program). Typically, members participate in a multifaceted approach, including activities such as cognitive-behavioral therapy and drug treatment, role-playing, and other forms of social development and education (Carlson, 2001). These programs have demonstrated some effectiveness based on empirical evaluations, though there are questions surrounding its efficacy beyond the prison setting (Carlson, 2001).

While a direct evaluation of intervention strategies used for gang members has not yet been conducted, two recent studies have attempted to examine the perceived effectiveness of interventions by surveying administrative officials. The first survey, conducted by Ruddell et al. (2006), sent out surveys to a random sample of jails asking administrators about special populations, including the mentally ill, chronic offenders, inmates serving long sentences, and gang members. In total, the responses of 134 surveys were analyzed, representing 39 different states; the average bed-size of the facilities was roughly 942 beds with a total of 125,259 beds (approximately 19% of all jail beds across the United States). Administrators identified gang members as being the second most disruptive group (mentally ill inmates were labeled as the most disruptive). Overall, administrators felt that isolating gang members, gathering information on gang members, and allocating intelligence between law-enforcement agencies were the most effective management strategies. In contrast, limiting program participation, legal punishments for gang behavior, and taking away "good time" credits were seen as the least effective. Interestingly, however, administrators were unlikely to rate *any* intervention as ineffective. These results suggest that administrators are aware that gang members pose a management problem in jails but may also have limited options. As noted by the authors, it may not be possible to transfer inmates due to the temporary nature of jails and the fact that some facilities are the only one in the area (Ruddell et al., 2006).

The second, authored by Winterdyk and Ruddell (2010), surveyed federal, state, and two private correctional company administrators, resulting in a sample of 37 jurisdictions representing a total of 1.19 million offenders (accounting for 72.6% of all inmates nationwide). Respondents were asked questions regarding the prevalence of prison gangs, the problems gangs and STGs posed in terms of running their facilities, and the effectiveness of intelligence tactics, intervention strategies for gang members, and the dissemination of intelligence between law-enforcement agencies. The majority of administrators (75%) indicated that segregation and isolation are very effective strategies for dealing with gang members, while approximately half felt that the use of SHUs is very effective. A slight majority of administrators (65%) responded that restricting visits is very effective.

Inversely, administrators identified restricting community access, participation in employment, and commissary access as the least effective strategies for managing gang member behavior. In terms of investigative techniques, searching mail and monitoring phone conversations and records were deemed very effective by most administrators. The majority of respondents identified sharing intelligence within prison systems as the most effective (78%), while a slight majority labeled sharing information with law enforcement as very effective (65%); information sharing with county jails and parole agencies was rated as least effective.

Taken together, these findings demonstrate that even though segregation and isolation haven't been empirically evaluated in their effectiveness with curbing the disruptive behavior of gang members, administrators in both jails and prisons feel that it works. However, the use of segregation can be problematic in the sense that it can increase the amount of time one spends in custody, impacting an offender's ability to transition out of the system (Winterdyk and Ruddell, 2010). Because of the stock that is placed in isolation tactics, there needs to be a formal examination of these practices to determine if they truly are effective, rather than just relying on anecdotal experience. These findings also indicate that prison administrators may not take the role of probation/parole and county jails in terms of sharing information. This is unfortunate because both of these agencies represent important roles in the trajectory of an offender. Jails can serve the role of initially investigating an inmate's gang affiliation. Probation and parole agencies may also uncover evidence of gang affiliation during the course of supervision and may need to adjust the way they deal with offenders in the face of their gang membership. Finally, there also appeared to be somewhat of a divergence in the perceived effectiveness of taking away privileges in prisons versus jails; while prison administrators felt taking away some privileges was an effective way to manage gang members, jail administrators did not feel as strongly and even felt some of these tactics were ineffective. This trend suggests that the amount of time gang members will spend in a respective institution (long-term for prison; short-term for jail) may affect their response to interventions affecting privileges.

In addition to adult prison gangs, the Outlaw Motorcycle Gangs (OMGs) represent the largest number of adult individuals who are gang affiliated outside the prison walls. Indeed, these gangs are a power in both prisons and communities in the United States. Their relationship to youth gangs almost always takes the form of using the younger groups to sell the OMGs' product: drugs (particularly methamphetamine).

BIKER GANGS

According to the National Highway Traffic Safety Administration (NHTSA), an estimated 7.1 million motorcycles were registered in the United States as of 2008 (National Highway Traffic Safety Administration [NHTSA], 2008). The vast majority of motorcycle riders are law-abiding citizens who enjoy motorcycles as a hobby or form of transportation. Some enthusiasts even belong to clubs or groups devoted to motorcyclists; for example, an estimated 230,000 riders belong to the American Motorcyclist Association, one of the largest motorcycle clubs in the United States (American Motorcyclist Association [AMA], 2011). However, a small proportion of motorcycle clubs function as gangs that embrace anti-social attitudes and engage in a variety of deviant behavior and criminal activities, rejecting the values of conventional organizations such as the AMA. Individual members of such clubs proudly call themselves "One Percenters," a nickname that originated from a comment made by the AMA that 99 percent of bikers follow the law (Glod, 2010). Formally, large groups or clubs of outlaw motorcyclists are classified by law enforcement as Outlaw Motorcycle Gangs (OMGs)[4], defined by the U.S. Department of Justice as "organizations whose members use their motorcycle clubs as conduits for criminal enterprises" (U.S. Department of Justice [U.S. DOJ], n.d.: para. 1).

As of 2008, law-enforcement organizations have determined that approximately 280 to 520 OMGs are in existence across the United States, with a total of roughly 20,000 confirmed members (NGIC, 2009). OMGs are known for their secrecy about the structure of their organizations, but they are infamous for the criminal activities they engage in, including drug and firearms trafficking, violent offenses, money laundering, theft, prostitution, gambling, and extortion (NGIC, 2009). Although they have been known to deal with a variety of illicit substances, OMGs have gained a reputation among law-enforcement agencies for their widespread distribution and personal use of methamphetamine (Drug Enforcement Administration [DEA], n.d.), as it is financially profitable, and many bikers use it to stay awake during lengthy trips. As is the case with other gangs, the crime associated with OMGs also extends well beyond the borders of the United States, as they have been known to traffic drugs and weapons to and from Canada as well as Mexico, and several OMGs now have chapters in various foreign countries (NGIC, 2009; DEA, n.d.). Thus, OMGs are seen as a dangerous threat because of their deep-seated involvement in crime on a national and global level, preference for violence, and their efforts to evade law enforcement (NIGC, 2009).

The One Percenters and the Other 99 Percent: A Comparison

To properly frame a discussion of OMGs, it is important to examine the characteristics that set OMGs apart from conventional motorcycle clubs and organizations as well as the qualities these groups share. To this end, Quinn and Forsyth (2009) characterize motorcycle organizations on a continuum, organized by the degree of criminal involvement of such groups and their devotion to OMGs: motorcycle associations, motorcycle clubs, supporter clubs, satellite/puppet clubs, and OMGs themselves. Motorcycle associations reach out to riders that own a specific bike model (e.g., Harley-Davidsons) as well as individuals characterized as RUBs (Rich Urban Bikers), but members are not heavily engaged in these types of groups (Quinn and Forsyth, 2009). Motorcycle clubs are more exclusive and organized in terms of leadership, with some clubs embracing the same values as One Percenters, while others are fairly benign and simply bring together people who enjoy riding motorcycles in a fraternal setting.

Motorcycle clubs that support One Percenters set themselves apart from other clubs and associations in that they may involve themselves in some degree of criminal activity and have ties to larger OMGs to boost their credibility, usually wearing the colors of the group they support and engaging in fraternization at events such as bike shows and races (Quinn and Forsyth, 2009). Clubs that go further in their support of OMGs are known as "satellite" or "puppet" clubs, and often do the criminal bidding of OMGs in an effort to prove their suitability for membership (Quinn and Forsyth, 2009: 239). Clubs, associations, and OMGs share some notable similarities such as their leadership structure (central leadership that dictates to loosely independent, locally based chapters), an emphasis on superficiality (e.g., making sure that one's bike is of superior quality), and a probable identification with "the iconography of the modern outlaw" (Quinn and Forsyth, 2009: 242). As a testament to the sometimes blurred line between One Percenters and their law-abiding counterparts, Quinn and Forsyth (2009) note:

> It is difficult to distinguish a modern One Percenter from other bikers unless the insignia is present. Further, the core traits of One Percenters and their clubs are merely the extreme of a continuum that runs from law-abiding to crime-immersed and from the countercultural gang member to the sophisticated subcultural entrepreneur. (Adapted from Quinn and Forsyth, 2007: 248)

According to Quinn and Koch (2003), motorcycle gangs are characterized by their general rebellious attitudes and refusal to adopt most mainstream values, with the exception of a desire to appear powerful. The culture of OMGs embraces masculinity, a sense of skill with mechanical tasks, and appearance as a dangerous, tough outlaw (Quinn and Koch, 2003) with a certain element of "romance" due to the risk taking that is inherent in riding a motorcycle (Quinn and Forsyth, 2009). While RUBs and other motorcyclists enjoy using their bikes as an occasional hobby, OMGs define themselves by riding their motorcycles as frequently as they can, with some groups even fining members for not riding their bike at least once per month (Quinn and Forsyth, 2009). One Percenters are often deeply embedded in their organizations and the fraternal bonds between fellow members, as well as with the appearance and performance of their motorcycles (Quinn and Forsyth, 2009). Bikers in OMGs also value respect and honor and are willing to go to great (and extremely violent) lengths to avenge acts of disrespect, evidenced by the bitter rivalries present among modern OMGs and confrontations with those who dare to challenge or otherwise affront OMGs.

The Criminality and Structure of OMGs

The criminality among OMGs is not uniform and, like other gangs, varies based on the situations that members find themselves in and the overarching goals of the organization. In a study of the criminality of biker gangs, Quinn and Koch (2003) outlined four distinct types of offending that can be observed within these groups: spontaneous expressive acts, planned expressive acts, short-term instrumental acts, and ongoing instrumental enterprises. *Spontaneous expressive acts* are typically violent crimes that arise between rivals in social settings and are committed by small numbers rather than the entire group (e.g., bar fights). *Planned expressive acts* are usually committed against adversaries (e.g., revenge for an affront via murder) and may be planned at the national or local level to represent the club's mission or interests. *Short-term instrumental acts* are those in which a small portion of members exploit a favorable situation to meet a goal for at least one member, such as stealing another's property or participating in the prostitution of an Old Lady (the girlfriend or wife of a biker), and may be either spur of the moment or carefully planned. Finally, *ongoing instrumental enterprises* generally consist of carefully planned criminal activities that demand a considerable amount of time and energy and are used to financially support the club (e.g., the widespread selling of drugs). One Percenters exude certain characteristics and behaviors that invite violent encounters, such as travelling with weapons in large groups, their code of honor and intolerance for disrespect, and their relative proficiency with violence (Quinn and Koch, 2003). Additionally, the incorporation of structural illegal crime is also commonplace because of the lack of separation between bikers and their respective OMG. As noted by the authors:

> … the creation and dissolution of illegal enterprises within a 1% club is a normal and natural phenomena occurring routinely under the umbrella of the club. For them it is no more or less independent of their membership than any other aspect of their lives. This highly integrated lifestyle that lacks boundaries between personal and collective spheres is quite distinct from the compartmentalized lives typical of modern citizens. (Quinn and Koch, 2003: 299–300)

Though law enforcement does not officially tally the crimes of OMGs, Barker and Human (2009) attempted to empirically examine the crimes of four OMGs (the Hells Angels, Outlaws, Bandidos, and Pagans) by performing a content analysis on newspaper articles depicting their criminal activities. A total of 631 articles were used, ranging from 1980 to 2005. The criminality of the OMGs was coded using the previously mentioned framework of Quinn and Koch (2003); incidents were classified as spontaneous expressive acts, planned expressive acts, short-term instrumental acts, and ongoing instrumental enterprises. Overall, a total of 89 criminal incidents were attributed to the OMGs. Most criminal incidents (50%) were ongoing instrumental enterprises, mostly comprised of the distribution of drugs and weapons. Planned aggressive acts (20%), such as the assault or murder of rival gang members, were roughly tied with spontaneous expressive acts (19%), such as bar fights with rivals or assaulting police officers. Short-term instrumental acts were less commonly observed (10%) and involved acts such as theft, rape, and extortion. Comparatively, the Hells Angels committed the most offenses (46%), followed by the Outlaws (29%), the Bandidos (18%), and the Pagans (7%). Notably, the Hells Angels also had the most ongoing criminal enterprises (26% of all criminal incidents) and planned aggressive acts (11% of all criminal incidents) compared to the other OMGs.

The Hells Angels were featured in 209 articles and a total of 41 criminal acts. The majority (23) featured ongoing criminal enterprises, followed by planned aggressive acts (10). Spontaneous expressive acts and short-term instrumental acts were less common (four incidents were observed for each category). The Outlaws had 204 criminal articles accounting for 26 different incidents. Approximately half were regarding ongoing criminal enterprises. The remainder focused on spontaneous expressive acts (six incidents), short-term instrumental acts (three incidents) and planned aggressive acts (three incidents). The Pagans had a total of 13 criminal articles. Four articles involved ongoing criminal enterprises, while one described a spontaneous aggressive act and a planned aggressive act. The Bandidos had 25 criminal articles featuring 6 spontaneous expressive acts, 5 ongoing instrumental enterprises, 4 planned expressive acts, and 1 short-term instrumental act. These findings call into question the decision not to collect official estimates of the crimes committed by OMGs, as the media does not report every criminal incident amassed by these groups (Barker and Human, 2009). More importantly, these findings also suggest that the reputation enjoyed by the OMGs for their prominent role in drug trafficking and violence are likely well-deserved, as many of these incidents were of a serious nature.

According to Quinn (2001), not all One Percenters can be lumped together; there are two distinct types of members in these groups that are vastly different in terms of their propensity for criminal activity: the conservatives and the radicals. While *conservative* members seek to enjoy the fraternal aspects of belonging to a club as well as the reckless abandon that comes with being a biker, they are not inherently criminal. *Radical* individuals, however, are committed to the criminal aspects of existing in an OMG. Though both radical and conservative individuals may exist within the same One Percenter club, one group is typically dominant and is greatly influential regarding the behavior and philosophies of the organization (Quinn, 2001). While most One Percenter groups are headed by conservative individuals who try to keep the group out of significant trouble, the major OMGs (such as the Hells Angels, Bandidos, and Outlaws) are led by radical individuals who steer the club in the direction of organized crime, such as racketeering and extortion, drug trafficking, prostitution, theft, and violence (Quinn, 2001). At different points in time, wars between rival gangs have contributed to an expansion of these OMGs, both in way of membership and organized crime to fund these costly inter-group battles (Quinn, 2001). After many of the major OMGs were condemned by law enforcement and the public, they eventually began to scale back their behavior to avoid negative publicity, a trend that endures today; the Hells Angels, for example, have attempted to sway the public by engaging in acts of charity for children and veterans (James, 2009). Though modern OMGs have evolved in the sense that they are more clandestine about their criminality, they are still very much involved in organized crime, as the culture of OMGs is one that embraces detachment from mainstream society and is a probable breeding ground for deviance. As Quinn (2001) notes:

> These clubs provide an outlet for the status frustration of their members that is facilitated by their isolation from the mainstream... Isolation

intensifies bonding processes while creating a world view and emotional tone that encourage violence. (2001: 395–396)

Due to their sophistication and structure, OMGs have long been compared to organized crime syndicates, such as the Mafia, both by researchers and law enforcement (Quinn and Koch, 2003). Abadinsky (2009) loosely defines organized crime as adhering to eight main characteristics:

1. Has no political goal
2. Is hierarchical
3. Has a limited or exclusive membership
4. Constitutes a unique subculture
5. Perpetuates itself
6. Exhibits a willingness to use illegal violence
7. Is monopolistic
8. Is governed by explicit rules and regulations (2009: 3)

The major modern OMGs exemplify each of these characteristics. In terms of political goals, as noted previously, OMGs define themselves by their abandonment of societal values and are involved in their organizations because of a pursuit of power (Quinn and Koch, 2003). These groups are also incredibly hierarchical, as in terms of leadership, OMGs generally follow the orders and requirements established by a national chapter (Quinn and Koch, 2003). Local chapters operate somewhat independently but must carefully adhere to national guidelines. Individual chapters are typically led by elected officers (e.g., a president, vice president, etc.) (Quinn and Koch, 2003). Attaining membership in an OMG is a difficult task; in general, those who want to be members must become "prospects" (potential members that often do undesirable tasks to prove their loyalty) for at least one year before they are "patched," or considered full-fledged members (Quinn and Koch, 2003). OMGs also participate in a unique subculture marked by machismo, freedom, and adherence to an outlaw persona (Quinn, 2001; Quinn and Koch, 2003; Quinn and Forsyth, 2009). OMGs attempt to perpetuate their organizations through the promotion of positive publicity via acts of charity (James, 2009), maintaining public Web sites to rally supporters (Barker, 2005), and soliciting new members to join.

OMGs have also been defined by their willingness to use violence against rivals and citizens (not One Percenters) alike. Like organized crime families, OMGs may use a team of "enforcers" to intimidate or harm others, such as rivals or disgraced club members (Quinn and Koch, 2003). One Percenter clubs have also displayed a liking for monopolist dominance, as there have been various wars between OMGs over turf; for years, the Hells Angels warred with the Mongols over their presence in northern California, which the Hells Angels had long claimed as their territory (LeDuff, 2002). Finally, OMGs adhere to an extensive repertoire of rules and regulations, usually determined by a national headquarters. Individual clubs have various rules regarding the display of logos, the upkeep of motorcycles, drug use (e.g., prohibiting the use of selected drugs, such as heroin), and respect for other members (Quinn and Koch, 2003). Despite the longstanding nature of the parallels between traditional organized crime and anecdotal and empirical evidence supporting the criminality of these groups (Barker and Human, 2009), OMGs such as the Hells Angels, have vehemently insisted that they are not criminal organizations (James, 2009).

Prominent Motorcycle Gangs

In this section, four of the largest OMGs will be discussed: the Hells Angels, the Bandidos, the Outlaws, and the Mongols. Although OMGs have taken to the Web and are attempting to promote positive publicity, they are still quite secretive about the exact nature, structure, and behavior of their organizations, as many OMG members have refused to be interviewed and law enforcement generally does not readily divulge extremely detailed information about these groups (Barker, 2005). Although they will not be discussed, countless other OMGs, including the Sons of Silence, the Pagans, the Iron Horses, and the Warlocks, exist across the United States, and even though they are smaller, still wield the force of hundreds of members and chapters (Barker, 2005).

    The Hells Angels Motorcycle Club (HAMC), nicknamed "The Mafia on Wheels" by some (Martin, 1992), was created in 1948 in San Bernardino, California, by veteran World War II pilots and went by the moniker "Pissed Off Bastards of Bloomington" (NDIC, 2002a: 1). An additional chapter was created in Oakland, California, which helped bring the club to prominence and eventually became the club's headquarters (NDIC, 2002a). The name "Hells Angels" was reportedly used because of its association with bomber squads (James, 2009). Over the next several decades, the HAMC continued to flourish, eventually expanding to other countries, including New Zealand, Canada, Africa, and Australia, and becoming the largest OMG (NDIC, 2002a). The HAMC has an approximate total of 2,000 to 2,500 members across the United States and 26 countries (NGIC, 2011). Nationwide, the HAMC has 900 to 950 members and nearly 70 chapters that span approximately 22 states (NGIC, 2009). It now has a presence on a total of six continents, with a particular stronghold in Canada through distribution of drugs, among other crimes (NGIC, 2009; CBCNews, 2011). The motto of the Hells Angels is telling: "When we do right nobody remembers, when we do wrong nobody forgets" (Hells Angels Motorcycle Club, n.d.).

    The process of becoming a Hells Angel is arduous; only white individuals over the age of 21 may apply and must have an approved bike (typically a Harley-Davidson) (Langton, 2009). After associating with the club anywhere from three months to two years, applicants are considered a "hangaround" and are tasked with protecting clubhouses (Langton, 2009). After they are approved by everyone in a chapter, they are promoted to a "prospect," a process in which individuals are on-call at all hours of the day and are at the mercy of other members who may ask them to commit dangerous or illegal acts (Langton, 2009). However, prospects are allowed to display the colors of the Hells Angels (red and white) as well as an incomplete set of patches, and they can use clubhouses (Langton, 2009). Eventually, prospects are "patched in," or initiated, and given a complete set of patches, displaying the symbol of the Hells Angels known as the "death's head" (James, 2009). According to Langton (2009), Hells Angels treat their colors with great respect, as:

> … the colors are said to be more important to a Hells Angel than any other possession or woman. The colors are precious and rules around them are complex and absolute. They cannot be touched by a non-member without punishment. A Hells Angel who forgets to wear his colors to a party or meeting will likely be beaten by other Angels. If he loses his colors, he will probably be exiled forever. To desecrate an Angel's colors is said to be an offense punishable by death, even when done by other Angels. (2009: ch.2)

Because there is no national leadership structure in charge of every HAMC chapter, individual chapters are organized by geographic region (West Coast and East Coast) and are headed by separate, elected leadership councils responsible for each region (NDIC, 2002a). Each HAMC chapter has a sophisticated leadership structure, complete with a president (a position with full authority over the HAMC, including the power to veto), vice president (the vice president runs the organization if the president cannot), sergeant-at-arms (an enforcer), and secretary/treasurer (an overseer of the financial transactions of the HAMC) (NDIC, 2002a). Members are required to follow rules set forth by the national chapter and attend meetings on a local and national level (NDIC, 2002a). To this day, members of the HAMC may have a military background, adding to their skill and dangerousness (NGIC, 2009). In terms of criminal activity, the HAMC is said to move and sell marijuana, methamphetamine, cocaine, hashish, heroin, LSD, PCP, ecstasy, and prescription drugs (NGIC, 2009). The HAMC has also attracted legal attention for fighting, motor vehicle theft, money laundering, and murder (NGIC, 2009).

The Bandidos Motorcycle Club, the second largest OMG, was founded in Texas in 1966 by an ex-marine (Coulthart and McNab, 2008; Bandidos MC Randers, 2011). While some have claimed that the Bandidos were created to exert influence over the markets of prostitution and drugs (Barker, 2005), others have advanced the idea that the Bandidos emulated Hells Angels in an attempt to outdo them (Coulthart and McNab, 2008). The Bandidos were named for "the Mexican bandits of the late nineteenth and early twentieth centuries, men who refused to 'live by anyone's rules but their own'" (Coulthart and McNab, 2008: 14). The Bandidos currently have 2,000 to 2,500 members worldwide (NGIC, 2009). In the United States, the Bandidos boast approximately 900 bikers in nearly 90 chapters across 16 states, an unknown amount of which have prior military experience; this OMG also has chapters in 13 foreign countries (NGIC, 2009). The club's colors are red and gold, the symbol is a figure donning a sombrero and holding a sword (Bandidos MC Randers, 2011), and revealingly, their motto is "Fuck the world. We are the people our parents warned us about" (Coulthart and McNab, 2008: 14).

The leadership of the Bandidos consists of an *el presidente*, or an international club president, who has authority over every chapter (Sims, 2009a). Independent chapters each have a president, vice president, sergeant-at-arms, road captain, and secretary/treasurer (Sims, 2009b). Members are expected to abide by certain by-laws, such as not wearing the club patch while riding in a car or truck, and the broad philosophy "All members are your brothers and your family" (Sims, 2009b: para. 5). They are also required to attend meetings (nicknamed "Church") four times a month and are penalized if they do not show up (Sims, 2009b). To join the Bandidos in the first place, potential members, or prospects, are required to serve the club for a period of at least one year before they are admitted (Sims, 2009b). Once admitted, the Bandidos reportedly engage in a particularly vile initiation process:

> New members were told to take their vest off and then his fellow
> members would urinate, defecate and vomit on it. The new member
> would then put the now moist vest back on, hop on his bike, and go
> motoring until the vest had dried. (Coulthart and McNab, 2008: 15)

Among law enforcement, the Bandidos are known to move and sell cocaine, marijuana, and methamphetamine (NGIC, 2009); it is also thought that they use "puppet" clubs to assist them with their criminal activities (NGIC, 2009). Additionally, as a testament to the violence of the Bandidos, there is an entire chapter, known as the Nomads, that is responsible for disciplining members (Barker, 2005). Strikingly, the Bandidos are friendly with the Outlaws and at one point, the two almost merged (Quinn and Forsyth, 2009); the Bandidos are said to obtain their drugs from the Outlaws (Barker, 2005). However, like several other OMGs, the Bandidos consider the Hells Angels enemies (Barker, 2005).

The Outlaws Motorcycle Club (also known as the American Outlaws Association, or A.O.A.) calls themselves the original OMG, claiming to have originated in Illinois in 1935 under the moniker McCook Outlaws Motorcycle Club (Barker, 2005: 105). Following a second name change, the club emerged as the Outlaws Motorcycle Club. Today, the Outlaws are said to have at least 1,700 members divided among 176 chapters worldwide (NGIC, 2009). The Outlaws have also expanded to 12 countries outside of the United States (NGIC, 2009). The colors of the Outlaws are black and white, while the logo is a white skull (named "Charlie") affixed to two pistons (NDIC, 2002b: 5). The motto of the club is "God forgives, Outlaws don't," which may be featured on patches in the form of "GFOD" (NDIC, 2002b). As is the case with several other OMGs, some members of the Outlaws are said to have military backgrounds (NGIC, 2009).

The Outlaws have an elaborate network of governance. The Outlaw Motorcycle Club is headed by an international and national president (NDIC, 2002b), while individuals regions (divided and named by color, such as the red and copper regions) are commanded by bosses that work with national leadership (Hench, 2010). Individual chapters are led by a president, vice president, treasurer, and sergeant-at-arms (enforcer) (Hench, 2010). Chapters follow guidelines that dictate election procedures, gatherings, and action against members who have disobeyed the rules (NDIC, 2002b). Members are required to pay dues of

$1,200 per year to finance activities such as memorials and group excursions and are instructed to attend meetings on the local and national level (Hench, 2010). To be eligible for membership, applicants must be white men over the age of 21 and also be in possession of an American motorcycle (preferably a Harley-Davidson) (NDIC, 2002b). To be formally inducted into this OMG, applicants begin as a hangaround and assist the chapter before being made a prospect; If he is approved by the club, then a prospect is moved up to probate status, a position in which he is required to demonstrate his commitment to the Outlaw Motorcycle Club (NDIC, 2002b).

According to law-enforcement officials, this OMG traffics and sells methamphetamine, cocaine, marijuana, and ecstasy, and it has been known to engage in "arson, assault, explosives operations, extortion, fraud, homicide, intimidation, kidnapping, money laundering, prostitution operations, robbery, theft, and weapons violations" (NGIC, 2009: 30) as well as violence in the name of expanding their organization (NDIC, 2002b). Furthering their criminality, the Outlaws do not get along with the HAMC and have violently warred regarding territory (NGIC, 2009), a far cry from the sense of camaraderie the two clubs shared during the 1960s (Barker, 2005).

The Mongols Nation Motorcycle Club, a predominantly Hispanic OMG, first originated in Montebello, California, in 1969; the club allegedly formed because the Hells Angels excluded Latinos (Mongols Nation Motorcycle Club, 2009a; Francis, 2008). Though smaller than some of the other OMGs in the United States, the Mongols are said to be the most brutal and treacherous (NGIC, 2009). The Mongols, headquartered in California, have approximately 800 to 850 members divided across 70 nationwide chapters (NGIC, 2009). The symbol of the Mongols is a caricature of Genghis Kahn, a tribute to the ferocity of the Mongol Empire (Quinn and Forsyth, 2009; Mongols Nation Motorcycle Club, 2009). The motto of the Mongols is "Respect few, fear none," a phrase that embodies their adherence to old-school, rebellious values (Queen, 2007). Members of the Mongols have been involved in the distribution of cocaine, methamphetamine, and marijuana as well as various violent crimes, particularly murder (NGIC, 2009; Queen, 2007). An undercover ATF (Alcohol, Tobacco, and Firearms) agent who infiltrated the Mongols succinctly describes them as "the most violent motorcycle gang in America, a tight-knit collective of crazies, unpredictable and unrepentant badasses" (Queen, 2007: 4).

The Mongols are organized in a hierarchical manner. Headed by a Mother Chapter (located in Commerce, California) and a national president, each individual Mongols chapter is led by a president, vice president, sergeant-at-arms, and a treasurer/secretary (Queen, 2007). Each chapter financially pays tribute to the Mother Chapter (Queen, 2007). Somewhat recently, the Mongols have undergone a leadership change in the Mother Chapter. Arrested in a law-enforcement operation known as "Black Rain," the former Mongols national president, Ruben "Doc" Cavazos, reportedly became an informant against the OMG and is accused of substantially involving the club in organized crime (Mongols Nation Motorcycle Club, 2009). Like other OMGs, the process of becoming a member of the Mongols is somewhat unpleasant:

As a prospect, you're a slave, the property of the club. You have to do everything a member tells you to do, from hauling drugs and guns to wiping a member's ass if he orders you to. Some members were good for simple orders like "Prospect, go get me a beer," or "Light my cigarette," or "Clean my bike." But others… took inordinate pleasure in making a prospect's life a living hell. (Queen, 2007: 4)

Members of the Mongols are required to give a monthly fee to the club and participate in chapter meetings (Queen, 2007). The Mongols have a lengthy constitution, spanning 70 pages, outlining the rules members are required to follow (Queen, 2007). For example, though likely adapted to appear law-abiding, as it is posted on a public Web site maintained by a Mongols chapter in Canada, 10 "Commandments[5]" are required of members in this particular chapter:

1. A Mongol never lies to another Mongol.
2. A Mongol never steals from another Mongol.
3. A Mongol never messes with another Mongol's ol' lady.
4. A Mongol never causes another Mongol to get arrested in any way, shape, or form.
5. A Mongol never uses his patch for any personal gain or any criminal or illegal activities.
6. A Mongol can never abuse or sell drugs period.
7. A Mongol should either be legitimately employed full time or actively seeking legitimate employment.
8. A Mongol (patch or no patch) should never use his patch for any personal gain and should never be involved in any criminal or illegal activities.
9. All Mongols should be brotherly and respectful to one another and a Mongol should never fight with another Mongol.
10. A Mongol should always be there for another Mongol.… A Mongol always has another Mongol's back. (Mongols MC Canada Inc., 2010: para. 3)

During their tenure, the Mongols have made enemies. The Mongols are fierce enemies of the Hells Angels; some members even bear a tattoo with the club's motto, "Respect few, fear none," an honor that is earned upon harming a Hells Angel (Garmire, 2008). Initially, the Hells Angels and Mongols warred over territory in Southern California, as the Hells Angels were infuriated that the Mongols were wearing a California rocker (a patch displayed on a biker's vest) (NGIC, 2009; Queen, 2007). A truce was made, with the Hells Angels yielding Southern California to the Bandidos (NGIC, 2009; LeDuff, 2002). Eventually, however, the Mongols defiantly moved into northern California (LeDuff, 2002), provoking the Hells Angels and culminating in a bloody brawl in a Laughlin Casino that left 3 gang members dead and wounded at least 12 (Associated Press, 2006). The violence has continued; in 2008, a Hells Angel president was murdered by a member of the Mongols (Van Derbeken, 2008). In contrast, the Mongols are currently on friendly terms with the Bandidos,

Outlaws, Sons of Silence, and Pagans (NGIC, 2009). The Mongols also have ties to the Mexican Mafia. In a bid to expand membership, the Mongols recruited street gang members into their gang, including the Sureños (Bell and Lucas, 2008). As tension increased between the two groups, the Mexican Mafia requested payment from the Mongols due to their increasing presence in the drug market; the Mongols refused, and a war erupted, resulting in bloodshed on both sides (Bell and Lucas, 2008). The gangs ended up resolving their differences, however, and currently cooperate with respect to drug trafficking (Bell and Lucas, 2008; Daniels, 2009).

SUMMARY

With a total of 147,000 known gang members behind bars, the authors would argue that prison gangs are the most ruthless and dangerous adult gangs in the United States. Prison gangs pose the most serious security threat to the institution, its employees, and other prisoners. Special housing is most often required for the separation of these groups. An entire prison has been built in California, Pelican Bay Prison, for gang members convicted of felonies. It is a super-maximum security facility with approximately 2,000 inmates. All of the major gangs are represented in this and other state and federal institutions, including OMGs (Outlaw Motorcycle Gangs), Bloods, Crips, Norteños, Sureños, MS-13—a real collection of violent adult gangs.

Members of street gangs and outlaw motorcycle clubs continue to conduct business from within the prison walls. Much the same as the Mafia bosses of old, the prison gang leaders continue to plan drug distribution and order or sanction murders of rivals in various communities.

As 95 percent of prison inmates are released from custody, prison gang members loom large in the communities to which they return. We have chosen to focus on the five major (in terms of the number of members and serious incidents reported) prison gangs: Mexican Mafia (La Eme), La Nuestra Familia, Texas Syndicate, Black Guerilla Family, and Aryan Brotherhood.

As noted by Pyrooz et al. (2011), prison gangs have superior organizational skills and leadership structure, unlike youth street gangs that typically lack real structure and are loosely organized.

Research conducted in prisons (state and federal) indicates gang membership was related to increased misconduct. There were more incidents of drug possession, property offenses, and more serious violence. In fact, prison gang members are most likely to be involved in the majority of violent misconduct occurrences.

Other research studies clearly indicated that prison gang members were uneducated or undereducated. One study found that 64 percent of these members did not have a high school diploma or a GED; 34 percent of nongang members had this deficiency. This is a significant component of low self-esteem, often underlying incidents of violence.

A current threat in corrections is the Muslim extremist groups, which are growing in numbers. With extreme budgetary cutbacks, there is less programming and job training available—which are critical to the successful reentry of inmates into the community—so the radicalization of inmates is occurring.

Institutions have attempted to control prison gang members through solitary confinement, secure housing units (SHU) and transferring leaders to different facilities. Convict files include notations of gang affiliation and programs that have been used to encourage individuals to leave the gang. However, none of these measures have been particularly successful.

Our other adult gang focus has been on the 280–520 Outlaw Motorcycle Gangs (OMGs). These gangs specialize in drugs and firearms trafficking. They are involved in crime on a national and global scale. They are risk-taking, preferring violence, and evading law enforcement. They will go to great, often violent, lengths to avenge any act of disrespect.

We chose to focus on the four largest OMGs: Hells Angels, Outlaws, Bandidos, and Mongols. The Hells Angels are the most well-known and the most active in criminal activities. These groups often "war" with each other regarding territory. Each group tries to "claim" an area as its own. This is most likely to occur when another gang attempts to sell drugs in this "claimed area."

These groups are detached from mainstream society having a highly integrated lifestyle. This lifestyle knows no boundaries between individuals and the collective. To these gang members, illegal acts are normal.

Each of the OMG organizations is hierarchical. There is a national chapter that sets the main rules for the organization, and the local chapters define their membership, plan activities, collect dues, and elect officers. Each chapter has a president, vice president, treasurer, sergeants-at-arms, and sometimes a secretary (depending on what the officers decide should be recorded). Meetings are held, usually at a highly secured "clubhouse," for members only.

While both prison gangs and motorcycle gangs share similarities with organized crime groups, the motorcycle gangs are the most reflective of those groups. They are involved in racketeering, extortion, drug trafficking, prostitution, theft, and violence.

These adult gangs command most of the attention of law enforcement and corrections. They pose serious challenges to these agencies as well as the communities in which they now, or will eventually, dwell.

NOTES

1. The authors extend their appreciation to University of Nevada, Las Vegas, graduate student Danielle Shields for the research and writing she did for this chapter.

2. It should be noted that while gangs account for the majority of STGs, other groups, (e.g., terrorist organizations, unorganized groups that are not necessarily a full-fledged gang) that pose a safety threat are also considered STGs.

3. The BGF is allied with several other gangs, such as the Crips (7,000 to 30,000 national members), the Bloods (30,000 to 35,000 national members), and the Black

Gangster Disciples (25,000 to 50,000 national members), significantly adding to their influence, as these members may be employed by the BGF (NGIC, 2009; Florida Department of Corrections, n.d.).

4. Unless otherwise indicated, the terms *One Percenter clubs/groups, motorcycle gangs,* and *OMGs* will be used interchangeably. Although the authors are aware that some (e.g., Quinn, 2001; Barker, 2005) reject the use of the term *OMG*, for the purpose of this chapter, this distinction is not made.

5. Note: To aid with the presentation of these commandments, they were slightly grammatically revised for the purpose of clarity and readability, but the content remains unchanged and unaltered.

Why Are There Gangs?

Explanations of why there are gangs are really part of a much larger concern with explaining crime and delinquency in general. In fact, some of the most popular sociological theories of crime and delinquency have actually been attempts to explain gang delinquency or crime (e.g., the theories of Cohen, Cloward, Ohlin, and Miller to be discussed here). Thus, in a sense, this chapter is really a summary of some of the major theories of crime and delinquency.

Multiple theories have been offered to explain crime, delinquency, and gangs. Some have taken a strictly sociological perspective; others have come from a purely psychological point of view; while others have been a combination of both of these perspectives. Space does not permit a complete review of all the theories of crime and delinquency and gangs, although the most common theories are included here, and these take a mostly sociological approach to the problem. We would be remiss, however, if we did not include a discussion of *deterrence*. It is important to understand deterrence theory as it relates to gangs if for no other reason than the fact that virtually all of the legal responses to this issue are based on this perspective. Deterrence theory originated in the Classical School of Criminology that began in the eighteenth century with the views of one of the most famous writers of the period, Cesare Beccaria (1738–1794).

THE THEORY OF DETERRENCE

Beccaria was part of a group of writers and artists who represented the period of Enlightenment. It is safe to say that just about everyone associated with this school of thought "affirmed their belief in the principles of reason, in the precision of the scientific method, and in the authority of nature" (Bierne, 1993: 20; see also Taylor, Walton, and Young, 1973). From the perspective of the Classical School, an unwritten "social contract" emerged during the Renaissance (1300–1600), a period during which a vast social movement swept away old customs and institutions and promoted intellectual development, while capitalism emerged throughout the Western world. The social contract, as described by philosophers such as Thomas Hobbes and Jean Rousseau, involves a *responsible* and *rational* person applying *reason*. Humans originally lived in a state of nature, grace, or innocence; escape from this state is the result of the ability to reason. Rational people have reasoning powers that place them above animals. This perspective also stressed that humans have *free will*. Theoretically, there is no limit to what they can accomplish. Furthermore, humans are essentially *hedonistic*. By their very *nature*, humans will choose actions that *maximize pleasure and minimize pain*. More importantly, social contract thinkers claim that the main instrument of the control of human behavior is *fear*, especially fear of *pain*. Fear of punishment and the pain it causes influence humans to make the right choice. Punishment is viewed as the logical means to control behavior. In addition, society has a right to punish the individual and to transfer this right to the state to ensure that it will be carried out.

Beccaria's book *On Crimes and Punishment* (1963), originally published in 1764, was based on the philosophical doctrine known as *utilitarianism*—the idea that punishment is based on its *usefulness* or *utility* or *practicality*. On the last page of his book, Beccaria noted:

> In order for punishment not to be, in every instance, an act of violence of one or of many against a private citizen, it must be essentially public, prompt, necessary, the least possible in the given circumstances, proportionate to the crimes, dictated by the laws. (1963: 99)

In other words, punishment should not be excessive; it should fit the crime (this is a key phrase, most commonly expressed as "let the punishment fit the crime"). Beccaria also argued that the punishment should closely follow the commission of a crime, making it more just and useful. The major thrust of the Classical School, however, is that the purpose of the criminal justice system should be to prevent crime through deterrence (discussed later in this section). A potential criminal, according to this line of thinking, will decide not to commit a crime because the punishment will be too costly.

According to the Classical School, to prevent crime, we must make the punishment (i.e., pain) greater than the criminal act. In summary, the Classical School assumes that 1) all people by nature are hedonistic and self-serving; they are likely to commit crime to get what they want; 2) to live in harmony and avoid a "war of all against all" (as Thomas Hobbes stressed), the people agree to give up certain freedoms to be protected by a strong central state; 3) punishment is necessary to deter crime, and the state has the prerogative (which has been granted to it by the people through a "social contract") to administer it; 4) punishment should "fit the crime" and not be used to rehabilitate the offender; 5) use of the law should be limited, and due process rights should be observed; 6) each individual is responsible for his or her actions so that mitigating circumstances or "excuses" are inadmissible (Taylor et al., 1973: 2).

Deterrence comes from the word *deter*, which the *Random House Dictionary* defines as "to discourage or restrain from acting or proceeding, as through fear or doubt." It also means "to prevent; check; arrest." It is synonymous with such words as "hinder" and "stop." In large part, the theory of deterrence is based on *fear*—fear of consequences. A young person might be warned by his or her parents, "if you stay out past midnight, you'll be grounded" or "if you do that again, we'll take the car away!"

Applying the deterrence idea to the prevention of crime, we have two variations. The first is known as *general deterrence*, which is used to "send a message" to would-be law violators about what will happen if they break a law. The assumption is that the general public will be discouraged from law-breaking behavior (Stafford and Warr, 1993).

The second variation is known as *special (or specific) deterrence*, in which the punishment will prevent a specific offender from reoffending. The offender will think twice the next time he or she considers committing a crime.

During the last half of the twentieth century, several variations to the classical approach appeared. One theory that became popular in the 1970s and 1980s took the position that crime was merely a product of "rational" choices and decisions that people made in their daily lives. Various terminologies have been used almost interchangeably, such as *criminal opportunity theory*, *routine activity theory*, and *situational choice model*.[1] This will be discussed later in the chapter.

SOCIOLOGICAL THEORIES

The theories to be reviewed during the remainder of this chapter can be grouped into eight general categories: 1) social disorganization/social ecology, 2) strain/anomie, 3) cultural deviance, 4) control theory (also known as social bond), 5) social learning, 6) rational choice, 7) labeling, and 8) critical/Marxist perspectives. Figure 7.1 provides a general summary of each of these perspectives. In the remainder of this chapter, we will provide a general overview of each of these perspectives.

Social Disorganization/Social Ecology Theory

Social disorganization theory has been one of the most popular and enduring sociological theories of crime and delinquency. Variations of this theory have been called the **social ecology** perspective because it has a lot to do with the *spatial or geographical distribution* of crime, delinquency, and gangs (Lanier and Henry, 1998: ch. 9; Stark, 1987). Modern versions of this perspective began with the work of several sociologists at the University of Chicago during the first three decades of the twentieth century. The original idea behind the spatial distribution of crime can be traced back to the mid-nineteenth century to the work of two rather obscure scientists, Adolphe Quetelet (1796–1874), a Belgian astronomer and mathematician, and a French lawyer and statistician named Michel Guerry (1802–1866). These two were actually the first scientists who collected and analyzed various crime data and examined the residences of

Theory	Major Points/Key Factors
1. Social disorganization	Crime stems from certain community or neighborhood characteristics, such as poverty, dilapidated housing, high density, high mobility, and high rates of unemployment. Concentric zone theory is a variation that argues that crime increases toward the inner city area.
2. Strain/anomie	Cultural norms of "success" emphasize such goals as money, status, and power, while the means to obtain such success are not equally distributed; as a result of blocked opportunities many among the disadvantaged resort to illegal means, which are more readily available.
3. Cultural deviance	Certain subcultures, including a gang subculture, exist within poor communities, which contain values, attitudes, beliefs, norms, and so on that are often counter to the prevailing middle class culture; an important feature of this culture is the absence of fathers, thus resulting in female-headed households, which tend to be poorer; youths get exposed to this subculture early in life and become embedded in it.
4. Control/social bond	Delinquency persists when a youth's bonds, or ties, to society are weak or broken, especially bonds with family, school, and other institutions; when this occurs, a youth is apt to seek bonds with other groups, including gangs, in order to get his or her needs met.
5. Learning	Delinquency is learned through association with others, especially gang members, over a period of time. This involves a process that includes the acquisition of attitudes and values, the instigation of a criminal act based on certain stimuli, and the maintenance or perpetuation of such behavior over time.
6. Labeling	Definitions of delinquency and crime stem from differences in power and status in the larger society, and those without power are the most likely to have their behaviors labeled as "delinquency"; delinquency may be generated, and especially perpetuated, through negative labeling by significant others and by the judicial system; one may associate with others similarly labeled, such as gangs.
7. Rational choice	People freely choose to commit crime based on self-interest because they are goal oriented and want to maximize their pleasure and minimize their pain. A variation is known as routine activities theory, which suggests that criminals plan very carefully by selecting specific targets based on such things as vulnerability (e.g., elderly citizens, unguarded premises, lack of police presence) and commit their crimes accordingly. However, choices are often not based on pure reason and rationality.
8. Critical/Marxist	Gangs are inevitable products of social (and racial) inequality brought about by capitalism itself; power is unequally distributed, and those without power often resort to criminal means to survive.

F I G U R E 7.1 Perspectives on delinquency, crime, and gangs.

offenders, matching them with various socioeconomic variables, such as poverty, infant mortality, unemployment, and other social indicators. This began what became known as the **Cartographic School** of criminology—in other words, mapmaking, which involved merely plotting on a city map the location of criminals and various social indicators (e.g., with colored dots, as police departments still do today when, for example, they plot the locations of certain crimes, such as serial rapes, or the locations of a series of muggings, auto thefts, etc.).[2]

This idea of mapmaking and the more general notion that crime is *spatially* distributed within a geographical area became one of the hallmarks of what came to be known as the **Chicago School** of sociology (named after the many researchers in the sociology department at the University of Chicago during the early twentieth century). Within the city of Chicago (and other major cities of the era), these researchers noticed that crime and delinquency rates varied by areas of the city (just as Guerry and Quetelet had done 50 years earlier). The researchers found that the highest rates of crime and delinquency were also found in the same areas exhibiting high rates of multiple other social problems, such as single-parent families, unemployment, multiple-family dwellings, welfare cases, and low levels of education. One of the key ideas of the social ecology of crime is the fact that high rates of crime and other problems persist within the same neighborhoods over long periods of time *regardless of who lives there.* As several gang researchers have noted, some gangs in certain neighborhoods have existed for as long as 50 or more years, often spanning three generations. This has been especially the case in East Los Angeles.[3] Thus there must be something about the places themselves, perhaps something about the neighborhoods rather than the people per se, that produces and perpetuates high crime rates (Stark, 1987).

The social ecology perspective borrows concepts from the field of plant biology, specifically studying human life and problems, using notions derived from studies of the interdependence of plant and animal life. From this perspective, people are seen as being in relationship to one another and to their physical environment. Further, just as plant and animal species tend to colonize their environment, humans colonize their geographical space.[4] The Chicago sociologists "argued that the urban topography of industry, railroads, crowded tenements, and vice districts influenced a person's alienation, detachment, and amorality" (Knupfer, 2001: 25). In contrast, the suburbs away from the city's core had boulevards, spacious parks, and manicured lawns that reflected community stability and organization.

One of the most important ideas originating from these Chicago sociologists (specifically Robert Park and Ernest Burgess) was the **concentric zone** model of city life (Burgess, 1925). This perspective on city life and land-use patterns identified specified zones emanating outward from the central part of the city. Five zones were identified: 1) central business district, or the "Loop"; 2) zone in transition; 3) zone of workingmen's homes; 4) residential zone; and 5) commuter zone.

According to this theory, growth is generated (from mostly political and economic forces) outward from the central business district. Such expansion occurs in concentric waves, or circles. Such expansion and movement affects neighborhood development and patterns of social problems. Studies of the rates of crime and delinquency, especially by sociologists Henry Shaw and David McKay, demonstrated that over an extended period of time, the highest rates were found within the first three zones *no matter who lived there.* These high rates were strongly correlated with such social problems as mental illness, unemployment, poverty, infant mortality, and many others.[5]

Such a distribution is caused by a breakdown of institutional, community-based controls, which in turn is caused by three general factors: industrialization, urbanization, and immigration. People living within these areas often lack a sense of community because the local institutions (e.g., schools, families, and churches) are not strong enough to provide nurturing and guidance for the area's children. It is important to note that there are important political and economic forces at work here. The concentration of human and social problems within these zones is not the inevitable natural result of some abstract laws of nature, but rather the actions of some of the most powerful groups in a city (urban planners, politicians, wealthy business leaders, etc.).

Within such environments, a subculture of criminal values and traditions develops that replaces conventional values and traditions. Such criminal values and traditions persist over time regardless of who lives in the area. (This is part of the cultural deviance theory, to be discussed shortly.) One of the classic works about gangs coming from a social disorganization perspective was that by Frederic Thrasher. His book *The Gang,* published in 1927, seems to be as relevant today as it was when originally published. For Thrasher, gangs originate from:

> … the spontaneous effort of boys to create a society for themselves where none adequate to their needs exists. What boys get out of such associations that they do not get otherwise under the conditions that adult society imposes is the thrill and zest of participation in common interests, more especially in corporate action, in hunting, capture, conflict, flight, and escape. Conflict with other gangs and the world about them furnishes the occasion for many of their exciting group activities. (Thrasher, 1927: 32–33)

Thrasher's view of gang causation was consistent with the social disorganization perspective. Specifically, gangs develop within the most impoverished areas of a city. More specifically, Thrasher noted that gangs tend to flourish in areas he called *interstitial.* These areas lie within the poverty belt within a city, "a region characterized by the deteriorating neighborhoods, shifting populations, and the mobility and disorganization of the slum…. Gangland represents a geographically and socially interstitial area in the city" (Thrasher, 1927: 20–21). Such an area has been called many names, such as the zone in transition, the slum, the ghetto, and the barrio.

Thrasher found evidence of at least 1,313 gangs in Chicago, with an estimated 25,000 members. No two of these gangs were alike; they reflected the great diversity characteristic of the city of Chicago in the 1920s (even today, Chicago itself and the gangs of Chicago reflect this diversification). Much like today, gang delinquency in Thrasher's day ranged from the petty (such as truancy and disturbing the peace) to the serious (serious property crime and violent crime).

His theory of why gangs exist and what functions they perform can be summarized in the following quotes:

> The failure of the normally directing and controlling customs and institutions to function efficiently in the boy's experience is indicated by the disintegration of family life, inefficiency of schools, formalism and externality of religion, corruption and indifference in local politics, low wages and monotony in occupational activities; unemployment; and lack of opportunity for wholesome recreation. All these factors enter into the picture of the moral and economic frontier, and, coupled with deterioration in the housing, sanitation, and other conditions of life in the slum, give the impression of general disorganization and decay.

> The gang functions with reference to these conditions in two ways: It offers a substitute for what society fails to give; and it provides a relief from suppression and distasteful behavior. It fills a gap and affords an escape. (Thrasher, 1927: 228–231)

According to Thrasher, by being in a gang, a young man acquires a personality and name for himself; he acquires a sort of status and has a role to play. Without the gang, the individual would lack a personality in the sense used here. The gang "not only defines for him his position in society ... but it becomes the basis for his conception of himself." The gang becomes the youth's reference group, that is, the group from which he obtains his main values, beliefs, and goals. In a sense, the gang becomes his family. Moreover, these groups of youths tend to progress from what Thrasher called "spontaneous play groups" to gangs when they begin to bring on disapproval from adults. When this occurs, particularly if coupled with legal intervention, the youths become closer and develop a "we" feeling.[6]

Thrasher clearly believed that gangs provided certain basic needs for growing boys, such as a sense of belonging and self-esteem. This perspective is consistent with Abraham Maslow's hierarchy of needs. Maslow's views will be discussed in a later section of this chapter.

Several subsequent studies have focused on the community or neighborhood as the primary unit of analysis. Such a focus begins with the assumption that crime and the extent of gang activities vary according to certain neighborhood or community characteristics. In a study called "Racketville, Slumtown and Haulberg," Spergel found that the three neighborhoods he studied varied according to a number of criteria and had different kinds of traditions, including delinquent and criminal norms. For example, Racketville, a mostly Italian neighborhood, had a long tradition of organized racketeering. Gangs in this neighborhood were mostly involved in the rackets because this was where the criminal opportunities were to be found (Spergel, 1964).

In contrast, the area Spergel called Slumtown was primarily a Puerto Rican neighborhood with a history of conflict and aggression. The gangs in this area were mostly involved in various conflict situations with rival gangs (usually over turf). Haulberg was a mixed ethnic neighborhood (Irish, German, Italian, and others) with a tradition of mostly property crimes; thus, a theft subculture flourished.

A more recent variation of this theme can be seen in the ethnographic fieldwork of Sullivan (1989). His study of three neighborhoods in Brooklyn (which he called Projectville, La Barriada, and Hamilton Park) provides important new information about the relationship between social, cultural, and economic factors and gangs.

The three neighborhoods studied by Sullivan varied according to several socioeconomic indicators. These neighborhoods also had significantly different patterns of crime. Hamilton Park had the lowest rate of all three neighborhoods, whereas Projectville ranked first, and La Barriada ranked second. La Barriada ranked the highest for crimes of violence.

La Barriada was a mixed Latino and white area; Projectville was a largely black neighborhood. The third area, Hamilton Park, was predominantly white. The two neighborhoods with the highest crime rates (Projectville and La Barriada) also had 1) the highest poverty level, with more than half the families receiving public assistance; 2) the highest percentage of single-parent families; 3) the highest rate of renter-occupied housing; 4) the highest rate of school dropouts; and 5) the lowest labor-force participation rates (and correspondingly highest levels of unemployment) (Sullivan, 1989: 21–27, 98).

Sullivan suggests that these differences can be explained by noting:

> The concentration in the two poor, minority neighborhoods [La Barriada and Projectville] of sustained involvement in high-risk, low-return theft as a primary source of income during the middle teens. The primary causes for their greater willingness to engage in desperate, highly exposed crimes for uncertain and meager monetary returns were the greater poverty of their households, the specific and severe lack of employment opportunities during these same mid-teen years, and the weakened local social control environment, itself a product of general poverty and joblessness among neighborhood residents. (1989: 203)

A key to understanding these differences, argues Sullivan, is that of personal networks rather than merely human capital. He explains:

> … personal networks derived from existing patterns of articulation between the local neighborhoods and particular sectors of the labor market. These effects of labor market segmentation were important for youth jobs both in the middle teens and during the ensuing period of work establishment. The Hamilton Park youths found a relatively plentiful supply of temporary, part-time, almost always off-the-books work through relatives, friends and local employers during the middle teens, most of it in the local vicinity. (1989: 103)

When these youths reached their late teens, they were able to make use of these same contacts to get more secure and better-paying jobs. The minority youths from Projectville and La Barriada never developed such networks.

Sullivan found that among the precursors to a criminal career among most of the youths studied was involvement in some gang or clique of youths. It typically began with fighting with and against other youths. Street fighting was motivated mostly by status and territory. Beginning in their early teens, these youths would spend a great amount of time within what they considered to be their own territory or turf. The cliques and gangs these youths belonged to "were quasi-familial groupings that served to protect their members from outsiders" (1989: 110).

Stark (1987) also suggested that criminal behavior persists within specific neighborhoods over time because of *certain characteristics of the neighborhoods*, rather than the people who inhabit them. He argued that there are five key characteristics of perpetually high-crime neighborhoods: 1) high density, 2) high rates of poverty, 3) mixed-use (poor dense neighborhoods mixed together with light industry and retail shops), 4) a high rate of transience among residents, and 5) dilapidation. His theory also incorporates the impact of these five characteristics on people's responses to the conditions. He identified 1) moral cynicism, 2) increased opportunities for crime, 3) an increase in the *motivation* to commit crime, and 4) diminished social control, especially among residents via informal methods of control. The neighborhood characteristics and people's responses to them drive away the least deviant people, further reducing social control and attracting "crime-prone" people into the area.

This theory impacts delinquency rates. In high-density neighborhoods, homes are crowded. As a result, more people congregate outside, and there is less supervision of children. Less supervision of children almost inevitably leads to poor school achievement, resulting in an increase in deviant behavior by such children. Moreover, with crowding in homes comes greater family conflict, further weakening attachments (see control theory, discussed later) (Stark, 1987: 896–97).

More recent studies have continued to confirm the connection between neighborhoods, especially lower socioeconomic areas, and delinquency, and in general support the work that began with Quetelet and Guerry and later the Chicago School.[7]

The *Los Angeles Times* incorporates this perspective in its continuing series on homicides in Los Angeles. The newspaper compares two neighborhoods in close proximity to one another in south central Los Angeles (where gangs are highly concentrated). During the past three years, one neighborhood (Vermont Knolls) has experienced no homicides. Another neighborhood about a mile away (Westmont) has had 28 homicides—a person "cannot walk a block outside its borders without coming across the site of a killing from the last three years" (Rubin and Pesce, 2010).

The explanation for this difference is that there has been a huge infusion of money for rebuilding in the Vermont Knolls area and the addition of several organizations, such as the Crenshaw Christian Center, a mega-church that now sits on the old Pepperdine University campus. "Most streets are lined with modest but appealing single-family houses. Front yards often have no fences, the lawns are green and well-maintained" (Rubin and Pesce, 2010). This area is also primarily inhabited by older residents.

The predominance of single-family homes instead of apartments means a less densely packed population and less turnover. And many in the neighborhood own their homes and have had roots in the area for generations. The result is a place where people know each other, have an emotional and financial investment and don't take kindly to anything that might disturb the peace. (2010)

In recent years, a substantial amount of research maps communities to show the geographic distribution of crime and criminals. James F. Austin and Associates is one organization that engages in this kind of research.[8] Also, a new academic journal began in 2009, called *Crime Mapping: A Journal of Research and Practice*, published within the Department of Criminal Justice at UNLV.[9]

Strain/Anomie Theory

Strain theory originated with Robert Merton, who borrowed the term *anomie* from the nineteenth-century French sociologist Émile Durkheim and applied it to the problem of crime in America (Merton, 1968). The concept of anomie refers to inconsistencies between societal conditions and opportunities for growth, fulfillment, and productivity within a society (the term *anomia* has been used to refer to those who experience personal frustration and alienation as a result of anomie within a society). It also involves the weakening of the normative order of society—that is, norms (rules, laws, etc.) lose their impact on people. The existence of anomie within a culture can also produce a high level of flexibility in the pursuit of goals, even suggesting that it may at times be appropriate to deviate from the norms concerning the methods of achieving success.

Durkheim, writing during the late nineteenth century, suggested that under capitalism, there is a more or less chronic state of deregulation and that industrialization had removed traditional social controls on aspirations. The capitalist culture produces in humans a constant dissatisfaction resulting in a never ending longing for more and more. And there is never enough—whether this be money, material things, or power. There is a morality under capitalism that dictates "anything goes," especially when it comes to making money (it certainly applies to the modern corporation).

What Durkheim was hinting at (but never coming right out and saying it—this was said very forcefully by Karl Marx) was that a very strong social structure is needed to offset or place limits on this morality. In other words, strong institutions, such as the family, religion, and education, are needed to place some limits on us. But the failure of these institutions can be seen in our high crime rates and the fact that the economic institution is so powerful that it has sort of "invaded" and become dominant over other institutions. (More will be said about this shortly.)

The basic thesis of strain theory is that crime stems from the lack of articulation or fit between two of the most basic components of society: *culture* and *social structure*.[10] Here we refer to culture as consisting of 1) the main value and goal orientations, or "ends," and 2) the institutionalized or legitimate means for attaining these goals. Social structure, as used here, consists of the basic social institutions of society, especially the economy, but also such institutions as the family, education, and politics, all of which are responsible for distributing *access* to the legitimate means for obtaining goals.

According to Merton, this "lack of fit" creates strain within individuals, who respond with various forms of deviance. Thus, people who find themselves at a disadvantage relative to legitimate economic activities are motivated to engage in illegitimate activities (perhaps because of unavailability of jobs, lack of job skills, education, and other factors). Within a capitalist society like the United States, the main emphasis is on the success goals, while less emphasis is on the legitimate means to achieve these goals. Moreover, these goals have become institutionalized in that they are deeply embedded into the psyches of everyone via a very powerful system of corporate propaganda.[11] At the same time, the legitimate means are not as well defined or as strongly ingrained. In other words, there is a lot of discretion and a lot of tolerance for deviance from the means but not the goals. One result of such a system is high levels of crime.

Another important point made by strain theory is that our culture contributes to crime because the opportunities to achieve success goals are not equally distributed. We have a strong class structure and incredible inequality within our society, which means that some have extreme disadvantages over others.[12] Another way of saying the same thing is that *culture promises what the social structure cannot deliver,* that being equal access to opportunities to achieve success. People dealing with this contradiction (one of many under capitalism) face pressures, or strains, to seek alternatives.

According to Merton, there are several possible alternatives, which he calls "modes of adaptation." In his now famous typology of adaptations (reproduced in almost every criminology textbook), Merton suggested several alternatives, which include the following:

- *Conformity*—accepting both the legitimate means and the success goals.

- *Ritualism*—accepting the means but rejecting the goals (one just goes to work every day but has given up the goal of "success").

- *Innovation*—where the person accepts the *goals* of success but rejects the legitimate *means* to obtain them.

- *Retreatism*—where one rejects both the goals *and* the means and more or less drops out of society (e.g., to become part of a drug subculture).

- *Rebellion*—where one rejects both the goals and the means but, instead of retreating, begins to substitute *new* definitions of success and means to obtain them.

Obviously, the adaptation known as *innovation* directly relates to criminal activity, including gang activities. Thus strain/anomie theory suggests that participating in gang-related activities is an example of being *innovative* in the pursuit of success.

According to Messner and Rosenfeld, in a recent revision of anomie theory, such strain explains high rates of crime not only among the disadvantaged but also among the more privileged because they are under "strains" to make more money, often "by any means necessary." This theory can certainly help explain the large amount of "corporate crime" in this country (Messner and Rosenfeld, 2007). Messner and Rosenfeld's revision of strain theory contains an important component that has usually been missing from writings on this particular theory. We are referring here to their emphasis on the importance of social institutions and the relationship with what is normally called the American dream. The next section pursues this idea in more detail.

Strain Theory and the Institutional Structure of Society: Crime and the American Dream. The American dream is a sort of ethos that is deeply embedded into our culture. Generally, it refers to a commitment to the goal of material success that is to be pursued by everyone. Within a capitalist society, everyone is supposed to act in his or her own self-interest (part of the creed of rugged individualism) in this pursuit (this has been part of the mythology of the free enterprise and the free market), and this, in turn, will automatically promote the common good. Somehow, the fruits of individual pursuits in this "free market" system will eventually "trickle down" to benefit others.

The American dream contains four core values that are deeply embedded within American culture. These are summarized in Figure 7.2. There is, however, a "dark side" to the American dream, which stems from a contradiction

1. *Achievement*—Often expressed by the phrase "Be all that you can be" (contained in a popular advertisement for the U.S. Army). According to this value, one's personal worth is typically evaluated in terms of one's monetary success and/or how "famous" one has become. This stems from a culture that emphasizes doing and having rather than being. Failure to achieve is equated with the failure to make a contribution to society. This value is highly conducive to the attitude "It's not how you play the game; it's whether you win or lose." A similar attitude is "Winning isn't everything; it's the only thing."

2. *Individualism*—According to this value, people are encouraged to "make it on your own." This value discourages one value that could (and has proven to successfully) reduce crime, namely cooperation and collective action. The so-called rugged individualist is perhaps the most famous representation of this cultural value. A corollary to this value is that "I don't need any help." Messner and Rosenfeld comment that "the intense individual competition to succeed pressures people to disregard normative restraints on behavior when these restraints threaten to interfere with the realization of personal goals."

3. *Universalism*—According to this value, everyone is supposed to strive for the American Dream. And, of course, everyone has the same opportunity to succeed, as long as he or she "works hard." Part of this stems from the famous Protestant work ethic.

4. *Fetishism of money*—Money is so important in our culture that it often overrides almost everything else. It is often worshiped like a god. Money is the currency for measuring just about everything. Moreover, there is no end, no final stopping point, for it is relentless. It has created what many call a consumerist culture, where everyone is being socialized, almost from the day they are born, to be first and foremost a consumer. (Witness the emergence of corporate-sponsored programs within elementary schools, including the ever-present McDonald's.)

F I G U R E 7.2 Core values of American culture (Messner and Rosenfeld, 2001:62–64).

in American capitalism: The same forces that promote progress and ambition also produce a lot of crime because there is such an incredible pressure to succeed at any cost. The emphasis on competition and achievement also produces selfishness and drives people apart, weakening a collective sense of community. The fact that monetary rewards are such a high priority causes tasks that are noneconomic to receive little cultural support (e.g., housewives and child-care workers). Even education is seen as a means to an end—the end being a high-paying job or any secure job (an advertisement for a local university that the senior author saw on a Boston subway encouraged people to "go back so you can get ahead" rather than encouraging people to obtain a degree for the sake of expanding their knowledge base and other noneconomic benefits). The existence of such a high degree of inequality produces feelings of unworthiness. Those who fail are looked down on, and their failure is too often seen as an *individual failure* rather than a failure attributed to institutional and cultural factors.

One of the keys to understanding the linkage of the American dream and crime is knowing the meaning and importance of the term **social institution**. Social institutions can be defined as a persistent set of organized methods of meeting basic human needs. If you think of fundamental human needs, then there are relatively stable groups and organizations, complete with various norms and values, statuses, and roles, that over time have become the human equivalent of "instincts" in lower forms of animal life (because humans do not have such instincts). The human needs that these institutions seek to meet revolve around the need to 1) "adapt to the environment," 2) to "mobilize and deploy resources for the achievement of collective goals," and 3) to "socialize members to accept the society's fundamental normative patterns" (Messner and Rosenfeld, 2007: 72). The most important of these institutions include 1) the economy, 2) the family, 3) education, and 4) politics. Other important institutions include health care, media, religion, and legal (many would place the legal within the much larger political institution).

It is important to understand that when these institutions fail to provide the needs of the members of society (at least of a sizable proportion of the population), then alternative institutions will begin to develop—not the "institution" per se but different forms, or methods, of meeting needs. For example, if the prevailing economic system is failing, more and more people will engage in alternative means of earning a living; if organized religion is not meeting such needs as answers to fundamental life questions, then people will seek out unorthodox religious forms (e.g., cults such as the Branch Davidians or Heaven's Gate); if the legal institution is not perceived as providing justice, then people may take the law into their own hands; and if the mainstream media provide too much disinformation and do not allow dissenting views, then we will see alternative media emerge. Given that our major institutions are not providing the needs of everyone, it is our contention that one of the functions of gangs is to provide what our social institutions have failed to deliver. This view is depicted in Figure 7.3.

As Messner and Rosenfeld suggest, what is unique about American society is that the economic institution almost completely dominates all other institutions.

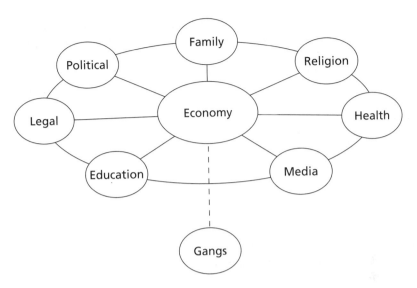

FIGURE 7.3 Social institutions and gangs.
© Cengage Learning 2013

This was once expressed by the famous American philosopher and educator John Dewey, who said something to the effect that "politics [or government] is the shadow that big business casts over society" (Chomsky, 1996: 29). American capitalism, unlike capitalism in other countries, emerged with virtually no interference from previously existing institutions. Unlike other societies, there were no other existing institutions that could tame or offset the economic imperatives. European and Japanese cultures, in contrast, place almost equal importance on the family, religion, education, and other institutional concerns. Under American capitalism, these other institutions become subordinate to the economic one (which is why in Figure 7.3 we have placed it in the middle). The goal is to make a profit, and everything else becomes secondary. Over time, this has become a market society in contrast to a market economy. In the former, the pursuit of private gain dominates all other pursuits (e.g., the arts or family support).[13]

As depicted in Figure 7.3, gangs fit into this scheme by providing some alternatives to the dominant institutions. Note that in this diagram, all of the major institutions shown here are connected by straight lines. This suggests what should be considered a truism, namely, that every institution is in some way connected with all the others; problems in one cause problems in another. And all the lines lead, eventually, to the center because the economic institution dominates all others.[14] As suggested in an earlier chapter, gangs function as sort of quasi-institutions in many ways. For example, many gang members feel that their homies are like a family. Gangs provide methods and incentives to seek alternative methods of earning money. They also provide an alternative media (graffiti) and an alternative religion (putting "RIP" style of graffiti on walls). They even have their own informal legal system. In short, gangs provide many of the needs that are supposed to be provided by mainstream institutions.

The emphasis on economics can have devastating consequences. The *New York Times* reported on an unpublished study called the Milwaukee Area Renters Study (MARS), which addresses the growing problem of evictions—a major issue since the 2008 recession.[15] "Eviction is a particular burden on low-income black women, often single mothers, who have an easier time renting apartments than their male counterparts but are vulnerable to losing them because their wages or public benefits have not kept up with the cost of housing." Matthew Desmond, a sociologist at the University of Wisconsin–Milwaukee, authored the study and states the problem succinctly: "Just as incarceration has become typical in the lives of poor black men, eviction has become typical in the lives of poor black women" (Eckholm, 2010). One out of every 25 renter-occupied households in Milwaukee as a whole is evicted, while in black neighborhoods, the rate is 1 in 14. Women in black neighborhoods constitute 13 percent of Milwaukee's population, but 40 percent of those evicted (Eckholm, 2010). Losing one's home can have a contagious effect. It can force a change in schools and perhaps threaten employment if the new residence is located too far from public transportation. This is one recent illustration of the links between institutions and the strain experienced by some members in society.

Differential Opportunity Structures.   A variation of strain theory comes from the work of Cloward and Ohlin in *Delinquency and Opportunity* (1960). These authors argued 1) that blocked opportunity aspirations cause poor self-concepts and feelings of frustration and 2) that these frustrations lead to delinquency, especially within a gang context. A key concept here is **differential opportunity structure**, which is an uneven distribution of legal and illegal means of achieving economic success, especially as they are unequally divided according to class and race. Cloward and Ohlin argued that while legitimate opportunities are blocked for significant numbers of lower-class youths, the same cannot be said for illegitimate opportunities (e.g., selling drugs and other crimes). Their major thesis was that

> ... the disparity between what lower class youth are led to want and what is actually available to them is the source of a major problem of adjustment. Adolescents who form delinquent subcultures, we suggest, have internalized an emphasis upon conventional goals. Faced with limitations on legitimate avenues of access to these goals, and unable to revise their aspirations downward, they experience intense frustrations; the exploration of nonconformist alternatives may be the result. (1960: 86)

Among the specific assumptions of this theory is that blocked opportunities (or aspirations) create feelings of frustration and low self-esteem, which in turn often lead to delinquency and frequently gang behavior. Cloward and Ohlin postulate that three different types of gangs emerge and that these types correspond with characteristics of the neighborhoods (which affect opportunities to commit different types of crimes) rather than of the individuals who live there. The three types of gangs are 1) **criminal gangs**, which are organized mainly around the commission of property crimes and exist in areas where there is already in existence relatively organized forms of adult criminal activity (thus, adult criminals are seen as successful role models by youths who live there); 2) **conflict gangs**, which engage mostly in violent behavior, such as gang fights over turf, and exist in neighborhoods where living conditions are for the most part unstable and transient, resulting in the lack of any adult role models, whether conventional or criminal; and 3) **retreatist gangs**, which engage mostly in illegal drug use and exist in those neighborhoods dominated by a great deal of illegal drug activity. These youths are described as double failures by Cloward and Ohlin (1960).

Social Embeddedness.   One of the most interesting new variations of strain theory comes from Hagan (1993: 465–491). Hagan borrows the term **social embeddedness** from economist Mark Granovetter (1992) to describe a developmental view of involvement in delinquency. Because much of the literature Hagan cites in support of this view pertains to gangs, it is obviously highly relevant here.

Hagan notes that instead of unemployment preceding involvement in criminal behavior (a common view in criminology), the reverse is actually the case for young offenders. For these youths, involvement in crime begins well before they can legally be involved in the labor market. According to Granovetter, becoming a regularly employed person involves much more than an individual's skills and education. It involves being connected to a social network of contacts that accrue over time and usually begins at a relatively early age. In other words, to become involved in the labor market, one needs to be socialized into this market starting at an early age. This means, among other things, that a youth begins to earn money doing odd jobs such as mowing lawns, babysitting, washing windows, shoveling snow, delivering papers, and so on long before turning 16. Through such activities, a youth begins a process of social embeddedness rather early in life. For those youths who do poorly in school and/or drop out, such contacts become difficult to establish.[16]

Hagan argues that, just as one can become socially embedded in the world of regular job contacts and the world of work, so too can one become embedded in a network of crime and deviance. In most of the high-crime, inner-city neighborhoods, the odd jobs of middle-class youths noted previously do not exist in large numbers (e.g., in the projects, there are no lawns to be mowed). He notes that parental involvement in crime will integrate youths into networks of criminal opportunities. Likewise, association with delinquent peers or contacts with drug dealers can also integrate youths into criminal networks. Moreover, delinquent acts tend to cause youths to become further isolated from networks of employment. A sort of snowballing effect takes place whereby each delinquent act and/or contact with the world of crime further distances a youth from the legitimate world of work. Thus the perspective of social embeddedness identifies "a process of separation and isolation from conventional employment networks" that has a time sequence with a "lagged accumulation of effect that should build over time" (Hagan, 1993: 469).

Hagan goes on to cite several examples of recent ethnographic research on delinquency (mostly work on gangs) that support this view (Anderson, 1990; Hagedorn 1998; Moore, 1991; Padilla, 1992; MacLeod, 2008; and Sullivan, 1989). Hagan quotes Anderson, who noted; "For many young men the drug economy is an employment agency....Young men who 'grew up' in the gang, but now are without clear opportunities, easily become involved; they fit themselves into its structure, manning its drug houses and selling drugs on street corners" (Anderson, 1990: 244). Similarly, Padilla noted that gang youths he studied "began turning to the gang in search of employment opportunities, believing that available conventional work would not sufficiently provide the kinds of material goods they wished to secure." Padilla also noted that these youths became involved in the gang world between the ages of 13 and 15. Increasing involvement in the gang further embedded them, and entry into the legitimate world of work became a serious problem for them later in life (Padilla, 1992: 101–102).

The process of estrangement from the legitimate world of work and consequent embeddedness in the world of criminal opportunities are further documented in Moore's study of Hispanic gangs in East Los Angeles, Hagedorn's work on Milwaukee gangs, Sullivan's study of three neighborhoods in New York (as reviewed in the previous section), and MacLeod's study of youths in a Chicago housing project. All of these studies found evidence of the socialization of inner-city youths (especially minority youths) into the world of criminal opportunities and their subsequent isolation from the social networks of legitimate work.

Cultural Deviance Theories

Cultural deviance theory proposes that delinquency is a result of a desire to conform to cultural values that are to some extent in conflict with those of conventional society. In part, this perspective is a direct offshoot of social disorganization theory because part of that theory (as noted previously) suggests that criminal values and traditions emerge within communities most affected by social disorganization.

Cohen's Culture of the Gang.   One of the most popular versions of cultural deviance theory was Albert Cohen's work, *Delinquent Boys: The Culture of the Gang* (1955). Although somewhat dated (he conducted his research in the 1950s), his perspective is still relevant today. Cohen's view incorporates the following assumptions: 1) a high proportion of lower-class youths (especially males) do poorly in school; 2) poor school performance relates to delinquency; 3) poor school performance stems from a conflict between dominant middle-class values of the school system and values of lower-class youths; and 4) most lower-class male delinquency is committed in a gang context, partly as a means of meeting some basic human needs, such as self-esteem and belonging.

There are two key concepts in Cohen's theory: 1) *reaction formation,* meaning that one openly rejects what he or she wants, or aspires to, but cannot achieve or obtain, and 2) *middle-class measuring rod* or evaluations of school performance *and* behavior within the school based on norms and values thought to be associated with the middle class, such as punctuality, neatness, cleanliness, nonviolent behavior, drive and ambition, achievement and success (especially at school), deferred gratification, and so on. Cohen argues that delinquents often develop a culture that is at odds with the norms and values of the middle class, which they turn upside down and rebel against.

This subculture remains real today, although with some variations, and it is important for those who deal with delinquents to understand it (Copes and Williams, 2007). One famous application of this theory to the treatment of delinquents was a program established in Provo, Utah (called Pine Hills), in the late 1950s. A form of group therapy was used whereby the offenders themselves actively participated in their own changes. The program proved to be somewhat successful (Empey and Rabow, 1961).

Lower Class Focal Concerns.   Still another variation of this perspective comes from the work of Walter B. Miller, an anthropologist from Harvard University, who has published extensively on the topic of gangs for the past 30 years. His theory includes an examination of what he calls the **focal concerns** of a distinctive lower-class culture (Miller, 1958: 5–19). Miller argues specifically that 1) there are clear-cut focal concerns (norms and values) within the lower-class culture and 2) that **female-dominated households** are an important feature within the lower class and are a major reason for the emergence of street-corner male adolescent groups in these neighborhoods.

Two key concepts here are 1) *focal concerns,* which include trouble, toughness, smartness, excitement, fate, and autonomy; and 2) *one-sex peer units,* which serve as alternative sources of companionship and male role model development outside the home. Such concerns are often at odds with mainstream middle-class society. The one-sex peer group is important to Miller's theory in the sense that gangs provide male members opportunities to prove their own masculinity in the absence of an adequate male role model within their family of origin. The principal unit in lower-class society is an age-graded, one-sex peer group constituting the major psychic focus and reference group for young people. The adolescent street-corner group is one variant of the lower-class structure, and the gang is a subtype distinguished by law-violating activities. For boys reared in female-headed households, the street-corner group provides the first real opportunity to learn essential aspects of the male role—by learning from other boys in the group with similar sex-role identification problems. The group also acts as a selection process in recruiting and retaining members. These concerns are illustrated in Figure 7.4.

Echoing Thrasher's work, Miller states that two central concerns of the adolescent street-corner group are belonging and status. One achieves belonging by adhering to the group's standards and values and continues to achieve belonging by demonstrating such characteristics as toughness, smartness, and autonomy. When there is conflict with other norms (e.g., middle-class norms), the norms of the group are far more compelling because failure to conform means expulsion from the group. Status is achieved by demonstrating qualities adolescents value

1. *Trouble* is a dominant feature of lower-class life. The major axis is law-abiding/ non-law-abiding behavior. Unlike the middle class, where judgment is usually based on one's achievements (e.g., education, career advancement), the lower-class concern is whether one will pursue the law-abiding route or its reverse. Further, membership in a gang is often contingent on demonstrating a commitment to law-violating behavior, acts that carry much prestige.

2. *Toughness* is associated with stereotypical masculine traits and behaviors, featuring mostly an emphasis on a concern for physical prowess, strength, fearless daring, and a general macho attitude and behavior (or machismo). It also includes a lack of sentimentality, a disdain for art and literature, and a view of women as sex objects. Concern over toughness may derive from being reared in a female-headed household and lack of male role models. The concern with toughness precludes males from assuming roles that might be seen as feminine, such as caring for one's children and acting responsibly toward fathering children out of wedlock.

3. *Smartness* revolves around the ability to con or outwit others, to engage in hustling activities. Skills in this area are continually being tested and honed, and the really skillful have great prestige. Many leaders of gangs are more valued for smartness than toughness, but the ideal leader possesses both qualities.

4. *Excitement* refers to the lifestyle within the lower class that involves a constant search for thrills or kicks to offset an otherwise boring existence. Alcohol, sex, and gambling play a large role here. The night on the town is a favorite pastime involving alcohol, sex, and music. Fights are frequent, so "going to town" is an expression of actively seeking risk and danger, hence excitement. Most of the time between episodes of excitement is spent doing nothing or hanging around—common for gang members.

5. *Fate* involves luck and fortune. According to Miller, most members of the lower class believe that they have little or no control over their lives, that their destiny is predetermined. Much of what happens is determined by luck, so if one is lucky, life will be rewarding; if one is unlucky—then nothing one does will change one's fate, so why bother working toward goals?

6. *Autonomy* is reflected in a contradiction of sorts. On the one hand there is overt resentment of external authority and controls ("No one is going to tell me what to do!"), and on the other hand there are covert behaviors that show that many members of the lower class do want such control. They recognize that external authority and controls provide a somewhat nurturing aspect to them. So, if one is imprisoned and subjected to rigid rules and regulations, one may overtly complain while locked up but on release may soon behave in such a way as to ensure reimprisonment and its corresponding nurturance. Rebellion over rules is really a testing of the firmness of the rules and an attempt to seek reassurance that nurturing will occur. Youngsters often misbehave in school because they do not get such reassurance.

FIGURE 7.4 W. B. Miller's "focal concerns" of lower-class culture.

© Cengage Learning 2013

(e.g., smartness, toughness, and others, as defined by lower-class culture). Status in the adolescent group requires *adultness*, that is, the material possessions and rights of adults (e.g., a car, the right to smoke and drink, etc.) but *not the responsibilities of adults*. The desire to act like an adult and avoid "kid stuff" results in gambling, drinking, and other deviant behaviors and compels the adolescent more than the adult to be smart, tough, and so on. He will seek out ways to demonstrate these qualities, even if they are illegal.

There is also a pecking order among different groups, defined by one's "rep" (reputation). Each group believes its safety depends on maintaining a solid rep for toughness compared with other groups. One's rep refers to both law-abiding and law-violating behavior. Which behavior will dominate depends on a complex set of factors, such as which community reference groups (criminals or police) are admired or respected or the individual needs of the gang members. Above all, having status is crucial and is far more important than the means selected in achieving it.

Violence is a learned behavior that can be unlearned. In desolate areas, pride becomes a fiercely guarded commodity and showing weakness invites trouble (Ahmed, 2010). Deanna Wilkinson of Ohio State University researches urban youth violence and notes that if youths in some subcultures walk away from a fight, they fear losing whatever status they had. Gary Slutkin of Chicago's Cease Fire program said his group targets changing the social norms that feed violence. Experts believe many factors put children at risk of falling into a pattern of violent thinking and behavior: "growing up in poverty, living in violent circumstances, failing to read at grade level by third grade, not graduating high school, and not being surrounded by caring, protective adults" (Shelton, 2010). Greg Boyle, a Jesuit priest in Los Angeles who runs Homeboy Industries (one of the nation's largest gang-intervention programs) comments: "It's not about thinking or behavior. It's about infusing a sense of hope so the kid starts to care. No one scares them straight—you care them straight" (Shelton, 2010; see also Boyle, 2010).

In her dissertation, Margaret Hughes of CSU–San Bernardino focused on turning points in the lives of young men who abandoned destructive behaviors, who identified alternatives to crime, made connections to neighborhoods, and understood the damage they were causing in their communities as pivotal factors for change. Hughes notes that organizations can work on changing thinking and behavior, but unless they can offer employment, violence and crime will remain in the background as alternatives (Shelton, 2010).

Several recent studies have found that lower-class offenders are often singled out for excessive punishments (especially minority males) by a court system that fails to take into account this subculture. Essentially, a mostly white, middle-class, bureaucratic subculture passes judgement on a very different subculture. Knowing that they will receive excessive punishment by the system, lower-class minority males are motivated not to get caught. At the same time, they believe they must live up to, and integrate, these focal concerns into their everyday lives.[17]

Control Theory

The essence of **control theory** (sometimes called **social bond theory**) is that the weakening, breakdown, or absence of effective social control accounts for delinquency. A unique feature of this perspective is that instead of asking why they do it, it asks why *don't* they do it. In other words, this theory wrestles with what it is that keeps or prevents people from committing crime. In this sense, control theory is really a theory of prevention.

The basic assumption of control theory is that proper social behavior requires socialization. Thus proper socialization leads to conformity, while improper socialization leads to nonconformity. Delinquency is one consequence of improper socialization. Carl Bell, director of the Institute for Juvenile Research at the University of Illinois at Chicago, says adults provide a protective shield in controlling youthful behavior. "To a great extent, children are all gasoline and no brakes. It's incumbent on parents, families, schools, and society to provide them with those brakes—with expectations, rules, monitoring, and social-emotional skills" (Shelton, 2010).

The essence of control theory is that delinquent behavior occurs because it is not prevented in the first place. There are several different versions of this theory. One states that the delinquent lacks either strong inner controls and/or strong outer controls (Reckless, 1961). The former refer to things such as a positive self-image or strong ego, while the latter refer to strong family controls, community controls, legal controls, and so on. Another version maintains that many youths commit delinquent acts because they rationalize deviance before it occurs —that is, they neutralize the normal moral beliefs they have learned while growing up. For example, they deny that there is a victim by saying things like "He had it coming," or they deny that there was any real harm by saying something like "No one was really hurt" or "They won't miss it" (Sykes and Matza, 1957).

The most popular version is the one put forth by sociologist Travis Hirschi (1969). According to Hirschi, all humans are basically anti-social, and all are capable of committing a crime. What keeps most of us in check (i.e., prevents us from deviating) is what he calls the "social bond to society," especially the norms of society that we have internalized. There are four major elements of this bond, as shown in Figure 7.5 (Hirschi, 1969: 16–34).

This theory is very popular (although many do not express it as "control theory"), as most people believe these traditional values about what is and is not appropriate role behavior for young people. Furthermore, juvenile justice workers practice this every day as they try to, in a sense, *reattach* delinquents to family, school, and so on; to get them to *commit* themselves to the demands of

1. *Attachment*—This refers to ties of affection and respect between kids and parents, teachers, and friends; attachment to parents is most important because it is from them that they obtain the norms and values of the surrounding society and internalize them (very similar to Freud's superego but more conscious than his term).

2. *Commitment*—Similar to Freud's concept of ego, except it is expressed in terms of the extent to which kids are committed to the ideal requirements of childhood, such as getting an education, postponing participation in adult activities (e.g., working full-time, living on your own, getting married), or dedication to long-term goals; if they develop a stake in conformity, then engaging in delinquent behavior would endanger their future.

3. *Involvement*—Similar to the conventional belief that "idle hands are the devil's workshop"; in other words, large amounts of unstructured time may decrease the ties to the social bond; those busy doing conventional things, such as chores at home, homework, sports, camping, working, or dating, do not have time for delinquency.

4. *Belief*—This refers simply to the belief in the law, especially the morality of the law (e.g., belief that stealing is just plain wrong).

FIGURE 7.5 Hirschi's four elements of the social bond.

childhood; to *involve* them in conventional activities; and to help them acquire a *belief* and respect for the law. This theory becomes an important starting point for the social development model and the risk-focused approach of delinquency prevention.

Johnstone, quoted earlier concerning strain theory, suggests that purely ecological explanations of gangs are limited "and cannot account for why gangs influence only some of the boys who live in gang neighborhoods...." Continuing, he notes that the opportunity to join a gang "is established by the external social environment, but the decision to do so is governed by social and institutional attachments and by definitions of self.... The transition from unaffiliated to gang-affiliated delinquency occurs at the point that a boy comes to believe that he has nothing further to gain by not joining a gang" (Johnstone, 1983: 297).

One recent study confirms control theory. Extensive studies of various ethnic gangs by Vigil and Yun led them to conclude that the common theme for all these gangs is that the weakening of the bonds identified by Hirschi sort of "frees" these youths "from social control and encourages deviant behavior." The study by Vigil and Yun, based on interviews of 150 incarcerated gang members from four ethnic groups (Vietnamese, Chicano, black, and Hispanic), confirms the social control thesis (Vigil and Yun, 1996).

Informal social control networks within communities contribute to social bonding. Todd Clear (2002) notes that three levels of informal social control lessen the extent of crime: 1) what people do privately within their intimate relationships; 2) what people do collectively in their relationships with others in the community; and 3) people's attitudes toward criminal behavior. The most common forms of social control originate in the privacy of child rearing. Collective methods of social control extend the lessons through a variety of associations and groups. These include churches, businesses, social clubs, volunteer groups, youth groups, neighborhood associations, and many more. Such social controls fall between the most formal controls (e.g., police) and family controls. Participation in these associations occupies a lot of free time for young people. This is one reason why after-school and summer activities are so important. In short, close bonding to these kinds of groups reduces the likelihood of delinquency (Clear, 2002). One study verified the assertion that students with low commitments to education are more likely to become delinquent (McCartan and Gunnison, 2007). Another study found that youths who participated in structured activities with adult leaders became better adjusted and were less likely to engage in delinquent behavior. This relates to the "involvement" part of the social bond (Persson, Kerr, and Stattin, 2007).

One variation of this perspective centers on the issue of self-control or lack thereof. Containment theory argues that there are both internal and external forces that influence the lives and behavior of juveniles. By internal, we mean personal factors such as anxiety, discontent, and hostility. By external factors, we are referring to various social forces, including significant others (especially the family) and the surrounding subculture. By developing both inner (e.g., self-control, positive self-concept) and outer (e.g., strong and supportive family) "containment," an individual will be able to resist involvement in delinquent behavior.[18] Several studies have supported this perspective, although most of them have focused on the individual delinquent's lack of self-control and low self-concept, rather than the surrounding culture and economic system (Hay and Forrest, 2006; Boutwell and Beaver, 2010).

Some have noted that parental criminality contributes to low self-esteem and in turn high levels of delinquency (Higgins, 2009; Coleman, 2008). Parental involvement in various kinds of criminal behavior has consistently been correlated with delinquency. This has been especially underscored through longitudinal studies of delinquency (Wilson, 1975; Farrington et al., 1996; Dryfoos, 1990).

Social Learning Theory

According to this theory, people become delinquent or criminal through the same kind of process as learning to become anything else. One learns behavior as one learns values, beliefs, and attitudes, through one's association with other human beings. One of the earliest variations of this theory as it applies to delinquency was the theory of **differential association** originally developed by Edwin Sutherland (Sutherland and Cressey, 1970). According to this theory, one becomes a delinquent not only through contact with others who are delinquent but also through contact with various values, beliefs, and attitudes supportive of criminal/delinquent behavior in addition to the various techniques used to commit such acts. One of the central points of this theory is the proposition that one becomes a delinquent/criminal "because of an excess of definitions favorable to violation of law over definitions unfavorable [to violation] of law" (Shoemaker, 1996: 152–153). In other words, a young person will become delinquent through his or her association with delinquent youths. Together they reinforce beliefs, values, and attitudes that lead to and perpetuate delinquency.

Social learning theory suggests that there are three related processes that lead one to become a delinquent or criminal: 1) acquisition, 2) instigation, and 3) maintenance (Goldstein, 1991: 55–61).

Acquisition refers to the original learning of behavior. The key to this process is that of reinforcement through the modeling influences of one's family, the immediate subculture (especially the peer subculture), and symbolic modeling (e.g., via television). In the case of learning aggression, a child who witnesses violence within the home is apt to engage in violence later in life. This is especially true if such violence within the home is rewarded or no sanctions are applied. Important here is the fact that children tend to acquire behaviors they observe in others and to see that these behaviors are rewarded.

Instigation refers to the process whereby once a person has acquired the behavior, certain factors work to cause or instigate a specific event—in this case, an act of delinquency. Learning theory suggests five key factors as major instigators:

- *Aversive events*—events characteristics such as frustration, relative deprivation, and, of particular importance in gang violence, verbal insults and actual assaults. For those who are especially violent, threats to one's reputation and status, especially those occurring in public, are very important instigators of violent acts.

- *Modeling influences*—actually observing delinquent or criminal behavior by someone who serves as a role model can be an immediate instigator.

- *Incentive inducements*—anticipated rewards. One can be motivated to commit a crime by some perceived reward, usually monetary.

- *Instructional control*—following orders from someone in authority. A gang member, for example, may obey a direct order from a leader within the gang.

- *Environmental control*—factors in one's immediate environment, which include crowded conditions (including traffic), extreme heat, pollution, and noise.

Each of these can cause someone to "lose it" and act out, sometimes in a violent manner.[19] For delinquent or criminal behavior to persist, there needs to be consistent **reinforcement** or **maintenance**. Social learning theory suggests four specific kinds of reinforcement:

- *Direct reinforcement* refers to extrinsic rewards that correspond to an act (e.g., money or recognition).

- *Vicarious reinforcement* includes seeing others get rewards and/or escape punishment for delinquent or criminal acts (e.g., a youth sees someone carrying a lot of money obtained by selling drugs).

- *Self-reinforcement* simply means that a person derives his self-worth or sense of pride as a result of criminal acts.

- *Neutralization of self-punishment* is the process whereby one justifies or rationalizes delinquent acts.

Concerning the last method of reinforcement, one long-standing sociological theory is commonly referred to as *techniques of neutralization* (Sykes and Matza, 1957). The authors of this perspective suggest that delinquents often come up with rationalizations or excuses that absolve them of guilt. Thus, for example, a youth may say that no one was harmed or that the victim deserved it ("He had it coming to him"), or he may condemn those who condemn him (e.g., by saying that adults do these kinds of things, too), appeal to higher loyalties (e.g., "I'm doing it for the 'hood"), or merely put the blame on various external factors. An important aspect of such techniques of neutralization is that during the process, the victim is dehumanized, and there is a gradual desensitization regarding the use of violence or other means of force to get one's way.

Gangs And Maslow's Hierarchy Of Needs Consistent with social learning theories is the view that humans pass through various stages in their lives. Relatedly, this view suggests that human problems do not emerge overnight, seemingly out of nowhere. Rather, life is a process, and humans go through life developmentally, through various stages of growth. There are numerous theories relating this process to human growth and fulfillment (e.g., those of Freud, Piaget, and Erikson), but space does not permit a complete summary of these views (see Santrock, 1981: 35–88; Cianci and Gambrel, 2003; Kenrick et al., 2010). While all of these views can be used to better understand the development of gangs, one perspective seems to relate to gangs better than most—namely, Maslow's hierarchy of needs (Maslow, 1951).

According to Maslow, there are five basic human needs that evolve in the following order: 1) physiological/biological, 2) safety and security, 3) love and belongingness, 4) self-esteem, and 5) self-actualization. Satisfying these needs is an essential part of everyday human struggles. Initial needs are those for basic survival, such as food and shelter, which should be met by one's parents during early childhood. The need for safety and security refers to stability, protection, freedom from fear, freedom from anxiety and chaos, and the need for structure, order, and limits.

The need for love and belongingness refers to the need to belong to some group or some individual, especially a family. If all three basic levels of needs are met, especially through the family, then the adolescent will be able to get along well with others and be motivated to satisfy the next level of need in the hierarchy. It should be noted that the need for love and belongingness becomes more problematic in an industrialized society with high geographic mobility, leading to the breakdown of traditional groupings. This often results in the formation of artificial groups, such as religious cults and gangs. (This is consistent with the social disorganization perspective.)

Self-esteem needs include self-respect, feeling good about oneself, and being held in esteem by others. It also includes the need for strength, achievement, adequacy, confidence, and a positive reputation. These needs can best be fulfilled by learning a skill, pursuing a profession, or otherwise engaging in conduct that elicits positive regard from others. Looking closely at youth gangs today, we can see how important reputation, or rep, is, and why an attack against one's reputation (often called "dissin'") is a serious offense calling for severe sanctions against the offending party (Vigil, 2010).

Finally, self-actualization needs are those that can be satisfied only when all the others are satisfied. Here the individual strives to become everything he or she is capable of becoming, to fulfill his or her potentiality. Self-actualized people can keep pessimistic doubts, wishes, fears, and so on from bothering them. They are very spontaneous and creative people. They accept themselves and others and are reasonably independent.

Clearly, gangs provide many of these developmental needs of adolescents, especially those from disadvantaged neighborhoods. Perkins suggests that some gangs (especially black gangs) provide members with housing, food, clothing, and other essentials (Perkins, 1987: 59). They are given a sense of security and power, a sense of belonging, identity, and discipline. Moore has noted that some gangs have functioned to help "order" adolescents' lives. They provided outlets for sociability, courtship, and other normal adolescent activities. More important, the legitimate institutions of socialization, such as schools and families, have become less important in adolescents' lives, and "street socialization" has begun to compete with, and often replace, these institutions (Moore, 1991: 6). In still another statement reminiscent of Thrasher, Moore further suggests that "institutions develop where there are gaps in the existing institutional structure. Gangs as youth groups develop among the socially marginal adolescents for whom school and family do not fill socialization needs." Moreover, gangs "persist as young-adult institutions in a changed society, in which the labor market is not filling the needs of the transition from adolescence to young adulthood. It is not that they are rebels, rather it is that they are left out of the credentialed, ordered society" (Moore, 1991: 9).

Bing provides an insightful look at what gangs provide for youths. A. C. Jones, a counselor at a youth camp in Southern California, puts it this way:

> What do you think happened when that kid there first began to seek
> out his masculinity? What happened when he first tried to assert himself?
> If he lived in any other community but Watts there would be legitimate
> ways to express those feelings. Little League. Pop Warner. But if you're
> a black kid living in Watts those options have been removed. You're
> not going to play Pop Warner. Not in Watts. Maybe if you live in
> Bellflower, maybe if you live in Agoura, but not in Watts—it's just not
> there, there's no funding for it. But you're at that prepubescent age, and
> you have all those aggressive tendencies and no legitimate way to get rid
> of them. And that's when the gang comes along, and the gang offers
> everything those legitimate organizations do. The gang serves emotional
> needs. You feel wanted. You feel welcome. You feel important. And
> there is discipline and there are rules. (Bing, 1991: 12)

Rational Choice Theory

Modern versions of the classical approach to crime learned from the mistakes of the original Classical School. Beccaria and Bentham erroneously assumed that all humans behave "rationally" all the time—that they consistently, carefully calculate the pros and cons of their behaviors. More recent examples of this view—including the *rational choice theory*—recognize that choices are often not based on pure reason and rationality; rather, they are determined by a host of factors. There are constraints on our choices because of lack of information, differing moral values, the social context of the situation, and other situational factors. In short, not everyone acts logically and rationally all the time, which may be especially true for young offenders. Indeed, it has been estimated that as many as two-thirds of delinquent acts are spur-of-the-moment acts with no advanced planning. Some planning does, of course occur, especially when the crimes are serious property crimes or systematic drug sales (Gove, 1994; Wolfgang, Thornberry, and Figlio, 1987).

Various terminology has been used, almost interchangeably, with this idea, such as *criminal opportunity theory* and *routine activity theory*.[20] Actually, these recent developments are merely a kind of "old wine in new bottles" since this kind of thinking originated with what has come to be called the **Classical School of Criminology**, starting with the writings of Cesare Beccaria and Jeremy Bentham in the late eighteenth and early nineteenth centuries.

For Beccaria and other liberal thinkers, the major principle that should govern legislation was that of "the greatest happiness for the greatest numbers" (this supports the view that government should be "of the people, by the people, for the people"), which is the basic philosophical doctrine known as *utilitarianism*, the idea that punishment was based on its usefulness or utility, or practicality. One of Beccaria's most famous statements in his book was as follows: "For a punishment to attain its end, the evil which it inflicts has only to exceed the advantages derivable from the crime." In other words, punishment should not be excessive; *it should fit the crime* (this is a key phrase, most commonly expressed as "let the punishment fit the crime," actually attributed to Bentham, the next author discussed).

Jeremy Bentham (1748–1832) was one of Beccaria's contemporaries. He suggested that criminal behavior (like all human behavior) is a rational choice, born of man's free will. To prevent crime, we must make the punishment (i.e., pain) greater than the criminal act.

Fast-forward to the last half of the twentieth century, and we have the reincarnation of the classical approach to crime. However, modern versions have usually learned from the mistakes of the original Classical School. The original statements from Beccaria and Bentham erroneously assumed that all humans behave "rationally" all the time, that they carefully calculate the pros and cons of their behaviors. More recent examples of this view—including the rational choice theory—recognize that choices are often not based on pure reason and rationality, but rather are determined by a host of factors. There are constraints on our choices because of lack of information, various moral values, the social context of the situation, and other situational factors. In short, not everyone acts logically and rationally all the time, which may be especially true for young offenders (Shelden, 2012).

Modern rational choice theory still makes the assumption that people freely choose to commit crime because they are goal oriented and want to maximize their pleasure and minimize their pain. In short, they are acting mostly out of self-interest. One modern variation, known as routine activities theory, suggests that criminals plan very carefully by selecting specific targets based on such things as vulnerability (e.g., elderly citizens, unguarded premises, lack of police presence) and commit their crimes accordingly. Thus people who engage in certain routine activities during the course of their daily lives place themselves at risk of being victimized, such as being out in high-crime areas at night, not locking their doors, leaving keys in their car, working at certain jobs during certain hours of the day (e.g., late-night clerk at a 7–11 store), and so on. Active criminals select such targets carefully, weighing the odds of getting caught accordingly. One flaw, among others, in such thinking is that there is an assumption that people should stay home more often to avoid being a victim when in fact certain groups (especially women and children) seem to be much more vulnerable at home than anywhere else (Maxfield, 1987; Messner and Tardiff, 1985).

As we saw in our discussion on socialization into the gang, there are many logical reasons why a youth may want to join a gang. Thus, rational choice theory may be quite suitable in explaining this. On the other hand, however, it does not logically follow that the threat of punishment (e.g., so-called enhancement statutes that increase the penalty for the commission of a crime if a person is a gang member) will deter such a youngster. One of the best comments on this problem comes from one of the most respected gang researchers, Malcolm Klein. Klein (1995) used a crackdown on gangs by the Los Angeles Police Department, known as Operation Hammer, to illustrate the problem of deterrence. This operation resulted in mass arrests of almost 1,500 individuals who were subsequently booked at a mobile booking unit next to the Los Angeles Memorial Coliseum. About 90 percent were released with no charges filed; there were only 60 felony arrests, and charges were eventually filed on about half of these. Klein uses a hypothetical situation of a gang member arrested and booked during such an operation. There are one of two possible scenarios as the gang member, immediately following his release, returns to his neighborhood and his gang. Klein writes as follows:

> Does he say to them [his homies],"Oh, gracious, I've been arrested and subjected to deterrence; I'm going to give up my gang affiliation." Or does he say, "Shit man, they're just jivin' us—can't hold us on any charges, and gotta let us go." Without hesitation, the gangbanger will turn the experience to his and the gang's advantage. Far from being deterred from membership or crime, his ties to the groups will be strengthened when the members group together to make light of the whole affair and heap ridicule on the police. (Klein, 1995: 163)

In other words, human behavior is far more complex than the rather simplistic notion that we all use our free will to make choices. Decisions hinge on the availability of alternative choices. A good analogy is that of a menu at a restaurant. Some restaurants have several items to choose from, while others have a limited selection. Likewise, some youths may have a variety of choices (stemming mostly from their environment), while others may have extremely limited selections. A youth growing up in a community with gangs may have the choice of joining or getting attacked. Other youths in other communities may have other options, such as moving with their parents to a new community (Agnew, 1995). Two researchers have proposed a *situational choice model* that asserts criminal behavior is a function of choices and decisions that are made within a surrounding context of various opportunities and constraints (Clarke and Cornish, 1983).

Each of the variations of the Classical School eventually is reduced to the key notion of *free will*, an idea that has been debated for several centuries among philosophers and scientists. It is beyond the scope of this chapter to deal with this topic in any detail, but we will briefly raise several issues.

Every event in life has a *cause*. Our world would be chaos, and science would not exist if there were effects without causes and effects. If a plane crashes, we immediately try to determine what caused the crash. No one would think of suggesting that it may be "causeless." If there is a new disease, an effective cure is possible only after we have identified the cause. If the police find a dead body, they will try to discover who and what caused it. All the laws of nature and all our scientific advances are possible *only* because *all* effects have causes. Modern life itself would be impossible if there were effects without causes. If there were effects without causes, the word "experience" would be nonsensical. Experience is all about the long slow process of learning which effects go with which causes.

When it comes to explaining certain human behaviors—especially crime— much of this kind of thinking is often tossed aside. For example, several years ago, Dr. Laura Schlessinger[21] discussed on her radio show the case of Susan Smith, the South Carolina woman who let her car slide into a pond with her two children in the back seat. Smith first blamed a black man, a complete stranger; eventually she confessed. Dr. Laura explained Susan Smith's actions by saying she was "evil." No further discussion was needed. To start to ask why she is "evil" opens you up to charges that you are some bleeding heart, soft-on-crime liberal, followed by the "abuse-excuse" mentality. It's almost as though trying to find a cause of this and similar tragedies is tantamount to approving Susan Smith's actions. To suggest that there is not a cause for what we describe as evil, however, is contrary to all the laws of science and logic. Quite often, people confuse "explanation" with "excuse."

Is Dr. Laura saying there is no cause for "evil"? If so, then there is no way to protect ourselves against it. There is nothing to be on the lookout for if it just happens without cause. It's like contracting some rare disease for which there are no preventive measures. Let's suppose that that is exactly what happens. How then can we hold people accountable? Are there people who are just born evil? What could that person have done to avoid being born evil?

Are there people who are not born evil but who then somehow become evil? That seems more likely. The question of how they became evil demands finding a cause. It is unlikely that they were not evil on January 18th, but they were evil on January 19 without something happening, some cause.

Do youngsters just suddenly choose to commit a delinquent act with no ante-cedent events leading up to it? If we take two youths growing up in the same neighborhood, and one joined a local gang and the other one didn't, do we simply say one "freely chose" to be in a gang and the other one "freely chose" not to? If so, then we must ask *why* they chose different paths. There have to be *causes* for each of the two courses of action. I often ask students why they are attending my university, rather than Harvard or Stanford. They often say they "freely chose" to attend my university, but when asked why they didn't "freely choose" Harvard or Stanford, they typically begin talking about their family back-grounds, the income level of their parents, the communities where they grew up, their grades in high school, and so on. Each of these variables in turn has its own *cause*, such as why one's parents are not rich or why the high school grades were not higher. If a peer received an athletic scholarship to a very prestigious school, we could ask why one person had athletic ability and the others did not.

The bottom line is that everything has a cause, and usually multiple causes. These causes can be simplified as being either genetic or environmental—the famous nature versus nurture debate. To reduce the complexities of human behavior, delinquent or otherwise, to some simple formula of "rational choice" is patently absurd. The Classical School perspective boxes us into a corner—it comes down to the idea that delinquent acts (and, in fact, all other acts) are merely "choices" we make with our "free will." Our entire legal system is based on deterrence. We have laws, police, and courts that mete out punishments for wrongdoing. All of these systems operate on the assumption that people make free choices to commit crime, and it is up to the legal system to prevent that from occurring by making the "pain" greater than the "pleasure" gained by committing a crime. Actions by the legal system—including the threat that legal agents may take action—are the foundation of the legal order. This system cannot handle the possibility that people may not have free will and that there are all sorts of causes beyond an individual's control.

It is important to note, however, that the basic thrust of the Classical School's vision of human beings and the proper response to crime was, for all practical purposes, left unchanged. Beccaria and Bentham's premises that criminals make willful decisions to commit crimes and thus must be held responsible continued to influence thinking about the criminal justice process. What began as a general theory of human behavior became a perspective on government crime control policy (Shichor, 2010). The administration of justice continued to be guided, as it is today, with one overriding principle: that human behavior, in this case criminal behavior, can be shaped, molded, changed, and so on, through the fear of punishment and that all that is needed is to make the punishment (or rather the pain that is associated with it) exceed the pleasure (or profit from the crime), to prevent people from committing crime.

Several competing theories emerged during the century after Beccaria published his views. Most of these were found within the "positivist" tradition of criminology. In the nineteenth century, a new trend emerged that used observation and measurement to study social phenomena. The *scientific method* represented a sharp break from the past. Rather than relying on religious beliefs or "armchair" philosophy, answers to fundamental questions about human beings and the universe around them were investigated through "objective" *science*.[22] Charles Darwin, in his book *On the Origin of Species* (published in 1859), presented evidence that "humans were the same general kind of creatures as the rest of the animals, except that they were more highly evolved or developed." Most importantly, humans were beginning to be "understood as creatures whose conduct was influenced, if not determined, by biological and cultural antecedents rather than as self-determining beings that were free to do what they wanted" (Kuhn, 1970: 36). The first "scientific" studies of crime and criminal behavior began at about the same time.

Positivism is a *method of inquiry* that attempts to answers questions through the scientific method. The researcher examines the "real world" of empirical facts by testing hypotheses, with the goal of arriving at the "truth" and deriving "laws" (e.g., the law of falling bodies, the law of relativity).[23] The positivist mode of inquiry gained respectability in the social sciences largely through the work of August Comte (1798–1857). "While Comte recognized that positive methods to study society cannot be completely identical to mathematical and physical science methods, he maintained that positive knowledge can be gained by using observation, experiment, comparison, and historical method" (Shichor, 2010: 214). Using the scientific approach, human beings are able to discover regularities among social phenomena resulting in the establishment of predict-ability and control (Bottomore et al., 1983: 382).

Most of the perspectives summarized previously have a tendency not to seriously question the nature of the existing social order (possible exceptions are social disorganization and strain theories, which to some extent provide at least an indirect critique of the existing order). Beginning with the labeling perspec-tive, some recent perspectives have focused on questioning the nature of the existing social order, specifically the social order of advanced capitalism in the late twentieth century. One result of the next two perspectives covered here is that instead of focusing on how offenders and potential offenders or at-risk youths can be made to accommodate to the existing social order, these views call for changing the nature of the existing social order so that fewer people will be drawn into criminal behavior in the first place.

The Labeling Perspective

The labeling perspective (also known as the *societal reaction* perspective) does not address in any direct way the causes of criminal/deviant behavior but rather focuses on three interrelated processes: 1) how and why certain behaviors are defined as criminal or deviant (in the case of gangs, why some groups and not others are labeled as gangs and why some crimes but not others are labeled as gang-related), 2) the response to crime or deviance on the part of authorities (e.g., the official processing of cases from arrest through sentencing), and 3) the effects of such definitions and official reactions on the person or persons so labeled (e.g., how official responses to groups of youths may cause them to come closer together and begin to call themselves a gang) (Schur, 1971). The key to this perspective is reflected in a statement by Becker, who wrote, "Social groups create deviance by making the rules whose infraction constitutes deviance, and by applying those rules to particular people and labeling them as outsiders" (1963: 8–9).

One key aspect of the labeling perspective is that the criminal justice system itself (including the legislation that creates laws and hence defines crime and criminals) helps to perpetuate crime and deviance. For example, several studies during the late 1960s and 1970s focused on the general issue of how agents of the criminal justice system (especially the police) helped to perpetuate certain kinds of criminal behavior.[24] In short, this perspective focuses on how gangs and gang-related behavior may be perpetuated by the criminal justice system's attempts to control the problem.

One of the most significant perspectives on crime and criminal behavior to emerge from the labeling tradition was Quinney's theory of the *social reality of crime*. In a truly landmark textbook on crime and criminal justice, Quinney organized his theory around six interrelated propositions:

1. Crime is a definition of human conduct that is created by authorized agents in a politically organized society.

2. Criminal definitions describe behaviors that conflict with the interests of the segments of society that have the power to shape public policy.

3. Criminal definitions are applied by the segments of society that have the power to shape the enforcement and administration of criminal law.

4. Behavior patterns are structured in segmentally organized society in relation to criminal definitions, and within this context persons engage in actions that have relative probabilities of being defined as criminal.

5. Conceptions of crime are constructed and diffused in the segments of society by various means of communication.

6. The social reality of crime is constructed by the formulation and application of criminal definitions, the development of behavior patterns related to criminal definitions, and the construction of criminal conceptions. (Quinney, 1970: 15–25)

An important component of Quinney's theory is four interrelated concepts: 1) process, 2) conflict, 3) power, and 4) action.[25] By *process,* Quinney is referring to the fact that "all social phenomena ... have duration and undergo change." The *conflict* view of society and the law is that in any society, "conflicts between persons, social units, or cultural elements are inevitable, the normal consequences of social life." Further, society "is held together by force and constraint and is characterized by ubiquitous conflicts that result in continuous change." *Power* is an elementary force in our society. Power, says Quinney, "is the ability of persons and groups to determine the conduct of other persons and groups. It is utilized not for its own sake but is the vehicle for the enforcement of scarce values in society, whether the values are material, moral, or otherwise." Power is important if we are to understand public policy. Public policy, including crime-control policies, is shaped by groups with special interests. In a class society, some groups have more power than others and therefore are able to have their interests represented in policy decisions, often at the expense of less powerful groups. Thus, for example, white, upper-class males have more power and their interests are more likely to be represented than those of working- or lower-class minorities and women. Finally, by *social action,* Quinney is referring to the fact that human beings engage in voluntary behavior, which is not completely determined by forces outside their control. From this perspective, human beings are "able to reason and choose courses of action" and are "changing and becoming, rather than merely being." It is true that humans are in fact shaped by their physical, social, and cultural experiences, but they also have the capacity to change and achieve maximum potential and fulfillment.

It is important to note the distinctions between primary and secondary deviance (Lemert, 1951). **Primary deviance** includes acts that the perpetrator and/ or others consider alien (i.e., not indicative, incidental) to one's true identity or character. In other words, an act is "out of character" (commonly expressed by others as "this is not like you"). These acts have only marginal implications for one's status and psychic structure. They remain primary deviance as long as one can rationalize or otherwise deal with the behavior and still maintain an acceptable self-image and an image acceptable to others. **Secondary deviance**, on the other hand, refers to a process whereby the deviance takes on self-identifying features; that is, deviant acts begin to be considered as indicative of one's true self, the way one "really" is. Deviance becomes secondary "when a person begins to employ his deviant behavior or a role based upon it as a means of defense, attack, or adjustment to the overt and covert problems created by the consequent societal reaction to him" (Lemert, 1951: 76).

This perspective eventually led some scholars to begin to question not only the criminal justice system but also the very social structure and institutions of society as a whole. In particular, some research in the labeling tradition directed attention to such factors as class, race, and sex in not only the formulation of criminal definitions (including the definition of *gang*) but also as major causes of crime itself. This in turn led to a critical examination of existing institutions of American society and to a critique of the capitalist system itself. A critical/Marxist criminology emerged from such efforts.

Critical/Marxist Perspectives

Quinney and Wildeman place the development of a critical/Marxist line of inquiry in the historical and social context of the late 1960s and early 1970s. They note that

> It is not by chance that the 1970s saw the birth of critical thought in the ranks of American criminologists. Not only did critical criminology challenge old ideas, but it went on to introduce new and liberating ideas and interpretations of America and of what America could become. If social justice is not for all in a democratic society—and it was clear that it was not—then there must be something radically wrong with the way our basic institutions are structured. (1991: 72)

In *Class, State, and Crime,* Quinney outlined his own version of a critical or Marxist theory of crime. Quinney linked crime and the reaction to crime to the modern capitalist political and economic system. This viewpoint suggests that the capitalist system itself produces a number of problems that are linked to various attempts by the capitalist class to maintain the basic institutions of the capitalist order. These attempts lead to various forms of accommodation and resistance by people who are oppressed by the system, especially the working class, the poor, and racial and ethnic minorities. In attempting to maintain the existing order, the powerful commit various crimes, which Quinney classified as crimes of control, crimes of economic domination, and crimes of government. At the same time, oppressed people engage in various kinds of crimes related to accommodation and resistance, including predatory crimes, personal crimes, and crimes of resistance (Quinney, 1977: 33–62).

Much of what is known as gang behavior, including gang-related crime, can therefore be understood as an attempt by oppressed people to accommodate and resist the problems created by capitalist institutions. Many gang members, as noted in Chapter 4, adapt to their disadvantaged positions by engaging in predatory and personal criminal behavior. Much of their behavior, moreover, is in many ways identical to normal capitalist entrepreneurial activity. Padilla's study, noted in Chapter 4, illustrates this.

A critical/Marxist perspective goes even further by focusing on "those social structures and forces that produce both the greed of the inside trader as well as the brutality of the rapist or the murderer. And it places those structures in their proper context: the material conditions of class struggle under a capitalist mode of production" (Quinney and Wildeman, 1991: 77). The material conditions include the class and racial inequalities produced by the contradictions of capitalism (which produce economic changes that negatively affect the lives of so many people, especially the working class and the poor).

According to Lanier and Henry, there are six central ideas common to critical/Marxist theories of crime and criminal justice (Lanier and Henry, 1998: 256–258):

1. *Capitalism shapes social institutions, social identities, and social action.* In other words, the actual "mode of production" in any given society tends to determine many other areas of social life, including divisions based on race, class, and gender plus the manner in which people behave and act toward one another.

2. *Capitalism creates class conflict and contradictions.* Because a relatively small group (a "ruling class" consisting of perhaps 1% to 2% of the population) owns and/or controls the "means of production," class divisions have resulted, as has the inevitable class conflict over control of resources. The contradiction is that workers need to consume the products of the capitalist system, but in order to do this, they need to have enough income to do so and thus increase growth in the economy. However, too much growth may cut into profits. One result is the creation of a *surplus population*—a more or less steady supply of able workers who are permanently unemployed or under-employed (also called the *underclass*).

3. *Crime is a response to capitalism and its contradictions.* This notion stems in part from the second theme in that the "surplus population" may commit crimes to survive. These can be described as *crimes of accommodation* (Quinney, 1980). Crimes among the more affluent can also result (see next point) in addition to *crimes of resistance* (e.g., sabotage and political violence).

4. *Capitalist law facilitates and conceals crimes of domination and repression.* The law and legal order can often be repressive toward certain groups and engage in the violation of human rights, which are referred to as *crimes of control and repression*. *Crimes of domination* also occur with great frequency as corporations and their representatives violate numerous laws (fraud, price-fixing, pollution, etc.) that cause widespread social harms but are virtually ignored by the criminal justice system.

5. *Crime is functional to capitalism.* There is a viable and fast-growing *crime control industry* that provides a sort of "Keynesian stimulus" to the economy by creating jobs and profits for corporations (e.g., building prisons, providing various products and services to prisons, jails, police departments, and

courthouses) (Shelden, 2008, 2010; Shelden and Brown, 2001; Shelden et al., 2008).

6. *Capitalism shapes society's response to crime by shaping law.* Those in power (especially legislators) define what is a "crime," what constitutes a threat to "social order," and, perhaps more importantly, *who* constitutes such a threat—which usually ends up being members of the underclass. Various problems that threaten the dominant mode of production become criminalized (e.g., the use of certain drugs used by minorities rather than drugs produced by corporations, such as cigarettes, prescription drugs, and of course alcohol).

The importance of the capitalist system in producing inequality and hence crime is apparent when examining recent economic changes in American society and the effects of these changes. In recent years particularly, many scholars have begun to seek an explanation of gangs (and crime in general) by examining changes in the economic structure of society and how such changes have contributed to the emergence of what some have called an underclass, which in many ways represent what Marx called the "surplus population" in addition to the *lumpenproletariat.*[26] In many ways, this perspective is an extension of some of the basic assumptions and key concepts of social disorganization/ecology, strain, and cultural deviance theories in addition to critical/Marxist perspectives.

SUMMARY

This chapter has reviewed several different theoretical explanations for the question "Why are there gangs?" Several key themes can be discerned from this review. First, with the exceptions of deterrence, rational choice, and social learning theory, the views discussed here stress the importance of the external socioeconomic environment in explaining gangs. Beginning with social disorganization/ecology (especially the early work of Thrasher), these theories link gangs to such environmental factors as poverty, social inequality, lack of community integration, and lack of meaningful employment and educational opportunities, along with the larger economic picture of a changing labor market and the corresponding emergence of a more or less permanent underclass mired in segregated communities. Little wonder that the overwhelming majority of gangs throughout history have been found in the most impoverished communities or what Thrasher called the "interstitial" areas of inner cities.

A second theme is that adolescents who grow up in such environments are faced with the daily struggles for self-esteem, a sense of belonging, protection from outside threats, and some sort of family-type structure. These and many other basic human needs are not being met by such primary social institutions as the family, the school, the church, and the community. Clearly, for significant numbers of youngsters, the gang fills many of these needs.

A third theme developed in this chapter is that becoming a gang member is a social process that involves learning various roles and social expectations within a given community. It involves the reinforcement of these expectations through various rationalizations or techniques of neutralization in addition to the perpetuation of various lifestyles, attitudes, and behaviors on the part of the significant others in the lives of these youths. Over time, a youth (actually beginning at a very early age) becomes embedded in his or her surrounding environment and cultural norms so that it becomes more and more difficult to leave the world of the gang.

A fourth theme is that delinquency in general and gang behavior in particular are shaped to a large degree by the societal reaction to such behavior and to the kinds of individuals who engage in such behavior. Such a response helps to perpetuate the very problem that the larger society is trying to solve.

A fifth theme is that gang behavior is often a quite rational response to the surrounding social conditions within one's environment. Rational choice theory, however, suggests that such a response might be offset by increasing the risks of being apprehended and punished by the juvenile or criminal justice system and specifically by increasing the degree of punishment. Given the context of gangs in American society, the deterrent effect of punishment is minimal, if not counterproductive. In fact, as punishments have become harsher during the past 20 years, the gang problem has escalated.

A sixth and final theme that emerges in this chapter is that one cannot possibly explain the phenomenon of gangs without considering the economic context of capitalism. As we have discussed in earlier chapters, most criminal activity of gang members is consistent with basic capitalist values, such as the law of supply and demand, the need to make money (profit), and the desire to accumulate consumer goods. And, like the larger capitalist system, there are many failures in the world of crime and gang activity.

Speaking of capitalism—and the economy in general—we are presently in the middle of the largest economic crisis since the Great Depression of the 1930s. This crisis has had a major impact on everyone, but especially those who were already living outside the mainstream of society, including gang members. This is the subject of the next chapter.

NOTES

1. Among the many examples are Cook (1986); Cohen and Felson (1979); Einstadter and Henry (1995); Cornish and Clarke (1987).

2. For a more detailed discussion of the work of Guerry and Quetelet, along with the Chicago School, see Lanier and Henry (1998: 183–192); see also Quinney and Wildeman (1991: 48–50).

3. See Moore (1978, 1991) for documentation of this phenomenon.

4. Lanier and Henry (1998: 182). Lanier and Henry also note that the term social or human ecology comes from the Greek word *oikos*, which translates roughly into "household" or "living space."

5. This is especially documented in Shaw and McKay (1972).

6. Vigil concludes that the gang provides many functions a family does. "The gang has become a 'spontaneous' street social unit that fills a void left by families under stress. Parents and other family members are preoccupied with their own problems, and thus the street group has arisen as a source of familial compensation." Vigil notes that about half of those he interviewed mentioned how important the group was to them, that the gang was something they needed, and that it gave them something in return. Close friends become like family to the gang member, especially when support, love, and nurturance are missing from one's real family (Vigil, 1988: 89–90).

7. Among others, see Sampson (1985); Sampson, Raudenbush, and Earls (1997); Laub and Sampson (2006); Sampson and Laub (1995).

8. See the following Web site: http://www.jfa-associates.com/publications/cjpm/JFA-JMC%20Mapping%20Gallery.pdf.

9. Retrieved from http://cacs.unlv.edu/CrimeMapping/.

10. The reader is encouraged to merely browse through any introductory sociology textbook to find numerous references to these two terms. In fact, one definition of sociology itself could easily be "the study of culture and social structure."

11. For an excellent discussion of the role of corporate propaganda, see the following: Herman and Chomsky (2002); Chomsky (1989); Fones-Wolf (1994); and Carey (1995).

12. For a quick and easy-to-read look at inequality, see Teller-Elsberg et al. (2006).

13. Messner and Rosenfeld (2007: 80) note that the United States lags far behind other countries (whose economic institutions are not nearly as dominant) in paid family leave.

14. A good illustration of this dominance is shown in Derber (1998).

15. See this Web site: http://www.uwsc.wisc.edu/projects.php.

16. Although not mentioned by Hagan, to become embedded in the labor market one also needs social or cultural capital. This term is discussed at length by MacLeod (2008) and is included in the next section. In summary, for those who lack the necessary social or cultural capital, being involved in the labor market with steady employment is quite difficult.

17. Hartley, Maddan, and Spohn (2007). Other studies addressing the same issue include Steffensmeier and Demuth. (2000); Steffensmeier and Demuth (2001); Steffensmeier, Ulmer, and Kramer (1998).

18. This view was originally formulated by Reckless (1961).

19. The movie *Falling Down*, starring Michael Douglas, illustrates how one can "lose it" because of some of these instigators.

20. Some illustrations of this approach can be found in Cook (1986) and Cohen and Felson (1979).

21. Some illustrations of her views can be seen on her Web site at http://drlaura.com/.

22. The "scientific method" consists, generally, of four main stages: 1) Identify a problem by observing something occurring in the universe (e.g., certain groups of people seem to commit more crime than others); 2) derive from this a hypothesis that

suggests a possible answer (e.g., those from single-family homes commit more crime than those from two-family homes); 3) test this hypothesis through an experiment or some other kind of observations (e.g., collect data on court cases); and 4) draw conclusions from your research. A possible fifth step is to modify your original hypothesis and derive a competing hypothesis. From this procedure, you eventually derive a "theory" to explain what you discovered. One of the great advantages of this method is that it is *unprejudiced* in that the conclusions are independent of religious persuasion, ideology, or the state of consciousness of the investigator and/ or the subject of the investigation. In direct contrast, faith refers to a belief in something that does not rest on any logical proof or material evidence. Faith does not determine whether a scientific theory is adopted or discarded. Knowledge based on faith was the dominant paradigm until the discovery of the scientific method. For an excellent book on the subject, see Kuhn (1970).

23. The word *empirical* is defined in the *Random House Dictionary* as "derived from or guided by experience or experiment"; a related term is *empiricism*, which means "the doctrine that all knowledge is derived from sense experience." A *hypothesis* is a key ingredient of the *scientific method*, and it can be defined as a proposition about the expected or anticipated relationship between two or more variables, usually expressed as the dependent and independent variable. When using the scientific method, you use a hypothesis to find out what causes something. It is sort of like testing a hunch you have about the cause of something, such as trying to determine why your car is not starting. In this case, the "car not starting" is the dependent variable in that it is dependent on some other variable—the independent variable. You might "hypothesize" that your car not starting is caused by its being out of gas.

24. Examples can be cited endlessly. A few are Chambliss (1975); Chambliss and Seidman (1971); Werthman (1967); and Werthman and Piliavin (1967).

25. The following quotes are taken from Quinney (1970: 8–15).

26. It is important to emphasize that Marx did distinguish between these two terms. The *lumpenproletariat* was seen by Marx as the bottom layer of society, the "social junk," "rotting scum," "rabble," and so on. In short, they were described as the "criminal class." The "surplus population" referred to working-class men and women who, because of various fluctuations in the market (caused chiefly by contradictions within the capitalist system), were excluded, either temporarily or permanently, from the labor market.

8

Gangs in Context: Inequality in American Society

In the previous chapter, we reviewed some theories, such as strain and critical/Marxist, that suggest the importance of the economic institution in generating not only crime but helping to create and sustain gang activity. Strong emphasis was placed on the salience of American capitalism in producing certain "strains" on its citizens. The changing economic structure of American capitalism and how this relates to crime in general and gangs in particular is the subject of this chapter.

SOME INTRODUCTORY COMMENTS

The sources and data we reported in the current chapter for the third edition of this book did not present a very rosy picture. The most recent data available at that time ended around 1996 or 1997. To say the least, since this time all hell has broken loose! The country—and the entire world—has experienced the worst economic crisis since the Great Depression, starting in 2008 (although there were clear indications that something was wrong as early as 2007).[1] This crisis has impacted not just the underclass but the middle class too, as life savings for millions decreased significantly; millions of jobs were lost; and, perhaps most devastating, the housing bubble burst and millions either lost or were close to losing their homes—arguably the bedrock of the "American dream." It is hard to predict when things will begin to turn around. In March 2011, the latest economic figures were not optimistic. The unemployment rate was 8.8 percent—8.6 percent for adult men, 7.7 percent for adult women, 24.5 percent for teenagers, 7.9 percent for whites, 15.5 percent for blacks, and 11.3 percent for Hispanics.[2] Another report broke the figures down further, noting that for blacks aged 16–19, the unemployment rate stood at 46.5 percent; for whites, it was 20.9 percent (Harvey, 2011). As these words are written (February, 2012), many economists have recently warned that another recession may be coming (Krugman, 2011; Baker, 2011; Barth, 2011). This will make matters especially worse for young black males living in the cities.

These are "official" unemployment figures, which leave out a lot.[3] There is also what is known as the "underemployment" rate, which is defined as the "unemployed; involuntarily part-time workers who want full-time work but have had to settle for part-time hours; and workers described as 'marginally attached,' who want and are available for a job, but have given up actively looking." In July 2010, underemployment was highest for young Americans (ages 18 to 29), at 28.4 percent. Among all adults in the workforce, a higher percentage of women were underemployed (21.6% vs. 15.6% for men) (Jacobe, 2010).

The Bureau of Labor Statistics (BLS) reports on "alternative measures of labor underutilization." One measure of unemployment (labeled as "U6") is known as "total unemployed, plus all persons marginally attached to the labor force, plus total employed part time for economic reasons, as a percent of the civilian labor force plus all persons marginally attached to the labor force." The percentage in February 2011 was 15.9%, down from 17.9% one year earlier (Bureau of Labor Statistics [BLS], 2011a).

Since the recession started, cases of reported runaway youth have been rising, stemming directly from the current crisis. Children will be negatively affected by the recession because it will increase the likelihood that they will be living under the poverty level, which in turn may increase the likelihood of doing poorly in school and dropping out, which can lead to crime.

> Children who fall into poverty during a recession will fare far worse along a range of variables, even well into adulthood, than will their peers who avoided poverty despite the downturn in the economy. These children will live in households with lower overall incomes, they will earn less themselves, and they will have a greater chance of living in or near poverty. They will achieve lower levels of education and will be less likely to be gainfully employed. Children who experience recession-induced poverty will even report poorer health than their peers who did not fall into poverty during the recession. These differences will persist for decades into their adult lives. (First Focus, 2009: 1)

About one out of nine children are living with an unemployed parent. "Children whose parents are unemployed are at increased risk for experiencing poverty, homelessness, and child abuse" (Isaacs, 2010). Children represent 24.5 percent of the overall population and 35.5 percent of people in poverty—and 31.3 percent of people 50 percent below the poverty threshold (6.9 million children) (DeNavas-Walt, Proctor, and Smith, 2010: 19).

> Half of the poor are now classified as in "extreme poverty"—described as living in families earning below 50 percent of the poverty line. The percent of children who are food insecure also increased to 18 percent

in 2010. This growth translates into an additional 750,000 children nationwide who are malnourished. (DiMaggio, 2010)

The 2010 Child and Youth Well-Being Index (CWI), created by the Foundation for Child Development (FCD), predicted that the effects of the recession will likely include: 1) a decline in prekindergarten enrollment, 2) an increase in the rate of those between the ages of 16 and 19 who are "detached" from mainstream institutions because they are not in school and do not have a job, and 3) an increase in "risky behavior" (violence, drugs, etc.) (Land, 2010). The key finding here is the decline in prekindergarten enrollment, as this is a leading predictor of child development in the early years, including delinquent behavior.

Before continuing, we believe it is necessary to provide a brief summary of the nature of capitalism, because we all live under this economic system, which is undergoing such a huge crisis. How this system and the current crisis relates to gangs will become clearer as we go along.

THE CAPITALIST ECONOMIC SYSTEM

Capitalism is one of several methods whereby societies attempt to meet the basic needs of citizens in terms of the production, distribution, and consumption of goods and services.[4] Often called the *mode of production*, this economic system consists of two essential parts: 1) the *forces* (or *means*) *of production* (the raw materials, tools, instruments, machines, buildings, and so on, plus the current state of science and technology, and the skills, abilities, and knowledge of the people themselves) and 2) the *relations of production*, which can be defined as "the specific manner in which the surplus is produced and then appropriated from the direct producers" (Edwards, Reich, and Weisskopf, 1986). These relations are essentially *class* relations, the most common of which are between the *owners/managers* and the *workers* (salary and wage earners). The more popular term is that of *social class*, which may be defined as "a group of individuals or families who occupy a similar position in the economic system of production, distribution, and consumption of goods and services in industrial societies" (Rothman, 1999: 5).

The most common indicator of social class position is one's occupation. Indeed, it can be said that the work people engage in limits their financial status (income and wealth), their social status or prestige, the stability of their employment, the chances for upward social mobility, and their general health and longevity. It plays a key role in the way they think of themselves, places them within the larger systems of power and authority, and has significant implications for the future of their children. Erik Wright has written an entire book, *Class Counts*, on the topic (1997). There is probably no other social variable that has a more significant bearing on one's lifestyle, including the probability of becoming defined as a criminal or delinquent.[5]

Several key questions immediately arise when analyzing capitalism, such as who owns the means of production and who decides how the *surplus* is to be distributed. The term *surplus* refers to the "difference between the volume of production needed to maintain the workforce and the volume of production the workforce produces"—meaning, very generally, the margin over and above what is required to meet basic needs (Heilbroner, 1985: 33).

Under most forms of capitalism in today's world, the relations of production are marked by an almost total separation of the workers (i.e., producers) from the means of production. One class (a small group, around 1–2% of the total population) owns most of the means of production—the factories, land, buildings, wealth, income, and other assets (see the upcoming "Changes in the U.S. Economy" section for a discussion of the current distribution of wealth and income). This *capitalist class*, or *ruling class*, has an enormous amount of power in society. Wealth frequently is not an end in itself; rather, it is a "means for gathering more wealth," which in turn serves "to augment the power of a dominant class" (Heilbroner, 1985: 35).

It is also important to note that inherent in this power relationship is the fact that typical workers have little choice but to sell their labor to the capitalist. Possessing "capital" in all of its forms and owning the means of production leads very directly to the most important ingredient in the relations of production, namely *domination*. Unlike other forms of domination in history (like the domination of the army, church, etc.), this form involves the power *to refuse* to sell commodities or buy labor power (Heilbroner, 1985: 39–40). A common example in recent years is the power the large corporations have to close production facilities in the United States and move to low-wage foreign countries.

Jeffrey Sachs, an economist and globalization expert at Columbia University, notes: "Companies will go where there are fast-growing markets and big profits" (Gogoi, 2010). Sales in international markets for some companies are growing at least twice as fast as domestically, and half of the revenue for companies in the S&P 500 in recent years has come from outside the United States. Corporations created 1.4 million jobs overseas in 2010, compared with fewer than 1 million in the United States, and they continue to build factories outside the United States to meet demand. According to Sachs, the United States is falling in most global rankings for higher education, while others are rising—leaving multinational corporations little choice in their hiring decisions. "We are not fulfilling the educational needs of our young people. In a globalized world, there are serious consequences to that" (Gogoi, 2010).

One crucial difference between the capitalist system and other systems is the *drive for profit*, which can be almost an obsession. Robert Heilbroner aptly defines this unique feature of capitalism as "the restless and insatiable drive to accumulate capital." The possession of capital "confers on its owners the ability to direct and mobilize the activities of society." Control over capital gives people more than prestige and distinction; access to capital is power. Moreover, wealth itself becomes a social category inseparable from power. "Wherever there is great property, there is great inequality. For one rich man, there must be at least five hundred poor, and the affluence of the rich supposes the indigence of the many" (Heilbroner, 1986: 42-46, quoting Smith, 1976: 709–710).

Power and control are distinctive characteristics in a capitalist system. The desire to have power and control over others permeates throughout the society, whether we are talking about owners of large multinational corporations or leaders of drug gangs trying to maintain power and control over their local "drug markets." It is essentially the same phenomenon, although on much different scales. There seems to be an insatiable desire to continue "converting money into commodities and commodities into money." Everything is turned into a commodity—from the simplest products (e.g., paper and pencil) to human beings (e.g., women's bodies, slaves). More importantly, the size of one's wealth has no bounds. "Daily life is scanned for possibilities that can be brought within the circuit of accumulation," since any aspect of society that can produce a profit will be exploited, including the misery and suffering of people who have been victimized by crime.[6] Life itself has been "commodified" (Heilbroner, 1986: 60).[7]

The accumulation of capital, and hence great wealth and inequality, would not be possible without the assistance of the state. Profits are secured with the assistance of the government, both state and local, in the form of tax loopholes, subsidies, and other forms of what is essentially taxpayer assistance. Big business could not exist (and has never existed) without strong support from the government—and hence taxpayers. For example, the U.S. government helped enrich several U.S. corporations by awarding "more than $107 billion in contract payments, grants and other benefits over the past decade to foreign and multinational American companies while they were doing business in Iran, despite Washington's efforts to discourage investment there. That includes nearly $15 billion paid to companies that defied American sanctions by making large investments that helped Iran develop its vast oil and gas reserves." The CEOs of the top 10 corporations that received funds distributed by the Troubled Asset Relief Program (TARP) earned a combined total of $242 million, which translates into about "$25 million per CEO to run companies that might have gone bankrupt if not for billions of dollars in taxpayer assistance" (AFL/CIO, 2009). Major banks in the United States paid employees a record amount in compensation and benefits—about $145.85 billion—a year after the government bailed out the U.S. financial system (Grocer, 2010; Baker, 2010). In the wake of the latest economic crisis, many commentators and scholars have documented the "myth of the free market" and have noted that literally billions of taxpayer dollars filter up to big business (Baker, 2009; Clarkson, 2009; Martens, 2008).

The key point is that capitalism, while bringing about a virtual cornucopia of goods and a standard of living that is the envy of the world, has its negative effects—namely, it produces a tremendous amount of inequality. Within a capitalist system, especially that which exists in U.S. society, such inequality is *inevitable* and a natural by product of the system itself. Despite the "economic boom" in the last decade of the twentieth century, inequality has become worse. This subject will be explored in more detail in the remainder of this chapter.

Class Distinctions

Karl Marx used the terms *reserve army* or *surplus population* to refer to a more or less chronically unemployed or underemployed segment of the population. The industrial revolution created the reserve workers who became "redundant" as mechanization increased. They were "superfluous" as far as producing profits were concerned. A closely related concept is what Marx and Engels called the *lumpenproletariat*. In the various English translations of *The Communist Manifesto* since the original publication in 1848, the term *dangerous class* has been used instead of *lumpenproletariat*. In its original usage, Marx and Engels referred to this segment of society as "the social scum, that passively rotting mass thrown off by the lowest layers of old society" Eastman, 1959: 332). Included in the *lumpenproletariat* were "thieves and criminals of all kinds, living on the crumbs of society, people without a definite trade, vagabonds, people without a hearth or home." Marx believed this segment of society was inevitable under capitalism because it was "not wholly integrated into the division of labor" (Giddens, 1971: 38).

There is, it should be noted, a dual character to the dangerous classes or surplus population. The surplus population has at times been viewed by those in power as a threat (viewed as social "junk" or "dynamite"—as was the case with almost the entire working class in the early years of the labor movement during the last half of the nineteenth century) or as a possible resource (e.g., a form of cheap labor or a group to exploit to keep wage levels down) (Spitzer, 1975). Moreover, the exact nature of this class has changed over the years, ranging from the working class in general in the nineteenth and early part of the twentieth centuries, to very specific categories in more recent years, such as racial minorities, the underclass, and gangs.

As Marx noted, the development of these class distinctions, especially the existence of a surplus population, is inevitable within a capitalist economic system. Capitalism produces several contradictions. One such contradiction occurs between capital and labor (owners and workers). Each group wants improved status. The owners want more profit, while workers want higher wages and/or more benefits (including better working conditions). This has been a continuous conflict throughout the history of capitalism; many believe *class conflict* is inevitable in capitalist societies. The battles have usually been won by the owners, although workers have made some very significant gains over the years (but not without constant struggles). The CEOs of large corporations have made the most gains. In 1980, the average CEO earned 42 times more than the average worker; in 1990, it was 107 times higher; in 2000, it was 525 times higher; and in 2009, it was 263 times higher. Although the ratio has declined since 2000, the gap remains much higher than in other countries.[8]

During the discussions of the emergence of the underclass that follow, keep in mind the comments about surplus population. It is my contention that the underclass, and especially those who belong to the gangs that flourish within this segment of the population, is an inevitable by product of U.S. capitalism. I emphasize *American* capitalism for an important reason: other capitalist democracies (e.g., France, Germany, Japan, the Scandinavian countries, etc.) do not have the high degree of inequality and poverty—and hence the crime—that exists in the United States, mainly because of the existence of strong institutions like the family and the church that are able to offset the excesses of capitalism.

Barbara Ehrenreich titled her best-selling book *Nickel and Dimed: On (Not) Getting by in America* (2001). Ehrenreich spent the better part of a year working at six different low-paying jobs and trying to make ends meet with the minimal wages earned. The stories she tells of the lives of herself and coworkers reveal the underside of the American dream and the failure of our so-called "market economy." The $6 or $8 an hour these workers earned put them all under the official poverty level. Most either had to augment their meager wages with a second job or depend on other workers in the household (usually a spouse, which in most cases was a husband, since most of the low-wage workers Ehrenreich worked with were women). Even with such additional help, they all struggled. In addition, their jobs required hard and rather boring labor.

Ehrenreich recently published a follow-up (2011) where she discusses this kind of work in the context of the recent economic downturn. She writes as follows:

> In 2000, I had been able to walk into a number of jobs pretty much off the street. Less than a decade later, many of these jobs had disappeared and there was stiff competition for those that remained. It would have been impossible to repeat my Nickel and Dimed "experiment," had I had been so inclined, because I would probably never have found a job. (2011: 2)

Further on, she says that the response of the government to the current crisis is spotty at best:

> We do of course have a collective way of ameliorating the hardships of individuals and families—a government safety net that is meant to save the poor from spiraling down all the way to destitution. But its response to the economic emergency of the last few years has been spotty at best. The food stamp program has responded to the crisis fairly well, to the point where it now reaches about 37 million people, up about 30 percent from pre-recession levels. But welfare—the traditional last resort for the down-and-out until it was "reformed" in 1996—expanded by only about 6 percent in the first two years of the recession. (2011: 4)

The so-called "safety-net" has become, in her words, like a "dragnet" in that recipients are controlled by a number of local ordinances that, in effect, criminalize poverty. In most cities, there are ordinances that prohibit the behavior of the poor—making it a crime to loiter, have in your possession a shopping cart, or sleep on park benches, and in some places it is against the law for a citizen to give a homeless person some food! It brings to mind the famous statement by Anatole France that "the law, in its majestic equality, forbids the rich as well as the poor to sleep under bridges."[9]

If Ehrenreich's picture is gloomy, think for a moment that these are the *working poor*. The *nonworking poor* are among what Julius Wilson has called the "truly disadvantaged" (see a discussion of his work later in this chapter). Moreover, the continuing economic woes facing the country, plus the growing deficits, impact millions of families, especially the nation's most marginalized populations. The spending on the "war on terrorism" and the continuing wars in Iraq and Afghanistan is estimated to be about $4 billion each month (the total defense budget is more than $533 billion, plus what is called "discretionary budget authority," which brings the total to $664 billion).[10] The inevitable cutbacks will have the most negative impact on the lives of ordinary people but especially the poorest of our citizens. Inequality in the richest of all nations in the history of the world is astoundingly high. One percent of the population possesses almost half of all the financial wealth in the country. Meanwhile, social supports that might reduce poverty and inequality somewhat have been either eliminated altogether or reduced so much that they barely make a difference.

Changes in the U.S. Economy

We are presently in the midst of an important era in history, the last stage of the Industrial Revolution (Eitzen, Zinn, and Smith, 2010). Several forces are producing this change: 1) technology, 2) the globalization of the economy, 3) the movement of capital, and 4) the overall shift of the economy away from manufacturing to information and services. Some have termed this stage *deindustrialization* (Bluestone and Harrison, 1982). Between 1998 and 2008, jobs in the production-of-goods sector declined from 17.3 percent to 14.2 percent; the projected percentage of manufacturing jobs in 2018 is 12.9. In contrast, the service-providing sector increased from 72.8 percent in 1998 to 77.2 percent in 2008, with a projection of 78.8 percent in 2018 (BLS, 2010a).

Cities like Rochester, Baltimore, Camden, Detroit, Memphis, and Richmond typify the deindustrialization process.[11] The movement of capital overseas, relocation of plants to countries with lower wages, and mergers with other corporations have all had the effect of eliminating the jobs of many workers. In *The End of Work*, Jeremy Rifkin takes a close look at economic changes and how they have affected the black community in particular. After the end of World War II, millions of blacks migrated to the North (as well as the West) in search of new job opportunities. Until 1954, the lot of the typical black worker steadily improved—until automation in the auto, steel, rubber, chemical, and other unskilled labor markets. Between 1953 and 1962, 1.6 million blue-collar jobs were lost in manufacturing industries. While unemployment among black workers never went higher than 8.5 percent between 1947 and 1953 (vs. 4.6% for whites), by 1964, the rate was 12.4 percent (vs. 5.9% for whites). Since this time, the unemployment rate for blacks has consistently been twice that for whites (Rifkin, 1995: 73–74).

A really significant change began in the 1950s with the growth of industrial parks in the suburbs. The first industry to feel the effects of these changes was the auto industry. The big Ford River Rouge plant in Detroit was the "flagship" of their operations and the location of the heaviest concentration of union power. Ford decided to move most of the production to the suburbs, where the new automated plants were located, even though there was plenty of room at the old site. Whereas in 1945 this plant had 85,000 workers, by 1960, it had just 30,000. GM and Chrysler made similar moves to the suburbs.

The many satellite businesses that served the auto industry (machine tools, tires, car parts, etc.) also began to move their operations to the suburbs. The bulk of the black population was left behind in the inner cities. Whereas in the 1950s black workers accounted for about one-fourth of the workers at GM and Chrysler, by 1960, there were 24 black workers in a workforce of 7,425 skilled workers at Chrysler; there were 67 blacks among the 11,000 skilled workers at GM. In fact, between 1957 and 1964, the manufacturing output doubled, while the number of blue-collar workers declined by 3 percent (Rifkin, 1995: 75). As businesses flocked to the suburbs, millions of middle- and working-class families (mostly white) moved too, so the inner cities became concentrated with poor, unemployed minorities.

The nature of work has changed. The proportion of workers (especially young workers) employed in high-paying manufacturing industries has declined. Meanwhile, the largest increases in the job market have been in the service industries of retail trade, finance, insurance, and real estate. There is increasing polarization into a low-wage/high-wage dichotomy. All of this has resulted in a drastic change in educational requirements for employment in industries paying the most money (job growth has generally been in areas requiring the most education) (U.S. Department of Commerce, Bureau of the Census, 2011).

Young blacks have found jobs in industries that generally pay the least. Those industries and occupations that pay the most require increasingly more education and skill levels (e.g., computer skills, knowledge of math and English).[12] Unemployment rates are consistently the highest for those who drop out of high school (BLS, 2011b; Alliance for Excellent Education, 2009). The average earnings for blacks without a high school diploma are lower than the earnings for whites without a diploma (Bureau of the Census, 2011). As of December 2010, the unemployment rate for black males 20 years of age and older was 16.5 percent (8.5% for whites); for blacks of both sexes between ages 16 and 19, the rate was 44.2 percent (compared to 22.5% for whites) (BLS, 2011c).

The average weekly wages ("real earnings" in 1982 dollars) in February 2011 were $351.89; the average hourly wage was $10.29. Six percent of workers paid by the hour—4.4 million people—earn the minimum wage of $7.25 (or less) (BLS, 2011d; *New York Times*, 2011). Adjusted for inflation, the minimum wage is about $1.50 an hour lower than it was in 1968. Figure 8.1 illustrates the changing distribution of wealth and income. In the post-World War II growth period (1947–1979), it was literally the case of a "rising tide lifts all boats." Since that time, it has been more like a "rising tide lifts all yachts."

The American dream generally holds out the promise that each generation will achieve more than the previous generation. "In the three decades following World War II, real earnings for workers grew by roughly 2 percent a year, nearly doubling incomes for each successive generation" (Greenstone and Looney, 2011). That has changed in recent decades—especially for men. Only 66 percent of men are employed full-time versus 80 percent in 1970; in contrast, the proportion of women in the labor force increased from 34 percent to over 55 percent (BLS, 2011e). A portion of the gains for women are attributable to an increase in the proportion of workers employed as *temporary* workers. As of 2009, 26.5 percent of women workers worked part-time, compared to 13.2 percent of the men; 19.5 percent of all workers were working part-time (BLS, 2010b).

Rising Together

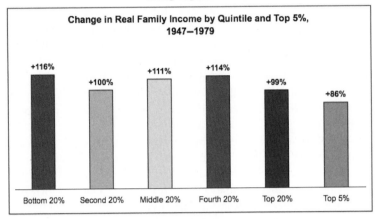

Change in Real Family Income by Quintile and Top 5%, 1947–1979

Bottom 20%: +116%
Second 20%: +100%
Middle 20%: +111%
Fourth 20%: +114%
Top 20%: +99%
Top 5%: +86%

Growing Apart

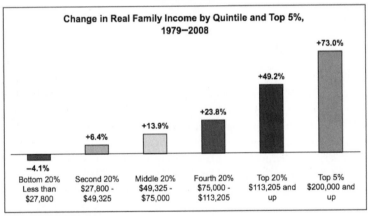

Change in Real Family Income by Quintile and Top 5%, 1979–2008

Bottom 20% Less than $27,800: −4.1%
Second 20% $27,800 - $49,325: +6.4%
Middle 20% $49,325 - $75,000: +13.9%
Fourth 20% $75,000 - $113,205: +23.8%
Top 20% $113,205 and up: +49.2%
Top 5% $200,000 and up: +73.0%

FIGURE 8.1 Income and Wealth Inequality in the United States

SOURCE: Working Group on Extreme Wealth, "How Unequal Are We?" http://extremeinequality
.org/?page_id=8. Based on the following: U.S. Census Bureau, Historical Income Tables,
Table F-3 (for income changes) and Table F-1 (for income ranges in 2008 dollars).

Temporary workers have been used more often in the past two decades, and the trend appears to be one that will continue.

For the less-educated, the percentages are worse: 57 percent of high school graduates have a full-time job today versus 79 percent in 1970. After adjusting for inflation, the median wage in 2009 was $49,777, which was roughly the same as in 1969. One analysis found that earnings have actually declined sharply, when adjusted for the fewer number of people working full-time—finding that the median wage has effectively declined $13,000 (28%) since 1969 (Greenstone and Looney, 2011).

According to the latest census report, there are 249.4 million people living in families. Of those, 31.2 million (12.5%) live below the poverty level (DeNavas-Walt et al., 2010). Female-headed households are the most likely to be living in poverty—sometimes described as the *feminization of poverty*. In 2009,

45.3 million lived in families with a female householder; 14.7 million (32.5%) lived below the poverty level. There were 14.5 million people living in black female-headed households; of those, 39.8 percent lived under the poverty level, in comparison to 23.8 percent in families with a white female householder and 40.6 percent of families with a Hispanic female householder.

In 2009, there were 78.9 million families; 10 million had incomes under $20,000, while 2 million earned more than $250,000 (U.S. Census Bureau, 2010a). Thirteen percent of all households earned under $15,000 per year, while 3.8 percent earned more than $200,000 (U.S. Census Bureau, 2010b). The amount of household income of the top 5 percent of earners in 2009 had increased 62.6 percent since 1979. For households in the lowest 20 percent of earnings, the amount had increased by less than 5 percent (U.S. Census Bureau, 2010c). In 1976, the percentage of total income that went to the top 1 percent of American households was about 9 percent; in 2007, that had grown to almost 24 percent. Meanwhile, adjusted for inflation, the average hourly wage for American workers went down by more than 7 percent (Frank, 2010).

The most recent figures on income inequality shows that the top 10 percent of income earners in the United States received 98 percent of all income growth between 1980 and 2008, while the rest got a mere 2 percent.[13] Furthermore, while the average pay of CEOs 30 years ago was about 42 times that of the average factory worker, by 2010, it was 319 times greater (Menendez et al., 2011).

Also, in 2007, the richest 1 percent of U.S. households owned one-third of all the private wealth in the nation, which is more than all the wealth of the bottom 90 percent combined (Working Group on Extreme Inequality, n.d.). The top 1 percent also own 50.9 percent of all stocks, bonds, and mutual fund assets.

Income inequality, measured by what is known as the *Gini Index of Inequality* (a value of 0 means perfect equality—everyone earns the same amount; and a value of 100 means perfect inequality—one person earns all), has gone up since the late 1960s. Whereas in 1970 the index for the United States was 35, in 2007, it was at 45, larger than any other industrialized nation (in contrast, the Gini for Canada is 31; the Netherlands is 31, while Sweden is the most equal with a score of 23).[14]

Over the last quarter of a century, many safeguards that people once counted on to shield them from financial harm have been weakened or completely lost. These include formal protections such as guaranteed corporate pensions and state and federal unemployment benefits. And they include informal ones, such as the loyalty that employers once showed their workers by offering secure jobs with relatively little prospect of long-term layoff. The informal social contract with corporate America that provided workers benefits in exchange for their production is no longer there. Part of the American dream is the financial stability that comes with a college education, which is too often beyond the reach of poor families today.

The proportion of people in the United States living in poverty has increased. As of 2009, 14.3 percent of Americans lived under the official poverty level (DeNavas-Walt et al., 2010: 14). As inequality has grown, the social conditions of the most disadvantaged sectors of society have worsened. The poverty rate for blacks was 25.8 percent, and for those under 18 it was 35.7 percent; in contrast, the rates for whites were 11.5 percent and 18 percent, respectively (U.S. Census

Bureau, 2010d). The Children's Defense Fund found that one in five children (15.5 million in 2009) lived in poverty—35 percent of black children and 12 percent of white children. Black children were three times more likely than white children to live in extreme poverty; 40 percent of black children were born poor compared to 8 percent of white children, and black children were seven times more likely to be persistently poor (Children's Defense Fund, 2011).

The Department of Health and Human Services has a complex formula for calculating poverty levels based on a subsistence level of living for individuals and families.[15] It is updated yearly and for 2009 it was $22,050 for a family of four; in contrast, it was $9,300 in 1982.[16] The minimal standard of living has been calculated on the same basis since the 1960s: the amount of money needed for a subsistence diet multiplied by three, updated for inflation. As many critics point out, food costs now represent a much smaller share of family budgets, while rent and transportation costs have increased and now constitute a larger share of household expenditures. Ehrenreich notes that when the original method for defining the poverty line was devised, 24 percent of the typical family budget went for food, while housing constituted 29 percent. By 1999, the food portion had decreased to 16 percent, while the housing portion rose to 37 percent (Ehrenreich, 2001: 200). Most critics contend that the official poverty rate should be raised by at least 50 percent. The Census Bureau publishes income to poverty ratios of 0.5 (incomes 50% below the poverty level), 1.0 (incomes below poverty level), and 1.25 (incomes 25 percent higher than the poverty level) based on official poverty thresholds. In 2009, 19 million people (6.3%) of the population fell under the 0.5 ratio; 43.7 percent of people in poverty were 50 percent below the poverty threshold (DeNavas-Walt et al., 2010: 19).

The Economic Policy Institute, after careful review of dozens of studies, arrived at an estimated "living wage" for a family of one adult and two children of about $30,000 per year (which translates to a wage of $14 per hour, full-time). The median weekly earnings in December 2010 were $751 per week ($39,052 annually). The median earnings for black men were $629 (73.4% of the median earnings for white men), while the median earnings for black women were $605 (versus $695 for white women). The median earnings for employees without a high school diploma were $438, $637 for those with a diploma, and $1,139 for those with a bachelor's degree (BLS, 2011f).

Michael Harrington wrote about the "invisible poor" in the early 1960s (1962). This underclass remains largely invisible today, unless they get "out of line." Plant closings, the movement of capital out of the central cities, the growth of suburbs, and many other changes have, in effect, made many youths superfluous within mainstream society. If underclass youth are unable to find jobs, they will not develop the work skills, attitudes, and habits that are appropriate and necessary in a competitive, highly technological economy. Without gainful employment, these youth are increasingly tempted to participate in the underground alternative economy of the urban ghettos—that is, the illegal system of barter in stolen goods, drugs, gambling, and prostitution.

All of this leads us to the subject of those who fall far below the just referenced "working poor."

THE DEVELOPMENT OF THE UNDERCLASS

The term *underclass* has been the subject of considerable debate. Herbert Gans refers to the term as an example of "new wine in old bottles." It has replaced terms such as "dangerous classes," the "undeserving poor," the "rabble," and so on. While it is synonymous with persistent and extreme poverty, it is also a "behavioral term invented by journalists and social scientists to describe poor people who are accused, rightly or wrongly, of failing to behave in the 'mainstream' ways of the numerically or culturally dominant American middle class" (1995: 2). The term essentially stigmatizes those who fall within the general category of the underclass—the homeless, those who live in "the projects," addicts, and young poor women with babies. The term is often used interchangeably with racial minorities. However, it is misleading to conclude that the underclass is synonymous with blacks and other minorities. In sheer numbers, whites comprise the majority of the underclass and the poor in general. In 2009, there were 18.5 million whites below the poverty line compared to 9.9 million blacks and 12.4 million Hispanics (DeNavas-Walt et al., 2010: 16).

Inner cities have been the most negatively affected by the economic changes discussed earlier. The movement of capital out of the inner cities corresponded with the exodus of many middle-class minorities. The tax base declined, while the concentration of the poor increased. Job opportunities disappeared. Federal funding for social programs, particularly those targeting the urban underclass, also decreased during the 1980s with the movement toward privatization—a system aimed at replacing federal assistance with private-sector methods of solving urban problems. Aid to disadvantaged school districts, housing assistance, financial aid to the poor, legal assistance to the poor, and social services in urban areas in general all declined (Cook, 2007).

A commission that studied the "riots" (the term "riot" is used by the white majority, whereas minorities are more likely to describe such events as a "rebellion," "civil disobedience," or "legitimate protest") after the verdicts in the trials of the police officers who beat Rodney King noted the declining investments in the inner city on the part of the federal government.[17] For example, between 1981 and 1992, the amount invested in job training fell from $23 billion to $8 billion, from $21 billion to $14 billion for local economic development, and from $6 billion to zero for "general revenue sharing"; federal support for housing was cut by 80 percent (Klein, 1995: 196).

The social and economic position of blacks—especially young black males, whom one author in the 1980s called an "endangered species"—has been tenuous (Gibbs, 1988). By the turn of the century, most young black men had become superfluous—part of the "surplus population." Although somewhat dated, William Julius Wilson's study of the black underclass in the late 1980s and mid-1990s is still relevant—in fact, the situation he reported on has grown worse (as noted earlier).

Wilson distinguished between inner-city ghettos of the 1980s and 1990s and those of an earlier era. Until the 1960s, these areas were inhabited by *different classes* of blacks (lower-class, working-class, and middle-class professionals), providing much stability and reinforcing dominant cultural norms and values (e.g., hard work, stability, importance of family, obeying the law). Youths growing up in these areas had a variety of stable role models:

> Even if the truly disadvantaged segments of an inner-city area experience a significant increase in long-term spells of joblessness, the basic institutions in that area (churches, schools, stores, recreational facilities, etc.) would remain viable if much of the base of their support comes from the more economically stable and secure families. Moreover, the very presence of these families during such periods provides mainstream role models that help keep alive the perception that education is meaningful, that steady employment is a viable alternative to welfare, and that family stability is the norm, not the exception. (Wilson, 1987: 56)

Wilson suggests that perceptive ghetto youngsters in a neighborhood that includes a good number of working and professional families may observe increasing joblessness and idleness but also witness many individuals regularly going to and from work; they may sense an increase in school dropouts but also see a connection between education and meaningful employment; they may detect a growth in single-parent families but also be aware of the presence of many married-couple families; they may notice an increase in welfare dependency but also see a significant number of families that are not on welfare; and they may be cognizant of an increase in crime but recognize that many residents in their neighborhood are not involved in criminal activity.

Unfortunately, this "social buffer" has practically disappeared, relocating to "better" neighborhoods. Blacks who are poor are far more likely than previously to live in areas where just about everyone else is poor. In contrast, whites who are poor are far more likely to be surrounded by the nonpoor, retaining the "social buffer." Inner-city residents have become more and more *isolated* from mainstream society. Such isolation includes being excluded from an informal job network that is found in other areas. One result of this is the growth of alternatives to the mainstream labor force, including welfare and crime, both of which have become more or less permanent alternatives in these areas. Wilson further notes that "the social transformation of the inner city has resulted in a disproportionate concentration of the most disadvantaged segments of the urban black population, creating a social milieu significantly different from the environment that existed in these communities several decades ago" (1987: 58).

The relatively new social subgroup of the disadvantaged who interact and live only with similarly situated people can be distinguished from the traditional "lower class" by its lack of mobility (Wilson, 1987: 8). The individuals who make up the underclass are mostly "the sons and daughters of previous generations of the poor" whose own children will remain poor. Many of them have more or less permanently dropped out of the lower class and lack skills and education to ever "make it" in conventional society. They survive mainly through options "ranging from private entrepreneurial schemes to working the welfare system. Hustling, quasi-legitimate schemes, and outright deviant activity are also alternatives to work" (Glasgow, 1981: 8–9).

A somewhat different interpretation was offered by Douglas Massey and Nancy Denton in their 1990s study appropriately called *American Apartheid*. They linked the origins and perpetuation of the black urban underclass to specific patterns of *segregation:*

> Residential segregation has been instrumental in creating a structural niche within which a deleterious set of attitudes and behaviors—a culture of segregation—has arisen and flourished. Segregation created the structural conditions for the emergence of an oppositional culture that devalues work, schooling, and marriage and that stresses attitudes and behaviors that are antithetical and often hostile to success in the larger economy. (1993: 8)

Because of segregation (especially within the housing market), blacks have been far less able than other minorities (e.g., Mexican Americans, Jews, Italians, Poles) to escape. Until about 1900, most blacks lived in areas that were largely white. Massey and Denton document the changes since that time, using five dimensions of segregation. *Unevenness* looks at overrepresentation and underrepresentation of blacks in an urban area. *Isolation* refers to blacks rarely sharing the same neighborhoods with whites. *Clustering* occurs when black neighborhoods are grouped together so that they either form one continuous enclave (occupying a large area of land) or are scattered about the city. *Concentrated* describes a focus in one small area or sparsely settled throughout a city. *Centralization* measures location within the central core of a city versus spread out along the periphery. Massey and Denton conclude that

> A high score on any single dimension is serious because it removes blacks from full participation in urban society and limits their access to its benefits. . . . Blacks . . . are more segregated than other groups on any single dimension of segregation, but they are also more segregated on all dimensions simultaneously; and in an important subset of U.S. metropolitan areas, they are very highly segregated on at least four of the five dimensions at once, a pattern we call hypersegregation. (1993: 74)

About one-third of all blacks currently live in *hypersegregated* areas. Massey and Denton conclude that quite often this isolation affects one's lifestyle and life chances:

> Typical inhabitants of one of these ghettos are not only unlikely to come into contact with whites within the particular neighborhood where they live; even if they traveled to the adjacent neighborhood they would still be unlikely to see a white face; and if they went to the next neighborhood beyond that, no whites would be there either. People growing up in such an environment have little direct experience with the white culture, norms, and behaviors of the rest of American society and few social contacts with members of other social groups. Ironically, within a large, diverse, and highly mobile post-industrial society such as the United States, blacks living in the heart of the ghetto are among the most isolated people on earth. (1993)

Poverty and Family Structure

Nearly every criminologist agrees that the family is probably the most critical factor related to crime and delinquency (Shelden, 2012). For more than 50 years, research has shown that three or four key family-related factors best distinguish the habitual delinquent from the rest of his or her peers. We have already noted that black families are far more likely to be headed by a female than are white families and that these families are far more likely to be living in poverty.

The percentage has increased for both racial groups since 1950; the gap between the two races has also increased. Wilson cited one major reason for the rise in black female-headed families was the "increasing difficulty of finding a marriage partner with stable employment." In other words, there is a "poor marriage market" for these young women. Wilson concludes that male unemployment is *the leading cause* of the rise in female-headed households (Wilson, 1996: 72–75). In addition, there has been a dramatic rise in the percentage of black children living with their mother only: 30 percent in 1970 to 50 percent in 2009; the proportion of black children under 18 living with a mother who *has never been married* went from a mere 4 percent in 1970 to 32 percent in 2009 (U.S. Census Bureau, 2009).

According to one recent report, educated black women are still finding it difficult to find a marriageable partner (Alexander, 2009). The reasons echo what Wilson said: unemployment, the drug war, and the growing imprisonment rate for black males. More than 2 percent of men of prime employment age (25 to 54) live in institutions, primarily prisons (Greenstone and Looney, 2011). One report concluded that a 1 percent increase in the male incarceration rate was associated with a 2.4 percent reduction in the proportion of women who would ever marry. "As incarceration rates exploded between 1970 and 2007, the proportion of U.S.-born black women aged 30–44 who were married plunged from 62 percent to 33 percent" (*The Economist,* 2010).

The effects on children have been devastating, contributing in large part to the increase in cases of abuse and neglect. Wilson found that by the time children born into single-parent families reach the age of 6, nearly two-thirds will have moved into different living arrangements. For black children, however, about two-thirds of these moves will be into female-headed families with no fathers; for white children, an almost identical percentage will move into families with two parents (Wilson, 1996: 71).

Current research reinforces Wilson's findings. Female-householder families with no husband present have the highest poverty rate among all types of households. One study suggested that "as a response to their high risks of poverty, female-headed households with children are increasingly found to include a cohabiting partner, or to be headed by a grandmother caring for her grandchildren" (Snyder, McLaughlin, and Findeis, 2006). Families headed by a grandparent who is caring for a grandchild are becoming increasingly more common, often because of financial hardships, drug or alcohol abuse by the parents, or incarceration. This is especially the case for minority children. Another study attributed the high rate of poverty within female-headed households to the fact that the women who work in such families are more likely to work in low-wage occupations (Lichtenwalter, 2005). Although 22.8 percent of all families with children lived in households with the mother only, these households represented 47 percent of poor families (U.S. Census Bureau, 2010e). "Children are the poorest age group in America—every fifth child is poor" (Children's Defense Fund, 2010).

In recent years, girls from single-parent households are far more likely than those from two-parent households to become unwed mothers. One recent study estimated that about 70 percent of black babies are born out of wedlock (*The Economist,* 2010). One of the main reasons for this is that it is more difficult to supervise the children's activities if there is only one parent in the household. Wilson's study in Chicago found that the highest rates of pregnancy among teens were in single-parent households in very poor and highly segregated neighborhoods (Wilson, 1996: 75). A study in London found that children living in single-parent families are far more likely to 1) have more trouble in school; 2) be at risk of suffering physical, emotional, or sexual abuse; 3) run away from home; 4) become teenage parents; 5) drink and take drugs; 6) drop out of school; and 7) get involved in criminal activities (O'Neill, 2002).

HOW THESE CHANGES RELATE
TO THE GROWTH IN GANGS

It would be misleading to conclude that the emergence of the underclass is the leading cause of crime. Clearly, there are some areas of the country that have suffered some of these same economic changes but have not shown a significant rise in crime. Nevertheless, the recent changes noted earlier have played a critical role in the perpetuation of the high rate of crime in many areas of the country. Moore has suggested that part of the problem stems from the existence of what is known as a *segmented labor market.* The theory behind this breaks sharply with conventional economic theory and popular conceptions. According to this view, the American labor market is *structurally segmented* according to such factors as job security, pay, and career opportunities. Jobs with good pay, security, and opportunities for advancement are relatively scarce. This is the *primary labor market.* Barrio and ghetto residents do not have ready access to these kinds of jobs. Instead, the majority are most likely to be found within the *secondary labor market,* which consists of unstable jobs with low wages (which are often only part-time jobs) and with little or no career advancement opportunities (Moore, 1978).

One consequence of this system is the existence of supplemental economic structures, specifically a welfare economy and an illegal economy. These economic structures supplement the more marginal or peripheral sectors of the secondary labor market. Individuals may move back and forth between the secondary market and this peripheral market. In many instances, the welfare and illegal economy "subsidizes" the marginal industries of the secondary labor market. These are "fall-back" sources of income, as minimum wages are not enough to support a family. Moore remarks:

> This is a world of limited opportunities, with legitimate jobs offering little prospect for lifetime satisfaction. In this respect, the segmented labor market becomes an essential concept for understanding the structure and context of the Chicano gang, the use and marketing of illegal drugs and stolen merchandise, and the prison involvements of the residents of the Los Angeles barrios. (1978: 33)

The geographic distribution of jobs tends to eliminate many minorities, making them part of the "surplus population" (Shelden, 2008). Most live within areas where industry has left; long commutes are required to try to find a job and to go to work if hired. High-tech jobs have replaced manufacturing jobs, leaving many minorities jobless. The good jobs of an earlier generation have been replaced by low-wage jobs with little security and no fringe benefits (the secondary labor market).

Urban decline contributes to social disorganization, weakening communities, and lessening social control. The poor, the unemployed, and the unemployable are left behind, while others leave the area for jobs, better schools, and better housing. Higher crime rates may be a by product of the changing socioeconomic factors, as illegal activities are some of the only options that remain for the uneducated and underemployed.

The most recent data on poverty among children is not encouraging. Henry Giroux, a frequent writer on youth, tells the story in harsh but truthful words:

> The hard currency of human suffering that impacts children is evident in some astounding statistics that suggest a profound moral and political contradiction at the heart of our culture: for example, the rate of child poverty is currently at 17.4 percent, boosting the number of poor children to 13 million. In addition, about one in three severely poor people are under age 17. Moreover, children make up 26 percent of the total population but constitute an astounding 39 percent of the poor. Just as alarming as this is the fact that 9.4 million children in America lack health insurance and millions lack affordable child care and decent early childhood education. Sadly, the United States ranks first in billionaires and defense expenditures and yet ranks an appalling twenty-fifth in infant mortality. As we might expect, behind these grave statistics lies a series of decisions that favor economically those already advantaged at the expense of the young. Savage cuts to education, nutritional assistance for impoverished mothers, veterans' medical care, and basic scientific research, are often cynically administered to help fund tax cuts for the already inordinately rich. (2008)

Another recent study, focusing on Chicago, found that black children suffer a great deal as a result of their exposure to "concentrated disadvantage" (living in extreme poverty, etc.), which has "had detrimental and long-lasting consequences for black children's cognitive ability, rivaling in magnitude the effects of missing 1 year of schooling" (Sampson, Sharkey, and Raudenbush, 2008).

In the Los Angeles area, two changes created problems. First, an increase in immigration (especially from Mexico) and, second, changes in the job market. As new Mexicans moved into the barrios, they displaced older Mexicans who were able to escape. High-tech jobs started to replace manufacturing jobs, and the unionized, good-paying steel and auto industries all but disappeared, leaving many minorities jobless. At the same time, the good white-collar jobs were taken mostly by white, educated classes.

Even so, many Mexican Americans were working, except that the jobs paid wages that placed many below the poverty level. Moore states that in 1980, in Mexican American husband-wife households in California, 16 percent (with full-time working husbands) fell below the poverty line, and 48 percent earned incomes that fell at less than twice the poverty level. Comparable figures for blacks were 5 percent and 27 percent and for whites, 4 percent and 15 percent. And nationally, 1 out of every 15 Hispanics who worked year-round and full-time fell below the poverty level in 1985, compared to 1 out of every 22 blacks and 1 out of every 40 whites (Moore, 1991: 20, 152).

During the 1960s, many community programs emerged to deal with the problems (e.g., the War on Poverty, and programs for dropouts, gangs, heroin users, etc.). Also, bilingual education increased. However, by the end of the 1970s and early 1980s, these programs had disappeared, even though the problems persisted (Moore, 1991: 21–22).

By the 1980s, the gang members and their families, compared with earlier generations, faced much greater competition for jobs. The good jobs of an earlier generation had been replaced by low-wage jobs with little security and no fringe benefits—in other words, the secondary labor market (1991: 22–23).

A study by Jackson documents the relationship between demographic and economic changes in the United States and the growth of gangs. Jackson writes that

> Demographic and economic transition seem to have some influence on crime and the presence of youth gangs in U.S. cities, even in the presence of controls for possibly competing explanations: opportunity factors related to the ease and profit of crime, age structure, racial and income heterogeneity, and economic and relative deprivation. (1991: 393)

Jackson's research suggests that crime and youth gangs "are likely consequences of the patterns of sociodemographic change recently experienced by urban areas in the United States . . . Urban decline, with its associated economic stress and social disorganization, may weaken the social cohesion and social control processes of cities . . . As a result, higher crime rates and more youth gangs may be among the unintended consequences of the nation's postindustrial growth and development" (1991: 395).

A similar process was at work in the area of Chicago where the gang studied by Padilla lived. The change here was the movement of key manufacturing jobs away from the inner city to the suburbs, rural areas, the Sunbelt regions of the United States, or even into Third World countries. Concomitant with this development was the growing militancy of the working class, which began winning some of its battles with the business owners. In response, many business owners simply moved to areas where there would be less worker resistance (Padilla, 1992: 32–33).

Adding to this process was a significant shift in the population, namely the so-called "white flight" into the suburbs, leaving behind the poor, the unemployed, the unemployable, and, in disproportionate numbers, the minorities. In the area studied by Padilla, Latinos represented the majority of the residents in virtually all the census tracts in the area. Within this relatively small area of Chicago, the unemployment rate went from 10 percent in 1970 to 18.7 percent in 1980; in some census tracts, the rate was as high as 30 percent (Padilla, 1992: 37–38). With these changes came the emergence of illegal opportunities to make money, in particular drug dealing, which is what occurred with the gang studied by Padilla (see chapter 3).

Malcolm Klein's research on gangs reinforces the preceding interpretations. He commented that "the effect of the increasing urban underclass, remains in my mind the foremost cause of the recent proliferation of gangs and the likely best predictor of its continuation" (Klein, 1995: 194). The effects of poverty are especially relevant here, and it is summarized nicely but crudely by a gang member Klein quotes, who bluntly states, "Bein' poor's a mother-fucker" (1995: 195). The effect of the changing labor market, as we have discussed here, does not escape the attention of Klein's conclusions, as he writes:

> Uneducated, underemployed young males turn to the illegal economies enhanced by gang membership, including selling drugs in some instances. Older males who in earlier decades would have "matured" into more steady jobs and family roles hang on to the gang structure by default. The newer gang cities like Milwaukee thus emerge, looking much like the traditional gang cities. (1995: 196–197)

It does not take much of a leap in logic to conclude there exists a strong correlation between the growth of gangs in the inner cities on the one hand and the growth in the gap between the rich and the poor on the other. While the following conclusion may be denied by some, to us it seems rather obvious: trillions of dollars have "trickled up" to the top 5 percent of the population during the past 20 years largely because of "corporate welfare," while millions suffer and join gangs to cope (Zepezauer, 2004; Slivinski, 2007).

The Death of Childhood in the Inner Cities

Children under the age of 18 constitute 39 percent of the homeless population—42 percent of the children are less than 5 years old (National Law Center on Homelessness and Poverty, 2009). The city of Los Angeles resembles many others in the United States; its "skid row" area is the largest in the United States. More than 11,000 adults and children are contained in its 55 square blocks. The failure of the American dream to satisfy the needs and wants of people can be clearly seen in downtown Los Angeles, literally a stone's throw from many symbols of wealth. (The city of Las Vegas, where the lead author lives, is perhaps the most extreme expression of massive symbols of wealth juxtaposed with signs of poverty.)

The United Coalition East Prevention Project began working with young people in the skid row area of Los Angeles in 2003, attempting to improve their environment and to provide opportunities for the future before the children—"succumb to illness, crime, despair, and death."

> They endure horrible living conditions, with no place to play, no sports, no chance for a good education. They have difficulty getting to school because of limited access to transportation, and once there, are often stigmatized by teachers and administrators. These young people are easy targets for the drug dealers and sexual predators. Yet the police rarely offer protection; instead they are quick to intimidate and cite these children for minor offenses like jaywalking. (United Coalition East Prevention Project, 2005)

The coalition reported that 45 percent of the youth on skid row had been cited by the police for jaywalking, not having enough money for a bus or train, and "loitering." In essence, the citations criminalize poverty. The citations do not reduce crime, but they are disastrous for the families that do not have the financial resources to pay fines. If the citations become warrants, children already facing daunting challenges will have a record, which will add more complications to completing school and or finding a job. The report described the circumstances of children they have encountered. Michael and Jamaica are two of hundreds of examples:

> Michael is multiracial. He has moved repeatedly since he was three years old. He lived for several years in a dilapidated "skid row" hotel with his aunt. When she died suddenly, he was detained in juvenile hall. His "crime": being young and poor with no family to take him in. He is currently living in a group home.

> Jamaica is 16 years old and multiracial. Her family—mother and four siblings—also live in a "skid row" hotel. It takes her two hours to get to school each day, where she is taunted by her classmates and singled out by teachers for not wearing the appropriate clothes. She is currently on probation for defending her younger brother from a drunk, violent man. (Cited in United Coalition East Prevention Project, 2005)

We create and sustain social conditions that give rise to predictable responses like gangs and violence—and then blame those who exhibit the behavior. To paraphrase seventeenth-century poet John Milton (author of *Paradise Lost*), "We punch people's eyes out and then reproach them for their blindness."

The correlation between economic conditions within urban areas and rates of delinquency has been noted for more than 150 years. Indeed, as the classic studies by Clifford Shaw and Henry McKay and others have noted (see Chapter 7), delinquency and crime cannot be separated from surrounding economic conditions. Solutions that fail to address these variables are doomed to be little more than "band-aids."

SUMMARY

In this chapter, we have discussed the role of American capitalism in relation to such important issues as poverty, inequality, and gangs. It was noted that under American capitalism, the "free market" is largely a myth, and a "surplus population" is constantly being created and reproduced. Most criminal activity of gang members is consistent with basic capitalist values, such as the law of supply and demand, the need to make money (profit), and the desire to accumulate consumer goods. And like the larger capitalist system, there are many failures in the world of crime and gang activity.

The term *underclass* was discussed, with the emphasis on how this term has become a sort of moral condemnation of various groups not falling within the mainstream of American society. Closely correlated with this term was the phenomenon of the "feminization of poverty" and the general economic decline of the inner cities. Important labor market changes have helped to perpetuate these problems, especially such processes as deindustrialization and capital flight.

Also discussed were certain specific labor market changes and the increasing segregation of minorities, especially blacks. This has led to increasing isolation of this segment of the population—isolated from mainstream society and the contacts that lead to a good education and decent jobs.

Finally, it was stated that there are many ways these changes are related to gangs and gang activity. Unemployment, poverty, and general despair lead young people to seek out economic opportunities in the growing illegal marketplace, often done within the context of gangs.

NOTES

1. The documentary *Inside Job* (winner of the 2011 Academy Award for best documentary) illustrates this point clearly.

2. Bureau of Labor Statistics (January 7, 2011). "News Release: The Employment Situation—December 2010). Retrieved from http://www.bls.gov/news.release/pdf/empsit.pdf.

3. Understanding unemployment statistics is a real challenge! A Google search found a variety of interpretations and also references to the "real" unemployment rate, which ranged from around 12% to more than 20% as of January 2011. For an overview, see the Bureau of Labor Statistics, "How the Government Measures Unemployment." Retrieved from http://www.bls.gov/cps/cps_htgm.htm.

4. Other modes of production have included mercantilism, feudalism, socialism, and communism. In primitive societies, the mode of production was hunting and gathering.

5. There is a wide body of literature documenting the relationship between social class and crime. Among other works, see *The Rich Get Richer and the Poor Get Prison* (Reiman, and Leighton, 2010) and *No Equal Justice: Race and Class in the American Criminal Justice System* (Cole, 1999).

6. Crime is indeed very profitable—for those who control it. It is not surprising that we have a multi-billion dollar "crime industry," which, like any other industry, seeks profits from crime in a variety of contexts—from those who build prisons to those who supply an infinite variety of goods and services to the institutions, to those who write the news stories and sell books about crime and criminals. See Shelden et al. (2008) for a discussion of this "crime control industry."

7. A fascinating slant on this process is described as the "McDonaldization" of U.S. society. This has been defined as "the process by which the principles of the fast-food restaurant are coming to dominate more and more sectors of American society as well as of the rest of the world." See Ritzer (1996: 1).

8. While the average pay for CEOs declined, retirement benefits increased 23% (AFL-CIO, 2010).

9. Examples are numerous, as the titles of these stories illustrate: "The Crime of Pushing a Shopping Cart" (Rhodes, 2006), and "Phoenix Church Ordered to Stop Feeding the Homeless" (Moriarty, 2009).

10. Department of Defense. Retrieved from http://www.whitehouse.gov/omb/assets/fy2010_new_era/Department_of_Defense.pdf. Another source puts the figure at about $965 billion because it includes the military portion from other budgets, money spent on the "war on terror," and past military spending (e.g., benefits). See the following: http://www.warresisters.org/pages/piechart.htm.

11. See Gonzales (2009) for a discussion of struggling former factory towns. Frank (2005) describes in some detail many once-thriving towns in Kansas now filled with many boarded-up former businesses; see especially pp. 60–63.

12. The latest figures show that more than a million students drop out of high school each year—about 71% finish high school on time with a regular diploma; about half of black and Hispanic students graduate on time (Alliance for Excellent Education, 2009).

13. Figures are from "The State of Working America." Retrieved from: http://www.stateofworkingamerica.org/pages/interactive#/?start=1980&end=2008.

14. This is taken from the CIA World Fact Book. Retrieved from https://www.cia.gov/library/publications/the-world-factbook/fields/2172.html.

15. For details, see the following Web site: http://aspe.hhs.gov/poverty/faq.shtml#differences.

16. See the following Web site: http://aspe.hhs.gov/poverty/figures-fed-reg.shtml.

17. For an insightful analysis of the Watts riots, see Conot (1967); unfortunately, this work is rarely cited. For an exceptional and brilliant review of the Los Angeles Police Department's response to gangs and riots, see Davis (1992), especially Chapter 5. Authors Shelden and Brown regularly show what they describe as a very "disturbing" historical film contrasting the Rodney King "riots" with the Watts uprising 25 years earlier, called *The Fire This Time*. It is "disturbing" because it implicates the federal and local government, especially law enforcement, in perpetuating the conditions that lead to rebellion and even to creating and sustaining gangs.

9

Legal Responses to the Gang Problem

INTRODUCTION

"Law enforcement and suppression tactics, already overtaxed as a solution to a problem they did not start, are having only moderate and uneven success in addressing the gang problem. It doesn't make any difference how many jails we build or how many cells are set aside for each new gang cohort, the strategy we now have has failed. It has failed because it is not based on facts, on science, on human development, or on common sense. We need to be honest in recognizing this fact and bold and courageous in charting a new course."

(VIGIL, 2010: 99)

James Diego Vigil hit the nail on the head. Since the first edition of this book, we have continuously pointed out the failures experienced by the legal system; starting with all sorts of repressive legislation, such as sentencing enhancements targeting gang-related crime, to "gang injunctions," to law enforcement "crackdowns," to the building of new prisons. Nothing has worked (for evidence of this, see Kaufman, 2010). After about 30 years of repression efforts, there are now more gangs and gang members than ever before (as we noted in Chapter 1).

In this era of getting tough, legislatures across the country continue to add stricter codes and harsher sentences for juveniles, especially those with gang affiliations and who commit acts of violence. Often legislative expenditures on incarceration as a result of sentencing statutes decrease the amount of funding for the reduction and prevention of crime. Legislators often allocate scarce resources and make value judgments about the impact or effectiveness of social and criminal justice policies based on their subjective perceptions, ideological preconceptions, political calculus, or wishful hopes rather than on objective data and informed policy analyses. Political slogans, rather than empirical evidence or evaluation research, often guide efforts to formulate youth crime, juvenile court waiver, and sentencing policies.

Responses to gang behavior can be grouped into three categories: 1) legislative—that is, local, state, and federal legislative bodies; 2) official—that is, the criminal justice system; and 3) public—that is, community/neighborhood-based programs (discussed in Chapter 10). Combined, these categories form an estranged cooperative, which is often a synthesis of antagonism, competition, mistrust, and self-interest. Mass media can be seen as a dispatcher or messenger for this contentious alliance. By capitalizing on sensational and peculiar events, the mass media have actually been able to shape public perceptions of youth gangs (Vago, 1994; Dorfman and Schiraldi, 2001; Esbensen and Tusinski, 2007) while simultaneously, and with shocking accuracy, predicting the responses of the cooperative (Reiman and Leighton, 2009). The mass media are able to produce and reproduce our perceptions of and responses to youth gang activities and behavior (Dorfman and Schiraldi, 2001; Esbensen and Tusinski, 2007; Hagedorn, 1998; Klein, 1995). In other words, the mass media may, on command (internal or external), create or re-create public interest in youth gangs while simultaneously orchestrating responses to this phenomenon by manipulating the extent and intensity of youth gang behavior.

Suppose for a moment that the public develops a perception that youth gangs are becoming increasingly troublesome, and assume that this perception is largely the result of the mass media—a phenomenon that is becoming more and more frequent. Following the cultivation of public interest/unrest (public response), policymakers scurry to introduce legislation (legislative response) they anticipate will appease the appetites of their disgruntled constituents (particularly those constituents who are most likely to vent their feelings in the voting booth). This legislation nearly always ignores the etiology and epidemiology of the youth gang phenomenon and falls far short of offering meaningful solutions to the alleged problem. It is difficult to discern whether this failure to consider the causes or extent of the youth gang phenomenon is intentional or unintentional. Nevertheless, the criminal justice apparatus responds (official response) by formulating and adopting policies and procedures in a frantic attempt to comply with legislative requirements. Often these policies and procedures (e.g., police performing general sweeps of targeted areas, prosecutors filing more conspiracy and enhancement charges, and judges handing down longer prison sentences mandated by legislated sentencing guidelines) are counterproductive. In many instances, these reflexive responses do little more than intensify existing tensions within the target communities, congest the courts, and fill the prisons. The heightening of tensions within communities is compounded when the extent of gang activity is grossly exaggerated or fabricated (Padilla, 1992). If the alleged problem persists, the mass media can instigate further pressure on both the criminal justice apparatus and legislators;

if the problem diminishes, the mass media can either change their focus (look for another potentially commercial phenomenon) or reproduce the initial production. Society's willingness to consume and ingest as much violence as is produced by the media renders it susceptible to this form of media manipulation.

The mass media capitalize on the public's appetite for violence by sensationalizing exciting stories related to youth gangs (e.g., drive-by shootings, alleged gang members caught with large amounts of cash and/or drugs, assaults that involve alleged gang members, robberies committed by alleged gang members, etc.). Regarding youth gangs, the mass media have the best of both worlds: 1) they have an addicted/interested audience (the public) for whom they perform, and 2) they are not bothered with the cumbersome responsibility of examining hard data, nor are they required to demonstrate the validity of their performance. A 10-year study of crime news in Hawaii found that coverage of gangs increased 40-fold, and the most frequent type of juvenile crime story reported by the newspapers was "gang activity." Yet the reality was quite different, as most offenses committed by juveniles were relatively minor ones, such as vandalism, running away from home, drug possession, and fighting (Dorfman and Schiraldi, 2001: 18). A study by Esbensen and Tusinski (2007) of 25 years of the three leading news magazines—*Newsweek, Time,* and *U.S. News and World Report*—found repeated exaggerations about the extent of the gang problem, along with racial and gender stereotypes.

A gang member in Detroit asked, "Where do they [newspaper and television reporters] get their information? I live on these fucking streets and don't see half the shit they say happens regular. How the fuck can it be regular if it hardly ever happens?" During an interview with one reporter at a major newspaper in Detroit, it was divulged, "Gang news is good news. It is reliable. Readers enjoy the story, and the circulation department is happy. It's good business. That's what counts."[1]

We are not suggesting that destruction and violence cannot be associated with youth gangs—there are casualties resulting from gang violence (e.g., drive-by shootings, assault, murder, rape, etc.) as well as victims of other forms of socially irresponsible behavior acted out by many of these youths (e.g., drug dealing, theft, vandalism, etc.). We do, however, support the notion that the two concepts—violence and youth gangs—are not necessarily synonymous. We further contend that by using these concepts interchangeably, the problem can be, and perhaps is, overstated and self-serving for commercial and political value.

THE LEGAL RESPONSE TO YOUTH GANGS

Three components of criminal processing as it relates to youth gangs are addressed in this chapter: 1) legislative action, 2) law enforcement, and 3) courts. Each component has a particular role in dealing with youth gangs. They all share common ground, and they are all subject to political pressures and mandates.

Legislatures

From a most naive perspective, legislative bodies act on the sentiment of society. Of course, most people 1) recognize that they are completely ignorant of legislation passed at the state and federal levels or 2) find that their representative voted contrary to what the constituents wanted or what their representative promised during the election cycle. This is probably best referred to as *politics*—supporting a candidate who supports legislation contrary to what he or she claimed to support during an election campaign. What is most interesting about this phenomenon is that the same people return to the polls and reelect their "nonrepresentatives." Political actors often wrap themselves around platforms that draw attention to episodes of youth gang activities.[2] The validity and extent of these indictments make little difference. Rarely do these actors address economic, social, and political factors that have a contributing causal link to delinquent behavior among many of society's youths (e.g., poverty, unemployment, discrimination in school funding, absence of constructive activities for youths, etc.). In fact, laws that govern political campaigns do little to discourage or restrict false information (this holds true for arguments between opposing candidates and for their distortions of social issues).

In their attempt to resolve the youth gang dilemma and appease disgruntled constituents, legislators across America have enacted new laws and revisions to existing ones. Frequently, their legislation begins with a consideration of the feasibility of existing laws. Legislators struggle with the troublesome question "What constitutes a gang?" Armed with arrogance, ignorance, and indifference, legislative bodies (federal, state, and local) spend much of their time reacting to the gang dilemma, preferring creative sanctions rather than a subscription to social justice or considering the social realities of youth gang members or affiliates and their families. In the process, many legislators believe it is necessary to fracture the U.S. Constitution; they begin by undoing many of the tenets set forth by the Founding Fathers, particularly in the area of due process. The concept of toughness stands in the way of more tolerant concepts such as individual rights, human rights, dignity, and compassion, which could be used to direct legislation.

In 1994, Governor John Engler of Michigan signed into law P.A. 328 of 1994, which mandates the permanent expulsion of public-school students (few black students, compared with white students, attend private schools) who are in possession of dangerous weapons as defined by the school code. These dangerous weapons include firearms, daggers, stilettos, knives with a blade over three inches long, pocket knives that are opened by a mechanical device, iron bars, and brass knuckles. When asked about the permanent expulsion law, several gang members in Detroit stated, "We can't believe it. Engler is actually recruiting for us."[3]

More recently, in December 2008, Christopher Hurst, a Democratic Party Washington state legislator from the 31st Legislative District, wrote an article for the *Enumclaw Courier Herald* titled "Legislature has to make life tough on gang members." Hurst, a former police officer of 25 years, noted that he had been the prime sponsor of the recent Omnibus Gang Bill that would hold gang members to higher levels of accountability when their crimes advanced the objectives of a gang. His follow-up proposals during the next legislative session included civil gang injunctions targeting violent gangs and their members. Essentially, civil gang injunctions include the suing of a gang and prohibiting members from engaging in organized activities in public. Violation of this injunction can result in immediate arrest and incarceration for the simple act of talking to another gang member (or alleged gang member) on a street corner (Hurst, 2008).

The National Gang Center (2011a) provides gang-related legislation produced by states across the country. After reviewing nearly 600 pages of current or recent legislation, we selected 12 legislative topics to address in this section:

- Enhanced Penalties—Sentencing
- Expert Testimony
- Gang-Related Clothing, Dress Codes, and School Uniforms
- Gang Participation and Forfeiture
- Gang Prevention
- Gang Prosecution
- Gang-Related Definitions
- Gang-Related Civil Causes of Action
- Gang Graffiti
- Juvenile Gang Members
- Public Nuisance/Premises Used by Gangs
- Law Enforcement Training

Enhanced Penalties—Sentencing.   Enhanced penalties—sentencing, as related to gangs, simply means that a criminal defendant who has pleaded guilty or been found guilty in court, and who is proven to be a member or associate of a gang, can receive an enhanced or increased sentence beyond the sentence limitation that a nongang member/affiliate would receive. In other words, a person convicted of robbery, who was found to be a gang member or affiliate, could receive a harsher sentence than a person convicted of robbery but who was not considered a gang member or affiliate. There are 29 states that have enhanced penalties-sentencing legislation related to gang members or affiliates.

Expert Testimony.   There are two standards that courts use to determine the level of expertise of an expert witness testifying in criminal cases involving gang members/affiliates. One standard is known as the *Frye Test*, which requires that the testimony offered by an expert witness must be consistent with the findings of the relevant scientific community. The other standard is known as the *Daubert Standard* and is used in all U.S. federal legal proceedings and about one-half of the state courts. While the Daubert Test is similar to the Frye Test in many ways, the Daubert Test focuses significant attention on methodology and hypotheses testing. Ideally, the foundation of the expert witness credentials is based on his or her knowledge, skill, experience, training, or education. Three states, Alaska,

Indiana, and Nevada, have legislation specifically addressing expert witness testimony issues in criminal courts involving cases where the defendants are alleged gang members. Depending on the jurisdiction, and the defense counsel for the defendant, expert witnesses can be used to educate the judge and jury about the social reality of youth gangs and their members, as well as the cultural artifacts associated within the communities where gang members reside. The legislation in Alaska, Indiana, and Nevada provides a list of topics that an expert witness may testify on, which include characteristics of gang members, social customs and behavior of members of criminal gangs, common practices and operations of criminal gangs, and terminology used by members of gangs. The term *culture* does not appear in any of this legislation.[4]

Gang-Related Clothing, Dress Codes, and School Uniforms.   Ten states have passed legislation that focuses on gang-related clothing, dress codes, and/or school uniforms. In California, legislation states, "Gang-related apparel is hazardous to the health and safety of the school environment."[5] Tennessee legislation, relevant to students in the sixth through twelfth grades, specifies that as "Wearing, while on school property, any type of clothing, apparel or accessory, including that which denotes such students' membership in or affiliation with any criminal gang."[6] Nevada legislation gives the board of trustees of each school district the authorization to develop clothing policies after consultation with local law-enforcement agencies, school police officers, individuals who have experience regarding the actions and activities of criminal gangs, and organizations that are dedicated to alleviating criminal gangs or assisting gang members who want to disassociate from a gang, and any other person the board of trustees deems appropriate.[7]

Gang Participation and Forfeiture.   Legislation that centers on gang participation and forfeiture has passed in 23 states. Florida legislation states:

> All profits, proceeds, and instrumentalities of criminal gang activity and all property used or intended or attempted to be used to facilitate the criminal activity of any criminal gang or of any criminal gang member; and all profits, proceeds, and instrumentalities of criminal gang recruitment and all property used or intended or attempted to be used to facilitate criminal gang recruitment are subject to seizure and forfeiture under the Florida Contraband Forfeiture Act.[8]

Nevada legislation stipulates that all personal property, including tools, substances, weapons, machines, computers, money, or security that is used as an instrumentality in the commission of any crime by a criminal gang, is subject to forfeiture.[9] Ohio legislation offers a provision for law enforcement to subsidize their efforts pertaining to criminal gangs with fines.[10]

Gang Prevention.   There are 24 states that have passed legislation related to gang prevention. Arizona's legislation of gang prevention tends to define gang prevention in the form of subsidies directed toward street gang enforcement and prosecution of gang members. State funding accommodates training for law enforcement and prosecutors as well as funding for investigation and prosecution of gang-affiliated offenses.[11] Legislation on gang prevention in states such as Colorado, Connecticut, and Illinois focuses more on education, which centers attention on the promotion of responsible citizenship and reduction of anti-social behavior.[12] States such as Michigan, South Carolina, and Washington have passed legislation that is a mixture for enforcement and prosecution of gang affiliates as well as counseling and other similar preventive approaches.[13] Legislation in the state of Washington actually focuses on education, employment, and culture awareness as a strategy for gang prevention.[14]

Gang Prosecution. Fourteen states have passed gang legislation related to prosecution. Arizona legislation outlines the procedure to pass along juveniles to the adult court system:

> If the judge finds by a preponderance of the evidence that probable cause exists to believe that the offense was committed, that the juvenile committed the offense, and that the public safety would best be served by the transfer of the juvenile for criminal prosecution, the judge shall order that the juvenile be transferred for criminal prosecution to the appropriate court having jurisdiction of the offense. The judge shall state on the record the reasons for transferring or not transferring the juvenile for criminal prosecution.[15]

California legislation related to gang prosecution includes enhanced prosecution provisions. This chapter of legislation stipulates that enhanced prosecution must include the following:

a. "Vertical" prosecutorial representation, whereby the prosecutor who makes the initial filing or appearance in a gang-related case will perform all subsequent court appearances on that particular case through its conclusion, including the sentencing phase

b. Assignment of highly qualified investigators and prosecutors to gang-related cases

c. Significant reduction of caseloads for investigators and prosecutors assigned to gang-related cases

d. Measures taken in coordination with law enforcement agencies to protect cooperating witnesses from intimidation or retribution at the hands of gang members or associates[16]

Georgia legislation stipulates that, "The commission of any offense enumerated in paragraph (1) of Code Section 16-15-3 by any member or associate of a criminal street gang shall be admissible in any trial or proceeding for the purpose of proving the existence of the criminal street gang and criminal gang activity."[17] These offenses include racketeering, stalking, rape and sodomy, escape from confinement, dangerous practices, state or county correctional facility security violations, helping or encouraging a child to escape from a correctional facility, graffiti, violent offenses and offenses involving a weapon, and participating in criminal street gang activities.[18]

In the state of Washington, legislation includes a provision providing for special allegation procedures involving minors in felony offenses. In felony offense prosecutions of crimes related to street gangs, the prosecutor may file a special allegation that the alleged felony offense involved compensation, threats, or solicitation of a minor in order to complete the offense. This legislation established the burden of proof for the special allegation.

> The state has the burden of proving a special allegation made under this section beyond a reasonable doubt. If a jury is had, the jury shall, if it finds the defendant guilty, also find a special verdict as to whether the criminal street gang-related felony offense involved the compensation, threatening, or solicitation of a minor in order to involve that minor in the commission of the felony offense. If no jury is had, the court shall make a finding of fact as to whether the criminal street gang-related felony offense involved the compensation, threatening, or solicitation of a minor in order to involve that minor in the commission of the felony offense.[19]

Gang-Related Definitions.   Forty-four states have passed legislation addressing gang-related definitions. Much of this legislation consists of defining what constitutes a gang or affiliation with a gang, the characteristics of a gang, including clothing worn by alleged gang members, hand signals, tattoos, and other alleged identifying characteristics. Much of this legislation also refers to specific offense categories applicable to their gang-related definitions. Alaska legislation defines a "criminal street gang" as

> A group of three or more persons (A) who have in common a name or identifying sign, symbol, tattoo or other physical marking, style of dress, or use of hand signs; and (B) who, individually, jointly, or in combination, have committed or attempted to commit, within the preceding three years, for the benefit of, at the direction of, or in association with the group, two or more offenses under any of, or any combination of, the following: (i) AS 11.41 (person offenses); (ii) AS 11.46 property offenses); or (iii) a felony offense.[20]

Arizona legislation defines a "criminal street gang" as

> An ongoing formal or informal association of persons in which members or associates individually or collectively engage in the commission, attempted commission, facilitation or solicitation of any felony act and that has at least one individual who is a criminal street gang member.[21]

Legislation in Colorado stipulates that, *gang* means a group of three or more individuals with a common interest, bond, or activity characterized by criminal or delinquent conduct, engaged in either collectively or individually."[22] Delaware legislation defines a "criminal street gang" as

> Any ongoing organization, association, or group of 3 or more persons, whether formal or informal, having as one of its primary activities the commission of one or more of the criminal acts enumerated in

Subdivision (a)(2) of this section, having a common name or common identifying sign or symbol, and whose members individually or collectively engage in or have engaged in a pattern of criminal gang activity.[23]

South Dakota legislation states that *reliable informants* can determine one's gang membership or affiliation.[24] Several states (Florida, Idaho, Illinois, and Texas) refer to terrorism in their gang definition legislation.[25]

Gang-Related Civil Causes of Action.   A cause of action typically surfaces from either a specific act, failing to perform a legal obligation, a violation of duty, or a violation/invasion of a right. Ten states have adopted legislation that focuses on gang-related civil causes of action. Illinois legislation stipulates:

> A civil cause of action is hereby created in favor of any pubic authority expending money, allocating or reallocating police, firefighting, emergency or other personnel or resources, or otherwise incurring any loss, deprivation, or injury, or sustaining any damage, impairment, or harm whatsoever, proximately caused by any course or pattern of criminal activity.[26]

This legislation further states that the cause of action shall be imposed on "any street gang in whose name, for whose benefit, on whose behalf, or under whose direction the act was committed," and "any gang officer or director who causes, orders, suggests, authorizes, consents to, agrees to, requests, acquiesces in, or ratifies any such act," as well as "any gang member who, in the furtherance of or in connection with, any gang-related activity, commits any such act."[27]

Nevada legislation gives authority to each board of county commissioners to protect public health, safety, and welfare of the residents of the county; to adopt procedures for district attorneys to file civil action in courts to seek relief, through temporary or permanent injunctions against any specific member of a criminal gang; and to recover monetary damages, attorney fees, and other costs from any member of a criminal gang who is engaged in criminal activities within the county. Additionally, the district attorney may also recover money from

> [t]he owner of a building or place located within the county that has been found to be a public nuisance because the building or place is regularly and continuously used by the members of a criminal gang to engage in, or facilitate the commission of, crimes by the criminal gang, but only if the owner has actual notice that the building or place is regularly and continuously used by the members of a criminal gang to engage in, or facilitate the commission of, crimes by the criminal gang.[28]

Under Texas legislation, a member of a street gang is liable to the state or any government entity injured by violating a temporary or permanent injunctive order. In any action brought against a member of a criminal gang, the plaintiff must demonstrate that the gang member violated the temporary or permanent injunction order. A district, county, or city attorney is authorized to sue for monetary damages on behalf of the state or local government entity. If the government attorney is successful, the state or government entity is authorized to recover the following:

- Actual damages

- A civil penalty not to exceed $20,000 for each violation

- Court costs and attorney fees[29]

Wisconsin legislation stipulates that the court is allowed to mandate a criminal gang member to dissociate himself or herself from any interest or involvement in any criminal gang activity. The court is authorized to restrict a criminal gang member from engaging in any future criminal gang activity.[30]

Gang Graffiti.   More than 30 states have passed legislation to address the issue of gang graffiti. Most state legislation definitions of graffiti are similar. For example, Nevada defines graffiti as an "unauthorized inscription, word, figure, or design that is marked, etched, scratched, drawn, painted on, or affixed to the public or private property, real or personal, of another, which defaces the property."[31] In New York, graffiti is defined as "the etching, painting, covering, drawing upon, or otherwise placing of a mark upon public or private property with intent to damage such property."[32]

Many states, such as Washington, have legislated protection to the owner of property defaced by graffiti. In Washington, a person defacing property with graffiti is liable for the actual damages and penalty damages to the owner of said property for up to $1,000, as well as an additional penalty not exceeding $200, and reasonable court costs and attorney's fees.[33] New Jersey legislation provides the court with the option to impose a penalty for defacing property with graffiti, reimbursement to the owner of said property for damages, and imposing community service obligations for the convicted individual.[34] Legislation in California and Hawaii stipulate that the parent or guardian having custody and control of a minor can be held jointly liable with the minor for graffiti damage.[35] In the District of Columbia, legislation authorizes holding the owner of property liable for not removing graffiti,[36] while Georgia legislation stipulates that graffiti removal will not be levied to property owners who are victims, and that inmates may be used to remove graffiti.[37]

Juvenile Gang Members.   Eighteen states have passed legislation that focuses on juvenile gang members. Much of this legislation directs attention to processing juveniles through either the juvenile or adult courts contingent upon their alleged gang activities. Indiana legislation stipulates that the juvenile court does not have jurisdiction over an individual who allegedly engaged in carjacking, criminal gang activity, or criminal gang intimidation.[38] Missouri legislation provides an option for prosecutors to transfer a defendant between the age of 14 and 17 to a court of general jurisdiction for offenses associated with criminal street gang activities, which include assault, robbery, murder, or certain illegal substance abuse activities.[39] Tennessee legislation states that children less than 16 years of age who are charged with first-degree murder, second-degree murder, rape, aggravated rape, aggravated robbery, and so on will be tried in adult court; however, the prosecution cannot seek the death penalty in these cases.[40] Texas legislation stipulates that a juvenile court in a disposition hearing of a juvenile who has been adjudicated to have engaged in gang-related conduct must order the child to participate in a criminal street gang intervention program. The program must be appropriate for the child—based on the child's level of involvement in criminal activities of a criminal street gang. The intervention program must include at least 12 hours of instruction, and it may also include voluntary tattoo removal. This legislation also states that if a child is sent to the authority of the Texas Youth Commission because of his or her gang-related conduct, the child must complete the gang intervention program before he or she can be released from custody or supervision by that commission.[41]

Public Nuisance/Premises Used by Gangs.   Twenty-four states have legislation focusing on public nuisance/premises used by gangs. Minnesota legislation stipulates, "A criminal gang that continuously or regularly engages in gang activities is a public nuisance."[42] California legislation proclaims, "By ordinance the city legislative body may declare what constitutes a nuisance."[43] Florida legislation authorizes the creation of administrative boards with authority to impose administrative fines and other noncriminal penalties relative to public nuisance/premises issues.[44] Iowa legislation lists an assortment of locations and behaviors that are considered nuisances. This list includes houses of ill fame, kept for the purpose of prostitution and lewdness; gambling houses; places resorted to by persons participating in gang activity; places used by persons engaged in controlled substances use; or houses where drunkenness, quarreling, fighting, or other breaches of the peace occur.[45] Relative to private property, Mississippi legislation states that every private building or place used by criminal street gang members for the commission of illegal activity may be subjected to injunction or cause of action damages or for the abatement of the nuisance.[46] In North Carolina, any real property that is used by a criminal street gang for the purpose of conducting gang activity is constituted a public nuisance, which may be abated.[47]

Law-Enforcement Training.   Only five states have legislation mandating or directing law-enforcement training related to gangs. In Connecticut, legislation mandates that each police basic and review training program must include training on gang-related violence. The Police Officer Standards and Training Council must provide training for security personnel employed in the public schools, and this training must be provided by a local or regional board of education. This training must include drug detection and gang identification.[48] Iowa legislation requires the police academy director, with the approval of the council, to give due consideration to varying factors and special requirements of law-enforcement agencies relative to the existing training curriculum, to include racial and cultural awareness and dealing with gang-affected youth.[49] Rhode Island legislation requires the commission on standards and training to provide instructions to police for identification, responding to, and reporting incidents involving criminal gang activity.[50] Texas legislation mandates training for parole officers who supervise members of gangs or other security threat groups.[51] Finally, Utah legislation requires sheriffs and police chiefs to ensure that officers enforcing gang laws must be trained in the identification of gang members and criminal street gangs.[52]

Law Enforcement

It has been argued that law enforcement represents society's first line of defense against crime. Subsequently, law enforcement is the first segment of the criminal justice system that responds to the youth gang dilemma. Obliged to cater to the whims of lawmakers who frequently underestimate the dynamics associated with youth gangs, law enforcement is faced with the question "What can we do?" Law enforcement has responded to youth gangs with a conglomeration of maneuvers. One of the most ambitious was a program known as the L.A. Plan that began in the 1980s, which in part continues to the present.

The L.A. Plan. This program was called the L.A. Plan by a federal agency, and its impetus came from the large increase in gang-related homicides in the 1980s. There were six different programs:

- Community Youth Gang Services (CYGS), which was a "youth outreach program" based in part on the familiar detached worker programs, but without having workers assigned to specific gangs. There was no evaluation, and eventually it was defunded, with the funds assigned to another program called L.A. Bridges (discussed later in this section).

- OSS and CRASH, which refer to Operation Safe Streets (an L.A. County Sheriff's Department program) and the LAPD's Community Resources Against Street Hoodlums. As the reader might conclude from these acronyms, these were purely suppression efforts.

- Operation Hammer (discussed further later in this section), which was a rather infamous LAPD action that amounted to street sweeps of gang members and was intended to "send a message" (general deterrence) to gangs. A total of 1,435 were arrested, but 1,350 were released with no charges filed (and among those charged, only 2% were felonies). Many were not even in gangs. LAPD soon abandoned the program.

- Operation Hardcore, which was instigated within the district attorney's office, where a group of prosecutors specifically targeted gang members, mostly homicide cases.

- A correctional gang caseloads program involving special gang units within the LAPD and the California Youth Authority (CYA), which involved surveillance of gang members on parole for the purpose of "violating" them and sending them back to prison if they were caught violating parole.

- An interagency task force, which was supposed to increase collaboration and coordination among various agencies involved in the preceding five programs. Mostly it was about sharing information about wanted suspects (as Klein and Maxson observed when they attended meetings), the telling of "war stories," and other informal contacts. (2006: 95)[53]

California's State Task Force (State Task Force on Youth Gang Violence, 1986: 37) offered a number of policy (and legislative) suggestions to combat youth gangs: 1) design and develop statewide gang information systems; 2) launch school-based gang and narcotics prevention programs; 3) provide technical assistance in gang analysis to local law-enforcement agencies; 4) identify gang members under the supervision of the California Youth Authority and intensify parole supervision; 5) establish and expand special units in probation to supervise gang members; 6) create a Southeast Asian youth gang prevention and intervention program; 7) establish standards throughout the correctional system that discourage gang membership; and 8) using ex-gang members and community street workers, establish a model gang intervention program. Although many of these suggestions do not affect law enforcement directly, they all have an impact on law enforcement's role in policing youth gangs.

In a desperate attempt to find solutions to the problem of youth gangs, violence, and drugs, law enforcement has embarked on a voyage from the proactive/policing approach of creating and sponsoring new programs with catchy acronyms such as DARE (Drug Awareness Resistance Education) and SANE (Substance Abuse Narcotics Education), to paying gang members to fight crime (*New York Times,* 1999).

The main underlying rationale of the law-enforcement approach is that of deterrence (reviewed in Chapter 7). In fact, all efforts that come under the more general banner of suppression are based on deterrence theory. Klein observes that the essence of suppression is that 1) there is little emphasis on prevention and treatment; 2) the highest priority is on street crimes, which typically means the most visible (e.g., drug crimes); and 3) there is a strong emphasis on surveillance and selective enforcement (meaning harassment) with 4) a corresponding assumption that gang members and potential gang members will respond in a rational manner and choose to refrain from continued involvement in gang activities (Klein, 1995: 160).

An example of suppression tactics can be seen in the case of Operation Hammer, mentioned previously, and similar police suppression tactics in Los Angeles during the late 1980s. This was a major police response to gangs in south-central Los Angeles under the administration of Police Chief Daryl Gates. The crackdown began in April 1988 and focused on 10 square miles in the south-central area. It was like a search and destroy mission in Vietnam (Miller, 1996). A total of 1,453 arrests were made, mostly for minor offenses such as curfew, disturbing the peace, and so on. Hundreds more had their names and addresses inserted into an electronic gang roster for future intelligence (Davis, 1992: 268). To aid in this repressive activity, the police used a special mobile booking operation next to the Los Angeles Coliseum. The overall purpose was merely social control (of black youth) rather than a serious attempt at reducing crime. Proof of this is the fact that out of the 1,453 arrests, 1,350 (93%) were released without any charges filed. More interesting is that half of them turned out *not* to be gang members. Only 60 felony arrests were made, and charges were filed on only 32 of these. Around 200 police officers were used, while during the same period there were two gang-related homicides (Klein, 1995: 162).

Similar suppression efforts in the war on gangs and war on drugs in Los Angeles have met with similar results. For example, Chief Gates launched the Gang Related Active Trafficker Suppression (GRATS) program in February and March 1988, just before Operation Hammer took place. This program targeted so-called drug neighborhoods for raids by 200 to 300 police officers. They stopped and interrogated anyone suspected of being a gang member based on how they dressed or the use of gang hand signals. Nine of these sweeps took place, resulting in 500 cars being impounded and around 1,500 arrests. Gates wanted to "get the message out to the cowards out there … that we're going to come and get them." Apparently the message did not get through, for after the chief gave a speech praising his sweeps, a few Crips fired on a crowd on a street corner in south-central Los Angeles, killing a 19-year-old woman (Davis, 1992: 268–274).

Such a crackdown was supported by many conservative leaders, including County Supervisor Kenneth Hahn, who asked for the use of the National Guard, suggesting that Los Angeles was "fighting the war on gang violence … that's worse than Beirut," while a state senator's press secretary argued that "when you have a state of war, civil rights are suspended for the duration of the conflict." Meanwhile, the NAACP reported that during these events there were hundreds of complaints about unlawful police conduct and that the police were in effect contributing to gang violence by leaving suspects stranded on enemy turf and even going so far as to write over Crip graffiti with Blood graffiti and vice versa (Davis, 1992: 274).

Moore notes a similar crackdown on gangs in Los Angeles that took place on four consecutive weekends in the late 1980s that netted a grand total of 563 arrests (mostly on outstanding warrants), 3 ounces of cocaine, and a total of $9,000 in cash related to the drug trade (Moore, 1991: 3–4). In San Diego, a similar sweep resulted in 146 arrests during a one-week period (mostly minor offenses, as usual), and only 17 were still in custody at the end of the week. Similar suppression efforts have been tried, with the same results, in such cities as Chicago, Milwaukee, Baltimore, and Boston (Klein, 1995: 162, 166).

In still another crackdown, Chief Gates ordered a raid that turned into what some called an "orgy of violence" as police punched and kicked residents, threw washing machines into bathtubs, smashed walls and furniture with sledgehammers and axes, and even spray-painted slogans on walls, including "LAPD Rules." The result was two minor drug arrests. The police took disciplinary action against 38 officers, including a captain who ordered his officers to level and "make uninhabitable" the apartments that were targeted (Davis, 1992: 276)—another example of a search and destroy type of activity, similar to that used in Vietnam.

Another Gates program was called CRASH (Community Resources Against Street Hoodlums), which was originally called TRASH, with the "T" standing for "Total," but the name was changed for obvious reasons. Under this program, the police engaged in "surveillance and harassment" with the explicit purpose being, to use one officer's words, to "jam" suspected gang members (i.e., harass and then move on, with no arrest being made in most cases). The officers were rotated out after two or three years and thus never had a real opportunity to develop detailed knowledge about the communities (Klein, 1995: 164–165).

Despite repeated failures, such as Operation Hammer, many police officials continue with similar suppression tactics, often based on the assumption that they are sending a message. Obviously the message is not getting through very clearly, as the number of gangs and gang members continues to grow.

Some individual police officers are more realistic than their superiors. One officer, who had worked with gang members for nearly eight years, in the course of his regular patrol duties stated, "Many of these kids have zero options. They live in a shit hole. I can arrest them. They may, in rare instances, actually do some time. When they get out, they are dumped back into the same shit hole."[54] Another officer pointed out that "these kids have no place to play. They find some structure (e.g., a street-light pole) to nail a backboard and hoop, and play basketball in the middle of the street. They disrupt traffic and make drivers mad. Pretty soon the kids just say fuck it and go find something else to do—they go banging." Most interesting is the reference to kids, suggesting an acknowledgment by these officers that these youths are not necessarily gangsters or criminals; rather, many are children. This language is qualitatively different from the rhetoric used by those who have transposed the term *kids* (a term frequently associated with a stage of the human development process) to other less flattering abstractions, such as *scavengers,* which is used by Taylor (1990b: 105). Of course, in a broader sense, these officers are drawing attention to structural issues germane to many neighborhoods in the inner city.

The interdiction dimension of law enforcement's response to youth gangs is a reflex of the tremendous pressure placed on police to produce results. Many law-enforcement agencies have come to rely on special units. Some scholars have pointed out advantages in the creation of these units (Skolnick, 1994; Skolnick and Bayley, 1986). Others are less than enthusiastic about the special-unit approach (Goldstein, 1991; Walker, 2001). With a nearly impossible mandate (to eradicate, or at least control, youth gangs), many law-enforcement administrators and local governments often find themselves financially driven to replenish insufficient resources.

During the past few years, the federal government has provided assistance in funding through block grants designated for youth gang interdiction. Most often, these grants are used to create and support social-control strategies rather than solution-oriented approaches. We found one law-enforcement agency that formed a special gang unit in order to compete for a piece of the block-grant pie. Surprisingly, we discovered that this particular jurisdiction did not have a youth gang problem at the time of application, nor does this jurisdiction have a gang problem now. During an interview with the detective in charge of the newly formed gang unit, it was revealed that "the mayor wanted a gang unit because he had heard that federal grant money was available for police departments that had adopted this sort of special unit." When asked what his gang unit did, he responded, "Nothing. We don't have any gangs in this community. We have some kids who play with spray paint. At best, we have a few gang wannabes."[55]

In Las Vegas, despite the lack of firm evidence that gangs are responsible for many serious crimes, the police department's gang unit was recently renamed a "gang bureau." With this categorization comes, not surprisingly, more money for more officers and equipment. Naturally, in recent years, the number of gangs and gang members has increased.[56]

These gang units have spread throughout the nation. A 2007 survey found that 365 of the nation's large police departments had specialized gang units employing more than 4,300 sworn officers. More than one-third (35%) were established between 2004 and 2007 (Langton, 2009). Most of the efforts of such units consist of surveillance and other intelligence gathering plus special attention devoted to drugs and graffiti.

One example is provided by the Detroit, Michigan, police department, which in the 1990s established a special gang unit consisting of more than 60 officers. This unit had five components: administrative, enforcement, investigative, intelligence, and surveillance.[57] On any given day, rarely were there more than four or five officers actually working on gang-specific cases within their jurisdictions. Typically, dealing with gangs for this unit was limited to conducting investigations when alleged gang members were possible suspects in a crime. Moreover, it was common knowledge among police officers throughout this department that assignment to the gang unit provides strong credentials for promotion—thus the gang unit in this jurisdiction was little more than a political position. Several officers agreed with one officer's perception: "Members of the gang unit profile around and play cowboy. When they do make contact with gang members they do little more than harass them." Another officer stated, "We [patrol officers] are the ones who work the gangs. We deal with them on a daily basis. The gang squad is too busy dealing with the media, and kissing the chief's ass." Suggesting that this perception may extend beyond this jurisdiction, a San Jose, California, police veteran of 22 years told Brown, "Gang units are like every other special unit in policing—full of bullshit and totally political."[58]

One of the best-known and widely duplicated law-enforcement programs is GREAT (Gang Resistance Education and Training). Developed by practitioners, the components of the program have been linked to control theory and social learning theory (Winfree, Esbensen, and Osgood, 1995). This is a curriculum taught by uniformed police officers to sixth and seventh graders in hourly sessions over an eight-week period. This program emphasizes skill training and information that may help youths resist peer pressure, improve self-esteem, shun violence, and ignore gang influences. The assessment of this program is mixed. GREAT has been found to modestly improve attitudes but may fall short of persuading adolescents not to join gangs, and participants have lower levels of gang affiliation and self-reported delinquency, including drug use, minor offending, property crimes, and crimes against persons (Howell, 1998: 13). The overall success has been limited (Esbensen et al., 2001; Klein and Maxson, 2006).

Gang suppression and reduction programs within police departments are numerous. Several of the most active are highlighted in the following discussion.

Boston's Youth Violence Strike Force employs a gun user reduction strategy in collaboration with police and probation officers. This strategy relies on the premise that guns are vital tools to gang members, especially in resolving gang conflicts. By removing guns from the street and from the possession of gang members, that vitality is effectively reduced (Lasley, 1998: 4).

Atlanta's police department has a model program, recognized by the Department of Justice's PACT (Pulling America's Communities Together). GANGIS, the Gang Intelligence System, is locally developed and supported by the federal government. Its goals are to improve and share intelligence and to support family ties and community values (Jackson and Gordon, 1995)—lofty in theory, but there is an indication (perhaps only perceived by citizens) that this unit has been effective in reducing the number of gang incidents in the community.

The Comprehensive Community-Wide Approach to Gang Prevention, Intervention, and Suppression Program, developed by Spergel and his colleagues (Spergel, 1995) contains 12 program components for the design and mobilization of community efforts by police, prosecutors, judges, probation and parole officers, corrections officers, school officials, employers, community-based agency staff such as street outreach workers, and a range of grassroots organizations' staff (Howell, 1998: 13–14). A pilot of this model is the Chicago Police Department's Gang Violence Reduction Project, which has been touted by city officials. The target of this project is Latino youth involved in serious gang crime and violence. "A core team of workers delivers relevant services, provides opportunities, and carries out suppression strategies in highly coordinated and integrated matters. The level of serious gang violence is decreasing; there are fewer arrests; gang members are referred to, or provided with a variety of counseling, crisis intervention, job placement, family, school, and special education programs and services" (Thornberry and Burch, 1997: 3).

A tactic used by the Los Angeles Police Department was Operation Cul de Sac, in which traffic barriers were placed in neighborhoods where gangs and gang violence had become a dominant force. The year before the project was implemented, these neighborhoods had seen the highest number of drive-by shootings, gang homicides, and street assaults in the city. Drugs were being sold in open disregard for the law. As automobile access to the area was reduced, crime was reduced; homicide and aggravated assault rates fell and were not displaced to other areas. This action, while measurably successful, was initiated and evaluated in this singular area (Lasley, 1998: 4). Lasley suggests that the lack of the displacement of gang-related crime "lies in the nature of gang ties to specific neighborhoods or turf ... [they] may have refrained from committing crimes in surrounding neighborhoods because these neighborhoods are the turf of rival gangs ... rival gangs traveling ... in the general vicinity of the site may have been given word to stay clear ... avoiding [the site] and contiguous neighborhoods altogether" (1998: 4).

This project makes the assumption that gang violence is partly the result of criminal opportunity. This program "directly challenged the popular notion that gang rivalries are so deep-seated, emotionally charged, and irrational that they cannot be mitigated or stopped by specific deterrence measures" (Lassley, 1998: 4).

Operation Cul de Sac did provide deterrence as opportunities were blocked by limited street access (see also Klein, 1995: 166).

Clark (1992) has further developed this notion of criminal opportunity by defining what he terms "situational crime prevention." This idea assumes that pinpointing and blocking the forces that facilitate would-be offenders' criminal acts can reduce crime. These individuals make rational choices in planning their acts, as Lasley (1998: 2) offers: "For example, gangs may choose a particular street to commit a crime because they rationally determine that the way the street is situated provides them with ready access and exit, thereby creating an opportunity to move easily and elude arrest."

Others would argue that these law-enforcement tactics are not effective. A 1999 ruling by the U.S. Supreme Court in striking down anti-loitering methods employed by law enforcement against gangs has curtailed this tactic. A Chicago loitering ordinance that had been enforced (45,000 arrests in three years) was ruled unconstitutional by the Court, which said, "If the loitering is in fact harmless and innocent, the dispersal order itself is an unjustified impairment of liberty" (Carellic, 1999: 4A). The ordinance required police to order any group of people standing around with no apparent purpose to move along if an officer believed any one of the members of the group belonged to a gang. Chicago's city attorney, Lawrence Rosenthal, said that gang crime is "different from every other form of criminal activity" because street gangs "rely on their ability to terrorize the community" with their mere presence. Gang members just "hang around" innocently by the time police arrive on the scene (Carellic, 1999).

More recent actions include so-called "zero tolerance" policies, such as those concerning wearing gang attire in schools. In California, many county law-enforcement agencies have created "Gang Strategy" groups to establish a uniform set of criteria intended to define a gang member and combat gang activities, such as those used in Santa Barbara County (Marshall, Tuttle, and Laurenzano, 2002).

Conducting sweeps, or rousts, of targeted areas is another strategy employed by police. Sweeps are tactics whereby many police officers converge on a target area for the purpose of eradicating (or relocating) specific forms of criminal or undesirable behavior. Similar methods were employed by the SS police to relocate the Jewish population in Nazi Germany (Miller, 1996) and to sweep and transfer Japanese Americans in World War II to concentration camps (Burns, 1974). However, we suspect that the American public, including political officials, are not willing to go quite that far to provide a solution to the youth gang problem. Following public outcries to local officials about prostitution, police have had some success in relocating prostitutes using these maneuvers. In the case of youth gang interdiction, this tactic is analogous to an attempt to put out a forest fire with a water bucket. While it is possible to remove prostitutes from a particular neighborhood (at least for a period of time), it is more difficult, and legally and morally questionable, to remove youth gang members from their neighborhoods, homes, and/or families. Often this tactic can do more harm than good; this is particularly true when local citizens view this approach as an example of racism (e.g., in Watts, Newark, and Detroit during the 1960s, and instrumental in events leading to the riots in south-central Los Angeles in 1992).

Ironically, one of America's gross social injustices (also believed to be a contributing factor in the proliferation of youth gangs)—racial segregation—may actually assist law enforcement in their quest for victory over youth gangs. There are social-control advantages reached through segregation. Jackson (1992: 90) writes, "Segregation may reduce the pressure on authorities to police minority populations, since segregation reduces interracial crime, the phenomenon most likely to result in pressure on crime control authorities." Moreover, she adds, "fear of crime, coupled with fear of loss of dominance, provides fertile ground for a mobilization of policing resources."

The FBI.   In 2011, the National Gang Threat Assessment, which was released by the National Gang Intelligence Center (NGIC), indicates that there are about 1.4 million gang members associated with more than 33,000 gangs that were criminally active throughout the United States.[59] The FBI states that gangs are poisoning our streets with drugs, violence, and all manner of crime.[60] In their fight against gang violence, the FBI claims that as of January 2011, there are 168 Safe Streets Task Forces (SSTFs) who focus on violent gangs in 55 of their field offices. In 2007, the FBI reports that the Violent Gang Safe Street Task Force accomplishments include 3,256 indictments and informations filed against gang members, compared to 3,845 filings. In 2007, there were 7,256 federal arrests of gang members compared to 7,184 federal arrests in 2010, and in 2007, there were 2,325 convictions of gang members compared to 3,176 in 2010. Over a 10-year period (2001–2010), the FBI reports totals of 29,273 indictments and informations, 57,106 arrests of gang members, and 23,094 gang member convictions.[61]

The overall effectiveness of police anti-gang efforts has not been demonstrated, despite law-enforcement claims to the contrary, usually based on dubious and typically anecdotal evidence (Spergel, 1995: 199). Assume there are 1.4 million gang members and more than 33,000 criminal gangs as suggested in the data provided by the FBI. These data suggest that the war on gangs is measured in much the same way as the progress of the Vietnam War—and we all know the outcome of the latter.

The Courts

The third segment of the legal response to youth gangs is the judiciary, of which there are three components. Of immediate interest to our work are 1) the juvenile court, 2) the adult court, and, 3) at the apex of the judiciary, the Supreme Court. Each component has played a role in the adjudication process of accused members of youth gangs. The juvenile courts have provided elevated statuses for convicted youths (Thrasher, 1927); adult courts have attempted to satisfy the public's voracious appetite for revenge by sending youths to prison; and the

Supreme Court has oscillated in its decisions regarding youths—mirroring changes in the political and public atmospheres.

There are three principle types of disputes (conflicts of claims or rights) brought before the court: 1) private dispute, which addresses civil matters; 2) public defendant dispute, which holds government officials and agencies accountable; and 3) public-initiated dispute, whereby the state holds norm violators accountable for their infractions (Goldman and Sarat, 1989). It is to the instance of public-initiated disputes that we turn our attention. The public-initiated dispute is a response by the state (also referred to as "the people") seeking to enforce social norms or to punish violators of those norms (Vago, 1994). The prosecutor, acting on behalf of the state (or people), brings these disputes to the attention of the courts. In more realistic terms, the prosecutor actually controls the court.

The Prosecutor. Prosecutors/district attorneys are a part of the executive branch of government, which makes them separate from the judiciary; they are the principal regulators within the criminal justice system. They have enormous discretionary powers, and the decisions they make are basically unsupervised (Shelden et al., 2008). Whereas law enforcement may be the first line of defense against crime in society, it is the prosecutor who actually establishes the parameters for that defense. The prosecutor has no direct regulatory authority over law enforcement; however, as Katzman (1991: 124) points out, "For an investigator, a primary goal is to develop cases which will be accepted by the prosecutor for prosecution." Thus, without support from the prosecutor, law enforcement has no means to process its product through the courts. Like law enforcement, the prosecution enjoys a substantial amount of discretion in processing criminal cases through the criminal justice system; in most instances, however, the law looks less favorably on the use of discretion employed by the police (LaFave and Israel, 1992). From an idealistic standpoint, the decision to prosecute a case is grounded in the concept of justice. In *Burger v. United States,* it was argued, "The United States Attorney is the representative not of an ordinary party to a controversy, but of a sovereignty whose obligation to govern impartially is as compelling as its obligation to govern at all; and whose interest, therefore, in a criminal prosecution is not that it shall win a case, but that justice shall be done."[62]

Realistically, the decision to prosecute a particular case is based on several factors: 1) the severity of the offense (more serious offenses are likely to be prosecuted), 2) public sentiment (political consideration), and 3) the strength of the evidence (whether the case can result in a conviction). Decisions to prosecute cases are rarely the subject of legal review (Chambliss and Seidman, 1971). The prosecutor with little animus usually carries out the prosecution of defendants; however, there have been instances of prosecutor vindictiveness brought before the higher courts (Zalman and Siegel, 1991).[63]

There is also the issue of the prosecutor exercising discretion not to prosecute. LaFave and Israel (1992) identified five general situations that may influence the prosecutor's decision not to prosecute a case: 1) when the victim expresses a desire that the offender not be prosecuted, 2) when the cost of prosecuting a case is too exorbitant, 3) when prosecution would result in undue harm to an offender, 4) when the offender is capable of assisting other enforcement goals, and 5) when the injury committed by the offender can be resolved without prosecution. Donald Black (1976) suggests that social stratification is a factor associated with the decision either to prosecute or decline prosecution. Others, such as Chambliss and Seidman (1971), Gordon (1990), Quinney (1970, 1974, 1977), Shelden (2010), and Reiman and Leighton (2009), suggest that social class and race are catalysts in the decision either to prosecute or decline prosecution.

Similar to law-enforcement agencies that have adopted special units to respond to the youth gang dilemma, prosecutors' offices have also designed and launched their own special prosecuting units to address this problem. Typically, the duties of these special units include designing and maintaining data banks that track gangs and their members, coordinating their efforts with law enforcement, and, most frequently, practicing vertical prosecution (the prosecutor initially assigned to a gang case remains with that case until final disposition).[64] In a study of gang prosecution in America conducted by the Institute for Law and Justice (1994: 2–13), it was reported that 32 percent of the large jurisdictions studied have gang units, whereas only 5 percent of the smaller jurisdictions have special units to deal with gangs.[65]

Characteristics of the strategies employed by prosecutors against youth gangs may be viewed in the context of either utilizing existing laws or employing a new set of gang statutes. Examples of the old legislation include certification (transferring jurisdiction of the juvenile to adult court), taking advantage of forfeiture laws (confiscation of vehicles used in drive-by shootings), and filing enhancement charges when the opportunity exists (e.g., crimes committed in or near a school, use of a weapon, elderly victim). New gang-directed legislation has provided prosecutors with additional tools. Prosecutors in many jurisdictions now confiscate weapons used by gang members, impose parental liability for damages caused by gang members, enhance penalties for vandalism (graffiti), and prosecute gang members who threaten or use coercive methods of intimidation on members who want to leave the gang or youths who do not join a gang. But new does not necessarily mean better or more efficient. It was found that prosecutors in many jurisdictions with statutory provisions for gangs have a broader range of problems. For example, "Prosecutors in gang-statute states complained in greater proportions about the lack of resources for various gang prosecutions than did their colleagues in nongang-statute states. The sharpest disparity is in lack of early intervention programs for youth at risk of gang involvement" (Institute for Law and Justice, 1994: 2–20).

One of the prototypical prosecutorial efforts was that of Operation Hardcore started in Los Angeles in the 1980s. Central to this is what is known as *vertical prosecution,* where one deputy district attorney is involved with the case from beginning to end. This operation also included special training given to both the police and members of the district attorney's investigation staff, use of witness protection programs, elimination of plea bargaining, use of high bail, and others. As usual, rather narrow and conspiratorial definitions of "gangs" were used. Although the operation in Los Angeles achieved a high rate of convictions (95%) and was copied all over the country, it narrowed the targets to mostly homicide cases. Also, the focus was clearly on special rather than general deterrence (Klein, 1995: 173). The special deterrence emphasis quite naturally resulted in a policy of incapacitation. However, while trying to send a message to gang members and wannabes (e.g., they created posters that read "Gangs—Prison! Think Twice"), there is no evidence that the intended recipients actually received the message, let alone paid any attention.

Unlike law enforcement, which is policy driven (i.e., by creating policies that conform to legislative activity, local government mandates, and prosecutor-established standards), the prosecutor is often guided by political realities or ambitions. The prosecutor is usually an elected public official and is frequently provided with access to an assortment of resources capable of promoting a desired public image that is politically marketable. The numbers of cases prosecuted, with particular attention to conviction rates, are the staples of reelection campaigns for prosecutors. Conversely, low numbers become targets for prosecutor wannabes. Youth gangs provide another commodity in which bargains can be made (plea bargains) and reputations constructed. This commodity is a component of the lower class, which is unable to purchase the "expensive spread" (private attorneys) of legal representation. In a way, prosecutors are analogous to journalists who cover youth gang stories. Neither is accountable for their decisions. Both can be viewed as being in the business (which, incidentally, justifies many types of behaviors) of marketing; one is marketing a tangible product (news), and the other is often marketing a political career.

The Bench.   The courts are presumed to consist of an independent judge applying preexisting legal norms after adversary proceedings in order to achieve a dichotomous decision in which one of the parties was assigned the legal right and the other found wrong (Shapiro, 1986: 1).

Beyond this idealistic perception is another collection of court functions. The courts legitimize government and its social-control apparatus—the criminal justice system (Heydebrand and Seron, 1990; Shelden et al., 2008). The media's presentation of the notion of judicial independence and adversarial proceedings is far from reality (Haltom and McCann 2004; Jewkes, 2011). According to Amy Bach's recent research:

> At times, judges abandon their neutrality and step into the adversarial void, acting like prosecutors, forcing defendants either to take a deal or wait in jail for a trial date. That, or they deny a defendant his rights altogether. (2009: 7)

In addition, the court has other functions, such as serving as trial referee (Frankel, 1975) and providing for the routinization of administrative legal procedures such as uncontested adoption cases and previously negotiated plea bargains (Spitzer, 1982) and lawmaking (Holmes, 1881; Shapiro, 1986; Vago, 1994). Many of these functions are relative to historical epochs (Hurst, 1950). In fact, the courts may be viewed as a forum that engages in the reification of the utility of criminal law. Reiman suggests:

> The criminal law enshrines institutions as equivalent to the minimum requirements for any decent social existence—and it brands the individual who attacks those institutions as one who has declared war on all organized society and who must therefore be met with the weapons of war. (Reiman, 1993: 141)

Judges, as a whole, attempt to present an image of objectivity and maintain a posture that is somewhat distanced from the youth gang issue. However, on an individual basis, some judges have begun to take a broader view of youth gangs.

The juvenile court, sometimes called family court, was founded on the principle that children must be treated differently from adults when their behavior is antithetical to standards adopted by society. In a quixotic sense, this court would provide the best of both worlds: 1) due process protection and 2) care and treatment during the dispositional phase. Of course, this has not always been the case (Faust and Brantingham, 1979). It was established that, through the juvenile court, every effort would be exhausted to return the delinquent child to a socially accepted status (1979). Of course, middle-class philanthropists were designated to establish the criteria for social acceptability (Platt, 1977; Shelden, 2010, 2012). Through *parens patriae*,[66] the state assumed the role of parent, acting on behalf of the delinquent child, and the juvenile court judge represented the state. Julian W. Mack notes:

> The problem for determination by the judge is not, has this boy or girl committed a specific wrong, but what is he, how has he become what he is, and what had best be done in his interest and in the interest of the state to save him from a downward career? (1989)

Mack also notes that the child who must be brought into court should, of course, be made to know that he is faced with the power of the state, but he should at the same time, and more emphatically, be made to feel that he is the object of its care and solicitude (1989)

In a similar vein, more than 60 years ago, Walter H. Beckham suggested:

> It should be understood that a juvenile court proceeding is not a trial of anyone on criminal charges but, according to the laws of most states, is an "investigation" into the conduct of a young citizen to determine not whether punishment should be inflicted, but what action or program should be adopted for the welfare of the child. (Beckham, 1989)[67]

Times have obviously changed.

Today, there is a tendency, particularly in the case of alleged youth gang members, to change the adjudication jurisdiction. In some states, a juvenile judge makes the determination whether the accused 1) committed a serious offense, in which case she or he is certified as an adult and referred to adult court for prosecution, or 2) can benefit from available rehabilitation facilities and programs established for juveniles. However, as noted at the beginning of this chapter, many state legislatures have removed this function from the juvenile courts. The difference between juvenile and adult jurisdiction over the individual is significant, particularly with the current application of capital punishment in most states. In the juvenile court, the child is subject to a relatively short period of incarceration, whereas in the adult court, the same child faces long-term incarceration or even death. Every state allows for transferring juveniles to adult court, some as young as 14 years of age or younger (Shelden, 2012: 386). Moreover, race appears to be a major factor in the certification process (2012: 387).

During a discussion with a midwestern district court judge about the certification process of youth gang members, the following information was revealed:

> I was trained in the logic and rationale of the law. Those are the two principle abstractions that accompanied me to the bench. Now, I see these youngsters [gang members] standing before me, and I realize the ineffectiveness of the system I have supported all my life. Although I am bound by statute to sentence many of these defendants to prison, I understand that it is to no avail. They simply return to the environment that manufactured the behavior, which brought them to me in the first place. Society has elected to accept this cycle; this defies all logic and rationale.[68]

When asked why society continues embracing its current retributive position, the judge replied:

> I want to believe that most of society is ignorant of the conditions in these environments; in which case they may be excused, in this instance, for their ignorance. In this instance, the solution lies with educating society. On the other hand, it may be that people who have the capacity to act in a positive manner do not feel obliged to act, and that means people will not be apprised of the situation. Of course, there is also the possibility that people just don't care anymore. (Brown, 1998)

As previously stated, the Supreme Court stands at the apex of America's judicial system. This judicial body is entrusted with the responsibility to ascertain the factual, procedural, and legal basis of criminal charges while simultaneously ensuring that stipulations set forth in the U.S. Constitution are observed by the entire court system. In other words, the latitude allowed and established by the Supreme Court operationally confines the lower courts. Thus, the Supreme Court has jurisdiction to review, either on appeal or by writ of *certiorari*, all the decisions of the lower federal courts and many of the decisions of the highest state courts (Scheb and Scheb, 2012: 38).

There is another aspect of the Supreme Court—a more politicized element that is generally masked from public consideration. This component is obscured behind an illusion of preoccupation with deference to evidence and fact-finding; both dimensions are subject to pressure from the legislative branch of government as well as from within the Supreme Court itself. The Supreme Court may reverse lower-court decisions on the facts in criminal cases but *only* when the lower court's record contains no evidence to support the conviction. The reason for this reluctance to overturn convictions is that the principal job of an appellate court is lawmaking.

The Supreme Court continually seeks to reiterate its connection with the basis of all judicial legitimacy: dispute settlement. As Shapiro notes:

> So long as the appellate courts do their lawmaking under the guise of doing substantial justice between man and man in particular cases—and they must do this if they are to be perceived as and supported as courts— they will keep clawing their way back towards the facts. (1986: 42–43)

Although the Supreme Court is frequently involved in political issues, it is not necessarily considered a factor in politics because of its low-key posture as an institution that enjoys much public support, even though the majority of the cases brought before the Supreme Court are not widely publicized in the general media (Zalman and Siegel, 1991). Moreover, the Supreme Court is most likely to cater to cases submitted for review by the government. O'Brien points out that

> … the government has a distinct advantage in getting cases accepted, but its higher rate is not surprising. Since the creation of the office in 1870, the solicitor general of the United States assumed responsibility for representing the federal government. From the Court's perspective, the solicitor general performs an invaluable service. He screens all pro- spective federal appeals and petitions and decides which should be taken to the Court…. Since he typically argues all government cases before the Court, the solicitor general has intimate knowledge of the justices and has been characterized as the Court's "ninth-and-a-half" member…. By contrast, indigents like Gideon are unlikely to have their cases given full consideration. (1990: 249–250)

The Supreme Court, responding largely to the demands of the criminal jus- tice apparatus and perhaps under political pressure because of public outcry, has heard cases pertaining to gangs. Supreme Court rulings date back at least to 1939. In the *Lanzetta et al. v. New Jersey* case, the Supreme Court overturned the conviction on the basis of ambiguity of the concept of *gang*, and its depen- dent term *gangster*, in the New Jersey law.[69] This definitional problem with the concept of gang would cause legislatures in the 1980s and 1990s to reconsider their statutory definitions of similar concepts. In another case, *Abel v. United States*, the question was raised whether belonging to a gang or organization that was involved in illegal activity could stand alone to justify criminal conviction.[70] The Supreme Court ruled that one might not be convicted merely for belonging to an organization that advocates illegal activity. To get a conviction, the gov- ernment must provide evidence that the individual knows of, and personally ac- cepts, the tenets of the organization or gang. To a large degree, the Supreme Court has allowed legislative bodies to redefine the law—tailoring it to meet society's demand for vengeance against criminal youths.

SUMMARY

The legal system's approach to controlling or eliminating gangs appears to be on the same track as that system's approach to controlling or eliminating illegal drugs. It seems as though much of the legislation that attempts to target gang activity is done so without any real understanding of youth gangs. For example, more prisons will simply mean that there will be more people in prison. When a gang member is imprisoned, similar to the incarceration of drug dealers, another takes his place on the street. During a two-year study of 79 gang members in Detroit, it was found that nearly 86 percent were not worried about legal sanctions or prison. More than 90 percent indicated that they were not particularly concerned about their own safety related to gang violence or encounters with authorities. These data are not surprising given that almost one-third of the subjects defined having fun as making money (which should be alarming when one considers that these youngsters ranged in age from 13 to 17).[71]

Most experts on youth gangs would agree that to understand this topic one must have a solid understanding of the culture of youth gangs. This understanding must include an understanding of the neighborhood and the broader culture. Perhaps the most disheartening aspect of the current gang legislation is the apparent ignorance on behalf of legislators regarding *culture*. Within the more than 600 pages of legislation reviewed, the term *culture* was absent, with the exception of one reference to the term *subculture* in the Louisiana legislation, and one reference to *race and culture* in Iowa's legislation related to police training.[72] Perhaps the failure of the war on gangs is a victim of legislative apathy or ignorance to culture.

If the goals of legislation, law enforcement, and the courts have been to control or eliminate youth gang activity across American, they have failed. In fact, the argument could be made that the legal approach has only expanded the prison population and actually promoted the proliferation of youth gangs. The foundation of these goals appears to have ignored the root factors that often influence the proliferation of gang activities, such as education, socioeconomic status, employment, and so on. For example, Oregon has passed gang-related legislation in the areas of drive-by shooting, unlawful use of a weapon, gang prevention, specific definitions of gangs, gangs and schools, and graffiti.[73] In a 2006 report from the Oregon Attorney General's Office, it was reported:

> Street gangs are responsible for a wide variety of crimes throughout the state and continue to pose a threat to citizens. With increasing frequency, some street gangs appear to be controlled by prison gangs and have been known to work with other organized criminal groups such as Mexican drug cartels and Asian and Eurasian organized crime groups. These groups often use street gangs to transport narcotics and carry out low-level crimes (Myers, 2006: 11).

In 2007, co-author Brown conducted a study of the Marion County Jail in Salem, Oregon, with 565 prisoners (87% response rate) participating. Of the participants, 103 (18.23%) of them (88 males and 15 females) said they had been involved with a youth gang, and 76 (13.45%) said they were actual gang members (75 males and 1 female). Among those who had been involved with a youth gang, 16 percent were American Indians, 16 percent were black, 32 percent were Hispanic, and nearly 43 percent were white. Those participants who said they were actual members of a gang were 18 percent American Indian, 8 percent black, 17 percent Hispanic, and 41 percent white. Fewer than 20 percent of those who had been involved with a gang and 17 percent of the gang members had received a high school diploma. When asked about their early family socioeconomic status, nearly 24 percent of the participants who said they were gang members said their families lived below the poverty line, while nearly 62 percent indicated they came from working-class families. When asked about their family's current socioeconomic status, almost 49 percent responded "below the poverty line," followed by 33 percent who said their current family's socioeconomic status was working class. Nearly 40 percent of those who had ever been involved with a gang and 54 percent of those who were gang members said they were unemployed prior to their arrest. Just over 55 percent of the gang member participants in the study were in jail waiting for court on felony charges, while nearly 45 percent were serving jail time for misdemeanor offenses.

Over 93 percent agreed with the statement that being a gang member is the same as being a family member. The majority of those participants who said they were gang members demonstrated a high level of commitment to the gang. There were a variety of answers when asked why they had become a gang member, but the primary reason was belonging. Most of the participants who were gang members became members following recruitment by relatives or close friends. Most of the gang member participants joined a gang when they were between the ages of 12 and 15 years old. All participant gang members said they had been involved in violence, and 58 (76.32%) participants said they had been victims of gang violence. Thirty gang member participants said they had seen a dead body resulting from gang violence, and 75 had witnessed a serious injury resulting from gang violence. Less than one-half of the gang member participants ever thought about leaving the gang, and when asked what would be necessary to persuade them to leave the gang, 60.53 percent answered "nothing," while 30.26 percent answered "a real alternative."[74]

Recent research by Cheryl Maxson and colleagues (2011) on the California Youth Authority echoes the previous findings. They found that 72 percent of the youth confined were gang members. The vast majority (90%) are black or Hispanic males. Only 36 percent had graduated from high school or received their GED. Three-fourths had family members who had been incarcerated. The median age of these gang members was 19. One has to wonder what kind of future awaits them and their counterparts in Salem, Oregon.

This chapter closes with the notion that perhaps the legal apparatus should seriously consider practical alternatives for individuals who are considering gang involvement. Understandably, those alternatives are likely not as "glamorous" as the current activities employed to curtail gang activities, but the overall outcomes are likely to be beneficial to society and to those gang members who seek a real alternative.

NOTES

1. Brown takes these quotes from an interview conducted during a study of youth gangs in Detroit, Michigan (1998).

2. In a campaign for county sheriff in Las Vegas, Nevada, in the early 1990s, the two major candidates focused on the local gang problem, almost to the total exclusion of any other major problem related to crime. The impression was given that gangs were responsible for almost all of the crime problems in this county, which is patently untrue. Nevertheless, these candidates kept trying to outdo each other with their own versions of a gang policy.

3. Interview by Brown of *Cash Flow Posse* members (1998).

4. Alaska § 12.45.037; Indiana § 35-50-2-15; Nevada § 193.168

5. California Ed Code § 35183

6. Tennessee § 49-6-4215

7. Nevada § 392.4635

8. Florida Contraband Forfeiture Act, s. 932.704

9. Nevada § 179.121

10. Ohio § 2923.44

11. Arizona § 41-191.07

12. Colorado § 22-25-104.5; Connecticut § 10-16b; Illinois § 20 ILCS 2605/2605-35

13. Michigan § 432.212 South Carolina § 16-8-340

14. Washington § 43.310.020

15. Arizona § 8-327

16. California Penal Code § 13826.2

17. Georgia § 16-15-9

18. Georgia § 16-15-3

19. Washington § 9.94A.833

20. Alaska § 11.81.900

21. Arizona: Arizona § 13-105

22. Colorado § 22-25-103

23. Delaware 11 § 616

24. South Dakota § 22-10A-1

25. Florida § 874.03; Idaho § 18-8502; Illinois § 725 ILCS 172/5-5; Texas Civ. Prac. & Rem. § 125.061

26. Illinois § 740 ILCS 147/15

27. Illinois § 740 ILCS 147/15

28. Nevada § 244.35705

29. Texas Civ. Prac. & Rem. § 125.070

30. Wisconsin § 895.444

31. Nevada § 206.005

32. New York Penal § 145.60

33. Washington § 4.24.330

34. New Jersey § 2C: 17-3

35. California Government Code § 38772; Hawaii § 577-3.5

36. District of Columbia § 22-3335

37. Georgia § 17-15A-4

38. Indiana § 31-30-1-4

39. Missouri § 578.423

40. Tennessee § 37-1-134

41. Texas Fam. Code § 54.0491

42. Minnesota § 617.92 Public Nuisance

43. California Government Code § 38771-38775

44. Florida § 893.138

45. Iowa § 657.2

46. Mississippi § 97-44-15

47. North Carolina § 14-50.24

48. Connecticut § 7-294l

49. Iowa § 80B.11

50. Rhode Island § 42-28.2-8.2

51. Texas Government Code § 508.1141

52. Utah § 76-9-907

53. The lead author was part of an evaluation team in Las Vegas in the 1990s for a program called Weed and Seed. He attended almost every meeting of the "task force," not unlike that described by Klein and Maxson, and came away with the same observations, especially the telling of "war stories."

54. This and subsequent quotes from police officers are from interviews by Brown during a study in Detroit, Michigan (1998).

55. Interview by Brown, at a suburban police station in Detroit (1998).

56. For an excellent critique of the official response to gangs in Nevada, see McCorkle and Miethe (2001).

57. Data provided to co-author Brown by a Detroit, Michigan, police department (1998).

58. Interview by Brown, 1998.

59. FBI Press Release, October 21, 2011, *2011 National Gang Threat Assessment Issued.* http://www.fbi.gov/news/pressrel/press-releases/2011-national-gang-threat-assessment-issued (December 11, 2011).

60. FBI: http://www.fbi.gov/about-us/investigate/vc_majorthefts/gangs (December 11, 2011).

61. FBI: http://www.fbi.gov/about-us/investigate/vc_majorthefts/gangs/recent-statistics (December 11, 2011).

62. 295 U.S. 78, 55 S. Ct. 629, 79 L.Ed. 1314, 1935.

63. See *Blackledge v. Perry* (417 U.S. 21, 94 S.Ct. 2098, 40 L.Ed. 628, 1974).

64. Prosecutor-led anti-gang programs include vertical prosecution, special gang units or prosecutors, victim/witness services, aggressive prosecution (i.e., the Street Terrorism Enforcement and Prevention [STEP] Acts that provide for sentencing enhancements

and civil forfeiture of street gang assets and criminal proceeds), and written policies and procedures to ensure cases are prosecuted efficiently and consistently for gang-related crimes (Gramckow and Tompkins, 1999).

65. The Los Angeles prosecutor's office was found to have the largest gang unit (48 lawyers).

66. *Parens patriae* is the philosophy that the state can assume the role of parent when parents are deemed unfit. For a detailed discussion of this philosophy within the context of the emergence of the juvenile justice system, see Shelden (2008).

67. Reprinted in McCarthy and Carr, 1989.

68. Interview by Brown with a Midwestern district court judge (1998).

69. 306 U.S. 451, 59 S.Ct. 618, 1939.

70. *Abel v. U.S.,* 362 U.S. 217, 80 S.Ct. 683, 1960.

71. Study by Brown of Detroit, Michigan, gang members (1998).

72. Louisiana § 15:1422. Legislative Findings and Declaration; Iowa § 80B.11.

73. Oregon § 163.707. Forfeiture of Motor Vehicle Used in Drive-By Shooting; Oregon § 166.220. Unlawful Use of Weapon; Oregon § 336.109. Policy to Reduce Gang Involvement, Violent Activities, and Drug Abuse; Oregon § 164.381. Definitions; Oregon § 137.131. Community Service As Condition of Probation for Offense Involving Graffiti; Oregon § 164.383. Unlawfully Applying Graffiti; Oregon § 164.386. Unlawfully Possessing Graffiti Implement; Oregon § 164.388. Preemption; Oregon § 419C.461. Disposition for Graffiti Related Offenses.

74. These data were included in a report submitted to the Marion County Sheriff's Office by William Brown in August 2007.

10

Community and National
Intervention Strategies

INTRODUCTION

It has become evident that many—if not most—traditional approaches to the prevention and treatment of gangs have not fared too well. It is time to think creatively. The authors have been involved in the study and teaching of the subject of crime and delinquency for more than 40 years (collectively much longer!), and we are convinced that some very fundamental changes need to be made in the way we live and think before we see any significant decrease in the gang problem. Adults have referred to the "problems" with youths in general—and gang members in particular—with such value-laden questions as "What's wrong with kids these days?"[1] The implication is that youths in trouble need to change their attitudes, their behaviors, their lifestyles, their methods of thinking, and so on. It seems that it is always *they* who have to change.

THE NEED FOR A NEW PARADIGM

Decades ago, a book by Thomas Kuhn, called *The Structure of Scientific Revolutions*, was published (1970). In this book, he argued that in the sciences certain paradigms or models serve to guide those who practice the scientific method. A paradigm can be defined as a collection of beliefs shared by scientists. They include general agreements, models, or theories about how problems are to be understood and resolved. These theories or models are used to measure success at explaining things, and they make note of certain anomalies that come up and can be used to guide improvements to the theory.

However, there are certain occasions when some of these anomalies may lead to what can be called a crisis in the paradigm itself. The prevailing paradigm cannot provide the answers to the questions being asked or problems to be solved; this is what Einstein meant with the quote that began this chapter. These are called "revolutions" in scientific thinking, and they usually lead to rather dramatic shifts in the thinking about a phenomenon. Classic examples include the discoveries of Copernicus, who challenged the conventional paradigm of viewing the sun revolving around the earth; Darwin's work on evolution; the work of Isaac Newton and Galileo; and the work of Noam Chomsky (often called the "Chomskian Revolution") in the field of linguistics. The development of Renaissance Humanism and the Reformation also come to mind. More recent examples include the Human Genome Project.

During these "revolutions," the prevailing paradigm always sort of runs into a brick wall in that there are some anomalies that cannot be explained via the prevailing models or paradigms. The answers to these tough questions must come out of a totally different paradigm, a new way of thinking. These paradigms come from people who think creatively and are unconstrained by convention.

The myopic view that youths are the only ones who need to change is usually accompanied with various labels that clearly describe the source of the problem. The labels keep changing, along with changing times. As Jerome Miller has noted, we began with "possessed" youths in the seventeenth century, moved to the "rabble" or "dangerous classes" in the eighteenth and late nineteenth centuries, and to the "moral imbeciles" and the "constitutional psychopathic inferiors" of the early twentieth century. We continued in the twentieth century with the "psychopath" of the 1940s, the "sociopath" of the 1950s, and more recently the "compulsive delinquent," the "unsocialized aggressive" (or even the "socialized aggressive"), and finally the "bored" delinquent. "With the growth of professionalism," continues Miller, "the number of labels has multiplied exponentially" (Miller, 1998: 234).

Miller asserts that the problem with these labels is that they maintain the existing order, buffering it from threats that might arise from its own internal contradictions. They reassure

> ... that the fault lies in the warped offender and takes everyone else off the hook. Moreover, it enables the professional diagnostician to enter the scene or withdraw at will, wearing success like a halo and placing failure around the neck of the client like a noose. (Miller, 1998)

More importantly, the labels reinforce the belief that harsh punishment works, especially the kind of punishment that includes some form of incarceration so that the offender is placed out of sight and, not coincidentally, out of mind.

A recurring problem in juvenile justice reform—and with other "reforms"—is that after so much political maneuvering, numerous reports and hearings in Senate chambers, and announcements that "change is coming," the end result is that nothing much has changed or that the changes are cosmetic. A review of juvenile justice "reforms" in San Francisco during the 1990s illustrates this problem. Males and Macallair note, "Despite the city's investment in juvenile justice reform from 1996–1999, there is no evidence of system change. Instead, it appears that new services and programs were simply marginalized. Marginalization occurs when new programs are designed as simple adjuncts to current operations, rather than intended to replace core system elements. San Francisco juvenile justice reforms during the period of this study did not reduce detention rates or disproportionate minority confinement. Instead, a wider pool of lower-risk youths was simply absorbed into the system in order to keep the juvenile hall population filled and the rolls of new programs filled." In other words, the end result was merely "net widening" (Macallair and Males, 2004).

GANGS ARE NOT JUST CRIMINAL JUSTICE PROBLEMS

Gangs are not strictly law-enforcement problems or, for that matter, criminal justice problems. Rather, they represent a problem that needs to be addressed at both the community and the societal level. As Cummings and Monti (1993: 310) note, economic issues are paramount because "the prevalence of gangs in nearly every American city is related to the same recessionary and industrial changes transforming urban and public policy." More recently, James Diego Vigil has advocated what he calls a "balance approach," which utilizes "prevention, intervention, and law enforcement as needed" (Vigil, 2010: ix). Notice that when referring to law enforcement, he said "as needed." As we will eventually note in this chapter and the concluding chapter, none of the solutions offered during the past several decades have even attempted to address these larger issues.

There is little question that unemployment and underemployment are the residuals after industry has abandoned a community. Many of our cities have suffered from the loss of industry, which has impacted minorities more than any other group. As the industries depart, middle-class workers move from the cities, leaving behind those who cannot afford to follow the job market, for at least a portion of these businesses relocate in outlying areas, along with the tax base. As poverty begins to encompass whole neighborhoods, urban blight and decay occur, providing a fertile breeding ground for the underclass youths to form gangs in answer to their despair, both economic and personal. As we saw in Chapter 8, the current recession has aggravated an already precarious situation. In fact, in most inner cities, it amounts to a depression rather than a recession, as unemployment is around 50 percent in some areas (Caldwell, 2010).

Further complicating the economic scenario is the adoption by many metropolitan areas of a gentrification policy. In these cases, the poor are further displaced as the middle class and wealthy return to the inner city and begin to restore and rehabilitate property. As the real estate values increase, the poor are driven farther from the core of public services designed in large part to accommodate them. The lack of resources to compete for the improved properties drives a solid economic wedge into poverty-ridden families, causing additional despair and frustration for the young people in these families. It is no wonder that these same youths resort to the sale and distribution of illegal drugs as a response.

During the late 1980s and early 1990s, the prevalence of guns in the hands of children, the apparent randomness of gang violence and drive-by shootings, the disproportionate racial minority role in homicides, and media depictions of callous youths' gratuitous violence inflamed public fear. Politicians exploited those fears, decried a coming generation of so-called "superpredators" suffering from moral poverty, and demonized young people to muster support for policies under which youths can be transferred to criminal court and incarcerated. Some analysts predicted a demographic time bomb of youth crime in the near future to which minority juveniles will contribute disproportionately (Bennett, DiIulio, and Walters, 1996; Fox, 1996; Zimring, 1998: 208). However, this contention was been refuted by subsequent research (Elikann, 1999; Males, 1999).

As we noted in previous editions of this book, the punitive model for dealing with gangs enjoys widespread support, and such support continues unabated with increasing expenditures for the criminal justice system (especially prisons) and, after 9/11, even more expenditures for security—in this case, Homeland Security. As of 2007 (latest figures available as of October 2011), expenditures for the criminal justice system are about $228 billion per year, up from about $11 billion per year in the early 1970s.[2] Expenditures for Homeland Security for fiscal year 2011 are $56.3 billion.[3] Despite these expenditures, the problems causing gangs continue, with no end in sight. It is also clearly evident that within this model, there is not only little rehabilitation occurring but also no significant positive change. The conditions within which gangs emerge have changed little since Thrasher (1927) wrote about them in the 1920s. If anything, they have worsened.

About 20 years ago, Walter Miller noted that there was an absence of any sort of national policy addressing the gang problem. At that time, Miller stated that this country "has failed to develop a comprehensive gang control strategy. The problem is viewed in local and parochial terms instead of from a national perspective. Programs are implemented in the absence of demonstrably valid theoretical rationales" (Miller, 1990: 274). While this remains a source of concern, at about the same time Spergel and Grossman (1997) noted that there was little systematic independent evaluation to measure the effectiveness of the programs; the federal government had initiated and completed a number of evaluations to measure program effectiveness and had established a National Youth Gang Center under the direction of noted gang researcher Irving Spergel. Attempts to draft a national policy were being made, but nothing much came of it. Vigil's quote at the start of Chapter 9 summarized nicely what we have at the start of the second decade of the twenty-first century.

However, Vigil does present a number of promising programs to deal with gangs. Later in this chapter, we will bring together a collection of general recommendations on the national level that address some of the issues raised by Miller. As has been noted at several junctures throughout this book, the problem of gangs cannot be addressed without dealing with much larger social issues facing American society. Before dealing with these more general issues, an overview will be presented of the varied gang-intervention strategies that have been offered historically.

TYPES OF INTERVENTION STRATEGIES

The discussion of intervention strategies will be divided into two sections. The first section begins with a general overview of several major categories of responses to the gang problem. The first typology to be discussed is based on the research conducted by Spergel and Curry during the 1980s. Following the outline of Spergel and Curry's typology, community-based responses—or what Spergel and Curry call community organization, social intervention, and opportunities provisions—will be reviewed. The previous chapter dealt with the legal response to the gang problem—or what Spergel and Curry call suppression efforts.

Spergel and Curry's Typology of Interventions

During the late 1980s, University of Chicago researchers surveyed 254 agencies (criminal justice and community agencies, along with schools) in 45 cities (Spergel and Curry, 1990). In this survey, they identified two major types of cities, based on the extent of the gang problem in the area. One type they called **chronic gang problem cities,** and the other they called **emerging gang problem cities.** As suggested by these terms, the former are those cities (e.g., Los Angeles, Chicago, and New York) that have had gang problems for many years, while the latter apply to cities (e.g., Milwaukee, Phoenix, and Atlanta) that have experienced such problems only in recent years (although not included in their survey, Las Vegas would be classified as an emerging gang problem city). The distinction between these two types of cities becomes important when considering the effectiveness of the various strategies used to deal with the current gang problem.

In their survey, Spergel and Curry found that the strategies used in these areas to deal with the problem of gangs could be grouped into four broad areas, which they labeled as 1) community organization, 2) social intervention, 3) opportunities provision, and 4) suppression or law-enforcement efforts.

These four strategies were found to be the most commonly used in the cities surveyed. In fact, they represent virtually every known type of method that has been tried in the past, is currently being used, and will likely be used in the future. It is within these broad areas that the risk factors noted previously can be reduced and the protective factors enhanced.

Community Organization.   This strategy refers to efforts to enhance, modify, or change relationships among different groups and organizations within a city to better cope with various problems. The researchers found that respondents in the areas surveyed used such terms as *networking* to refer to this specific strategy. Essentially, such a strategy involves cooperation among the community organizations, to take advantage of the various skills and knowledge such groups have and to try to avoid duplication of services. It is an attempt to combine all available resources to solve a community problem involving all citizens, not just those directly affected.

Spergel and Curry identified such specific strategies as mobilizing the community, building community trust, educating the community, involving the schools, and involving parent groups in community programs.

Social Intervention.   Within this category are some very common methods that have been used for many years to deal with youth and related problems. They include the very popular (and, incidentally, not very successful) strategies of youth outreach and street-work counseling. This general strategy has been defined as follows: "It is the systematic effort of an agency worker, through social work or treatment techniques within the neighborhood context, to help a group of young people who are described as delinquent or potentially delinquent to achieve a conventional adaptation" (Spergel and Curry, 1990: 295).

Social intervention is much broader in scope than the traditional youth outreach efforts. Among the more common strategies identified by the respondents to the survey by Spergel and Curry included the following: crisis intervention, providing role models for youths, inter-gang mediation, referrals for services, counseling of gang members, drug-use prevention and treatment, helping members leave the gang, and more general diversion and outreach activities. The general goal of social intervention is "to change the values of youths in such a way as to make gang involvement less likely" (Spergel and Curry, 1990: 296).

Opportunities Provision.   This strategy is an attempt to provide jobs, job training, and education, particularly for the most at-risk youths. Within this category, Spergel and Curry found "efforts to stimulate the development of new and improved schools, special training, job programs, and business and industry involvement in the social and economic advancement of people, including and targeting gang youth" (Spergel and Curry, 1990: 297). More-specific strategies include helping prepare youths to enter the job market (e.g., teaching interviewing skills and how to write a resume), job training, placement of youths in jobs (e.g., via a youth employment agency), and assisting youths with school problems (e.g., special tutors and alternative schooling).

Suppression.   The term *suppression* is used by Spergel and Curry to describe a variety of strictly law-enforcement strategies, including special patrols by police gang units, special prosecution efforts within the district attorney's office, legislation that targets gang activities, and development and implementation of information systems (e.g., the GREAT program, which stands for Gang Reporting, Evaluation, and Tracking).

The Perceived Effectiveness of These Strategies

The respondents in the survey conducted by Spergel and Curry and their colleagues were asked to rank each of these strategies according to which was most often used and which they perceived to be the most effective. The effectiveness of these strategies is based on the opinions or perceptions of those responding to Spergel and Curry's survey, rather than on empirical evidence. The effectiveness varied according to whether the respondents lived in a chronic gang problem city or an emerging gang problem city. In emerging gang problem cities, the perception was that the most effective strategies were the various efforts classified as community organization. Ranked second in effectiveness was that of opportunities provision, with social intervention and suppression ranked third and fourth, respectively. From a statistical standpoint (based on the method used in this survey—analysis of covariance), only community organization was found to be statistically significant.

In chronic gang problem cities, the most effective methods were found within opportunities provision, with community organization ranked second. Ranked third and fourth were suppression and social intervention, respectively. From a statistical standpoint, only opportunities provision was statistically significant.

This survey shows that if communities rely solely on suppression efforts, the gang problem will not be reduced to any significant degree, regardless of whether the area is a chronic or an emerging gang problem city. Organizing communities and providing opportunities to at-risk youths appear to be the most promising strategies.

What is important to stress is that various components of each of these major strategies should be used in combination. This is because it is erroneous to assume from the data presented by Spergel and Curry that an *entire category* of various strategies will not work. Each specific type of strategy needs to be examined within each broad category to see which one is most effective.

This type of research has not been done as yet. It may be found, for example, that certain specific kinds of law-enforcement procedures are more effective than others (e.g., various forms of community policing may be more effective than traditional police procedures) or that certain specific types of social intervention may be more effective than traditional youth outreach (e.g., providing role models or inter-gang mediation may be very effective).

Each community needs to study in detail each kind of strategy in use to see which is most effective (see the discussion of the risk-focused approach in a later section of this chapter). The effectiveness of a specific strategy may vary according to the type of community where it is used (e.g., providing role models may be more effective than gang mediation in Las Vegas, but the opposite may be true in Phoenix). Such a research effort must necessarily arise from a strong mobilization effort to organize a community and combine both human and non-human resources.

Note that the preceding section originally appeared in the first edition of this book, published in 1997. Most of the research that went into the first edition culminated around 1995, so it has been 17 years since the section was written. Since this time, the bulk of the "programs" have fallen either into the "suppression" category or have had a law-enforcement presence. Unfortunately, as Klein and Maxson review six major gang control programs across the county, they find little to be positive about. We will briefly review their assessment shortly.

Other Intervention Typologies

One of the most comprehensive overviews of delinquency-prevention programs is the text by Dryfoos (1990). In this book, she addresses four interrelated problems: delinquency, teen pregnancy, drug abuse, and school failure.

Although not aimed specifically at gangs, these problems and program typologies can nevertheless be easily adapted to the gang problem. Her review of the research found that the majority of prevention programs fall into one of three broad categories: 1) early childhood and family interventions, 2) school-based interventions, and 3) community-based and/or multicomponent interventions (Dryfoos, 1990: 116). Programs that fall within the early childhood and family intervention category include two major types: 1) preschool/Head Start programs and 2) parent training/support programs. Programs found within the school-based intervention category include three main types: 1) curricula, 2) organization of the school (teacher training, school team, and alternative schools), and 3) special services (counseling and mentoring programs, health services, and volunteer work). Community-based interventions include three main types: 1) school–community collaboration programs, 2) community education, and 3) multicomponent comprehensive programs.

Several recent studies have confirmed the success of early intervention programs such as Head Start and similar preschool programs. A follow-up of the original participants in the Ypsilanti Head Start program to the age of 40 found continued success for the treatment group, including higher income and lower involvement in the criminal justice system (Belfield et al., 2006; Schweinhart et al., 2005). For instance, a longitudinal study of a preschool intervention program in Chicago of more than 1,500 low-income youths (93% of whom were black) found that there were significant reductions in not only the incidence of delinquency but its frequency and severity, by age 18 (Mann and Reynolds, 2006). The most comprehensive was a meta-analysis of 123 comparative studies of early childhood interventions. Positive effects were found for children who attend a preschool program prior to entering kindergarten. The most significant impact was on the children's cognitive behaviors, social skills, and school progress—all of which are correlated with reduced rates of delinquency (Camilli et al., 2010).

Often overlooked partners in combating gang problems are social service agencies, which are often the only point of contact with troubled youth. These agencies, including state and local juvenile justice agencies, continue to target males for programmatic services as their numbers demand attention. Again, unfortunately, for many females social service agencies provide scant aid; the only help they may receive from these agencies is pregnancy counseling. Many of these agencies have recognized that because recipients of their programs are frequently gang members or in a family with gang members, appropriate services for this population are necessary. Mandated services and funding resources help to drive these agencies to address the problem.

Intervention programs must begin with some general assumptions or basic principles to serve as both a practical and a theoretical guide. The Dryfoos over- view is one such example of linking interventions with empirical data on the various risk factors associated with delinquency and related problems. Another example was provided by the Office of Juvenile Justice and Delinquency Preven- tion back in the early 1990s in its review of efforts to combat serious, violent, and chronic juvenile offenders (Wilson and Howell, 1994). Wilson and Howell note that the research on these types of offenders has concluded that there are several interrelated social and personal factors that serve as basic correlates. These include delinquent peer groups, poor school performance, living in high-crime neighborhoods, weak family attachments, lack of consistent discipline within the home, and physical or sexual abuse. Prevention programs should obviously address these factors. A nationwide comprehensive strategy must follow these five guidelines: 1) Strengthen the family; 2) support core institutions (schools, churches, and community organizations); 3) promote delinquency prevention in general (because it is the most cost-effective method of dealing with the prob- lem); 4) intervene immediately and effectively when delinquent behavior occurs; and 5) identify and control the small group of serious, violent, and chronic juve- nile offenders.

Borrowing heavily from the social development model devised by Hawkins and Catalano, the Office of Juvenile Justice and Delinquency Prevention suggests that programs should focus on the key risk factors that strongly correlate with serious and chronic delinquency. Five major types of risk factors are identified: 1) individual characteristics, 2) family influences, 3) school experiences, 4) peer- group influences, and 5) neighborhood and community influences. Within each of these five key factors, several different types of programs are identified (Hawkins, Catalano, and Miller, 1992).

One of the major problems with many community-based interventions is the lack of any consistent theoretical rationale behind the programs implemen- ted. Without a stated rationale, it is difficult to evaluate such programs. One promising theoretical rationale is the risk-focused approach discussed in the next section.

A RISK-FOCUSED APPROACH

Risk-focused prevention is based on the assumption that trying to prevent a problem from occurring in the first place is better than trying to deal with it after the fact (similar to the old saying "an ounce of prevention is worth a pound of cure"). More specifically, this approach suggests that the most effective way to prevent a problem is, first, to identify the factors that tend to increase the probability or risk that the problem will emerge in the first place and, second, to find methods to reduce the risks, thereby increasing the protective or resiliency factors. One of the most noteworthy examples is the Seattle Social Development Project. This project is described as follows:

> The Seattle Social Development Project (SSDP) was a multi-year, school-based intervention that used a risk-reduction and skill-development strategy to improve outcomes for participating children and youths. The program was guided theoretically by the social development model, which hypothesizes that youths who are provided with opportunities for greater involvement with their schools and families, who develop the competency or skills they need for fuller participation with their schools and families, and for whom skillful participation is constantly reinforced, ultimately develop strong bonds with their families and schools. Further, the model proposes that these strong bonds set children on a positive developmental trajectory, resulting in more positive outcomes and fewer health-risk behaviors later in life. (Seattle Social Development Project, 2011)

This project is connected to the work during the past three decades of several researchers at the University of Washington. The researchers have found that similar factors tend to be associated with a core of serious problem behaviors among youths—delinquency, substance abuse, school problems, teen pregnancy, and gangs. These factors, which they label as "risk factors," are grouped into four major categories: 1) community, 2) family, 3) school, and 4) individual/peer (Hawkins and Weis, 1985; Hawkins, Catalano, and Miller, 1992).

The Seattle project began in 1981, and it "combined teacher, child, and parent components with the goal of enhancing children's bonding with their families and schools" (Seattle Social Development Project, 2011). An important concept in this model is that of protective factors. These are those factors in young people's lives that act as buffers against the risk factors found within their environments. These buffers protect the person by either reducing the impact the risk factor has on the person or altering how a person responds. The goal is to strengthen these protective factors for youths who are at risk. These protective factors are grouped into three major areas: 1) individual characteristics (e.g., gender, a resilient temperament, a positive social orientation, and intelligence), 2) bonding (to family, school, etc.), and 3) healthy beliefs and clear standards (e.g., parents having high expectations and showing good modeling and clear standards for good behavior).

The Social Development Strategy

Hawkins and his associates at the University of Washington describe the "social development strategy" as building strong bonding with the long-term goal of assisting children in developing into healthy adults. It is their contention that to build bonding, three main conditions are necessary: 1) opportunities, 2) skills, and 3) recognition (Developmental Research and Programs, 1993: 13).

To begin with, children need to be given opportunities to make a contribution to their schools, their communities, and their families. If these opportunities are beyond their abilities, they will likely experience failure and frustration. On the other hand, if the opportunities are too easy, they will likely become bored.

Second, children should develop the skills needed to take advantage of the opportunities provided to them. The most important skills are cognitive ones such as problem-solving and reading, along with communication, the ability to be assertive, and the ability to ask for support.

Finally, children need to be recognized and acknowledged for what they have done, even if they have not done everything perfectly. Such recognition gives them the incentive to contribute more and reinforces their successes. Supportive teachers and recognition from parents are especially important.

The social development strategy recognizes that certain individual characteristics make it easier for children to develop skills, make a contribution, and be recognized. Children with a resilient temperament, for example, are less likely to be frustrated by blocked opportunities and will keep on trying. Those children with high intelligence will tend to develop a variety of skills to help them. Children who are sociable will stand a greater chance to be recognized by adults. Although these traits are often innate, they can be taught and nurtured so that the shy child can become more sociable, the less resilient child can be taught to deal better with blocked opportunities, and the less intelligent child can be helped in improving his or her intelligence.

The social development strategy suggests that increasing opportunities, skills, and recognition leads to greater bonding, which in turn leads to healthier beliefs and clear standards, which in turn lead to healthy behaviors. Thus, prevention programs need to focus especially on providing opportunities, skills, and recognition. Prevention programs also need to develop clear and consistent standards for behavior and to teach skills that will help to develop such standards.

A key ingredient of the social development strategy is community mobilization (a strategy proven to be quite successful in solving the gang problem, as noted in the next section). The authors of this strategy borrowed from two very successful models: the Stanford Heart Disease Prevention Program and the Minnesota Heart Health Program. These programs used the mass media very extensively; they used volunteers and educational strategies; and they mobilized the community. The result was a reduction in risks associated with heart disease.

The community approach, as the name suggests, reaches out to include a broad spectrum of individuals, groups, and organizations. The community itself makes it clear that certain unhealthy behaviors are unacceptable and will not be tolerated (e.g., children carrying guns to school, boys harassing girls at school, and drinking and driving). This approach takes advantage of existing community resources in the broadest sense and pools them to develop a communitywide strategy. The mobilization process involves four specific steps: 1) involving key community leaders, 2) forming a community board or task force, 3) conducting a community risk and resource assessment, and 4) planning the program and deciding on evaluation methods. This model is based in part on the assumption that problems such as drug abuse, teen pregnancy, and gangs are community problems rather than problems that affect just specific individuals.

Evaluations

While there have been several evaluations of programs stemming from the social development strategy, unfortunately there have been mixed results when it comes to reducing serious delinquency and gang involvement. Several studies are particularly relevant for gang prevention. These evaluated the effects of the intervention on "school bonding" (related to control/social bond theory discussed in Chapter 7) (Battin et al., 1998; Hawkins et al., 2001). While Battin et al. did not find any significant differences between a control and experiment group, research by Hawkins et al. (1999) found that at the age of 18, program participants were significantly less likely to have committed violent delinquent acts than the control group (48% vs. 60%). On the other hand, there were no significant differences between lifetime rates of nonviolent delinquency, arrests, court charges, and use of drugs. A follow-up to age 21 (Hawkins et al., 2005) found that program participants were more likely to graduate from high school than the control group (91% vs. 81%). Yet there were no significant differences when it came to the use of illegal drugs and arrests. Overall, researchers suggested that focusing on "full intervention" (on children from first through sixth grade) may be more effective than the "late intervention" (fifth and sixth grade only) (Seattle Social Development Project, 2011).

One offspring of the Social Development Strategy is a program called the National Guard Youth ChalleNGe Program. This program is "an intensive residential program that aims to 'reclaim the lives of at-risk youth' who have dropped out of high school and give them the skills and values to succeed as adults" (National Guard Youth ChalleNGe Program, 2011).

National Guard Youth ChalleNGe Program

This program got underway in 1993 and was developed by the National Guard Bureau in the U.S. Department of Defense. So far, more than 100,000 children and youth have participated. The following description is provided by its Web site:

> The program is 17 months long and divided into three phases: a two-week Pre-ChalleNGe Phase, which is a demanding orientation and assessment period; a 20-week Residential Phase; and a one-year Post-Residential Phase. The participants live at the program site, often a military base, during the first two phases. The curriculum for the Residential Phase focuses on eight core components of positive youth development: leadership/fellowship, responsible citizenship, service to community, life-coping skills, physical fitness, health and hygiene, job skills, and academic excellence. At the end of the Residential Phase, participants work with staff to arrange post-residential placement, such as employment, education, or military service. During the

Post-Residential Phase, participants return to their families and receive structured mentoring from qualified mentors identified by themselves within their own community. While the program environment is described as "quasi-military," participation in ChalleNGe is voluntary, and there are no requirements for military service during the program or afterward. (National Guard Youth ChalleNGe Program, 2011; Millenky, Bloom, and Dillon, 2011)

An evaluation began with a nine-month follow-up. This found that, first, the treatment group (14.6%) was more likely than the control group to have obtained a high school diploma (14.6% vs. 2.6%). Also, the treatment groups were more likely to be employed, to be taking college courses, and less likely to have been arrested and convicted.

However, after 21 months, even though the treatment group was more likely to have taken college courses or vocational courses and to be employed, there were no significant differences as far as being arrested and charged with a crime during the previous year, although the treatment group was less likely to be convicted. On the other hand, as far as self-reported delinquency was concerned, while both groups were about equally as likely to report a violent incident and drug use in the past year, the treatment group was less likely to report property damage incidents.

A three-year follow-up found that although the treatment group was still more likely to have completed college courses and to have been working, there were no significant differences as far as being charged or convicted of a crime, or self-reported crime (National Guard Youth ChalleNGe Program, 2011; Millenky et al., 2011).

COMPONENTS OF SUCCESSFUL PROGRAMS

Research on the subject of community intervention has covered a wide variety of programs dealing with an equally wide variety of problems, ranging from drug abuse and delinquency to teen pregnancy and school failure. What are the ingredients of programs that have had some success? Do these successful programs have certain features that set them apart from others?

Successful delinquency treatment and prevention programs have several key ingredients, which have been identified by several researchers (Chesney-Lind and Shelden, 2004; Dryfoos, 1990; Falco, 1992; Gendreau, 1991; Hollin, 1993; Schorr, 1989; Lipsey, 2009). First, as Falco (1992) and Huff (1990a) suggest with regard to the community's awareness of drug and/or gang problems, there is a need for communities to avoid denial of a problem. Second, programs should target medium- to high-risk youths with intensive, multifaceted approaches that focus especially on the development of social skills (e.g., conflict resolution) and address the attitudes, values, and beliefs that reinforce anti-social behaviors. Third, programs should offer alternatives to gang involvement (recreational programs, school events, jobs, etc.).

Gendreau (1991) has urged that programs provide explicit reinforcement and modeling of alternatives to pro-criminal styles of thinking, feeling, and acting. Fourth, programs should be conducted within the community, with a special focus on families and schools (in an attempt to promote bonding with these two institutions). Fifth, the staff should be well trained and consist of skilled individuals who have developed empathy and an understanding of a youth's own subculture and who do not patronize or discredit his or her beliefs. Sixth, the program should be linked with the world of work by assisting youths in developing job skills. Seventh, the goals of the program should be specific and culminate in some kind of award (e.g., a diploma). Eighth, it must be understood that relapse is normal (whether we are dealing with drug or alcohol abuse or any pattern of negative antisocial behavior) and that treatment is a continual process rather than a single episode; relapse-prevention techniques should always be employed to prepare for community adaptation. Schorr concludes, "In short, the programs that succeed in helping the children and families ... are intensive, comprehensive, and flexible.... Their climate is created by skilled, committed professionals who establish respectful and trusting relationships and respond to the individual needs of those they serve" (1989: 259).

These components have recently been underscored in a recent meta-analysis[4] by Mark Lipsey who found that the most successful programs had the following ingredients: the program had a "therapeutic" intervention philosophy, it served "high-risk" offenders, and it had a high quality of implementation (2009). Lipsey grouped evaluations into seven categories: counseling, deterrence, discipline, multiple coordinated services, restorative programs, skill building, and surveillance. Comparing the effects, he found that interventions based on punishment and deterrence appeared to increase criminal recidivism, whereas therapeutic approaches based on counseling, skill building, and multiple services had the greatest impact in reducing further criminal behavior. Cognitive behavioral skill building approaches were more effective in reducing further criminal behavior than any other intervention. The Missouri Model, discussed later, has been highly successful and employs the elements Lipsey identified as most effective.

Some Specific Illustrations of Community-Based Interventions

Much of the public response to the problem of youth gangs has been the creation of "programs." Many of these programs are operated by communities themselves or by nonprofit organizations. Against seemingly insurmountable forces (e.g., underfunding, limited power to change economic and social structures), a number of communities have initiated programs that attempted to resolve their local youth gang problems. Ironically, many of the people who live in these communities have themselves been blamed for the youth gang dilemma (e.g., because of having poor parenting skills, failure to produce acceptable role models, being derelict in transferring socially preferred values to their children, etc.). Yet, they continue seeking ways to salvage their communities and their children.

Several public programs designed to abate youth gang activity and violence in their respective communities have been examined (Dryfoos, 1990; Goldstein and Huff, 1993; Martin, 1992; Vigil, 2010). Although many of these programs share common ground in defining their goals (e.g., reduction in drug abuse, violence, and gang membership), they have adopted strategies that range from increased education about violence prevention to community-based centers that provide an array of services (e.g., self-esteem enhancement, job training, drug counseling, crisis intervention, etc.). Some offer recreational alternatives to gang activities (e.g., basketball, football, etc.). The strategies adopted by these programs frequently overlap. Nearly all of these programs suffer from sporadic and insufficient funding, more and more a result of legislative priority shifts from community-based services to law-enforcement intervention. Many of these programs were propagated from community grassroots movements, while others have religious foundations, and some have formed alliances with components of the criminal justice system (Martin, 1992).

One of the most popular and long-lasting gang intervention programs has been the "detached worker" program (Goldstein, 1993: 22–32). Such efforts date as far back as the mid-nineteenth century with settlement houses, Boy Scouts, Boys Clubs, and others. The Chicago Area Projects of the 1920s and 1930s utilized various kinds of detached worker programs. By the 1960s, such programs could be found in most large urban areas (New York, Boston, Los Angeles, Chicago, and San Francisco, among others). Unfortunately, the results of these kinds of programs have been disappointing. The theoretical rationale of such programs is that instead of bringing gang youths to programs, the programs should be brought to the gang youths themselves, in their own community or turf. Detached worker programs have typically involved various kinds of social work and counseling interventions, including recreational activities, tutoring, family and individual counseling, casework, and job training. These programs have also included various kinds of control efforts (e.g., surveillance), treatment (usually based on psychoanalytic perspectives), providing various opportunities (educational, recreational, and/or employment), and changing values. The last (changing values), which over time became one of the main goals of these programs, involved a rechanneling of the beliefs, attitudes, and behaviors of gang youths in more positive directions.

The results of detached worker programs have been mostly negative. For example, the Roxbury Project evaluated by W. B. Miller (1974) failed to significantly alter the anti-social behavior of the gang youths who participated. The Los Angeles Group Guidance Project actually made things worse, as delinquency among gang members increased, especially for those who received the most attention from the detached workers (Klein, 1968, 1995). One of the main reasons for the failure of most of these programs is the lack of program integrity.

As Goldstein (1993: 27–32) notes, many programs suffer from high staff turnover, low or inadequate funding, low staff morale, bureaucratic red tape, and extremely high caseloads (sometimes as high as 1 caseworker to 92 youths), among other problems. Many programs suffer from the fact that the workers are not as "detached" as the theory suggests they should be, with many spending the bulk of their time in the office or traveling alone from one spot to another. Further, most programs failed to have direct delinquency-reduction techniques and offered no techniques tailored to different kinds of gang youths (e.g., hard-core versus marginal members, aggressive youths versus nonaggressive youths). Finally, detached worker programs have not been comprehensive enough; the workers were not adequately trained and were often overworked.

Another common type of gang-intervention program is one that involves opportunities provisions. Such programs have attempted to attack the multiple problems facing gang youths—unemployment, low wages, lack of recreational and educational opportunities, poor health, inadequate housing, and other problems. Among the most popular programs addressing these factors have been Mobilization for Youth (a New York program based on Cloward and Ohlin's [1960] theory), the Ladino Hills Projects (Miller, 1974), the Citywide Mural Project (Albuquerque), the New York City Police Probation Diversion Project, the House of Umoja (Philadelphia), and the Community Access Team, Youth Enterprises, and SEY Yes programs (all in the Southern California area) (Goldstein, 1993: 34–35). Opportunities provisions programs have not been systematically evaluated. There is a great deal of anecdotal and impressionistic evidence that such programs are effective, as the survey by Spergel and Curry (1990) found.

Some Major Gang-Control Programs.   In this section, we briefly summarize six major gang control programs identified by Klein and Maxson (2006, Ch. 3). They selected these programs because they were major multi-million dollar efforts that included full-scale evaluations. What is interesting about their discussion is that Klein and Maxson conceptualized these programs as ideological, political, or bureaucratic. The "ideological" programs were all initiated by law-enforcement agencies, which led to "a narrow conception of street gangs and yielded an uncompromising police presence in the program, without recourse to alternative social and community resources" (Klein and Maxson, 2006: 89). The L.A. Plan and the Gang Resistance, Education, and Training (G.R.E.A.T.) program are included within the ideological category. The one "political" program was initiated by the attorney general of Illinois (a program that included "a number of easy-to-swallow social and educational initiatives quite devoid of gang-related reasoning"), which ended up with no evaluation (Klein and Maxson, 2006).

The "bureaucratic" programs included L.A. Bridges (set up by a city bureaucracy called the Community Development Department of Los Angeles) and the Safe Futures program (a branch of the U.S. Department of Justice).

What do these programs have in common? What connects them (aside from the obvious concern with gangs) "is their reliance on conventional wisdom, albeit quite different versions thereof." By "conventional wisdom" Klein and Maxson mean "the combination of untested assumptions and relatively unchallenged facts that we normally take to represent truth" (2006: 90). For the most part, the convention wisdom of these programs was rooted in the deterrence theory that became so popular in the 1980s and 1990s.

The L.A. Plan consisted of six different programs: 1) Community Youth Gang Services, 2) Operation Safe Streets (OSS) and Community Resources

Against Street Hoodlums (CRASH), 3) Operation Hammer, 4) Operation Hard-core, 5) Correctional gang caseloads, and 6) Interagency task force. Only one could be construed as anything other than suppression efforts, namely what was called the Community Youth Gang Services, which was a "youth outreach program" based in part on the familiar detached worker programs but without having workers assigned to specific gangs. There was no evaluation, and eventually it was defunded, with the funds assigned to another program called L.A. Bridges (discussed later). The G.R.E.A.T program was just another version of D.A.R.E. (both funded and operated by law-enforcement agencies).

Gang Resistance, Education, and Training (G.R.E.A.T.)

This program was modeled in part after the famous D.A.R.E. program (Drug Awareness, Resistance, and Education), which has been praised as a cure-all for drug addictions yet a proven failure based on several evaluations over the past couple of decades (see the meta-analysis of eight evaluations by Ennett et al., 1994; see also Rosenbaum and Hanson, 1998). The difference with the G.R.E.A.T program is that it focused on gangs (instead of drugs), and it was aimed at youths who were in the seventh grade but not necessarily "at risk" of becoming gang members. Local police were in charge of the program (as they are in D.A.R.E.), and it was funded by the Bureau of Alcohol, Tobacco and Firearms (ATF). A series of standardized lessons were given by police officers to seventh graders starting in 1991, and by 2000, around 3,500 officers in every state in the country were trained. The goal was to reduce gang activity and educate youth about the consequences of joining a gang. The lessons were supposed to teach kids skills that would enable them to resist gangs (just like D.A.R.E.). Evaluations sampled 22 schools and more than 3,500 students. Control groups were included (Esbensen et al., 2001).

So what have the evaluations found? Although there were some positive attitude changes among the seventh graders (but even these were negligible because out of 24 attitudinal variables, only 4 resulted in significant changes), the impact on delinquency in general and gang activity in particular was negative. This was supposed to be a gang-*prevention* program, but there has been no evidence that the program had any impact on the likelihood of gang involvement. One of the main reasons for the failure of this program is that it did not target those most at risk of becoming a gang member (as Klein and Maxson [2007: 101] note, about 90% of those targeted would not have become gang members whether they participated or not).

L.A. Bridges

A rather ambitious effort was undertaken in Los Angeles starting in 1997 called L.A. Bridges. The goal was for the city to fund a variety of anti-gang programs in selected areas, providing much needed services to at-risk children and youth, especially those in middle schools. After-school programs, sports programs, tutoring, counseling, anger-management classes, and parenting classes were provided. It had included in its budget an independent evaluation. A recent report observes that after six years and $50 million in expenditures, nothing much has changed. The program was supposed to serve 5,200 students a year in 26 middle schools, but an evaluation has shown very low participation by parents and students and, moreover, a lack of any sort of documentation of the results of these efforts. An audit concluded that the program ought to be shut down entirely because of mismanagement, high administrative costs, and even "lack of proof that it was reducing gang-related crime" (McGreevy, 2003). The program originally required each contractor to maintain a caseload of a minimum of 50 students who were high risk for becoming gang members and another 150 lower-risk youths. Further, each agency that was contracted was supposed to provide documentation that showed these youths were being served. However, 1 of the agencies had to be terminated and another 14 had serious problems.

Despite this negative evaluation, the city budgeted $13 million during the fiscal year ending June 30, 2003. Apparently nothing succeeds like failure! According to a spokesperson of the Community Development Department, which oversees the program, "The evaluation showed that certainly there are areas that need improvement, but overall we are able to quantify improvement in the performances" (McGreevy, 2003). No evidence was provided.

At the beginning, Malcolm Klein was part of a special panel that created the program. Klein wrote a strong critique of the proposal, stating that to be successful it must target specific gangs in specific parts of the city, who are actually being recruited, and then target them with services. He commented that this was "$50 million down the drain if what the city wanted was a gang-prevention program." Since that time, Klein says he's been "out of the loop" (McGreevy, 2003). Klein and Maxson note that Klein's exclusion from the evaluation was symptomatic of the "avoidance of academic expertise in program development" (2006: 108).[5]

We suspect that L.A. Bridges is just another in a long line of programs ostensibly set up to do something about a problem but that instead serves the interests of some groups who are the recipients of the funds. McGreevy and Winton (2007) reported that more than $100 million has been spent on L.A. Bridges, with no proven results.[6]

In March 2011, the state of California awarded 10 grants totaling about $5 million to "expand education, job training and placement programs for 900 at-risk youth in eight counties as part of the California Gang Reduction, Intervention and Prevention Initiative" (Employment Development Department, 2011). This money brings the total to $20 million since the program was launched in 2007. Most of the $5 million is going toward job training and was distributed to agencies such as the Riverside County Economic Development Agency, the Jewish Vocational Service of Los Angeles, and the Oakland Private Industry Council. It remains to be seen what the impact will be.

This is common throughout the country, as all this money is poured into these kinds of programs every year, with few positive results, while little of the money trickles down to those who need it the most. Who has benefited, other than those running the programs? The number of gangs and gang members continues to grow despite the money spent and the programs developed.

An exception can be found in a program located in the heart of gang territory in East Los Angeles, known as Homeboy Industries.

Homeboys Industries: A Unique Program

The motto of this program is as follows: "Homeboy Industries is the living example of our mission statement, 'nothing stops a bullet like a job.'"[7] This program began with the goal of helping gang members find jobs. These youths lived in one of the toughest neighborhoods in Los Angeles, the area around East L.A., where gangs have become an entrenched institution (Moore, 1991). The program consisted of counseling, education, tattoo removal, substance abuse and addiction assistance, job training, and job placement. It began under the leadership of Father Greg Boyle, who has been a fixture within the community for many years (Fremon, 2004).

What makes this program distinct is the businesses they have established, not unlike what has been accomplished in Delancey Street in San Francisco.[8] These businesses are Homeboy Bakery, Homeboy Silkscreen & Embroidery, the Homegirl Café, Homeboy/Homegirl Merchandise, Homeboy Diner (located on the second floor of Los Angeles City Hall), and Homeboy Farmers Markets.

Homeboy Industries began in 1998 as a "Jobs For A Future" (JFF) program created by Father Gregory Boyle while he was pastor of the Dolores Mission parish in Boyle Heights (a neighborhood within East Los Angeles). It became a nonprofit institution in 2001.

Unfortunately, the recent recession dealt the program a heavy blow. According to a story in the *Los Angeles Times* (Becerra, 2010, 2010a), 300 people (about three-fourths of the staff, including Gregory Boyle) had to be laid off because they could not raise enough money to remain open, and sales from their businesses were falling. However, some persistence has perhaps paid off, for in February 2011, they introduced a new product called Homeboy Salsa. The logo reads "Jobs Not Jails." It soon became the hottest selling snack at Ralph's supermarket deli sections throughout the Los Angeles area (Hallock, 2011). This became possible through "collaboration with Ralphs, which waived slotting fees—what food manufacturers sometimes pay grocery companies to carry a new product—and donated $50,000 to the project." The program has made a comeback in the past year, largely because of some large private donations, which resulted in hiring back about 100 employees who had been laid off the previous year. The *Times* story further notes:

> Meanwhile, Homegirl Café plans to expand to Los Angeles International Airport, and a Homeboy General Store is slated to open this spring in City Hall downtown. The bakery, Homeboy's original business and the employer of about 40 people, turns out more than 3,000 breads and pastries a day—croissants, cookies, tarts, baguettes and sourdough loaves that are sold at 17 farmers markets and

increasingly at "foodie" spots such as Intelligentsia coffee houses in Silver Lake and Pasadena and the new Black Cat Bakery on Fairfax Avenue. (Hallock, 2011)

One of the unique aspects of this program is that it targets gangs within their own turf, as it is located in an area that has one of "the highest concentration of gang activity in all of Los Angeles." In fact, it "is a sanctuary for former gang members who yearn to become functioning members of society" (Vigil, 2010: 93–94).

The most recent news about this program is that a screenwriter has adapted Father Greg Boyle's book *Tattoos on the Heart* (Boyle, 2010) as a play at the Casa 0101 Theater in Boyle Heights under the leadership of Josefina López (Johnson, 2011).

This program is an illustration of what can be accomplished when thinking unconventionally, because the program is not funded by the government and not operated by the criminal justice system (such as those reviewed earlier). We sincerely hope that it continues to be successful.

A Model Program: The Detention Diversion Advocacy Project. One of the major problems with most programs reviewed here (with the exception of Homeboy Industries) is that they rarely target kids who are seriously at risk of joining gangs or are in gangs. They far too often target kids who are only marginally at risk and would probably go straight with little or no intervention. What is required is going to what Miller has called the "deep end" of the system, targeting those at the highest risk (1998). A program that started in San Francisco, known as the Detention Diversion Advocacy Project (DDAP), illustrates this idea. The senior author of this book conducted an evaluation of this program. The success of this program, plus the fact that it has been replicated in two other parts of the country (Washington, D.C., and Montgomery County, Maryland) and the fact that the evaluation was published by the Office of Juvenile Justice and Delinquency Prevention (Shelden, 1999b), warrants a special section in this chapter. Even though it was not originally established to deal with gangs, it is still worth considering because so many offenders who have participated have been involved in gangs or at least lived in areas where gangs are prevalent.

The original DDAP was begun in 1993 by the Center on Juvenile and Criminal Justice (CJCJ) in San Francisco, California. The program's major goal is to reduce the number of youth in court-ordered detention and provide them with culturally relevant community-based services and supervision. Youths selected are those that are likely to be detained pending their adjudication. DDAP provides an intensive level of community-based monitoring and advocacy that is not presently available. **Disposition case advocacy** is the concept that describes the type of approach being used in this program. This method has been defined as "the efforts of lay persons or non-legal experts acting on behalf of youthful offenders at disposition hearings" (Macallair, 1994: 84). It is based in part on the more general concept of "case management," which has been

defined as a "client-level strategy for promoting the coordination of human services, opportunities, or benefits." Case management seeks to achieve two major
outcomes: 1) "the integration of services across a cluster of organizations" and 2)
continuity of care (Moxley, 1989: 11). The main focus of case management is to
develop a network of human services that integrates the development of client
skills and the involvement of different social networks and multiple service providers (Moxley, 1989: 21).

The goals the program is designed to accomplish include the following: 1)
Provide multilevel interventions to divert youth from secure detention facilities;
2) demonstrate that community-based interventions are an effective alternative to
secure custody and that the needs of both the youths and the community can be
met at a cost savings to the public; and 3) reduce disproportionate minority
incarceration.[9]

The DDAP program involves two primary components:

- *Detention Advocacy*—This component involves identifying youth likely to
  be detained pending their adjudication. After a potential client is identified,
  DDAP case managers present a release plan to the judge. The plan includes
  a list of appropriate community services that will be accessed on the
  youth's behalf. Additionally, the plan includes specified objectives as a
  means to evaluate the youth's progress while in the program. Emphasis is
  placed on maintaining the youth at home, and if the home is not a viable
  option, the project staff will identify and secure a suitable alternative. If the
  plan is deemed acceptable by a judge, the youth is released to DDAP's
  supervision.

- *Case Management*—The case management model provides frequent and
  consistent support and supervision to youth and their families. The purpose
  of case management is to link youths to community-based services and
  closely monitor their progress. Case management services are field
  oriented, requiring the case manager to have daily contact with the
  youth, his or her family, and significant others. Contact includes a
  minimum of three in-person meetings a week. Additional services are
  provided to the youth's family members, particularly parents and guardians,
  in areas such as securing employment, day care, drug treatment services,
  and income support.

Clients are identified primarily through referrals from the public defender's
office, the probation department, community agencies, and parents. Admission
to DDAP is restricted to youths currently held, or likely to be held, in secure
detention. The youths selected are those deemed to be "high risk" in terms of
their chance of engaging in subsequent criminal activity. The selection is based
on a risk-assessment instrument developed by the National Council on Crime
and Delinquency. The target population consists of those whose risk-assessment
scores indicate that they would ordinarily be detained. This is what Jerome
Miller has termed the "deep-end" approach (1998). This is very important, for
by focusing on *detained* youths, the project ensures that it remains a true diversion

alternative rather than "net widening." Youths are screened by DDAP staff to determine whether they are likely to be detained and whether they present an acceptable risk to the community.

Client screening involves gathering background information from probation reports, psychological evaluations, police reports, school reports, and other pertinent documents. Interviews are conducted with youths, family members, and adult professionals to determine the types of services required. After a potential client is evaluated, a DDAP staff member presents a comprehensive community service plan at the detention hearing and requests that the judge release the youth to DDAP custody.

Because the project deals only with youths who are awaiting adjudication or final disposition, their appropriateness for the project is based on whether they can reside in the community under supervision without unreasonable risk and their likelihood of attending their court hearings. This is similar in principle to what often occurs in the adult system when someone is released on bail pending their court hearings (e.g., arraignments, trial).

The primary goal of the project is to design and implement individualized community service plans that address a wide range of personal and social needs. Services that address specific linguistic or medical needs are located by case managers. Along with the youth's participation, the quality and level of services are monitored by DDAP staff. It should be noted that the purpose of multiple collaboratives is to ensure that the project is able to represent and address the needs of the various communities within San Francisco in the most culturally appropriate manner. Because youth services in San Francisco have been historically fragmented by ethnicity, race, and community, a more unified approach is being tried with DDAP in that it has become a neutral site within the city and staffed by representatives from CJCJ and several other community-based service agencies (e.g., Horizon's Unlimited, Potrero Hill Neighborhood House, Vietnamese Youth Development Center).

More specific goals include 1) ensuring that a high proportion of the program clients are not rearrested while participating in the program, 2) achieving a high court reappearance rate, 3) reducing the population of the Youth Guidance Center, and 4) reducing the proportion of minority youths in detention. Currently, the Youth Guidance Center is the only place of detention in the city. It has a capacity of 137, but the daily population typically ranges from 140 to 150. The average length of stay is around 11 to 12 days.

The evaluation consisted of comparing a group of youths referred to DDAP with a similarly matched control group that remained within the juvenile justice system (for a complete overview of the evaluation, see Shelden, 1999b). The results showed that after a three-year follow-up, the recidivism rate for the DDAP group was 34 percent, compared to a 60 percent rate for the control group. Detailed comparisons holding several variables constant (e.g., prior record, race, age, gender, etc.) and examining several different measures of recidivism (e.g., subsequent commitments, referrals for violent offenses) showed that the DDAP youths still had a significantly lower recidivism rate.

There may be several reasons for the apparent success of this program. From the data collected here and information from previous research, three reasons seem of paramount importance.

First, the caseloads of the DDAP caseworkers are extremely low in comparison to normal probation officers. The DDAP workers average about 10 cases each. Regular probation officers in major urban areas have caseloads ranging from 50 to 150. Smaller caseloads typically result in more intensive supervision, and more intensive supervision means that caseworkers are constantly on top of things with regard to their clients. Indeed, with small caseloads, they can spend more quality time with their clients *in the field* (e.g., in their homes, on the street corners, at school) rather than endless hours in an office doing paperwork, on the phone, and doing other bureaucratic chores.

Second, DDAP is a program that is out of the mainstream of the juvenile justice system; that is, it is a true alternative rather than one of many bureaucratic extensions of the system. This means that normal bureaucratic restrictions do not generally apply. For example, the qualifications for being a caseworker with DDAP are not as strict as one might find within the juvenile justice system (e.g., age restrictions, educational requirements, arrest records, "street" experience, etc.). From casual observations of some of these caseworkers, this researcher was impressed with their dedication and passion to helping youth. Moreover, the backgrounds of these workers were similar to the backgrounds of some of their clients (e.g., similar race, neighborhood of origin, language, etc.).

Third, the physical location of DDAP seemed to this observer user friendly and lacked the usual macho appearance of the formal system. There are no bars, no concrete buildings, no devices for screening for weapons as one enters the building, no cells for lockdown, and so on. Further, the DDAP workers are not officers of the court with powers of arrest and the usual accoutrements of such occupations (e.g., badges, guns).

There could also be a possible fourth explanation, but one we can only speculate on at this time because we lack the data to draw such a conclusion. It could be that given the low caseloads, DDAP caseworkers are more likely than regular probation officers to be on top of the case, that is, to be in constant contact with the youth and thus be able to nip in the bud potential problems. Also, some police officers, when facing a possible arrest situation and learning that the youth is a DDAP case (presuming the officer knows about DDAP), may be in a position to contact the caseworker, who might be able to persuade the officer that the situation could be handled without a formal arrest. We have no way of knowing whether this occurs with any degree of regularity. Even if it did, such a procedure may be a positive sign because youths from more privileged backgrounds are often treated this way by the police if it is believed that someone in authority can handle the youth informally. Many youths have been saved the stigma of formal juvenile processing by such intervention by significant adults in their lives.

Since this evaluation was completed, DDAP has expanded into several new locations, notably in Baltimore; Washington, D.C., and Philadelphia. An evaluation was conducted on the program in Philadelphia, also showing positive results (Feldman and Jubrin, 2002).

Evidence-Based Practices

The Rand Corporation conducted a study of what it called "evidence-based" programs that address the problem of gangs and youth violence. The programs they reviewed had been subjected to rigorous evaluation research (Greenwood, 2010). Space does not permit a complete discussion of each of these programs, so we will merely list them here. They are divided into the following categories:

- *Proven programs*—These are programs that have been subjected to rigorous evaluations that showed positive results. They include such programs as the Nurse Family Partnership, Functional Family Therapy, Multidimensional Treatment Foster Care, Aggression Replacement Training, and Multisystemic Therapy.

- *Proven strategies*—These include a group of generic strategies that have been shown via meta-analysis of evaluations to be successful in reducing recidivism. Among these are 25 specific strategies that include cognitive behavioral programs and various diversion programs.

- *Promising programs*—These are what the Rand study calls "brand name programs" that have been shown to be successful but have not been replicated. These include a total of 16 programs such as the Seattle Social Development Project (noted earlier) and Family Integrated Transitions.

The Rand study also included a list of programs that have been proven to be ineffective. Some examples include D.A.R.E., Guided Group Interaction, boot camps, intensive probation, Scared Straight, regular surveillance-oriented parole, and deterrence programs (intervention dramatizing the negative consequences of certain kinds of behavior).

BROAD-BASED NATIONAL STRATEGIES

Addressing the delinquency problem will require a national strategy; the problem is not just local in nature. More than 20 years ago, criminologist Elliot Currie (1989) suggested five general categories for a national strategy to address the general problem of crime. These are just as relevant today; the nine tenets detailed earlier urge similar reform.

1. *Early educational interventions*—These would include programs such as Head Start, based on the assumption that delinquency is related to poor school performance and dropping out, which in turn are related to a lack of preparedness for school, especially among lower-class minorities.

2. *Expanded health and mental health services*—Such services would focus on high-risk youths and include prenatal care and postnatal care. This is based on evidence that the most violent youths suffer from childhood traumas of the central nervous system, exhibit multiple psychotic symptoms, and have also experienced severe physical and/or sexual abuse (see also Dryfoos, 1990).

3. *Family support programs*—Programs should be designed to address child abuse and other forms of domestic violence. Abused children are far more likely than nonabused children to become abusers themselves. Some recent research indicates that the majority of prison inmates, especially violent ones, experienced severe physical, emotional, or sexual abuse, or some combination of all three.

4. *Reentry programs*—There should be careful planning for helping offenders after they have broken the law, rather than merely warehousing them in a correctional setting. The key ingredient in virtually all successful rehabilitation programs is improving skills—work skills, reading and verbal skills, problem-solving skills, and so on.

5. *Drug and alcohol abuse treatment programs*—The war on drugs targets the manufacturing and distribution (the supply side) of drugs, rather than the use (the demand side). The nation needs to emphasize treatment of addictions.

About the same time Currie wrote his proposals, sociologist Mark Colvin (1991) also wrote about the need for national strategies. He focuses on the concept of social reproduction—the process through which institutions (primarily families and schools) prepare children for productive roles in society. His main thesis is that these institutions have largely failed to establish the necessary social bonds to link young people to legitimate avenues to adulthood. The result is that many are becoming marginal to the country's economic institutions. This has been caused by a failure to invest in human development and human capital. This failure has resulted in a growing crime rate and increasing expenditures for welfare and prisons. There is a need for a "national comprehensive program aimed at spurring economic growth, human development, and grass-roots, democratic participation in the major institutions affecting our lives and those of our children" (Colvin, 1991: 437).

Crime may be less likely to occur in communities with stronger social capital. Higher levels of community participation create social networks, consensus, and an environment of mutual support and trust.

> Improving social capital through volunteerism and political activism could alter the social norms surrounding crime and a community's reaction to crime. Civic engagement seems to mitigate those cultural norms that allow violence and crime to take root. Increasing youth participation in community activities could be an important tool in stemming the adverse effects of crime, as well as keeping individual youth more bonded to conventional social norms. (Butts et al., 2010: 27)

A comprehensive approach must aim at broader economic and human-development programs that affect large segments of the population (e.g., the Social Security system versus welfare for the poor). The country must do what other industrialized nations do and consider seriously the need to develop human capital for the continued overall well-being of society. In the United States, the system is so privatized that public or social needs are often undermined by private investment decisions that result in moving capital all over the world but eliminate jobs at home. Education is the key here. However, as Colvin notes, education must be more than what the term has traditionally meant—namely, formalized public schooling leading to a diploma. Education should be a comprehensive policy that includes families, schools, workplaces, and communities working to reduce the marginalization of young people. "For youth, who often feel the effects of social exclusion, social capital can be as simple as a positive relationship or affiliation with neighborhood and community associations. Thus, collective as well as personal efficacy can be achieved through volunteerism and political participation" (Colvin, 1991: 26).

Another national strategy that has attracted attention is positive youth development (PYD). For most of the twentieth century, adolescence was viewed as a period of turmoil. The deficit-based approach to adolescence focused on what could go wrong in a young person's development. The individual treatment philosophy of the original juvenile court movement was based on this approach. Studies, however, noted that most youth succeed even in the presence of multiple risk factors and applied the label "resilience" to describe qualities that promote healthy development in the face of adversity. Youth advocates began to see adolescence as a process of positive opportunities for youth to learn, serve, and benefit from interactions with pro-social adults and communities.

The strength-based, resilience-oriented perspective on adolescence of PYD is "a comprehensive way of thinking about the development of adolescents and the factors that facilitate their successful transition from adolescence to adulthood" (Butts et al., 2010: 9):

> The basic premise of PYD is that even the most disadvantaged young
> person can develop positively when connected to the right mix of
> opportunities, supports, positive roles, and relationships. Having a wide
> range of pro-social experiences during adolescence allows a young per-
> son to practice and demonstrate competency and to embrace his or her
> responsibilities and value to the larger community. The central purpose
> of PYD is action. Communities are encouraged to break down barriers
> to opportunity, and provide positive roles and relationships for all youth,
> including the most disadvantaged and disconnected. (2010)

PYD involves building connections, valuing community, and emphasizing learning/doing and attaching/belonging. A key concept involves changing the frame—looking at youth as resources rather than as victims of villains. People are beginning to question the rationale for interventions based solely on the punishment or individual treatment model:

- If delinquent behavior stems from a lack of integration and habilitation, why do correctional strategies focus on isolation of offenders?

- If the goal is to make offenders more responsible and accountable, why do we place them in positions (e.g., in most treatment programs) where others assume responsibility for their activities and behaviors?

- If many sources of delinquency are to be found in communities, families, and schools, why do probation strategies often target only the individual offender?

- If youth justice professionals are experts in delinquent behavior, why are youth justice agencies so often viewed by policymakers as an all-purpose "dumping ground" for troubled youth rather than a resource for resolving problems in schools and communities? (Butts et al., 2010: 15)

Addressing the Problem of Social Inequality

As noted in Chapter 8, the problem of gangs is strongly related to social inequality. Social inequality in America has reached its highest point since the start of the Great Depression. Yet, most commentary in recent years has focused almost exclusively on the impact the current economic crisis has had on the "middle class," while ignoring the poor and especially the growing marginality of the urban underclass, which has been ever more devastating (simply put, they are already experiencing a "depression"). One important function of the punishment business is processing this underclass into the prison system. Indeed, as a study by Bruce Western clearly shows, there is, as noted in Chapter 9, a kind of "pipeline" from the inner-city black underclass to the prison system. The prison system has become, in short, little more than a dumping ground for this class of people (2006).

To break this "pipeline," we might very well need something like what Paul Krugman has called a "New, New Deal" (Krugman, 2007; see also Dodd, 2008). He suggests starting with universal health care and continuing onto job creation and other reform measures, just like FDR did with the original "New Deal." Perhaps a kind of public works program like the WPA in the 1930s would be required. Some have suggested instituting a kind of "Marshall Plan" for the inner cities (McGreevy, 2007).[10] Doing this requires reversing the trends begun during the Reagan years, which means reversing the tax cuts that have lined the pockets of the super-rich (Kamin and Shapiro, 2004). As one recent study concluded, the "broken economy" has been a case of "failure by design" by those who run the economy and political system (Bivens, 2012). As of this writing (February 2012), the "stimulus package" that rivaled the one put together during the 1930s is more than two years old, so it is still too soon to tell what overall impact it might have. Despite this stimulus, the national unemployment rate remains at just over 8 percent.[11] In September 2011, a new jobs stimulus plan (costing about $447 billion) was proposed by the Obama administration (Dorning, 2011).

SUMMARY

Throughout this chapter, the focus has been on intervention strategies for the gang problem at the community and societal levels. These strategies solicit mobilization of community members (e.g., parents and concerned citizens), schools (e.g., teachers), social service agencies (e.g., mental health agencies), and other components germane to the community (e.g., churches) to participate in activities that focus on the family, supervision, and creating opportunities. On a more macro (national) level, policymakers and administrators must make decisions that provide leadership and place prevention before reaction. Policies must be adopted and administered that provide some degree of hope for at-risk youths.

We also reviewed some programs that theoretically targeted gang prevention, such the G.R.E.A.T. program and L.A. Bridges. As we noted, these are among many illustrations of programs that failed despite the expenditures of millions of dollars.

Many of the programs reviewed here have demonstrated some effectiveness in the containment of gang activities and delinquency in general (e.g., DDAP). Such programs, however, have limitations. They cannot do much in regard to the social and economic environments from which most gangs are spawned. Thus, a more concerted national program is needed to correct slum injustices that plague our inner cities. Obviously, we must first discover a way in which such a program can be less political and more humanistic.

NOTES

1. For an excellent discussion of this subject, see Sternheimer (2006).
2. Bureau of Justice Statistics: http://bjs.ojp.usdoj.gov/content/glance/tables/exptyptab.cfm.
3. From the Homeland Security Web site: http://www.dhs.gov/xlibrary/assets/budget_bib_fy2011.pdf.
4. Hollin (1993: 72) defines *meta-analysis* (quoting from Izzo and Ross 1990: 135) as "a technique that enables a reviewer to objectively and statistically analyze the findings of each study as data points ... The procedure of meta-analysis involves collecting summary statistics, using the summary statistics from each study as units of analysis, and then analyzing the aggregated data in a quantitative manner using statistical tests."
5. Each of the authors of this book has had a similar experience, as have many other academic people we know.
6. For a more detailed discussion of L.A. Bridges, see Klein and Maxson (2006: Ch. 3).
7. Much of this information is taken from their Web site: http://www.homeboy-industries.org/.
8. http://www.delanceystreetfoundation.org/
9. The ability of case advocacy and case management to promote detention alternatives was demonstrated by the National Center on Institutions and Alternatives (NCIA). Under contract with New York City's Spofford Detention Center, NCIA significantly augmented the efforts of that city's Department of Juvenile Justice to reduce the number of youths in detention and expand the range of alternative options (Jefferson and Associates, 1987; this is also documented in Krisberg and Austin, 1993: 178–181).

A similar case management system has been in use in Florida through the Associated Marine Institutes (Krisberg and Austin, 1993). The Key Program, Inc., also uses the case management approach where, in this instance, the youth are *closely supervised*, meaning that they are monitored on a 24-hour basis and must conform to some very strict rules concerning work, school, counseling, victim restitution, and so on (1993).

Additional evidence in support of the use of case advocacy comes from a study by the Rand Corporation (Greenwood and Turner, 1991). This study compared two groups of randomly selected youths, a control group that was recommended by their probation officers for incarceration, and an experimental group that received disposition reports by case advocates. Of those who received case advocacy disposition reports, 72 percent were diverted from institutional care, compared to 49 percent of the control group. The Rand study also found tremendous resistance from juvenile justice officials, especially probation officers, to alternative dispositions, especially those coming from case advocates. It appeared that the probation staff resented the intrusion into what had heretofore been considered their own "turf" (Greenwood and Turner, 1991: 92).

10. For more details on the Marshall Plan, see the following Web site: http://www.marshallfoundation.org/TheMarshallPlan.htm.

11. http://www.bls.gov/cps/

11

Conclusions

We begin with a fundamental realization: No amount of
thinking and no amount of public policy have brought us any
closer to understanding and solving the problem of crime. The
more we have reacted to crime, the farther we have removed
ourselves from any understanding and any reduction of
the problem. In recent years, we have reformulated the law,
punished the offender, and quantified our knowledge. Yet the
United States remains one of the most crime-ridden nations. In
spite of all its wealth, economic development, and scientific
advances, this country has one of the worst crime
records in the world.

(QUINNEY AND WILDEMAN, 1991: VII).

"We can't solve problems by using the same kind of thinking
we used when we created them."

– ALBERT EINSTEIN

The first quote was written in 1991 and was used to begin this chapter in the
second and third editions of this book, published in 2001. It remains just as
relevant today. It should send us an important message, and we should all remember it and seriously reflect on it. It must be said at the outset that the prospects
for the future are not very good as long as we stay in the past. To paraphrase
George Santyana (1863–1952), those who fail to study history are doomed to
repeat it. There is a tendency in American society to not give enough attention
to the study of history; thus we often do repeat it. Such is the case in our response
to the problem of crime and delinquency in general and of gangs in particular.
And, in this era of post-9/11, these words remain significant. Success is, as we

have noted, measured using military-type criteria—arrests made, weapons seized, drugs confiscated, "enemy" areas "secured," and so on. Questions of larger issues, such as social justice, continue to be ignored at our peril.

The Albert Einstein quote has been added for this fourth edition. It was written about a century before the first quote. To us, it summarizes the current state of affairs in this country. We keep doing the same thing over and over again, expecting different results. This is the popular definition of insanity. From our review of the literature on (and the history of) gangs, it seems that nothing succeeds like failure, to borrow from Reiman's popular book *The Rich Get Richer and the Poor Get Prison* (Reiman and Leighton, 2009).

This book has offered a comprehensive review of youth gangs in America. We may be no closer to an answer as to what we as a society can do to stem the criminal actions and violence of these groups, but our intent at the outset was to provide an understanding of the phenomenon of gangs. We are convinced that we have added to the knowledge base regarding this phenomenon. We are somewhat less frustrated over the inability of gangs and their communities to communicate with one another. But it is not because people are not trying. A flurry of activity takes place throughout the country every day of the week— board meetings, seminars, lectures, discussions, projects, and programs. These are actions that are driven by youth gangs. They capture the time and energy of many individuals and groups who focus mostly on getting rid of youth gangs. The focus is on what to do and how to do it now; most often this takes the form of a new policy for law-enforcement agencies to implement. Politicians and administrators are continually participating in a search for methods of eradicating gangs and restoring safe and secure streets for the remainder of the population. Despite the recent influx of research on gangs, there is still much to be learned. This is especially true when considering the wide variations in gang structures from one city to another. More than a dozen years ago, Hagedorn made the following persuasive observation:

> A major conclusion of this study is the uniqueness and variability of
> modern gangs and the importance of local factors in understanding and
> fashioning a flexible response. But on another level, this book is a chal-
> lenge for both sociologists and practitioners to go beyond the law
> enforcement paradigm in both theory and policy. The development of
> an urban minority underclass in the last decades, first in large cities and
> more recently in middle and small sized cities, has altered the nature of
> gangs and demands new investigation and new policies. (1998: 33)

In a similar vein, Horowitz concludes that

> …. gang research has progressed substantially in the last several years,
> though the results are difficult to compare in part because of the small
> number of cases included in most of the studies. It may not be possible
> yet to develop a general theory of gangs. We do not know the

parameters of what makes up a "gang" and enough about the nature of the gangs as social/business organizations or the relationships among gang organizations and ethnicity, the local community and its institutions, the wider society, and the legal and illegal activities of members. (Horowitz 1990: 52–53)

But do we really need more data from scientific research on the problem of gangs? Is there something missing from our usual analyses of social problems? Richard Quinney has written that "we of the West live in an age of lost meaning. The ethos of the Enlightenment has come to an end. We can no longer believe fully in scientific rationalism as the source of all knowledge and human progress. The Enlightenment liberated us from the tradition of one era only to be captured by the materialistic ethic of another" (1991: 108–109).

Perhaps it is time to seek new levels of understanding. Indeed, in this era of materialism and selfishness, there is an emptiness to so many lives. Little wonder that so many of our youths, desperate for some recognition and a place in the world, seek out similarly situated young people for protection and a sense of belonging and empowerment. Seeing the greed and search for power and control among the adults of the world, is it any wonder that so many youths have been caught up in a similar search for power and control? And should we be surprised that so many young people (especially urban minorities) have little hope for the future or at least have some serious doubts about it? Two personal stories told by one of the authors (Brown) highlight what we are talking about here. The stories are from his own personal experiences and are taken from two seemingly different social contexts—Vietnam and Detroit, Michigan. But a closer examination of these two stories will reveal that the two contexts are more similar than different.

The first story is about an experience Brown had several years ago while giving a lecture to a group of social science students at a university in Ho Chi Minh City, Vietnam.[1] We will let Brown tell the story in his own words:

During the lecture, several students raised questions about homelessness in America. They were unable to understand how, in a country with so much prosperity, there could actually be people without a place to live. To be certain, there were many without homes in Ho Chi Minh City during the early 1990s. And for Vietnam, it was relatively simple to explain this phenomenon. Vietnam was one of the poorest countries in the world. Western businesses, with their advanced technology, were beginning to displace a form of labor which had dominated Vietnam for centuries. People were migrating from the countryside to the city in search of work.

I spent several hours walking those streets late at night and observing people huddled in corners, some lying beside cooking fires trying to keep warm. Yet, in this classroom, I found it difficult to explain why there were so many homeless people in America. I attempted to explain changes in the American economy, and the displacement of workers in recent years. "But America is rich with resources," replied several knowledgeable students. "How can it be that these people have nowhere to live?" Clearly, this was one of the most difficult discussions I had ever encountered. My lecture turned to the topics of fear, complacency, insensitivity, competition, greed, power, and hate, and eventually discussing issues related to human rights.

The second story is about a 15-year-old black youth named Jimmy.[2] (The following is reproduced exactly as it was for the first two editions of this book.) Brown met Jimmy as a result of his observations of gang life in Detroit. Brown relates his story as follows:

> My wife and I had previously discussed the prospects of taking Jimmy somewhere for his birthday. The difficulty, however, was where does a white, middle-class couple take a black, soon-to-be-15 gang member for his birthday? Drawing from our limited middle-class options, and recalling the interests of our two daughters who have since grown up, we decided that the Detroit Zoo, followed by a movie, and perhaps dinner, would be both appropriate and appreciated. Having made our decision, I had obtained permission from Jimmy's sister (Jimmy's mother was in prison, and he had never met his father) to take him on an outing for his birthday. The irony, of course, was that several months earlier Jimmy had introduced me to a contact who arranged my first visit to a crack house (in and of itself, a zoo-like environment). Unknowingly, I was now going to introduce Jimmy, who had been born and raised in this city, to the Detroit Zoo. It had never occurred to me, nor to my wife, that an inner-city child, soon to be 15, had never visited a city zoo.
>
> The day was absolutely perfect, given the unpredictability of late spring in southeastern Michigan. The sky was clear, and a slight breeze carried the pleasant scent of Lake St. Clair across the city. Jimmy was "hanging" outside his apartment, located in a complex that many would be inclined to label "the projects." Although attempting to maintain the normal attitude of a streetwise kid, there was a hint of excitement in Jimmy's voice as we exchanged greetings. His sister had already left for work (she also received food stamps due to the low wages she received), so we got into the car and drove to Woodward, turned left, and traveled north to Ten Mile Road.

The Detroit Zoo is located off of Woodward at Ten Mile Road. Those who are familiar with Detroit are aware that, as one drives north out of the inner city, Eight Mile Road represents the Mason-Dixon line of this city. North of Eight Mile Road is white country, and south of this "line of ignorance" is black country. Although some suburban and state policymakers attempt to deny this fact, one need only to look at the occupants of vehicles and at people on the streets. The social reality of racial segregation is self-evident at the Eight Mile Road boundary.

Although I knew that Jimmy had been involved in illegal drug sales, and I suspected he was still involved in this enterprise to some extent, he was, as usual, broke. Many people believe that these kids make large amounts of money running drugs, but I had found that most of the youngsters I have studied have little or no money. This observation has also been noted by others who have conducted ethnographic studies of youth gangs (Padilla, 1992). I gave Jimmy $20 so that he could have some sense of independence. As we paid for our tickets (Jimmy paid for his own from the $20 I had given him) and walked into the zoo, my wife reached out to hold Jimmy's hand in a protective sort of way. For a moment he did not resist, then politely withdrew his hand. My wife was concerned about Jimmy's safety in this very secure setting, yet Jimmy had been taking care of himself on the streets of Detroit for several years now! We walked around the zoo for nearly six hours. It was interesting, to say the least, to watch Jimmy eat cotton candy, ice cream bars, popcorn, and so on like a normal kid on an outing. I had seen him navigate around a crack house and stand up for himself, on many occasions, in less than calm situations.

Following the zoo experience, we went to a movie. I welcomed the rest. Jimmy ate two more boxes of popcorn and one ice cream sandwich and drank an extra-large drink. I attempted to calculate the transition of calories into pounds had I attempted this quest to devour these treats.

After the movie we went to a preselected restaurant. At the restaurant we encountered many stares and subtle examples of disapproval from many of the occupants. There were instances during our visit to this restaurant when I wanted to respond to some of the rude onlookers, but this was Jimmy's day. I am certain that Jimmy was aware of the ugliness associated with those demonstrations of white ignorance, but it didn't have much impact on his appetite—after ordering, and eating, a prime rib dinner, he ate an obscene slice of chocolate cream pie. Before leaving the restaurant, I telephoned Jimmy's sister and told her we were on our way home.

Obviously concerned, and now relieved, she asked how Jimmy had behaved (in direct contradiction of those who think parental interest and family values are lacking in the inner city), specifically drawing attention to his manners. I told her that he had been absolutely wonderful, and I really meant it. Returning to our table, I found Jimmy and my wife engaged in deep conversation about basketball—an activity about which she has neither knowledge, nor interest to acquire knowledge. Later, when I asked her about their discussion, she replied, "I just wanted him to be able to talk about whatever he wanted to talk about. I felt very sad because I realized that we had to take him home soon."

We left the restaurant about 10 o'clock and began our journey back to Jimmy's home. Jimmy had also realized that the day had come to a close. In retrospect, my wife and I developed an analogy about this event. Imagine a delicate flower kept in a refrigerator. The petals are drawn closely together in defense against the cold—trying desperately to survive. This represents Jimmy on the morning that we drove toward the zoo. At some point during our tour of the zoo, Jimmy, responding very much like that delicate flower when warmth entered that cold environment, began to open his petals. Throughout the day that flower remained in full bloom. Looking across the seat on the way home, it became obvious that the closer we got to Eight Mile Road, the more the flower began to close. By the time we arrived at Jimmy's apartment, the petals had closed—realizing that survival was foremost.

My wife and I will never forget Jimmy's 15th birthday. It was a day filled with good intentions. We both wanted that day to be special for Jimmy—and it was. That day was also filled with cruelty. We removed Jimmy, for a day, from "the projects." We showed him what life would be like if he were white or middle class. We gave him a glimpse of life outside his natural environment. But Jimmy is not white, nor is he middle class. He is black. He lives, like so many other black kids, in poverty. The future is very uncertain for him. The probability of escape for Jimmy, and the thousands of "Jimmys" like him, is very low—despite all the political rhetoric of "American opportunity."

I have seen Jimmy many times since his 15th birthday. Each time he talks about our outing. In his own way, he always expresses his gratitude for that day. But, like any delicate flower, he has come to accept his lot in life. While it may be very cold in his environment of poverty, he feels that it is better than the pain of experiencing brief encounters in an environment that he believes is beyond his reach. Thus, he has never asked to repeat the experience.

As we noted in the third edition of this book, Jimmy's life changed for the worse. He was sent to prison (one of several in the northern peninsula of Michigan) following a conviction for burglary and drugs. Then about two years ago, he was killed. A young man who had just committed a robbery shot him. Jimmy's sister said that while he obviously remembered the celebration of his 15th birthday he "always knew that is was just a dream."

Jimmy's story is not unusual for black youths growing up in today's inner cities. According to one estimate, more than one-fourth (28.5%) of all black children will end up in prison some time in their lifetime (Shelden, 2010). About one-third of all black males in their 20s are somewhere in the criminal justice system—in prison or jail, on probation, or on parole (Mauer, 2006). The incarceration rate for blacks is more than 6,000 (per 100,000 population), more than eight times greater than for whites (Shelden, 2010).

It seems that there is either a lack of interest or an absence in effort in truly understanding what is going on in our inner cities—beyond the reflexive responses of repressed people. Understandably, the "haves" desire to retain that which they perceive to be legally theirs. There are vested interests that continue to repress the "have nots." This, it has been suggested, is human nature. Adoption of this perspective is understandable, albeit inexcusable, for policymakers who desire only to be reelected and to continue their careers as power brokers. But it is unconscionable for social scientists, in constant pursuit of government grants, to ignore social facts (the plight of inner-city youth) and continue focusing on, and perpetuating, social control. Many social scientists may argue that their work is objective research conducted in the name of science (part of the "publish or perish" doctrine within academia).[3] Many social scientists may argue that they are not necessarily responsible for the actions of policymakers and social-control agents who respond to the findings of their research. Richard Quinney points out that

> ... as social scientists (as we are called in this age), we give witness to the possibility of social existence. The tragic character of our project is the continuing disparity between our interpretive constructions and the knowledge of the symbols that are necessary in the struggle for social existence. That there are moments when our efforts are appropriate is the hope and objective of critical reflection. We are in the long tradition of the world coming to know itself. The meaning of social existence is being revealed to us. (Quinney 1982: 15)

Jimmy is a human being—not a social statistic. Jimmy, although he definitely engaged in criminal activity during the few years of his existence, is a victim—he is neither a variable nor a numerical digit keyed into a database. Jimmy does not need a program;[4] like thousands of kids in similar situations, he needs hope. This is an ideal that every human should expect to possess. It is not a new concept, not a fad, not wishful thinking; it can be found in a Christian religious promise given nearly 2,000 years ago: "Love ... hopeth all things. ... But now abideth faith, hope, love, these three" (I Corinthians 13:7–13). Yet the concept is something that is hard to grasp and to hold on to when the reality of the neighborhood in which one lives speaks to something other than hope; it speaks to despair and dismay, to frustration and failure. This is the environment for the youths who comprise most of the gangs in our society today; still, we—the middle class, the professionals, the politicians—too often believe that the responses of these youths should nevertheless be positive, conforming, and decent. We need to return hope to these youths in the form of education, job skills, decent housing, and adequate health care. David Dawley spoke powerfully as he issued the following challenge to all of us who are sincere about ending the suffering:

> In foreign affairs, Desert Storm demonstrated the power of defined
> goals, massive force and political resolve. Now the question is: Can we
> mobilize similar political commitment and economic investment in a
> coordinated campaign to bring opportunity, hope, and justice to the
> Third World within our own borders? (1992: 198)

The story of Jimmy begs an answer to the question What would these kids be like if meaningful environmental changes were introduced to the inner cities of America? Yet we seem preoccupied with asking questions that support more social control on the streets, efficiency in the courtrooms, easier methods to certify juveniles as adults, and how long we can "lock 'em up." We (social scientists, policymakers, social-control agents, and all others who make up humanity) must begin to open our eyes and recognize the social existence of the youths who are members of gangs, those who are contemplating membership, and those who will inevitably join existing and future gangs. It is irrational to declare war on a symptom while the causes are ignored.

Classifying all gang members as garbage, scum, or other such epithets denies their humanity. It is clear that most of the youths who join gangs are "the people society gave up on—the bottom of the barrel." Yet they are "also people who want love, respect, responsibility, and friendship. They are like most young people, growing up with many of the same personal needs. For most, the gang is the only real family they know; the gang is survival, protection, recognition, education" (Dawley, 1992: 189).

What we also need is a truly progressive criminology for the new millennium, a criminology that must be a combination of enlightenment, empowerment, and reinforcement. It is a criminology that strives for peace and social justice (Quinney and Wildeman 1991: 110–119; Shelden et al., 2008). A progressive criminology must have, at its core, an appreciation for human rights. Human rights must be viewed as nonnegotiable. People must replace statistics. It is not likely, looking at much of the conservative and liberal publications that fill our professional journals, that assistance will be forthcoming from conventional criminologists or sociologists. Many criminology and criminal justice programs situated in major universities appear to be breeding grounds for conservative social and criminological thought. Many have grown accustomed to the Bureau of Justice funding trough. A progressive criminology must, as Quinney suggests, come from within concerned parties, regardless of their discipline. Members of a progressive criminology must not become involved for the purpose of radicalism or self-promotion; rather, they must be devoted to social change that empowers the disenfranchised and strives to improve the quality of life for all people.

Looking back 1,000 years to the dawn of the modern age, we have certainly improved not only social conditions in general but also our system of justice. Yet it is ironic that at the beginning of this new age what passes for a system of "justice" still tends to concentrate mostly on punishing the "dangerous classes" (Shelden, 2008). And we continue our relentless attack on "dangerous classes" all over the globe. In this sense, domestic policy merges with foreign policies. Despite the vast amount of knowledge about crime and the enormous sums of money available, sometimes our methods of social control seem like what occurred at the start of the old millennium. We are, as Elliott Currie has remarked, "at one of those critical watersheds in our history when it comes to crime and justice." On the one hand, writes Currie, "there are tremendous opportunities for serious reform." On the other hand, "there is also the very real danger that things could get much worse—especially if the recent era of economic prosperity comes to a halt." We could easily find ourselves in "a country where, even more than today, endemic tendencies toward social disintegration are held in check by an increasingly pervasive penal system and an increasingly militarized and uncontrolled police." Currie suggests that criminologists must be willing to "stick their necks out" and "do a better job of public education and public advocacy than we've been able to muster in the last quarter-century" (1999: 18).

SOME FINAL WORDS

The United States is arguably the richest and most powerful country in the world, yet in many ways we are impoverished. Literally trillions of dollars have been spent on the wars in Iraq and Afghanistan, while trillions more have been funneled to the top 1 percent of the population via tax cuts and other giveaways (Cooper, 2011; Alden, 2011; Baker, 2006).[5] Meanwhile, millions suffer from abject poverty, home foreclosures, job losses, and educational failure. The infrastructure of our cities has been crumbling while schools continue to deteriorate, all because of the loss of money that gets shifted upward. At the same time, we spend billions of dollars buttressing the criminal justice system while approaching what amounts to a police state given the militarization of law enforcement (Kraska, 1999). This is all part of what amounts to a policy of "containment" of the underclass, as the criminal justice system engages in punishing the poor (Wacquant, 2009).

Meanwhile, it could easily be argued that the biggest "gang" of all is Wall Street. As these words are being written (February, 2012), the movement known as Occupy Wall Street is in full force all over the country. The central message of this movement is too often buried inside the news media as the main focus seems to be the various police actions against the demonstrators.[6] Not too many would note the irony that while police make hundreds of arrests for relatively minor offenses (e.g., disturbing the peace)—which usually end up being dismissed in court—within the confines of the buildings high above the protesters, there is rampant criminality. We mean this literally, for over the years the "top 1 percent" has indeed engaged in some of the worst crimes, destroying millions of lives while raiding the U.S. treasury of trillions of dollars. As thousands of protestors are carted off to jail in handcuffs, few of the corporate crooks ever see the inside of a jail. They literally are getting away with murder.

Several of the components of the common definitions of "gangs" given earlier in this book (e.g., those provided by the National Gang Center) can be used to describe the general organization and behavior of those who can be identified as part of what is generally labeled as "Wall Street." There are certainly three or more members, although their ages are considerably older than those of youth gangs. They certainly have a common identity as financiers, brokers, hedge fund operators, bankers, and so on. The name "Wall Street" is a common denominator. While they may not consider themselves as a "gang" in the usual sense of the word, they do have some "permanence and a degree of organization." Finally, without a doubt this "gang" has consistently been involved in a persistent and high rate of criminality that, from a purely financial standpoint, makes ordinary street gangs look like petty amateur thieves.

Indeed, a few years ago, it was estimated by two of the authors of this book (Shelden et al., 2008) that the cost of corporate and white collar crime came to more than $1.5 trillion per year. The recent financial meltdown that led to the current recession is estimated to involve several trillion dollars in outright fraud. A report by *The Economist* (2011) listed the top 10 examples of "insider trading" cases between 2000 and 2010 (based upon the amount stolen). The total estimated amount of money involved in these fraudulent cases amounted to just over $400 million. In its 2009 report called the "2009 Financial Crimes Report," the FBI reported that corporate fraud cases alone went from 423 in FY 2005 to 692 in FY 2009. The amount of money involved came to an estimated $1 billion.

Where are the headlines about these crimes?

Any attempt to "reform" the criminal justice system, to make it "better" at achieving "justice" or reducing crime by any significant amount must confront the existence of the crime-control industry and all the profits made off the existence of crime. In short, the criminal justice system—the crime-control industry —has, ironically, a vested interested in not reducing crime to any great extent. True, we may try to make the current system more "efficient" at capturing and convicting criminals, but that does not generally result in any significant reduction in the overall rate of crime.

Saul Alinsky, the social reformer and agitator of the early twentieth century (and a name that became part of the 2008 election), offered a parable that is highly informative for readers who need a perspective to guide their own individual efforts to seek change. Imagine a large river with a high waterfall. At the bottom of this waterfall, hundreds of people are working frantically to rescue those who have fallen into the river. One individual looks up and sees a seemingly neverending stream of people cascading down the waterfall, and he begins to run upstream. One of his fellow rescuers hollers, "Where are you going? There are so many people that need help here." The man replied, "I'm going upstream to find out why so many people are falling into the river."

Now imagine that the scene at the bottom of the waterfall represents the criminal justice system responding to crimes that have been committed and dealing with both victims and offenders. If you look more closely, you will begin to notice that there are more people at the bottom of the stream, that they work in relatively new buildings with all sorts of modern technology, and that those working here get paid rather well, with excellent benefits. And the money keeps flowing into this area, with all sorts of businesses lined up to provide various services and technical assistance. If you look upstream, you will find something far different. There are not too many people; the buildings are not as modern; the technology is old or nonexistent. The people working upstream are not paid very much, have few benefits, and the turnover is quite high. Businesses do not offer assistance. Budgets are insufficient, and workers constantly need to beg for money. More women work upstream, and the culture does not value their work as highly as the work of men (men are in charge downstream). Prevention does not seem to be very macho in this culture, and it is not linked to profits.

Some people choose to respond to problems related to crime and delinquency by working downstream. This is certainly a noble goal, and good people are always needed. As for the authors of this text, we picture ourselves among those who are constantly running upstream, asking "why?" Which way you want to go is up to you. You just have to be able to look yourself in the mirror each day and be able to say, "I tried." A lot of work lies ahead. The answer begins and ends with people—with "highly motivated, highly trained staff constantly interacting with youth to create an environment of trust and respect" (Mendel, 2010: 28).

The first order of business, however, is to end the strangulation of the country by the corporate elite that rules. The trillions of tax dollars filtering in their direction needs to be redirected the other way.

Many criminologists, especially those of us affiliated with universities, where we have at our disposal such vast amounts of information and the leisure time to pursue the truth, must take seriously Noam Chomsky's "call to action" more than 30 years ago, when he wrote of the "responsibilities of intellectuals." In this classic statement, Chomsky said that this responsibility is quite simple: "It is the responsibility of intellectuals to speak the truth and to expose lies"(Chomsky 1987: 60). Thus, it is our responsibility to expose the lies about gangs, about who they are and who they are not, about what kinds of social conditions create and perpetuate gangs and gang activities, and about what should and should not be done about the problem. We hope that in this book we have contributed, in some small way, to a more enlightened view of this problem and that we have been responsible.

NOTES

1. For a more detailed discussion of Brown's experiences in Vietnam, see Brown (1994).

2. Jimmy is a pseudonym for a Detroit gang member who is included in Brown's study of youth gangs.

3. Historian Howard Zinn put it well when he wrote, "We publish while others perish" (1990: 5).

4. During a discussion with one gang member, focusing on possible programs to get kids out of the gang, Brown was told, "The only thing programs do is try to make 'good niggas' out of us. There's no difference between a 'good nigga' and a 'bad nigga.' You're still just a 'nigga.' I'm a person. Society don't give a shit, my brothers do."

5. For a good look at what kinds of programs get cut because of these massive tax cuts, see Cooper, 2011.

6. http://occupywallst.org/

Bibliography

Abadinsky, H. 1993. *Drug Abuse: An Introduction,* 2d ed. Chicago: Nelson-Hall.

_____. 2009. *Organized Crime.* Belmont, CA: Wadsworth and Cengage Learning.

Abel, R. (Ed.). 1982. *The Politics of Informal Justice.* New York: Academic Press.

Adamson, C. 2000. "Defensive Localism in White and Black: A Comparative History of European-American and African-American Youth Gangs." *Ethnic and Racial Studies* 23: 272–298.

Adler, F. 1975. *Sisters in Crime.* New York: McGraw-Hill.

AFL/CIO. 2009. "Runaway Executive Pay and the Wall Street Bailout," March 26. Retrieved from http://www.aflcio.org/corporatewatch/paywatch/tarp.cfm.

_____. 2010. "Trends in Executive Pay." Retrieved from http://www.aflcio.org/corporatewatch/paywatch/pay/.

Agnew, R. 1995. "Determinism, Indeterminism, and Crime: An Empirical Exploration." *Criminology* 33: 87–88.

Ahmed, A. 2010. "No Backing Down." *Chicago Tribune,* February 21: 1, 10.

Albeda, R., N. Folbre, and the Center for Popular Economics. 1996. *The War on the Poor.* New York: The New Press.

Alden, W. 2011. "Cost of Tax Cuts For America's Rich Exceeds Value of Budget Cuts." Huffington Post, April 18. Retrieved from http://www.huffingtonpost.com/2011/04/18/tax-cuts-rich_n_848933.html.

Alexander, B. 2009. "Marriage Eludes High-Achieving Black Women." MSNBC, August 13. Retrieved from http://www.msnbc.msn.com/id/32379727.

Allegro, D. B. 1989. "Police Tactics, Drug Trafficking, and Gang Violence: Why the No-Knock Warrant Is an Idea Whose Time Has Come." *Notre Dame Law Review* 64: 552–570.

Alliance for Excellent Education. 2009. "High School Dropouts in America." Retrieved from http://www.all4ed.org/files/GraduationRates_FactSheet.pdf.

Alonzo, A. 2003. "New Anti-Gang Strategy Is Introduced by Chief Bratton." Streetgangs.com Magazine (January 15). Retrieved from http://www.streetgangs.com/features/011503_bratton.

_____. 2004. "Racialized Identities and the Formation of Black Gangs in Los Angeles." *Urban Geography* 25, 658–674.

Alsaybar, B. 1999. "Deconstructing Deviance: Filipino American Youth Gangs, 'Party Culture,' and Ethnic Identity in Los Angeles." *Amerasia Journal* 25(1): 116–138.

American Civil Liberties Union (ACLU). 2010. "School to Prison Pipeline." Retrieved from http://www.nyclu.org/issues/racial-justice/school-prison-pipeline.

American Motorcyclist Association. 2011. "AMA Facts and Figures." Retrieved from http://www.americanmotorcyclist.com/about/Media/FactsAndFigures.aspx.

Anderson, E. 1978. *A Place on the Corner.* Chicago: University of Chicago Press.

_____. 1990. *Streetwise: Race, Class and Change in an Urban Community.* Chicago: University of Chicago Press.

_____. 1994. "The Code of the Streets." *The Atlantic Monthly*, May: 81–94.

Anderson, J. F., W. Brooks, A. Langsam, and L. Dyson. 2003. "The 'New' Female Gang Member: Anomaly or Evolution? *Journal of Gang Research* 10: 47–65.

Andrews, D. A., I. Zinger, R. D. Hoge, J. Bonta, P. Gendreau, and F. T. Cullen. 1990. "Does Correctional Treatment Work? A Clinically Relevant and Psychologically Informed Meta-Analysis." *Criminology* 28: 369–404.

Annie Casey Foundation. 2008. "Missouri Juvenile Justice System Honored by Harvard University & Casey Foundation." December. Retrieved from http://www.aecf.org/MajorInitiatives/JuvenileDetentionAlternativesInitiative/Resources/Dec08newsletter/JJNews5.aspx.

Anti-Defamation League (ADL). 2001. "Bigotry Behind Bars: Racist Groups in U.S. Prisons." Retrieved from http://www.adl.org/special_reports/racist_groups_in_prisons/prisons_racist_gangs.asp.

Asbury, H. 1927. *The Gangs of New York*. New York: Alfred Knopf.

Associated Press. 1999. "Whites Leaving Welfare Faster than Minorities, Survey Reveals." March 30. Retrieved from http://www.ncpa.org/sub/dpd/index.php?Article_ID=12311.

_____. 2006. "11 Hells Angels Start Trial for Deadly Biker Brawl." Fox News.com, September 26. Retrieved from http://www.foxnews.com/story/0%2C2933%2C215761%2C00.html#ixzz1Okdk1zPF.

Atlanta Gang Conference. 1992. "Gangs Prevention Training." Sponsored by Carondelet Management Institute. Atlanta, GA. October 9–10.

Auletta, K. 1983. *The Underclass*. New York: Vintage Books.

Austin, J., and J. Irwin. 2001. *It's About Time: America's Imprisonment Binge*, 3d ed. Belmont, CA: Wadsworth.

Austin, J., and K. McGinnis. 2004. *Classification of High-Risk and Special Management Prisoners: A National Assessment of Current Practices* (no. 019468). Washington, DC: U.S. Department of Justice, National Institute of Corrections.

Bach, A. 2009. *Ordinary Injustice*. New York: Metropolitan Books.

Bagdikian, B. 2004. *The New Media Monopoly*. Boston: Beacon Press.

Baker, B. 1988a. "Tough Boss Shows Gang Members New Way of Life." *Los Angeles Times*, April 15.

_____. 1988b. "Gang Murder Rates Get Worse." *Los Angeles Times*, April 10.

_____. 1988c. "Homeboys: Players in a Deadly Drama." *Los Angeles Times*, June 26.

Baker, D. 2006. *The Conservative Nanny State: How the Wealthy Use the Government to Stay Rich and Get Richer*. Washington, DC: Center for Economic and Policy Research.

_____. 2009. "Free Market Myth." Z Net, January 7. Retrieved from http://www.zmag.org/znet/viewArticle/20181.

_____. 2010. "The Big Bank Theory: How Government Helps Financial Giants Get Richer." *Boston Review*, January/February. Retrieved from http://bostonreview.net/BR35.1/baker.php.

_____. 2011. "Disaster Not Averted: The Latest Jobs Numbers and the Very Real Chance of Another Great Depression." *The New Republic*, June 6. Retrieved from http://www.tnr.com/article/politics/89460/jobs-may-umemployment-second-great-depression.

Barnhart, T. 2009, November. The Aryan brotherhood. *The Corrections Connection*, November. Retrieved from http://www.corrections.com/tracy_barnhart/?p=500.

Bandidos MC Randers. 2011. "History of Bandidos MC." Retrieved from http://bandidosranders.dk/bmc/index.php?option=com_content&view=article&id=3:histry&catid=1:artcat&Itemid=2.

Barker, T. 2005. "One Percent Bikers Clubs: A Description." *Trends in Organized Crime* 9: 101–112.

_____, and K. Human. 2009. "Crimes of the Big Four Motorcycle Gangs." *Journal of Criminal Justice*, 37(2): 174–179.

Barnard, L. 2002. "Are You the Parent of a Tagger?" Oxnard (CA) Police Department, pamphlet, March 23.

Barrows, J., and C. R. Huff. 2009. Gangs and Public Policy: Constructing & Deconstructing Gang Databases. *Criminology & Public Policy* 8: 675–703.

Barth, C. 2012. "U.S. Is Headed for Recession in 2012 Says Shilling." *Forbes*, June 8. Retrieved from http://www.forbes.com/sites/chrisbarth/2011/06/08/u-s-is-headed-for-recession-in-2012-says-shilling/.

Bartlett, D. L., and J. B. Steele. 1992. *America: What Went Wrong?* Kansas City, MO: Andrews and McMeel.

Battin, S. R., K. G. Hill, R. D. Abbott, R. Catalano, and J. D. Hawkins. 1998. "The Contribution of Gang Membership to Delinquency Beyond Delinquent Friends." *Criminology* 36: 93–115.

Beccaria, C. 1963. *On Crimes and Punishment*. New York: Bobbs-Merrill.

Becerra, H. 2010. "L.A.'s Homeboy Industries Lays Off Most Employees." *Los Angeles Times*, May 14. Retrieved from http://www.latimes.com/news/local/la-me-0514-homeboy-industries-20100514,0,1924697.story.

————. 2010a. "Money Woes Come at Boyle and Homeboy High Points." *Los Angeles Times*, May 15. Retrieved from http://www.latimes.com/news/custom/topofthetimes/callocal/la-me-0515-homeboy-boyle-20100515,0,6499219.story.

Beck, A. J., J. C. Karberg, and P. M. Harrison. 2002. "Prison and Jail Inmates at Mid-Year, 2001." Washington, DC: Bureau of Justice Statistics.

Beck, A. J., D. Gilliard, L. Greenfeld, C. Harlow, T. Hester, L. Jankowski, T. Snell, J. Stephan, and D. Mortan. 1993. *Survey of State Prison Inmates, 1991*. Washington, DC: Bureau of Justice Statistics. Retrieved from http://bjs.ojp.usdoj.gov/content/pub/pdf/SOSPI91.PDF.

Becker, H. S. 1963. *Outsiders: Studies in the Sociology of Deviance*. New York: Free Press.

Beckham, W. H. 1989. "Helpful Practices in Juvenile Court Hearings." In F. B. McCarthy, W. W. Patton, and J. G. Carr (Eds.), *Juvenile Law and Its Processes*. Los Angeles, CA: LexisNexis.

Beeghley, L. 2003. *Homicide: A Sociological Explanation*. Landham, MD: Roman and Littlefield.

Belenko, S., J. Sprott, and C. Petersen. 2004. "Drug and Alcohol Involvement among Minority and Female Juvenile Offenders: Treatment and Policy Issues." *Criminal Justice Policy Review* 15: 3–36.

Belfield, C. R., N. Milagros, S. Barnett, and L. Schweinhart. 2006. "The High/Scope Perry Preschool Program: Cost-Benefit Analysis Using Data from the Age-40 Follow-up." *Journal of Human Resources* 41(1): 162–190.

Bell, D. 1987. *And We Are Not Saved*. New York: Basic Books.

Bell, K., and F. Lucas (producers). 2008. *Mongol nation* [DVD]. United States: The History Channel.

Bellair, P. E., and T. L. McNulty. 2009. "Gang Membership, Drug Selling, and Violence in Neighborhood Context." Washington, DC: National Institute of Drug Abuse. Retrieved from https://harrisschool.uchicago.edu/Research/conferences/NLSYConf/pdf/Bellair_Neighborhood_Disadvantage.pdf.

Bennett, W., J. DiIulio, and J. P. Walters. 1996. *Body Count: Moral Poverty and How to Win America's War against Crime and Drugs*. New York: Simon and Schuster.

Bensinger, G. 1984. "Chicago Youth Gangs: A New Old Problem." *Crime and Justice*. 7: 1–16.

Beres, L. S., and T. D. Griffith. 2005. "Gangs, Schools and Stereotypes." *Loyola of Los Angeles Law Review* 37: 935–978. Retrieved from http://llr.lls.edu/volumes/v37-issue4/documents/beres.pdf.

Berlin, I. 1978. "The Hedgehog and the Fox." In H. Hardy and A. Kelly (Eds.), *Russian Thinkers*. New York: Viking.

Bernstein, J., C. Brocht, and M. Spade-Aguilar. 2000. "How Much Is Enough? Basic Family Budgets for Working Families." Washington, DC: Economic Policy Institute.

Berrick, J. D. 1995. *Faces of Poverty: Portraits of Women and Children on Welfare*. New York: Oxford University Press.

Bierne, P. 1993. *Inventing Criminology*. Albany: SUNY Press

Bing, L. 1991. *Do or Die*. New York: Harper Collins.

Bischof, G. 2005. "Katrina Journal: What We Need Is a Marshall Plan in Reverse." History News Network, October 17. Retrieved from http://hnn.us/articles/16874.html.

Bishop, D., C. E. Frazier, L. Lanza-Kaduce, and L. Winner. 1996. "The Transfer of Juveniles to Criminal Court: Does It Make a Difference?" *Crime and Delinquency* 42: 187–202.

Bivens, J. 2012. *Failure by Design: The Story Behind America's Broken Economy*. Ithaca, New York: Economic Policy Institute.

Bjerregaard, B., and C. Smith. 1993. "Gender Differences in Gang Participation, Delinquency, and Substance Abuse." *Journal of Quantitative Criminology* 4: 329–355.

Black, D. 1976. *The Behavior of the Law*. New York: Academic Press.

Blankstein, A. 2011. "Bystander Shot in Buttocks by Taggers." *Los Angeles Times*, July 18. Retrieved from http://latimesblogs.latimes.com/lanow/2011/07/bystander-shot-in-buttocks-by-taggers.html.

Blazak, R. 2009. "The Prison Hate Machine." *Criminology & Public Policy* 8: 633–640.

————. 2011. "Essay: The Racist Skinhead Movement." Retrieved from http://www.splcenter.org/get-informed/intelligence-files/ideology/racist-skinhead/racist-skinheads.

Block, C. R., and R. Block. 1993. *Street Gang Crime in Chicago*. Washington, DC: U.S. Department of Justice, National Institute of Justice, Research in Brief.

Block, C. R., A. Christakos, A. Jacob, and R. Przybylski. 1996. *Street Gangs and Crime: Patterns and Trends in Chicago*. Research Bulletin. Chicago: Illinois Criminal Justice Information Authority.

Bluestone, B., and B. Harrison. 1982. *The Dein-dustrialization of America.* New York: Basic Books.

Blumberg, A. (Ed.). 1974. *Current Perspectives on Criminal Behavior.* New York: Knopf.

Bobrowski, L. J. 1988. *Collecting, Organizing and Reporting Street Gang Crime.* Chicago: Chicago Police Department, Special Functions Group.

Bogardus, E. 1943. "Gangs of Mexican-American Youth." *Sociology and Social Research* 28: 55–56.

Bonfante, J. 1995. "Entrepreneurs of Crack." *Time,* February 27, pp. 22–23.

Bookin-Weiner, H., and R. Horowitz. 1983. "The End of the Youth Gang: Fad or Fact?" *Criminology* 21: 585–602.

_____. 1961. "Delinquent Subcultures: Socio-logical Interpretations of Gang Delinquency." *Annals of the American Academy of Social Science* 338: 119–136.

Bordua, D. J. (Ed.). 1967. *The Police: Six Sociological Essays.* New York: Wiley.

Bottomore, T., L. Harris, V. G. Kiernan, and R. Miliband (Eds.). 1983. *A Dictionary of Marxist Thought.* Cambridge, MA: Harvard University Press.

Bourdieu, P. 1986. "Forms of Capital." In J. G. Richardson (Ed.), *Handbook of Theory and Research for the Sociology of Education.* New York: Greenwood Press.

Bourgois, P. 2002. *In Search of Respect: Selling Crack in El Barrio.* Oxford: Cambridge University Press.

Boutwell, B. B., and K. M. Beaver. 2010. "The Intergenerational Transmission of Low Self-Control." *Journal of Research in Crime and Delinquency* 47: 174–209.

Bowker, L. (Ed.). 1978. *Women, Crime and the Criminal Justice System.* Lexington, MA: Lexington Books.

Bowker, L., and M. Klein. 1983. "The Etiology of Female Juvenile Delinquency and Gang Membership: A Test of Psychological and Social Structural Explanations." *Adolescence* 13: 739–751.

Boyle, G. 2010. *Tattoos on the Heart: The Power of Boundless Compassion.* New York: Free Press (Kindle edition.).

Boyle, J., and A. Gonzales. 1989. "Using Proactive Programs to Impact Gangs and Drugs." *Law and Order* 37(8): 62–64.

Brace, C. L. 1872. *The Dangerous Classes of New York.* New York: Wynkoop and Hallenbeck.

Bradshaw, P. 2005. *Terrors and Young Teams: Youth Gangs and Delinquency in Edinburgh.* In S. H. Decker and F. M. Weerman (Eds.), *European Street Gangs and Troublesome Youth Groups.* Walnut Creek, CA: Alta Mira.

Brotherton, D. C., and L. Barrios. 2002. *Between Black and Gold: The Street Politics of the Almighty Latin King and Queen Nation.* New York: Columbia Univ. Press.

Brown, W. B. 1994. "Reconciliation in a Back-Alley Cafe of Saigon." *Humanity and Society* 18: 75–84.

_____. 1998. "The Fight for Survival: African-American Gang Members and Their Families in a Segregated Society." *Juvenile and Family Court Journal* 49: 1–14.

_____. 1999. "Surviving Against Insurmountable Odds: African American Mothers and Their Gang Affiliated Daughters." *Humanity and Society* 23: 102–124.

Brown, W. B., and R. Shelden. 1994. "Gangs and Gang Members as Victims and Victimizers." February. Berkeley, CA: Western Society of Criminology.

Brown, W. B., R. Shelden, and A. Kiesz-Mrozewska. 1994. "Social, Economic, Political, and Legal Quandaries Following Solidarity: Changes in Crime and Delinquent Behavior in Poland." March. Chicago: Academy of Criminal Justice Sciences.

Brown, W. K. 1977. "Black Female Gangs in Philadelphia." *International Journal of Offender Therapy and Comparative Criminology* 21: 221–228.

_____. 1978. "Black Gangs as Family Extensions" and "Graffiti, Identity, and the Delinquent Gang." *International Journal of Offender Therapy and Comparative Criminology* 22: 39–48.

Bureau of the Census. 2011. "Mean Earnings by Highest Degree Earned," Table 228. *Statistical Abstract of the United States, 2011.* Retrieved from http://www.census.gov/compendia/statab/2011/tables/11s0228.pdf.

Bureau of Justice Statistics. 2009. Expanded Homicide Data, Table 12. U.S. Washington, DC: Department of Justice. Retrieved from http://www2.fbi.gov/ucr/cius2009/offenses/exp&ed_information/data/shrtable_12.html.

Bureau of Labor Statistics (BLS). 2010a. "Employment by major industry sector, 1998, 2008, and projected 2018," Table 2. Retrieved from http://www.bls.gov/news.release/ecopro.t02.htm.

_____. 2010b. "Women in the Labor Force: A Databook (2010 edition)," Table 20. Retrieved from http://www.bls.gov/cps/wlf-table20-2010.pdf.

_____. 2011a. "Alternative Measures of Labor Utilization," Table A-15. Retrieved from http://www.bls.gov/news.release/empsit.t15. htm.

_____. 2011b. "Employment Status of the Civilian Population 25 Years and Over by Educational Attainment," Table A-4. Retrieved from http://www.bls.gov/news. release/empsit.t04.htm.

_____. 2011c. "Employment Status of the Civilian Population by Race, Sex, and Age," Table A-2, January 7. Retrieved from http:// www.bls.gov/news.release/empsit.t02.htm.

_____. 2011d. "Real Earnings News Release," Table A-1, March 17. Retrieved from http:// www.bls.gov/news.release/realer.htm.

_____. 2011e. "Employment Situation Release," Table A-1. Retrieved from http:// www.bls.gov/news.release/empsit.t01.htm.

_____. 2011f. "Usual Weekly Earnings of Wage and Salary Workers Fourth Quarter 2010." Retrieved from http://www.bls.gov/ news.release/pdf/wkyeng.pdf.

Burgess, E. W. 1925. "The Growth of the City." In R. E. Park, E. W. Burgess, and R. D. McKenzie (Eds.), *The City.* Chicago: University of Chicago Press.

Burns, H. 1974. "Racism and American Law." In R. Quinney (Ed.), *Criminal Justice in America.* Boston: Little, Brown.

Butts, J. A., G. Bazemore, and A. S. Meroe. 2010. "Positive Youth Justice—Framing Justice Interventions Using the Concepts of Positive Youth Development." May. Washington, DC: Coalition for Juvenile Justice, p. 14. Retrieved from http://juvjustice.org/media/ resources/public/resource_390.pdf.

Caldwell, R. 2010. "Inner City Black Male Unemployment at 50 Percent." *West Orlando News,* August 24. Retrieved from http:// westorlandonews.com/2009/08/24/ inner-city-black-male-unemployment-at-50-percent/.

Camilli, G., S. Vargas, S. Ryan, and W. S. Barnett. 2010. "Meta-Analysis of the Effects of Early Education Interventions on Cognitive and Social Development." *Teachers College Record* 112: 579–620. Retrieved from http://www. tcrecord.org.

Campbell, A. 1984a. *The Girls in the Gang.* Cambridge, MA: Basil Blackwell.

_____. 1984b. "Girls' Talk: The Social Re-presentation of Aggression by Female Gang Members." *Criminal Justice and Behavior* 11: 139–156.

_____. 1990. "Female Participation in Gangs." In C. R. Huff, *Gangs in America,* 2d ed. Newbury Park, CA: Sage.

_____. 1993. *Men, Women, and Aggression.* New York: Basic Books.

Carellic, R. 1999. "Supreme Court Strikes Down Anti-Loitering Law Aimed at Gangs." *Savannah Morning News.* Savannah, GA. June 11: 4A.

Carey, A. 1995. *Taking the Risk Out of Democracy.* Chicago: University of Illinois Press.

Carlson, P. M. 2001. "Prison Interventions: Evolving Strategies to Control Security Threat Groups." *Corrections Management Quarterly* 5: 10–22.

Carp, S. 2009. "Black Male Conundrum." *Catalyst Chicago,* June. Retrieved from http://www. catalyst-chicago.org/news/index.php? item=2593&cat=23.

Catalano, R., R. Loeber, and K. McKinney. 1999. "School and Community Intervention to Prevent Serious and Violent Offending." Office of Juvenile Justice and Delinquency Prevention. Washington, DC: U.S. Department of Justice.

CBCNews.com 2011. *31 Hells Angels-Linked Drug Cases Dropped in Que.* Retrieved from http:// www.cbc.ca/news/canada/montreal/story/ 2011/05/31/alleged-hells-angels-drug-charges-thrown-out-of-court.html.

CBS. 1992. "Girls in the Hood." *Street Stories.* August 6.

_____. 2006. "13-Year-Old Cadet Dies At Boot Camp." August 13. Retrieved from http://www.cbsnews.com/stories/2006/08/ 13/national/main1890432.shtml.

Cernkovich, S., and P. Giordano 1987. "Family Relationships and Delinquency." *Criminology* 16: 295–321.

Chambliss, W. J. 1975. "The Saints and the Roughnecks." In Chambliss, W. J. (Ed.), *Criminal Law in Action.* New York: Wiley.

_____. 1993. "State Organized Crime." In W. Chambliss and M. Zatz (Eds.), *Making Law: The State, the Law and Structural Contradictions.* Bloomington: Indiana University Press.

_____, and R. B. Seidman 1971. *Law, Order, and Power.* Reading, MA: Addison-Wesley.

Champion, D. J. 1998. *The Juvenile Justice System,* 2d ed. Upper Saddle River, NJ: Prentice-Hall.

Chan, S. 2009. "A Sociologist's Look at Graffiti." *New York Times,* February 17. Retrieved from http://cityroom.blogs.nytimes.com/ 2009/02/17/a-new-look-at-graffiti-writers-lives/?hp.

Chaney, K. 2009. "Gang-Related Crime More Visible, Not More Prevalent." *Chicago Defender.* August 26. Retrieved from http:// www.chicagodefender.com/article-6185-gang-related-crime-more-visible-not-more-prevalent.html.

Chesney-Lind, M. 1993. "Girls, Gangs and Violence: Reinventing the

Liberated Female Crook." *Humanity and Society* 17: 321–344.

———. 1986. "Women and Crime: The Female Offender." *Signs* 12: 78–96.

Chesney-Lind, M., and R. G. Shelden. 2004. *Girls, Delinquency and Juvenile Justice*, 3d ed. Belmont, CA: Wadsworth.

Chesney-Lind, M., R. Shelden, and K. Joe. 1996. "Girls, Delinquency and Gang Membership." In C. R. Huff, *Gangs in America*, 2d ed. Newbury Park, CA: Sage.

Chesney-Lind, M., A. Rockhill, N. Marker, and H. Reyes. 1994. "Gangs and Delinquency: Exploring Police Estimates of Gang Membership." *Crime, Law and Social Change* 21: 210–228.

Chicago Crime Commission. 1995. *Gangs: Public Enemy Number One, 75 Years of Fighting Crime in Chicagoland*. Chicago: Report of the Chicago Crime Commission.

———. 2009. *The Chicago Crime Commission Gang Book*. Chicago: Chicago Crime Commission.

Chicago Police Department. 1999. *Special Crime Report: The Continuing Fight Against Gangs, Guns and Drugs or the Record, Building Safe Neighborhoods in Chicago*. Chicago Police Department.

Chicago Tribune. 2005. "Six Camp Counselors Charged in Death." July 20: 17.

Children & Family Justice Center of Northwestern University School of Law. 2005. *Education on Lockdown: The Schoolhouse to Jailhouse Track*. Retrieved from http://www.mindfully.org/Reform/2005/Schoolhouse-Jailhouse-Track24mar05.htm.

Children's Defense Fund. 2010. "State of America's Children—2010," p. B–1. Retrieved from http://www.childrensdefense.org/child-research-data-publications/data/state-of-americas-children-2010-report-child-poverty.pdf.

———. 2011. "Portrait of Inequality 2011: Black Children in America." Retrieved from http://www.childrensdefense.org/programs-campaigns/black-community-crusade-for-children-II/bccc-assets/portrait-of-inequality.pdf.

Chin, L. 1990. "Chinese Gangs and Extortion." In C. R. Huff, *Gangs in America*, 2d ed. Newbury Park, CA: Sage.

———. 1996. "Gang Violence in Chinatown." In C. R. Huff, *Gangs in America*, 2d ed. Newbury Park, CA: Sage.

Chin, K. 1990. *Chinese Subculture and Criminality*. Westport, CT: Greenwood Press.

———. 1995. *Chinatown Gangs*. New York: Oxford University Press.

Chomsky, N. 1987. "On the Responsibility of Intellectuals." In E. Peck (Ed.), *The Chomsky Reader*. New York: Pantheon Books.

———. 1989. *Necessary Illusions: Thought Control in Democratic Societies*. Boston: South End Press.

———. 1993. *Year 501: The Conquest Continues*. Boston: South End Press.

———. 1996. *Class Warfare*. Monroe, ME: Common Courage Press.

———. 1998. *The Common Good*. Monroe, ME: Odonian Press.

———. 1999. "Domestic Terrorism: Notes on the State System of Oppression." *New Political Science* 21: 303–324.

Cianci, R., and P. A. Gambrel. 2003. "Maslow's Hierarchy of Needs: Does It Apply in a Collectivist Culture." *Journal of Applied Management and Entrepreneurship* 8: 143–161.

Clark, R. (Ed.) 1992. *Situational Crime Prevention: Successful Case Studies*. New York: Harrow and Heston.

Clarke, R. V., and D. B. Cornish (Eds.). 1983. *Crime Control in Britain: A Review of Policy and Research*. Albany: SUNY Press.

Clarkson, C. A. 2009. "AIG Anger and the Free Market Myth." *Huffington Post*, March 26. Retrieved from http://www.huffingtonpost.com/charles-a-clarkson/aig-anger-and-the-free-ma_b_179632.html.

Clear, T. 2002. "Addition by Subtraction." In M. Mauer and M. Chesney-Lind (Eds.), *Invisible Punishment: The Collateral Consequences of Mass Imprisonment*. New York: New Press.

Cleeland, N. 1999. "Temps Become Full-Time Factor in Industry." *Los Angeles Times*, May 29: A1, A12.

Clemmer, D. 1958. *The Prison Community*. New York: Holt, Rinehart and Winston.

Cloward, R., and L. Ohlin. 1960. *Delinquency and Opportunity*. New York: Free Press.

Cloyd, J. W. 1982. *Drugs and Information Control: The Role of Men and Manipulation in the Control of Drug Trafficking*. Westport, CT: Greenwood Press.

Cohen, A. 1955. *Delinquent Boys: The Culture of the Gang*. New York: Free Press.

———. 1990. "Foreword and Overview." In C. R. Huff, *Gangs in America*, 2d ed. Newbury Park, CA: Sage.

Cohen, L., and M. Felson. 1979. "Social Change and Crime Rate Trends: A 'Routine Activities' Approach." *American Sociological Review* 44: 588–608.

Cohen, S. 1980. *Folk Devils and Moral Panics: The Creation of the Mods and Rockers*, 2d ed. New York: St. Martin's Press.

Cole, D. 1999. *No Equal Justice: Race and Class in the American Criminal Justice System*. New York: The New Press.

Coleman, S. 2008. "The Impact of Parental Criminality on Individual Delinquency." Paper presented at the ASC Annual Meeting, St. Louis, Missouri, November 12.

Collins, P. H. 1990. *Black Feminist Thought: Knowledge, Consciousness, and the Politics of Empowerment*. New York: Rutledge.

Collins, C., and F. Yeskel. 2000. *Economic Apartheid in America*. New York: The New Press.

Colvin, M. 1991. "Crime and Social Reproduction: A Response to the Call for 'Outrageous' Proposals." *Crime and Delinquency* 37: 436–448.

Commission on Behavioral and Social Sciences and Education. 1993. *Losing Generations: Adolescents in High-Risk Settings*. Washington, DC: National Academy Press.

Connell, R. W. 1987. *Gender and Power*. Palo Alto, CA: Stanford University Press.

Conot, R. 1967. *Rivers of Blood, Years of Darkness*. New York: Bantam.

Cook, P. J. 1986. "The Demand and Supply of Criminal Opportunities." In M. Tonry and N. Morris (Eds.), *Crime and Justice*, vol. 7. Chicago: University of Chicago Press.

Cook, R. C. 2007. "Progressive Schemes to Reduce Poverty Will Fail without Monetary Reform." Center for Research on Globalization. Retrieved from http://www.globalresearch.ca/index.php?context=va&aid=5905.

Cook, T. D., H. Cooper, D. S. Cordray, H. Hartmann, L. V. Hedges, R. I. Light, T. A. Lewis, and S. M. Mosteller (Eds.). 1992. *Meta-Analysis for Explanation: A Casebook*. New York: Russell Sage Foundation.

Coontz, S. 1992. *The Way We Never Were: American Families and the Nostalgia Trap*. New York: Harper Collins.

_____. 1997. *The Way We Really Are: Coming to Terms with America's Changing Families*. New York: Basic Books.

Cooper, D. 2011. "Infographic: Tax Breaks vs. Budget Cuts." Center for American Progress, February 22. Retrieved from http://www.americanprogress.org/issues/2011/02/tax_breaks_infographic.html.

Copes, A., and J. P. Williams. 2007. "Techniques of Alienation: Deviant Behavior, Moral Commitment, and Subcultural Identity." *Deviant Behavior* 28: 247–272.

COPS. 2010. "Secure Our Schools," September. Retrieved from http://www.cops.usdoj.gov/pdf/fact_sheets/e091028312-SOS-FactSheet_093010.pdf.

_____. 2011. "FY2011 Secure Our Schools Program." Retrieved from http://www.cops.usdoj.gov/Default.asp?Item=2368.

Cornish, D. B., and R. V. Clarke (Eds). 1987. *The Reasoning Criminal*. New York: Springer-Verlag.

Cottingham, C. (Ed.). 1982. *Race, Poverty, and the Urban Underclass*. Lexington, MA: Lexington Books.

Coughlin, B. C., and S. A. Venkatesh. 2003. "The Urban Street Gang After 1970." *Annual Review of Sociology* 29: 41–64.

Coulthart, R., and D. McNab. 2008. *Dead Man Running: An Insider's Story on One of the World's Most Feared Outlaw Motorcycle Gangs … the Bandidos*. Australia: Allen & Unwin.

Covey, C., S. Menard, and R. Franzese. 1992. *Juvenile Gangs*. Springfield, IL: Charles S. Thomas.

Covington, J., and R. B. Taylor. 1991. "Fear of Crime in Urban Residential Neighborhoods: Implications of Between- and Within-Neighborhood Sources for Current Models." *Sociological Quarterly* 32: 231–249.

Crittenden, D. 1990. "You've Come a Long Way, Moll." *Wall Street Journal*, January 25: A14.

Cullen, L. 2002. *A Job to Die For*. Monroe, ME: Common Courage Press.

Cummings, S., and D. J. Monti (Eds.). 1993. *Gangs: The Origins and Impact of Contemporary Youth Gangs in the United States*. Albany, NY: SUNY Press.

Cunningham, R. M. 1994. "Implications for Treating the Female Gang Member." *Progress: Family Systems Research and Therapy* 3: 91–102.

Cureton, S. R. 2009. "Something Wicked This Way Comes: A Historical Account of Black Gangsterism Offers Wisdom and Warning for African American Leadership." *Journal of Black Studies* 40: 347–361.

Curran, D., and S. Cook. 1993. "Growing Fears, Rising Crime: Juveniles and China's Justice System." *Crime and Delinquency* 39: 296–315.

Currie, E. 1985. *Confronting Crime*. New York: Pantheon.

_____. 1989. "Confronting Crime: Looking Toward the Twenty-First Century." *Justice Quarterly* 6: 5–25.

_____. 1998. *Crime and Punishment in America*. New York: Metropolitan Books.

_____. 1999. "Radical Criminology—or Just Criminology—Then and Now." *Social Justice* 26: 16–18.

Curry, G. D. 1998. "Female Gang Involvement." *Journal of Research in Crime and Delinquency* 35: 100–118.

_____. 2000. "Self-Reported Gang Involvement and Officially Recorded Delinquency." *Criminology* 38: 1253–1274.

_____, C. Maxson, and J. Howell. 2001. *Gang Homicides in the 1990s*. Fact Sheet. March. Washington, DC: Office of Juvenile Justice and Delinquency Prevention.

_____, and S. H. Decker. 1998. *Confronting Gangs: Crime and Community*. Los Angeles: Roxbury Press.

_____, and I. A. Spergel. 1988. "Gang Homicide, Delinquency, and Community." *Criminology* 26: 381–405.

_____, R. A. Ball, and R. J. Fox. 1994. "Gang Crime and Law Enforcement Recordkeeping." *National Institute of Justice, Research in Brief.* August: 1–11.

_____ and S. Decker. 1996. "Estimating the National Scope of Gang Crime from Law Enforcement Data." In C. R. Huff, *Gangs in America*, 2d ed. Newbury Park, CA: Sage.

Curtis, L. A. 1985. *American Violence and Public Policy*. New Haven, CT: Yale University Press.

Daniels, S. M. 2009. "Leader of Mongol Motorcycle Gang Faces 20 Years in Prison." *The Orange County Register*, July 8. Retrieved from http://articles.ocregister.com/2009–0708/cities/24654629_1_mongols-motorcycle-gang-drug-trafficking.

Datesman, S. K., and F. R. Scarpitti (Eds.). 1980. *Women, Crime, and Justice*. New York, Oxford University Press.

Davis, J. R. 1982. *Street Gangs: Youth, Biker, and Prison Groups*. Dubuque, IA: Kendall/Hunt.

Davis, M. 1992. *City of Quartz*. New York, NY: Vintage Books.

Davis, N. 1999. *Youth Crisis*. Westport, CT: Praeger.

_____. 2008. "Foreword" to J. M. Hagedorn, *A World of Gangs: Armed Young Men and Gangsta Culture*. Minneapolis, MN: University of Minnesota Press.

Dawley, D. 1992. *A Nation of Lords: The Autobiography of the Vice Lords*, 2d ed. Prospect Heights, IL: Waveland Press.

Decker, S. H. 2007. "Youth Gangs and Violent Behavior." In D. J. Flannery, A. T. Vazsonyi, and I. D. Waldman (Eds.), *The Cambridge Handbook of Violent Behavior and Aggression*. Cambridge, MA: Cambridge University Press.

_____, C. M. Katz, and V. J. Webb. 2008. "Understanding the Black Box of Gang Organization: Implications for Involvement in Violent Crime, Drug Sales, and Violent Victimization." *Crime & Delinquency* 54: 153–172.

_____, F. Gemert, and D. C. Pyrooz. 2009. "Gangs, Migration, and Crime: The Changing Landscape in Europe and the USA." *International Migration and Integration*. Retrieved from http://www.streetgangs.com/bibliography/2009/2009_decker_gemert_101509.pdf.

_____, and J. L. Lauritsen. 1996. "Breaking the Bonds of Membership: Leaving the Gang." In C. R. Huff, *Gangs in America*, 2d ed. Newbury Park, CA: Sage.

_____, and G. D. Curry. 2000. "Addressing Key Features of Gang Membership: Measuring the Involvement of Young Members." *Journal of Criminal Justice* 28: 473–482.

_____. 2002. "Gangs, Gang Homicides, and Gang Loyalty: Organized Crimes of Disorganized Criminals?" *Journal of Criminal Justice* 30: 1–10.

DeLisi, M., M. T. Berg, and A. Hochstetler. 2004. "Gang Members, Career Criminals and Prison Violence: Further Specification of the Importation Model of Inmate Behavior." *Criminal Justice Studies* 17: 369–383.

DeNavas-Walt, C., B. Proctor, and J. Smith. 2010. *Income, Poverty, and Health Insurance Coverage in the United States: 2009*. U.S. Census Bureau, Current Population Reports, P60–238. Retrieved from http://www.census.gov/prod/2010pubs/p60-238.pdf.

Derber, C. 1998. *Corporation Nation*. New York: St. Martin's Press.

Developmental Research and Programs. 1993. *Communities That Care: Risk-Focused Prevention Using the Social Development Strategy*. Seattle, WA: Developmental Research and Programs.

Deykin, E., and S. Buka. 1994. "Suicidal Ideation and Attempts among Chemically Dependent Adolescents." *American Journal of Public Health* 84(4) (April).

Dickey, W. 1996. "The Impact of 'Three Strikes and You're Out' Laws: What We Have Learned." *Overcrowded Times* 7(5) (October).

Dickey, W., and P. S. Hollenhorst. 1998. "Three-Strikes Laws: Massive Impact in California and Georgia, Little Elsewhere." *Overcrowded Times* 9(6) (December).

DiMaggio, A. 2010. "Forgotten Casualties of the Recession: Child Poverty in the Age of Neoliberalism." *Counterpunch*, July 7. Retrieved from http://www.counterpunch.org/dimaggio07072010.html.

Dodd, R. 2008. "Politically Incorrect Solutions: What about a New Deal-Style Jobs Program?" *Dollars and Sense*, April 16. Retrieved from http://www.alternet.org/story/81921/.

Dokoupil, T. 2010. "'Zero Tolerance' Trouble in New York." *Newsweek*, June 7.

Dolan, E. F., and S. Finney. 1984. *Youth Gangs.* New York: Simon and Schuster.

Domhoff, G. W. 1998. *Who Rules America? Power and Politics in the Year 2000,* 3d ed. Mountain View, CA: Mayfield.

Donnermeyer, J. 1994. "Crime and Violence in Rural Communities." Columbus, OH: North Central Regional Education Laboratory, Ohio State University.

Dorfman, L., and V. Schiraldi. 2001. *Off Balance: Youth, Race & Crime in the News.* Building Blocks for Youth. Retrieved from: http://www.justicepolicy.org/research/2060.

Dorning, M. 2011. "Obama Channels Economic Frustration with $447 Billion Plan to Boost Jobs." *Bloomberg,* September 9. Retrieved from http://www.bloomberg.com/news/2011-09-08/obama-proposes-cutting-payroll-taxes-in-half.html.

Drowns, R., and K. Hess. 1995. *Juvenile Justice.* Belmont, CA: Wadsworth.

Drug Enforcement Administration. 2012. *Production and Trafficking.* U.S. Department of Justice. Retrieved from http://www.fas.org/irp/agency/doj/dea/product/meth/production.htm.

Drury, A. J., and M. DeLisi. 2011. "Gangkill: An Exploratory Empirical Assessment of Gang Membership, Homicide Offending, and Prison Misconduct." *Crime & Delinquency* 57: 130–146.

Dryfoos, J. 1990. *Adolescents at Risk.* New York: Oxford University Press.

Durkheim, E. 1950. *Rule of the Sociological Method.* Glencoe, IL: Free Press (originally published in 1895).

Duster, T. 1987. "Crime, Youth Employment and the Underclass." *Crime and Delinquency* 33: 300–316.

Dyer, J. 2000. *The Perpetual Prisoner Machine: How America Profits from Crime.* Boulder, CO: Westview Press.

Eastman, M. (Trans. and ed.). 1959. *Capital, The Communist Manifesto and Other Writings.* New York: The Modern Library.

Easton, A. 1991. *Adolescent Culture.* New York: New York University Press.

Eckholm, E. 2010. "A Sight All Too Familiar in Poor Neighborhoods." *New York Times,* February 18. Retrieved from http://www.nytimes.com/2010/02/19/us/19evict.html?scp=2&sq=evictions&st=cse.

The Economist. 2010. "Sex and the Single Black Woman: How the Mass Incarceration of Black Men Hurts Black Women." April 8. Retrieved from http://www.economist.com/world/united-states/displaystory.cfm?story_id=15867956.

————. 2011. "America's biggest cases of insider trading." May 12. Retrieved from http://www.economist.com/blogs/dailychart/2011/05/insider_trading.

Edwards, R. W. 1994. "Links among Violence, Drug Use and Gang Involvement." Columbus, OH: North Central Regional Education Laboratory, Ohio State University.

Edwards, R. C., M. Reich, and T. E. Weisskopf (Eds.). 1986. *The Capitalist System,* 3d ed. Englewood Cliffs, NJ: Prentice-Hall.

Egley, A. J. 2000. *Highlights of the 1999 National Youth Gang Survey.* Fact Sheet. Washington, DC: Office of Juvenile Justice and Delinquency Prevention.

————, and M. Arjunan. 2002. *Highlights of the 1999 National Youth Gang Survey.* Fact Sheet. Washington, DC: Office of Juvenile Justice and Delinquency Prevention.

————, and C. E. Ritz. 2006. *Highlights of the 2004 National Youth Gang Survey.* Fact Sheet No. 2006-01. Washington, DC: U.S. Department of Justice, Office of Juvenile Justice and Delinquency Prevention. Retrieved from http://www.ncjrs.gov/pdffiles1/ojjdp/fs200601.pdf.

————, and J. C. Howell. 2011. *Highlights of the 2009 National Youth Gang Survey.* Washington, DC: Department of Justice, Juvenile Justice Fact Sheet, June. Retrieved from https://www.ncjrs.gov/pdffiles1/ojjdp/233581.pdf.

————, J. C. Howell, and J. Moore. 2010. *Highlights of the 2008 National Youth Gang Survey,* March. Retrieved from http://www.ncjrs.gov/pdffiles1/ojjdp/229249.pdf.

Ehrenreich, B. 2001. *Nickel and Dimed: On (Not) Getting By in America.* New York: Henry Holt.

————. 2011. "Turning Poverty into an American Crime." *The Nation,* August 9. Retrieved from http://www.thenation.com/article/162632/turning-poverty-american-crime.

Einstadter, W., and S. Henry. 1995. *Criminological Theory: An Analysis of Its Underlying Assumptions.* Fort Worth, TX: Harcourt Brace.

Eitzen, D. S., M. B. Zinn, and K. E. Smith. 2010. *In Conflict and Order: Understanding Society,* 12th ed. Boston: Allyn and Bacon.

Elikann, P. 1999. *Superpredators: The Demonization of Our Children.* Reading, MA: Perseus Books.

Elliott, D. S., D. Huiziinga, and S. S. Ageton. 1985. *Explaining Delinquency and Drug Use.* Beverly Hills, CA: Sage.

Empey, L., and J. Rabow. 1961. "The Provo Experiment in Delinquency Rehabilitation." *American Sociological Review* 26: 679–695.

Employment Development Department of California. 2011. "State Grants Nearly $5 Million to Combat Gang Violence and Provide Job Training for At-Risk Youth." News release, retrieved from http://www.calgrip.ca.gov/documents/EDD_OGYVP_CalGRIP_Awards_Press_Release_032311.pdf.

Engels, F. 1993 [1845]. *The Condition of the Working Class in England.* New York: Oxford University Press.

Ennett, S. T., N. S. Tobler, C. L. Ringwalt, and R. Flewelling. 1994. "How Effective Is Drug Abuse Resistance Education? A Meta-Analysis of Project D.A.R.E. Outcome Evaluations." *American Journal of Public Health* 84: 1394–1401.

Erlanger, H. S. 1979. "Estrangement, Machismo and Gang Violence." *Social Science Quarterly* 60: 235–249.

Esbensen, F. A., and D. Huizinga. 1993. "Gangs, Drugs, and Delinquency in a Survey of Urban Youth." *Criminology* 31: 565–589.

_____, E. P. Deschenes, and L. T. Winfree. 1999. "Differences Between Gang Girls and Gang Boys." *Youth and Society* 31: 27–53.

_____, and D. Huizinga. 1993. "Gangs, Drugs, and Delinquency in a Survey of Urban Youth." *Criminology* 31: 565–589.

_____, and D. W. Osgood. 1997. "National Evaluation of G.R.E.A.T.: Research in Brief." Washington, DC: Department of Justice.

_____, and Winfree Jr., L. T. 1998. "Race and gender differences between gang and non-gang youths: Results from a multisite survey." *Justice Quarterly* 15: 505–526.

_____ and Lynskey, D. P. 2001. "Youth gang members in a school survey." In M. W. E. P. Deschenes, and L. T. Winfree, "Differences Between Gang Girls and Gang Boys." *Youth and Society* 31: 27–53.

_____, D. W. Osgood, T. J. Taylor, D. Peterson, and A. Freng. 2001. "How Great Is G.R.E.A.T.? Results from the Longitudinal Quasi-Experimental Design." *Criminology and Public Policy* 1: 87–118.

_____, and F. M. Weerman. 2005. "Youth Gangs and Troublesome Youth Groups in the United States and the Netherlands: A Cross-National Comparison." *European Journal of Criminology* 2: 5–37.

_____, and K. E. Tusinski. 2007. "Youth Gangs in the Print Media." *Journal of Criminal Justice and Popular Culture* 14: 21–38.

Estevao, M., and S. Lach. 2001. *Measuring Temporary Labor Outsourcing in U.S. Manufacturing: A Study by the Employment Policies Institute.* Washington, DC: Employment Policies Institute.

Evans, W. P., C. Fitzgerald, D. Weigel, and S. Chvilicek. 1999. "Are Rural Gang Members Similar to Their Urban Peers: Implications for Rural Communities." *Youth and Society* 30: 267–282.

Fagan, J. A. 1989. "The Social Organization of Drug Use and Drug Dealing Among Urban Gangs." *Criminology* 27: 633–667.

_____. 1990. "Social Processes of Delinquency and Drug Use among Urban Gangs." In C. R. Huff, *Gangs in America*, 2d ed. Newbury Park, CA: Sage.

_____. 1996. "Gangs, Drugs, and Neighborhood Change." In C. R. Huff, *Gangs in America*, 2d ed. Newbury Park, CA: Sage.

Fagan, J. A., E. S. Piper, and M. Moore. 1986. "Violent Delinquents and Urban Youth." *Criminology* 23: 439–466.

Falco, M. 1992. *The Making of a Drug-Free America.* New York: Times Books.

Farrington, D., L. Ohlin, and J. Q. Wilson. 1986. *Understanding and Controlling Crime: Toward a New Research Strategy.* New York: Springer-Verlag.

Farrington, D., R. Loeber, M. Stouthamer-Loeber, W. Van Kammen, and L. Schmidt. 1996. "Self-Reported Delinquency and a Combined Delinquency Seriousness Scale Based on Boys, Mothers, and Teachers: Concurrent and Predictive Validity for African-Americans and Caucasians." *Criminology* 34: 501–25.

Faust, F. L., and P. J. Brantingham. 1979. *Juvenile Justice Philosophy.* St. Paul, MN: West.

Federal Bureau of Investigation (FBI). 1995, 2000, 2009. *Crime in America: Uniform Crime Reports.* Washington, DC: U.S. Department of Justice.

_____. 2011. The Mexican Mafia. *FBI Records Vault.* Retrieved from http://vault.fbi.gov/Mexican%20Mafia.

Feldman, L. B., and C. E. Jubrin. 2002. *Evaluation Findings: The Detention Diversion Advocacy Program Philadelphia, Pennsylvania.* Washington, DC: Center for Excellence in Municipal Management, George Washington University.

Field J. 2003. *Social Capital.* New York: Routledge.

First Focus. 2009. "Turning Point: The Long-Term Effects of Recession-Induced Poverty." Retrieved from http://www.firstfocus.net/sites/default/files/r.2009-5.12.ff_.pdf.

Fishman, L. T. 1988. "The Vice Queens: An Ethnographic Study of Black Female Gang

Behavior." Paper presented at American Society of Criminology annual meeting.

Fleisher, M. S. 1995. *Beggars and Thieves: Lives of Urban Street Criminals*. Madison, WI: University of Wisconsin Press.

_____, and S. H. Decker. 2001. An overview of the challenge of prison gangs. *Corrections Management Quarterly* 5: 1–9.

_____, and J. L. Krienert. 2004. Life-Course Events, Social Networks, and the Emergence of Violence among Female Gang Members. *Journal of Community Psychology* 32: 607–622.

Florida Department of Corrections. (n.d.). *Gang and Security Threat Group Awareness*. Retrieved from http://www.dc.state.fl.us/pub/gangs/prison2.html.

Flowers, R. B. 1987. *Women and Criminality*. New York: Greenwood Press.

Folbre, N., and the Center for Popular Economics. 1995. *The New Field Guide to the U.S. Economy*. New York: New Press.

Fones-Wolf, E. 1994. *Selling Free Enterprise*. Indianapolis, IN: University of Indiana Press.

Fong, R. 1990. "The Organizational Structure of Prison Gangs." *Federal Probation* 54: 36–43.

Foote, D. 2008a. "Rewriting the Locke Story." *Los Angeles Times*, May 20. Retrieved from http://articles.latimes.com/2008/may/20/opinion/oe-foote20.

Foote, D. 2008b. *Relentless Pursuit, a Year in the Trenches with Teach for America*. New York: Vintage Books.

Ford, R. 1998. "Razor's Edge." *Boston Globe Magazine*, May 24: 3, 22–28.

"Fort Worth Pays Gangs to Fight Crime." 1994. *New York Times*, May 13: A13.

Fox, J. 1996. *Trends in Juvenile Violence: A Report for the U.S. Attorney General on Current and Future Rates of Juvenile Offending*. Washington, DC: U.S. Department of Justice.

Fox, K., J. Lane, and R. Akers. 2010. "Understanding Gang Membership and Crime Victimization among Jail Inmates: Testing the Effects of Self-Control." *Crime & Delinquency*, December 12.

Fox, R. L., R. W. Van Sickel, and T. L. Steiger. 2007. *Tabloid Justice: Criminal Justice in an Age of Media Frenzy*. Boulder, CO: Lynne Reinner.

Fradette, R. 1992. "Gang Graffiti and Tattoos." Unpublished seminar paper. Department of Criminal Justice, University of Nevada, Las Vegas.

Francis, R. 2008. "Mongols Motorcycle Gang Members Arrested." *USA Today*, October. Retrieved from http://www.usatoday.com/news/nation/2008-10-21-mongols_N.htm.

Frank, R. 2010. "Income Inequality: Too Big to Ignore." *New York Times*, October 16. Retrieved from http://www.nytimes.com/2010/10/17/business/17view.html.

Frank, T. 2005. *What's the Matter with Kansas?* New York: Henry Holt and Company.

_____. 2007. "School Security Cameras Go Cutting Edge." *USA Today*, November 1. Retrieved from http://www.usatoday.com/news/nation/2007-11-01-school-cameras_n.htm.

Frankel, M. 1975. "The Search for Truth: An Empirical View." *University of Pennsylvania Law Review* 123: 1031.

Fremon, C. 2004. *Father Greg and the Homeboys*, rev. ed. Albuquerque, NM: University of New Mexico Press.

Frias, G. 1982. *Barrio Warriors: Homeboys of Peace*. Los Angeles, CA: Diaz Publications.

Frieden, T. 2009. "43 criminal investigations of Wall Street." *CNN Justice Producer*, March 20. Retrieved from http://money.cnn.com/2009/03/20/news/economy/fraud_probes/index.htm.

Friedrichs, D. O. 2009. *Trusted Criminals: White Collar Crime in Contemporary Society*, 3d ed. Belmont, CA: Cengage.

Fritsch, E. J., T. J. Caeti, and R. W. Taylor. 2003. "Gang Suppression Through Saturation Patrol and Aggressive Curfew and Truancy Enforcement: A Quasi-Experimental Test of the Dallas Anti-Gang Initiative." In Decker, S. H. (Ed.), *Policing Gangs and Youth Violence*. Belmont, CA: Wadsworth.

Fuentes, N. 2006. *The Rise and Fall of the Nuestra Familia: The Biography of Robert L. Gratton, One of California's Highest-Ranking Prison Gang Members*. United States: Know Gangs Publishing.

Gaes, G. G., S. Wallace, E. Gilman, J. Klein-Saffran, and S. Suppa. 2002. The Influence of Prison Gang Affiliation on Violence and Other Prison Misconduct. *The Prison Journal* 82: 359–385.

Gans, H. 1995. *The War Against the Poor: The Underclass and Antipoverty Policy*. New York: Basic Books.

Garabedian, P. G., and D. C. Gibbons (Eds.). 1967. *Becoming Delinquent*. Chicago: Aldine.

Garcia, J. 2006. "Teen's New Autopsy Shows He Suffocated." *Orlando Sentinel*, May 6. Retrieved from http://articles.latimes.com/2006/may/06/nation/na-bootcamp6.

Garmire, S. 2008. "Expert Links Shooting Suspects to Mongols Motorcycle Gang." *The Times-Standard*, December. Retrieved from http://www.times-standard.com/localnews/ci_11251602.

Garrett, C. J. 1985. "Effects of Residential Treatment on Adjudicated Adolescents: A Meta-Analysis." *Journal of Research in Crime and Delinquency* 25: 463–489.

Garvey, M. 2005. "Deputies Not Keeping Pace with L.A. Gangs." *Los Angeles Times*, December 12. Retrieved from http://articles.latimes.com/2005/dec/12/local/me-homicide12.

Gatti, U., R. E. Tremblay, F. Vitaro, and P. McDuff. 2005. "Youth Gangs, Delinquency and Drug Use: A Test of the Selection, Facilitation and Enhancement Hypothesis." *Journal of Child Psychology and Psychiatry* 46: 1178–1190.

Gendreau, P. 1991. "General Principles of Effective Programming." Paper delivered at National Coalition of State Juvenile Justice Advisory Groups, April.

Gibbs, J. T. (Ed.). 1988. *Young, Black, and Male in America: An Endangered Species*. Dover, MA: Andover House.

Giddens, A. 1971. *Capitalism and Modern Social Theory*. New York: Cambridge University Press.

——. 1990. *Introduction to Sociology*. New York: Norton.

Gilbert, D. 1998. *The American Class Structure*, 5th ed. Belmont, CA: Wadsworth.

Gillespie, E., and B. Schellhas (Eds.). 1994. *Contract with America*. New York: Random House.

Gilligan, C. 1991. *Women's Psychological Development: Implications for Psychotherapy*. New York: Haworth Press.

Giordano, P. 1978. "Girls, Guys and Gangs: The Changing Social Context of Female Delinquency." *Journal of Criminal Law and Criminology* 69: 126–132.

——, S. Cernkovich, and M. Pugh. 1986. "Friendships and Delinquency." *American Journal of Sociology* 5: 1170–1202.

Giroux, H. 2001. *Public Spaces, Private Lives: Beyond the Culture of Cynicism*. Lanham, MD: Rowman & Littlefield.

——. 2008. "Disposable Youth in a Suspect Society: A Challenge for the Obama Administration," November 28. Retrieved from http://www.zcommunications.org/disposable-youth-in-a-suspect-society-a-challenge-for-the-obama-administration-by-henry-a-giroux.

Glascow, D. C. 1981. *The Black Underclass*. New York: Vintage Books.

Glaze, L. E. 2010. *Correctional Populations in the United States, 2009* (no. NCJ 231681). Washington, DC: Bureau of Justice Statistics. Retrieved from http://bjs.ojp.usdoj.gov/content/pub/pdf/cpus09.pdf.

Glod, M. 2005. Outlaws Motorcycle Gang Members Indicted in Virginia. *Washington Post*, June. Retrieved from http://www.washingtonpost.com/wp-dyn/content/article/2010/06/15/AR2010061505407.html.

Glueck, S., and E. Glueck. 1950. *Unraveling Juvenile Delinquency*. Cambridge, MA: Harvard University Press.

Gogoi, P. 2010. "Job Market Booming Overseas for Many American Companies." *Associated Press*, December 28. Retrieved from http://www.huffingtonpost.com/2010/12/28/job-market-booming-overseas_n_801839.html.

Golden, R. 1997. *Disposable Children: America's Welfare System*. Belmont, CA: Wadsworth.

Goldman, S., and A. Sarat (Eds.). 1989. *American Court Systems: Readings in Judicial Process and Behavior*. New York: Longman.

Goldstein, A. P. 1991. *Delinquent Gangs: A Psychological Perspective*. Champaign, IL: Research Press.

——. 1993. "Gang Intervention: A Historical Review." In A. P. Goldstein and C. R. Huff (Eds.), *The Gang Intervention Handbook*. Champaign, IL: Research Press.

——, and C. R. Huff (Eds.). 1993. *The Gang Intervention Handbook*. Champaign, IL: Research Press.

——, and B. Glick. 1994. *The Prosocial Gang: Implementing Aggression Replacement Training*. Newbury Park, CA: Sage.

Goldstein, H. 1990. *Problem Oriented Policing*. New York: McGraw-Hill.

Gonzales, J. M. 2009. "Ailing Factory Towns Face Tougher Recovery." Manufacturing.net, June 16. Retrieved from http://www.manufacturing.net/Article-Ailing-Factory-Towns-Face-Tougher-Recovery-061609.aspx?menuid=242.

Gonzales, R. 2004. "Asian Gangs Latest Threat Sweeping the Neighborhood." Retrieved from http://lang.dailynews.com/socal/gangs/articles/sgvnp1_asian.asp.

Goode, E., and N. Ben-Yahuda. 1994. *Moral Panics: The Social Construction of Deviance*. Cambridge, MA: Blackwell.

Gora, J. 1982. *The New Female Criminal: Empirical Reality or Social Myth*. New York: Praeger.

Gordon, D. R. 1990. *The Justice Juggernaut: Fighting Street Crime, Controlling Citizens*. New Brunswick, NJ: Rutgers University Press.

——. 1994. *The Return of the Dangerous Classes: Drug Prohibition and Policy Politics*. New York: W. W. Norton.

Gove, W. R. 1994. "Why We Do What We Do: A Biopsychosocial Theory of Human Motivation." *Social Forces* 73: 374–75.

Gover, A. R., W. G. Jennings, and R. Tewksbury. 2009. "Adolescent Male and Female Gang Members' Experiences with Violent Victimization, Dating Violence, and Sexual Assault." *American Journal of Criminal Justice*. (Online version, January.) Retrieved from http://www.springerlink.com/content/j28g2507mw614128/fulltext.html.

Gramckow, H., and E. Tompkins. 1999. *Enabling Prosecutors to Address Drug, Gang, and Youth Violence: Juvenile Accountability Incentive Block Grants Program*. Washington, DC: Office of Juvenile Justice and Delinquency Prevention Bulletin, December.

Granovetter, M. 1992. "The Sociological and Economic Approaches to Labour Market Analysis: A Social Structural View." In M. Granovetter and R. Swedberg (Eds.), *The Sociology of Economic Life*. Boulder, CO: Westview Press.

Green Dot Public Schools. 2010, August 11. "Transformation of Locke High School." Retrieved from http://www.greendot.org/green_dot039s_ transformation_of_locke_high_school_yields_impressive_retention_and_enrollment_rates.

Greenburg, D. (Ed.). 1991. *Crime and Capitalism*, 2d ed. Palo Alto, CA: Mayfield.

Greene, J., and K. Pranis. 2007. "Gang Wars: The Failure of Enforcement Tactics and the Need for Effective Public Safety Strategies." *Justice Policy Institute*: 33. Retrieved from http://www.justicepolicy.org/content-hmID=1811&smID=1581&ssmID=22.htm.

Greenstone, M., and A. Looney. 2011, March 4. "Have Earnings Actually Declined?" Retrieved from http://www.brookings.edu/opinions/2011/0304_jobs_greenstone_looney.aspx.

Greenwood, P. 2010. *Preventing and Reducing Youth Crime and Violence: Using Evidence-Based Practices*. Sacramento, CA: Governor's Office of Gang and Youth Violence Policy. Retrieved from http://advancingebp.org/wp-content/uploads/2010/02/GreenwoodPaper_FINAL_1-27-10.pdf.

Greenwood, P. W., and S. Turner. 1991. *Implementing and Managing Innovative Correctional Programs: Lessons from OJJDP's Private Sector Initiative*. Santa Monica, CA: Rand Corporation.

Griffin, M. L., and J. R. Hepburn. 2006. The Effect of Gang Affiliation on Violent Misconduct among Inmates during the Early Years of Confinement. *Criminal Justice & Behavior* 33: 419–466.

Grocer, S. 2010. "Banks Set for Record Pay." *Wall Street Journal*, January 14. Retrieved from http://online.wsj.com/article/SB10001424052748704281204575003351773983136.html?mod=djemalertNEWS.

Guerrero, A. P., S. T. Nishimura, J. Y. Chang, C. Ona, V. L. Cunanan, and E. S. Hishinuma. 2010. "Low Cultural Identification, Low Parental Involvement and Adverse Peer Influences as Risk Factors for Delinquent Behaviour among Filipino Youth in Hawaii." *International Journal of Social Psychiatry* 56: 371–387.

Hagan, J. 1993. "The Social Embeddedness of Crime and Unemployment." *Criminology* 31: 465–491.

_____, and B. McCarthy. 1992. "Streetlife and Delinquency." *British Journal of Criminology* 43: 533–561.

Hagedorn, J. M. 1990. "Back in the Field Again: Gang Research in the Nineties." In C. R. Huff, *Gangs in America*, 2d ed. Newbury Park, CA: Sage.

_____. 1991. "Gangs, Neighborhoods, and Public Policy." *Social Problems* 38: 529–542.

_____. 1994. "Neighborhoods, Markets and Gang Drug Organization." *Journal of Research in Crime and Delinquency* 31: 264–294.

_____. 1998. *People and Folks: Gangs, Crime and the Underclass in a Rustbelt City*, 2d ed. Chicago: Lakeview Press.

_____. 2008. *A World of Gangs: Armed Young Men and Gangsta Culture*. Minneapolis: University of Minnesota Press.

Hallock, B. 2011. "Homeboy Industries Pins Hopes on Chips and Salsa." *Los Angeles Times*, February 17. Retrieved from http://www.latimes.com/features/food/la-fo-homeboy-chips-20110217,0,7678132.story.

Haltom, W., and M. McCann. 2004. *Distorting the Law: Politics, Media, and the Litigation Crisis*. Chicago: University Of Chicago Press.

Hamm, M. S. 2008. Prisoner Radicalization: Assessing the Threat in U.S. Correctional Institutions. *National Institute of Justice Journal* 261: 14–19.

Haney, C. 2003. Mental Health Issues in Long-Term Solitary and "Supermax" Confinement. *Crime & Delinquency*, 49: 124–156.

Hanson, K. 1964. *Rebels in the Streets: The Story of New York's Girl Gangs*. Englewood Cliffs, NJ: Prentice-Hall.

Harper, G. W., J. Davidson and S. G. Hosek (2008). "Influence of Gang Membership on Negative Affect, Substance Use, and Antisocial Behavior Among Homeless African American Male Youth." *American Journal of Men's Health* 2: 229–243.

Harper, G., and W. L. Robinson. 1999. "Pathways to Risk among Inner-City African American

Adolescent Females: The Influence of Gang Membership." *American Journal of Community Psychology* 27: 383–404.

Harrington, M. 1962. *The Other America: Poverty in the United States.* Baltimore, MD: Penguin Books.

————. 1984. *The New American Poverty.* New York: Penguin Books.

Harris, M. G. 1988. *Cholas: Latino Girls and Gangs.* New York: AMS Press.

————. 1997. "Cholas, Mexican-American Girls, and Gangs." In L. Mays (Ed.), *Gangs and Gang Behavior.* Chicago: Nelson-Hall.

Hartley, R. D., S. Maddan, and C. C. Spohn. 2007. "Concerning Conceptualization and Operationalization: Sentencing Data and the Focal Concerns Perspective" *Southwest Journal of Criminal Justice* 4: 58–78.

Harvey, P. 2011. *Back to Work: A Public Jobs Proposal for Economic Recovery.* New York: Demos. Retrieved from http://www.demos.org/pubs/BackToWork.pdf.

Hasenauer, H. 1996. "Gang Awareness." Soldiers Online, 1996. Retrieved from http://www.dtic.mil/soldiers.

Hawkins, J. D., and J. G. Weis. 1985. "The Social Development Model: An Integrated Approach to Delinquency Prevention." *Journal of Primary Prevention* 6: 73–79.

————, R. F. Catalano, and J. Y. Miller. 1992. "Risk and Protective Factors for Alcohol and Other Drug Problems in Adolescence and Early Adulthood: Implications for Substance Abuse Prevention." *Psychological Bulletin* 112: 64–105.

————, R. F. Catalano, D. M. Morrison, J. O'Donnell, R. D. Abbott, and L. E. Day. 1992. "The Seattle Social Development Project: Effects on the First Four Years on Protective Factors and Problem Behaviors." In McCord and Tremblay, *The Prevention of Antisocial Behavior in Children.* New York: Guilford.

————, J. Guo, K. G. Hill, S. Battin-Pearson, and R. D. Abbott. 2001. "Long-Term Effects of the Seattle Social Development Intervention on School Bonding Trajectories." *Applied Developmental Science: Special Issue: Prevention as Altering the Course of Development* 5: 225–236.

————, R. Kosterman, R. F. Catalano, K. G. Hill, and R. D. Abbott. 2005. "Promoting Positive Adult Functioning Through Social Development Intervention in Childhood: Long-Term Effects from the Seattle Social Development Project." *Archives of Pediatrics & Adolescent Medicine* 159: 25–31.

Hay, C., and W. Forrest. 2006. "The Development of Self-Control: Examining Self-Control Theory's Stability Thesis." *Criminology* 44: 739–774.

Hay, D., P. Linebaugh, J. Rule, E. P. Thompson, and C. Winslow (Eds.). 1975. *Albion's Fatal Tree: Crime and Society in Eighteenth-Century England.* New York: Pantheon.

Heilbroner, R. L. 1985. *The Nature and Logic of Capitalism.* New York: W. W. Norton.

Heinz, A., H. Jacob, and R. L. Lineberry. 1983. *Crime in City Politics.* New York: Longman.

Helfand, D. 2008. "Gang Violence, Political Fights." *Los Angeles Times*, March 10. Retrieved from http://www.streetgangs.com/topics/2008/031008gangviolence.html.

Hells Angels Motorcycle Club. (n.d.). Hells Angels Motorcycle Club World. Retrieved from http://www.hells-angels.com/.

Helmer, J. 1975. *Drugs and Minority Oppression.* New York: Seabury Press.

Hench, D. 2010. Indictment Sheds Light on Motorcycle Club. *The Morning Sentinel*, June 21. Retrieved from http://www.onlinesentinel.com/news/indictment-sheds-light-on-motorcycle-club_2010-06-20.html.

Herbert, B. 2010. "Cops vs. Kids." *New York Times*, March 5. Retrieved from http://www.nytimes.com/2010/03/06/opinion/06herbert.html.

Herman, E., and N. Chomsky. 2002. *Manufacturing Consent: The Political Economy of the Mass Media*, 2d ed. New York: Pantheon.

Hernstein, R. J., and C. Murray. 1996. *Bell Curve: Intelligence and Class Structure in American Life.* New York: Free Press.

Heydebrand, W., and C. Seron. 1990. *Rationalizing Justice: The Political Economy of Federal District Courts.* Albany: State University Press of New York.

Higgins, G. E. 2009. "Parental Criminality and Low Self-Control: An Examination of Delinquency." *Criminal Justice Studies* 22: 141–152.

Hindelang, M. J., M. R. Gottfredson, and T. J. Flanigan (Eds.). 1981. *Sourcebook of Criminal Justice Statistics, 1980.* Washington, DC: U.S. Department of Justice, Bureau of Justice Statistics.

Hirschi, T. 1969. *Causes of Delinquency.* Berkeley: University of California Press.

————. 1983. "Crime and the Family." In J. Q. Wilson (Ed.), *Crime and Public Policy.* San Francisco, CA: Institute for Contemporary Studies.

Hochhaus, C., and F. Sousa. 1988. "Why Children Belong to Gangs: A Comparison of Expectations and Reality." *The High School Journal*, December–January: 74–77.

Hollin, C. 1993. "Cognitive-Behavioral Interventions." In A.P. Goldstein and C. R.

Huff, *The Gang Intervention Handbook.* Champaign, IL: Research Press.

Holmes Jr., O. W. 1881. *The Common Law.* 58th printing. Boston: Little, Brown.

Holthouse, D. 2005. Smashing the Shamrock. *Southern Poverty Law Center Intelligence Report* 119. Retrieved from http://www.splcenter. org.

Holvey, R. 2005, October. "Fighting Gangs in Our Prisons and in Our Neighborhoods." *New Jersey Municipalities.* Retrieved from http://www.njslom.org/magart1005_page46. html.

Hooks, B. 1995. *Killing Rage: Ending Racism.* New York: Henry Holt.

Horowitz, J. 1960. *The Inhabitants.* New York: World.

Horowitz, R. 1982. "Masked Intimacy and Marginality: Adult Delinquent Gangs in a Chicano Community." *Urban Life* 11: 3–26.

––––––––. 1983a. "The End of the Youth Gang." *Criminology* 21: 585–600.

––––––––. 1983b. *Honor and the American Dream.* New Brunswick, NJ: Rutgers University Press.

––––––––. 1987. "Community Tolerance of Gang Violence." *Social Problems* 34: 437–450.

––––––––. 1990. "Sociological Perspectives on Gangs: Conflicting Definitions and Concepts." In C. R. Huff, *Gangs in America,* 2d ed. Newbury Park, CA: Sage.

––––––––, and G. Schwartz. 1974. "Honor, Normative Ambiguity and Gang Violence." *American Sociological Review* 39: 238–251.

Howell, J. C. 1997. "Youth Gangs, Drug Trafficking and Homicide: Policy and Program Implications." *Juvenile Justice* 4: 9–20.

––––––––. 1998. "Youth Gangs: An Overview." Washington, DC: U.S. Department of Justice, Office of Juvenile Justice and Delinquency Prevention.

––––––––. 2007. "Menacing or Mimicking? Realities of Youth Gangs." *Juvenile and Family Court Journal* 58: 39–50. Retrieved from http://www.nationalgangcenter.gov/Content/Documents/Menacing-or-Mimicking. pdf.

––––––––, and J. P. Moore. 2010. "History of Street Gangs in the United States." *National Gang Center Bulletin* 4. Retrieved from http://www.nationalgangcenter.gov/Content/Documents/History-of-Street-Gangs.pdf.

––––––––, and J. P. Lynch. 2000. *Youth Gangs in Schools.* Washington, DC: Office of Juvenile Justice and Delinquency Prevention.

––––––––, A. Egley Jr., and D. K. Gleason. 2002. *Modern Day Youth Gangs. Youth Gang Series*

Bulletin. Washington, DC: Office of Juvenile Justice and Delinquency Prevention.

––––––––, J. P. Moore, and A. Egley Jr. 2002. "The Changing Boundaries of Youth Gangs." 2002. In C. R. Huff, *Gangs in America,* 3d ed. Thousand Oaks, CA: Sage.

Huang, H. 2007. "From the Asian Boyz to the Zhu Lian Bang (the Bamboo Union Gang): A Typological Analysis of Asian Gangs." *Asian Criminology* 2: 127–143.

Huebner, B. M. 2003. Administrative Determinants of Inmate Violence: A Multilevel Analysis. *Journal of Criminal Justice* 31: 107–117.

––––––––, S. P. Varano, and T. Bynum. 2007. "Gangs, Guns, and Drugs: Recidivism among Serious, Young Offenders." *Criminology and Public Policy* 6: 187–221.

Huff, C. R. 1989. "Youth Gangs and Public Policy." *Crime and Delinquency* 35: 524–537.

––––––––. (Ed.) 1990a. *Gangs in America.* Newbury Park, CA: Sage.

––––––––. 1990b. "Denial, Overreaction, and Misidentification: A Postscript on Public Policy." In C. R. Huff, *Gangs in America,* 2d ed. Newbury Park, CA: Sage.

––––––––. 1993. "Gangs in the United States." In A. P. Goldstein and C. R. Huff (Eds.), *The Gang Intervention Handbook.* Champaign, IL: Research Press.

––––––––. (Ed.). 1996. *Gangs in America,* 2d ed. Thousand Oaks, CA: Sage.

––––––––. 1998. "Criminal Behavior of Gang Members and At-Risk Youth." National Institute of Justice, Research in Brief. Washington, DC: U.S. Department of Justice.

––––––––. (Ed.). 2002. *Gangs in America,* 3d ed. Thousand Oaks, CA: Sage.

––––––––, and K. S. Trump. 1996. "Youth Violence and Gangs." *Education and Urban Society* 28: 492–503.

Hughes, T., and D. J. Wilson. 2005. *Reentry Trends in the United States.* Washington, DC: Department of Justice, Bureau of Justice Statistics.

Hunt, G., K. Joe-Laidler, and K. MacKenzie. 2005. "Moving into Motherhood: Gang Girls and Controlled Risk." *Youth & Society* 36: 333–373.

Hurst, C. 2008. "Legislature Has to Make Life Tough on Gang Members." *Enumclaw Courier-Herald,* December 9. Retrieved from http://www.courierherald.com/opinion/35789034.html.

Hurst, J. W. 1950. *The Growth of American Law: The Lawmakers.* Boston, MA: Little, Brown.

Hutchinson, R. 1993. "Blazon Nouveau: Gang Graffiti in the Barrios of Los Angeles and

Chicago." In S. Cummings, and D. J. Monti (Eds.), *Gangs: The Origins and Impact of Contemporary Youth Gangs in the United States.* Albany, NY: SUNY Press.

Ignatieff, M. 1978. *A Just Measure of Pain.* New York: Columbia University Press.

Inciardi, J. A., R. Horowitz, and A. E. Pottieger. 1993. *Street Kids, Street Drugs, Street Crime.* Belmont, CA: Wadsworth.

Institute for Law and Justice. 1994. *Gang Prosecution in the United States.* Washington, DC: U.S. Department of Justice, National Institute of Justice.

Isaacs, J. B. 2010. "The Recession's Impact on Children." The Brookings Institute. Retrieved from http://www.brookings.edu/opinions/2010/0115_recession_children_isaacs.aspx.

Iselin, A. 2010. "Research on School Suspension." *Center for Child and Family Policy*, April 27. Retrieved from http://www.childandfamily-policy.duke.edu/pdfs/familyimpact/2010/Suspension_Research_Brief_2010-04-27.pdf.

Izzo, R. L., and R. R. Ross. 1990. "Meta-Analysis of Rehabilitation Programs for Juvenile Delinquents: A Brief Report." *Criminal Justice and Behavior* 17: 134–142.

Jablon, R. 2000. "L.A. Prepares for Worst as Police Scandal Grows." Associated Press, February 19.

Jackson, C. B., and J. Gordon. 1995. "Atlanta's GANGIS Advances Fight Against Crime." *The Police Chief*, May 11.

Jackson, P. G. 1989. "Theories and Findings about Youth Gangs." *Criminal Justice Abstracts*, June: 313–329.

————. 1991. "Crime, Youth Gangs, and Urban Transition: The Social Dislocations of Postindustrial Economic Development." *Justice Quarterly* 8: 379–398.

————. 1992. "Minority Group Threat, Social Context, and Policing" In A. E. Liska, *Social Threat and Social Control.* Albany: State University of New York Press.

Jackson, R., and W. D. McBride. 1992. *Understanding Street Gangs.* Placerville, CA: Copperhouse.

Jacobe, D. 2010. "U.S. Underemployment Steady at 18.4% in July." Retrieved from http://www.gallup.com/poll/141770/underemployment-steady-july.aspx.

Jacobs, J. B. 2009. Gang Databases: Contexts and Questions. *Criminology & Public Policy*, 8: 705–709.

Jaffe, I. 2006, July. Aryan Brotherhood Leaders Convicted of Murder. *National Public Radio.* Retrieved from http://www.npr.org/templates/story/story.php?storyId=5591170.

James, R. 2009. The Hells Angels. *Time Magazine*, August 3. Retrieved from http://www.time.com/time/nation/article/0,8599,1914201,00.html.

Jankowski, M. S. 1990. *Islands in the Street: Gangs and American Urban Society.* Berkeley: University of California Press.

Jealous, B. T., R. M. Brock, and A. Huffman. 2011. "Misplaced Priorities: Over Incarcerate, Under Educate. NAACP Smart and Safe Campaign. Retrieved from http://naacp.3cdn.net/01d6f368edbe135234_bq0m68x5h.pdf.

Jefferson and Associates, and Community Research and Associates. 1987. *Creating a New Agenda for the Care and Treatment of San Francisco's Youthful Offenders: A Model Program.* San Francisco: Jefferson and Associates.

Jewkes, Y. 2011. *Media and Crime: Key Approaches to Criminology*, 2d ed. Thousand Oaks, CA: Sage.

Joe, D., and N. Robinson. 1980. "Chinatown's Immigrant Gangs." *Criminology* 18: 337–345.

Joe, K., and M. Chesney-Lind. 1995. "'Just Every Mother's Angel': An Analysis of Gender and Ethnic Variations in Youth Gang Membership." *Gender and Society* 9: 408–431.

Johnson, B. D., P. J. Goldstein, E. Preble, J. Schmeidler, D. Lipton, B. Spunt, and T. Miller. 1985. *Taking Care of Business: The Economics of Crime by Heroin Abusers.* Lexington, MA: Lexington Books.

Johnson, R. 2011. "Casa 0101 Brings Art to the Eastside." *Los Angeles Times*, September 25. Retrieved from http://www.latimes.com/entertainment/news/la-ca-josefina-lopez-20110925,0,6459426.story.

Johnstone, J. C. 1983. "Youth Gangs and Black Suburbs." *Pacific Sociological Review* 24: 355–373.

Judd, D. R. 1999. "Symbolic Politics and Urban Policies." In A. Reed Jr. (Ed.), *Without Justice For All.* Boulder, CO: Westview Press.

Kamin, D., and I. Shapiro. 2004. "Studies Shed New Light on Effects of Administration's Tax Cuts." Washington, DC: Center on Budget and Policy Priorities, September 13. Retrieved from http://www.cbpp.org/8-25-04tax.htm.

Kataoka, S. H. 2001. "Mental Health Problems and Service Use among Female Juvenile Offenders: Their Relationship to Criminal History." *Journal of the American Academy of Child and Adolescent Psychiatry* 40: 549–555.

Katzman, G. S. 1991. *Inside the Criminal Process.* New York: W. W. Norton.

Kaufman, P. 2010. "The Long View of Crime." National Institute of Justice, *NIJ Journal* 265,

April. Retrieved from http://www.nij.gov/journals/265/crime.htm.

Keiser, R. L. 1969. *The Vice Lords: Warriors of the Streets*. New York: Holt, Rinehart and Winston.

Kelly, D. H. (Ed.). 1993. *Deviant Behavior*. New York: St. Martin's Press.

Kelly, J. 2010. "Weekly Notes." *Youth Today*, November 12. Retrieved from http://www.youthtoday.org/view_blog.cfm?blog_id=420.

Kennedy, D. M. 2009. Gangs and Public Policy: Constructing and Deconstructing Gang Databases Policy Essay. *Criminology & Public Policy* 8: 711–716.

Kenrick, D. T., V. Griskevicius, S. L. Neuberg, and M. Schaller. 2010. "Renovating the Pyramid of Needs: Contemporary Extensions Built upon Ancient Foundations." *Perspectives on Psychological Science* 5. Retrieved from http://www.csom.umn.edu/assets/144040.pdf.

Kent, D., S. Donaldson, P. Wyrick, and P. Smith. 2000. "Evaluating Criminal Justice Programs Designed to Reduce Crime by Targeting Repeat Gang Offenders." *Evaluation and Program Planning* 23: 115–124.

Kent, D. R., and G. T. Felkenes. 1998. *Cultural Explanations for Vietnamese Youth Involvement in Street Gangs*. Westminster, CA: Westminster Police Department, Office of Research and Planning. Retrieved from http://www.hawaii.edu/hivandaids/Cultural_Explanations_for_Vietnamese_Youth_Involvement_in_Street_Gangs.pdf.

"Kids Who Kill." 1991. *U.S. News and World Report*, April 8: 26–34.

Kim, H. (n.d.). "The Origin of Asian and Chinese Gangs in Chicago's Chinatown." Retrieved from http://www.gangresearch.net/ChicagoGangs/tongs/kimpri.html.

Kitchen, D. B. 1995. *Sisters in the Hood*. Ph. D. dissertation, Western Michigan University.

Klein, M. 1968. *The Ladino Hills Project. Final Report*. Washington, DC: Office of Juvenile Delinquency and Youth Development.

———. 1971. *Street Gangs and Street Workers*. Englewood Cliffs, NJ: Prentice-Hall.

———. 1985. "Differences between Gang and Non-Gang Homicides." *Criminology* 23: 209–220.

———. 1995. *The American Street Gang*. New York: Oxford University Press.

———. 1989. "Street Gang Violence." In M. E. Wolfgang and N. A. Weiner (Eds.), *Violent Crime, Violent Criminals*. Newbury Park, CA: Sage.

———. 1990. *Street Gangs and Drug Sales*. Los Angeles: University of Southern California,

Center for Research on Crime and Social Control.

———. 2006. *Street Gang Patterns and Policies*. New York: Oxford University Press (Kindle edition).

Klein, M., C. Maxson, and M. A. Gordon. 1984. *Evaluation of an Imported Gang Violence Deterrence Program: Final Report*. Los Angeles: University of Southern California, Social Science Research Institute.

Klein, M., H. Kerner, C. L. Maxson, and E. Weitekampf (Eds.). 2000. *The Eurogang Paradox: Street Gangs and Youth Groups in the U.S. and Europe*. Amsterdam: Kluwer Academic Publishers.

Klivans, G. 2008, August/July. "Gang Codes: Not Hiding in Plain Sight." *American Jails Magazine* 22: 57–59.

Kluegel, J. R. (Ed.). 1983. *Evaluating Contemporary Juvenile Justice*. Beverly Hills, CA: Sage.

Knox, G. (n.d.). Gangs, Guerilla Warfare, and Social Conflict: The Potential Terrorism Threat from Gangs in America. *National Gang Crime Research Center*. Retrieved from http://www.ngcrc.com/introcha.html#N_39_.

———. 2004. "The Problem of Gangs and Security Threat Groups." Retrieved from http://www.ngcrc.com/ngcrc/corr2006.html.

Knupfer, A. M. 2001. *Reform and Resistance: Gender, Delinquency, and America's First Juvenile Court*. New York: Routledge.

Knutson, R. 2010. "Blast at BP Texas Refinery in '05 Foreshadowed Gulf Disaster." Frontline, PBS, July 27. Retrieved from http://www.propublica.org/article/blast-at-bp-texas-refinery-in-05-foreshadowed-gulf-disaster.

Kobrin, S., J. Puntil, and E. Peluso. 1987. "Criteria of Status among Street Groups." *Journal of Research in Crime and Delinquency* 4: 98–118.

Kontos, L., D. C. Brotherton, and L. Barrios (Eds.). 2003. *Gangs and Society: Alternative Perspectives*. New York: Columbia University Press.

Korem, D. *Suburban Gangs—The Affluent Rebels*. Richardson, TX: International Focus Press.

Kornblum, W. 1987. "Ganging Together: Helping Gangs Go Straight." *Social Issues and Health Review* 2: 99–104.

Kotlowitz, A. 1991. *There Are No Children Here*. New York: Doubleday.

Kozol, J. 1992. *Savage Inequalities: Children in America's Schools*. New York: Harper Perennial.

———. 2005. *The Shame of the Nation: The Restoration of Apartheid Schooling in America*. New York: Three Rivers Press.

Krajicek, D. J. 1999. "Time to Stick a Fork in America's Correctional Boot Camp

Boondoggle." MSNBC, December 23. Retrieved from http://www.nospank.net/n-j37.htm.

Kraska, P. B. 1999. "Militarizing Criminal Justice: Exploring the Possibilities." *Journal of Political and Military Sociology* 27: 205–216.

Krienert, J. L., and Fleisher, M. S. 2001. Gang Membership as a Proxy for Social Deficiencies: A Study of Nebraska Inmates. *Corrections Management Quarterly* 3: 47–58.

Krisberg, B., and J. Austin. 1993. *Reinventing Juvenile Justice*. Newbury Park, CA: Sage.

Krohn, M. D., N. M. Schmidt, A. J. Lizotte, and J. M. Baldwin. 2011. "The Impact of Multiple Marginality on Gang Membership and Delinquent Behavior for Hispanic, African American, and White Male Adolescents." *Journal of Contemporary Criminal Justice* 27: 18–42.

Krugman, P. 2007. *The Conscience of a Liberal*. New York: W.W. Norton.

————. 2011. "The Wrong Worries." *New York Times*, August 4. Retrieved from http://www.nytimes.com/2011/08/05/opinion/the-wrong-worries.html?_r=1&partner=rssnyt&emc=rss.

Kuhn, T. 1970. *The Structure of Scientific Revolutions*, 2d ed. Chicago: University of Chicago Press.

LaCourse, E., D. Nagin, R. E. Tremblay, F. Vitaro, and M. Claes. 2003. "Developmental Trajectories of Boys' Delinquent Group Membership and Facilitation of Violent Behaviors during Adolescence." *Development and Psychopathology* 15: 183–197.

LaFave, W. R., and J. H. Israel. 1992. *Criminal Procedure*, 2d ed. St. Paul, MN: West.

Laidler, K. A., and G. Hunt. 1997. "Violence and Social Organization in Female Gangs." *Social Justice* 24: 148–169.

Lam, K. D. 2009. *Reppin' 4 Life: The Formation and Racialization of Vietnamese Youth Gangs in Southern California*. Doctoral dissertation, University of Illinois at Urbana-Champaign.

Land, K. 2010. "The 2009 Foundation for Child Development and Youth Well-Being Index (CWI) Report." Retrieved from http://www.soc.duke.edu/~cwi/2009CWIReport.pdf.

Langton, J. 2009. *Fallen Angel: The Unlikely Rise of Walter Stadnick and the Canadian Hells Angels*. Ontario, CA: John Wiley & Sons Canada, Ltd.

Lanier, M. M., and S. Henry. 1998. *Essential Criminology*. Boulder, CO: Westview Press.

Laongo, T. 1994. "I Was a Gang Girl." *Mademoiselle*. July.

Lapham, L. 2000. "School Bells." *Harper's Magazine* 301: 7–9.

Lasley, J. 1998. *Designing Out: Gang Homicides and Street Assaults*. Washington, DC: National Institute of Justice.

Latimer, D., and J. Goldberg. 1981. *Flowers in the Blood: The Story of Opium*. New York: Franklin Watts.

Laub, J., and R. J. Sampson. 2006. *Shared Beginnings, Divergent Lives: Delinquent Boys to Age 70*. Cambridge, MA: Harvard University Press.

Lauderback, D., J. Hansen, and D. Waldorf. 1992. "'Sisters Are Doin' It for Themselves': A Black Female Gang in San Francisco." *The Gang Journal* 1: 57–72.

Lavigne, Y. 1993. *Good Guy, Bad Guy*. Toronto, Random House.

Le, C. H. 2011. "Asian Gangs." Retrieved from http://www.asian-nation.org/gangs.shtml.

LeDuff, C. 2002. A Biker Shot Dead Is Laid to Rest, and a Bloody Turf War Rages On. *The New York Times*, May 5. Retrieved from http://www.nytimes.com/2002/05/05/us/a-biker-shot-dead-is-laid-to-rest-and-a-bloody-turf-war-rages-on.html.

Lee, F. R. 1991. "For Gold Earrings and Protection, More Girls Take the Road to Violence." *New York Times*, November 25: A1.

Lemert, E. 1951. *Social Pathology*. New York: McGraw-Hill.

Leovy, J. 2003. "Crime Edges Up, Led by 10% Jump in Homicides." *Los Angeles Times*, January 1.

Lerner, S., 1986. *Bodily Harm: The Pattern of Fear and Violence at the California Youth Authority*. Bolinas, CA: Common Knowledge Press.

Levitt, S. D., and S. J. Dubner. 2005. *Freakonomics*. New York: Harper Perennial.

Lewis, N. 1992. "Delinquent Girls Achieving a Violent Equality in D.C." *Washington Post*. December 23: A1, A14.

Libit, H. 2002. "State Approves $4.6 Million for Former Boot Camp Inmates. Settlement Likely to Play Role in Governor's Race." *Baltimore Sun*, August 8.

Lichtenwalter, S. 2005. "Gender Poverty Disparity in US Cities: Evidence Exonerating Female-Headed Families." *Journal of Sociology and Social Welfare*, June. Retrieved from http://findarticles.com/p/articles/mi_m0CYZ/is_2_32/ai_n14711313/?tag=content;col1.

Lieberman, T. 2003. "Bruised and Broken: U.S. Health System." *AARP Bulletin* 44 (March): 3–4.

"Life and Death with the Gangs." 1987. *Time*, August 24: 21–22.

Lipsey, M. 1992. "Juvenile Delinquency Treatment: A Meta-Analysis Inquiry into the Variability of Effects." In T. D. Cook et al., *Meta-analysis for Explanation: A Casebook*. New York: Russell Sage Foundation.

_____. 2009. "The Primary Factors that Characterize Effective Interventions with Juvenile Offenders: A Meta-Analytic Overview." *Victims and Offenders* 4: 124–147.

Lipton, E. 2009. "Ex-Leaders of Countrywide Profit from Bad Loans." *New York Times*, March 3. Retrieved from http://www.nytimes.com/2009/03/04/business/04penny.html?_r=1&hp.

Liska, A. E. (Ed.). 1992. *Social Threat and Social Control*. Albany: State University of New York Press.

Loeber, R., and M. Stouthamer-Loeber. 1986. "Family Factors as Correlates and Predictors of Juvenile Conduct Problems and Delinquency." In M. Tonry and N. Morris (Eds.), *Crime and Justice: An Annual Review*. Chicago: University of Chicago Press.

Long, D. P., and L. Ricaud. 1997. *The Dream Shattered: Vietnamese Gangs in America*. Boston: Northeastern University Press.

Loper, A. B., and D. G. Cornell. 1995. "Homicide by Girls." Paper presented at the National Girls Caucus Annual Meeting, Orlando, Florida.

Los Angeles County. 1992. *L. A. Style: A Street Gang Manual of the Los Angeles County Sheriff's Department*. Los Angeles: Los Angeles County Sheriff's Department.

_____. 1999, August. *Gangs*. Santa Clarita Valley, Cobra Unit, Los Angeles County Sheriff's Department.

Losen, D. J., and R. J. Skiba. 2010. "Suspended Education: Urban Middle Schools in Crisis." *Southern Poverty Law Center*. Retrieved from http://www.splcenter.org/get-informed/publications/suspended-education.

Lour, G. C. 1987. "The Family as Context for Delinquency Prevention: Demographic Trends and Political Realities." In J. Q. Wilson and G.C. Loury (Eds.), *From Children to Citizens, Volume III: Families, Schools, and Delinquency Prevention*. New York: Springer-Verlag.

Loury, G. C. 1985. "The Moral Quandary of the Black Community." *Public Interest* 79: 11.

Lovell, D., and R. Jemelka. 1996. "When Inmates Misbehave: The Costs of Discipline." *The Prison Journal* 76: 165–179.

Lydersen, K. 2003. "Zero Tolerance for Teens." *AlterNet*, July 1. Retrieved from http://www.alternet.org/story/16305/.

Macallair, D. 1994. "Disposition Case Advocacy in San Francisco's Juvenile Justice System: A New Approach to Deinstitutionalization." *Crime and Delinquency* 40: 84–95.

_____. 2002. "Boot Camp Blunder." San Francisco: Center on Juvenile and Criminal Justice. Retrieved from http://www.cjcj.org.

_____, and M. Males. 2004. "A Failure of Good Intentions: An Analysis of Juvenile Justice Reform in San Francisco during the 1990s." *Review of Policy Research* 21: 63–78.

Machiavelli, N. 1950. *The Prince and the Discourses*. New York: Modern Library.

Mack, J. W. 1989. "The Juvenile Court." In F. B. McCarthy and J. Carr (Eds.), *Juvenile Law and Its Processes*, 2d ed. Charlottesville, VA: Michie Company Law Publishers.

MacKenzie, D. L., A. R. Gover, G. S. Armstrong, and O. Mitchell. 2001. *A National Study Comparing the Environments of Boot Camps with Traditional Facilities for Juvenile Offenders*. Washington, DC: National Institute of Justice.

MacLeod, J. 2008. *Ain't No Makin' It: Leveled Aspirations in a Low-Income Neighborhood*, 3d ed. Boulder, CO: Westview Press.

Maguire, K., and A. L. Pastore (Eds.). 1998. *Sourcebook on Criminal Justice Statistics—1997*. Washington, DC: U.S. Department of Justice, Bureau of Justice Statistics.

Maguire, K., A. L. Pastore, and T. J. Flanagan. 1993. *Sourcebook of Criminal Justice Statistics, 1992*. Washington, DC: U.S. Department of Justice, Bureau of Justice Statistics.

Males, M. 1999. *Framing Youth: Ten Myths about the Next Generation*. Monroe, ME: Common Courage Press.

_____, and D. Macallair. 2000. "Dispelling the Myth: An Analysis of Youth and Adult Crime Patterns in California over the Past 20 Years." San Francisco: Justice Policy Institute. Retrieved from http://www.cjcj.org/files/Dispelling.pdf.

_____, D. Macallair, and K. Taqi-Eddin. 1999. "California's Three-Strikes Law Ineffective." *Overcrowded Times*, August 10: 4.

Mann, C. R. 1984. *Female Crime and Delinquency*. Tuscaloosa, AL: University of Alabama Press.

Mann, E. A., and A. J. Reynolds. 2006. "Early Intervention and Juvenile Delinquency Prevention: Evidence from the Chicago Longitudinal Study." *Social Work Research* 30: 153–167.

Marinucci, C., S. Winokur, and G. Lewis. 1994. "Ruthless Girlz." *San Francisco Examiner*, December 12: A1.

Marshall, J., R. Tuttle, and H. Laurenzano. 2002. "Gangs: Behind the Headlines." *Santa Maria Times*, February 25.

Martens, P. 2008. "The Free Market Myth Dissolves into Chaos." *Counterpunch*, January 3. Retrieved from http://www.counterpunch.org/martens01032008.html.

Martin, D. E. 1992. *Promising Programs Addressing Youth Violence*. Detroit, MI: Wayne State University, Center for Urban Studies, Urban Safety Program.

Martin, P. 1992. "Look Homeward Angel Cycle Icon Sonny Barger Kick-Starts Life as a Free Man by Violating Parole." *Phoenix Newtimes News*, December. Retrieved from http://www.phoenixnewtimes.com/1992-12-02/news/look-homeward-angelcycle-icon-sonny-barger-kick-starts-life-as-a-free-man-by-violating-parole/.

Marx, K. 1964. *The Economic and Philosophic Manuscripts of 1844*. New York: International.

———, and F. Engels. 1947. *The German Ideology* [1845–46]. New York: International.

Maslow, A. H. 1951. *Motivation and Personality*. New York: Harper and Row.

Massey, D. S. 2007. "Residential Segregation and Persistent Urban Poverty." In M. T. Martin and M. Yaquinto (Eds.), *Redress for Historical Injustices in the United States: On Reparations for Slavery, Jim Crow, and Their Legacies*. Durham, NC: Duke University Press.

———, and N. A. Denton. 1993. *American Apartheid: Segregation and the Making of the Underclass*. Cambridge, MA: Harvard University Press.

Matza, D. 1964. *Delinquency and Drift*. New York: Wiley.

Mauer, M. 2006. *Race to Incarcerate*, 2d ed. New York: New Press.

Maxfield, M. 1987. "Household Composition, Routine Activities, and Victimization: A Comparative Analysis." *Journal of Quantitative Criminology* 3: 301–320.

Maxson, C. L. 1998. *Gang Members on the Move*. Bulletin. Washington, DC: U.S. Department of Justice, Office of Justice Programs, Office of Juvenile Justice and Delinquency Prevention.

———. 1995. *Street Gangs and Drug Sales in Two Suburban Cities*. Washington, DC: National Institute of Justice, Research Brief, September.

———, C. Bradstreet, D. Gascón. J. Gerlinger, J. Grebenkemper, D. Haerle, J. Kang-Brown, M. Omori, S. Reid, and D. Scott. 2011. "Developing Effective Gang Policies for California's Division of Juvenile Justice: Preliminary Findings Draft Report." Irvine,

CA: University of California-Irvine, Department of Criminology, Law and Society, August 29.

———, and M. W. Klein. 1983a. "Agency Versus Agency: Disputes in the Gang Deterrence Model." In J. Kluegel, *Evaluating Contemporary Juvenile Justice*. Beverly Hills, CA: Sage.

———. 1983b. "Gangs: Why We Couldn't Stay Away." In J. Kluegel, *Evaluating Contemporary Juvenile Justice*. Beverly Hills, CA: Sage.

———. 1990. "Street Gang Violence: Twice as Great or Half as Great?" In C. R. Huff, *Gangs in America*, 2d ed. Newbury Park, CA: Sage.

———, K. J. Woods, and M. W. Klein. 1996. "Street Gang Migration: How Big a Threat?" *National Institute of Justice Journal* 230: 26–31.

———, and M. Whitlock. 2002. "Joining the Gang: Gender Differences in Risk Factors for Gang Membership." In C. R. Huff (Ed.), *Gangs in America*, 3d ed. Thousand Oaks, CA: Sage.

Mays, L. 1997. *Gangs and Gang Behavior*. Chicago: Nelson-Hall.

McCartan, L. K., and E. Gunnison. 2007. "Examining the Origins and Influence of Low Self-Control." *Journal of Crime and Justice* 30: 35–62.

McCarthy, F. B., and J. Carr (Eds.). 1989. *Juvenile Law and Its Processes*, 2d ed. Charlottesville, VA: Michie Company Law Publishers.

McChesney, R. 2004. *The Problem of the Media: U.S. Communication Politics in the Twenty-First Century*. New York: Monthly Review Press.

McCord, J., and R. Tremblay (Eds.). 1992. *The Prevention of Antisocial Behavior in Children*. New York: Guilford.

McCorkle, R., and T. Miethe. 1998. "The Political and Organizational Response to Gangs: An Examination of a Moral Panic." *Justice Quarterly* 15: 41–64.

———. 2001. *Panic: Rhetoric and Reality in the War on Street Gangs*. Saddle River, NJ: Prentice-Hall.

McGloin, J. M. 2005. "Policy and Intervention Considerations of a Network Analysis of Street Gangs." *Criminology and Public Policy* 4(3): 607–636.

———. 2007. "The Continued Relevance of Gang Membership." *Criminology and Public Policy* 6: 231–240.

McGreevy, P. 2003. "Effort to Fight Gangs Faulted." *Los Angeles Times*, January 5. Retrieved from http://articles.latimes.com/2003/jan/05/local/me-bridges5.

_____. 2007. "Study Fails to Stem Gangs Debate." *Los Angeles Times*, February 23. Retrieved from http://articles.latimes.com/2007/feb/23/local/me-gangs23.

_____, and R. Winton. 2007. "L.A. Anti-Gang Project Lacks Proof of Progress." Retrieved from http://articles.latimes.com/2007/mar/06/local/me-bridges6.

McNaught, S. 1999. "Gangsta Girls." *The Boston Phoenix*, May 20–27.

McRobbie, A., and J. Garber. 1975. "Girls and Subcultures." In S. Hall and T. Jefferson (Eds.), *Resistance through Rituals: Youth Subculture in Post-War Britain*. New York: Holmes and Meier.

Mendel, R. A. 2010. "The Missouri Model: Reinventing the Practice of Rehabilitating Youthful Offenders." The Annie E. Casey Foundation. Retrieved from http://www.aecf.org/~/media/Pubs/Initiatives/Juvenile%20Detention%20Alternatives%20Initiative/MOModel/MO_Fullreport_webfinal.pdf.

Mendez, D. 1996. "More and More Girls Joining Violent Male Gangs." *The Seattle Times*, October 27: A7.

Menendez, R., T. Harkin, S. Brown, and C. Levin. 2011. U.S. Senate Letter to Charles Tharp, CEO, Center on Executive Compensation, Washington, DC. Retrieved from https://s3.amazonaws.com/s3.documentcloud.org/documents/237892/col-ceo-menendez-letter-defending-provision.pdf.

Merton, R. K. 1968. *Social Theory and Social Structure*. New York: Free Press.

Messerschmidt, J. 1993. *Masculinities and Crime*. Baltimore, MD: Rowman and Littlefield.

Messner, S., and K. Tardiff. 1985. "The Social Ecology of Urban Homicide: An Application of the Routine Activities Approach." *Criminology* 23: 241–267.

_____, R. Rosenfeld. 2007. Crime and the American Dream, 4th ed. Belmont, CA: Wadsworth.

Mieczkowski, T. 1986. "Geeking Up and Throwing Down: Heroin Street Life in Detroit." *Criminology* 24: 645–666.

Miethe, T., R. McCorkle, and S. Listwan. 2005. *Crime Profiles: The Anatomy of Dangerous Persons, Places, and Situations*. New York: Oxford University Press.

_____, W. C. Regoeczi, and K. Drass. 2004. *Rethinking Homicide: Exploring the Structure and Process Underlying Deadly Situations*. Oxford: Cambridge University Press.

Millenky, M., D. Bloom, and C. Dillon. 2010. *Making the Transition: Interim Results of the National Guard Youth ChalleNGe Evaluation*. New York: MDRC.

Miller, J. 2001. *One of the Guys: Girls, Gangs, and Gender*. New York: Oxford University Press.

_____. 2008. *Getting Played: African American Girls, Urban Inequality and Gendered Violence*. New York: New York University Press.

_____, and R. Brunson. 2000. Gender Dynamics in Youth Gangs: A Comparison of Males' and Females' Accounts. *Justice Quarterly* 17: 419–448.

Miller, J. G. 1996. *Search and Destroy: African-American Males in the Criminal Justice System*. New York: Cambridge University Press.

_____. 1998. *Last One Over the Wall: The Massachusetts Experiment in Closing Reform Schools*, 2d ed. Columbus, OH: Ohio State University Press.

Miller, J. M., and A. Cohen. 1995. "A Brief History of Gang Theories and Their Policy Implications." In J. M. Miller and J. P. Rush (Eds.), *A Criminal Justice Approach to Gangs: From Explanation to Response*. Cincinnati, OH: ACJS/Anderson Monograph Series.

Miller, J. M., and J. P. Rush (Eds.). 1995. *A Criminal Justice Approach to Gangs: From Explanation to Response*. Cincinnati, OH: ACJS/Anderson Monograph Series.

Miller, R. L. 1996. *Drug Warriors and Their Prey: From Police Power to Police State*. Westport, CT: Praeger.

Miller, W. B. 1958. "Lower Class Culture as a Generating Milieu of Gang Delinquency." *Journal of Social Issues* 14: 5–19.

_____. 1974. "American Youth Gangs: Past and Present." In A. Blumberg (Ed.), *Current Perspectives on Criminal Behavior*. New York: Knopf.

_____. 1975. *Violence by Youth Gangs and Youth Groups as a Crime Problem in Major American Cities*. Washington, DC: U.S. Department of Justice.

_____. 1980a. "The Molls." In S. K. Datesman and F. R. Scarpitti (Eds.), *Women, Crime, and Justice*. New York: Oxford University Press.

_____. 1980b. "Gangs, Groups, and Serious Youth Crime." In D. Schichor and D. Kelly (Eds.), *Critical Issues in Juvenile Delinquency*. Lexington, MA: D.C. Heath.

_____. 1982. *Crime by Youth Gangs and Groups in the United States*. Washington, DC: U.S. Department of Justice.

_____. 1990. "Why the United States Has Failed to Solve Its Youth Gang Problem." In C. R. Huff, *Gangs in America*, 2d ed. Newbury Park, CA: Sage.

_____. 2001. *The Growth of Youth Gang Problems in the United States, 1970–98*.

Washington, DC: Office of Juvenile Justice and Delinquency Prevention.

Mills, N. 1997. *The Triumph of Meanness: America's War Against Its Better Self*. New York: Houghton Mifflin.

Mintz, H. 2003. "California Case Tugs at Key Parts of Death Penalty Debate." *Las Vegas Review Journal*, February 23.

Miringoff, M., and M. Miringoff. 1999. *The Social Health of the Nation*. New York: Oxford University Press.

Mock, B. 2006. *L.A. Blackout*. *Southern Poverty Law Center Intelligence Report* 124. Retrieved from http://www.splcenter.org.

Mokhiber, R. 2005. "Crime without Conviction: The Rise of Deferred and Non-Prosecution Agreements." *Corporate Crime Reporter*, December 28. Retrieved from http://www.corporatecrimereporter.com/deferredreport.htm.

Molidor, C. 1996. "Female Gang Members: A Profile of Aggression and Victimization." *Social Work* 41: 251–257.

Mollenkamp, C. 2009. "UBS Makes a Change at the Top." *Wall Street Journal*, February 27. Retrieved from http://online.wsj.com/article/SB123562945194379899.html?mod=djemalertNEWS.

Molnar, B. E., A. Browne, M. Cerda, and S. L. Buka. 2005. "Violent Behavior by Girls Reporting Violent Victimization." *Archives of Pediatric and Adolescent Medicine* 159: 731–39.

Mongols MC Canada, Inc. 2010. *Mongols Canada*. Mongols Canada Website. Retrieved from http://mongolsmccanada.com/main.html.

Mongols Nation Motorcycle Club. 2009a. *Mongols MC – Est. 1969*. Retrieved from http://www.mongolsmc.com/sub/history.

Mongols Nation Motorcycle Club 2009b. *Out-Bad*. Retrieved from http://www.mongolsmc.com/sub/outbad.

Montgomery, M. 2008. September. Gangster Reveals Mexican Mafia Secrets. *National Public Radio*. Retrieved from http://www.npr.org/templates/story/story.php?storyId=94333325.

Moore, J. W. 1978. *Homeboys: Gangs, Drugs, and Prisons in the Barrio of Los Angeles*. Philadelphia: Temple University Press.

_____. 1985. "Isolation and Stigmatization in the Development of an Underclass: The Case of Chicano Gangs in East Los Angeles." *Social Problems* 33: 1–10.

_____. 1988. "Gangs and the Underclass: A Comparative Perspective." Introductory chapter in J. M. Hagedorn, *People and Folks: Gangs, Crime and the Underclass in a Rustbelt City*, 2d ed. Chicago: Lakeview Press.

_____. 1991. *Going Down to the Barrio: Homeboys and Homegirls in Change*. Philadelphia: Temple University Press.

_____. 1993. "Gangs, Drugs, and Violence." In S. Cummings and D. J. Monti (Eds.), *Gangs: The Origins and Impact of Contemporary Youth Gangs in the United States*. Albany, NY: SUNY Press.

_____. J. D. Vigil, and J. Levy. 1995. "Huisas of the Street: Chicana Gang Members." *Latino Studies Journal* 6: 27–48.

_____. J. D. Vigil, and R. Garcia. 1983. "Residence and Territoriality in Chicano Gangs." *Social Problems* 31: 182–194.

Moore, M. 2007. "Blacks and Latinos Are Suspended More Often." Retrieved from http://www.gazette.net/stories/052307/montnew221126_32333.shtml.

Moore, M. T. 2010. "For DC, Hope in Treating Young Offenders." *USA Today*, May 28. Retrieved from http://www.usatoday.com/news/nation/2010-05-18-offenders_N.htm?csp=obinsite.

Moore, S. 2009. "Missouri System Treats Juvenile Offenders with Lighter Hand." *New York Times*, March 27. Retrieved from http://www.nytimes.com/2009/03/27/us/27juvenile.html.

Morash, M., S. Park, and J. Kim. 2010. "The Importance of Context in the Production of Girls' Violence: Implications for the Focus of Interventions." In M. Chesney-Lind and n. Jones (Eds.), *Fighting for Girls: New Perspectives on Gender and Violence*. New York: SUNY Press. (Kindle edition.)

Moriarty, S. 2009. "Phoenix Church Ordered to Stop Feeding the Homeless." November 12. Retrieved from http://homelessness.change.org/blog/view/phoenix_church_ordered_to_stop_feeding_the_homeless.

Morris, E. W. 2005. "Tuck in that Shirt!" Race, Class, Gender, and Discipline in an Urban School." *Sociological Perspectives* 48: 25–48.

Morris, N., and M. Tonry (Eds.). 1989. *Crime and Justice: An Annual Review of Research*, vol. 12. Chicago: University of Chicago Press.

Morrison, R. D. 1992. "Gangs: Police Strategies for the Nineties." *The Police Marksman* 17: 30–31.

Moxley, R. 1989. *Case Management*. Beverly Hills, CA: Sage.

Murray, C. 1993. "Tomorrow's Underclass." *Wall Street Journal*, October 29.

Musto, D. 1973. *The American Disease: Origins of Narcotics Control*. New Haven, CT: Yale University Press.

Myers, H. 2006. *Organized Crime in Oregon*. State of Oregon, Department of Justice.

National Alliance of Gang Investigators Associations. 2003. "Getting Out of Gangs, Staying Out of Gangs." Washington, DC: NAGIA, January 14.

National Drug Intelligence Center (NDIC). 1996. *National Street Gang Survey Report*. Johnstown, PA: National Drug Intelligence Center.

_____. 2002a. *Drugs and Crime Outlaw Motorcycle Gang Profile: Hells Angels Motorcycle Club* (no. 2002-M0148-003). Washington, DC: United States Department of Justice.

_____. 2002b. *Drugs and Crime Outlaw Motorcycle Gang Profile: Outlaws Motorcycle Gang* (no. 2002-M0148-005). Washington, DC: United States Department of Justice.

_____. 2005. Gangs in the United States. *Narcotics Digest Weekly* 4: 1–12.

National Gang Center. 2010. "National Youth Gang Survey Analysis." Retrieved from http://www.nationalgangcenter.gov/Survey-Analysis/Demographics.

_____. 2011a. "Compilation of Gang-Related Legislation." December 5. Retrieved from http://www.nationalgangcenter.gov/Legislation.

_____. 2012. Retrieved from http://www.nationalgangcenter.gov/.

National Gang Intelligence Center (NGIC). 2009. *National Gang Threat Assessment, 2009* (No. 2009 M0335-001). Washington, DC: National Drug Intelligence Center.

_____. 2011. *National Gang Threat Assessment 201*, January. Retrieved from https://www.csoroundtable.org/sites/csoroundtable.org/files/National%20Gang%20Intelligence%20Center%202011%20Report.pdf.

National Guard Youth ChalleNGe Program. 2011. Retrieved from http://www.promisingpractices.net/program.asp?programid=275.

National Highway Traffic Safety Administration (NHTSA). 2010. *Traffic Safety Facts, 2008 Data: Motorcycles* (no. DOT HS 811 159). Washington, DC: NHTSA's National Center for Statistics and Analysis. Retrieved from http://www-nrd.nhtsa.dot.gov/Pubs/811159.pdf.

National Law Center on Homelessness and Poverty. 2009. "Children and Youth: Fact Sheets." Retrieved from http://www.nlchp.org/program_factsheets.cfm?prog=2.

National Law Enforcement Institute. 1992. *Gang Manual*. Santa Rosa, CA: National Law Enforcement Institute.

National Youth Gang Center. 2012. *National Youth Gang Survey Analysis*. Retrieved from http://www.nationalgangcenter.gov/Survey-Analysis.

NBC. 1993. "Diana Koricke in East Los Angeles." *World News Tonight*. March 29.

Needle, J. A., and W. V. Stapleton. 1983. *Police Handling of Youth Gangs*. Washington, DC: American Justice Institute.

New York Times. 1999. "Bold Effort Leaves Much Unchanged For The Poor." December 30.

_____. 2007. "The Right Model for Juvenile Justice." (Editorial), October 28. Retrieved from http://www.nytimes.com/2007/10/28/opinion/28sun2.html.

_____. 2011. "A Minimum Wage Increase." (Editorial), March 26. Retrieved from http://www.nytimes.com/2011/03/27/opinion/27sun2.html?src=twrhp.

Newsweek. 1998. "God and Gangs." June 1: 21–24.

Neufeld, S., and A. Linskey. 2008. "Baltimore Study Links Truancy and Street Violence." *Baltimore Sun*, May 9. Retrieved from http://www.latimes.com/news/nationworld/nation/la-na-skippingschool9-2008may09,0,3627757.story.

Nguyen, K. 2002. *The Unwanted: A Memoir of Childhood*. Boston: Back Bay Books.

Nuestra Familia. (n.d.). *Nuestra Familia Constitution*. Gangs187.com. Retrieved from http://www.gangs187.com/NFConstitution.pdf.

O'Brien, D. M. 1990. *Storm Center: The Supreme Court in American Politics*, 2d ed. New York: W. W. Norton.

O'Connor, A. 2000. "Police Scandal Clouds List of Gang Members." *Los Angeles Times*, March 25.

O'Neill, R. 2002. "Experiments in Living: The Fatherless Family." London: The Institute for the Study of Civil Society, September. Retrieved from http://www.civitas.org.uk/pdf/Experiments.pdf.

Office for Victims of Crime. 1996. *Victims of Gang Violence: A New Frontier in Victim Services*. New York: Office for Victims of Crime.

Olson, D. E., B. Dooley, and C. M. Kane. 2004. The Relationship Between Gang Membership and Inmate Recidivism. Illinois Criminal Justice Information Authority. Retrieved from http://www.icjia.state.il.us/public/pdf/Bulletins/gangrecidivism.pdf.

Orlando-Morningstar, D. 1997. Prison Gangs. *Federal Judicial Center Special Needs Offenders Bulletin* 2: 1–12.

Osgood, D. W., and J. M. Chambers. 2000. "Social Disorganization Outside the Metropolis: An Analysis of Rural Youth Violence." *Criminology* 38: 81–115.

Ostner, I. 1986. "Die Entdeckung der Madchen: Neue Perspecktiven für die." *Kolner Zeitschrift für Soziologie und Sozialpsychologie* 38: 352–371.

Padilla, F. 1992. *The Gang as an American Enterprise.* New Brunswick, NJ: Rutgers University Press.

Paige, C. 2008. "'Big Brother' Concerns over School Cameras." *Boston Globe,* October 19. Retrieved from http://www.boston.com/news/local/articles/2008/10/19/big_brother_concerns_over_school_cameras/.

Parent, D. G. 2003. *Correctional Boot Camps: Lessons from a Decade of Research.* Washington, DC: National Institute of Justice.

Parker, B. 2009. "High School Tightens Security." *Boston Globe,* October 22. Retrieved from http://www.boston.com/news/local/articles/2009/10/22/lexington_high_school_to_install_125_surveillance_cameras/.

Pasko, L. 2010. "Damaged Daughters: The History of Girls: Sexuality and the Juvenile Justice System." *Journal of Criminal Law and Criminology* 100: 1099–1130.

Pasko, L., and Chesney-Lind, M. 2010. Under Lock and Key: Trauma, Marginalization, and Girls' Juvenile Justice Involvement. *Justice Research and Policy* 12: 25–49.

Patterson, G. R., P. Chamberlain, and J. B. Reid. 1982. "A Comparative Evaluation of a Parent-Training Program." *Behavior Therapy* 13: 636–650.

Pearson, G. 1983. *Hooligan: A History of Reportable Fears.* New York: Schoeken Books.

————. 1991. "Goths and the Vandals: Crime in History." In D. Greenburg, *Crime and Capitalism,* 2d ed. Palo Alto, CA: Mayfield.

Pelz, M. E., J. W. Marquart, and C. T. Pelz. 1991. "Right-Wing Extremism in the Texas Prisons: The Rise and Fall of the Aryan Brotherhood of Texas." *Prison Journal* 71: 23–37.

Pennell, S., and C. Curtis. 1982. *Juvenile Violence and Gang Related Crime.* San Diego, CA: San Diego Association of Governments.

Perkins, U. E. 1987. *Explosion of Chicago's Black Street Gangs: 1900 to the Present.* Chicago: Third World Press.

Perrucci, R., and E. Wysong. 2003. *The New Class Society,* 2d ed. New York: Roman and Littlefield.

Persson, A., M. Kerr, and H. Stattin. 2007. "Staying In or Moving Away from Structured Activities: Explanations Involving Parents and Peers." *Developmental Psychology* 43: 197–207.

Peterson, D., J. Miller, and F. Esbensen. 2001. The Impact of Sex Composition on Gangs and Gang Delinquency. *Criminology* 39: 411–439.

Phillips, K. 1990. *The Politics of the Rich and the Poor.* New York: Random House.

————. 2002. *Wealth and Democracy.* New York: Broadway Books.

Phillips, M. B. 1991. "A Hedgehog Proposal." *Crime and Delinquency* 37: 555–574.

Pih, K., M. De La Rosa, D. Rugh, and K. Mao. 2008. Different Strokes for Different Gangs? An Analysis of Capital among Latino and Asian Gang Members." NIH Public Access. Retrieved from http://www.ncbi.nlm.nih.gov/pmc/articles/PMC2705161/.

Piven, F. F., and R. A. Cloward. 1971. *Regulating the Poor: The Functions of Public Welfare.* New York: Vintage Books.

Platt, A. M. 1977. *The Child Savers,* 2d ed. Chicago: University of Chicago Press.

Pogrebin, R. 2007. "Rebuilding New Orleans, Post-Katrina Style." *New York Times,* November 6.

Polakow, V. 1993. *Lives on the Edge: Single Mothers and Their Children in the Other America.* Chicago: University of Chicago Press.

Polk, K. 1984. "The New Marginal Youth." *Crime and Delinquency* 30: 462–479.

Portillos, L., and M. Zatz. 1995. "Not to Die For: Positive and Negative Aspects of Chicano Youth Gangs." Paper presented at the American Society of Criminology Annual Meeting, Boston.

Proband, S. C. 1997. "Black Men Face 29 percent Lifetime Chance of Prison." *Overcrowded Times* 8: 1.

Project TEAM. 1991. *Report to the Community.* Sierra Vista, AZ: Sierra Vista New Turf Project.

Prothrow-Stith, D. 1991. *Deadly Consequences.* New York: Harper Collins.

Provine, D. 2007. *Unequal Under Law: Race in the War on Drugs.* Chicago: University Of Chicago Press.

Pyrooz, D. C., S. H. Decker, and M. Fleisher. 2011. "From the Street to the Prison, from the Prison to the Street: Understanding and Responding to Prison Gangs." *Journal of Aggression, Conflict and Peace Research* 3: 12–24.

Quadegno, J. 1994. *The Color of Welfare: How Racism Undermined the War on Poverty.* New York: Oxford University Press.

Queen, W. 2007. *Under and Alone: The True Story of the Undercover Agent Who Infiltrated America's Most Violent Outlaw Motorcycle Gang.* New York: Ballantine Books.

Quicker, J. C. 1983. *Homegirls: Characterizing Chicana Gangs.* San Pedro, CA: International University Press.

Quinn, J. F. 2001. Angels, Bandidos, Outlaws, and Pagans: The Evolution of Organized Crime among the Big Four 1% Motorcycle Clubs. *Deviant Behavior* 22: 379–399.

————, and B. Downs. 1995. "Predictors of Gang Violence: The Impact of Drugs and Guns on Police Perceptions in Nine States." *Journal of Gang Research* 23: 15–27.

————, and C. J. Forsyth. 2009. Leathers and Rolexs: The Symbolism and Values of the Motorcycle Club. *Deviant Behavior* 30: 235–265.

————, and D. S. Koch. 2003. The Nature of Criminality within One-Percent Motorcycle Clubs. *Deviant Behavior* 24: 281–305.

Quinney, R. 1970. *The Social Reality of Crime.* Boston: Little, Brown.

————. 1974. *Critique of Legal Order: Crime Control in Capitalist Society.* Boston: Little, Brown.

————. 1980. *Class, State, and Crime: On the Theory and Practice of Criminal Justice,* 2d ed. New York: David McKay.

————. 1982. *Social Existence: Metaphysics, Marxism, and the Social Sciences.* Beverly Hills, CA: Sage.

————. 1991. *Journey to a Far Place: Autobiographical Reflections.* Philadelphia: Temple University Press.

————. 2002. *Critique of Legal Order: Crime Control in Capitalist Society.* New Brunswick, NJ: Transaction Books.

————, and J. Wildeman. 1991. *The Problem of Crime: A Peace and Social Justice Perspective,* 3d ed. Mountain View, CA: Mayfield.

Quinones, S. 2007. "Gang Rivalry Grows into Race War." *Los Angeles Times,* October 18. Retrieved from http://www.latimes.com/news/local/la-me-firestone18oct18,0,6500817.story?coll=la-home-center.

Rafael, T. 2009. *The Mexican Mafia.* New York: Encounter Books.

Ratcliffe, J. H., and T. A. Taniguchi. 2008. "Is Crime Higher Around Drug-Gang Street Corners? Two Spatial Approaches to the Relationship between Gang Set Spaces and Local Crime Levels." *Crime Patterns and Analysis* 1: 23–46.

Reckless, W. 1961. *The Crime Problem,* 3d ed. New York: Appleton-Century-Crofts.

Regoli, R. M., and J. D. Hewitt. 2000. *Delinquency in Society,* 4th ed. New York: McGraw-Hill.

Reich, R. B. 1991. "The Real Economy." *The Atlantic* 267: 35–52.

Reiman, J. 1993. "A Radical Perspective on Crime." In D. H. Kelly (Ed.), *Deviant Behavior.* New York: St. Martin's Press.

————, and P. Leighton. 2009. *The Rich Get Richer and the Poor Get Prison: Ideology, Crime, and Criminal Justice,* 9th ed. Saddle River, NJ: Prentice Hall.

Reinarman, C. and H. G. Levine (Eds.). 1997. *Crack in America: Demon Drugs and Social Justice.* Berkeley, CA: University of California Press.

Reiner, I. 1992. *Gangs, Crime and Violence in Los Angeles: Findings and Proposals from the District Attorney's Office.* Arlington, VA: National Youth Gang Information Center.

Rhodes, M. 2006. "The Crime of Pushing a Shopping Cart." September 19. Retrieved from http://www.indybay.org/newsitems/2006/09/19/18312750.php.

————. 2010. "War on the Poor… Continues in Fresno." February 5. Retrieved from http://www.indybay.org/newsitems/2010/02/05/18637084.php.

Rice, R. 1963. "A Reporter at Large: The Persian Queens." *The New Yorker* 39, October 19.

Rifkin, J. 1995. *The End of Work.* New York: G. P. Putnam.

Riis, J. A. 1969. *The Battle with the Slum.* Montclair, NJ: Paterson Smith (originally published in 1902).

Ritzer, G. 1996. *The McDonaldization of Society,* rev. ed. Thousand Oaks, CA: Pine Forge Press.

Roberts, S. 1972. "Crime Rate of Women Up Sharply Over Men's." *New York Times,* June 13.

Roberts, S., J. Zhang, and J. Truman. 2010. *Indicators of School Crime and Safety: 2010.* National Center for Education Statistics, November. Retrieved from http://nces.ed.gov/pubs2011/2011002.pdf.

Robins, L. 1966. *Deviant Children Grown Up.* Baltimore, MD: Williams and Wilkins.

Romero, D. 2011. "L.A. Launches Graffiti Database to Track Taggers, Keep Evidence on File." *LA Weekly,* March 4. Retrieved from http://blogs.laweekly.com/informer/2011/03/lapd_tagger_database.php.

Rosenbaum, D. P. and G. S. Hanson. 1998. "Assessing the Effects of School-Based Drug Education: a Six-Year Multi-Level Analysis of Project D.A.R.E." *Journal of Research in Crime and Delinquency* 35: 381–412.

Rosoff, S. M., H. N. Pontell, and R. Tillman. 2009. *Profit without Honor: White Collar Crime and the Looting of America,* 5th ed. Saddleback, NJ: Prentice-Hall.

Rothman, R. A. 1999. *Inequality and Stratification: Race, Class, and Gender,* 3d ed. Upper Saddle River, NJ: Prentice-Hall.

Rubin, J., and A. Pesce. 2010. "Within South L.A.'s Killing Zone, a Haven from Violence." *Los Angeles Times,* January 26. Retrieved from http://www.streetgangs.com/news/ 012610_south_la_killzone.

Rubin, L. B. 1994. *Families on the Fault Line*. New York: Harper/Collins.

Ruddell, R., S. H. Decker, and A. Egley. 2006. Gang Interventions in Jails: A National Analysis. *Criminal Justice Review* 31: 33–46.

Ruigrok, W., and R. van Tulder. 1995. *The Logic of International Restructuring*. London: Rutledge.

Rusche, G., and O. Kirchheimer. 1968. *Punishment and Social Structure*. New York: Russell and Russell. (Originally published 1938.)

Rutten, T. 2008. "Who'll Stop the Gangs?" *Los Angeles Times*, February 27. Retrieved from http://www.latimes.com/news/printedition/ asection/la-oe-rutten27feb27,0,1538722. column.

Sachs, S. L. 1997. *Street Gang Awareness*. Minneapolis, MN: Fairview Press.

Sagan, L. A. 1989. *The Health of Nations*. New York: Basic Books.

Sampson, R. J. 1985. "Neighborhood and Crime: The Structural Determinants of Personal Victimization." *Journal of Research in Crime and Delinquency* 22: 7–40.

———. 1986. "Effects of Socioeconomic Context on Official Reaction to Juvenile Delinquency." *American Sociological Review* 5: 876–885.

———, and B. W. Groves. 1989. "Community Structure and Crime: Testing Social-Disorganization Theory." *American Journal of Sociology* 94: 774–802.

———, and J. Laub. 1995. *Crime in the Making: Pathways and Turning Points through Life*. Cambridge, MA: Harvard University Press.

———, S. W. Raudenbush, and F. Earls. 1997. "Neighborhoods and Violent Crime: A Multilevel Study of Collective Efficacy." *Science* 277: 918–924.

———, J. P. Sharkey, and S. W. Raudenbush. 2008. "Durable Effects of Concentrated Disadvantage on Verbal Ability among African-American Children." *National Academy of Sciences*, January. Retrieved from http:// www.pnas.org/content/105/3/845.full. pdf+html.

Sanders, W. 1994. *Gangbangs and Drivebys*. New York: Aldine DeGruyter.

Sanders, W. B. 1970. *Juvenile Offenders for a Thousand Years*. Chapel Hill: University of North Carolina Press.

Santa Cruz, N. 2011. "For Chronic Truants, a GPS Program Can Help Them Make the Grade." *Los Angeles Times*, February 25. Retrieved from http://www.latimes.com/news/local/ la-me-0225-gps-kids-20110225,0,5243827. story.

Sante, L. 1991. *Low Life: Lures and Snares of Old New York*. New York: Vintage Books

Santiago, D. 1992. "Random Victims of Vengeance Show Teen Crime." *The Philadelphia Inquirer*, February 23: A1.

Santrock, J. W. 1981. *Adolescence: An Introduction*. Dubuque, IA: William C. Brown.

Sapolsky, R. M. 1988. "Lessons of the Serengeti: Why Some of Us Are More Susceptible to Stress." *The Sciences*, May/June: 38–42.

Savage, D. 2010. "Justices Take Up Kids' Rights." *Chicago Tribune*, November 2.

Savitz, L. D., L. Rosen, and M. Lalli. 1980. "Delinquency and Gang Membership as Related to Victimization." *Victimology* 5: 152–160.

Scelfo, J. 2005. "Bad Girls Go Wild." *Newsweek*, June 13: 66.

Scheb, J. M., and J. M. Scheb II. 1994. *Criminal Law and Procedure*, 2d ed. Minneapolis/St. Paul, MN: West.

Scheer, R. 2011. *The Great American Stickup*. New York: Nation Books.

Scheinfeld, D. H. 1983. "Family Relationships and School Achievement among Boys of Lower-Income Black Families." *American Journal of Orthopsychiatry* 53.

Schichor, D., and D. Kelly (Eds.). 1980. *Critical Issues in Juvenile Delinquency*. Lexington, MA: D.C. Heath.

Schiraldi, V., and T. Ambrosio. 1997 "Striking Out: The Crime Control Impact of Three Strikes Laws." *Justice Policy Institute*, March.

Schmid, R. E. 2003. "Uninsured Strain Communities." *Las Vegas Review-Journal*, March.

Schnurer, E. B., and C. R. Lyons. 2004. "Juvenile Boot Camps: Experiment in Trouble." Washington, DC: Center for National Policy. Retrieved from http://www.cnponline.org/ Issue%20Briefs/Statelines/ statelin0200.htm.

Schorr, L. 1989. *Within Our Reach: Breaking the Cycle of Disadvantage*. New York: Anchor.

Schott 50 State Report. 2008. Retrieved from http://blackboysreport.org/node/9.

Schur, E. 1971. *Labeling Deviant Behavior*. New York: Harper and Row.

Schweinhart, L. J., J. Montie, Z. Xiang, W. S. Barnett, C. R. Belfield, and M. Nores. 2005. *LIFETIME effects: The HighScope Perry Preschool Study through Age 40*. (Monographs of the HighScope Educational Research Foundation, 14). Ypsilanti, MI: HighScope Press.

Schwendinger, H., and J. Schwendinger. 1985. *Adolescent Subcultures and Delinquency*. New York: Praeger.

Seagal, D. 1993 "Tales from the Cutting-Room Floor: The Reality of 'Reality-Based'

Television." *Harper's Magazine*, November. Retrieved from http://www.d.umn.edu/~jmaahs/Crime%20and%20Media/pdf%20files/tales_cutting_room_floor_Harpers.pdf.

Seattle Social Development Project. 2011. Retrieved from http://www.promisingpractices.net/program.asp?programid=64#reviewed.

Selmon, D., and P. Leighton. 2010. *Punishment for Sale: Private Prisons, Big Business, and the Incarceration Binge*. Lantham, MD: Rowman and Littlefield.

Shapiro, I., and R. Greenstein. 1997. "Trends in the Distribution of After-Tax Income: An Analysis of Congressional Budget Office Data." Washington, DC: Center on Budget and Policy Priorities, August 14.

Shapiro, M. 1986. *Courts: A Comparative Political Analysis*. Chicago: University of Chicago Press.

Shaw, C., and H. D. McKay. 1972. *Juvenile Delinquency in Urban Areas*. Chicago: University of Chicago Press. (Originally published in 1942.)

Shaxson, N. 2011. *Treasure Islands: Uncovering the Damage of Offshore Banking and Tax Havens*. New York: Macmillan.

Shelden, R. G. 1991. A Comparison of Gang Members and Non-Gang Members in a Prison Setting. *The Prison Journal* 71: 50–60.

_____. 1999a. "The Prison Industrial Complex." *The Progressive Populist* 5(11), November 1.

_____. 1999b. *Detention Diversion Advocacy: An Evaluation*. Washington, DC: U.S. Department of Justice, Office of Juvenile Justice and Delinquency Prevention, Juvenile Justice Bulletin.

_____. 2002. "Round Up the Usual Suspects." Paper presented at the Western Society of Criminology annual meeting, February, San Diego, California.

_____. 2008. *Controlling the Dangerous Classes: A History of Criminal Justice in America*, 2d ed. Boston, MA: Allyn and Bacon.

_____. 2010. *Our Punitive Society*. Long Grove, IL: Waveland Press.

_____. 2012. *Delinquency and Juvenile Justice in American Society*, 2d ed. Long Grove, IL: Waveland Press.

_____, and W. B. Brown. 2001. "The Crime Control Industry and the Management of the Surplus Population." *Critical Criminology* 9: 39–62.

_____, W. B. Brown, K. Millerm, and R. Fritzler. 2008. *Crime and Criminal Justice in American Society*. Long Grove, IL: Waveland Press.

_____, W. B. Brown, and S. Listwan. 2003. "The New American Apartheid: The Incarceration of African-Americans." In S. L. Browning, R. R. Miller, and R. D. Coates (Eds.), *The Common Good: A Critical Examination of Law and Social Control*. Chapel Hill: Carolina Academic Press.

_____, T. Snodgrass, and P. Snodgrass. 1992. "Comparing Gang and Non-Gang Offenders: Some Tentative Findings." *Gang Journal* 1: 73–85.

Shellety, J. E. 1993. "Residents Speak Out on Growing Gang Presence." *Salt Lake Tribune*, October 3.

Shelton, D. 2010. "Changing the Hard Cases." *Chicago Tribune*, February 22. Retrieved from http://newsletter.csbs.csusb.edu/archive/March2010/9590_margret_hughes.pdf.

Shichor, D. 2010. "The French-Italian Controversy: A Neglected Historical Topic in Criminological Literacy." *Journal of Criminal Justice Education* 21(3): 211–228.

Shoemaker, D. J. 1996. *Theories of Delinquency* (3d ed.). New York: Oxford University Press.

Short, J. F. (Ed.). 1968. *Gang Delinquency and Delinquent Subcultures*. New York: Harper and Row.

_____. 1990a. "Gangs, Neighborhoods, and Youth Crime." *Criminal Justice Research*, Bulletin 5.

_____. 1990b. "New Wine in Old Bottles? Change and Continuity in American Gangs." In C. R. Huff, *Gangs in America*, 2d ed. Newbury Park, CA: Sage.

_____. 1996. "Gangs and Adolescent Violence." Unpublished report. Boulder, CO: Center for the Study and Prevention of Violence.

_____, and F. Strodtbeck. 1965. *Group Process and Gang Delinquency*. Chicago: University of Chicago Press.

Siegel, L., and J. Senna. 2000. *Juvenile Delinquency*, 7th ed. Belmont, CA: Wadsworth.

Sikes, G. 1997. *Eight Ball Chicks*. New York: Anchor Books.

Silverberg, M. 2006. Wahhabism in the American Prison System. Marksilverberg.com. Retrieved from http://www.marksilverberg.com/article/WahhabisminAmerica/67/.

Simi, P. 2003. "Rage in the City of Angels: The Historical Development of the Skinhead Subculture in Los Angeles." Doctoral dissertation, Department of Sociology, University of Nevada–Las Vegas.

Simon, R. 1975. *Women and Crime*. Lexington, MA: Lexington Books.

Sims, J. 2009a. "Order to Kill Came from Top Bandidos Trial." *The London Free Press*, October 15. Retrieved from http://www.lfpress.com/news/bandidos/2009/10/15/11415256.html.

————. 2009b. Bandidos Creed Big on Club Rules. *The London Free Press*, May 6. Retrieved from http://pbdba.lfpress.com/perl-bin/publish.cgi?x= articles&p=264282&s= bandidos_ trial.

Sipchen, B. 1993. *Baby Insane and the Buddha*. New York: Bantam Books.

Skarbek, D. 2008. "Putting the 'Con' into Constitutions: The Economics of Prison Gangs." *The Journal of Law, Economics, and Organization* 26: 183–211.

Skiba, R. J., S. C. Eckes, and K. Brown. 2009/2010. "African American Disproportionality in School Discipline: The Divide between Best Evidence and Legal Remedy." *New York Law School Law Review* 54: 1071–1112. Retrieved from http://www.nyls.edu/user_files/1/3/4/17/49/1001/Skiba%20et%20al%2054.4.pdf.

Sklar, H. 1998. "Let Them Eat Cake." *Z Magazine*. November: 29–32.

————. 1999. "For CEO's, a Minimum Wage in the Millions." *Z Magazine*. July/August: 63–66.

Skogan, W. G. 1990. *Disorder and Decline: Crime and the Spiral of Decay in American Neighborhoods*. Berkeley: University of California Press.

Skolnick, J. H. 1990. Draft paper. *Gang Organization and Migration*. Berkeley, CA: Center for the Study of Law and Society.

————. 1994. *Justice Without Trial: Law Enforcement in Democratic Society*, 3d ed. New York: Macmillan College.

————, and D. H. Bayley. 1986. *The New Blue Line: Police Innovation in Six American Cities*. New York: Free Press.

————, T. Correl, E. Navarro, and R. Rabb. 1990. "The Social Structure of Street Drug Dealing." *American Journal of Police* 9: 1–41.

Slivinski, S. 2007. "The Corporate Welfare State: How the Federal Government Subsidizes U.S. Businesses." *Cato Institute*. Retrieved from http://www.cato.org/pub_display.php?pub_id=8230.

Slovan, M. 2010. "State Lawmakers Want to Rid Schools of Gangs, But Will Their Proposals Hurt Kids More Than They Help?" Olympia Newswire, January 28. Retrieved from http://www.olympianews.org/2010/01/28/state-lawmakers-want-to-rid-schools-of-gangs-but-will-their-proposals-hurt-more-schools-than-they-help/.

Smith, A. 1976. *The Wealth of Nations*. Oxford: Clarendon Press.

Snyder, H. N., and M. Sickmund. 2006. *Juvenile Offenders and Victims: 2006 National Report*. Washington, DC: U.S. Department of Justice, Office of Juvenile Justice and Delinquency Prevention. Retrieved from http://www.ojjdp.gov/ojstatbb/nr2006/.

Snyder, A. R., D. K. McLaughlin, and J. Findeis. 2006. "Household Composition and Poverty among Female-Headed Households with Children: Differences by Race and Residence." *Rural Sociology* 71: 597–624. Retrieved from http://www.uwec.edu/bonstemj/GenderWork/women.bottom.pdf.

Society of African American Professionals. 2006. "Status of Black Males in America." Retrieved from http://www.soaap.org/newsletter/?newsID=11.

Soss, J. 2002. "TANF Reauthorization: Where Is the Language of Racial Justice? Race and Welfare in the U.S." Presentation to the CHN Welfare Advocates Meeting, American University, January 15.

Speir, H. 1994. "Folks Nation, Inc., Apply Within." *Gwinnett Loaf* 2, September 10: 7–9.

Spergel, I. A. 1964. *Racketville, Slumtown and Haulberg*. Chicago: University of Chicago Press.

————. 1984. "Violent Gangs in Chicago: In Search of Social Policy." *Social Service Review* 58: 199–225.

————. 1989. "Youth Gangs: Continuity and Change." In N. Morris and M. Tonry (Eds.), *Crime and Justice: An Annual Review of Research,* vol. 12. Chicago: University of Chicago Press.

————. 1990. *Youth Gangs: Problem and Response*. Chicago: University of Chicago, School of Social Service Administration.

————. 1995. *The Youth Gang Problem: A Community Approach*. New York: Oxford University Press.

————, and G. D. Curry. 1990. "Strategies and Perceived Agency Effectiveness in Dealing with the Youth Gang Problem." In C. R. Huff, *Gangs in America*, 2d ed. Newbury Park, CA: Sage.

————, and S. F. Grossman. 1997. "The Little Village Project: A Community Approach to the Gang Problem." *Social Work* 42: 456–470.

Spitzer, S. 1975. "Toward a Marxian Theory of Deviance." *Social Problems* 22: 638–651.

————. 1982. "The Dialectics of Formal and Informal Control." In R. Abel (Ed.), *The Politics of Informal Justice*. New York: Academic Press.

Stabile, C. A. 1995. "Feminism without Guarantees: The Misalliances and Missed Alliances of Postmodernist Social Theory." In A. Callari, S. Cullenberg, and C. Biewener (Eds.), *Marxism in the Postmodern Age*. New York: Guilford Press.

Stafford, M. R., and M. Warr. 1993. "A Reconceptualization of General and Specific Deterrence." *Journal of Research in Crime and Delinquency* 30: 123–135.

Starbuck, D., J. Howell, and D. Lindquist. 2001. *Hybrid and Other Modern Gangs*. Washington, DC: Office of Juvenile Justice and Delinquency Prevention, Juvenile Justice Bulletin, December.

Stark, R. 1987. "Deviant Places: A Theory of the Ecology of Crime." *Criminology* 25: 893–909.

State Task Force on Youth Gang Violence. 1986. *Final Report*. Sacramento: California Council on Criminal Justice.

Steffensmeier, D. J., and R. H. Steffensmeier. 1980. "Trends in Female Delinquency: An Examination of Arrest, Juvenile Court, Self-Report, and Field Data." *Criminology* 18: 62–85.

_____, and S. Demuth. 2000. "Ethnicity and Sentencing Outcomes in U.S. Federal Courts: Who Is Punished More Harshly?" *American Sociological Review* 65: 705–729.

_____, and S. Demuth 2001. "Ethnicity and Judges' Sentencing Decisions: Hispanic-Black-White Comparisons." *Criminology* 39: 145–178.

_____, J. Ulmer, and J. Kramer. 1998. "The Interaction of Race, Gender, and Age in Criminal Sentencing: The Punishment Cost of Being Young, Black, and Male." *Criminology* 36: 763–797.

Steiner, B., M. D. Markarios, and L. F. Travis. 2011. "Examining the Effects of Residential Situations and Residential Mobility on Offender Recidivism." *Crime and Delinquency*, February 18. Retrieved from http://cad.sagepub.com/content/early/2011/02/17/0011128711399409.abstract?rss=1.

Sternheimer, K. 2006. *Kids These Days: Facts and Fictions about Today's Youth*. Landham, MD: Rowman & Littlefield.

Stolzenberg, L., and S. J. D'Alessio. 1997. "Three Strikes and You're Out: The Impact of California's New Mandatory Sentencing Law on Serious Crime Rates." *Crime and Delinquency* 43: 457–469.

Story, L., and E. Dash. 2009. "Undisclosed Losses at Merrill Lynch Lead to a Trading Inquiry." *New York Times*, March 6. Retrieved from http://www.nytimes.com/2009/03/06/business/06wall.html?em.

Stover, D. 1986. "A New Breed of Youth Gangs Is on the Prowl and a Bigger Threat Than

Ever." *American School Board Journal* 173: 19–24, 35.

Stryker, S. 1980. *Symbolic Interactionism*. Menlo Park, CA: Benjamin/Cummings.

Sullivan, E. L. 2007. "A Critical Policy Analysis: The Impact of Zero Tolerance on Out-of-School Suspensions and Expulsions of Students of Color in the State of Texas by Gender and School Level." Doctoral dissertation, Texas A&M University.

Sullivan, M. L. 1989. *Getting Paid: Youth Crime and Work in the Inner City*. Ithaca, NY: Cornell University Press.

Sutherland, E. H., and D. R. Cressey. 1970. *Criminology*, 8th ed. Philadelphia: Lippincott.

Suttles, G. 1968. *The Social Order of the Slum*. Chicago: University of Chicago Press.

Swahn, M. H., R. M. Bossarte, B. West, and V. Topalli. 2010. "Alcohol and Drug Use among Gang Members: Experiences of Adolescents Who Attend School." *Journal of School Health* 80: 353–360.

Sykes, G., and D. Matza. 1957. "Techniques of Neutralization." *American Journal of Sociology* 22: 664–670.

Takata, S. R., and S. D. Baskin. 1987. "Kenosha Gang Project." Rockville, MD: National Institute of Justice.

Taylor, C. S. 1990a. *Dangerous Society*. East Lansing: Michigan State University Press.

_____. 1990b. "Gang Imperialism." In C. R. Huff, *Gangs in America*, 2d ed. Newbury Park, CA: Sage.

_____. 1993. *Girls, Gangs, Women, and Drugs*. East Lansing: Michigan State University Press.

Taylor, I., P. Walton, and J. Young. 1973. *The New Criminology*. London: Routledge & Kegan Paul.

Taylor, M. C., and G. A. Foster. 2007. "Bad Boys and School Suspensions: Public Policy Implications for Black Males." *Sociological Inquiry* 56: 498–506.

Teller-Elsberg, J., N. Folbre, J. Heintz, and the Center for Popular Economics. 2006. *Field Guide to the U. S. Economy*. New York: The New Press.

Texas Appleseed. 2010. *Texas' School-to-Prison Pipeline: School Expulsion—The Path from Lockout to Dropout*. Austin, TX. Retrieved from http://www.texasappleseed.net/index.php?option=com_docman&task=doc_download&gid= 309&Itemid=.

Texas Syndicate. 2012. Retrieved from http://www.prisonoffenders.com/texas_syndicate.html.

Thompson, D. W., and L. A. Jason. 1997. "Street Gangs and Preventive Interventions."

In L. Mays (Ed.), *Gangs and Gang Behavior*. Chicago: Nelson-Hall.

Thornberry, T., D. Huizinga, and R. Loeber. 2004. The Causes and Correlates Studies: Findings and Policy Implications. *Juvenile Justice Journal* 9: 3–19.

Thornberry, T. P., and J. H. Burch. 1997. "Gang Members and Delinquent Behavior." Office of Juvenile Justice and Delinquency Programs. Washington, DC: U.S. Department of Justice. Office of Justice Programs.

Thornberry, T. P., M. Krohn, A. Lizotte, and D. Chard-Wierschem. 1993. "The Role of Juvenile Gangs in Facilitating Delinquent Behavior." *Journal of Research in Crime and Delinquency* 30: 55–87.

Thornberry, T. P., M. Krohn, A. Lizotte, C. A. Smith, and K. Tobin. 2003. *Gangs and Delinquency in Developmental Perspective*. New York: Cambridge University Press.

Thrasher, F. 1927. *The Gang*. Chicago: University of Chicago Press.

Toy, C. 1992. "A Short History of Asian Gangs in San Francisco." *Justice Quarterly* 9: 647–665.

Tracy, S. T. 2003. "Gang-Banging Comes to the Country." Paper presented at the annual meeting of the American Academy of Criminal Justice Sciences, March 7, Boston.

Trout, C. H. 1992. Taking a New Look at an Old Problem. *Corrections Today* 54: 62–66.

Trulson, C. R., J. W. Marquart, and S. K. Kawucha. 2008. Gang Suppression and Institutional Control. *Corrections Today*, 68(2): 26–30.

Truman, J. 2011. "Criminal Victimization, 2010." Washington, DC: U. S. Department of Justice, Bureau of Justice Statistics. Retrieved from http://bjs.ojp.usdoj.gov/content/pub/pdf/cv10.pdf.

Turner, M. G., J. L. Sundt, B. K. Applegate, and F. T. Cullen. 1995. "Three Strikes and You're Out Legislation: A National Assessment." *Federal Probation* LIX: 16–35.

United Coalition East Prevention Project. 2005. "Toxic Playground: Growing Up In Skid Row." Retrieved from http://www.socialmodelrecovery.org/sites/default/files/Toxic%20Playground.pdf.

U.S. Department of Commerce, Bureau of the Census. 1989. *Statistical Abstract of the United States: 1994*. Washington, DC: U.S. Government Printing Office.

_____. 1990. *1990 Census, Summary Tape, File 3C*. Washington, DC: U.S. Government Printing Office.

_____. 1994. *Statistical Abstract of the United States: 1994*. Washington, DC: U.S. Government Printing Office.

_____. 1995. *Statistical Abstract of the United States, 1995*. Washington, DC: U.S. Government Printing Office.

_____. 2000a. "From Birth to Seventeen: The Living Arrangements of Children, 2000; Population Profile of the United States, 2000." (Internet release), pp. 6.1–6.5.

_____. 2000b. "Scholars of All Ages: School Enrollment, 2000." (Internet release), pp. 8.1–8.4.

_____. 2000c. "Identifying Need: Poverty 2000." (Internet release), pp. 13.1–13.4.

_____. 2000d. "Paying the Bills: Meeting Basic Needs, 1995." (Internet release), pp. 14.1–14.2.

_____. 2000e. "People at Risk: Health Insurance Coverage, 2000." (Internet release), pp. 15.1–15.2.

_____. 2001. *Statistical Abstract of the United States, 2001*. Washington, DC: U.S. Government Printing Office.

_____. 2011. *Statistical Abstract of the United States, 2011*. Washington, DC: U.S. Government Printing Office, Table 642. Retrieved from http://www.census.gov/compendia/statab/2011/tables/11s0642.pdf.

U.S. Census Bureau. 2009. "America's Families and Living Arrangements, 2009," Table C3. Retrieved from http://www.census.gov/population/www/socdemo/hh-fam/cps2009.html.

U.S. Census Bureau. 2010a. "Income Distribution to $250,000 or More for Families: 2009." Current Population Survey, Annual Social and Economic Supplement, Table FINC-07. Retrieved from http://www.census.gov/hhes/www/cpstables/032010/faminc/new07_000.htm.

_____. 2010b. "Households by Total Money Income, Race, and Hispanic Origin of Householder: 1967 to 2009," Table H-17. Retrieved from http://www.census.gov/hhes/www/income/data/historical/household/index.html.

_____. 2010c. "Mean Household Income Received by Each Fifth and Top 5 Percent," table H-3. Retrieved from http://www.census.gov/hhes/www/income/data/historical/household/index.html.

_____. 2010d. "Annual Social and Economic (ASEC) Supplement." Retrieved from http://www.census.gov/hhes/www/cpstables/032010/pov/new01_100.htm.

_____. 2010e. "America's Families and Living Arrangements." Current Population Survey, table 3-C. Retrieved from http://www.census.gov/population/www/socdemo/hh-fam/cps2010.html.

U.S. Department of Justice. (n.d.). *Motorcycle Gangs. Organized Crime and Gang Section.* Retrieved from http://www.justice.gov/criminal/ocgs/gangs/motorcycle.html.

————. 1998. *Addressing Community Gang Problems: A Practical Guide.* Washington, DC: Office of Juvenile Justice and Delinquency Prevention.

————. 1999. *1996 National Youth Gang Survey.* Washington, DC: Office of Juvenile Justice and Delinquency Prevention.

————. 2001. *2000 National Youth Gang Survey.* Washington, DC: Office of Juvenile Justice and Delinquency Prevention.

U.S. Department of Justice. 2008, April. "Estimated Gang Membership." National Drug Intelligence Center Attorney General's Report to Congress on the Growth of Violent Street Gangs in Suburban Areas. Retrieved from http://www.justice.gov/ndic/pubs27/27612/estimate.htm.

U.S. Department of Labor, Bureau of Labor Statistics. 2003. *Employment Status of the Civilian Population by Sex and Age*, Table A-1.

USA Today. 2002. "Gang Bloodshed Surging in Some U.S. Cities," Nation, December 11. Retrieved from http://www.usatoday.com/news/nation/2002-12-11-gang-violence_x.htm.

Vago, S. 1994. *Law and Society*, 4th ed. Englewood Cliffs, NJ: Prentice Hall.

Valdez, A. 2007a. *Gangs: A Guide to Understanding Street Gangs*, 5th ed. San Clemente, CA: LawTech Publishing.

————. 2007b. Mexican American Girls and Gang Violence: Beyond Risk. New York: Palgrave Macmillan. (Kindle edition.)

————. February 2009. Prison Gangs 101. *Corrections Today* 71(1): 40–43.

————. 2003. "Toward a Typology of Contemporary Youth Gangs." In L. Kontos et al. (Eds.), *Gangs and Society: Alternative Perspectives.* New York: Columbia University Press.

Valentine, B. 1978. *Hustling and Other Hard Work: Life Styles in the Ghetto.* New York: Free Press.

Van Derbeken, J. 2008. Rival Sought in Slaying of Hells Angels Leader. *San Francisco Chronicle*, September 11. Retrieved from http://www.sfgate.com/cgi-bin/article.cgi?f=/c/a/2008/09/11/BAU812SG0D.DTL.

Van Do, P. 2002. "Between Two Cultures: Struggles of Vietnamese Adolescents." *The Review of Vietnamese Studies* 2: 1–19.

Venkatesh, S. 2003. "A Note on Social Theory and the American Street Gang." In L. Kontos, D. Brotherton, and L. Barrios. *Gangs and Society: Alternative Perspectives.* New York: Columbia University Press.

————. 2008. *Gang Leader for a Day.* New York: Penguin Press.

Vigil, J. D. 1983. "Chicano Gangs: One Response to Mexican Urban Adaption." *Urban Anthropology* 12: 45–68.

————. 1988. *Barrio Gangs.* Austin: University of Texas Press.

————. 1990. "Cholos and Gangs: Culture Change and Street Youths in Los Angeles." In C. R. Huff, *Gangs in America*, 2d ed. Newbury Park, CA: Sage.

————. 2002. *A Rainbow of Gangs: Street Cultures in the Mega-City.* Austin, TX: University of Texas Press.

————. 2007. *The Projects: Gang and Non-Gang Families in East Los Angeles.* Austin: University of Texas Press. (Kindle edition)

————. 2010. *Gang Redux: A Balanced Anti-Gang Strategy.* Long Grove, IL: Waveland Press.

————, and S. C. Yun. 1996. "Southern California Gangs: Comparative Ethnicity and Social Control." In C. R. Huff, *Gangs in America*, 2d ed. Newbury Park, CA: Sage.

————, and J. M. Long. 1990. "Emic and Etic Perspectives on Gang Culture: The Chicano Case." In C. R. Huff, *Gangs in America*, 2d ed. Newbury Park, CA: Sage.

————, and S. C. Yun. 1996. "Vietnamese Youth Gangs in Southern California." In C. R. Huff, *Gangs in America*, 2d ed. Newbury Park, CA: Sage.

Voisin, D. R., B. Torsten, L. Neilands, F. Salazar, R. Crosby, and R. J. DiClemente. 2008. "Pathways to Drug and Sexual Risk Behaviors among Detained Adolescents." *Social Work Research* 32: 147–157.

Wacquant, L. 2009. *Punishing the Poor: The Neoliberal Government of Social Insecurity.* Durham, NC: Duke University Press.

Waldorf, D. 1993. "When the Crips Invaded San Francisco: Gang Migration." *Gang Journal.* 1(4): 11–16.

Walker, S. 2001. *Sense and Nonsense about Crime and Drugs*, 5th ed. Belmont, CA: Wadsworth.

Wallace Jr., J. M., S. Goodkind, C. M. Wallace, and J. G. Bachman. 2008." Racial, Ethnic, and Gender Differences in School Discipline among U.S. High School Students: 1991–2005." *Negro Educational Review* 59: 47–62.

Wang, Z. 1995. "Gang Affiliation among Asian-American High School Students: A Path Analysis of Social Developmental Model." *Journal of Gang Research* 2: 1–13.

Warnick, B. R. 2008. "Surveillance Cameras in Schools: An Ethical Analysis." *Harvard Educational Review* 77: 317–343.

Warr, M. 1996. "Organization and Instigation in Delinquent Groups." *Criminology* 34: 11–37.

Warren, J. 2004. "Spare the Rod, Save the Child." *Los Angeles Times*, July 1. Retrieved from http://articles.latimes.com/2004/jul/01/local/me-juvie1.

———, and M. Dolan. 2005. "Tookie Williams Is Executed." *Los Angeles Times*, December 13.

Warren, J., and G. Krikorian. 2005. "Prisons Weigh Threat of Radical Islamist Gangs." *Los Angeles Times*, September 4. Retrieved from http://articles.latimes.com/2005/sep/04/local/me-prisons4.

Washington Post. 2004. "How Much More Abuse?" Editorial, *The Washington Post*, June 3. Retrieved from http://www.washingtonpost.com/wp-dyn/articles/A11237-2004Jun2.html.

Weber, M. 1946. *From Max Weber: Essays in Sociology*. H. Gerth and C. W. Mills (trans.). New York: Oxford University Press.

———. 1958. *The Protestant Ethic and the Spirit of Capitalism*. New York: Charles Scribner.

Weinstein, H. 2001. "3-Strikes Sentence is Ruled Cruel." *Los Angeles Times*, November 4.

Weisheit, R., and L. Edward Wells. 2001. "The Perception of Gangs as a Problem in Non-metropolitan Areas." *Criminal Justice Review* 26: 170–192.

Weisheit, R., L. E. Wells, and D. N. Falcone. 1994. "Community Policing in Small Town and Rural America." *Crime and Delinquency* 40: 549–567.

Werner, E. E., and R. S. Smith. 1982. *Vulnerable, but Invincible: A Longitudinal Study of Resilient Children and Youth*. New York: McGraw-Hill.

Werthman, C. 1967. "The Function of Social Definitions in the Development of Delinquent Careers." In P. G. Garabedian and D. C. Gibbons (Eds.), *Becoming Delinquent*. Chicago: Aldine.

———, and I. Piliavin. 1967. "Gang Members and the Police." In D. J. Bordua (Ed.), *The Police: Six Sociological Essays*. New York: Wiley.

West, D. J., and D. P. Farrington. 1977. *The Delinquent Way of Life*. London: Heinemann.

———. 1973. *Who Becomes Delinquent?* London: Heinemann.

Western, B. 2006. *Punishment and Inequality in America*. New York: Russell Sage Foundation.

Wheatley, T. 2011. "Vandals and Taggers, Beware." *Creative Loafing*. Retrieved from http://clatl.com/atlanta/atlantas-graffiti-task-force-begins-investigating-removing-vandalism/Content?oid=3161169.

Whitehead, J. T., and S. P. Lab. 1989. "A Meta-Analysis of Juvenile Correctional Treatment." *Journal of Research in Crime and Delinquency* 26: 276–295.

Whyte, W. F. 1943. *Street Corner Society*. Chicago: University of Chicago Press.

Wilkinson, K. 1974. "The Broken Home and Juvenile Delinquency: Scientific Explanation or Ideology?" *Social Problems* 21: 726–739.

Williams, K., M. Cohen, and G. D. Curry. 1994. "Evaluation of Female Gang Prevention Programs." Paper presented at the American Society of Criminology annual meeting, Miami, FL.

Williams, K., G. D. Curry, and M. I. Cohen. 2002. "Gang Prevention Programs for Female Adolescents: An Evaluation." In W. L. Reed and S. H. Decker (Eds.), *Responding to Gangs: Evaluation and Research*. Washington, DC: U.S. Department of Justice, National Institute of Justice. Retrieved from https://www.ncjrs.gov/pdffiles1/nij/190351.pdf.

Williams, P., and J. Dickinson. 1993. "Fear of Crime: Read All About It? The Relationship between Newspaper Crime Reporting and Fear of Crime." *British Journal of Criminology* 33: 33–56.

Williams, T. 1989. *The Cocaine Kids: The Inside Story of a Teenage Drug Ring*. Menlo Park, CA: Addison-Wesley.

Wilson, H. 1975. "Juvenile Delinquency, Parental Criminality and Social Handicap." *British Journal of Criminology* 15: 241–250.

———. 1980. "Parental Supervision: A Neglected Aspect of Delinquency." *British Journal of Criminology* 20: 203–235.

Wilson, J. J., and J. C. Howell. 1994. *Comprehensive Strategy for Serious, Violent, and Chronic Juvenile Offenders*. Washington, DC: Office of Juvenile Justice and Delinquency Prevention.

Wilson, J. Q., and G. L. Kelling. 1989. "Making Neighborhoods Safe." *Atlantic Monthly*, February: 46–52.

———, and R. Herrnstein, 1985. *Crime and Human Nature*. New York: Simon and Schuster.

Wilson, W. J. 1987. *The Truly Disadvantaged*. Chicago: University of Chicago Press.

———. 1996. *When Work Disappears: The World of the New Urban Poor*. New York: Vintage Books.

Wilson-Brewer, R., S. Cohen, L. O'Donnell, and I. F. Goodman. 1991. *Violence Prevention for Young Adolescents: A Survey of the State of the Art*. Washington, DC: Carnegie Corporation of New York.

Winfree Jr., L. T., F. Esbensen, and D. W. Osgood. 1995. "On Becoming a Youth Gang Member: Low Self-Control or Learned Behavior?" Paper presented at the Academy of Criminal Justice Sciences annual meeting, Boston.

Winterdyk, J., and Ruddell, R. 2010. Managing Prison Gangs: Results from a Survey of U.S.

Prison Systems. *Journal of Criminal Justice* 38: 730–736.

Wolff, E. 1995. *Top Heavy: A Study of Increasing Inequality of Wealth in America.* New York: Twentieth Century Fund Press.

Wolfgang, M. E. 1958. *Patterns in Criminal Homicide.* Philadelphia: University of Pennsylvania Press.

_____, R. Figlio, and T. Sellin. 1972. *Delinquency in a Birth Cohort.* Chicago: University of Chicago Press.

_____, T. P. Thornberry, and R. M. Figlio. 1987. *From Boy to Man: From Delinquency to Crime.* Chicago: University of Chicago Press.

_____, and N. A. Weiner (Eds.). 1989. *Violent Crime, Violent Criminals.* Newbury Park, CA: Sage.

Wooden, W. S. 1995. *Renegade Kids, Suburban Outlaws.* Belmont, CA: Wadsworth.

Woodson, R. L. 1985. "Self-Help, Not Big Daddy, Must Rescue the Black Underclass." *Washington Post,* May 12: B-1+.

Working Group on Extreme Inequality. (n.d.). "How Unequal Are We?" Retrieved from http://extremeinequality.org/?page_id=8.

Wortley, S., and J. Tanner. 2006. "Immigration, Social Disadvantage and Urban Youth Gangs: Results of a Toronto-Area Survey." *Canadian Journal of Urban Research* 15: 18–37. Retrieved from http://coyote.uwinnipeg.ca/bitstream/handle/10680/383/b-wortley-eng.pdf?sequence=1.

Wright, E. O. 1997. *Class Counts.* London: New Left Books.

Wright, M. E. 2010. "Juvenile Justice Reform: Making the 'Missouri Model' an American Model." *Huffington Post,* March 15. Retrieved from http://www.huffingtonpost.com/marian-wright-edelman/juvenile-justice-reform-m_b_498976.html.

Yablonski, L. 1962. *The Violent Gang.* New York: Macmillan.

Yarborough, T. 2005. *Surviving Twice: Amerasian Children of the Vietnam War.* Herndon, VA: Potomac Books.

Youth Transition Funders Group. 2006, Spring. *A Blueprint for Juvenile Justice Reform,* 2d ed. Retrieved from http://www.ytfg.org/documents/Platform_Juvenile_Justice.pdf.

Zalman, M., and L. Siegel. 1991. *Criminal Procedure: Constitution and Society.* New York: West.

Zatz, M. S. 1987. "Chicano Youth Gangs and Crime: The Creation of a Moral Panic." *Contemporary Crises* 11: 129–158.

_____. 1985. "Los Cholos: Legal Processing of Chicano Gang Members." *Social Problems* 33: 13–30.

Zepezauer, M. 2004. *Take the Rich Off Welfare.* Boston: South End Press.

Zimring, F. 1998. *American Youth Violence.* New York: Oxford University Press.

_____, and G. J. Hawkins. 1973. *Deterrence: The Legal Threat in Crime Control.* Chicago: University of Chicago Press.

Zinn, H. 1990. *The Politics of History,* 2d ed. Urbana: University of Illinois Press.

_____. 1994. *You Can't Be Neutral on a Moving Train.* Boston: Beacon Press.

Zopf Jr., P. E. 1989. *American Women in Poverty.* New York: Greenwood Press.

Index

Note: Pages followed by an "f" denote figures; an "n" denote notes; a "t" denote tables.